Fodor's 2001

Scotland

S0-CFK-506

CONTENTS

MAPS

Circled letters in text correspond to letters on the photographs. For more information on the sights pictured, turn to
the indicated page number Ⓐ on each photograph.

DESTINATION SCOTLAND

Many travel destinations, including the most visited and famous, merely impress you. Scotland is different; it sweeps you off your feet. Then it imprints itself on your heart. North Sea to Irish Sea, Highlands to Lowlands to islands, the landscapes of Scotland—lush woodlands, windswept moors, lochs as deep as the imagination—take your breath away, whether resplendent in sunlight or mysterious under the nation's storied, brooding skies. Urban travelers celebrate the stately vistas of Edinburgh and the Victorian mien of Glasgow. Mere minutes from both lies open land scattered with glorious gardens and distilleries and rich with castles and grand country hotels such as golden, battlemented Inverlochy. Amid the antiques, crafts, fine woolens, and tartans for which Scotland is famous, shoppers rejoice. Tipplers toast the nation's many distilleries. And to anglers and golfers, heaven may be better than Scotland, but they'd need to see it to believe it.

There may be no more gloriously dignified city in the world than Scotland's capital. It was outside the walls of looming Edinburgh Castle, on heights

Ⓐ▷ 43

such as Ⓐ**Castlehill** that Scotland began. Up here, witches burned in the days when faith could be ferocious. Today, the narrow walkways of the Old Town twist across this ridge, and along the area's Ⓔ**Royal Mile** you'll find fine shopping and views that take in, among other splendors, Ⓓ**Princes Street,**

EDINBURGH

Ⓑ▷ 49

a main drag of the classical Ⓑ**New Town** down below. The New Town's planned squares and regular facades make a perfect stage for buskers during summer's three-week-long Edinburgh International Festival, one of the world's great arts celebrations. Creative ferment abounds during this event, spilling over into the Edinburgh Festival Fringe, the unofficial, sassy offspring of the festival proper (and often an easier ticket). At any time, the promontory known as Arthur's Seat is an obligatory climb. And, except when the royal family is in, the Ⓒ**Palace of Holyroodhouse** is a must, with its fine paneling and plasterwork. Guided tours take you not only through some of the most imposing of these spaces but also down the corridors of Scottish and British history, and the

Ⓒ▷ 47

story of Mary, Queen of Scots, comes stirringly alive—intrigues, murders, and all. With all the sights, museums, and shops worth frequenting by day you may want to retire early. Do so, and you'll miss the city's vibrant arts and nightlife. Sleep when you get home.

E > 38

GLASGOW

Warm as a pint with friends, but also bold and exuberant, Glasgow used to call itself the Second City—not of Scotland but of the British Empire. It was a claim Glaswegians could back up. Commerce hummed and prosperity ruled through Victorian times, when the Ⓐ**City Chambers** went up, a reflection of Glasgow's self-confidence—just before a long depression humbled the city's pride. These days the mood is upbeat again. Glasgow crackles with the energy of urban renaissance, complete with trendy stores and a thriving cultural life. Ⓑ**George Square,** at the heart of town,

Ⓐ 98

Ⓑ 99

©>105

is a launch point for explorations that can yield surprises, such as the Art Nouveau ©**Glasgow School of Art,** designed by the great Charles Rennie Mackintosh while Glaswegians were still enthralled by Victorian pomp. The restaurant scene offers more surprises—from around the world and, at the sterling Ⓓ**Ubiquitous Chip,** from closer to home (try the venison haggis). With Glasgow less than an hour from Loch Lomond, Burns Country, and great golf on the Clyde Coast, it's easy to crown a day trip with a sumptuous, sophisticated dinner.

Ⓓ>115

BORDERS AND SOUTHWEST

Ⓐ❯333

Enter Scotland by car from England, and you enter it though the Borders. Here, England could be 500 miles away. The names of places, even of beers, are all inimitably Scottish. Sir Walter Scott, champion of Scotland, lived at Ⓓ**Abbotsford House,** and transformed a local farmhouse into a romantic baronial mansion filled with Scottish artifacts. Here, in the pastoral reaches between the great Tweed and Teviot rivers, livestock clog the roads and seem to outnumber the occasionally kilted humans; fields are dotted by ruins such as those of Ⓒ**Jedburgh Abbey,** razed by the English

Ⓑ❯158

© > 144

Ⓓ > 148

during Henry VIII's attempt to marry off his son to the infant Mary, Queen of Scots. In the highlands of Galloway, Scotland's southwest corner—deeper yet into the Scottish past—stands Ⓑ**Threave Castle,** the remains of the former bastion of the Black Douglases, earls of Nithsdale and lords of Galloway. Poet Robert Burns spent the gloaming of his life in perfectly preserved Ⓔ**Dumfries,** nearby. Your deepest glimpse into the Scottish soul may come on the golf course. This part of Scotland is home to Prestwick, Royal Troon, Western Gailes, and Ⓐ**Turnberry,** hallowed names to any golfer, and hallowed ground in the land where golf was born.

Ⓔ > 156

FIFE AND ANGUS

While not exactly Scotland's answer to Spain's Costa del Sol, Fife can at least lay claim to being Scotland's driest and sunniest region—a good thing, too, considering all the golf played here. You can hardly go wrong on any course in Scotland, but

Ⓐ 182

some 30 layouts grace Fife, many of them seaside links with few if any windbreaks; the North Sea weather, ball-gobbling gorse, and fiendishly placed, seemingly bottomless fairway bunkers test North American golfers in ways they've only dreamed of (sometimes in nightmares). Fife is also home to the *ultimate* golf experience: a round on the Ⓒ**Old Course** at the Royal & Ancient Golf Club of St. Andrews. If you don't know a putter from a flagstick, you'll still love this well-groomed university town for its first-rate restaurants, varied shopping, and splendid sightseeing.

Ⓑ 171

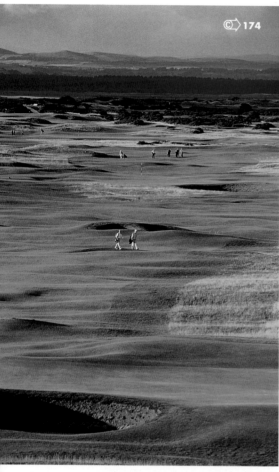

Start with the poignant remains of its once magnificent ⒷCathedral, begun in 1160, and the ruined St. Andrews Castle and St. Rule's Tower, which rewards those who climb it with glorious views of the compact town. Just down the road is ⒺCrail, by acclamation the prettiest village on the Fife coast. As you move north from Fife, crossing the Firth of Tay, you come to Angus. Renowned for its long glens, perfect for scenic hikes though secluded plateaus surrounded by hills and mountains, Angus also offers lovely seacoast views and a generous helping of things old, atmospheric, and quintessentially Scottish. Two of the finest are the ⒶHouse of Dun, an 18th-century mansion lovingly maintained by the National Trust for Scotland, and ⒹGlamis Castle, a 1,000-year-old gem where Shakespeare's complex villain Macbeth, Thane of Glamis, is remembered. Fair-sized Dundee, the handy urban gateway into Angus (and the nation's fourth-largest city), wins the affection of many for its unaffected ways.

The counties of Perthshire and Stirlingshire, which make up the Central Highlands, are sometimes known as Scotland's waist, for here the country is cinched narrow. Yet the area could as easily be called Scotland's heart. Stretching north from Glasgow, this is a magical place of lush woodlands, rolling hills, and deep, shimmering lochs—among them the celebrated ⒜**Loch Lomond,** its "bonnie, bonnie banks" immortalized in a famous lament (composed, it is said, by a Jacobite prisoner in English hands). The countryside surrounding Scotland's largest loch is where William Wallace, or Braveheart, battled the English and where Rob Roy MacGregor entered into legend. Robert the Bruce won Scotland 400 years of independence on a field near Stirling Castle.

CENTRAL HIGHLANDS

⒜ 204

⒝ 208

Ⓒ▷ 205

Ⓓ**Blair Castle** is another must if you love beauty, history, or both. Nearby in Pitlochry stands the tiny Ⓑ**Edradour Distillery,** whose single-malt product is a Scottish icon, just like the Ⓔ**Highland Games,**

Ⓓ▷ 209

which still showcase Scottish grit, brawn, and bravery. Great romantic poet Sir Walter Scott used the landscapes of the Trossachs as the backdrop to his *Lady of the Lake.* Modern-day romantics ride vintage steam trains here. As you chug over the glorious 19th-century Horseshoe Curve Viaduct in Ⓒ**Perthshire,** remember: The open hills are called "forests" in these parts. Though Scotland's big cities are never far away—occasionally you can see Glasgow and Edinburgh—it may feel as if you knew them only in dreams.

Ⓔ▷ 383

ABERDEEN AND THE NORTHEAST

Ⓐ▷232

Though no one keeps track officially, the northeast may have more postcard views than any other corner of Scotland. To the west of handsome Aberdeen, with its ever-so-Scottish Ⓔ**Mercat Cross** and its urban pleasures, so many castles grace the pine- and moor-cloaked valley of the blue River Dee, known as Royal Deeside, that together with the area to the north it is called Castle Country. The sobriquet may be uninspired; the castles, hardly. Enchanted by the setting, Victoria and

C ➤ 240

Albert built a hideaway here, Balmoral, which became a favorite royal home away from home and still is. When Ⓐ**Kildrummy Castle** paid dearly, at the wrecker's hand, for being rebel headquarters in the Jacobite rising of 1715, it had already stood for 500 years. A grand late-Victorian country house hotel nearby will take good care of you. Ten miles on and built for comfort, not combat, turreted Ⓑ**Craigievar Castle** looks younger than its nearly 400 years and always will, thanks to tender care. The same is true of Ⓒ**Pitmedden Garden** to the north, a faithful version of a 17th-century garden, created by the National Trust. A drive west brings you to Ⓓ**Glenfiddich Distillery,** most famous of several Speyside producers and, with its visitor center and show, a kind of a theme park of spirits. The northeast is glorious, from its Grampian heights to some of Scotland's wildest shores, so amid all the man-made diversions, don't miss the scenery (don't worry, no one has yet).

Ⓔ ➤ 222

Ⓓ ➤ 234

17

ARGYLL AND THE ISLES

Divided by the peninsula of Kintyre, the west of Scotland is a scenic treasure—if occasionally a wet one, thanks to weather that rolls in off the North Atlantic. Here, fine castles decorate a lush, rugged landscape poked by slender fingers of sea. ©**Kilchurn Castle,** an early property of the Campbell clan that is now ruined and somehow all the lovelier for it, and ⒟**Dunstaffnage Castle,** a former bastion of the Mac-Dougalls, can be seen on the same day. A good jumping-off point for both is Ⓐ**Inveraray,** an 18th-century planned town with a turreted castle, the seat of the current Campbell duke. Because of the proximity of the Gulf Stream swinging past, flowers odd to such high latitudes do well in these parts, as you can see in the town's Ardkinglas Woodland Gardens, known for their collection of conifers, and nearby Crarae Gardens, where azaleas and magnolias bloom. Perhaps the most distinctive feature of the

Ⓐ▷ 252

© 252

Argyll region are the islands just offshore. The Isle of Arran recalls 1950s seaside holidays. Jura is quiet and empty. The ®**Isle of Mull** stands out for the brightly painted houses in Tobermory, its capital. ©**Islay** may have more distilleries per capita than any comparable area on earth, each producing its own subtle, peaty whisky. Iona was a burial ground for kings and clan chiefs long before missionary monks arrived in A.D. 563; today it's home to a religious retreat. Here and elsewhere on this coast, Scotland is at its rural best.

Ⓓ 250

Ⓔ 257

AROUND
THE GREAT GLEN

Rugged beauty and wide open spaces define the Great Glen—a rift valley along which the northern end of Scotland appears to be sliding southwestward and off the rest of the country by millimeters per millennium. Laced with rivers and streams, ringed by Scotland's tallest mountains, including the ©**Cairngorms,** and containing Scotland's greatest lochs, this geological tear in the southern Highlands is grand and dramatic—a fitting backdrop for red deer, golden eagles, and shaggy Highland cattle alike. The best-known beast in these parts, however, is the Loch Ness monster, and the town of Drumnadrochit is base

camp for Nessie watchers. (It's fun watching *them*.) You have a far better chance of seeing something ancient at ruined Ⓑ**Urquhart Castle** nearby, and a far better chance of seeing something surprising at the Cairngorms Reindeer Centre. The magnificent loch should be reward enough. Get to it from tourist-friendly Inverness, but first honor Culloden Moor, in 1646 the site of the last land battle fought on British soil—and one of the bloodiest in the

Ⓓ 280

history of war. Fort William, at the Glen's western end, makes a good hub for exploring the region—and for climbing 4,406-foot Ben Nevis, Britain's tallest peak. To the north, in Arisaig, you can catch a boat to the diminutive Small Isles, among them Ⓐ**Muck,** Ⓓ**Canna,** and Ⓔ**Eigg,** where you can slip into the gentle rhythms of island life. Alternatively, from Arisaig, you might take a steam train through wild country to Glenfinnan, where Bonnie Prince Charlie's backers forged their cause, or just go trekking—and let the Great Glen's grandeur renew you.

Ⓔ 280

You haven't seen Scotland until you've visited the Northern Highlands. The lore of the clans, the echoes of Bonnie Prince Charlie, the wildness of the landscape, the big skies, the immensity of the rolling moors —Scotland seems richer here, as if captured in concentrated form. Nature is at its most miraculous. At the limestone confection called Ⓐ**Smoo Cave**, amid tropical plantings at

THE NORTHERN HIGHLANDS

Ⓒ**Inverewe Gardens,** on a Caribbean-looking beach on the Ⓕ**Isle of Harris,** or anywhere on the Ⓓ**Isle of Skye,** you may be excused for thinking you're in Brigadoon. Nor is the spell broken at a castle

that's often called Scotland's most perfect, Ⓔ**Eilean Donan Castle,** set near the Kyle of Lochalsh and accessible via a stone footbridge. On Skye, across the narrow water, soft mists drape haunting mountains; June sunsets last half the night. It's unforgettable. Quite the opposite, for many, are thoughts of the duke of Sutherland, who built Ⓑ**Dunrobin Castle**—forever linked to a man who brutalized the native Gaels. Find happier thoughts elsewhere in the Northern Highlands. The opportunities are plentiful.

THE NORTHERN ISLES

Ⓐ 324

Travelers who like the untrodden path, archaeology buffs, and poetic souls for whom bleak is beautiful are drawn north in Scotland to the Orkney and Shetland Islands. Stone circles and other antiquities recall centuries of settlement in the Orkneys. Eight centuries after Vikings looted Ⓐ**Maes Howe,** a 4,500-year-old burial mound on Mainland, the principal island, their Norse graffiti is a treasure in its own right. A mile away, good for a brisk walk, 36 of the original 60 megaliths that

Ⓑ 324

form the Ⓑ**Ring of Brogar** still stand, even more powerful when aswirl in fog. The Neolithic village of Skara Brae, complete with stone beds, and the Unstan Chambered Tomb are 5,000 years old; the Norman Ⓓ**St. Magnus Cathedral,** in the town of Kirkwall, is a toddler by comparison, built between 1137 and 1200. The Shetland Islands have ancient treasures, too, Ⓒ**Jarlshof** prime among them. Thousands of years of continuous human settlement, from Stone Age to Norse, have been excavated here. Reflecting on the hard lives that were lived in this place, you will be moved. But the ancient stones don't make the Northern Isles musty. Lodging and dining are commendable; the seafood is superb. Anglers and divers love it here; shoppers may love it even more—for the local crafts and jewelry on Orkney, and for Shetland's handmade knitwear and woolens. Don your new wool sweater, throw on some fine Celtic gewgaws for luck, and you may preen like a puffin.

Ⓓ 326

25

GREAT ITINERARIES

A Heritage in Stone

7 to 10 days

Stone is a distinctive element of the Scottish landscape. On this tour you see it in many forms, on 18th-century Edinburgh streetscapes and in Aberdeen castles, in rural Angus and on Orkney in prehistoric monuments, some of Europe's finest. Distilleries flourish, too: the stony soil makes for clear, mineral-rich water that is the basis for the nation's distinctive whiskies.

SOUTH OF ABERDEEN

2 or 3 days. Head toward Dundee to spectacular 17th-century ⒶGlamis Castle, the Queen Mother's childhood home. Heading north you'll see the remarkable Aberlemno sculptured stones on your way to Brechin, a market town whose cathedral is filled with antiquities. Stonehaven is the site of clifftop Dunnottar Castle. Crathes Castle, inland, has a classic tower and a garden of clipped yews. The south Deeside road, the B976 west of Banchory, is a much quieter alternative to the busier A93 heading west toward Balmoral Castle, a Victorian fantasy designed by Prince Albert and now a beloved retreat of Queen Elizabeth II. From there go north at Dinnet and drive west through Strathdon. Nearby are the ruined 13th-century Kildrummy Castle and its gardens, and to the north-

east, across rich farmland, Oyne and the fascinating Archaeolink Prehistory Park. En route to Aberdeen, note the Maiden Stone and the mysterious Easter Aquhorthies stone circle just off the A96.
☞ *Dundee and Angus in Chapter 5 and Royal Deeside in Chapter 7.*

ORKNEY

3 or 4 days. From Aberdeen, take the eight-hour ferry ride north to Stromness on Mainland ⒸOrkney. North of town are reminders of the areas long history, including the huge Maes Howe Burial Mound (circa 2500 BC) and Ring of Brodgar, with three dozen immense standing stones. Nearby Skara Brae is a Neolithic village of stone houses first occupied three millennia ago; theyre complete with stone beds, cupboards, and fireplaces. The Brough of Birsay, the ruined Earl's Palace, and the Gurness Brough, an Iron Age tower, are on your way as you circle back to Kirkwall, which has a magnificent cathedral and a distillery. To the south, causeways link Orkney to the island of South Ronaldsay, site of the 5,000-year-old Tomb of the Eagles. From Stromness, ferry back to the mainland town of Scrabster, past the magnificent cliffs of Hoy.
☞ *Around Orkney in Chapter 11.*

SOUTH TO EDINBURGH

2 or 3 days. From Scrabster drive south toward Wick, but follow signs for the Grey Cairns of Camster, two Neolithic chambered burial cairns. Proceed south to the behemoth Dunrobin Castle just south of unassuming Golspie, then on to Inverness. East of town, not far from the infamous battlefield at ⒷCulloden Moor, are the well-preserved early Bronze Age Clava Cairns, a burial complex, and Cawdor Castle, associated with Shakespeare's *Macbeth*. Travel south via Grantown-on-Spey over wild moorland to the main Deeside route close to the holiday resort of Ballater, where the buildings are all silver-gray stone. To the west, beyond 19th-century Balmoral Castle, is walled 17th-century Braemar Castle. Drive south from Braemar over the highest main road in Britain and down to Blairgowrie. Continue to Perth and Scone Palace, where early Scottish kings were crowned. Then it's back to Edinburgh.
☞ *The Northern Highlands in Chapter 10, Speyside and Loch Ness in Chapter 9, Royal Deeside and Castle Country in Chapter 7, Perthshire in Chapter 6.*

Ⓐ 183

Loch Linnhe, A828, A82, Craignure, Mull, Kilchurn Castle, A85, Oban, Iona, Fionnphort, 36 mi., A849, Firth of Lorn, Loch Awe, 96 mi., Inverary, A83, Tarbet, ARGYLE, 136 mi., Colonsay, Jura, Islay, Kintyre, Arran, Firth of Clyde

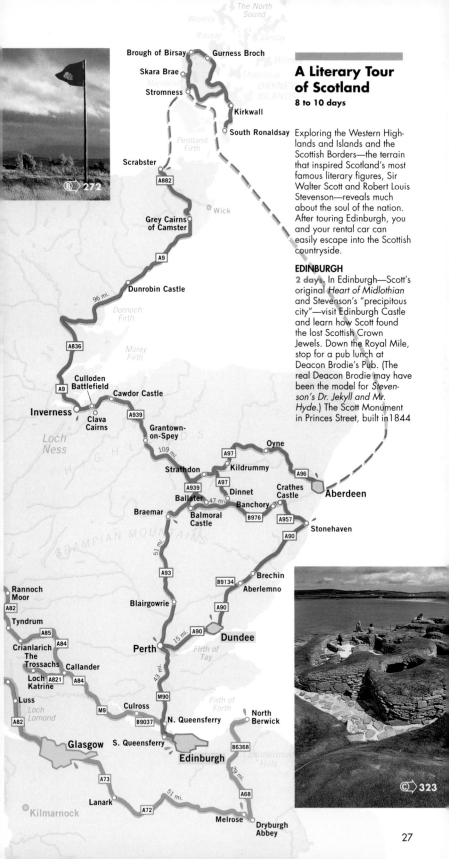

Map labels

The North Sound
Westray
Rousay
Stronsay
Sanday
ORKNEY ISLANDS
Shapinsay
Mainland

Brough of Birsay
Gurness Broch
Skara Brae
Stromness
Kirkwall
South Ronaldsay

Pentland Firth

Scrabster

B ⟩ 272

A882

Wick

Grey Cairns of Camster

A9

96 mi.

Dornoch Firth

Dunrobin Castle

A836

Moray Firth

Culloden Battlefield
A9
Inverness
Cawdor Castle
A939
Clava Cairns
Grantown-on-Spey
Loch Ness
HIGHLANDS

109 mi.

Oyne
A97
Kildrummy
Strathdon
A97
Dinnet
A939
Ballater
Crathes Castle
Braemar
Banchory
Balmoral Castle
B976
Aberdeen
A96
A957
Stonehaven
47 mi.
A90

GRAMPIAN MOUNTAINS

51 mi.

A93

Brechin
B9134
Aberlemno
Blairgowrie
A90

15 mi.
A90
Dundee
Perth
Firth of Tay
43 mi.

Rannoch Moor
A82
Tyndrum
A85
Crianlarich
A84
The Trossachs
Callander
Loch Katrine
A821
A84
Luss
Loch Lomond
A82

M90
Culross
M9
B9037
N. Queensferry
North Berwick
S. Queensferry
Glasgow
Firth of Forth
Edinburgh
B6368

A73
Lammermuir Hills
3 mi.
Lanark
A72
51 mi.
A68
Kilmarnock
Melrose
Dryburgh Abbey

Article

A Literary Tour of Scotland
8 to 10 days

Exploring the Western Highlands and Islands and the Scottish Borders—the terrain that inspired Scotland's most famous literary figures, Sir Walter Scott and Robert Louis Stevenson—reveals much about the soul of the nation. After touring Edinburgh, you and your rental car can easily escape into the Scottish countryside.

EDINBURGH

2 days. In Edinburgh—Scott's original *Heart of Midlothian* and Stevenson's "precipitous city"—visit Edinburgh Castle and learn how Scott found the lost Scottish Crown Jewels. Down the Royal Mile, stop for a pub lunch at Deacon Brodie's Pub. (The real Deacon Brodie may have been the model for *Stevenson's Dr. Jekyll and Mr. Hyde.*) The Scott Monument in Princes Street, built in 1844

C ⟩ 323

27

to commemorate the author, is an Edinburgh landmark. A superb view of the city is the reward for the steep climb to the top. In the New Town, pass by 17 Heriot Row, the Stevenson family home, and tour the Palace of Holyroodhouse, the Queen's official residence in Scotland and scene of the triumphant visit by George IV in 1822, with Sir Walter Scott in charge of the publicity.
☞ *Exploring Edinburgh and the Lothians in Chapter 2.*

INTO THE TROSSACHS

2 days. Drive to Queensferry for magnificent views of the bridge over the Firth of Forth, and visit the 16th-century Hawes Inn, which put in an appearance in Stevenson's *Kidnapped.* To the west is 18th-century Culross, another setting from *Kidnapped.* At Callander you are near the Trossachs. Scott's popular *The Lady of the Lake,* published in 1810, put the place firmly on the map. *Rob Roy,* on the other hand, was set in countryside you can identify from cruises aboard the steam-powered SS *Sir Walter*

Scott, which has sailed from the Trossachs Pier on Loch Katrine for a century. Spend a couple of hours enjoying the peaceful scenery from the deck. To the north, past Crianlarich and Tyndrum, you cross Rannoch Moor. In Stevenson's *Kidnapped,* redcoats pursued David Balfour and Alan Breck here, amid dramatic highland scenery.
☞ *The Trossachs and Loch Lomond in Chapter 6.*

AROUND ARGYLL

2 to 3 days. From Oban, the busy ferry port, cross over to the Isle of Mull. Near Fionnphort, to the southwest, is an area of Mull described in *Kidnapped.* The tiny Isle of Iona, accessible via ferry, was the burial place of Scottish kings in ancient times. Back on the mainland, en route to the head of Loch Awe, you'll pass ruined Kilchurn Castle. The drive south passes through beautiful countryside en route to the 18th-century planned town of Inveraray.
☞ *Around Argyll and Iona and the Isle of Mull in Chapter 8.*

MELROSE AND EAST LOTHIAN

2 to 3 days. Passing through Glasgow and Lanark, visit the market town of Melrose, epicenter of Scott Country. Here you will find the famous ruined Ⓔabbey that was the setting for Scott's *The Lay of the Last Minstrel,* and the poet's country home, Ⓓ Abbotsford House. Nearby Scott's View offers a panorama of the River Tweed and Eildon Hills. Dryburgh Abbey is also a must; the author is buried in this atmospheric ruin. The Lammermuir Hills extend north, into East Lothian, and the countryside east of Edinburgh is sometimes known as the Garden of Scotland. Stevenson set his novel *Catriona* along the coast here, around the small resort of North Berwick.
☞ *Side Trips from Glasgow in Chapter 3, the Borders in Chapter 4, and Side Trips from Edinburgh in Chapter 2.*

Island-Hopping on the Western Seaboard

7 to 9 days

This island-hopping tour takes in landfalls that are accessible even if you start your trip in Glasgow and don't have time to go farther north. Here distilleries and beaches are set amid mountain scenery, and you can experience the rhythm of island life.

Ⓔ 148

Culross
B9037 N. Queensferry
S. Queensferry
Edinburgh
B6368
29 mi.
51 mi.
A68
A72
Melrose Dryburgh Abbey
Firth of Forth
North Berwick
Lammermuir Hills
Berwick-upon-Tweed
R. Tweed

ARRAN

2 or 3 days. In the port of Ardrossan catch the car ferry to Brodick. The surrounding Isle of Arran is the biggest island in the Clyde, and there's plenty to see. A mile north of the ferry pier is red-sandstone Brodick Castle, with beautiful interiors and gardens that are astonishingly yellow when rhododendrons bloom, in late spring and early summer. The road that circles the island, the String, leads to a beach and palm trees at the holiday resort of Lamlash—the climate is that mild—and on to Blackwaterfoot and the Machrie Moor Stone Circle, where there are mysterious red monoliths. The area is full of hut circles, chambered cairns, and other prehistoric sites. On Arran's northern tip is Lochranza, site of Scotland's newest distillery, as well as ruined Lochranza Castle. Also on the island is Goatfell, which at 2,866 ft is the highest mountain on Arran. Allow five hours to climb it.
☞ *Arran in Chapter 8.*

KINTYRE PENINSULA, ISLAY, JURA

3 or 4 days. From Lochranza take the ferry to Claonaig on the Kintyre Peninsula. The B842 down the eastern shore of the peninsula is the quieter way to Campbeltown, where there is a heritage center and museum. The main A83 heads back to Tayinloan. Take a 20-minute ferry ride from here to the balmy Island of Gigha. The quiet roads make for great biking, and rentals are available. There are lovely beaches, and tender shrubs flourish in the gardens at Achamore. Back in Tayinloan head north to Kennacraig, where you can catch a ferry to Port Ellen on the unspoiled Isle of Islay. Beaches here are deserted, especially at Machir Bay on the west coast. You'll find good bird-watching at the reserve at Loch Gruinart: rare red-legged, red-beaked crows known as choughs can be found here. And there are excellent golf courses, photogenic villages such as Port Charlotte, and, most famously, distilleries that

make the peaty local malt whisky. Laphroaig and Lagavulin are near Port Ellen, Bowmore is in the center of the island, and Bunnahabhain and Caol Ila are in the east, at Port Askaig.
A short ferry crossing at Port Askaig takes you to mountainous Jura, a good place for experienced walkers. Novelist George Orwell wrote *1984* while he lived on this island, in the late 1940s. The single good road takes you north past the impressive Jura House Garden and on to Craighouse, the main village, where there is a hotel and a distillery. You can catch a ferry back to Kennacraig from Port Askaig or Port Ellen.
☞ *Argyll and Islay in Chapter 8.*

INVERARY AND LOCH LOMOND

2 days. From Kennacraig return to Glasgow via Lochgilphead and Inveraray, an 18th-century town on the shores of Loch Fyne. In the Loch Fyne Oyster Bar you can

Ⓕ 204

buy your fill to take out or eat the briny delicacies on the spot. A drive through Glen Croe reveals the magnificent mountains near Tarbet at the head of Ⓕ Loch Lomond, the largest lake in Scotland in terms of surface area. There are great views of the loch from the A82 south, and the village of Luss, a half hour from Glasgow, makes a scenic stop.
☞ *Around Argyll in Chapter 8 and the Trossachs and Loch Lomond in Chapter 6.*

FODOR'S
CHOICE

Even with so many special places in Scotland, Fodor's writers and editors have their favorites. Here are a few that stand out.

BUILDINGS AND MONUMENTS

Ⓓ **Cawdor Castle, Nairn (Great Glen).** Shakespeare's *Macbeth* was Thane of Cawdor, but this 14th-century castle exudes 600 years of real, not fictional, history. ☞ p. 275

Georgian House, Edinburgh. In New Town's Charlotte Square, this house is decorated in period style to demonstrate the lifestyle of an affluent 18th-century family. ☞ p. 52

Marischal College, Aberdeen. This ornate facade, built in 1891, is part of the second-largest granite building in the world. ☞ p. 222

Ⓘ **Calanais Standing Stones, Lewis (Northern Highlands).** This series of monoliths is considered second only to Stonehenge, in England, and is thought to have been used for astronomical observations. ☞ p. 310

Torosay Castle, Isle of Mull (Argyll and the Isles). At one of Mull's best-known castles, you'll find a friendly air, and you'll have the run of the place. ☞ p. 261

Ⓐ **Traquair House, near Walkerburn (Borders).** This is said to be the oldest continually occupied house in Scotland. Be sure to sample the ale brewed on-site in an 18th-century brewhouse. ☞ p. 152

DINING

Ⓔ **Auchterarder House, Auchterarder (Central Highlands).** This dining room, filled with sparkling glassware, is attached to a fine hotel and serves excellent cuisine. ££££ ☞ p. 211

Ⓙ **Witchery by the Castle, Edinburgh.** Pierce Brosnan was the most recent star to be spotted at this spooky haunt, which comes complete with flickering candlelight. The lugubrious, cavernous interior is festooned with cauldrons and broomsticks—but there's nothing spooky about the Scottish-accented French food. ££££ ☞ p. 55

Old Monastery, Buckie (Aberdeen). The setting is a Victorian former religious establishment, and the theme is ever present, from the Cloisters bar to the Chapel restaurant. Local specialties include fresh river fish and Aberdeen Angus beef. £££–££££ ☞ p. 239

Ⓑ **Yes, Glasgow.** This stylish restaurant belies its basement location, with careful lighting and mirrors setting off the dramatic red, purple, and cream color scheme. Try the Surprise Menu: an eclectic four-course selection reflecting the best fresh produce available that day. ££–£££ ☞ p. 111

The Cellar, Anstruther (Fife). That this place is popular with locals is a good sign. Come here for top-quality fish, beef, and lamb, cooked in a simple, straightforward fashion. ££ ☞ p. 175

LODGING

Channings, Edinburgh. This elegant hotel comprises five Edwardian terraced houses, some with wonderful views of Fife. ££££ ☞ p. 65

Ⓗ **Cringletie House, Peebles (Borders).** Turrets and crow-step gables lend a Scottish baronial style to this hotel, whose accommodations are simple and comfortable; the food is its major achievement. ££££ ☞ p. 152

Kildrummy Castle Hotel, Kildrummy (Aberdeen and the Northeast). The castle offers a peaceful setting for attentive service and award-winning cuisine. ££££ ☞ p. 233

Ⓒ **Clifton House, Nairn (Great Glen).** Original works of art, antique furnishings, regular musical and theatrical performances, and famed cuisine make this hotel unique. £££ ☞ p. 275

Talisker House, Skye (Northern Highlands). This secluded country mansion offers spacious bedrooms with elegant furnishings, excellent cuisine, and views seaward. ££ ☞ p. 307

22 Murrayfield Gardens, Edinburgh. An exceptionally friendly and comfortable B&B in a well-heeled suburb has as its hosts a couple who will be delighted to help you get the most out of your visit. ££ ☞ p. 66

MUSEUMS

Auchindrain Museum, near Inveraray (Argyll). Here, an 18th-century communal tenancy farm has been restored to illustrate early farming life in the Highlands. ☞ p. 253

Ⓖ **Burrell Collection, Glasgow.** Pollock County Park is the setting for one of Scotland's finest art collections, with exhibits ranging from Egyptian, Greek, and Roman artifacts to stained glass and French Impressionist paintings. ☞ p. 107

Carnegie Birthplace Museum, Dunfermline (Edinburgh and the Lothians). The birthplace of Andrew Carnegie tells his life story. ☞ p. 80

Ⓕ **Paisley Museum and Art Gallery, Paisley (Glasgow).** A town in the Glasgow suburbs is home to this museum, which tells the story of the woolen Paisley shawl and describes the famous Paisley pattern and weaving techniques. ☞ p. 124

Scottish Fisheries Museum, Anstruther (Fife). This museum illustrates the life of Scottish fishermen through documents, artifacts, paintings, and quayside floating exhibits. ☞ p. 175

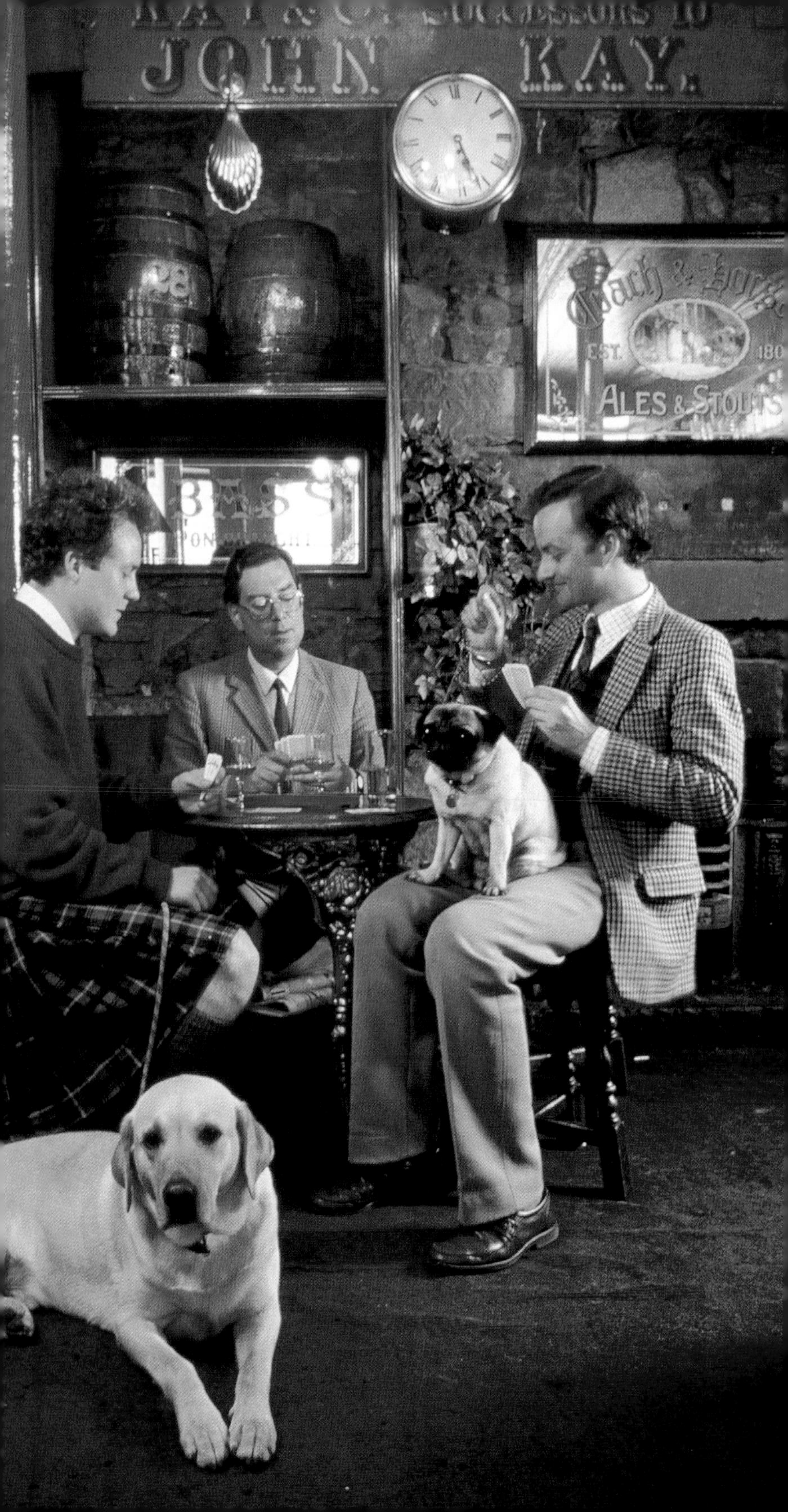
JOHN KAY.
ALES & STOUTS

1 EDINBURGH AND THE LOTHIANS

Edinburgh is to London as poetry is to prose, as Charlotte Brontë once wrote. One of the world's stateliest cities and proudest capitals, it is built—like Rome—on seven hills, making the perfect setting for the ancient pageant of history. Explore its streets—peopled by the spirits of Mary, Queen of Scots, Sir Walter Scott, and Robert Louis Stevenson—marvel at brooding Edinburgh Castle, then pay your respects to the "wur-r-rld's best" terrier, Greyfriars Bobby. Come evening, enjoy candlelit restaurants or a folk *ceilidh*. And remember—you're not worth your porridge until you've climbed Arthur's Seat.

By Gilbert
Summers

Updated by
Stewart
Hennessey

I
N A SKYLINE OF SHEER DRAMA, EDINBURGH CASTLE watches over
Scotland's capital city, frowning down on Princes Street, now the main
downtown shopping area, as if disapproving of its modern razzmatazz.
Its ramparts still echo with gunfire each day when the traditional one
o'clock gun booms out over the city, startling unwary shoppers. But nearly
everywhere in Edinburgh (the *burgh* is always pronounced *burra* in Scots)
there are spectacular buildings, whose Doric, Ionic, and Corinthian pillars add touches of neoclassical grandeur to the largely Presbyterian backdrop. The most notable examples are perched amid the greenery of Calton
Hill, which overlooks the city center from the east.

Large gardens and greenery are a strong feature in central Edinburgh,
where the council is one of the most stridently conservationist in Europe.
Conspicuous from Princes Street is Arthur's Seat, a mountain of bright
green and yellow furze rearing up behind the spires of the Old Town.
This child-size mountain jutting 800 ft above its surroundings has steep
slopes and little crags, like a miniature Highlands set down in the middle of the busy city. Appropriately, these theatrical elements give a unique
identity to Edinburgh's skyline—after all, the city has been a stage that
has seen its fair share of romance, violence, tragedy, and triumph.

In fact, the curtain is currently going up on a spectacular new act, as
nearly 300 years after the Union of Parliaments, Edinburgh is once again
the seat of a Scottish parliament. Of course, the first-time visitor to Scotland may be surprised that the country still has a capital city, perhaps
believing the seat of government was drained of its resources and
power after the union with England in 1707—far from it. The Union
of Parliaments brought with it a set of political partnerships—such as
separate legal, ecclesiastical, and educational systems—which Edinburgh
assimilated and integrated with its own surviving institutions.

But now Scotland is on the verge of having significantly more control
over its government than at any time since 1707. The first 129 Members of the Scottish Parliament (MSPs) were elected on May 6, 1999,
and have wide-ranging powers in Scotland over education, health,
housing, transport, training, economic development, the environment,
and agriculture (foreign policy, defense and economic policy remain
with the U.K. government at Westminster, London). The parliament
now sits in temporary accommodations at the Assembly Hall of the
Church of Scotland, on the Mound, but in 2002 will move into a brand-
new structure, designed by Spanish architect Enric Miralles, at the foot
of the Royal Mile, adjacent to the Palace of Holyroodhouse.

Towering above it, as nearly everywhere throughout the city, will be
Edinburgh Castle, the symbolic heart of the country. Perhaps not surprisingly, this structure was actually built over the plug of an ancient
volcano. Many thousands of years ago, an eastward-grinding glacier
encountered the tough basalt core of the volcano and swept around
the core, scouring steep cliffs and leaving a trail of matter, like the tail
of a comet. This material formed a ramp gently leading down from
the rocky summit. On this *crag* and *tail*—now the setting for the city
castle—would grow Edinburgh.

The lands that rolled down to the sea were for centuries open country,
sitting between Castle Rock and the tiny community clustered by the shore
that grew into Leith, Edinburgh's seaport. By the 12th century Edinburgh
had become a walled town, still perched on the hill. Its shape was becoming clearer: like a fish with its head at the castle, its backbone running down the ridge, and its ribs leading briefly off on either side. The
backbone gradually became the continuous thoroughfare now known

as the Royal Mile, and the ribs became the closes (alleyways), some still surviving, that were the scene of many historic incidents.

By the early 15th century Edinburgh had become the undisputed capital of Scotland. The bitter defeat of Scotland at Flodden in 1513, when Scotland aligned itself with France against England, caused a new defensive city wall to be built. Though the castle escaped destruction, the city was burned by the English earl of Hertford under orders from King Henry VIII (1491–1547) of England. By 1561, when Mary, Queen of Scots (1542–87), returned from France already widowed, the guest house of the Abbey of Holyrood had grown to become the Palace of Holyroodhouse. Mary's legacy to the city included the destruction of most of the earliest buildings of Edinburgh Castle, held by her supporters after she was forced to flee her homeland.

In the trying decades after the union with England in 1707, many influential Scots, both in Edinburgh and elsewhere, went through an identity crisis, but out of the 18th-century difficulties grew the Scottish Enlightenment, during which educated Scots made great strides in medicine, economics, and science.

Changes, too, came to the cityscape itself. By the mid-18th century it had become the custom for wealthy Scottish landowners to spend the winter in the Old Town of Edinburgh, in town houses huddled between the high castle rock and the Royal Palace below. In the tall, crowded buildings of old Edinburgh, the well-to-do tended to have their rooms on the middle floors, while the "lower orders" occupied dwellings on the top and ground floors. Uniquely cross-fertilized in the coffeehouses and taverns, intellectual notions flourished among a people determined to remain Scottish despite their parliament having voted to dissolve itself. One result was a campaign to expand and beautify the city, to give it a look worthy of its future nickname, the Athens of the North. Thus was the New Town of Edinburgh built, whose broad streets and gracious buildings created a harmony that even today's throbbing traffic cannot obscure.

Today's Edinburgh is the second most important financial center in the United Kingdom, one of many reasons its residents come from all over Britain. Not the least of these reasons is the city's regularly being ranked near the top in surveys measuring "quality of life"; thus New Town apartments on fashionable streets sell for considerable sums. In some senses the city is showy and materialistic, but Edinburgh still supports learned societies, some of which have their roots in the Scottish Enlightenment: the Royal Society of Edinburgh, for example, established in 1783 "for the advancement of learning and useful knowledge," is still an important forum for interdisciplinary activities, both in Edinburgh and in Scotland as a whole.

Hand in hand with the city's academic and scientific life is a rich cultural force, with the Edinburgh International Festival attracting lovers of all the arts. Running for three weeks from mid-August into September, this is the biggest arts festival in the world. It attracts talent from all parts of the globe: first-tier orchestras and conductors, international dance troupes and ballet companies, and leading opera and theater performers.

But even as Edinburgh enters the 21st century, the guardian castle remains the focal point of the city and its venerable history. Princes Street—a master stroke in city planning—was built up only on one side, allowing magnificent views of the great rock on which the fortress stands. Turn a corner off, say, George Street, however, and you will see not an endless cityscape, but the blue sea and a patchwork of fields. This is the county of Fife, beyond the inlet of the North Sea called the Firth of Forth—a reminder, like the mountains to the northwest, which can be glimpsed from Edinburgh's highest points, that the rest of Scotland lies within easy reach.

Pleasures and Pastimes

Dining

Although Edinburgh's restaurants now offer a sophisticated, diverse mix of exotic and foreign cuisines, from Mexican to Thai, from Chinese to Greek and Russian, perhaps the most exotic of all is genuine Scottish cuisine. When in Edinburgh, look out for the traditional and nouvelle versions of the classic favorites, such as marvelous salmon and venison, and of course the spicy haggis, usually served with *neeps and tatties* (mashed turnips and potatoes).

Other culinary delights await—including newer-than-now variations on old Scottish dishes like *partan bree* (a rich crab soup), and Loch Fyne herring. Remember that Scotland is traditionally the "land o' cakes," so be sure to enjoy some of those delicious buns, pancakes, scones, and biscuits for breakfast or high tea.

Not so long ago the standards of cooking and service too often betrayed that puritanical Scottish conviction that enjoying yourself is a sin. Today Scottish game and seafood are often presented with great flair; all the best restaurants deal directly with local boats and producers, so freshness is guaranteed. After the feast, other delicacies await: Handmade chocolates, often with whisky or Drambuie fillings, and the traditional "petticoat tail" shortbread are good choices, or try some of the boiled sweets in jars, such as Edinburgh rock. Oatmeal, local cheeses, and even malt whisky (turning up in any course) amplify the Scottish dimension. And speaking of whisky, try a "wee dram" of a single malt—the pale, unblended spirit—when you visit Scotland's capital.

The Great Outdoors

Edinburgh is a fairly compact, if hilly, city, and biking is a good way to get around, though careful route planning may be needed to avoid traffic. The East Lothian countryside, with its miles of twisting roads and light traffic, is within cycling distance of the city. You won't have to go far afield for golf—there are about 30 courses within or close to the city (not including the easily accessible East Lothian courses), many of which welcome visitors (☞ Chapter 11).

Lodging

From grand hotel suites done up in tartan fabrics to personal-touch B&Bs, Edinburgh is splendidly served by a wide variety of guest accommodations. Some of the best are in lovely traditional Georgian or Victorian properties, some of which are even in the New Town, only a few minutes from downtown. There are also a number of upscale hotels in the downtown area, each with an international flavor.

Nightlife and the Arts

Edinburgh's nightlife is quite varied and includes dinner dances, discos, Scottish musical evenings, and *ceilidhs* (a mix of country dancing, music, and song; pronounced *kay*-lees). Jazz and folk music in general are wide-ranging. Edinburgh is world renowned for its flagship arts event, the Edinburgh International Festival, and there is no escaping a theater buzz if you visit the city from August to early September. The annual festival has attracted all sorts of international performers since its inception in 1947. Even more obvious to the casual stroller during this time is the refreshingly irreverent Edinburgh Festival Fringe, unruly child of the official festival, which spills out of halls and theaters and onto the streets all over town. Film and book festivals are also regulars on the calendar. At other times throughout the year, professional and amateur groups alike offer a range of cultural performances appropriate to a capital city, even if Edinburgh's neighbor and rival city, Glasgow, has the reputation of being more lively.

Shopping

To make the most of shopping in Edinburgh, you will need at least two days, in part because the city's most interesting shops are scattered among several districts. Edinburgh's downtown has the usual chain stores, lined up shoulder to shoulder and offering identical goods. But within a few yards, along some of the side streets, you'll find shops offering more exclusive wares, such as designer clothing, unique craft items, 18th-century silverware, and wild-caught, smoked Scottish salmon.

As the capital city and an important tourist center, Edinburgh features a cross section of Scottish specialties, such as tartans and tweeds, rather than products peculiar to the Edinburgh area. Once you venture into Edinburgh's "villages"—perhaps Stockbridge, Bruntsfield, Morningside, or even the Old Town itself—you will find many unusual stores specializing in single items, such as antique clocks or designer knitwear using the finest Scottish wool or cashmere. In many cases the goods sold in these stores are unavailable elsewhere in Scotland.

If you are interested in antiques, Edinburgh is a fruitful hunting ground. Scotland has a strong tradition of distinctive furniture makers, silversmiths, and artists; top-quality examples of their work can still be found, but at a price. Most reputable dealers are able to arrange transport abroad for your purchases if you buy something too bulky to fit into your luggage.

EXPLORING EDINBURGH AND THE LOTHIANS

The Old Town, which bears a great measure of symbolic weight as the "heart of Scotland's capital," is a boon for lovers of atmosphere and history. In contrast, if you appreciate the unique architectural heritage of Edinburgh's Enlightenment, then the New Town's for you. If you belong in both categories, don't worry—the Old and the New Towns are only yards apart. The Princes Street Gardens roughly divide Edinburgh into two areas: the winding, congested streets of Old Town, to the south, and the orderly, Georgian architecture of New Town, to the north. Princes Street runs east–west along the north edge of the Princes Street Gardens. Explore the main thoroughfares but also don't forget to get lost among the tiny *wynds* and *closes* (old medieval alleys that connect the winding streets). Away from Edinburgh's central core, Victorian expansion and urban sprawl have greatly increased the city's dimensions, but Edinburgh, as cities go, is still compact, and much of the city center can be covered on foot.

The hills, green fields, beaches, and historic houses and castles in the countryside outside Edinburgh—Midlothian, West Lothian, and East Lothian, collectively called the Lothians—can be reached quickly by bus or car, a welcome escape from the festival crush at the height of summer.

Numbers in the text correspond to numbers in the margin and on the Exploring Edinburgh, West Lothian and the Forth Valley, and Midlothian and East Lothian maps.

Great Itineraries

Edinburgh's spectacular setting usually means a good first impression. You can be there for a day and think you know the place, as even a cursory bus tour will enable you to grasp the layout of the castle, Royal Mile, Old Town, New Town, and so on. However, if your taste is more for leisurely strolling through the nooks and crannies of the Old Town closes, then allow three or four days for exploring.

IF YOU HAVE 2 DAYS

To start off, make your way to Edinburgh Castle—not just the battlements—and spend some time there, if only to revel in its sense of history. Certainly, take a city bus tour as well. Your list of must-sees should also include the National Gallery of Scotland and, unless it is winter, the Georgian House for an idea of life in the New Town.

IF YOU HAVE 5 DAYS

Five days allow plenty of time for Old Town exploration, including the important museums of Huntly House and the People's Story (in the Canongate Tolbooth), and for a walk around the New Town, with its Scottish National Portrait Gallery and the Scottish National Gallery of Modern Art, both well worth an hour or two. You should also have plenty of time for shopping, not only in areas close to the city center, such as Rose Street and Victoria Street, but also in some of the less touristy areas, like Bruntsfield. Make a foray to Leith to visit the former royal yacht *Britannia;* then check out Leith's array of eating places. You could also get out of town: hop on a bus out to Midlothian to see the stunning stone carving in Rosslyn Chapel, at Roslin, and visit the Edinburgh Crystal Visitor Centre, at Penicuik, for crystal bargains. Consider spending another half day traveling out to South Queensferry to admire the Forth road and rail bridges; then visit palatial Hopetoun House, with its wealth of portraits and fine furniture.

IF YOU HAVE 8 DAYS

In eight days, in addition to a thorough exploration of Edinburgh's Old and New towns, museums, and galleries and a shopping trip or two, you will not only have time to explore Leith, Roslin, and South Queensferry but will also be able to take a couple of side trips from the city. Allow at least a day for each trip so you have time to enjoy stately homes, such as Dalmeny House for its Rothschild collection of sumptuous French furniture; a historic ruin such as Linlithgow Palace, with its Mary, Queen of Scots, connection; or the magnificently sited Castle Campbell. At Gullane, with its splendid East Lothian beach, you can walk in the footsteps of Robert Louis Stevenson. Andrew Carnegie's Birthplace Museum, at Dunfermline; Dunbar, with its John Muir Country Park; or the delightful market town of Haddington, with the nearby Lennoxlove House (which also boasts Mary, Queen of Scots, associations) are other gems beyond the city limits. If it is festival time, however, you can probably take in shows, concerts, and exhibitions for eight solid days and hardly stray from the city center.

Old Town

Eastward of Edinburgh Castle, the historic castle ramp becomes the street known as the Royal Mile, the backbone of the Old Town, leading from the castle down to the Palace of Holyroodhouse. The Mile, as it is called, is actually made up of one thoroughfare that bears, in consecutive sequence, different names—the Esplanade, Castle Hill, Lawnmarket, Parliament Square, High Street, and Canongate. The streets and passages winding into their tenements or "lands" and crammed onto the ridge back of the Mile really *were* Edinburgh until the 18th century saw expansions to the south and north. Everybody lived here, the richer folk on the lower floors of houses, with less well-to-do families on the upper floors—the higher up, the poorer. Time and progress (of a sort) have swept away some of the narrow closes (alleyways) and tall tenements of the Old Town, but enough survive for you to be able to imagine the original profile of Scotland's capital, and there is now refurbishment under way to make many of these surviving closes more inviting to explore. Sir Walter Scott (1771–1832), David Hume (1711–76), the painter Allan Ramsay (1713–84), and many other well-known names are associated with the Old Town. But perhaps three are more famous than any others—John Knox (1513–72); Mary, Queen of Scots (1542–87); and Prince Charles Edward Stuart (1720–88).

A Good Walk

A perfect place to begin your exploration of the Old Town is **Edinburgh Castle** ①. After exploring its extensive complex of buildings and admiring the armchair-worthy view from the battlements, set off down the first part of Royal Mile, stopping en route at your choice of museums and other interesting ports of call: To the left of **Castlehill** ②, the **Outlook Tower** ③ offers more splendid views of the city from its camera obscura. Opposite, the **Scotch Whisky Heritage Centre** ④ offers an unusual chance to discover Scotland's liquid gold—stop off for a sample. The six-story tenement known as **Gladstone's Land** ⑤, a survivor of 16th-century domestic life, is on the left walking down. Near Gladstone's Land, down yet another close is the **Writers' Museum** ⑥, housed in a fine example of 17th-century urban architecture. Farther down on the left is the Tolbooth Kirk (a *tolbooth* was a town hall or prison, and *kirk* means "church") and Upper Bow.

From the **Lawnmarket** ⑦ you can start your discovery of the Old Town closes, the alleyways that spread like ribs from the Royal Mile backbone. For a worthwhile shopping diversion, turn right down **George IV Bridge** ⑧, then to the right down Victoria Street, a 19th-century addition to the Old Town. Its shops offer antiques, old prints, clothing, and quality giftware. Down in the historic **Grassmarket** ⑨, where parts of the old city walls still stand, the shopping continues. Retrace your steps to George IV Bridge, then detour again southward to see the **National Library of Scotland** ⑩, the **Kirk of the Greyfriars** ⑪, and the little statue of the faithful Greyfriars Bobby. On Chambers Street, at the foot of George IV Bridge, the impressive galleries of the **Royal Museum of Scotland and Museum of Scotland** ⑫, housed in a lavish Victorian building, interest visitors of all ages.

Returning to the junction of George IV Bridge with the Royal Mile, turn right (eastward) down **High Street** ⑬ for the old **Parliament House** ⑭, the **High Kirk of St. Giles** ⑮, the Mercat Cross—still the site of royal proclamations—and the elegant City Chambers, bringing a flavor of the New Town's neoclassicism to the Old Town's severity. Farther down on the right is the Tron Kirk, with the **Museum of Childhood** ⑯ and **Brass Rubbing Centre** ⑰ beyond, providing the opportunity for an unusual souvenir. **John Knox House** ⑱, associated with Scotland's severe 16th-century religious reformer, and the **Netherbow Arts Centre** ⑲ are on this section of the Royal Mile, which immediately afterward becomes **Canongate** ⑳.

A short distance down Canongate on the left is **Canongate Tolbooth** ㉑; **Huntly House** ㉒ is opposite, and the **Canongate Kirk** ㉓ and Acheson House are nearby. This walk ends, as it started, on a high point: the **Palace of Holyroodhouse** ㉔, full of historic and architectural interest and some fine paintings, tapestries, and furnishings to admire, in Holyrood Park. Being erected nearby is the new **Scottish Parliament Building** ㉕, scheduled to be completed by 2002.

TIMING

The walk could be accomplished in a day, but to give the major sights—the castle, Palace of Holyroodhouse, and Royal Museum of Scotland—the time they deserve and also to see at least some of the other

Edinburgh

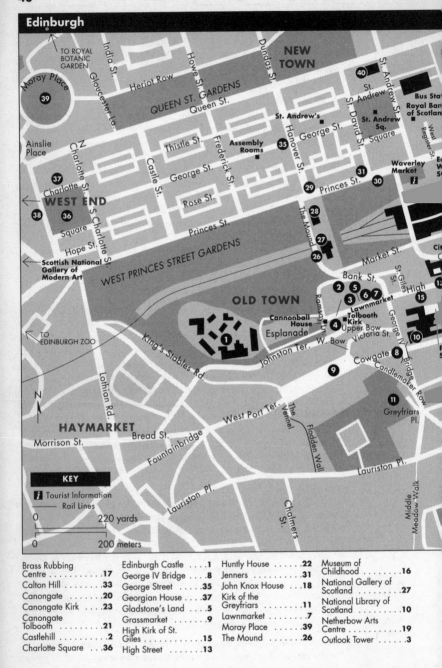

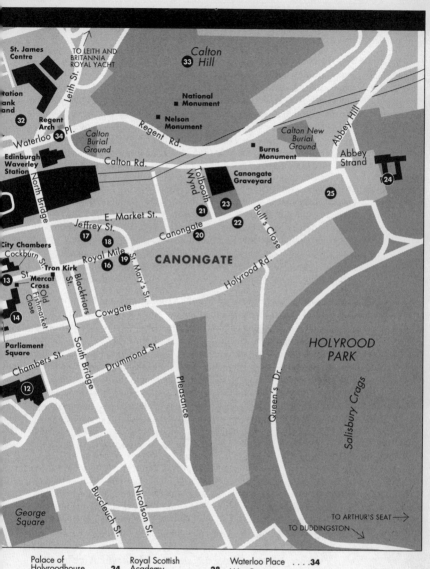

St. James Centre

TO LEITH AND BRITANNIA ROYAL YACHT

Leith St.

Calton Hill 33

tation ank and

32 Regent Arch

National Monument ■

Nelson Monument ■

34 Pl.

Waterloo

Calton Burial Ground

Regent Rd.

Calton New Burial Ground

Burns Monument ■

Abbey Hill

Edinburgh Waverley Station

North Bridge

Calton Rd.

Tolbooth Wynd

Canongate Graveyard

Abbey Strand

24

Bull's Close

25

E. Market St.

21 23 22

City Chambers

Jeffrey St.

Cockburn St.

17 18

Canongate 20

Royal Mile

Tron Kirk

16 19

St. Mary's St.

Blackfriars St.

CANONGATE

Holyrood Rd.

13 Mercat Cross

St.

Old Fishmarket Close

14

Cowgate

Parliament Square

Chambers St.

South Bridge

Drummond St.

Pleasance

HOLYROOD PARK

Queen's Dr.

Salisbury Crags

12

Buccleuch St.

Nicolson St.

George Square

TO ARTHUR'S SEAT →

TO DUDDINGSTON

attractions properly, you should allow two days. We suggest that you end the first day with an afternoon in the Royal Museum of Scotland and spend the second afternoon at Holyroodhouse.

Sights to See

🖑 ⑰ **Brass Rubbing Centre.** A delightfully hands-on way to explore the past, brass rubbing attracts more and more serious tourists every year. No experience is needed to create do-it-yourself replicas from original Pictish stones and markers, rare Scottish brasses, and medieval church brasses. All the materials are here, and children find the pastime quite absorbing. It's down a close opposite the Museum of Childhood. ⊠ *Trinity Apse, Chalmers Close,* ☎ *0131/556–4364.* 🖃 *Free, rubbings 90p–£15 each.* ⊙ *Mon.–Sat. 10–5, Sun. (during festival only) noon–5.*

⑳ **Canongate.** Named for the canons who once ran the abbey at Holyrood, Canongate is now the site of the Palace of Holyroodhouse. In Scots, *gate* means "street." Canongate itself was originally an independent *burgh,* another Scottish term used to refer to a community with trading rights granted by the monarch. Canongate is home to the Canongate Kirk and Graveyard, Canongate Tolbooth, Huntly House, and Acheson House (☞ *below*). ⊠ *Section of Royal Mile from end of High St. to Abbey Strand at entrance to Palace of Holyroodhouse.*

㉓ **Canongate Kirk.** The graveyard of the Canongate Kirk, built in 1688, is the burial place of some notable Scots, including Adam Smith (1723–90), author of *The Wealth of Nations* (1776), who once lived in the nearby 17th-century Panmure House. You can also visit the grave of the undervalued Scots poet Robert Fergusson (1750–74). That Fergusson's grave is even marked is the result of efforts by the much more famous Robert Burns (1759–96). On a visit to the city Burns was dismayed to find the grave had no headstone, so he commissioned an architect—by the name of Robert Burn—to design one. (Burn reportedly took two years to complete the commission, so Burns, in turn, took two years to pay.) Burn also designed the Nelson Monument, the tall column on Calton Hill (☞ *below*) to the north, which you can see from the graveyard.

Against the eastern wall of the graveyard is a bronze sculpture of the head of Mrs. Agnes McLehose, the "Clarinda" of the copious correspondence in which Robert Burns engaged while confined to his lodgings with an injured leg in 1788. Burns and McLehose—an attractive and talented woman who had been abandoned by her husband—exchanged passionate letters for some six weeks that year, Burns signing his name "Sylvander," Mrs. McLehose "Clarinda." The missives were dispatched across town by a postal service that delivered them within the hour for one penny. The curiously literary affair ended when Burns left Edinburgh in 1788 to take up a farm tenancy and to marry Jean Armour.

Opposite the Canongate graveyard is **Acheson House** (circa 1633), once a fine town mansion, which, like so much of the property in the Canongate, fell on hard times. It has been restored, as has the 1628 **Moray House,** a little farther up the street. ⊠ *Canongate,* ☎ *0131/556–3515.* ⊙ *June–Sept., Mon.–Sat. 10:30–4:30, Sun. services 10 and 11:15.*

㉑ **Canongate Tolbooth.** Nearly every city and town in Scotland once had a tolbooth. Originally a customs house where tolls were gathered, a tolbooth came to mean "town hall" and later "prison" because detention cells were housed in the basement. The building where Canongate's town council once met now houses a museum, the **People's Story,** which focuses on the lives of "ordinary" people from the 18th century to today. Exhibits describe how this in some ways rather sterile street, Canongate, once bustled with the activities of the various tradesmen needed to supply life's essentials in the days before superstores. Special displays include a reconstruction of a cooper's workshop and a 1940s kitchen. ⊠ *Canongate,* ☎ *0131/529–4057.* ⌷ *Free.* ☉ *Mon.– Sat. 10–5, Sun. (during festival only) 2–5.*

<table>
<tr><td>NEED A
BREAK?</td><td>You can get a good cup of tea and a sticky cake, a quintessentially Scottish indulgence, from **Clarinda's** (⊠ 69 Canongate, ☎ 0131/557–1888) or the **Abbey Strand Tearoom** (⊠ The Sanctuary, Abbey Strand, ☎ no phone), near the palace gates.</td></tr>
</table>

❷ Castlehill. In the late 16th century witches were brought to what is now a street in the Royal Mile to be burned at the stake, as a bronze plaque recalls. The cannonball embedded in the west gable of Castlehill's **Cannonball House** was, according to legend, fired from the castle during the Jacobite Rebellion of 1745, led by Charles Edward Stuart (also known as Bonnie Prince Charlie, 1720–88), the most romantic of the Stuart pretenders to the British throne. Most authorities agree on a more prosaic explanation, however; they say it was a height marker for Edinburgh's first piped-water supply system, installed in 1681. Atop the Gothic **Tolbooth Kirk,** built in 1842–44 for the General Assembly of the Church of Scotland, is, at 240 ft, the tallest spire in the city. It is the home of the Edinburgh Festival offices, the **Festival Centre** (⊠ Castlehill).

The **Upper Bow,** running from Lawnmarket to Victoria Street, was once the main route westward from the town and castle. Before Victoria Street (☞ *below*) was built in the late 19th century, the Upper Bow led down into a narrow dark thoroughfare coursing between a canyon of tenements. All traffic struggled up and down this steep slope from the Grassmarket, which joins the now-truncated West Bow at its lower end. ⊠ *East of the Esplanade and west of Lawnmarket.*

<table>
<tr><td>NEED A
BREAK?</td><td>A number of atmospheric pubs and restaurants bustle on this section of the Royal Mile. Try the friendly pub **Jolly Judge** (⊠ James Ct., ☎ 0131/ 225–2669), where firelight brightens the dark-wood beams.</td></tr>
</table>

<table>
<tr><td>OFF THE
BEATEN PATH</td><td>**DUDDINGSTON** – Tucked behind Arthur's Seat, and about a one-hour walk from Princes Street via Holyrood Park, this little community, formerly of brewers and weavers, has the interesting Duddingston Kirk, with a Norman doorway and a watchtower that was built to keep body snatchers out of the graveyard. The church overlooks Duddingston Loch, popular with bird-watchers, and moments away is an old-style pub called the Sheep's Heid Inn, which offers a variety of beers and the oldest skittle (bowling) alley in Scotland. ⊠ *Take LRT Bus 42 or 46.*</td></tr>
</table>

❶ Edinburgh Castle. The crowning glory of the Scottish capital, Edinburgh Castle is popular not only because of its symbolic value as the heart of Scotland but also due to the views from its battlements: on a clear day the vistas—stretching to the "kingdom" of Fife—are of breathtaking loveliness. Clear days are frequent now; Edinburgh is officially smokeless and the nickname "Auld Reekie" no longer applies.

The castle opens the chronicle of Scottish history, which will engulf you from now until you leave the country. Archaeological investigations have established that the rock on which the castle stands was inhabited as far back as 1000 BC, in the latter part of the Bronze Age. There have been fortifications here since the mysterious people called the Picts first used it as a stronghold in the 3rd and 4th centuries AD. The Picts were dislodged by Saxon invaders from northern England in AD 452, and for the next 1,300 years the site saw countless battles and skirmishes. You will hear the story of how Randolph, earl of Moray, nephew of freedom-fighter Robert the Bruce, scaled the heights one dark night in 1313, surprised the English guard, and recaptured the castle for the Scots. At the same time he destroyed every one of its buildings except for St. Margaret's Chapel, dating from around 1076, so that successive Stuart kings had to rebuild the place bit by bit.

The castle has been held over time by Scots and Englishmen, Catholics and Protestants, soldiers and royalty. In the 16th century Mary, Queen of Scots, chose to give birth there to the future James VI of Scotland, who was also to rule England as James I. In 1573 it was the last fortress to support Mary's claim as the rightful Catholic queen of Britain, causing the castle to be virtually destroyed by English artillery fire.

You enter across the **Esplanade,** the huge forecourt, which was built in the 18th century as a parade ground and now serves as the castle parking lot. It comes alive with color each August when it is used for the Tattoo, a magnificent military display, with the massed pipes and drums of the Scottish regiments beating retreat on the floodlit heights. Heading over the drawbridge and through the gatehouse, past the guardsmen, you'll find the rough stone walls of the **Half Moon Battery,** where the one o'-clock gun is fired every day in an impressively anachronistic ceremony. Climb up through a second gateway, and you come to the oldest surviving building in the complex, the tiny 11th-century **St. Margaret's Chapel,** named in honor of Saxon queen Margaret (1046–93), who had persuaded her husband, King Malcolm III (circa 1031–93), to move his court from Dunfermline to Edinburgh because the latter's environs—the Lothians—were occupied by Saxon settlers with whom she felt more at home, or so the story goes (Dunfermline was surrounded by Celts). The chapel was the only building spared when the castle was razed in 1313 by the Scots, having won it back from their English foes. The **Crown Room** contains the **Honours of Scotland—**the crown, scepter, and sword that once graced the Scottish monarch. Upon the **Stone of Scone,** in the Crown Room, Scottish monarchs once sat to be crowned. In the section now called **Queen Mary's Apartments,** Mary, Queen of Scots, gave birth to James VI of Scotland (1566–1625). The **Great Hall** displays arms and armor under an impressive vaulted, beamed ceiling. Scottish parliament meetings were conducted here until 1840. During the Napoleonic Wars (1803–15), the castle held French prisoners of war, whose carvings can still be seen on the vaults under the Great Hall.

Several military features of interest include the **Scottish National War Memorial,** the **Scottish United Services Museum,** and the famous 15th-century Belgian-made cannon *Mons Meg.* This enormous piece of artillery has been silent since 1682, when it exploded while firing a salute for the duke of York; it now stands in an ancient hall behind the Half-Moon Battery, the curving ramparts that give Edinburgh Castle its distinctive appearance from miles away. Contrary to what you may hear from locals, it is not *Mons Meg* but the battery's time gun that goes off with a bang every weekday at 1 PM, frightening visitors and reminding Edinburghers to check their watches. ☎ *0131/668–8800 for Edinburgh Castle, 0131/225–7393 for War Memorial,* FAX *0131/ 225–8920 (War Memorial).* ⌧ *£7.* ⊙ *Apr.–Sept., daily 9:30–5:15; Oct.– Mar., daily 9:30–4:15.*

NEED A
BREAK?   At the castle, **Mills Mount Restaurant** (⌧ Edinburgh Castle, ☎ 0131/ 668–8800) serves coffee, light lunches, and afternoon tea in bright premises with panoramic views over the city.

⑧ George IV Bridge. It is not immediately obvious that this is in fact a bridge, as buildings are closely packed most of the way along both sides.

But these buildings descend several stories below street level, as can be seen by looking over the short lengths of parapet.

At the corner of George IV Bridge and Candlemaker Row, near the Greyfriars Church, stands one of the most photographed sculptures in Scotland, *Greyfriars Bobby*. This famous Skye terrier kept vigil beside his master's grave in the churchyard for 14 years, after 1848, leaving only for a short time each day to be fed at a nearby pub after the one-o'clock salute from the castle. Make a point of renting a tape of the memorable Walt Disney 1961 film *Greyfriars Bobby*—it shows the poverty of Scottish life back then (unusual for a Disney presentation), as well as being a moving interpretation of an enthralling story. ⊠ *Between Bank St. and intersection with Candlemaker Row.*

❺ Gladstone's Land. A standout for those in search of the authentic atmosphere of old Edinburgh, this narrow, six-story tenement, next to the Assembly Hall on Lawnmarket, is a survivor from the 17th century. Typical Scottish architectural features are on show here, including an arcaded ground floor (believe it or not, even here—in the city center—livestock sometimes inhabited the ground floor). The house itself is furnished in the style of a 17th-century merchant's house and displays magnificent painted ceilings. ⊠ *377B Lawnmarket*, ☎ *0131/226–5856.* ⊠ *£3.20.* ☉ *Easter–Oct., Mon.–Sat. 10–5, Sun. 2–5 (last admission 4:30).*

❾ Grassmarket. An area that was for centuries an agricultural market now hosts numerous shops, bars, and restaurants, making it a hive of activity at night. Sections of the Old Town wall can be traced approximately on the north (castle) side by a series of steps that run steeply up from Grassmarket to Johnston Terrace above. By far the best-preserved section of the wall, however, is to be found by crossing to the south side and climbing the steps of the lane called the Vennel. Here you can see a section of the 16th-century **Flodden Wall**, which comes in from the east and turns southward at Telfer's Wall, a 17th-century extension. From here there are outstanding views northward to the castle. Grassmarket's history is long and fabulous. Body snatchers Burke and Hare lived here, and the **cobbled cross** marks the site of the town gallows. Among those hanged here were many 17th-century Covenanters. Judges were known to issue the death sentence for these religious reformers with the words, "Let them glorify God in the Grassmarket."

From the northeast corner of the Grassmarket, **Victoria Street,** a 19th-century addition to the Old Town, leads up to George IV Bridge. Shops sell antiques, new designer clothing, and high-quality gifts.

❺ High Kirk of St. Giles. Sometime called St. Giles's Cathedral (it was briefly a cathedral in the mid-17th century), St. Giles is about one-third of the way along the Royal Mile from Edinburgh Castle. This is one of the city's principal churches, but anyone expecting a rival to Paris's Notre Dame or London's Westminster Abbey will be disappointed: St. Giles is more like a large parish church than a great European cathedral. There has been a church here since AD 854, although most of the present structure dates from 1829. The spire, however, was completed in 1495. Outside, the building is dominated by this stone crown, towering 161 ft above the ground; inside, the atmosphere is dark and forbidding. At the far end of the church you'll find a life-size bronze statue of the Scot whose spirit still dominates the place, the great religious reformer and preacher John Knox, before whose zeal all Scotland once trembled. The most elaborate feature is the **Chapel of the Order of the Thistle,** bearing the belligerent national motto NEMO ME IMPUNE LACESSIT ("No one provokes me with impunity"), which was added in 1911. ⊠ *High St.,* ☎ *0131/225–4363.* ⊠ *Kirk free, Thistle Chapel* *suggested donation £1.* ⊘ *Mon.–Sat. 9–5 (until 7 in summer), Sun. 1–5. Services: Sun. 8, 10, and 11:30* AM, *6 and 8* PM *(music program only at 6); weekdays 8* AM, *noon; Sat. noon, 6* PM.

⓭ High Street. One of the four streets making up the Royal Mile, High Street contains some of the Old Town's most impressive buildings and sights, which merit individual entries. However, there are also other, less obvious historic relics to be seen. Near Parliament Square, look on the west side for a **heart** set in cobbles. This marks the site of the vanished Tolbooth, the center of city life from the 15th century until the building's demolition in 1817. This ancient civic edifice, formerly housing the Scottish parliament and used as a prison from 1640 onward, inspired Sir Walter Scott's (1771–1832) novel *The Heart of Midlothian.*

Just outside Parliament House is the **Mercat Cross** (*mercat* means "market"), a focus of public attention for centuries. A great landmark of Old Town life, this was an old mercantile center, and in the early days this area also saw executions and was the spot where royal proclamations were—and are still—read. Most of the present cross is comparatively modern, dating from the time of Gladstone, the great Victorian prime minister and rival of Disraeli. Across High Street from St. Giles's Cathedral are the **City Chambers,** now the seat of local government. Built by John Fergus, who adapted a design of John Adam in 1753, the chambers were originally known as the Royal Exchange and intended to be where merchants and lawyers could conduct business. Note that the building drops 11 stories to Cockburn Street on its north side.

A *tron* is a weigh beam used in public weigh houses, and the **Tron Kirk** was named after a salt tron that used to stand nearby. The kirk itself was built after 1633, when St. Giles's became an Episcopal cathedral for a brief time. In this church in 1693 a minister offered an often-quoted prayer for the local government: "Lord, hae mercy on aa [every] fool and idiot, and particularly on the Magistrates of Edinburgh."

You would once have passed out of the safety of the town walls through a gate called the **Netherbow Port.** Look for the brass studs in the street cobbles that mark its location. A plaque outside the Netherbow Arts Centre (☞ *below*) depicts the gate. ⊠ *Between Lawnmarket and Canongate.*

㉒ Huntly House. A must for those interested in the details of Old Town life, this attractive timber-front building, dating from 1570, houses a fascinating museum of local history, displaying Scottish pottery and Edinburgh silver and glassware. ⊠ *142 Canongate,* ☏ *0131/529–4143.* ▤ *Free.* ⊘ *Mon.–Sat. 10–5, Sun. (during festival only) 2–5.*

⓲ John Knox House. It is not certain that Scotland's severe religious reformer John Knox (1514–72) ever lived here, but mementos of his life are on view inside. This distinctive dwelling offers a glimpse of what Old Town life was like in the 16th century. The projecting upper stories were once commonplace along the Royal Mile, darkening and further closing in the already narrow passage. Look for the initials of former owner James Mossman and his wife, carved into the stonework on the "marriage lintel." Mossman was goldsmith to Mary, Queen of Scots, and was hanged in 1573 for his allegiance to her. ⊠ *45 High St.,* ☏ *0131/556–2647.* ▤ *£1.95.* ⊘ *Mon.–Sat. 10–4:30.*

⓫ Kirk of the Greyfriars. Built (circa 1620) on the site of a medieval monastery, the Gothic Greyfriars Church was where the National Covenant, declaring the independence of the Presbyterian Church in Scotland from government control, was signed in 1638. The covenant plunged Scotland into decades of civil war. Informative panels tell the story, and there's a visitor center on-site. Be sure to search out the grave-yard—one of the most evocative in Europe; nearby, at the corner of George IV Bridge and Candlemaker Row, stands one of the most pho-tographed sites in Scotland, the Greyfriars Bobby statue (☞ George IV Bridge, *above*). ⊠ *Greyfriars Pl.,* ☎ *0131/225–1900.* ☜ *Free.* ☉ *Easter–Oct., weekdays 10:30–4:30, Sat. 10:30–2:30; Nov.–Easter, Thurs. 1:30–3:30; groups by appointment.*

❼ Lawnmarket. The second of the streets that make up the Royal Mile was formerly the site of the produce market for the city, with a once-a-week special cloth sale of wool and linen. Now it's home to Gladstone's Land (☞ *above*) and the Writers' Museum (☞ *below*). At different times the Lawnmarket Courts housed James Boswell, David Hume, and Robert Burns. In nearby Brodie's Close in the 1770s lived the infamous Deacon Brodie, pillar of society by day and a murdering gang leader by night. Robert Louis Stevenson may well have used him as the inspiration for his *Jekyll and Hyde.* ⊠ *Between Castlehill and High St.*

❣ ⑯ Museum of Childhood. Even adults enjoy this cheerfully noisy museum—a cacophony of childhood memorabilia, vintage toys, and dolls, as well as a reconstructed schoolroom, street scene, fancy-dress party, and nurs-ery—the first in the world to be devoted solely to the history of child-hood. It's two blocks past the North Bridge–South Bridge junction on High Street. ⊠ *42 High St.,* ☎ *0131/529–4142.* ☜ *Free.* ☉ *Mon.–Sat. 10–5, Sun. (during festival only) 2–5.*

⑩ National Library of Scotland. Founded in 1689, this library has a su-perb collection of books and manuscripts on the history and culture of Scotland and also mounts regular exhibitions. Situated on George IV Bridge, this library is a special magnet for genealogists investigat-ing family trees. Even amateur family sleuths will find the staff help-ful in their research. ⊠ *George IV Bridge,* ☎ *0131/226–4531.* ☜ *Exhibitions free.* ☉ *Mon., Tues. and Thurs., Fri. 9:30–8:30; Wed. 10–8:30; Sat. 9:30–1; exhibitions Mon.–Sat. 10–5.*

⑲ Netherbow Arts Centre. The gallery and theater here host a regular pro-gram of exhibitions and productions. The café serves breakfast coffee with home-baked goods, full lunches, and afternoon teas. ⊠ *43 High St.,* ☎ *0131/556–9579.* ☜ *£1.95.* ☉ *Mon.–Sat. 10–5 (last admission 4:30) and for evening performances.*

❸ Outlook Tower. Want to view Edinburgh as Victorian travelers once did? Head for the 17th-century Outlook Tower's **camera obscura,** where you'll find this optical instrument—a sort of projecting telescope—which offers bird's-eye views of the whole city (on a clear day, that is) illuminated onto a concave table. The structure was significantly al-tered in the 1840s and 1850s with the installation of the telescopic "magic lantern." ⊠ *Castlehill,* ☎ *0131/226–3709.* ☜ *£3.95.* ☉ *Apr.–Oct., weekdays 9:30–6, weekends 10–6; Nov.–Mar., daily 10–5.*

㉔ Palace of Holyroodhouse. The haunt of Mary, Queen of Scots, and the setting for high drama—including at least one notorious murder, a spec-tacular funeral, several major fires, and centuries of the colorful lifestyles of larger-than-life, power-hungry personalities—this is now Queen Elizabeth's official residence in Scotland. A doughty and im-pressive palace standing at the foot of the Royal Mile in a hilly pub-lic park, it is built around a graceful, lawned central court at the end of Canongate. When the Queen or Royal Family is not in residence, you can take a conducted tour. Many monarchs, including Charles II, Queen Victoria, and George V, have left their mark on its rooms, but it is Mary, Queen of Scots, whose spirit looms largest. For some visi-tors the most memorable room here is the little chamber in which in

1566 David Rizzio, secretary to Mary, Queen of Scots, met an unhappy end. Partly because Rizzio was hated at court for his social-climbing ways, Mary's second husband, Lord Darnley, burst into the queen's rooms with his henchmen, dragged Rizzio into an antechamber, and stabbed him more than 50 times (a bronze plaque marks the spot). Darnley himself was murdered in Edinburgh the next year to make way for the queen's marriage to her lover, Bothwell.

The **King James Tower** is the oldest surviving section, containing the rooms of Mary, Queen of Scots, on the second floor, and Lord Darnley's (a.k.a. Henry Stewart, 1545–65) rooms below. Though much has been altered, there are fine fireplaces, paneling, plasterwork, tapestries, and 18th- and 19th-century furniture throughout. Along the front of the palace, between the two main towers, are the duchess of Hamilton's room and the Adam-style dining room. Along the south side of the palace are the **Throne Room** and other drawing rooms now used for social and ceremonial occasions.

At the back of the palace is the **King's Bedchamber.** The **Great Picture Gallery,** 150 ft long, is hung with the portraits of 111 Scottish monarchs. These were commissioned by Charles II, eager to demonstrate his Scottish ancestry (some of the royal figures here are fictional and the likenesses of others imaginary). All the portraits were painted by a Dutch artist, Jacob De Witt, who signed a contract in 1684 with the Queen's cash keeper, Hugh Wallace, which bound him to deliver 110 pictures within two years, for which he received an annual stipend of £120. Surely one of the most desperate scenes in the palace's history is that of the Dutch artist feverishly turning out potboiler portraits at the rate of one a week for two years.

The palace came into existence originally as a guest house for the Abbey of Holyrood, which was founded in 1128 by Scottish king David I (1082–1153). Look for the brass letters sss set into the road at the beginning of Abbey Strand (the continuation of the Royal Mile beyond the traffic circle). The letters stand for "sanctuary" and recall the days when the former abbey served as a retreat for debtors, which it was until 1880, when the government stopped imprisoning people for debt. Curiously, the area of sanctuary extended across what is now Holyrood Park, so debtors could get some fresh air without fear of being caught by their creditors. Oddest of all, however, was the agreement that after debtors checked in at Holyrood they were able to go anywhere in the city on Sunday. This made for great entertainment on Sunday evening as midnight approached: the debtors raced back to Holyrood before the stroke of 12, often hotly pursued by their creditors. The poet Thomas de Quincey (1785–1859) and the comte d'Artois (a.k.a. Charles X, 1757–1836), brother of the deposed king of France, Louis XVIII (1755–1824), were only two of the more exotic of Holyrood's denizens.

After the Union of the Crowns in 1603, when the Scottish royal court packed its bags and decamped for England, the building fell into decline. Oliver Cromwell (1599–1658), the Protestant Lord Protector of England who had conquered Scotland, ordered the palace rebuilt after a fire in 1650, but the work was poorly carried out. When the monarchy was restored, with the ascension of Charles II (1630–85) to the British throne in 1660, Holyrood was rebuilt in the architectural style of Louis XIV (alias the Sun King, 1638–1715), and this is the style you see today.

In 1688 an anti-Catholic faction ran riot within the palace, and in 1745, during the last Jacobite campaign, the palace was occupied by Charles Edward Stuart. After the 1822 visit of King George IV (1762–1830), at a more peaceable time, the palace sank into decline once again. But Queen

Victoria (1819–1901) and her grandson King George V (1865–1936) renewed interest in the palace: The buildings were once more refurbished and made suitable for royal residence. Behind the palace lie the open grounds and looming crags of Holyrood Park, the hunting ground of early Scottish kings. At Edinburgh's minimountain, **Arthur's Seat** (822 ft), views are breathtaking. ⊠ *Abbey Strand*, ☎ *0131/556–7371, 0131/ 556–1096 for recorded information.* 🎟 *£5.50.* ☉ *Apr.–Oct., daily, 9:30–5:15; Nov.–Mar., daily 9:30–3:45; closed during royal visits.*

⑭ Parliament House. The seat of Scottish government until 1707, when the governments of Scotland and England were united, Parliament House is partially hidden by the bulk of St. Giles's. It's now the home of the Supreme Law Courts of Scotland. Parliament Hall, inside, is remarkable for its hammer-beam roof and its display of portraits by major Scottish artists. ⊠ *Parliament Sq.,* ☎ *0131/225–2595.* 🎟 *Free.* ☉ *Weekdays 10–4.*

⑫ Royal Museum of Scotland and Museum of Scotland. Occupying an imposing Victorian building on Chambers Street, the Royal Museum of Scotland covers a broad spectrum, from natural history and archaeology to scientific and industrial history. The great Main Hall, with its soaring roof, is architecturally interesting in its own right. A striking new building adjacent to it, which opened in late November 1998, houses the **Museum of Scotland,** with displays concentrating on Scotland's own heritage. This edifice, rather sadly, overshadows the traditional old Royal next door. As a state-of-the-art and no-expense-spared modern museum, it is full of playful models, intricate reconstructions, and paraphernalia stretching from the Bronze Age to the latest Scottish pop stars. ⊠ *Chambers St.,* ☎ *0131/225–7534.* 🎟 *£3 (entry to both museums).* ☉ *Mon. and Wed.–Sat. 10–5, Tues. 10–8, Sun. noon–5.*

❹ Scotch Whisky Heritage Centre. The mysterious process that turns malted barley and spring water into one of Scotland's most important exports is revealed in this museum. Although whisky making is not in itself packed with drama, the center manages an imaginative presentation using models and tableaux viewed while riding in low-speed barrel-cars. At one point you'll find yourself inside a huge vat surrounded by bubbling sounds and malty smells. ⊠ *354 Castlehill,* ☎ *0131/220– 0441.* 🎟 *£5.50.* ☉ *Daily 10–6 (last tour 5; extended hrs in summer).*

㉕ Scottish Parliament Building. Under erection at the foot of the Royal Mile, this will house the 129 MSPs of Scotland's parliament. It is due for completion at the end of 2001 and has been designed by Barcelona architect Enric Miralles, in association with Edinburgh's RMJM Architects. ⊠ *Currently under construction.*

❻ Writers' Museum. Down a close off Lawnmarket is Lady Stair's House, built in 1622 and a good example of 17th-century urban architecture. The museum housed here evokes Scotland's literary past, with exhibits on Sir Walter Scott (1771–1832), Robert Louis Stevenson (1850– 94), and Robert Burns (1759–96). ⊠ *Off Lawnmarket,* ☎ *0131/529– 4901.* 🎟 *Free.* ☉ *Mon.–Sat. 10–5, Sun. (during festival only) 2–5.*

New Town

It was not until the Scottish Enlightenment, a civilizing time of expansion in the 1700s, that the city fathers decided to break away from the Royal Mile's rocky slope and create a new Edinburgh below the castle, a little to the north. This was to become the New Town, with elegant squares, classical facades, wide streets, and harmonious proportions. Clearly, change had to come. For at the dawn of the 18th century, Edinburgh's unsanitary environment—primarily a result of the crowded conditions in which most people lived—was becoming notorious. The well-known

Scots fiddle tune "The Flooers (flowers) of Edinburgh" was only one of many ironic references to the capital's unpleasant atmosphere, which greatly embarrassed the Scot James Boswell (1740–95), biographer and companion of the English lexicographer Dr. Samuel Johnson (1709–84). In his *Journal of a Tour of the Hebrides,* Boswell recalled that on retrieving the newly arrived Johnson from his grubby inn in the Canongate, "I could not prevent his being assailed by the evening effluvia of Edinburgh . . . Walking the streets at night was pretty perilous and a good deal odoriferous. . . ."

To help remedy this sorry state of affairs, in 1767 James Drummond, the city's lord provost (the Scots term for mayor), urged the town council to hold a competition to design a new district for Edinburgh. The winner was an unknown young architect named James Craig (1744–95). His plan called for a grid of three main east–west streets, balanced at either end by two grand squares. These streets survive today, though some of the buildings that line them have been altered by later development. Princes Street is the southernmost, with Queen Street to the north and George Street as the axis, punctuated by St. Andrew and Charlotte squares. A look at the map will reveal a geometric symmetry unusual in Britain. Even Princes Street Gardens are balanced by Queen Street Gardens, to the north. Princes Street was conceived as an exclusive residential address, with an open vista facing the castle. It has since been altered by the demands of business and shopping, but the vista remains.

The New Town was expanded several times after Craig's death and now covers an area about three times larger than Craig envisioned. Indeed, some of the most elegant facades came later and can be found by strolling north of Queen Street Gardens.

A Good Walk

Start your walk on the **Mound** ㉖, the sloping street that joins the Old and New towns. Two galleries immediately east of this great linking ramp, the **National Gallery of Scotland** ㉗ and the **Royal Scottish Academy** ㉘, are the work of William Playfair (1789–1857), an architect whose neoclassical buildings contributed greatly to Edinburgh's title: the Athens of the North.

At the foot of the Mound is Edinburgh's most famous street, **Princes Street** ㉙, the humming center of modern-day Edinburgh—a ceaseless promenade of natives and visitors alike patter along its mile or so of retail establishments. Natives lament the disappearance of the dignified old shops that once lined this street; now a long sequence of chain stores on the north side has replaced them, although the south side still offers a grand vista of the castle to the south. Walk east until you reach the soaring Gothic spire of the **Scott Monument** ㉚. Opposite is that most Edinburgh of institutions, **Jenners** ㉛ department store. **Register House** ㉜, an elegant neoclassical treasure designed by Robert Adam (1728–92), stands opposite the main post office and marks the east end of Princes Street. Immediately west of Register House is the Café Royal, at 17 Register Street, one of the city's most interesting pubs. It has good beer and great character, with ornate tiles and stained glass contributing to the atmosphere.

The monuments on **Calton Hill** ㉝, growing ever more noticeable ahead as you walk east along Princes Street, can be reached by first continuing along **Waterloo Place** ㉞, the eastern extension of Princes Street, from which you can get to the Regent Bridge. Waterloo Place then continues in a single sweep through the Calton Burial Ground to the screen walling at the base of Calton Hill. On the left you'll see steps that lead to the hilltop. If you're walking and don't feel up to the steep climb, you can take the road farther on to the left, which loops up the hill at a more leisurely pace.

Leaving Calton Hill, you may wish to continue east along Regent Road, perhaps as far as the Burns Monument, to admire the views westward of the castle and of the facade of the former Royal High School (directly above you). Then retrace your steps to the Waterloo Place traffic lights and make your way to St. Andrew Square by cutting through the St. James Centre shopping mall (across Leith Street) and then through the bus station. After admiring the lavish interior of the Royal Bank of Scotland, on the eastern side of the square—the building was originally the town house of the immensely rich Sir Lawrence Dundas, one of Chippendale's most lavish patrons—walk west along **George Street** ㉟, with its variety of shops.

The essence of the New Town spirit survives in **Charlotte Square** ㊱, at the west end of George Street, and especially in the beautiful **Georgian House** ㊲ and **West Register House** ㊳. To explore further, choose your own route northward, down to the wide and elegant streets centering on **Moray Place** ㊴, a fine example of an 1820s development. Then make your way back eastward along Queen Street to visit the **Scottish National Portrait Gallery** ㊵, which has exceptional paintings and a fine restaurant. Another attraction within reach of the New Town is the 70-acre **Royal Botanic Garden.** Walk down Dundas Street, the continuation of Hanover Street, and turn left and across the bridge over the Water of Leith, Edinburgh's small-scale river. You will reach the gardens, still one of the most cherished spots for residents as well as an important center for scientific research.

TIMING

This walk could be done in a morning if you start early, but if you want to get the most out of the National Gallery of Scotland and the Scottish National Portrait Gallery, take the whole day and allow at least an hour for each museum. The Portrait Gallery has a good restaurant, so one option is to arrive in time for lunch, then spend the afternoon there.

Sights to See

㉝ Calton Hill. Robert Louis Stevenson's favorite view of his beloved city was from the top of this hill, and you will be rewarded, too, if you make the climb. The architectural styles represented by the extraordinary collection of monuments include mock Gothic—the Old Observatory, for example—and neoclassical. Under the latter category falls William Playfair's monument to his talented uncle, the geologist and mathematician John Playfair (1748–1819), as well as his cruciform **New Observatory.** The piece that commands the most attention, however, is the so-called **National Monument,** often referred to as "Edinburgh's [or Scotland's] Disgrace." Intended to copy Athens's Parthenon, this monument for the dead of the Napoleonic Wars was started in 1822 to the specifications of a design by Playfair. But in 1830, only 12 columns later, money ran out, and the columned facade became a monument to high aspirations and poor fund-raising. The tallest monument on Calton Hill is the 100-ft-high **Nelson Monument,** completed in 1814 in honor of Britain's naval hero Horatio Nelson (1758–1805). The **Burns Monument** is the circular Corinthian temple below Regent Road. Devotees of Robert Burns will want to visit one other grave (☞ Canongate Kirk, *above*)—that of Mrs. Agnes McLehose, or "Clarinda," in the Canongate Graveyard. ✉ *Bounded by Leith St. to the west and Regent Rd. to the south,* ☎ *0131/ 556–2716.* ⬙ *Nelson Monument £2.* ☉ *Apr.–Sept., Mon. 1–6, Tues.– Sat. 10–6; Oct.–Mar., Mon.–Sat. 10–3.*

㊱ Charlotte Square. The New Town's centerpiece opens out at the west end of George Street—an 18th-century square that is home to one of the proudest achievements of Robert Adam, Scotland's noted neoclassical architect. On the north side, Adam designed a palatial facade to unite three separate town houses of such sublime simplicity and perfect proportions that architects come from all over the world to study it. Happily, the Age-of-Enlightenment grace notes continue within, as the center town house is now occupied by the Georgian House museum (☞ *below*), and to the west is West Register House (☞ *below*). ⊠ *West end of George St.*

OFF THE BEATEN PATH	**EDINBURGH ZOO –** On an 80-acre site on the slopes of Corstorphine Hill, Edinburgh's zoo offers traditional zoo delights plus animal contact and handling sessions in the main season, as well as its ever-popular Penguin Parade (held daily in summer). ⊠ *Corstorphine Rd., next to Post House Hotel (4 mi west of city)*, ☎ *0131/334–9171.* ☞ *£7.* ☉ *Daily 9–6.*

③⑤ **George Street.** With its variety of upmarket shops and handsome Georgian frontages, this is a more pleasant, less crowded street for you to wander along than Princes Street (☞ *below*). The **statue of King George IV,** at the intersection of George and Hanover streets, recalls the visit of George IV to Scotland in 1822. He was the first British monarch to do so since King Charles II, in the 17th century. By the 19th century Scotland was perceived at Westminster, the distant English seat of parliament, as being almost civilized enough for a monarch to visit safely.

The ubiquitous Sir Walter Scott turns up farther down the street. It was at a grand dinner in the **Assembly Rooms,** between Hanover and Frederick streets, that Scott acknowledged having written the *Waverley* novels (the name of the author had hitherto been a secret). You can meet Scott once again, in the form of a plaque just downhill, at 39 Castle Street, where he lived from 1797 until his death in 1832. ⊠ *Between Charlotte and St. Andrew Sqs.*

NEED A BREAK?	The little restaurant on the upper floor at the **James Thin** bookstore (⊠ 57 George St., ☎ 0131/225–4495) is ideally placed for enjoying a cup of coffee or light lunch while reading your latest vacation purchase.

★ ③⑦ **Georgian House.** The National Trust for Scotland has furnished the house in period style to show the elegant domestic arrangements of an affluent family of the late 18th century. The hallway was designed to accommodate sedan chairs, in which 18th-century grandees were carried through the streets. ⊠ *7 Charlotte Sq.,* ☎ *0131/225–2160.* ☞ *£4.40.* ☉ *Apr.–Oct., Mon.–Sat. 10–5, Sun. 2–5 (last admission 4:30).*

③① **Jenners.** Edinburgh's equivalent of London's Harrods department store, Jenners is noteworthy not only for its high-quality wares and good restaurants, but also because of the building's interesting architectural detail—baroque on the outside, with a mock-Jacobean central well inside. It was one of the earliest department stores ever to be established, in 1838. The caryatids decorating the exterior were said to have been placed in honor of the store's predominantly female customers. ⊠ *48 Princes St.,* ☎ *0131/225–2442.* ☉ *Mon., Wed., Fri., Sat. 9–5:30; Tues. 9:30–5:30; Thurs. 9–7:30.*

OFF THE BEATEN PATH	**LEITH –** Edinburgh's ancient seaport has been revitalized in recent years, with the restoration of those fine commercial buildings that survived an earlier, and insensitive, redevelopment phase. It is worth exploring the lowest reaches of the Water of Leith, an area where pubs and restaurants now proliferate. The major attraction for visitors here, however, is the former royal yacht *Britannia*, moored at Leith Docks (it costs £6.50 and is open daily 10:30–6), where you can wander round the ship that Queen Elizabeth called "the one place where I can truly relax," then check in at the shore-based visitor center, which tells the ship's sometimes fabled story. ⊠ *Reach Leith by walking down Leith St. and Leith Walk, from east end of Princes St. (20- to 30-min); or take Bus 7, 10,*

14, 16, 17, 22, 25, 32/52, 34/35, 42/46, or 87, Circle Route 87 or 2/12, or special Britannia Bus X50 from Waverley Bridge.

③⑨ Moray Place. Twelve-sided Moray Place—with its "pendants," Ainslie Place and Randolph Crescent—was laid out in 1822 by the earl of Moray. It is a fine example of an 1820s development, with imposing porticos and a central secluded garden (for residents only). From the start the houses were planned to be of particularly high quality, and the curving facades are still pleasant today. ✉ *Between Charlotte Sq. and the Water of Leith.*

②⑥ The Mound. The Mound originated from the need for a dry-shod crossing of the muddy quagmire left behind when Nor' Loch, the body of water below the castle, was drained (the railway now cuts through this area). The work is said to have been started by a local tailor, George Boyd, who tired of struggling through the mud en route from his New Town house to his Old Town shop. The building of a ramp was under way by 1781, and by the time of its completion, in 1830, "Geordie Boyd's mud brig [bridge]," as the street was first known, had been built up with an estimated 2 million cartloads of earth dug from the foundations of the New Town.

②⑦ National Gallery of Scotland. Opened to the public in 1859 in a grand neoclassical building designed by William Playfair—renovated in the late 1980s at vast expense to show the original gilding and rich color schemes of reds and greens within the galleries—the National Gallery has a wide selection of paintings, from the Renaissance to the postimpressionist period. It is most famous for the Old Master paintings bequeathed by the duke of Sutherland, including Titian's *Three Ages of Man.* All the great names are here; works by Velázquez, El Greco, Rembrandt, Goya, Poussin, Clouet, Turner, Degas, Monet, and van Gogh, among others, complement a fine collection of Scottish art, including Sir Henry Raeburn's *Reverend Robert Walker Skating on Duddingston Loch* and other masterworks by Ramsay, Raeburn, and Wilkie. ✉ *The Mound,* ☎ *0131/ 624–6200.* 🎫 *Free.* ☼ *Mon.–Sat. 10–5, Sun. 2–5 (extended hrs during festival); Print Room: weekdays 10–noon and 2–4 by appointment.*

②⑨ Princes Street. The north side of this well-planned street is now one long sequence of chain stores whose unappealing modern fronts can be seen in almost any large British town. Luckily the other side of the street is occupied by the well-kept Princes Street Gardens, which act as a wide green moat to the castle on its rock. ✉ *Running east–west from Lothian Rd. to Waterloo Pl.*

NEED A BREAK?   Immediately west of Register House is the **Café Royal** (✉ 17 W. Register St., ☎ 0131/557–4792), which has good beer and lots of character, with ornate tiles and stained glass contributing to the atmosphere.

③② Register House. Scotland's first custom-built archives depository, Register House—designed by the great Robert Adam—was partly funded by the sale of estates forfeited by Jacobite landowners, after their last rebellion in Britain (1745–46). Work on the building, which marks the end of Princes Street, started in 1774. The statue in front is of the first duke of Wellington (1769–1852). ✉ *Princes St.,* ☎ *0131/535–1314.* 🎫 *Free.* ☼ *Weekdays 9–4:30.*

OFF THE BEATEN PATH   **ROYAL BOTANIC GARDEN** – Just north of the city center, this 70-acre garden is second only to Kew Gardens in London for the variety of plants it contains and for the charm of its setting. An immense array of species is on show, from tropical to Nordic, including Britain's largest rhododendron and azalea collection. A highlight is an impressive Chinese garden. There are also a convenient cafeteria and a shop on the premises. To reach the gardens, only a 10- to 15-minute walk from the New Town, walk down Dundas Street, the continuation of Hanover Street, and turn left across the bridge over the Water of Leith, Edinburgh's small-scale river. ⊠ *Inverleith Row,* ☎ *0131/552–7171.* ☎ *Free (donation for greenhouses appreciated).* ☉ *Gardens: Nov.–Jan., daily 9:30–4; Feb. and Oct., daily 9:30–5; Mar. and Sept., daily 9:30–6; Apr.–Aug., daily 9:30–7. Shop, café, and exhibition areas: Mar.–Oct., daily 10–5; Nov.–Feb., daily 10–3:30.*

㉘ Royal Scottish Academy. This most imposing neoclassic temple, with columned facade overlooking Princes Street, is used for the RSA Annual Exhibition of paintings, sculpture, and prints from late April through July. Immediately before the annual exhibition, art students have their own exhibition, and the various Scottish societies of artists—watercolorists, landscapists, portraitists—hold exhibitions at other times during the year. ⊠ *Princes St.,* ☎ *0131/225–6671.* ☎ *Fees vary depending on exhibit.* ☉ *Annual Exhibition: late Apr.–July, Mon.–Sat. 10–5, Sun. 2–5.*

㉚ Scott Monument. What appears to be a Gothic cathedral spire chopped off and planted in the east of the Princes Street Gardens is the nation's tribute to Sir Walter—a 200-ft-high monument looming over Princes Street. Built in 1844 in honor of Scotland's most famous author, Sir Walter Scott (1771–1832), the author of *Ivanhoe, Waverley,* and many other novels and poems, it is centered on a marble statue of Scott and his favorite dog, Maida. Take the time to explore the immediate setting, Princes Street Gardens, one of the prettiest city parks in Britain. In the open-air theater, amid the park's trim flower beds, stately trees, and carefully tended lawns, brass bands occasionally play. Here, too, is the famous **monument to David Livingstone,** whose African meeting with H. M. Stanley is part of Scot-American history. ⊠ *Princes St.,* ☎ *0131/529–4068.*

OFF THE
BEATEN PATH
SCOTTISH NATIONAL GALLERY OF MODERN ART – Close to the New Town in a handsome former school building on Belford Road, this gallery features paintings and sculpture, including works by Pablo Picasso (1881–1973), Georges Braque (1882–1963), Henri Matisse (1869–1954), and André Derain (1880–1954). The gallery also has an excellent restaurant in the basement. ⊠ *Belford Rd.,* ☎ *0131/556–8921.* ☎ *Free.* ☉ *Mon.–Sat. 10–5, Sun. 2–5 (extended hrs during the festival).*

㊵ Scottish National Portrait Gallery. A magnificent red-sandstone Gothic building on Queen Street houses this must-visit institution. The gallery contains a superb Thomas Gainsborough (1727–88) and portraits by the Scottish artists Allan Ramsay and Sir Henry Raeburn (1756–1823), among many others. The building's beautiful murals themselves are worthy of study. ⊠ *Queen St.,* ☎ *0131/624–6200.* ☎ *Free (charge for special exhibitions).* ☉ *Mon.–Sat. 10–5, Sun. 2–5.*

㉞ Waterloo Place. The fine neoclassically inspired architecture on this street was designed as a piece by Archibald Elliot (d. 1823) in 1815. Waterloo Place extends over Regent Bridge, bounded by the 1815 **Regent Arch,** a simple, triumphal Corinthian-column war memorial at the center of Ionic screens bordering the bridge. ⊠ *Eastern extension of Princes St.*

㊳ West Register House. In the middle of the west side of Charlotte Square, the former St. George's Church today fulfills a different role, as an extension of the original Register House on Princes Street. ⊠ *Charlotte Sq.,* ☎ *0131/535–1400.* ☎ *Free.* ☉ *Weekdays 9–4:30.*

DINING

Updated by
Stewart
Hennessey

As befits one of the richest cities in Britain, Edinburgh has a huge number of restaurants, including the predictable cosmopolitan range, but there is a strong emphasis on traditional style. This tends to mean the Scottish-French style that harks back to the historical "Auld Alliance," founded on—not to mince any words here—a shared loathing for the English. The Scots element is the preference for plain and fresh foodstuffs; the French supply the sauces, often to be poured on after cooking. This equation has now been taken to a high art in many Edinburgh eateries.

On the whole, restaurants tend to be fairly small to medium size, and it is therefore best to make reservations at the more popular ones, even during midweek and definitely at Festival time. This being an unusually small capital, most of the good restaurants are within easy walking distance of the main streets, Princes Street and the Royal Mile.

It is possible to eat well in Edinburgh without spending a fortune. Even at those restaurants ranked in the top price category, two people could often squeeze by for under £30 if they ordered prudently. A service charge of 10% may be added to your bill, though this practice is not adhered to uniformly. If no charge has been added and you are satisfied with the service, a 10% tip is appropriate. Dining in Edinburgh is slightly different from much of Britain because the City Council has uniquely relaxed those arcane British licensing laws, so people often eat a bit later into the evening in Scotland than in England, or rather they finish eating and then drink on in a leisurely Scottish fashion. Speaking of which, for bars and pub grub, *see* Nightlife and the Arts, *below*.

CATEGORY	COST*
££££	over £30
£££	£20–£30
££	£15–£20
£	under £15

per person for a three-course meal, including VAT and excluding drinks and service

Old Town

French

££££
★
✕ Witchery by the Castle. The inspiration for this spooky haunt—complete with flickering candlelight—derives from the fact that some 300 years ago hundreds of witches were executed on the Castlehill, just yards from where you will be seated. The lugubrious, cavernous interior is festooned with cabalistic insignia and Tarot card characters. There's nothing spooky about the Scottish-accented French food, however, with fine venison, duck, lamb, salmon, and fillet steak among the specialties. Before and after peak dinner hours (5:30 to 6:30 and 10:30 to 11:30 PM) £9.95 two-course specials are offered, but this is largely one of the most expensive, yet best-value, restaurants in Edinburgh. Pierce Brosnan was one star spotted here recently. ⊠ *352 Castlehill, Royal Mile,* ☎ *0131/225–5613. Reservations essential. AE, DC, MC, V.*

£–££ **✕ Le Sept.** Tucked discreetly down a cobbled lane off the Royal Mile, this low-arched restaurant in the center of the city is a refined gem and an understated local institution. It's friendly, lively, unfussy, and famed for its crepes with adventurous fillings, but the daily changing menu also features simple staples like delicately cooked salmon fillets and succulent lamb stew. The wine list is similarly select and the service is always charming, especially by British standards. For set lunches it offers unbeatable value, with three courses costing £6. Within 500 yards

Easter 8PM

there are umpteen restaurants charging double for inferior fodder. ⊠ *7 Old Fishmarket Close,* ☎ *0131/225–5428. AE, MC.*

£–££   ✗ **Merchants.** Beneath the dramatic arch of George IV Bridge and only moments from the Grassmarket, Merchants is a bustling, cheery cavern of bright scarlet walls, mirrors, plants, and a nonstop jazz sound track. The menu ranges from simple haggis and beef to a mille-feuille of scallops and lamb chops with raspberry-and-mint sauce. Its ambitious dishes are reminiscent of old-fashioned nouvelle, but it really does the basics best. Set lunches run from £8.50, while set dinners start at £16.50 ⊠ *17 Merchant St.,* ☎ *0131/225–4009. AE, DC, MC, V.*

Scottish

£££   ✗ **The Tower.** Housed in the nation's National Museum, this no-smoking eatery set out to be the city's trendiest restaurant when it opened last year, and it achieved its goal, narrowly. It has a high-powered ambience, a space-age design, and a view of Edinburgh Castle so magnificent it ennobles the rather over-sociable seating arrangement. The menu is plain and straightforward, ranging wildly from good old unhealthy Scottish grills to posh-as-you-like lobster. The service improved immensely during its first few months and although it may still be pushing its luck on the price front, it's a fun novelty. ⊠ *Museum of Scotland, Chambers St.,* ☎ *0131/225–3003. Reservations essential. AE, MC, DC, V.*

££   ✗ **Tuscan Square.** This bright, pristine restaurant took a year or so to get off the ground but now offers some of the best food—and service—in Edinburgh. Situated beside The Royal Lyceum Theatre, it attracts the smartly dressed on a night out, yet charges considerably less than that would suggest. The dishes are imaginative Scots with a Continental slant, such that chicken liver parfait comes with warm brioche and apple chutney—these marriages work wonderfully. An excellent wine list and a healthy array of malts adds a more time-honored sensibility. ⊠ *30b Grindlay St.,* ☎ *0131/229–9895. AE, MC, V.*

£–££   ✗ **Beehive Inn.** Something of an institution, the Beehive snuggles in the Grassmarket, under the majestic shadow of the castle. Some 400 years ago the Beehive was a coaching inn, and outside the pub's doors once stood the main set of city gallows. Recently refurbished with an open grill, it presents such delights as pork wrapped with bacon in phyllo pastry. Open only for dinner, the upstairs Rafters restaurant is strewn with fascinating period junk. Reservations are advised. ⊠ *18/20 Grassmarket,* ☎ *0131/225–7171. AE, DC, MC, V.*

£–££   ✗ **Doric Tavern.** Beyond this café–bistro bar's rather tatty entrance staircase plastered with posters and playbills, the stripped wood floor, dark-wood tables, and navy velvet curtains create a superbly subdued, languid atmosphere. The menu always features a daily special—like roast pigeon salad with raspberry vinegar dressing—and a selection of fresh fish and meat dishes, always accompanied by vegetarian options. Try the lavish choices from the fixed-price lunch (£13.50) or dinner (£19.50), both excellent value. ⊠ *15/16 Market St.,* ☎ *0131/225–1084. Reservations essential. AE, MC, V.*

Vegetarian

£   ✗ **Banns Vegetarian Cafe.** Just off the Royal Mile in the heart of the Old Town, Banns serves a tasty range of nonmeat fare in a light and airy room with sturdy wooden furniture. Enjoy a cup of coffee with a decadently sinful cake delivered daily by a local French patisserie, or dine on a phyllo basket of cream cheese, herbs, and vegetables, or enchiladas. Allow plenty of time at lunchtime, as service can be slow. ⊠ *5 Hunter Sq.,* ☎ *0131/226–1112. AE, MC, V.*

New Town

Chinese

££ ✕ **Kweilin.** This pleasant family-run restaurant in Edinburgh's sedate New Town is popular with the city's Chinese community. Amid the traditional Chinese decor are several large paintings depicting scenes from the Kwangsi province, of which Kweilin is the capital. The lunchtime special menu is a pricey-sounding £10 but worth it, and the special menus tailored for two, three, or four evening guests are even better value, starting at £18 per person. Two à la carte highlights are the deep-fried crispy chicken on the bone and the meat-stuffed eggplant on a hot plate. ⊠ *19–21 Dundas St.,* ☎ *0131/557–1875. AE, MC, V. Closed Mon. except in Dec.*

Eclectic

££ ✕ **The Dome.** The splendid interior of this former bank, with its painted plasterwork and central dome, provides an elegant but faintly camp backdrop for relaxed dining or just a drink at the central bar, where sophisticated professional types wind down after work. The toasted BLT sandwiches are almost big enough for two, but if you are feeling hungrier, the eclectic menu offers many other options: try the *penne rigate* (pasta tubes) sautéed in a basil cream sauce with fresh mussels, or the smoked chicken salad on a bed of watercress. ⊠ *14 George St.,* ☎ *0131/624–8624. AE, MC, V.*

French

££££ ✕ **Pompadour.** As may be expected of a restaurant named after the
★ king's mistress, Madame de Pompadour, the decor here is inspired by the court of Louis XV, with subtle plasterwork and rich murals. The cuisine is also classic French, with top-quality Scottish produce completing the happiest of alliances. The extensive, well-chosen wine list complements such dishes as sea bass with crispy leeks and caviar butter sauce, whole lobster with mustard and cheese, or loin of venison with potato pancakes. This is the place to go if you want a festive night out, and it's ideal for the formal lunch that needs lightening up. ⊠ *Caledonian Hotel, Princes St.,* ☎ *0131/459–9988. Jacket and tie. AE, DC, MC, V. No lunch weekends.*

Italian

£–££ ✕ **La Rusticana.** Hanover Street exists to confuse lovers of Italian
★ food; all the best pasta and pizza restaurants compete here but, mostly, La Rusticana wins the day. Stronger on pasta than pizza, this cellar restaurant does the taste-bud trick best, while being only marginally above average in price. Along with its sister restaurant in the Old Town, on Cockburn Street, it is a fundamental part of Edinburgh's food culture, a favorite for business meetings and a generous patron of charity events. It's in the city center, two minutes from Princes Street. ⊠ *90 Hanover St.,* ☎ *0131/225–2227. AE, DC, MC, V.*

£ ✕ **Bar Napoli.** This only just loses to La Rusticana as the Italian pride of Hanover Street, although it may have the edge for pizza, and it stays open exceptionally late, sometimes until 2:45 AM. Certainly the chef's promise of a "genuine Italian experience" is justified. The pizza *"rusticana"* (with tomatoes, mozzarella cheese, fried red peppers, mushrooms, chopped chicken, artichokes, black olives, and oregano) is the chef's "greatest work of art," and there is an extensive menu of other pizzas and pasta dishes, all made with fresh, local produce. The lunchtime menu is a mere £3.95. ⊠ *75 Hanover St.,* ☎ *0131/225–2600. AE, MC, V.*

Scottish

££££ ✕ **Grill Room.** Set in the Edwardian splendor of the Balmoral Hotel (☞ Lodging, *below*), the Grill Room has established itself at the top end

58

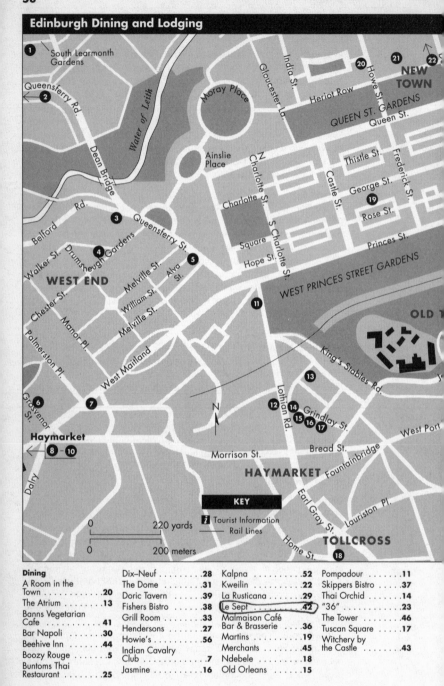

Dining

A Room in the Town	.20	Dix–Neuf	.28	Kalpna	.52	Pompadour	.11
The Atrium	.13	The Dome	.31	Kweilin	.22	Skippers Bistro	.37
Banns Vegetarian Cafe	.41	Doric Tavern	.39	La Rusticana	.29	Thai Orchid	.14
Bar Napoli	.30	Fishers Bistro	.38	Le Sept	.42	"36"	.23
Beehive Inn	.44	Grill Room	.33	Malmaison Café Bar & Brasserie	.36	The Tower	.46
Boozy Rouge	.5	Hendersons	.27	Martins	.19	Tuscan Square	.17
Buntoms Thai Restaurant	.25	Howie's	.56	Merchants	.45	Witchery by the Castle	.43
		Indian Cavalry Club	.7	Ndebele	.18		
		Jasmine	.16	Old Orleans	.15		

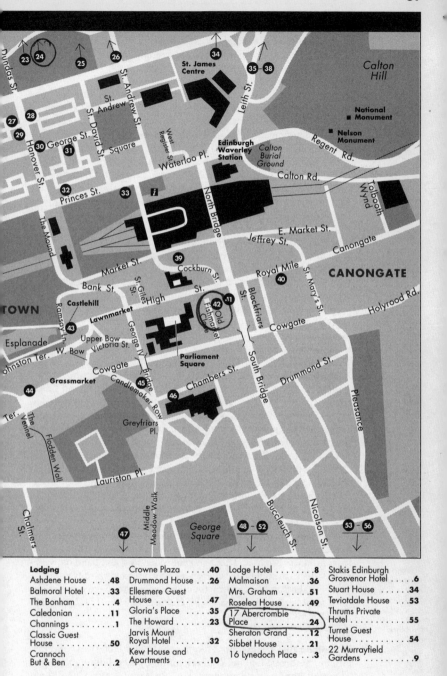

of Edinburgh's dining scene. The Asian-theme room has a luxurious ambience created by a green marble floor, Chinese lacquer wall panels, and an abundance of silver and crystal. The service is formal but relaxed and unhurried. As its name suggests, the restaurant specializes in grills, but the à la carte menu is extensive. ⊠ *Princes St.,* ☎ *0131/556–2414. Reservations essential. Jacket and tie. AE, DC, MC, V.*

£££   ✗ **"36."** This exclusive basement restaurant is in The Howard hotel (☞ Lodging, *below*), on one of Edinburgh's most elegant residential streets in the New Town. It applies the same principle to decor and cuisine, determinedly retaining old-fashioned simplicity but subtly using a wide variety of contemporary influences. Thus the food begins with basic and snappingly fresh ingredients but adds sauces and garnishes that truly surprise. Similarly you enter through a beautiful and beautifully preserved neoclassical entryway to find yourself in a very light, modern interior. ⊠ *36 Great King St.,* ☎ *0131/557–3500. Reservations essential. AE, DC, MC, V.*

££–£££   ✗ **A Room in the Town.** This newish restaurant, opened by one of Edinburgh's most experienced hands in the trade, was a hit overnight. It is small but spaciously seated, just the sedate and friendly place you'd want if seeking a quiet romantic nook. The food is classic Scots-French, with a strong emphasis on local fresh meat, with the Scottish touch accounting for slightly sweeter-than-usual sauces. The slightly high prices are offset by a BYOB policy (there's an excellent wine shop a block away), but wine is also offered at standard restaurant prices, plus very nice brandy. Scottishly plain but Continentally cheerful, it's perfect for a special occasion. ⊠ *18 Howe St.,* ☎ *0131/225–8204. Reservations essential. AE, DC, MC, V.*

££–£££   ✗ **Martins.** Don't be put off by the off-the-beaten-path location of this spot, tucked away in a little back alley between Frederick and Castle streets, for all's well that end's well when it comes to fine Scottish dining. The menu emphasizes organically grown local products and wild-caught foods. Typical modern Scottish dishes include fillet of turbot, panfried with fennel, shiitake mushrooms, and green peppercorn sauce, or charred lamb fillet with couscous, spinach, and an anise sauce. The cheese board, famed far and wide, has a sampling of Scottish and Irish cheeses. Lunches are an excellent value. The wine list includes an excellent choice of half-bottles. Smoking is not permitted. ⊠ *70 Rose St. North La.,* ☎ *0131/225–3106. Reservations essential. AE, DC, MC, V. Closed Sun. and Mon. No lunch Sat.*

££   ✗ **Dix-Neuf.** This fairly new restaurant-cum-bar celebrates the historic French-Scots connection in cuisine, with rich sauces adorning fresh, local produce. Bright and airy, and enlivened by a jazz band on weekends, it walks the tight line between friendly buzz and warmly intimate. The appealing ambience attracts enough people to make reservations for a meal here a good idea. ⊠ *97 Hanover St.,* ☎ *0131/220–6119. AE, DC, MC, V.*

Thai

££   ✗ **Buntoms Thai Restaurant.** A room in the Linden Hotel was converted into this authentic-looking Thai restaurant by the addition of genuine Thai wall coverings and antiques. You can leave Georgian New Town at the door and be transported halfway around the world with such savory delights as hot-and-sour squid and mushroom salad, seafood with broccoli in oyster sauce, or spiced chicken fried with cashews and onions (one of this restaurant's best offerings). Don't come here if you're on a tight schedule—each dish is prepared fresh, but it's definitely worth the wait. ⊠ *Linden Hotel, 9–13 Nelson St.,* ☎ *0131/557–4344. Reservations essential. AE, DC, MC, V. No lunch Sun.*

Vegetarian

£–££ ✕ **Hendersons.** This was Edinburgh's original vegetarian restaurant long before it was fashionable to offer healthy, meatless creations. Tasty options include eggplant, tomato, and chickpea curry, or leek and Stilton pie. If you haven't summoned the courage to try an authentic haggis while in Scotland, come here to sample a vegetarian version. The **Bistro Bar,** owned by the same proprietors, around the corner on Thistle Street is also open daily in the evening. ✉ *94 Hanover St.,* ☎ *0131/225–2131. AE, DC, MC, V. Closed Sun. (except during festival).*

Haymarket

Cajun

£–££ ✕ **Old Orleans.** The finest Cajun cooking in Edinburgh (no, it's not the *only* Cajun cooking here), Old Orleans serves up its dishes with real Southern extravagance. There are also Mexican and regional American dishes that with the Cajun items include red snapper, swordfish, smothered turkey, traditional jambalaya, and spareribs (they come with a large bib and finger bowl). Decor consists of amusing New Orleans kitsch: trellis and metalwork, brass instruments, and travel-related mementos; the music is blues and jazz; and the (constantly changing) lunchtime menu is equally welcoming, coming in at less than £8. ✉ *30 Grindlay St.,* ☎ *0131/229–1511. AE, DC, MC, V.*

Chinese

£–££ ✕ **Jasmine.** Seafood is the specialty of this small, friendly, candlelit Cantonese restaurant, with rapid service to deal with the constant stream of customers, even in midweek. The subdued cream decor with wooden screens is relaxing, although tables are quite closely spaced. Delicious dishes include crispy monkfish with honey sauce, baked crabs in black bean sauce, and fried oysters with ginger and spring onions. For two or more people, the set menus are a good value. A take-out menu is available. ✉ *32 Grindlay St.,* ☎ *0131/229–5757. AE, MC, V.*

Scottish

£££ ✕ **The Atrium.** With its cream-color tented fabric ceiling, smart cream
★ cotton chair covers, and wrought-iron candlesticks and unusual candelabra, the Atrium is a distinctive setting for pre- or post-theater dinner (the Traverse Theatre is right next door). A head chef has helped the place live up to its prices, as inventive Scots-French dishes and adventurous sauces now dazzle patrons. Try the seared scallops with artichoke-and-crab salad. For a lighter snack, try the upstairs café-restaurant **Blue** (☎ 0131/221–1222), under the same ownership. ✉ *10 Cambridge St. (beneath Saltire Ct.),* ☎ *0131/228–8882. AE, DC, MC, V. Closed Sun. (except during festival) and last wk of Dec. No lunch Sat. (except during festival).*

Thai

£–££ ✕ **Thai Orchid.** The theme is green at this bowfront restaurant, where green walls and brightly colored Thai silks set off Thai statues and gold masks. The food is a genuine taste of Thailand: the first king of Thailand once enjoyed *gaeng masaman* (beef or chicken slow cooked with roasted peanuts and potatoes), and other menu options include *goong nung* (king prawns steamed with lemongrass, white wine, lime juice, and coriander), and *gai yang* (chicken breast marinated with ground rice, garlic, soy sauce, and ground herbs, char-grilled and served with sticky rice and chili pepper dip). ✉ *44 Grindlay St.,* ☎ *0141/228–4438. AE, MC, V. Closed Sun. No lunch Sat.*

West End and Points West

Eclectic

££–£££ ✕ **Boozy Rouge.** The decor at this fashionable restaurant is cheery and simple—wood tables, bright tiles, and modern art—and the food is exceptional. The imaginative combinations can sound pretentious but they are actually a treat. For a strangely satisfying meal, try the saddle of Perthsire venison with blueberry and cinnamon coulis followed by butterscotch-stuffed, red wine–poached pear with citrus sorbet. ⊠ *1 Alva St.,* ☎ *0131/225–9594. AE, DC, MC, V.*

Indian

££££ ✕ **Indian Cavalry Club.** A very strong postimperial Raj atmosphere and excellent food are two of the staples at this cool and sophisticated Indian restaurant. The dishes have a confident, up-to-date flair with steamed specialties approaching nouvelle Indian. This place has the kind of historic atmosphere that inspires formal, respectful attire among the clientele—no denim here. The Club Tent in the basement serves light meals. ⊠ *3 Atholl Pl.,* ☎ *0131/228–3282. AE, DC, MC, V.*

South Side

African

£ ✕ **Ndebele.** This small, very friendly café—named after the colorful tribe from South Africa and Zimbabwe who have maintained the customs and language of their Zulu ancestors—is ideally placed for a snack before a trip to the Cameo cinema opposite. The wood-paneled, geometric-patterned walls in bright shades of purple and orange are hung with African art. The large range of interesting sandwiches on a choice of breads, the tasty *boerewors* (South African sausage), or smoked ostrich can be eaten on the spot or ordered out, and there is also a large selection of deli products for sale, including *biltong* (strips of cured, air-dried meat). A small art gallery downstairs has changing exhibitions of African artwork for sale. The lunchtime menu regularly features fish, meat, or vegetables and comes in at an endearing £6. ⊠ *57 Home St., Tollcross,* ☎ *0131/221–1141. No credit cards.*

French

£–££ ✕ **Howie's.** The steaks at this lively chain of simple neighborhood, French-style bistros are tender Aberdeen beef, and the Loch Fyne herring are sweet-cured to Howie's own recipe. All three restaurants are licensed, but you can bring your own bottle if you want to. All branches are closed Monday lunch, except for Bruntsfield Place. ⊠ *75 St. Leonard's St.,* ☎ *0131/668–2917;* ⊠ *208 Bruntsfield Pl.,* ☎ *0131/221–1777;* ⊠ *63 Dalry Rd.,* ☎ *0131/313–3334. AE, MC, V. No lunch Mon.*

Indian

£–££ ✕ **Kalpna.** This vegetarian Indian restaurant is on the city's South Side,
★   close to the university. The unremarkable facade amid an ordinary row of shops and the low-key decor enlivened by Indian prints and fabric pictures belie the food—unlike anything you are likely to encounter elsewhere in the city. For the unsure palate, a lunchtime buffet allows you to pick and mix for only £5, and again on Wednesday evenings for £8.95. ⊠ *2/3 St. Patricks Sq.,* ☎ *0131/667–9890. MC, V. Closed Sun. except in the summer season.*

Leith

French

£–££ ✕ **Malmaison Café Bar and Brasserie.** Freshly made soups, crunchy salads, inventive sandwiches (try the roasted red pepper and pesto), and gooey pastries are the choices in this eatery, part of the stylish Malmaison Hotel (☞ Lodging, *below*) in Edinburgh's rejuvenated dock-side area. Extremely popular are the Malmaison fish cakes with chips, buttered spinach, and parsley sauce; if you fancy something more substantial (and more expensive), try the Brasserie (reservations essential), which offers traditional French and modern British cuisine. ⊠ *1 Tower Pl., Leith,* ☎ *0131/555–6868. AE, DC, MC, V.*

Seafood

££ ✕ **Fishers Bistro.** This pub-cum-bistro down on the waterfront in Leith is popular with both locals and visitors (reservations advised). Bar meals are served, but for more comfort and elegance sit in the cozy green-walled dining room. Seafood is a specialty: watch the blackboard for the daily special, perhaps spicy sweet-potato and turnip soup followed by seared swordfish steak with sweet chili pepper sauce. ⊠ *1 The Shore,* ☎ *0131/554–5666. AE, DC, MC, V.*

££ ✕ **Skippers Bistro.** Don't miss this superb seafood restaurant, tucked away in a corner of Leith. It has a traditional, snug, cluttered ambience, with dark wood, shining brass, and lots of pictures and seafaring ephemera. As a starter the delectable homemade fish cakes can't be beat. Main dishes change daily but might feature halibut, salmon, monkfish, or sea bass in delicious sauces. ⊠ *1A Dock Pl.,* ☎ *0131/554–1018. Reservations essential. AE, MC, V.*

LODGING

It used to be that Scottish hotels were considered either rather better or much worse than their English counterparts; the good ones were very good, and the bad ones horrid. Today these distinctions no longer exist, and Scotland's capital features a wide array of delightful hotel accommodations. The inexpensive Scottish hotel, once reviled, is now at least the equal of anything that might be found in England. If you are planning to stay in Edinburgh during the annual summer arts festival, be sure to reserve several months in advance. Also note that weekend rates in the larger hotels are always much cheaper than midweek rates, so if you want to stay in a plush hotel, come on the weekend.

CATEGORY	COST*
££££	over £150
£££	£100–£150
££	£60–£100
£	under £60

All prices are for a standard double room, including service, breakfast, and VAT.

Old Town

££££ 🏨 **Crowne Plaza.** Although it was built late in the 1980s, this well-located modern hotel blends into its surroundings among the ancient buildings on the Royal Mile. Guest rooms are spacious, neat, and plain—practical rather than luxurious. ⊠ *80 High St., Royal Mile, EH1 1TH,* ☎ *0131/557–9797,* 🖷 *0131/557–9789. 238 rooms with bath. Restaurant, indoor pool, health club, meeting rooms, parking (fee). AE, DC, MC, V.*

New Town

££££ 🏨 **Balmoral Hotel.** The attention to detail in the elegant rooms and the
★ sheer élan of a re-created Edwardian heyday both contribute to the growing popularity of this grand former railroad hotel. Staying here, below the impressive clock tower marking the east end of Princes Street, gives you a strong sense of being at the center of Edinburgh life. The

hotel's main restaurant is the plush and stylish Grill Room (☞ Dining, *above*). ⊠ *1 Princes St., EH2 2EQ,* ☎ *0131/556–2414,* FAX *0131/ 557–3747. 184 rooms with bath, 21 suites. 2 restaurants, bar, indoor pool, beauty salon, health club, parking (fee). AE, DC, MC, V.*

££££   ⊞ **Caledonian.** A conspicuous block of red sandstone beyond the west
★   end of West Princes Street Gardens, the "Caley" was built 1898–1902 as the flagship hotel of the Caledonian Railway, and its imposing Victorian decor has been faithfully preserved. The public area has marbled green columns and an ornate stairwell with a burnished-metalwork balustrade. Rooms are exceptionally large and well appointed, and the generous width of the corridors reminds guests that this establishment was designed in a more sumptuous age. ⊠ *Princes St., EH1 2AB,* ☎ *0131/459–9988,* FAX *0131/225–6632. 246 rooms with bath. 2 restaurants, parking (fee). AE, DC, MC, V.*

££££   ⊞ **The Howard.** The Howard, close to Drummond Place, is a classic
★   New Town building, elegant and superbly proportioned. It is also small enough to offer personal attention. You'll like it if you enjoy a swank private club atmosphere. All guest rooms are spacious and furnished with antiques and original works of art, and some overlook the garden. The hotel's acclaimed contemporary restaurant, called 36, features innately Scottish dishes with worldly influences. ⊠ *34 Great King St., EH3 6QH,* ☎ *0131/557–3500,* FAX *0131/557–6515. 15 rooms with bath. Restaurant, free parking. AE, DC, MC, V.*

££££   ⊞ **Jarvis Mount Royal Hotel.** Perched above the ground-floor shops on Princes Street, overlooking Edinburgh Castle and the West Princes Street Gardens, the Mount Royal (and its entrance) is almost hidden between two of the city's major stores (Jenners and Marks & Spencer) and could easily be overlooked. Guest rooms have wood furnishings and pastel colors; the best views are from the rooms at the front of the hotel. ⊠ *53 Princes St., EH2 2DG,* ☎ *0131/225–7161,* FAX *0131/ 220–4671. 158 rooms with bath. Restaurant. AE, DC, MC, V.*

££–£££   ⊞ **Drummond House.** Many hotels would be put to shame by the ac-
★   commodations at this top-of-the-heap guest house in the heart of the New Town, within walking distance of the city center. The Georgian terraced house has spacious rooms, sumptuously decorated and furnished with swagged curtains, canopied beds, and antique furniture— all in elegant taste to suit the age of the house. Smoking is not permitted inside Drummond House, but guests can smoke while strolling through the several acres of private gardens across the road, open only to Drummond Place residents and hotel guests. ⊠ *17 Drummond Pl., EH3 6PL,* ☎ FAX *0131/557–9189. 4 rooms with bath. MC, V.*

££   ⊞ **Gloria's Place.** This luxurious Georgian B&B (built before George Washington was president) is a 10-minute walk from the city center. Well-equipped bedrooms (including direct-dial phone and laptop computer outlets) are complemented by the comfortable sitting room with its wall of books. Smoking is not permitted. ⊠ *20 London St., EH3 6NA,* ☎ *0131/557–0216,* FAX *0131/315–3375. 3 rooms with bath and shower. AE, MC, V.*

££   ⊞ **17 Abercrombie Place.** An exceptional standard is set at this bed-and-
★   breakfast in the center of the New Town. Stunning views can be had from the top-floor rooms of this Georgian terraced house characterized by shuttered windows and antique furniture and rugs (some used as wall hangings). Your hostess—a lawyer—enjoys meeting guests and is very helpful. Dinner can be provided (for guests only) by prior arrangement. This house is unusual for the area, as it has parking spaces for seven cars. ⊠ *17 Abercrombie Pl., EH3 6LB,* ☎ *0131/557–8036,* FAX *0131/558–3453. 9 rooms with bath or shower. Dining room, free parking. MC, V.*

££   ⊞ **Sibbet House.** The late-18th-century Georgian elegance of this small
★   terraced town house in Edinburgh's New Town has been enhanced by

careful attention to drapery, decor, and period antique furniture. Prices are reasonable, it is nonsmoking throughout, and breakfasts are traditionally Scottish and sustaining, to say the least. You must eat out in the evenings, but all kinds of restaurants are only a few minutes' stroll. Two self-catering apartments are also available. ✉ *26 Northumberland St., EH3 6LS,* ☎ *0131/556–1078,* 𝔽𝔸𝕏 *0131/557–9445. 4 rooms with bath or shower, 1 suite, 2 apartments. MC, V.*

££ 🏨 **Stuart House.** Within a 15-minute walk from the city center, this
★ B&B is in a Victorian terraced house with some fine plasterwork. The decor suits the structure: bold colors, floral fabrics, and generously curtained windows combine with antique and traditional-style furniture and chandeliers to create an opulent ambience. Smoking is not permitted. ✉ *12 E. Claremont St., EH7 4JP,* ☎ *0131/557–9030,* 𝔽𝔸𝕏 *0131/557–0563. 7 rooms with bath or shower. AE, DC, MC, V.*

Haymarket

££££ 🏨 **Sheraton Grand.** Beyond the reception area and sweeping grand staircase, you'll find the guest rooms, which are well above average size; many are traditionally decorated, with tartan furnishings and prints of old Edinburgh. The grandest rooms face the castle. This property has two fine restaurants: the brasserie-style Terrace, overlooking Edinburgh Castle and Festival Square, and the intimate Grill Room, serving fine fish, game, and Scottish beef. The hotel's popularity with locals, especially after work and in the evening before and after concerts at Usher Hall, across the street, testifies to its continuing role in Edinburgh's social life. ✉ *1 Festival Sq., Lothian Rd., EH3 9SR,* ☎ *0131/229–9131,* 𝔽𝔸𝕏 *0131/228–4510. 264 rooms with bath. 2 restaurants, bar, indoor pool, health club, free parking. AE, DC, MC, V.*

West End and Points West

££££ 🏨 **The Bonham.** This contemporary hotel in a traditional town-house space boldly mixes sleek design with state-of-the-art business accommodation. Beyond unassuming white hallways, each room is done in a unique minimalist concept, with modern pieces from local artists, geometric furnishings, and attractive lighting. The modern restaurant—in chic unadorned style with oversize mirrors and a central catwalk of light—serves Californian twists on Scottish specialties. Leisure and business travelers alike will feel well cared for with the thorough yet unobtrusive service. ✉ *35 Drumsheugh Gardens, EH3 7RN,* ☎ *0131/226–6050, 0131/623–6060 reservations,* 𝔽𝔸𝕏 *0131/226–6080. 50 rooms with bath. Restaurant, meeting rooms. AE, DC, MC, V. Closed Dec. 24–27.*

££££ 🏨 **Channings.** Five Edwardian terraced town houses make up this inti-
★ mate, elegant hotel in an upscale West End neighborhood just minutes from the west end of Princes Street. Beyond the clubby, oak-paneled lobby lounge are the quiet guest rooms, with restrained colors, antiques, marble baths, and great views of Fife (from those facing north), setting a stylish, refined tone. The Brasserie offers excellent value in traditional Scottish and Continental cooking, especially at lunchtime; try the hot smoked salmon with coriander and saffron risotto. ✉ *12–16 S. Learmonth Gardens, EH4 IEZ,* ☎ *0131/315–2226 or 0131/332–3232,* 𝔽𝔸𝕏 *0131/332–9631. 48 rooms with bath or shower. Restaurant. AE, DC, MC, V.*

££££ 🏨 **Stakis Edinburgh Grosvenor Hotel.** This attractive, comfortable hotel in the West End comprises several converted terrace houses and is distinguished by an elegant Victorian facade. Guests are pampered as soon as they enter the large reception area, furnished with ample Chesterfield armchairs. The single rooms are fairly small, and the doubles are just adequate. All are brightly decorated with peach curtains and floral bedspreads; the furniture is made of dark wood. First- and second-floor bedrooms have high ceilings with attractive plaster cornices. Just a short walk from the West End's shopping district, the hotel is convenient to the Haymarket railway station. ⊠ *Grosvenor St., EH12 5EF,* ☎ *0131/226–6001,* FAX *0131/220–2387. 188 rooms with bath. Restaurant, 2 bars. AE, DC, MC, V.*

££   ★   ⊡ **Kew House and Apartments.** This establishment is about as sumptuous as a guest house can be without being classified a full-service hotel. Inside the elegant terrace, dating from 1860, are six tastefully modernized rooms with all the usual luxuries—hair dryer, trouser press, and fresh flowers—plus chocolates, shortbread, and a decanter of sherry on arrival. There is also, unusual for a guest house, a bar and a restaurant. It's 15-minute stroll from the center of town. This is a no-smoking property. ⊠ *1 Kew Terr., EH12 5JE,* ☎ *0131/313–0700,* FAX *0131/313–0747. 6 rooms with shower, 2 apartments with bath and shower. Restaurant, bar, free parking. AE, DC, MC, V.*

££   ★   ⊡ **Lodge Hotel.** This detached Georgian stone house, a 15-minute walk from Princes Street, is easy to find on the main A8 Edinburgh–Glasgow road. Spacious rooms—all nonsmoking—are furnished in period style, with swagged curtains and canopied beds, and are stocked with fresh flowers and fruit as well as a decanter of sherry. Downstairs, there are a cocktail bar and peaceful gold-and-blue sitting room. The dining room has well-spaced tables covered with crisp white cloths and a menu heavy on fresh Scottish produce. ⊠ *6 Hampton Terr., West Coates, EH12 5JD,* ☎ *0131/337–3682,* FAX *0131/313–1700. 12 rooms with shower. Dining room. MC, V.*

££   ⊡ **16 Lynedoch Place.** You'll find considerate hosts in Andrew and Susie Hamilton (and Gertrude, the lovable dog), who have opened up their beautiful Georgian terraced house as a B&B, a five-minute walk from the center. Rooms (one single and two doubles, all no-smoking) are tasteful, with rosy pinks, cool yellows, terra-cotta oranges, and floral patterns. Breakfast is served in a magnificent hunter green dining room with antiques and family pictures, and Susie goes all out. In a pinch, they will open up the twin and single rooms upstairs for a family. ⊠ *16 Lynedoch Pl., EH3 7PY,* ☎ *0131/225–5507,* FAX *0131/226–4185. 3 rooms, 1 with bath, 2 with shower. Dining room, library, free parking. MC, V. Closed Dec. 23–27.*

££   ★   ⊡ **22 Murrayfield Gardens.** A handsome stone detached house with easy parking in an upscale residential area called Murrayfield just a 10-minute bus ride from downtown, this is an impressive B&B on all counts, with a particularly friendly host and hostess. Warm yellows are used in the elegant decor of the first-floor lounge, in the sunny dining room, and in the bedrooms with their panoramic views. With prior notice, dinner will be provided. ⊠ *22 Murrayfield Gardens, EH12 6DF,* ☎ *0131/337–3569,* FAX *0131/337–3803. 3 rooms, 2 with bath and shower, 1 with shower. Dining room, free parking. MC, V. Closed during Christmas and 2 wks Feb.*

£   ⊡ **Crannoch But & Ben.** This tip-top (no-smoking) B&B offers private baths, a comfortable residents' lounge, and good hearty breakfasts. Only 3 mi from the city and on a good bus route, it's also particularly convenient to the airport. ⊠ *467 Queensferry Rd., EH4 7ND,* ☎ *0131/336–5688. 2 rooms with bath. Free parking. No credit cards.*

South Side

££   ⊡ **Ashdene House.** On a quiet residential street on the South Side, only 10 minutes from the city center by bus, this Edwardian house is a first-class B&B, where smoking is forbidden. Bedrooms are decorated with country-style reproduction pine furniture and vividly colored fabrics, while in the downstairs public areas, turn-of-the-century shades of pink complement the age of the house. The owners are particularly helpful in arranging tours and evening theater entertainment, and they will recommend local restaurants. There is ample parking on the street and in a lot. ⊠ *23 Fountainhall Rd., EH9 2LN,* ☎ *0131/667–6026. 5 rooms with shower. Free parking. MC, V.*

££ ⊞ **Classic Guest House.** It is easy to find this Victorian terraced house, on a main route into Edinburgh from the south. The decor is modern classic: stripped pine floors throughout, elegant chinoiserie in the dining room, and pastel florals in the warm bedrooms. Smoking is not permitted. Note that three of the four rooms have en suite showers only. ⊠ *50 Mayfield Rd., EH9 2NH,* ☎ *0131/667–5847,* FAX *0131/662–1016. 4 rooms with bath or shower. Dining room. MC, V.*

££ ⊞ **Ellesmere Guest House.** Yet another Victorian terraced house, this B&B is close to the King's Theatre and several good restaurants. Its first-class rooms have modern furniture with pleasant pastel floral bedspreads and curtains; one room has a four-poster bed. Guests can relax in the comfortable sitting room, but the owners prefer that they not smoke. Ellesmere is stocked with brochures covering things to do in Edinburgh. ⊠ *11 Glengyle Terr., EH3 9LN,* ☎ *0131/229–4823,* FAX *0131/229–5285. 6 rooms, 1 with bath, 5 with shower. No credit cards.*

££ ⊞ **Roselea House.** Another South Side B&B guest house, on the main route from the south, the Roselea is easy to find. The Victorian house is decorated with "a touch of tartan," and there is a sitting room for guests. ⊠ *11 Mayfield Rd., EH9 2NG,* ☎ *0131/667–6115,* FAX *0131/ 667–3556. 5 rooms with bath or shower. Free parking. AE, MC, V.*

££ ⊞ **Thrums Private Hotel.** There is a pleasing mix of the modern and traditional in this detached Victorian house. It is small, cozy, and quiet, yet surprisingly close to downtown. ⊠ *14–15 Minto St., EH9 1RQ,* ☎ *0131/667–5545,* FAX *0131/667–8707. 15 rooms, 8 with bath, 7 with shower. Restaurant, bar, free parking. MC, V.*

£–££ ⊞ **Teviotdale House.** This is a small family-run and -owned hotel in the genteel South Side. The friendly Covilles are the hosts, and the house is a warm retreat on a tree-lined street away from but within reach of city-center bustle (a 10-minute bus ride). Individually decorated rooms and innovative, appetizing home cooking make this a pleasant, reasonable budget alternative to center-city hotels. The establishment is entirely no-smoking. Note that six of the rooms have en suite showers only. ⊠ *53 Grange Loan, EH9 2ER,* ☎ FAX *0131/667–4376. 7 rooms with bath or shower. Dining room. AE, MC, V.*

£ ⊞ **Mrs. Graham.** Parking is relatively easy (and unmetered) on the quiet
★ back street where this Victorian terraced house is situated (South Side/Newington), but it's also easy enough to get here taking Bus 3, 31, 69, 80, or 81 south from the city center. The spotlessly clean B&B has antique furniture complemented by beautiful kilim rugs and wall hangings. The two rooms share one bath. ⊠ *18 Moston Terr., EH9 2DE,* ☎ *0131/667–3466. 2 rooms without bath. No credit cards. Closed Sept.–Apr.*

£ ⊞ **Turret Guest House.** On a quiet residential street on the South Side, this B&B is close to bus routes as well as the Commonwealth Pool and Holyrood Park. Cheerful and cozy, it has modern furnishings, but many of the building's Victorian cornices, paneled doors, and high ceilings remain. ⊠ *8 Kilmaurs Terr., EH16 5DR,* ☎ *0131/667–6704,* FAX *0131/668–1368. 6 rooms, 4 with shower. MC, V.*

Leith

£££ ⊞ **Malmaison.** Once a seamen's hostel, the Malmaison in the heart of Leith offers good value yet stylish digs only 10 minutes by bus from the city center. Public areas are swathed in dramatic black, cream, and taupe color schemes. King-size beds, CD players, and satellite TV are standard in all bedrooms, decorated in a chic, bold modern style. The French theme of the hotel (sister to the Malmaison in Glasgow) is emphasized in the Café Bar and Brasserie (☞ Dining, *above*), serving all day. ⊠ *1 Tower Pl., Leith, EH6 7DB, ☎ 0131/468–5000, FAX 0131/468–5002. 60 rooms with bath. Restaurant, bar, café, free parking. AE, DC, MC, V.*

NIGHTLIFE AND THE ARTS

The Arts

To those who think Edinburgh's arts scene is made up of just the elegiac wail of a bagpipe and the twang of a fiddle or two, hundreds of performing arts options will prove them wrong. The crown in the jewel, of course, is the famed Edinburgh International Festival of Music, Drama, and Art, which now attracts the best in music, dance, theater, painting, and sculpture from all over the globe during three weeks from mid-August to early September.

The *List*, available from newsagents throughout the city, the *Day by Day List*, and *Events 2000*, available from the **Information Centre** (⊠ 3 Princes St., ☎ 0131/473–3800), carry the most up-to-date details about cultural events. The *Scotsman*, an Edinburgh daily, also carries reviews in its arts pages on Monday and Wednesday and daily during the festival. Tickets are generally available from box offices in advance; in some cases, they are also available from certain designated travel agents or at the door, although concerts by national orchestras often sell out long before the day of the performance.

Dance
Edinburgh has no ballet or modern dance companies of its own, but visiting companies perform from time to time at the Festival Theatre or Royal Lyceum (☞ *below*).

Festivals
The **Edinburgh International Festival** (⊠ Edinburgh Festival Office, Festival Centre, Castlehill, EH1 1ND, ☎ 0131/473–2001, FAX 0131/473–2003), the premier arts event of the year, has since 1947 attracted performing artists of international caliber to a celebration of music, dance, and drama.

The **Edinburgh Festival Fringe** (⊠ Edinburgh Festival Fringe Office, 180 High St., EH1 1QS, ☎ 0131/226–5257, 0131/226–5259 during festival only, FAX 0131/220–4205) offers many theatrical and musical events, some by amateur groups (you have been warned), and is more of a grab bag than the official festival. During festival time (roughly the same as the International Festival) it's possible to arrange your own entertainment program from morning to midnight and beyond, if you do not feel overwhelmed by the variety available.

The **Edinburgh Film Festival** (⊠ Edinburgh Film Festival Office, at the Filmhouse, 88 Lothian Rd., EH3 9BZ, ☎ 0131/228–4051, FAX 0131/229–5501) is yet another aspect of this busy summer festival logjam.

The **Edinburgh Military Tattoo** (⊠ Edinburgh Military Tattoo Office, 32 Market St., EH1 1QB, ☎ 0131/225–1188, FAX 0131/225–8627) may not be art, but it is certainly entertainment. It is sometimes confused with the festival itself, partly because the dates overlap. This celebration of martial music and skills with bands, gymnastics, and stunt motorcycle teams is set on the castle esplanade, and the dramatic backdrop augments the spectacle. Dress warmly for late-evening performances. Even if it rains, the show most definitely goes on.

If you're a jazz enthusiast, you may delight in the August **International Jazz Festival** (⌧ 29 St. Stephen St., EH3 5AN, ☎ 0131/467–5200).

In an entirely different vein, the **Edinburgh International Science Festival** (☎ 0131/220–3977), held around Easter each year, aims to make science accessible, interesting, but above all fun. Children's events turn science into entertainment and are especially popular.

Film

Apart from cinema chains, Edinburgh has the excellent two-screen **Filmhouse** (⌧ 88 Lothian Rd., ☎ 0131/228–2688 box office), the best venue for modern, foreign-language, offbeat, or simply less-commercial films. Its diverse monthly program is available from the box office and at a variety of other locations throughout the city (at the Tourist Centre, for example, or in theater foyers).

The **Cameo** (⌧ 38 Home St., ☎ 0131/228–4141) has three extremely comfortable theaters, a bar, and late-night specials; it's open Thursday–Saturday from 11:30 PM on. The family-owned and -run **Dominion** (⌧ Newbattle Terr., ☎ 0131/447–4771) offers one of the most pleasant alternatives to the larger commercial cinemas.

Music

The **Festival Theatre** (⌧ 13–29 Nicolson St., ☎ 0131/529–6000) hosts ballet, opera, and concerts, including performances by the Royal Scottish National Orchestra in season. The **Playhouse** (⌧ Greenside Pl., ☎ 0131/557–2692) leans toward popular artists and musicals. The **Queen's Hall** (⌧ Clerk St., ☎ 0131/668–2019) is more intimate in scale and hosts smaller recitals. **Usher Hall** (⌧ Lothian Rd., ☎ 0131/228–1155) is Edinburgh's grandest venue but is currently closed for an extensive renovation.

Theater

MODERN

The **Netherbow Arts Centre** (⌧ 43 High St., ☎ 0131/556–9579) includes modern plays in its program of music, drama, and cabaret. The **Theatre Workshop** (⌧ 34 Hamilton Pl., ☎ 0131/226–5425) hosts fringe events during the Edinburgh Festival and modern, community-based theater all year. The **Traverse Theatre** (⌧ 10 Cambridge St., ☎ 0131/228–1404) has developed a solid reputation for new, stimulating Scottish plays, performed in a specially designed flexible space.

TRADITIONAL

Edinburgh has three main theaters. The **Edinburgh Festival Theatre** (⌧ 13–29 Nicolson St., ☎ 0131/529–6000) is the city's newest theater and hosts a variety of opera and ballet, and excellent occasional tours. The **King's** (⌧ 2 Leven St., ☎ 0131/529–6000) has a program of contemporary and traditional dramatic works. The **Royal Lyceum** (⌧ Grindlay St., ☎ 0131/248–4848) shows traditional plays and contemporary works, often transferred from or prior to their London West End showings.

At Musselburgh, on the eastern outskirts of Edinburgh, the **Brunton Theatre** (⌧ Ladywell Way, Musselburgh, ☎ 0131/665–2240) offers a regular program of repertory, touring, and amateur performances. At the **Church Hill Theatre** (⌧ Morningside Rd., ☎ 0131/447–7597), local dramatic societies mount productions of a high standard. The **Playhouse** (⌧ Greenside Pl., ☎ 0131/557–2692) hosts mostly popular artists and musicals.

Nightlife

The **Edinburgh and Scotland Information Centre** above Waverley Market (⌧ 3 Princes St., ☎ 0131/473–3800) can supply information on various types of nightlife, especially on spots offering dinner dances. The *List* provides a lot of information on the music scene.

Bars and Pubs

Edinburgh's 400-odd pubs are a study in themselves. In the eastern and northern districts of the city you will find some grim, inhospitable-looking places that proclaim that drinking, for the Scot, is no laughing matter. But throughout Edinburgh many pubs have deliberately traded in their old spit-and-sawdust images for atmospheric revivals of the warm, oak-paneled, leather-chaired *howffs* of a more leisurely age.

Abbotsford (⊠ 3 Rose St., New Town, ☎ 0131/225–1894) offers an ever-changing selection of five real ales, bar lunches, and lots of Victorian atmosphere. **Cask and Barrel** (⊠ 115 Broughton St., New Town, ☎ 0131/556–3132) is a spacious, busy pub in which to sample hand-pulled ales at the horseshoe bar, reflected in a collection of brewery mirrors. **Cloisters** (⊠ 26 Brougham St., Tollcross, West End, ☎ 0131/221–9997) is a West End pub priding itself on the absence of music, gaming machines, and any other modern pub gimmicks and specializing in real ales, malt whiskies, and good food, all at reasonable prices. **Cumberland Bar** (⊠ 1–3 Cumberland St., New Town, ☎ 0131/558–3134) is not to be missed, with 11 ales on tap, wood trim, typical pub mirrors, and a comfy sitting room.

Drum and Monkey (⊠ 80 Queen St., New Town, ☎ 0131/538–8111), with cozy, dark-wood booths and a maroon color scheme, is just the place for soup-and-sandwich lunches with a pint of draught beer. **Guildford Arms** (⊠ 1 W. Register St., east end of Princes St., New Town, ☎ 0131/556–4312) is worth a visit for its interior alone: ornate plasterwork, cornices, friezes, and wood paneling are the setting for some excellent draft ales, including Orkney Dark Island. **Harry's Bar** (⊠ 7B Randolph Pl., New Town, ☎ 0131/539–8100), an Americana-decorated basement bar with disco music, is hugely popular with locals. **Kay's Bar** (⊠ 39 Jamaica St., New Town, ☎ 0131/225–1858) is another friendly, comfortable New Town spot that's a good place for a bar lunch. Don't miss the selection of 50 single-malt whiskies in addition to the real ales on draft. **Leslie's Bar** (⊠ 45 Ratcliffe Terr., South Side, ☎ 0131/667–7205) is convenient to the hotels and guest houses of Newington, with superb Victorian decor in its small saloon and public bars.

Madogs (⊠ 38A George St., New Town, ☎ 0131/225–3408) was one of Edinburgh's first all-American cocktail bar-restaurants; it remains popular with professionals after work, with live music most weeknights. The 260-year-old **Malt and Hops** (⊠ 45 The Shore, Leith, ☎ 0131/555–0083), with its own ghost and a choice of real ales, overlooks the waterfront down in Leith. **Milne's Bar** (⊠ 35 Hanover St., New Town, ☎ 0131/225–6738) is known as the poets' pub because of its popularity with the Edinburgh literati. Pies and baked potatoes go well with seven real ales and varying guest beers (beers not of the house brewery). Victorian advertisements and photos of old Edinburgh give it an old-time feel. **Southsider** (⊠ 3–7 W. Richmond St., South Side, ☎ 0131/667–2003), convenient to the antiques and junk shops of Causewayside, is a busy, sometimes smoky bar popular with locals and students.

Standing Order (⊠ 62–66 George St., New Town, ☎ 0131/225–4460), in a former banking hall with a magnificent painted-plasterwork ceiling, is one of the popular and expanding J. D. Wetherspoon chain of pubs, priding itself on friendly, music-free watering holes with cheap beer and ample nonsmoking areas—you can even lounge on leather sofas. **Tiles** (⊠ 1 St. Andrew Sq., New Town, ☎ 0131/558–1507), which is closed Sunday, is a converted banking hall and gets its name from the wealth of tiles covering the walls, which are topped by elaborate plasterwork. The large selection of real ales is complemented by a choice of bar meals or a table d'hôte menu specializing in fresh Scottish poultry, game, and fish.

Casinos

The following casinos are private, but membership can be granted with 24 hours' notice. All have American roulette, poker, blackjack, and slot machines and are open 2 PM–4 AM. You must be at least 18 years old to enter. **Stanley Berkeley** (⊠ 2 Rutland Pl., ☎ 0131/228–4446). **Stanley Martell** (⊠ 7 Newington Rd., ☎ 0131/667–7763). **Stanley Edinburgh** (⊠ 5B York Pl., ☎ 0131/624–2121). **Stakis Maybury Casino** (⊠ 5 South Maybury, ☎ 0131/338–4444) has a highly rated restaurant.

Ceilidhs and Scottish Evenings

For those who feel a trip to Scotland is not complete without hearing the "Braes of Yarrow" or "Auld Robin Gray," several hotels feature traditional Scottish-music evenings in the summer season, including the **Carlton Highland Hotel** (⊠ North Bridge, ☎ 0131/556–7277) and the **Edinburgh Thistle Hotel** (⊠ Leith St., ☎ 0131/556–0111), which produces Jamie's Scottish Evening. Contact the hotels for information.

Folk Clubs

There are always folk performers in various pubs throughout the city, especially at the **Tron** (⊠ Hunter Sq., ☎ 0131/220–1591) and the **Green Tree** (⊠ Cowgate, ☎ 0131/225–1294). The *List* has details.

Nightclubs

For the young and footloose, many Edinburgh discos offer reduced admission and/or less expensive drinks for early revelers. Consult the *List* for special events.

L'Attaché Nightclub (⊠ Beneath the Rutland Hotel, 1 Rutland St., West End, ☎ 0131/229–3402), which is open Friday and Saturday, features DJs spinning mainstream '60s–'90s sounds. The popular **Club Mercado** (⊠ 36–39 Market St., Old Town, ☎ 0131/226–4224; closed Mon.–Thurs.) offers theme nights covering the full spectrum of musical sounds. **The Honeycomb** (⊠ 36–38 Blair St., off High St., Old Town, ☎ 0131/220–4381; closed Mon.–Thurs.) is a hot spot with funky DJ sounds.

Minus One (⊠ Carlton Highland Hotel, North Bridge, Old Town, ☎ 0131/556–7277; closed Sun.–Thurs.) specializes in mainstream sounds with a DJ both nights. **Po Na Na Souk Bar** (⊠ 43b Frederick St., ☎ 0131/226–2224) is a dance club where you can hear yourself think and where the age ranges from teens to people who could be their parents. Laid-back yet very slickly run, the place gets rather crowded on weekend evenings. The **Venue** (⊠ 15 Calton Rd., New Town, ☎ 0131/557–3073) blares varying beats, including techno and progressive house.

OUTDOOR ACTIVITIES AND SPORTS

Participant Sports

Biking

Rates in summer are £50 per week for up to a 21-speed and £60 for a mountain bike. Bicycles may be rented at **Sandy Gilchrist Cycles** (⊠ 1 Cadzow Pl., ☎ FAX 0131/652–1760) and **Bike Trax** (⊠ 13 Lochrin Pl., ☎ 0131/228–6333). **Recycling** (⊠ 276 Leith Walk, ☎ FAX 0131/553–1130 or 0131/467–7775), with the motto "Great Bikes, No Bull," runs a sell-and-buy-back scheme for longer periods (say, more than two weeks), which can save you money, and also offers especially good deals on weekly rates.

Golf

The Scottish Tourist Board offers a free leaflet on golf in Scotland, available from the **Edinburgh and Scotland Information Centre** (⊠ 3 Princes St., ☎ 0131/473–3800). *SSS* indicates the "standard scratch score," or average score. For information on golfing throughout Scotland, *see* Chapter 11. The following courses are open to visitors.

Braids (⊠ 3 mi south of city, ☎ 0131/447–6666): Course 1, 18 holes, 5,731 yards, SSS 67; Course 2, 18 holes, 4,832 yards, SSS 63. **Bruntsfield Links** (⊠ 2 mi south of city, ☎ 0131/336–4050, FAX 0131/336–5538): 18 holes, 6,407 yards, SSS 71. **Craigentinny** (⊠ 3 mi east of city, ☎ 0131/554–7501): 18 holes, 5,407 yards, SSS 67. **Duddingston** (⊠ 4 mi east of city, ☎ FAX 0131/661–4301): 18 holes, 6,420 yards, SSS 71.

Liberton (⊠ Kingston Grange, 297 Gilmerton Rd., 4 mi south of city, ☎ 0131/664–8580, FAX 0131/666–0853): 18 holes, 5,412 yards, SSS 70. **Lothianburn** (⊠ Biggar Rd., 6 mi south of city, ☎ 0131/445–5067): 18 holes, 5,568 yards, SSS 68. **Portobello** (⊠ Stanley St., 2 mi north of city, ☎ 0131/669–4361): 9 holes, 2,410 yards, SSS 32. **Silverknowes** (⊠ Silverknowes Pkwy., 4 mi northwest of city, ☎ 0131/336–3843): 18 holes, 6,210 yards, SSS 71. **Torphin Hill** (⊠ Torphin Rd., 3 mi west of city, ☎ 0131/441–1100): 18 holes, 4,580 yards, SSS 66.

Health Clubs

Some of the larger Edinburgh hotels have their own fitness centers. Most facilities are free to guests, though there may be a charge for snooker and squash. Unless otherwise stated, the facilities are open to nonguests only through private membership. These include the **Carlton Highland** (⊠ North Bridge, ☎ 0131/556–7277), with pool, gymnasium, squash, and massage; **Sheraton Grand** (⊠ 1 Festival Sq., Lothian Rd., ☎ 0131/229–9131), with pool, gymnasium, and £15/day charge for nonresidents; **Royal Scot Swallow** (⊠ Glasgow Rd., ☎ 0131/334–9191), with pool, gymnasium, and £10/day charge for nonresidents; and **Forth Bridges** (⊠ S. Queensferry, ☎ 0131/469–9955), with pool, gymnasium, snooker, and squash.

Running and Track Sports

At **Holyrood Park,** at almost any time of day or night, joggers run the circuit around Arthur's Seat. **Meadowbank Stadium** (⊠ Northeast of city center, ☎ 0131/661–5351) has facilities for more than 30 track and indoor sports.

Skiing

Hillend (⊠ Biggar Rd., ☎ 0131/445–4433, ⌖ chairlift £1.10; ⊙ Apr.–Aug., weekdays 9:30–9, weekends 9:30–7; Sept.–Mar., Mon.–Sat. 9:30–9, Sun. 9:30–7), on the southern edge of the city, is the longest artificial ski slope in the United Kingdom—go either to ski (equipment can be rented on the spot) or to ride the chairlift for fine city views.

Swimming

The **Royal Commonwealth Pool** (⊠ Dalkeith Rd., ☎ 0131/667–7211, ⌖ £2.35), the largest swimming pool in the city, is part of a complex that includes a fitness center and a cafeteria.

Spectator Sports

Rugby

At Murrayfield Stadium, home of the **Scottish Rugby Union** (☎ 0131/346–5000), Scotland's international rugby matches are played in early spring. During that time of year, crowds of good-humored rugby fans from Ireland and Wales add greatly to the atmosphere in the streets of Edinburgh.

Soccer

Like Glasgow, Edinburgh is soccer-mad, and there is a tense rivalry between the city's two professional teams, the mostly Protestant **Heart of Midlothian Football Club ("Hearts")** based at Tynecastle (☎ 0131/200–7255), and the predominantly Catholic **Hibernian ("Hibs")** club, which plays its home matches at Easter Road (☎ 0131/661–2159).

SHOPPING

Arcades and Shopping Centers

Like most large towns, Edinburgh has succumbed to the fashion for under-one-roof shopping. If you dislike a breath of fresh air (or a wonderful view) between shops—or if it's raining—try the upscale **Waverley Market** (⊠ East end of Princes St.), with a fast-food area, designer-label boutiques, and shops that sell Scottish woolens and tweeds, whisky, and confections. The **St. James Centre** (⊠ East end of Princes St.) has unremarkable chain stores. **Cameron Toll** (⊠ Bottom of Dalkeith Rd.) shopping center, on the city's South Side, caters to local residents, with food stores and High Street brand names. The newest shopping center at **South Gyle** (⊠ On outskirts of city, near airport) is based on a typical U.S.-style shopping mall. Here you will find the High Street brand names again, including a huge Marks & Spencer.

Department Stores

In contrast to other major cities, Edinburgh has few true department stores. **Aitken and Niven** (⊠ 77–79 George St., ☎ 0131/225–1461) is an Edinburgh institution: a small department store where the well-heeled come to buy upscale clothing, shoes, and accessories. In the city center you will find **Jenners** (⊠ 48 Princes St., ☎ 0131/225–2442), which specializes in traditional china and glassware and Scottish clothing (upmarket tweeds and tartans) and has a justly famous food hall—selling shortbreads and Dundee cakes, honeys, and marmalades—as well as a range of high-quality groceries. **Frasers** (⊠ West end of Princes St., ☎ 0131/225–2472) is a part of Britain's largest chain of department stores. **John Lewis** (⊠ 69 St. James Centre, ☎ 0131/556–9121), specializing in furniture and household goods, pledges they are "never knowingly undersold." Frasers and John Lewis are not local, independently owned firms, and the goods are similar to those carried in other, United Kingdom–wide branches.

The High Street multiples, **Marks & Spencer** (⊠ 54, 91, and 104–106 Princes St., ☎ 0131/225–2301), **British Home Stores** (⊠ 64 Princes St., ☎ 0131/226–2621), and so on, are also represented on Princes Street. However, even given the competition, if you plan on a morning or a whole day of wandering from department to department, trying on beautiful clothes, buying crystal or china, or stocking up on Scottish food specialties, with a break for lunch at an in-store restaurant, then Jenners is the store to choose.

Shopping Districts

Despite its renown as a shopping street, **Princes Street** in the New Town may disappoint many visitors with its dull, anonymous modern architecture, average chain stores, and fast-food outlets. It is, however, one of the best spots to shop for tartans, tweeds, and knitwear, especially if your time is limited. One block north of Princes Street, **Rose Street** has many smaller specialty shops; part of the street is a pedestrian zone, so it's a pleasant place to browse. The shops on **George Street** tend to be fairly upscale. London names, such as Laura Ashley and Waterstones bookstore, are prominent, though some of the older independent stores continue to do good business.

The streets crossing George Street—Hanover, Frederick, and Castle—are also worth exploring. **Dundas Street,** the northern extension of Hanover Street, beyond Queen Street Gardens, features several antiques shops. **Thistle Street,** originally George Street's "back lane," or service area, has several boutiques and more antiques shops. As may be expected, many shops along the **Royal Mile** sell what may be politely or euphemistically described as tourist-ware—whiskies, tartans, and tweeds. Careful exploration, however, will reveal some worthwhile establishments. Shops here also cater to highly specialized interests and hobbies.

Close to the castle end of the Royal Mile, just off George IV Bridge, the specialty shops of **Victoria Street** are contained within a small area. Follow the tiny West Bow to **Grassmarket** for more specialty stores. North of Princes Street, on the way to the Royal Botanic Garden, **Stockbridge** is an oddball shopping area of some charm, particularly on St. Stephen Street. To get there, walk north down Frederick Street and Howe Street, away from Princes Street, then turn left onto North West Circus Place. **Stafford and William streets** comprise a small, upscale shopping area in a Georgian setting. Walk to the west end of Princes Street and then along its continuation, Shandwick Place, then turn right into Stafford Street. William Street crosses Stafford halfway down.

Specialty Shops

Antiques

Antiques dealers tend to cluster together, so it may be easier to concentrate on one area—St. Stephen Street, Bruntsfield Place, Causewayside, or Dundas Street, for example—if you are short of time. Try **Byzantium** (⊠ 9A Victoria St., ☎ 0131/225–1768) for an eclectic mix of antiques, crafts, clothes—and an excellent coffee shop on the top level.

Books, Paper, Maps, and Games

As a university city and cultural center, Edinburgh is endowed with excellent bookstores. All keep a wide range of guides and books giving information about every aspect of Edinburgh life, and all have extended opening hours (until 10 PM on certain nights), including Sundays. Some of the most central are **James Thin** (⊠ 57 George St., ☎ 0131/225–4495; ⊠ 53 S. Bridge, ☎ 0131/556–6743) and **Waterstones** (⊠ 83 George St., ☎ 0131/225–3436; ⊠ 13–14 Princes St., ☎ 0131/556–3034; ⊠ 128 Princes St., ☎ 0131/226–2666).

Try **George Waterston** (⊠ 35 George St., ☎ 0131/225–5690) not only for stationery but also for an excellent selection of small gift items. **R. Somerville of Edinburgh** (⊠ 82 Canongate, ☎ 0131/556–5225) is a dealer of a large variety of playing cards. **Carson Clark Gallery** (⊠ 181–183 Canongate, ☎ 0131/556–4710) is a specialist in antique maps, sea charts, and prints.

Clothing Boutiques

Edinburgh is home to several top-quality designers (although, it must be said, probably not as many as are found in Glasgow, the country's fashion center), some of whom make a point of using Scottish materials in their creations. **Bill Baber's Sheepish Looks** (⊠ 66 Grassmarket, ☎ 0131/225–3249) is one of the most imaginative of the many Scottish knitwear designers, and a long way from the conservative pastel "woolies" sold at some of the large mill shops. Well-heeled Edinburgh also has a branch of **D and B by Angela Holmes** (⊠ 37–39 Frederick St., ☎ 0131/225–1019), whose distinctive clothing—from silk ball gowns and wedding dresses to flowing corduroy skirts with matching jackets and pretty cotton print summer dresses—is guaranteed to make you stand out from the crowd. **Judith Glue** (⊠ 60 and 64 High St., ☎ 0131/558–1866) has brilliantly patterned Orkney knitwear, as well as distinctive crafts, cards, jewelry, and paintings.

If you are shopping for children, especially those who fit the tousled-tomboy mold, try **Baggins** (⊠ 12 Deanhaugh St., Stockbridge, ☎ 0131/315–2011) for practical, reasonably priced clothes made from natural fibers, as well as toys and fancy dress items. All clothes here are made to the owner's design in the store's on-site workshop. **Burberrys and the Scotch House** (⊠ 39–41 Princes St., ☎ 0131/556–1252) is popular with overseas visitors for its top-quality (if top-price) clothing and accessories. **The Extra Inch** (⊠ 12 William St., ☎ 0131/226–3303) has a full selection of clothes European size 38 and over.

Jewelry
Joseph Bonnar (⊠ 72 Thistle St., ☎ 0131/226–2811), in the heart of New Town, is a specialist in antique jewelry. **Alistir Tait** (⊠ 116a Rose St., ☎ 0131/225–4105) offers a collection of high-quality antique and fine jewelry, silver, and clocks. The jeweler **Hamilton and Inches** (⊠ 87 George St., ☎ 0131/225–4898), established in 1866, is a silver- and goldsmith worth visiting not only for its modern and antique gift possibilities, but also for its late-Georgian interior, designed by David Bryce in 1834—all gilded columns and elaborate plasterwork.

Linens, Textiles, and Home Furnishings
Go to **And So To Bed** (⊠ 22 Howe St., ☎ 0131/225–6998) for a wonderful selection of embroidered and embellished bed linens, cushion covers, and such. **In House** (⊠ 28 Howe St., ☎ 0131/225–2888) has designer furnishings and collectibles at the forefront of modern design in the house. The interior design shop **Ampersand** (⊠ 18 Victoria St., ☎ 0131/226–2734) stocks a large selection of sundry collectibles, mostly jugs, plates, lamps, and vases, as well as unusual fabric sold by the meter. **Studio One** (⊠ 10–16 Stafford St., ☎ 0131/226–5812) has a well-established and comprehensive inventory of kitchen goods and gift articles.

Outdoor Sports Gear
If you plan to do a lot of hiking or camping in the Highlands or the Islands, you may want to look over the selection of outdoor clothing, boots, jackets, and heavy- and lightweight gear at **Tiso** (⊠ 121 Rose St., ☎ 0131/225–9486).

Scottish Specialties
If you want to identify a particular tartan, several shops on Princes Street will be pleased to assist. The **Clan Tartan Centre** (⊠ 70–74 Bangor Rd., Leith, ☎ 0131/553–5100) has extensive displays of various aspects of tartanry. At the **Edinburgh Old Town Weaving Company** (⊠ 555 Castlehill, ☎ 0131/226–1555), you can talk to the cloth- and tapestry weavers as they work, then buy the products. **Geoffrey (Tailor) Highland Crafts** (⊠ 57–59 High St., ☎ 0131/557–0256) can clothe you in full Highland dress, with kilts made in its own workshops. **Edinburgh Crystal** (⊠ Eastfield, Penicuik, ☎ 01968/675128) makes fine glassware stocked by many large stores and gift shops in the city center, but you can also visit its premises (visitor center, restaurant, and shops, including a seconds and discontinued-lines store for real bargains), in Penicuik (☞ Side Trips from Edinburgh, *below*).

SIDE TRIPS FROM EDINBURGH

If you stand on an Edinburgh eminence—the castle ramparts, Arthur's Seat, Corstorphine Hill—you can plan a few Lothian excursions without even the aid of a map. The Lothians is the collective name given to the swath of countryside south of the Firth of Forth and surrounding Edinburgh. This region was home to many courtly and aristocratic families and has the castles and mansions to prove it. The rich arrived and with them, deer parks, gardens in the French style, and Lothian's fame as a seed plot for Lowland gentility. Although the region has always provided rich pickings for the historian, it also used to offer even richer pickings for coal miners—for a century after the industrial revolution gentle streams in fairy glens (so the old writings describe them) steamed and stank with pollution. Although some black spots still remain, most of the rural countryside is now once again a fitting setting for excursions. When the coal miners left, admirals came here to retire, and today the "land of Lud" happily offers many delights to the traveler. The 70-mi round-trip exploring the historic houses and castles of West Lothian and the Forth Valley and some territory north of the River Forth can be accomplished in a full day with select stops. Stretching east to the sea and south to the Lowlands from Edinburgh, the sights in Midlothian and East Lothian are no more than one hour from Edinburgh. The inland river valleys, hills, and castles of Midlothian and East Lothian's delightful waterfronts, dunes, and golf links offer a taste of Scotland in close proximity to the capital.

West Lothian and the Forth Valley

West Lothian skirts the edge of the Central Highlands and comprises a good bit of Scotland's central belt. The River Forth snakes across a widening floodplain on its descent from the Highlands, and by the time it reaches the western extremities of Edinburgh, it has already passed below the mighty Forth bridges and become a broad estuary. Castles and stately homes sprout thickly on both sides of the Forth.

Cramond

41 At this compact settlement on the coast west of the city (4 mi northwest of the city center), you can watch summer sunsets over the Firth of Forth, joined by the River Almond. The river's banks, once the site of mills and industrial works, now offer pleasant, leafy walks.

DINING

£–££ ✕ **Cramond Inn.** In this dark village inn dating from the 1600s—once the haunt of Robert Louis Stevenson—you can stop for a pint at the bar or a selection from the small but varied pub menu: grilled halibut and new potatoes, sole and salmon rolls, chicken with mango chutney and rice, or a steak. ⊠ *Cramond Glebe Rd., Cramond Village,* ☎ *0131/ 336–2035. DC, MC, V.*

Dalmeny House

42 The first of the stately homes clustered on the western edge of Edinburgh, Dalmeny House is the home of the earl and countess of Rosebery. This 1815 Tudor Gothic mansion displays among its sumptuous contents the best of the family's famous collection of 18th-century French furniture. (Much of this collection was formerly displayed at Mentmore, the country seat 40 mi north of London, which belonged to the present earl's grandfather, Baron Mayer Rothschild [1840–1915]). Highlights include the library; the drawing room, with its tapestries and highly wrought French furniture; the Napoléon Room; and the Vincennes and Sevres porcelain collections. ⊠ *B924, by South Queensferry (7 mi west of city center),* ☎ *0131/331–1888.* ⊡ *£3.80.* ☉ *July– Aug., Sun. 1–5:30, Mon., Tues. noon–5:30 (last admission 4:45).*

West Lothian and the Forth Valley

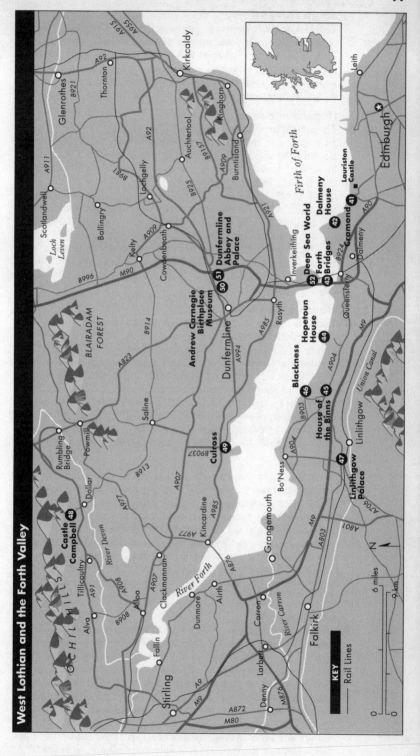

Kirkcaldy

Glenrothes

Thornton

Auchtertool

Kinghorn

Burntisland

Scotlandwell

Loch
Leven

Ballingry

Lochgelly

Kelty

Cowdenbeath

Inverkeithing

Firth of Forth

Edinburgh

Leith

Lauriston
Castle

Dalmeny
House

Deep Sea World

Cramond

Dalmeny

Forth
Bridges

Queensferry

Andrew Carnegie
Birthplace
Museum

Dunfermline Abbey
and Palace

Dunfermline

BLAIRADAM
FOREST

Saline

Rosyth

Hopetoun
House

Blackness

Powmill

Rumbling
Bridge

Dollar

Culross

House of
the Binns

Linlithgow

Union Canal

Castle
Campbell

OCHIL HILLS

Tillicoultry

Alva

Bo'Ness

Linlithgow
Palace

Grangemouth

River Devon

Alloa

Clackmannan

Dunmore

Airth

River Forth

Kincardine

Falkirk

River Carron

Carron

Larbert

Stirling

Fallin

Denny

KEY

—— Rail Lines

N

50
51
52
43
42
41
44
46
45
47
49
48

6 miles
9 km

South Queensferry

★ ❹❸ This pleasant little waterside community, a former ferry port 9 mi west of the city, is totally dominated by the **Forth bridges,** which cross the Firth of Forth here. The **Forth Rail Bridge** was opened in 1890 and is 2,765 yards long, except on a hot summer's day when it expands by about another yard! Its neighbor is the 1,993-yard-long **Forth Road Bridge,** in operation since 1964.

Hopetoun House

❹❹ The palatial premises of Hopetoun House, probably Scotland's grandest courtly seat and home of the marquesses of Linlithgow, are considered to be among the Adam family's finest designs. The enormous house was started in 1699 to the original plans of Sir William Bruce (1630–1710), then enlarged between 1721 and 1754 by William Adam (1689–1748) and his son Robert. There is a notable painting collection, and the house has decorative work of the highest order, plus all the trappings to keep you entertained: a nature trail, a restaurant in the former stables, and a museum. Much of the wealth that created this sumptuous building came from the family's mining interests in the surrounding regions. ✉ *6 mi west of South Queensferry, off A904,* ☎ *0131/331–2451.* 💷 *£5.* ◷ *Apr.–Sept., daily 10–5:30; Oct., weekends 10–5:30 (last admission 4:30).*

House of the Binns

❹❺ The 17th-century General Tam Dalyell (circa 1599–1685) transformed a fortified stronghold into a gracious mansion, the House of the Binns (the name derives from *ben,* the Scottish word for *hill*). The present exterior dates from around 1810 and shows a remodeling into a kind of mock fort with crenellated battlements and turrets. Inside there are magnificent plaster ceilings done in the Elizabethan style. The house is cared for by the National Trust for Scotland. ✉ *Off A904, 4 mi east of Linlithgow,* ☎ *01506/834255.* 💷 *£3.90.* ◷ *House: May–Sept., Sat.–Thurs. 1:30–5:30 (last tour 5). Parkland: Apr.–Oct., daily 10–7; Nov.–Mar., daily 10–4 (last admission 30 mins before closing).*

Blackness

❹❻ The castle of Blackness stands like a grounded gray hulk on the very edge of the Forth. A curious 15th-century structure, it has had a varied career as a strategic fortress, state prison, powder magazine, and youth hostel. The countryside is gently green and cultivated, and open views extend across the blue Forth to the distant ramparts of the Ochil Hills. The castle is run by Historic Scotland, a government organization that looks after many, but not all, historic properties in Scotland. ✉ *B903, 4 mi northeast of Linlithgow,* ☎ *0131/668–8800.* 💷 *£1.80.* ◷ *Apr.–Sept., daily 9:30–6; Oct.–Mar., Mon.–Wed. and Sat. 9:30–4, Thurs. 9:30–noon, Sun. 2–4.*

Linlithgow

❹❼ On the edge of Linlithgow Loch stands the splendid ruin of **Linlithgow Palace,** birthplace of Mary, Queen of Scots (1542). Burned, perhaps by accident, by Hanoverian troops during the last Jacobite rebellion in 1746, this impressive shell stands on a site of great antiquity, though nothing for certain survived an earlier fire in 1424. The palace gatehouse is from the early 16th century, and the central courtyard's elaborate fountain dates from around 1535, but the halls and great rooms are cold, echoing stone husks now in Historic Scotland's care. ✉ *A706, south shore of Linlithgow Loch,* ☎ *0131/668–8800.* 💷 *£2.50.* ◷ *Apr.–Sept., daily 9:30–6; Oct.–Mar., Mon.–Sat. 9:30–4, Sun. 2–4.*

En Route From the M9 you will begin to gain tempting glimpses of the Highland hills to the northwest and the long, humped wall of the Ochil Hills, across the river plain to the north. The **River Carron,** which flows under the M9, gave its name to the *carronade,* a kind of cannon manufactured in Falkirk, a few minutes to the southwest. You will also notice the apocalyptic complex of Grangemouth Refinery (impressive by night), which you may also smell if the wind is right—or wrong! The refinery processes North Sea crude oil but was originally sited here because of the now-extinct oil-shale extraction industry of West Lothian, pioneered by a Scot, James "Paraffin" Young. This landscape may not be the most scenic in Scotland, but it has certainly played its role in the nation's industrial history.

Ochil Hills

The scarp face of the Ochil Hills looms unmistakably. It is an old fault line that yields up hard volcanic rocks and contrasts with the quantities of softer coal immediately around the River Forth. The steep Ochils provided grazing land and water power for Scotland's second-largest textile area. Some mills still survive in the so-called Hillfoots towns, on the scarp edge east of Stirling. Several hikers' routes run into the narrow chinks of glens here. Behind Alva is **Alva Glen,** a park near the converted Strude Mill, at the top and eastern end of the little town. A little farther east is the **Ochil Hills Woodland Park,** which provides access to Silver Glen. The **Mill Glen,** behind Tillicoultry (pronounced tilly-*coot*-ree), with its giant quarry, fine waterfalls, and interesting plants, is another hiking option for energetic explorers.

Dollar

This *douce* (Scots for well-mannered or gentle) and tidy town below the Ochil Hills slopes lies at the mouth of Dollar Glen. By following signs for **Castle Campbell,** however, you will find a road that angles sharply up the east side of the wooded defile. The narrow road ends in a parking lot from which it's only a short walk to Castle Campbell, high on a great sloping mound in the center of the glen. With the green woods below, bracken hills above, and a view that on a clear day stretches right across the Forth Valley to the tip of Tinto Hill near Lanark, this is certainly the most atmospheric fortress within easy reach of Edinburgh. Formerly known as Castle Gloom, Castle Campbell stands out among Scottish castles for the sheer drama of its setting. The sturdy square of the tower house survives from the 15th century, when this site was first fortified by the first earl of Argyll (d. 1493). Other buildings and enclosures were subsequently added, but the sheer lack of space on this rocky eminence ensured that there would never be any drastic changes. The castle is associated with the earls of Argyll, as well as with John Knox, the fiery religious reformer, who preached here. It also played a role in the religious wars of the 17th century, having been captured by Oliver Cromwell in 1654 and garrisoned with English troops. It is now cared for by Historic Scotland. ⊠ *Dollar Glen, 1 mi north of Dollar (30 mi northwest of Edinburgh),* ☎ *0131/ 668–8800.* ⊒ *£2.50.* ⊙ *Apr.–Sept., daily 9:30–6; Oct.–Mar., Mon.–Wed. and Sat. 9:30–4, Thurs. 9:30–noon, Sun. 2–4.*

Culross

On the muddy shores of the Forth, **Culross** is one of the most remarkable little towns in all of Scotland. It once had a thriving industry and export trade in coal and salt (the coal was used in the salt-panning process). It also had, curiously, a trade monopoly in the manufacture of baking *girdles* (griddles). But as local coal became exhausted, the impetus of the industrial revolution passed it by, and other parts of the Forth Valley prospered. Culross became a backwater town, and the merchants' houses of the 17th and 18th centuries were never replaced by Victorian developments or modern architecture. In the 1930s the then-new and also very poor National Trust for Scotland started to buy up the decaying properties. With the help of a variety of other agencies, these buildings were conserved and brought to life. Today ordinary citizens live in many of the National Trust properties. A few—the Palace, Study, and Town House—are open to the public. With its Mercat Cross, cobbled streets, tolbooth, and narrow wynds, Culross is now a living museum of a 17th-century town. ⊠ *25 mi northwest of Edinburgh,* ☎ *01383/880359.* ☞ *Palace, Study, and Town House £4.40.* ☉ *Study and Town House: Apr.–Sept., daily 1:30–5; Oct., weekends 11–5 (last admission 4:30); Palace: Apr.–Sept., daily 11–5 (last admission 4).*

Dunfermline

This town 16 mi northwest of Edinburgh was once the world center for the production of damask linen; the **Dunfermline Museum** (⊠ Viewfield Terr., ☎ 01383/313838, ☞ £2, ☉ Apr.–Oct., Mon.–Sat. 11–5, Sun. 2–5) tells the full story. Today the town is better known as the birthplace of millionaire philanthropist Andrew Carnegie (1835–1919). Undoubtedly Dunfermline's most famous son, Carnegie endowed the town with a library, health and fitness center, spacious park, and, naturally, a Carnegie Hall, still the focus of culture and entertainment. The ★ ⑤⓪ 1835 weaver's cottage in which Carnegie was born is now the **Andrew Carnegie Birthplace Museum.** Don't be misled by the cottage's exterior. Inside it opens into a larger hall, where documents, photographs, and artifacts tell Carnegie's fascinating life story. You will learn such obscure details as the claim that Carnegie was one of only three men in the United States then able to translate Morse code by ear as it came down the wire. ⊠ *Moodie St.,* ☎ *01383/724302.* ☞ *£1.50.* ☉ *Apr.–May and Sept.–Oct., Mon.–Sat. 11–5, Sun. 2–5; June–Aug., Mon.–Sat. 10–5, Sun. 2–5; Nov.–Mar., daily 2–4.*

⑤① Also in Dunfermline is the **Dunfermline Abbey and Palace.** The abbey complex was founded by Queen Margaret, the English wife of the Scots king Malcolm III (circa 1031–93). Some Norman work can be seen in the present church, where Robert the Bruce (1274–1329) lies buried. The palace grew from the abbey guest house and was the birthplace of Charles I (1600–49). Dunfermline was the seat of the royal court of Scotland until the end of the 11th century, and its central role in Scottish affairs is explored by means of display panels dotted around the drafty but hallowed buildings. ⊠ *Monastery St.,* ☎ *0131/668–8800.* ☞ *£1.80.* ☉ *Apr.–Sept., daily 9:30–6; Oct.–Mar., Mon.–Wed. and Sat. 9:30–4, Thurs. 9:30–noon, Sun. 2–4.*

North Queensferry

The former ferry port on the north side of the Forth dropped almost into oblivion after the Forth Road Bridge opened but was dragged ⑤② abruptly back into the limelight when the hugely popular **Deep Sea World** arrived in the early 1990s. This sophisticated "aquarium"—for want of a better word—on the Firth of Forth offers a fascinating view of underwater life. Go down a clear acrylic tunnel for a diver's-eye look at more than 5,000 fish, including a posse of 9-ft sharks, and visit the exhibition hall, which has an audiovisual presentation on local marine life, an Amazon jungle display, and various other creatures. Nervous ichthyophobes will feel more at ease in the adjacent café and gift shop. ⊠ *North Queensferry,* ☎ *01383/411880.* ☞ *£6.15.* ☉ *Apr.–June and Sept.–Oct., daily 10–6; July–Aug., daily 10–6:30; Nov.–Mar., weekdays 11–5, weekends 10–6.*

West Lothian and the Forth Valley A to Z

ARRIVING AND DEPARTING

By Bus: First Midland Bluebird (☎ 01324/613777) bus services link most of this area, but working out a detailed itinerary by bus would be best left to your travel agent or guide.

By Car: Leave Edinburgh by Queensferry Road—the A90—and follow signs for the Forth Bridge. Beyond the city boundary at Cramond take the slip road, B924, for South Queensferry, watching for signs to Dalmeny House. From Dalmeny follow the B924 for the descent to South Queensferry. The B924 continues westward under the approaches to the suspension bridge and then meets the A904. On turning right onto A904, follow signs for Hopetoun House, House of the Binns, and Blackness Castle. From Blackness take the B903 to its junction with the A904. Turn left for Linlithgow on the A803. At this point it's best to join the M9, which will speed you westward. Follow Kincardine Bridge signs off the motorway, cross the Forth and take the A977 north from Kincardine, formerly a trading port and distillery center. Take the A907 to Alloa, get on the A908 (marked TILLICOULTRY) for a short stretch, and then pick up the B908 (marked ALVA).

At this point you'll be leaving the industrial northern shore of the Forth behind and entering the Ochil Hills, which you can explore by following the A91 eastward at Alva; squeezed between the gentle River Devon and the steep slopes above, the road continues to Dollar, where you should follow signs to Castle Campbell. From the castle, retrace your route to A91 and turn left. Just a few minutes outside Dollar, turn right onto a minor road (signposted RUMBLING BRIDGE). Then turn right onto the A823. Follow A823 through Powmill (follow the signs for Dunfermline); turn right off A823, following the signs for Saline (a pleasant if undistinguished village), and take an unclassified road due south to join the A907. Turn right, and then within a mile go left on the B9037, which leads down to Culross. Take the B9037 east to join the A994, which leads to Dunfermline. From here follow the Edinburgh signs to the A823 and return via North Queensferry and the Forth Road Bridge (toll 40p).

By Train: Dalmeny, Linlithgow, and Dunfermline all have rail stations and can be reached from Edinburgh Waverley station. For information call the **National Train Enquiry Line** (☎ 0345/484950).

VISITOR INFORMATION
The tourist information office in the **Mill Trail Visitor Centre** (☎ 01259/ 769696), at Alva, can provide information on the region's textile establishments as well as a *Mill Trail* brochure, which can lead you to mill shops offering bargain woolen and tweed goods.

Midlothian and East Lothian

In spite of the finest stone carving in Scotland at Rosslyn Chapel, associations with Sir Walter Scott, outstanding castles, and miles of varied rolling countryside, Midlothian, the area immediately south of Edinburgh, for years remained off the beaten tourist path. Perhaps a little in awe of sophisticated Edinburgh to the north and the well-manicured charm of the stockbroker belt of nearby upmarket East Lothian, Midlothian remained quietly preoccupied with its own workaday little towns and dormitory suburbs.

As for East Lothian, it started with the advantage of golf courses of world rank, most notably Muirfield, plus a scattering of stately homes and interesting hotels. Red-pantiled and decidedly middle class, it is an area of glowing grain fields in summer and quite a few discreetly polite STRICTLY PRIVATE signs at the end of driveways. Still, it has plenty of interest for you, including photogenic villages, active fishing harbors, and vistas of pastoral Lowland Scotland, seemingly a world away (but much less than an hour by car) from bustling Edinburgh.

Roslin

★ ⑤ A pretty little U-shape miners' village, with its rows of stone-built terraced cottages, Roslin is famous for the extraordinary **Rosslyn Chapel.** Conceived by Sir William Sinclair (circa 1404–80) and dedicated to St. Matthew in 1450, the chapel is outstanding for the quality and variety of the stone carving inside. Covering almost every square inch of stonework are human figures, animals, and plants. The chapel was actually never finished. The original design called for a cruciform structure, but only the choir and parts of the east transept walls were completed. ✉ *Roslin, off A703, 7½ mi south of Edinburgh,* ☎ *0131/ 440–2159.* 🎟 *£3.* ⊙ *Mon.–Sat. 10–5, Sun. noon–4:45.*

Penicuik

⑤ There are fine views of the Pentland Hills beyond this town, but its chief attraction for the tourist is the **Edinburgh Crystal Visitor Centre,** with crystal pieces and an audiovisual exhibition on the production of crystal. Guided tours reveal the stages involved in the manufacture of cut crystal. In addition, groups of 6–10 people can prebook a VIP tour (adults over 18 only), which includes an opportunity for you to blow a glass bubble and cut your own piece of glass, later polished and given to you as a keepsake. Advance booking is essential for this tour. The Visitor Centre also has a coffee shop and gift shops. ✉ *Eastfield, Penicuik, 10 mi south of Edinburgh,* ☎ *01968/675128.* 🎟 *Center free, tours £3, VIP tour £10.* ⊙ *Mon.–Sat. 9–5, Sun. 11–5. Factory tours: Oct.–Mar., weekdays 9:15–3:30; Apr.–Sept., weekdays 9:15–3:30, weekends 11–2:30 (shorter demonstration tour offered).*

The Pentlands

This unmistakable range of hills immediately south of Edinburgh has the longest artificial ski slope in Britain, at Hillend, and an all-year chairlift that provides magnificent views (even to nonskiers). There are several other access points along the A702 running parallel to the hills—the best is Flotterstone, where you'll find a parking lot, pub, and quiet roads for walking.

DINING

£ ✕ **Old Bakehouse.** Here you will find home-cooked fare in quaint, wood-beamed rooms. Danish open sandwiches are the specialty, but homemade soups and hot main courses are also included on the menu. ✉ *West Linton, southwest of Penicuik on A702,* ☎ *01968/660830. AE, MC, V. Closed Mon. No dinner Tues., Thurs., and Sun.*

Newtongrange

⑤ This former mining community 6 mi southeast of Edinburgh is home to the **Scottish Mining Museum,** where, in a visitor center newly completed for the year 2000, you can learn something about the history of Scotland's mining industry and its mining communities. Go on shift as a coal miner and experience life at the (virtual reality) coal face. There are also interactive displays and "magic helmets" that bring the tour to life and relate the power that the mining company had over the lives of the individual workers in a frighteningly autocratic system that survived well into the 1930s; the mining company owned the houses, shops, and even the pub. Newtongrange was in fact the largest planned mining village in Scotland. The scenery is no more attractive than you would expect, though the green Pentland Hills are still hovering in the distance. ☎ *0131/663–7519.* 🎟 *£4.* ⊙ *Daily 10–5.*

Borthwick

⑤ Set in green countryside with scattered woods and lush hedgerows, the little village of Borthwick, 13 mi southeast of Edinburgh, is dominated by **Borthwick Castle,** which dates from the 15th century and is still oc-

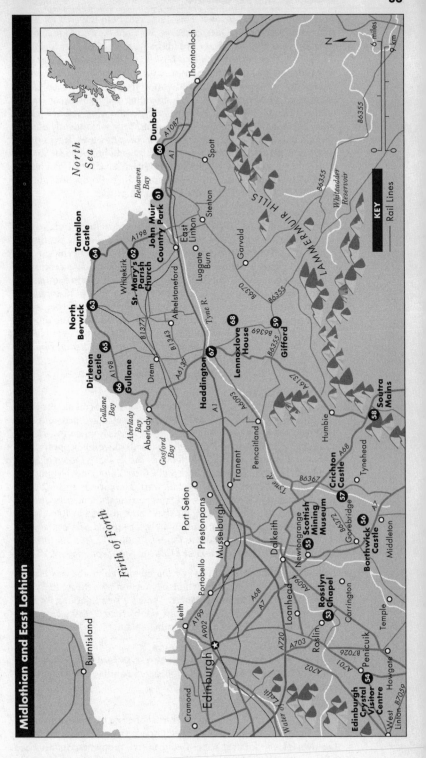

Midlothian and East Lothian

cupied (☞ Lodging, *below*). This stark, tall, twin-towered fortress is associated with Mary, Queen of Scots. She came here on a kind of honeymoon with her ill-starred third husband, the earl of Bothwell (circa 1535–78). Their already-dubious bliss was interrupted by Mary's political opponents, often referred to as the Lords of the Congregation, a confederacy of powerful nobles who were against the queen's latest liaison and who instead favored the crowning of her young son, James. Rather insensitively, they laid siege to the castle while the newlyweds were there. The history books relate that Mary subsequently escaped disguised as a man. She was not free for long, however. It was only a short time before she was defeated in battle and imprisoned. She languished in prison for 21 years before Queen Elizabeth I of England (1558–1603) signed her death warrant (1587). Bothwell's fate was equally gloomy: He died insane in a Danish prison.

LODGING

££££ **Borthwick Castle.** There are hotels with castle names; and there are hotels inside what once were castles; and then there is Borthwick, which is still first a castle and only second a place where you can stay. This 15th-century fortress was already taking guests half a century before Columbus discovered the Americas. Nowhere else in Scotland offers the extraordinary experience of staying as a part of history. Your "bedchamber," be reassured, is warm and comfortable, fully equipped with bath or shower (the plumbing is not 15th century). You dine not in a restaurant but in a magnificent vaulted room, the Great Hall, lit by candles and the gleam of a log fire. ✉ *North Middleton, Midlothian EH23 4QY,* ☎ *01875/820514,* FAX *01875/821702. 10 rooms, 1 with bath, 9 with shower. AE, DC, MC, V. Closed Jan.–mid-Mar.*

Crichton Castle

57 Like Borthwick Castle, Crichton Castle (a Historic Scotland property) is set in attractive, rolling Lowland scenery, interrupted here and there with patches of woodland. You can reach this castle from Borthwick Castle by taking a peaceful walk through the woods (there are signposts along the way). Crichton was a Bothwell family castle; Mary, Queen of Scots, attended the wedding here of Bothwell's sister, Lady Janet Hepburn, to Mary's natural brother, Lord John Stewart. The curious arcaded range reveals diamond-faceted stonework; this particular geometric pattern is unique in Scotland and is thought to have been inspired by Renaissance styles on the Continent, particularly Italy. The oldest part of the work is the 14th-century keep (square tower). ✉ *B6367, 7 mi southeast of Dalkeith,* ☎ *0131/668–8800.* *£1.80.* ⏲ *Apr.–Sept., daily 9:30–6.*

En Route Follow the A68 5 mi south, away from Edinburgh, to the very edge of the Lammermuir Hills. Just beyond the junction with the A6137 you'll 58 come to a spot called **Soutra Mains.** There's a small parking lot here, from which you can enjoy glorious unobstructed views extending northward over the whole of the Lothian plain.

Gifford

59 With its 18th-century kirk and Mercat Cross, **Gifford** is a good example of a tweedily respectable, well-scrubbed, red-pantile-roofed East Lothian village, 25 mi east of Edinburgh.

Dunbar

In the days before tour companies started offering package deals to the 60 Mediterranean, **Dunbar** was a popular holiday resort. Now a bit faded, the town is lovely for its spacious Georgian-style properties, characterized by the astragals, or fan-shape windows, above the doors; the symmetry of the house fronts; and the parapeted roof lines. Though not the popular seaside playground it once was, Dunbar, 30 mi east of Edinburgh, does still have an attractive beach and a picturesque harbor.

John Muir Country Park

61 Taking in the estuary of the River Tyne winding down from the Moorfoot Hills, the John Muir Country Park offers varied coastal scenery: rocky shoreline, golden sands, and the mixed woodlands of Tyninghame, teeming with wildlife. Dunbar-born John Muir (1838–1914), whose family emigrated to the United States when he was a child, helped found the Yosemite and Sequoia national parks. Only recently has the work of this early conservationist been acknowledged in his native Scotland. ⊠ *28 mi east of Edinburgh.*

Whitekirk

62 The unmistakable red-sandstone **St. Mary's Parish Church** with its Norman tower stands on a site occupied since the 6th century. It was a place of pilgrimage in medieval times because of its healing well. Behind the kirk, in a field, stands a tithe barn. Tithe barns originated in the practice of giving to the church a proportion of local produce, which then required storage space. At one end of the structure is a 16th-century tower house, which at one point in its history accommodated visiting pilgrims. The large three-story barn was added to the tower house in the 17th century. ⊠ *A198; 27 mi east of Edinburgh.* 🔄 *Free.* ☉ *Daily, early morning–late evening.*

North Berwick

63 The pleasant little seaside resort of **North Berwick,** 26 mi northeast of Edinburgh, manages to retain a small-town personality even when it's thronged with city visitors on warm summer Sunday afternoons. Munching on ice cream, the city folk stroll on the beach and in the narrow streets or gape at the sailing craft in the small harbor.

64 Rising on a cliff beyond the flat fields east of North Berwick, **Tantallon Castle** is a substantial ruin defending a headland with the sea on three sides. The red sandstone is pitted and eaten by time and sea spray, with the earliest surviving stonework dating from the late 14th century. The fortress was besieged in 1529 by the cannons of King James V (1512–42). (Rather inconveniently, the besieging forces ran out of gunpowder.) Cannons were used again, to deadlier effect, in a later siege during the Civil War in 1651. Twelve days of battering with the heavy guns of Cromwell's General Monk greatly damaged the flanking towers. However, much of the curtain wall of this former Douglas stronghold (now cared for by Historic Scotland) survives. ⊠ *A198, 3 mi east of North Berwick,* ☎ *0131/668–8800.* 🔄 *£2.50.* ☉ *Apr.–Sept., daily 9:30–6; Oct.–Mar., Mon.–Wed. and Sat. 9:30–4, Thurs. 9:30–noon, Sun. 2–4.*

Dirleton

65 Set right in the center of this small village is the 12th-century **Dirleton Castle,** surrounded by a high outer wall. Within the wall you'll find a 17th-century bowling green, set in the shade of yew trees and surrounded by a herbaceous flower border that comes ablaze with color in high summer. Dirleton Castle (now in Historic Scotland's care) was occupied in 1298 by King Edward I of England as part of his campaign for the continued subjugation of the unruly Scots. ⊠ *A198, 22 mi northeast of Edinburgh,* ☎ *0131/668–8800.* 🔄 *£2.50.* ☉ *Apr.–Sept., daily 9:30–6; Oct.–Mar., Mon.–Sat. 9:30–4, Sun. 2–4.*

Gullane

66 Very noticeable along this coastline are the golf courses of East Lothian, laid out wherever there is available links space. **Gullane,** surrounded by them, is ultrarespectable, its inhabitants clad mostly in expensive golfing sweaters. **Muirfield,** venue for the Open Championship, is nearby, as is **Greywalls,** now a hotel (☞ Lodging, *below*) but originally a private house, designed by Sir Edwin Lutyens (1869–1944).

Apart from golf, at Gullane's beach, well within driving distance of the city, you can enjoy restful summer evening strolls.

LODGING

££££ ☒ **Greywalls.** This is the ideal hotel for a golfing vacation: comfortable, with attentive service and award-winning modern British cuisine that makes the most of local produce. The house itself is an architectural treasure. Edward VII used to stay here, as have Nicklaus, Trevino, Palmer, and a host of other golfing greats. Shades of restful green predominate in the stylish fabrics from the likes of Nina Campbell, Colefax and Fowler, and Osborne and Little. ✉ *Muirfield, Gullane EH31 2EG,* ☎ *01620/842144,* FAX *01620/842241. 23 rooms with bath. Restaurant, putting green, tennis court. AE, DC, MC, V. Closed Nov.–Mar.*

Haddington

One of the best-preserved medieval street plans in the country can be
⑥⑦ explored in **Haddington,** 15 mi east of Edinburgh. Among the many buildings of architectural or historical interest is the Town House, designed by William Adam in 1748 and enlarged in 1830. A wall plaque at the Sidegate recalls the great heights of floods from the River Tyne. Beyond is the medieval Nungate footbridge, with the Church of St. Mary a little way upstream.

⑥⑧ Just to the south of Haddington is **Lennoxlove House,** the grand ancestral home of the very grand dukes of Hamilton and Lennox, which displays items associated with Mary, Queen of Scots. A turreted country house, part of it dating from the 15th century, Lennoxlove is a cheerful mix of family life and Scottish history. Housed in the beautifully decorated rooms are collections of portraits, furniture, and porcelain. ✉ *B6369, 1 mi south of Haddington,* ☎ *01620/823720.* ☞ *£3.50.* ☉ *Easter–Oct., Wed., Thurs., bank holidays, and weekends 2–4:30.*

Midlothian and East Lothian A to Z

ARRIVING AND DEPARTING

By Bus: City bus services run out as far as Swanston and the Pentland Hills. **First Lowland** (☎ 0131/663–9233) buses run to towns and villages throughout Midlothian and East Lothian. For details of all services, inquire at the St. Andrew Square bus station in Edinburgh.

By Car: Leave Edinburgh via the A701 (Liberton Rd.). At the not-very-picturesque community of Bilston, turn left to Roslin on the B7006. From Roslin return to the A701 for Penicuik. From Penicuik take the A766 to A702, which runs beneath the Pentland Hills to West Linton. Then follow the B7059 and the A701 to Leadburn and then Howgate. Get onto the A6094 for a few minutes, then turn right onto the B6372, and continue past Temple, an attractive village on the edge of the Moorfoot Hills, toward Gorebridge.

At the junction of B6372 with A7, just before Gorebridge, you have a choice. If your interests tend toward social history, turn left and drive 2 mi to reach Newtongrange. If your interests lie elsewhere, turn right instead, and after a few moments' travel south you will see a sign for Borthwick. Take a left onto an unclassified road off A7, and a few minutes later Borthwick Castle appears. From Borthwick take the B6372 and turn right onto the A68. Just beyond the village of Pathhead you'll see signs to Crichton Castle. Having detoured to the castle, follow the A68 south, away from Edinburgh, to the very edge of the Lammermuir Hills. Just beyond the junction with the A6137, at Soutra Mains, there's a small parking lot from which to enjoy the view. Make your way back to the A6137 and turn right onto it; turn right again onto the B6355, go through Gifford, and head east for the junction with the B6370, which leads to Dunbar.

West of Dunbar, on the way back to Edinburgh, the A1087 leads to the sandy reaches of Belhaven Bay, signposted from the main road, and to the John Muir Country Park. From the park drive north on the A198 (a right turn off the A1), to reach Whitekirk, Tantallon Castle, and North Berwick. Dirleton, with its own massive castle, and Gullane, surrounded by golf courses, follow. A198 eventually leads to Aberlady, from which you can take the A6137 south to the former county town of Haddington and, by way of the B6369, to Lennoxlove House. Return to the A1 at Haddington and head west back to Edinburgh. From Haddington it's about 15 mi back to center city.

By Train: There is no train service in Midlothian. In East Lothian, the towns of North Berwick, Drem, and Dunbar have train stations with regular service from Edinburgh.

EDINBURGH AND THE LOTHIANS A TO Z

Arriving and Departing

By Bus
National Express (☎ 0990/808080) provides bus service to and from London and other major towns and cities. The main terminal, St. Andrew Square Bus bus station, is only a couple of minutes (on foot) north of Waverley station, immediately east of St. Andrew Square. Long-distance coaches must be booked in advance from the booking office in the terminal. Edinburgh is approximately eight hours by bus from London.

By Car
Downtown Edinburgh centers on Princes Street, which runs east–west. Drivers from the east coast will come in on A1, with Meadowbank Stadium serving as a landmark. The highway bypasses the suburbs of Musselburgh and Tranent; therefore, any bottlenecks will occur close to downtown. From the Borders the approach to Princes Street is by A7/A68 through Newington, an area offering a wide choice of accommodations. From Newington the east end of Princes Street is reached by North Bridge and South Bridge. Approaching from the southwest, drivers will join the west end of Princes Street (Lothian Road) via A701 and A702, and those coming west from Glasgow or Stirling will meet Princes Street from M8 or M9, respectively. A slightly more complicated approach is via M90—from Forth Road Bridge/Perth/east coast; the key road for getting downtown is Queensferry Road, which joins Charlotte Square close to the west end of Princes Street.

By Plane
At present, **Edinburgh Airport** (☎ 0131/333–1000), 7 mi west of the city center, offers no transatlantic flights. It does, however, have air connections throughout the United Kingdom—London (Heathrow, Gatwick, Stansted, Luton, and City), Aberdeen, Birmingham, Bournemouth, Bristol, Dundee, East Midlands, Kirkwall (Orkney), Leeds/Bradford, Manchester, Norwich, Shetland, Southampton, and Belfast (in Northern Ireland)—as well as with a number of European cities, including Amsterdam, Brussels, Copenhagen, Dublin, Dusseldorf, Munich, Paris, and Zurich. There are flights to Edinburgh Airport virtually every hour from London's Gatwick and Heathrow airports; it's usually faster and less complicated to fly through Gatwick (which has excellent rail service from London's Victoria Station). Airlines serving Edinburgh include Aer Lingus, Air France, British Airways, British Midland, Crossair, EasyJet, Euroscot, Gill Air, KLM, Sabena, Servisair, and Suckling Airways.

Glasgow Airport (☎ 0141/887–1111), 50 mi west of Edinburgh, is now the major point of entry into Edinburgh for transatlantic flights (☞ Glasgow A to Z *in* Chapter 2).

Prestwick Airport (☎ 01292/479822), 30 mi southwest of Glasgow, after some years of eclipse by Glasgow Airport, is beginning to be part of the reckoning, not least because of the activities of **Ryanair** (☎ 01292/ 678000), a company that has sparked a major price war on the Anglo-Scottish routes (e.g., between London and Glasgow/Edinburgh). It offers unbeatable, no-frills, rock-bottom air fares between Prestwick and London's Stansted Airport.

BETWEEN EDINBURGH AIRPORT AND THE CITY CENTER

There are no rail links to the city center, despite the fact that the airport sits between two main lines. By bus or car you can usually make it to Edinburgh in a comfortable half hour, unless you hit the morning or evening rush hours (7:30–9 and 4–6).

By Bus: Lothian Regional Transport (☎ 0131/555–6363) and **Guide Friday** (☎ 0131/556–2244) run buses between Edinburgh Airport's main terminal building and Waverley Bridge, in the city center and within easy reach of several hotels. The buses run every 15 minutes daily (9–5) and less frequently (roughly every hour) during off-peak hours. The trip takes about 30 minutes (about 45 minutes during rush hour). A single-fare ticket on a Lothian Regional Transport bus costs £3.30, on Guide Friday £3.60.

By Limousine: The following Edinburgh firms provide chauffeur-driven limousines to meet flights at Edinburgh Airport: **David Grieve Chauffeur Drive** (✉ 9/7 Lower Gilmour Pl., ☎ 0131/229–8666), for about £32; **Little's Chauffeur Drive** (✉ 5 St. Ninian's Dr., ☎ 0131/334–2177), £46 plus VAT; and **Sleigh Ltd.** (✉ 6 Devon Pl., ☎ 0131/337–3171), £50 plus VAT.

By Rental Car: There is a good choice of car-rental companies operating from the terminal building (☞ Contacts and Resources, *below*). The cost is from £40 a day, depending on the firm. If you choose to plunge yourself into Edinburgh's traffic system, take care on the first couple of traffic circles (called roundabouts) you encounter on the way into town from the airport—even the most experienced drivers find them challenging. By car the airport is about 7 mi west of Princes Street downtown and is clearly marked from A8. The usual route to downtown is via the suburb of Corstorphine.

By Taxi: These are readily available outside the terminal. The trip takes 20–30 minutes to the city center, 15 minutes longer during morning and evening rush hours. The fare is roughly £15. Note that because of a local regulation, airport taxis picking up fares from the terminal are any color, not the typical black cabs, although these also take fares going to the airport.

BETWEEN GLASGOW AIRPORT AND EDINBURGH

By Bus and Train: Scottish Citylink (☎ 0990/505050) buses leave Glasgow Airport every 15 minutes to travel to Glasgow's Buchanan Street (journey time is 25 minutes), where you must transfer to an Edinburgh bus (leaving every 20 minutes). The trip to Edinburgh takes 70 minutes and costs £7 round-trip and £4.50 one-way. A somewhat more pleasant option is to take a cab from Glasgow Airport to Glasgow's Queen Street train station (lasts 20 minutes and costs about £15) and then take the train to Waverley Station in Edinburgh. Trains leave about every 30 minutes; the trip takes 50 minutes and costs £7.30. Check times on weekends. Another, less expensive alternative—best for those with little luggage—is to take the bus from Glasgow Airport to Glasgow's Buchanan bus station, walk five minutes to the Queen Street train station, and catch the train to Edinburgh.

By Taxi: Taxis (☎ 0141/848–4900) from Glasgow Airport to downtown Edinburgh take about 70 minutes and cost around £70–£80.

By Train
Edinburgh's main train hub, **Waverley Station,** is downtown, below Waverley Bridge and around the corner from the unmistakable spire of the Scott Monument. For information call the **National Train Enquiry Line** (☎ 0345/484950). Travel time from Edinburgh to London by train is as little as 4½ hours for the fastest service.

Edinburgh's other main station is **Haymarket,** about four minutes (by rail) west of Waverley. Most Glasgow and other western and northern services stop here. Haymarket can be slightly more convenient for visitors staying in hotels beyond the west end of Princes Street.

Getting Around

By Bus
Lothian Regional Transport (LRT; ✉ 27 Hanover St., ☎ 0131/555–6363; ⊙ Mon.–Sat. 8:30–6; ✉ Waverley Bridge, ☎ 0131/555–6363 or 0131/554–4494), operating burgundy-and-white buses, is the main operator within Edinburgh. You can buy tickets on the bus. The Day Saver Ticket (£2.40), allowing unlimited one-day travel on the city's buses, can be purchased in advance or from the driver on any LRT bus (exact money is required when purchasing on a bus). The Rider Card (for which you will need a photo) is valid on all buses for seven days (beginning Sunday through Saturday night) and costs £10.50, while the four-week Rider costs £30.50.

First Lowland (✉ St. Andrew Square bus station, ☎ 0131/663–9233), operating green-and-cream buses, provides much of the service between Edinburgh and the Lothians and offers day tours around and beyond the city. You will also see other bus companies, most of which are part of First Bus Company.

By Car
Driving in Edinburgh has its quirks and pitfalls, but competent drivers should not be intimidated. Metered parking in the center city is scarce and expensive, and the local traffic wardens are a feisty, alert bunch. Note that illegally parked cars are routinely wheel-clamped ("booted") and towed away, and getting your car back will be expensive. After 6 PM the parking situation improves considerably, and you may manage to find a space quite near your hotel, even downtown. If you park on a yellow line or in a resident's parking bay, be prepared to move your car by 8 the following morning, when the rush hour gets under way. Parking lots are clearly signposted; overnight parking is expensive and not permitted in all lots.

Princes Street in New Town is usually considered the city center. The street runs east–west; motorists using the A1 east-coast road enter the city from the east end of Princes Street. Using the city bypass, you can reach key points to the west, such as the airport or the Forth Road Bridge (gateway to the north), from many parts of the outskirts and from East Lothian without getting tangled up in downtown traffic.

By Taxi
Taxi stands can be found throughout the downtown area; the following are the most convenient: the west end of Princes Street, South St. David Street, and North St. Andrew Street (both just off St. Andrew

Square), Waverley Market, Waterloo Place, and Lauriston Place. Alternatively, hail any taxi displaying an illuminated FOR HIRE sign.

By Train

Edinburgh has no urban or suburban rail systems.

Contacts and Resources

Car Rentals

Major companies have booths at the airport. **Avis** (☎ 0131/333–1866). **Europcar** (☎ 0131/344–3114). **Hertz** (☎ 0131/333–1019). **National Car Rentals** (☎ 0131/344–3250).

Consulates

American Consulate General (⌧ 3 Regent Terr., ☎ 0131/556–8315). The London office of the **Canadian High Commission** (☎ 0171/258–6316) can provide local information for visitors.

Emergencies

Ambulance, police, or fire: ☎ 999. (No coins are needed for emergency calls made from pay phones.) **Edinburgh Royal Infirmary** (⌧ 51 Lauriston Pl., ☎ 0131/536–1000) is south of the city center—down George IV Bridge and then to the right.

Guided Tours

EXCURSIONS

Both **Lothian Regional Transport** and **Scotline Tours** (☞ Orientation Tours, *below*) and limousine companies (☞ Between Edinburgh Airport and the City Center, *above*) offer day trips to destinations such as St. Andrews and Fife or the Trossachs and Loch Lomond.

ORIENTATION TOURS

Scottish Tourist Guides (contact Kate Anderson, ⌧ 2/4 Dumbryden Gardens, Edinburgh EH14 2NG, ☎ FAX 0131/453–1297), endorsed by the Scottish Tourist Board, offers knowledgeable guides appropriate for an individual or a group. The tours are wide-ranging and flexible.

Lothian Regional Transport (☎ 0131/555–6363) offers the "Edinburgh Classic Tour," a worthwhile introduction to the Old and New Towns. The ticket (🎫 £6) is a bargain because it is valid on any other "Classic Tour" bus for the rest of the day. There are frequent departures from Waverley Bridge (outside the rail station) and other points around the city. Open-top buses operate in suitable weather. This is a flexible, show-up-and-hop-on service, meaning that you can get off the bus at any attractions you may want to see more closely and then get on another open-top bus later. Allow an hour for the complete tour. You can buy tickets from the Lothian Regional Transport offices on Hanover Street or Waverley Bridge, or you can buy them from the driver.

The "City Tour" offered by **Scotline Tours** (⌧ 87 High St., ☎ 0131/557–0162 8 AM–9 PM for reservations) costs £10 and is a comprehensive introduction to the city that includes visits to Edinburgh Castle, the High Kirk of St. Giles, and the Palace of Holyroodhouse. Allow at least four hours for the entire tour. Scotline also offers a range of day tours to points beyond the city.

Guide Friday, Ltd. (⌧ 133–135 Canongate, ☎ 0131/556–2244) also offers an orientation tour (£6.50), this time in cheerful open-top, double-decker buses. The commentaries provided tend to be more colorful than accurate. The minimum tour time is one hour, and buses leave from Waverley Bridge. This company also operates a shuttle bus service to see the former royal yacht *Britannia*, moored in Leith Docks; the bus runs every 40 minutes from Waverley Bridge (cost £3).

PERSONAL GUIDES

Scottish Tourist Guides (☎ 0131/453–1297; ☞ Orientation Tours, *above*) can supply guides (in 19 languages) who are fully qualified and will meet clients at any point of entry into the United Kingdom or Scotland.

SPECIAL-INTEREST TOURS

Scottish Tourist Guides (☞ Orientation Tours, *above*) will design tours tailored to your interests; it also offers its special "Nightlife" tour. The **Cadies and Witchery Tours** (✉ 352 Castlehill, ☎ 0131/225–6745) operates a "Ghosts and Gore" tour (£7) through the narrow Old Town alleyways and closes, with costumed guides and other theatrical characters showing up en route.

Robin's Edinburgh Tours (✉ 66 Willowbrae Rd., ☎ 0131/661–0125) run by an Edinburgh native, offers a number of tours (from £5 up) every day: "Grand City Tour" 10 AM; "Royal Mile Tour" 11 AM; "Ghosts and Witches" 7 PM; "Dr. Jekyll's Tour" (April–October only) 9 PM.

WALKING TOURS

The **Cadies and Witchery Tours** (☞ *above*), fully qualified members of the Scottish Tourist Guides Association, has since 1983 steadily built a reputation for combining entertainment and historical accuracy in its lively and enthusiastic "Ghosts and Gore Tour" and "Witchery Murder and Mystery Tour."

Late-Night Pharmacies

You can find out which pharmacy is open late on a given night by looking at the notice posted on every pharmacy door. A pharmacy—or dispensing chemist, as it is called here—is easily identified by its sign, showing a green cross on a white background. **Boots** (✉ 48 Shandwick Pl., west end of Princes St., ☎ 0131/225–6757) is open Monday–Friday 8 AM–9 PM, Saturday 8 AM–7 PM, Sunday 10–5.

Lost and Found

To retrieve lost property, try the **Lothian and Borders police headquarters** (✉ Fettes Ave., ☎ 0131/311–3131).

Maps

Several excellent city maps are available at bookstores. Particularly recommended is the *Bartholomew Edinburgh Plan,* with a scale of approximately 4 inches to 1 mi, by the once-independent and long-established Edinburgh cartographic company John Bartholomew and Sons, Ltd.

Money

Most city-center banks have a bureau de change (usual banking hours are weekdays 9:30–4:45). The bureau de change at the Tourist Centre, Waverley Market, is open daily. There are also bureaux de change at Waverley Station, Edinburgh Airport, and Frasers department store, at the west end of Princes Street.

Post Offices

The post office in the **St. James Centre** (✉ St. Andrew Sq., ☎ 0131/556–0478) is the most central and is open Monday 9–5:30, Tuesday–Friday 8:30–5:30, and Saturday 8:30–6. Other main **post offices** in the city center are at ✉ 40 Frederick St.; ✉ 7 Hope St. Many newsagents also sell stamps.

Travel Agencies

American Express (✉ 139 Princes St., ☎ 0131/225–7881).

Visitor Information

The **Edinburgh and Scotland Information Centre** (✉ 3 Princes St., ☎ 0131/473–3800, FAX 0131/473–3881; ☉ May, June, and Sept., Mon.–Sat. 9–7, Sun. 10–7; July and Aug., Mon.–Sat. 9–8, Sun. 10–8; Oct.–Apr.,

Mon.–Sat. 9–6, Sun. 10–6), adjacent to Waverley Station (follow the TIC signs in the station and throughout the city), offers an accommodations service (Book-A-Bed-Ahead) in addition to the more typical services.

Complete information is also available at the **airport information desk** at the Edinburgh Airport.

The *List,* a publication available from city-center bookstores and newsagents, and the *Day by Day List* and *Events 2000* from the Edinburgh and Scotland Information Centre, all list information about all types of events, from movies and theater to sports. The *Scotsman,* a national newspaper published in Edinburgh, is good for both national and international news coverage, as well as for reviews and notices of upcoming events in Edinburgh and elsewhere in Scotland.

2 GLASGOW

If Edinburgh is proud, age-of-elegance, and reserved, Glasgow is aggressive, industrial-revolution, and exuberant—and never more so than now, since cultural renewal has restored much of Glasgow's 19th-century grandeur. Today a busy metropolis with a thriving artistic life and cityscape à la Charles Rennie Mackintosh and Alexander "Greek" Thomson, Scotland's largest city was named the 1999 U.K. City of Architecture and Design. Visitors will find the "dear green place" more vibrant than ever.

By John
Hutchinson

Updated by
Beth Ingpen

IN THE DAYS WHEN BRITAIN still ruled over an empire, Glasgow pronounced itself the Second City of the Empire. Its people were justifiably proud of Glasgow, since it was here that Britain's great steamships, including the 80,000-ton *Queen Elizabeth,* were built. The term "Clyde-built" (from Glasgow's River Clyde) became synonymous with good workmanship and lasting quality. Scots engineers were to be found wherever there were engines—Glaswegians built the railway locomotives that opened up the Canadian prairies, the South African veldt, the Australian plains, and the Indian subcontinent. It was perhaps no coincidence that even Captain Kirk, on the starship *Enterprise,* always said to his Scottish engineer, "Beam me up, Scotty."

A 16th-century traveler described Glasgow as "a flourishing cathedral city reminiscent of the beautiful fabrics and florid fields of England." Daniel Defoe in 1727 described it as "the cleanest and beautifullest and best-built of cities." Booming prosperity, however, created a Glasgow less clean and less beautiful.

Stretching along both banks of the widening River Clyde, Glasgow was transformed into a depressed city in the early 20th century, and a half century ago its slums of dockland and the Clyde banks were infamous for their time. "All Glasgow needs," said an architecture pundit then, "is a bath and a little loving care." In the past two decades, happily, it got both. Modern Glasgow has undergone an urban renaissance: trendy downtown stores, a booming and diverse cultural life, stylish restaurants, and an air of confidence make it Scotland's most exciting city.

The city's development has been unashamedly commercial, tied up with the wealth of its manufacturers and merchants, who constructed a vast number of civic buildings throughout the 19th century. Many of these have been preserved, and Glasgow claims to be Britain's greatest Victorian city. The work of Glasgow architect Alexander "Greek" Thomson (1817–75) is increasingly recognized as central to the quality of the cityscape from this era, although many of his buildings have only recently begun to be appreciated and are still in disrepair. But Glasgow, always at the forefront of change, boasts, side by side with the overly Victorian, an architectural vision of the future in the work of Charles Rennie Mackintosh (1868–1928). The Glasgow School of Art, the Willow Tearoom, the *Glasgow Herald* building (now home to the Lighthouse architecture and design center), and the churches and schools he designed point clearly to the clarity and simplicity of the best of 20th-century design.

Glasgow first came into prominence in Scottish history somewhere around 1,400 years ago, and typically for this rambunctious city it was all to do with an argument between a husband and his wife. The king of Strathclyde gave his wife a ring that she was rash enough to present to an admirer. The king got it back by a ruse and threw it into the Clyde, then asked his wife what she had done with it. In her distress, the queen went to her confessor, St. Mungo, and asked his advice. He instructed her to fish in the river and—surprise—the first salmon she landed had the ring in its jaws. If you study the Glasgow coat of arms you'll see that the supporters are three salmon, one with a ring in its mouth. Not so surprisingly, Mungo is now the city's patron saint, and you'll find his tomb in the mighty medieval cathedral that bears his name.

Glasgow led a fairly quiet existence in the Middle Ages. Its cathedral was the center of religious life, and although the city was made a Royal Burgh in 1175 by King William the Lion, its population never numbered more than a few thousand people. What changed Glasgow irrevocably was the Treaty of Union between Scotland and England, in 1707. This allowed Scotland to trade with the essentially English colonies in America, and with their expansion Glasgow prospered. In came cotton, tobacco, and rum; out went various Scottish manufactured goods and clothing. The key to it all was tobacco. The prosperous merchants known as tobacco lords ran the city, and their wealth laid the foundation for the manufacturing industries of the 19th century.

As Glasgow prospered, its population grew. The "dear green place" became built over. The original medieval city, around the cathedral and High Street, expanded westward. The 18th-century Merchant City, today undergoing much refurbishment, lies just to the south and west of George Square, and the houses of the merchants are even farther west along the gridiron pattern of Glasgow's streets, up the hill toward Blytheswood Square. But the city isn't known as an 18th-century city; that honor is left to Edinburgh, in the east. Rather, Glasgow is most famous for its Victorian cityscapes. During the 19th century, the population grew from 80,000 to more than 700,000, and along with this enormous growth there developed a sense of exuberance and confidence that's still reflected in its public buildings. The City Chambers, built in 1888, are an extravaganza of marble and red sandstone, a clear symbol of the Victorian merchants' hopes for the future.

Today, as always, Glasgow's eye is trained on the future. Still, it has learned to take the best of its past and adapt it for the needs of the present day. The dear green places still remain in the city-center parks; the medieval cathedral stands proud, as it has done for 800 years; the Merchant City is revived and thriving; the Victorian splendor has been cleansed of its grime; and the cultural legacy of museums and performing arts is stronger than ever. To cap it all, Glasgow is a nexus of rail routes and motorways that can deliver you in less than an hour to Edinburgh, Stirling, Loch Lomond, the Burns Country, and the Clyde coast golfing resorts. The city is an excellent place to get out of—but, of course, is also a great place to get into.

Pleasures and Pastimes

Dining
You'll find Chinese, Italian, and Indian food in addition to the usual French and Scottish offerings. Glasgow also has a strong café culture: visit one or two to get a feel for this important feature of the city. Pubs are also good bets for cheap lunches.

Lodging
Glasgow has become a major business destination in the past several years, with the Scottish Conference and Exhibition Centre serving as the hub of activity. There are now some big city-center hotels of both expensive and moderate character, and you'll find some good and reasonable small hotels and guest houses with a more pronounced character in the suburbs, convenient to the city by public transport. All the large hotels have restaurants open to nonguests.

Shopping
Glaswegians are clotheshorses, and you'll find some of the world's best clothes at the many stores and malls that helped in April 2000 to win Glasgow a top place (second only to London's West End) in a U.K.-wide survey of shoppers' favorite cities. Princes Square is a good place to enhance your wardrobe (if you're willing to break the bank to do so). The newest additions to the shopping scene—the Buchanan Galleries and the Braehead shopping center—are also very popular with serious shoppers.

EXPLORING GLASGOW

You can't read Glasgow's layout in a single glance. However, the city center is relatively flat and set along a straightforward grid of streets, making it easy to walk around Glasgow Cathedral and Provand's Lordship, High Street, and the Merchant City. The River Clyde, on which Glasgow's trade across the Atlantic developed, is always at the center of the city—literally cutting it in two and offering intriguing views of buildings on the other side. In Glasgow, always look up: your reward is much ornate detailing visible above eye level.

In the quieter, slightly hillier western part of the city is Glasgow University and that other, "forgotten" side of Glasgow, unjustly perceived as a grimy center of heavy industry.

Numbers in the text correspond to numbers in the margin and on the Glasgow and Glasgow Excursions: Ayrshire and the Clyde Valley maps.

Great Itineraries

To take advantage of Glasgow's wealth of cultural sites and shopping, you could easily spend four or five days, but you can see the city's greatest hits in only two days.

IF YOU HAVE 2 DAYS

Glaswegians are particularly proud of the Burrell Collection in Pollok Country Park, so it should top your list of must-sees. On the first day, explore the core of historic Glasgow—the medieval area and Merchant City. Glasgow Cathedral gives a glimpse into history and an impression of St. Mungo. Buchanan Street, including the Princes Square development and the new Buchanan Galleries, offers the best shopping. On the second day, see the West End, including the painting, sculpture, and Charles Rennie Mackintosh furniture at the Hunterian Art Gallery. If you haven't yet seen the city-center parks, venture to Glasgow Green and the art collections at Pollok Country Park and Bellahouston Park. Remember that Glasgow's pubs and clubs offer great entertainment until late in the evening.

IF YOU HAVE 5 DAYS

Five days allows enough time to add to your brief tour more of Glasgow's key museums and cultural attractions: the Glasgow Gallery of Modern Art, in the city center, or the St. Mungo Museum, to the east. You could easily take a full day to see the cluster of West End museums by Kelvingrove Park (Kelvingrove Museum and Art Gallery, Hunterian Art Gallery and Hunterian Museum, and Museum of Transport). For a good day trip, take the hour-long train ride to Wemyss Bay, and from there take the ferry to the Isle of Bute, home to the spectacular Victorian Gothic Mount Stuart House.

IF YOU HAVE 10 DAYS

Ten days will allow you to thoroughly explore all the museums (you may want to visit the Burrell Collection more than once). Shopping in Princes Square can easily occupy a morning; Buchanan Street and Sauchiehall Street will also reward inveterate shoppers. Make time for at least one side trip. Ayrshire and the Clyde coast need at least two days—possibly three if you want to see everything: Mount Stuart House, on the Isle of Bute; Ayr and Alloway, which will delight Robert Burns enthusiasts; and Culzean Castle, whose Georgian elegance provides sharp contrast to the Gothic spirit of Mount Stuart. Travel up the Clyde Valley to Lanark for a morning at New Lanark, the restored site of an 18th-century social experiment in improving the lives of mill workers; you can also enjoy beautiful walks along the waterfall-dotted River Clyde here. Biggar will fill an afternoon or more with its fascinating museums, including Moat Park, which has a fine embroidery collection.

Medieval Glasgow and the Merchant City

In this central part of the city there are not only surviving medieval buildings, but also some of the best examples of the architectural confidence and exuberance that so characterized the Glasgow of 100 years ago. Today this revitalized area is enjoying a newfound appreciation.

A Good Walk

George Square ①, the focal point of Glasgow's business district, is the natural starting point. It's in the very heart of Glasgow and is convenient to the Buchanan Street bus and underground stations and parking lot, as well as to the Queen Street railway station. After viewing the **City Chambers** ②, on the square's east side, leave by the northeast corner and head eastward through a not particularly pretty part of the city along George Street, past Strathclyde University. Turn left at High Street, then go up the hill to **Glasgow Cathedral** ③, the **St. Mungo Museum and Cathedral Visitor Center** ④, and the fascinating if macabre **Necropolis** ⑤, just off Cathedral Square.

Opposite the cathedral, across Castle Street, is **Provand's Lordship** ⑥, Glasgow's oldest house. Retrace your steps down Castle Street and High Street. Look for the Greek goddess Pallas atop the imposing gray-sandstone building on the right, the former Bank of Scotland, before reaching the Tolbooth Steeple at **Glasgow Cross** ⑦. Continue east along London Road (under the bridge) about a quarter of a mile, and you'll come to the **Barras** ⑧, Scotland's largest indoor market. Turn right down Greendyke Street from London Road to reach **Glasgow Green** ⑨ by the River Clyde, with the **People's Palace** ⑩ museum of social history as its centerpiece.

Go back to Greendyke Street, past the new St. Andrew's Square development—with the magnificent St. Andrew's Church (1750)—then go via Saltmarket northward to Tolbooth Steeple. Continue westward along Trongate. This is where the powerful tobacco lords who traded with the Americas presided. On the right, down Albion Street, are the offices of Glasgow's daily papers, the *Herald* and the *Evening Times*. On the left, jutting out into Trongate, is the Tron Steeple, all that remains of a church burned down in 1793 when a joke by the local chapter of the Hell-Fire Club (young aristocratic troublemakers) got out of hand. The rebuilt church has now been converted into the Tron Theatre.

Continue along the Trongate, then turn right on Hutcheson Street. This is Glasgow's **Merchant City,** with many handsome restored Georgian and Victorian buildings. At the end of the street, just south of George Square, look for **Hutcheson's Hall** ⑪, a National Trust for Scotland visitor center and shop. Continue up John Street, take a left on Cochrane Street, and a right on South Frederick Street; on the west side of George Square, on the corner with West George Street, is the **Merchants' House** ⑫. Return to Ingram Street and walk down Glassford Street; on the right is the Trades House, whose 1791 facade was designed by Robert Adam. Turn right along Wilson Street to reach Virginia Street, another favorite haunt of Glasgow's tobacco merchants. At Number 33 a former tobacco exchange survives, now an indoor shopping center. Walk northward up Virginia Street back to Ingram Street. To the left you'll have a good view down to the elegant Royal Exchange Square and the Royal Exchange itself. Once a meeting place for merchants and traders, it's now the **Glasgow Gallery of Modern Art** ⑬. Royal Exchange Square leads you westward to the pedestrian-zone shopping area of Buchanan Street. The Princes Square shopping mall, on the east side, has a good selection of specialty shops. Just off Buchanan Street to the west, in Mitchell Lane, is **The Lighthouse** ⑭, Glasgow's impressive new homage to architecture, housed in a Charles Rennie Mackintosh–designed building.

Make your way down to Argyle Street. Looking to the west, you'll see the large railway bridge supporting the tracks going into **Central Station** ⑮. Note the lovely iron arcading of Gardner's Warehouse, at 36 Jamaica Street. Head north up Union Street to see the extraordinary architecture of Numbers 84–100, Alexander "Greek" Thomson's so-called **Egyptian Halls** ⑯, now sadly semi-derelict.

From here continue north to St. Vincent Street and turn right to reach Nelson Mandela Place, also called St. George's Place. Here is the **Scottish Stock Exchange** ⑰, with its ornate "French Venetian"–style exterior. To see a famous example of Alexander Thomson's Greek Revival churches, walk west on St. Vincent Street about eight blocks to Pitt Street and the **St. Vincent's Street Church** ⑱.

TIMING

This walk covers a lot of ground, but can be done comfortably in a day, leaving time to browse in the People's Palace and the Glasgow Gallery of Modern Art. Start after the morning rush hour, say at 10, and finish before the evening rush starts, about 4. Remember that the Barras is only open on weekends and the City Chambers only on weekdays.

Sights to See

✎ *following the text of a review is your signal that the property has a Web site, where you will find details and, usually, images; for a link, visit www.fodors.com/urls.*

⑧ Barras. Scotland's largest indoor market—named for the barrows, or pushcarts, formerly used by the stall holders—is a mecca for anyone addicted to searching through piles of junk for bargains. The approximately 80-year-old institution, open weekends only, is made up of nine markets. The atmosphere is always good-humored, and you can find just about anything here, in any condition, from old model railroads to cheese rolls. You can reach the Barras by walking from ScotRail's Argyle Street station, or take any of the various buses to Glasgow Cross at the foot of the Gallowgate. ⊠ *¼ mi east of Glasgow Cross,* ☎ *0141/552–7258.* ☞ *Free.* ⊙ *Weekends 9–5.*

⑮ Central Station. The depot is known as the Heilanman's Umbrella because it was the point of meeting and shelter for so many Highlanders who had moved to Glasgow in the last century in search of better economic opportunities. ⊠ *Bounded by Gordon, Union, Argyle, Jamaica, Clyde, Oswald, and Hope Sts.*

★ **❷ City Chambers.** Dominating the east side of George Square, this exuberant expression of Victorian confidence, built by William Young, was opened by Queen Victoria (1819–1901) in 1888. Among the interior's outstanding features are the entrance hall's vaulted ceiling, the marble-and-alabaster staircases, and the banqueting hall. Several smaller suites are furnished in different woods. ⊠ *George Sq.,* ☎ *0141/287–2000.* ☞ *Free guided tours weekdays at 10:30 and 2:30 (may be closed for occasional civic functions).* ✎

⑯ Egyptian Halls. This somewhat dilapidated building was designed and built in 1871 by Victorian architect Alexander "Greek" Thomson, whose nickname came from his penchant for incorporating Egyptian and Greek elements into his work. ⊠ *84–100 Union St.*

❶ George Square. The focal point of Glasgow's business district is lined with an impressive array of statues of worthies: Queen Victoria; Scotland's national poet, Robert Burns (1759–96); the inventor and developer of the steam engine, James Watt (1736–1819); Prime Minister William Gladstone (1809–98); and towering above them all, Scotland's foremost writer, Sir Walter Scott (1771–1832). The column was intended for George III (1738–1820), after whom the square is named, but his statue wasn't erected after he was found to be insane toward the end of his reign. On the square's east side stands the magnificent Italian Renaissance–style **City Chambers** (☞ *above*), and the handsome **Merchants' House** (☞ *below*) fills the corner with West George Street.

Off and around George Square, several streets—Virginia Street, Miller Street, Glassford Street—recall the yesterdays of mercantile wealth. The French-style palaces, with their steep mansard roofs and cupolas, were once tobacco warehouses. Inside them are shops and offices; here and there you may trace the elaborately carved mahogany galleries where the auctions took place. Two of the grandest structures, Stirling's Glasgow Gallery of Modern Art (☞ *below*) and the Mitchell Library (☞ *below*), enshrine the fame of two 18th-century tobacco barons who built them as residences. ⊠ *Between George and St. Vincent Sts.*

★ **❸ Glasgow Cathedral.** The most complete of Scotland's cathedrals (it would have been more complete if 19th-century vandals hadn't pulled down its two graceful towers), this is an unusual double church, one above the other, and dedicated to Glasgow's patron saint, St. Mungo. Begun in the 12th century, consecrated in 1136, and completed about 300 years later, it was spared the ravages of the Reformation, which destroyed so many of Scotland's medieval churches, because Glasgow's trade guilds defended it. In the lower church is the splendid crypt of St. Mungo, who's sometimes also called St. Kentigern (*kentigern* means "chief word," while Mungo is perhaps a nickname meaning "dear name"). The site of the tomb has been revered since the 6th century, when St. Mungo founded a church here. Mungo features prominently in local legends; one is about a pet bird that he nursed back to life, and another tells of a bush or tree, the branches of which he used to relight a fire. Tree, bird, and the salmon with a ring in its mouth (from the famous tale dealing with the king and queen of Strathclyde, related in the introduction above) are all to be found on the city of Glasgow's coat of arms, together with a bell that Mungo brought from Rome. ⊠ *Cathedral St.,* ☎ *0131/ 668–8800.* ⬚ *Free.* ☉ *Apr.–Sept., Mon.–Sat. 9:30–6, Sun. 2–6; Oct.– Mar., Mon.–Sat. 9:30–4, Sun. 2–4 and for services.* ☙

❼ Glasgow Cross. This crossroads was the very center of the medieval city. The Mercat Cross (*mercat* means "market"), topped by a unicorn, marked the spot where merchants met, where the market was held, and where criminals were executed. Here, too, was the *tron*, or weigh beam, that merchants used to check weights, installed in 1491. The Tolbooth Steeple dates from 1626 and served as the civic center and the place where travelers paid tolls. ⊠ *Intersection of Saltmarket, Trongate, Gallowgate, and London Rd.*

⓭ Glasgow Gallery of Modern Art. The newest (1996) of Glasgow's many excellent galleries occupies the former Royal Exchange building. Designed by David Hamilton and finished in 1829, the Exchange was a meeting place for merchants and traders; later it became Stirling's Library. It incorporates the mansion built in 1780 by William Cunninghame, one of the wealthiest tobacco lords. The modern art, craft, and design collections contained within this handsome building include Scottish figurative art, works by Scottish artists such as Peter Howson and John Bellany, and also paintings and sculpture from else-

Glasgow

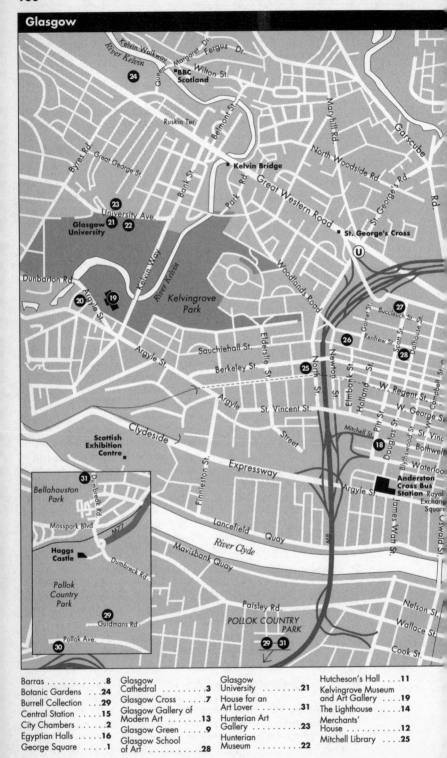

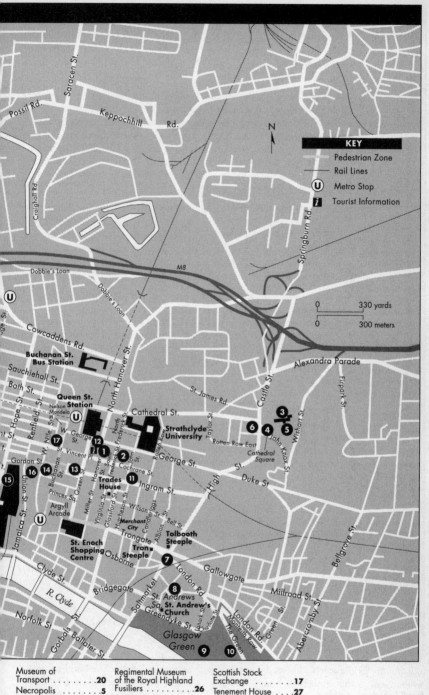

where in the world, including Papua New Guinea, Ethiopia, and Mexico. The display scheme is designed for each floor to reflect one of the four elements—earth, air, fire, and water—which creates some unexpected juxtapositions and also allows for various interactive exhibits. ☒ *Queen St.,* ☎ *0141/229–1996.* ☞ *Free.* ☉ *Mon.–Thurs. and Sat. 10–5, Fri. and Sun. 11–5.*

❾ Glasgow Green. Glasgow's oldest park, on the northeast side of the River Clyde, has a long history as a favorite spot for public recreation and political demonstrations. Note the Nelson Column, erected long before London's; the Arch, now the finish line for the thousands of runners of the Glasgow Half Marathon; and the Templeton Business Centre, once a carpet factory, built in the late 19th century in the style of the Doge's Palace in Venice. The most significant building in the park is the **People's Palace** (☞ *below*).

★ ⓫ Hutcheson's Hall. Now a visitor center and shop for the National Trust for Scotland, this elegant neoclassical building was designed by David Hamilton (1768–1843) in 1802. The hall was originally a hospice founded by two brothers, George and Thomas Hutcheson; you can see their statues in niches in the facade. ☒ *158 Ingram St.,* ☎ *0141/552–8391.* ☞ *Free.* ☉ *Mon.–Sat. 10–5.* ✎

⓮ The Lighthouse. Housed in the former offices of the *Glasgow Herald* newspaper, which were designed by Charles Rennie Mackintosh in 1893, the Lighthouse opened in mid-1999. Mackintosh's building is a fitting setting for Scotland's **Centre for Architecture, Design and the City,** which celebrates all facets of the architectural profession with exhibitions. ☒ *11 Mitchell La.,* ☎ *0141/221–6362.* ☞ *Free; £1 charge for exhibition areas; £2.50 charge for Mackintosh Interpretation Centre.* ☉ *Mon., Wed., and Fri.–Sat. 10:30–5:30; Tues. 11–5:30; Thurs. 10:30–7; Sun. noon–5.*

Merchant City. This once run-down area around Hutcheson Street is being renovated. Among the preserved Georgian and Victorian buildings are elegant designer boutiques. The **City and County buildings** were built in 1842 to house civil servants; note the impressive arrangement of bays and Corinthian columns.

⓬ Merchants' House. This handsome 1874 Victorian building, home to Glasgow's chamber of commerce, is topped by a golden sailing ship, a reminder of the importance of sea trade to Glasgow's prosperity. Inside is the fine **Merchants' Hall,** embellished with stained-glass windows and many portraits. ☒ *West side of George Sq.,* ☎ *0141/221–8272.* ☞ *Free.* ☉ *Hall and anterooms, weekdays 10–noon and 2–5 (unless closed for meetings) or by appointment.*

❺ Necropolis. A burying ground since the beginning of recorded history, the Necropolis contains some extraordinarily elaborate Victorian graves, watched over by a statue of John Knox (1514–72). It includes the tomb of 19th-century Glasgow merchant William Miller (1810–72), author of the "Wee Willie Winkie" nursery rhyme. ☒ *Behind Glasgow Cathedral.*

★ ❿ People's Palace. An impressive Victorian red-sandstone building dating from 1894 houses an intriguing museum dedicated to the city's social history; included among the exhibits is one devoted to the ordinary folk of Glasgow, called the *People's Story.* Also on show are the writing desk of John McLean (1879–1923), the "Red Clydeside" political activist who came to Lenin's notice, and the famous "banana boots" worn on stage by the famous Glasgow-born comedian, Billy Connolly. Behind the museum are the well-restored Winter Gardens, a relatively sheltered spot where you can escape the often chilly winds whistling across the green. ⊠ *Glasgow Green,* ☎ *0141/554–0223.* 🖻 *Free.* ☉ *Mon.–Thurs. and Sat. 10–5, Fri. and Sun. 11–5.* ✧

6 Provand's Lordship. Glasgow's oldest house was built in 1471 by Bishop Andrew Muirhead as a residence for churchmen. Mary, Queen of Scots (1542–87) is said to have stayed here. After her day, however, the house fell into decline and was used as a sweets shop, a soft-drink factory, the home of the city hangman, and a junk shop. The city rescued it and turned it into a museum. Exhibits show the house as it might have looked in its heyday, with period rooms and an ambience of ancient dustiness. Because the house lodged three Scottish monarchs (James II and James IV also stayed here), it's allegedly haunted as well. ⊠ *Castle St.,* ☎ *0141/552–8819.* 🖻 *Free.* ☉ *Mon.–Thurs. and Sat. 10–5, Fri. and Sun. 11–5.*

4 St. Mungo Museum and Cathedral Visitor Center. An outstanding collection of artifacts speaks for the many religious groups who have settled throughout the centuries in Glasgow and the west of Scotland. The centerpiece is surrealist Salvador Dalí's (1904–89) magnificent painting *Christ of St. John of the Cross.* Inside are a gift shop and a café. ⊠ *2 Castle St.,* ☎ *0141/553–2557.* 🖻 *Free.* ☉ *Mon.–Thurs. and Sat. 10–5, Fri. and Sun. 11–5.*

18 St. Vincent's Street Church. Dating from 1859, this church, the work of Alexander Thomson, exemplifies his Greek Revival style, replete with Ionic temple, sphinx-esque heads, Greek ornamentation, and rich interior color. ⊠ *Pitt and St. Vincent Sts.*

17 Scottish Stock Exchange. Scotland's hub of commerce was built in 1877 in French Venetian style by John Burnet, who was inspired by London's Law Courts in the Strand, designed by William Burges (1827–81). Burges is said to have been flattered rather than perturbed by Burnet's close imitation. ⊠ *7 Nelson Mandela Pl. Not open to public.*

The West End

Glasgow's West End offers a stellar mix of education, culture, art, and parkland. The neighborhood is dominated by Glasgow University, founded in 1451, making it the third oldest in Scotland, after St. Andrews and Aberdeen, and at least 130 years ahead of the University of Edinburgh. It has thrived as a center of educational excellence, particularly in the sciences. The university buildings are set in parkland, reminding you that Glasgow is a city with more green space per citizen than any other in Europe. It's also a city of museums and art galleries, having benefited from the generosity of industrial and commercial philanthropists and from the deep-seated desire of the city fathers to place Glasgow at the forefront of British cities.

A Good Walk

Start at the city's main art gallery and museum, **Kelvingrove Museum and Art Gallery** ⑲, in Kelvingrove Park, west of the M8 beltway, at the junction of Sauchiehall (pronounced *socky*-hall) and Argyle streets. There are parking facilities, and plenty of buses come here from downtown. Across Argyle Street in the Old Kelvin Hall exhibition center is the **Museum of Transport** ⑳.

As you walk up Kelvin Way through the trees, the skyline to your left is dominated by the Gilbert Scott Building, **Glasgow University**'s ㉑ main edifice. Turn left up University Avenue, past the Memorial Gates, which were erected in 1951 to celebrate the university's 500th birthday. On either side of the road are two important galleries, both maintained by the university. On the south side of University Avenue, in the

Victorian part of the university, is the **Hunterian Museum** ㉒. Across University Avenue, in an unremarkable building from the 1970s, is the even more interesting **Hunterian Art Gallery** ㉓.

The walk from the university to the **Botanic Gardens** ㉔ isn't very exciting, but it's worth the effort. Continue along University Avenue and turn right at Byres Road, going as far as Great Western Road and the Grosvenor Hotel. The 40 acres of gardens are across the busy Great Western Road.

After leaving the gardens, cross the River Kelvin on Queen Margaret Drive and walk past the BBC Scotland building, just after Hamilton Drive. Turn right, then right again down the steps to the Kelvin Walkway, on the north bank of the river. (Farther upstream the Kelvin Walkway connects with the West Highland Way, an official long-distance footpath leading to Fort William, approximately 100 mi away.) The walkway headed downstream back toward the city center first crosses a footbridge, then passes old mill buildings, and then goes under Belmont Street and the Great Western Road at Kelvinbridge. Here it passes the Kelvinbridge underground station and goes under the Gibson Street Bridge, then back into Kelvingrove Park.

At this point, you can choose to take one of the paths up the hill and explore the stately Victorian crescents and streets of the park area, or you can take the lower road past the fountain and head directly back to Sauchiehall Street. Whichever way you choose, you should end up, having walked eastward, at the point where Sauchiehall Street crosses the M8 motorway. Down North Street to your right (southward) you'll see the front of **Mitchell Library** ㉕. Cross the M8 motorway and continue down Sauchiehall Street to the **Regimental Museum of the Royal Highland Fusiliers** ㉖. Turn up Garnet Street and go to the top, then right on Buccleuch (pronounced buck-*loo*) Street. On the left is the **Tenement House** ㉗, tucked away from normal tourist routes. Coming out of the Tenement House, turn east on Buccleuch Street to Scott Street. As you turn south on Scott Street, notice the mural that reflects the name of the area, Garnethill, then turn left onto Renfrew Street to reach Charles Rennie Mackintosh's masterpiece, the **Glasgow School of Art** ㉘. Nearby is his equally celebrated **Willow Tearoom,** where you can enjoy a cup of Earl Grey. To return to the city center, either continue down Scott Street, then east on Sauchiehall Street, or turn south down Blythswood Street, noting the elegant Blythswood Square (constructed 1823–29).

TIMING

You need at least a day for this walk, and even then you won't manage to see all you want to at the Kelvingrove and Hunterian museums; if you anticipate lingering at the museums and galleries, plan at least two days since each could take up an enjoyable day in itself.

Sights to See

㉔ **Botanic Gardens.** Begun by the Royal Botanical Institute of Glasgow in 1842, the displays here include an herb garden, a wide range of tropical plants, and a world-famous collection of orchids. The most spectacular building in the complex is the **Kibble Palace,** built in 1873 and originally the conservatory of a Victorian eccentric named John Kibble. Its domed, interlinked greenhouses contain tree ferns, palm trees, temperate plants, and the Tropicarium, where you can experience the lushness of a tropical rain forest. Elsewhere on the grounds are more conventional greenhouses, as well as well-maintained lawns and colorful flower beds. ⊠ *Great Western Rd.,* ☎ *0141/334–2422.* ▧ *Free.* ☉ *Gardens: daily 7–dusk; Kibble Palace and other greenhouses: daily 10–4:45. All close at 4:15 in winter.*

★ ㉘ **Glasgow School of Art.** The exterior and interior, structure, furnishings, and decoration of this art nouveau building form a unified whole, reflecting the inventive genius of Charles Rennie Mackintosh, who was only 28 years old when he won the competition for its design. Architects and designers from all over the world come to admire it, but because it's a working school of art, general visitor access is sometimes limited. Guided tours are available (it's best to make reservations). The art school shop has an interesting selection of Mackintosh prints, postcards, and books, together with a selection of contemporary art by students and graduates. A block away is Mackintosh's Willow Tearoom (☞ *below*). ⊠ *167 Renfrew St.,* ☎ *0141/353–4500.* ☞ *£5.* ☉ *Tours weekdays 11 AM and 2 PM, Sat. 10:30 AM.* ☜

NEED A BREAK? | The **Willow Tearoom** (⊠ 217 Sauchiehall St., ☎ 0141/332–0521) has been restored to its original, archetypal Charles Rennie Mackintosh art nouveau design, right down to the decorated tables and chairs. The building was designed by Mackintosh in 1903 for Kate Cranston, who ran a chain of tearooms. The tree motifs are echoed in the street address, since *sauchie* is an old Scots word for *willow*. For a review of the fine tearoom restaurant, ☞ Dining, *below*.

㉑ **Glasgow University.** The Gilbert Scott Building, the university's main edifice, was built just over a century ago and is a good example of the Gothic Revival style. **Glasgow University Visitor Centre** has exhibits on the university, a coffee bar, and a gift shop and is the starting point for one-hour guided walking tours of the campus. ⊠ *University Ave.,* ☎ *0141/330–5511.* ☞ *Free; guided tour £2.* ☉ *Oct.–Apr., Mon.–Sat. 9:30–5; May–Sept., Mon.–Sat. 9:30–5, Sun. 2–5. Tours: May–Sept., Wed. and Fri.–Sat. 11 and 2; Oct.–Apr., Wed. 2.*

★ ㉓ **Hunterian Art Gallery.** Part of Glasgow University, this gallery houses William Hunter's (1718–83) collection of paintings (his antiquarian collection is housed in the nearby **Hunterian Museum;** [☞ *below*]), together with prints and drawings by Tintoretto (1518–94), Rembrandt (1606–69), Sir Joshua Reynolds (1723–92), and Auguste Rodin (1840–1917), as well as a major collection of paintings by James McNeill Whistler (1834–1903), who had a great affection for the city that bought one of his earliest paintings. Also in the gallery is a replica of **Charles Rennie Mackintosh's town house,** which used to stand nearby. The rooms contain Mackintosh's distinctive art nouveau chairs, tables, beds, and cupboards, and the walls are decorated in the equally distinctive style devised by him and his wife, Margaret. ⊠ *Glasgow University, Hillhead St.,* ☎ *0141/330–5431.* ☞ *Free.* ☉ *Mon.–Sat. 9:30–5. Mackintosh house closed for lunch 12:30–1:30.* ☜

㉒ **Hunterian Museum.** The city's oldest museum (1807) and part of Glasgow University, the Hunterian houses part of the collections of William Hunter, an 18th-century Glasgow doctor who assembled a staggering quantity of valuable material. (The doctor's art treasures are housed in the nearby **Hunterian Art Gallery;** [☞ *above*].) The museum displays Hunter's hoards of coins, manuscripts, scientific instruments, and archaeological artifacts in a striking Gothic building. ⊠ *Glasgow University,* ☎ *0141/330–4221.* ☞ *Free.* ☉ *Mon.–Sat. 9:30–5.*

★ ⑲ **Kelvingrove Museum and Art Gallery.** Looking like a combination of cathedral and castle, this magnificently ornamented red-sandstone edifice dating from the early 20th century contains Glasgow's main museum and art gallery. There has always been debate as to which facade is the front and which is the back. However you enter, Kelvingrove houses what's claimed to be Britain's finest civic collection of British and

Continental paintings, with 17th-century Dutch art, a selection from the French Barbizon school, French Impressionism, Scottish art from the 17th century to the present, silver, ceramics, European armor, and even Egyptian archaeological finds. Be sure to pause at Rembrandt's *The Man in Armor.* ⊠ *Kelvingrove Park,* ☎ 0141/287–2699. ⬚ *Free.* ☉ *Mon.–Thurs. and Sat. 10–5, Fri. and Sun. 11–5.*

Kelvingrove Park. Taking its name from the River Kelvin, which flows through it, this peaceful retreat was purchased by the city in 1852. Apart from the abundance of statues of prominent Glaswegians, including Lord Kelvin (1824–1907), the Scottish mathematician and physicist who pioneered a great deal of work in electricity, the park has a massive fountain commemorating a Lord Provost of Glasgow from the 1850s, a duck pond, play area, small open-air theater, and lots of exotic trees. ⊠ *Northwest of city center, bounded roughly by Sauchiehall St., Woodlands Rd., and Kelvin Way.*

㉕ Mitchell Library. The largest public reference library in Europe houses more than a million volumes, including what's claimed to be the world's largest collection on Robert Burns. The library's founder, Stephen Mitchell, who died in 1874 (the same year the library was founded), is commemorated by a bust in the entrance hall. Minerva, goddess of wisdom, looks down from the library's dome, encouraging the library's users and frowning at the drivers thundering along the motorway just in front of her. The western facade (at the back) is particularly beautiful. ⊠ *North St.,* ☎ 0141/287–2931. ⬚ *Free.* ☉ *Mon.– Thurs. 9–8, Fri.–Sat. 9–5.*

★ **㉔ Museum of Transport.** Here Glasgow's history of locomotive building is dramatically displayed with full-size exhibits. The collection of Clyde-built ship models is world famous. Anyone who remembers Britain in the 1950s will wax nostalgic at the re-created street scene from that era. ⊠ *Kelvin Hall, 1 Bunhouse Rd.,* ☎ 0141/287–2720. ⬚ *Free.* ☉ *Mon.–Thurs. and Sat. 10–5, Fri. and Sun. 11–5.*

OFF THE
BEATEN PATH

QUEEN'S CROSS CHURCH – To learn about the Glasgow-born designer Mackintosh, head for the Charles Rennie Mackintosh Society Headquarters, housed in a church that he designed. Although one of the leading lights in the turn-of-the-century art nouveau movement, Mackintosh died in 1928 with his name scarcely known. Today, he's widely confirmed as a brilliant innovator. This off-the-beaten-track center provides further insight into Glasgow's other Mackintosh-designed buildings, which include Scotland Street School, the Martyrs Public School, the Glasgow School of Art, and reconstructed interiors in the Hunterian Art Gallery. The church is on the corner of Springbank Street at the junction of Garscube Road with Maryhill Road; a cab ride can get you here, or take a bus toward Queen's Cross from stops along Hope Street. ⊠ *870 Garscube Rd.,* ☎ 0141/946–6600. ⬚ *Suggested donation £2.* ☉ *Weekdays 10–5, Sat. 10–2, Sun. 2–5 (or by arrangement).*

㉖ Regimental Museum of the Royal Highland Fusiliers. The history of a famous regiment and the men who served in it is told with exhibits of medals, badges, and uniforms. ⊠ *518 Sauchiehall St.,* ☎ 0141/332– 0961. ⬚ *Free.* ☉ *Mon.–Thurs. 9–4:30, Fri. 9–4, weekends by appointment only.*

★ **㉗ Tenement House.** This ordinary, simple city-center apartment is anything but ordinary inside: it was occupied from 1911 to 1965 by Agnes Toward, who seems never to have thrown anything away. What's left is a fascinating time capsule, painstakingly preserved with her everyday furniture and belongings. The red-sandstone building itself dates from 1892 and can be found in the Garnethill area north of Charing Cross station. ⊠ *145 Buccleuch St.,* ☎ *0141/333–0183.* 🎫 *£3.50.* ⊙ *Mar.–Oct., daily 2–5 (last admission 4:30).* 🐾

The South Side: Art-Filled Parks West

Just southwest of the city center in the South Side, two of Glasgow's dear green places—Bellahouston Park and Pollok Country Park—have important art collections: Charles Rennie Mackintosh's House for an Art Lover, the Burrell Collection, and Pollok House. A respite from the buzz of the city can also be found in the parks, where you can have a picnic or ramble through greenery and gardens. Both parks are off Paisley Road, about 3 mi southwest of the city center. You can take a taxi or car, city bus, or a train from Glasgow Central Station to Pollokshaws West Station or Dumbreck.

A Good Tour

Traveling either by car, taxi, bus, or train, start your art exploration at the **Burrell Collection** ㉙, its diverse collections displayed in a super-modern structure. Repair to the museum's good café-restaurant for a bite, or plan to pack a picnic lunch to enjoy in one of the parks. **Pollok House** ㉚, with the Stirling Maxwell Collection of painting and fine art, is just a walk of a few hundred yards beyond the Burrell. Head north on Haggs Road and Dumbreck Road to Bellahouston Park and Charles Rennie Mackintosh's art nouveau **House for an Art Lover** ㉛, based on the architect's entry into a 1901 competition.

TIMING

Allow the good part of a day for seeing the three collections, strolls through the parks, and a picnic or lunch. Note that the House for an Art Lover is usually open on weekends (and some weekdays).

Sights to See

㉙ **Burrell Collection.** Set in Pollok Country Park, a custom-built, ultra-modern (1983), yet elegant building of pink sandstone and stainless steel houses 8,000 exhibits of all descriptions, from ancient Egyptian, Greek, and Roman artifacts to Chinese ceramics, bronzes, and jade, to medieval tapestries, stained glass, Rodin sculptures, and exquisite French Impressionist paintings—Degas's *The Rehearsal* and Sir Henry Raeburn's *Miss Macartney,* to name a few. The magpie collection was donated to the city in 1944 by eccentric millionaire Sir William Burrell (1861–1958). The exterior and interior were designed with large glass walls so that the items on display could relate to their surroundings: art and nature, supposedly in perfect harmony. It does, however, seem an incongruous setting for Chinese porcelain and the reconstruction of medieval castle rooms. ⊠ *Buses 45, 48, and 57 from Union St.,* ☎ *0141/287–2550.* 🎫 *Free.* ⊙ *Mon.–Thurs. and Sat. 10–5, Fri. and Sun. 11–5.*

㉛ **House for an Art Lover.** Set in Bellahouston Park is a "new" Mackintosh house: based on a competition entry Charles Rennie Mackintosh submitted in 1901, but which was never built in his lifetime, it was completed in 1996 and now houses permanent exhibitions—consisting of designs for the various rooms and decorative pieces he and his wife, Margaret, created—and Glasgow School of Art's postgraduate study center. ⊠ *Bellahouston Park, Dumbreck Rd.; Buses 9, 53, and 54 from Union St.,* ☎ *0141/353–4770.* 🎫 *£3.50.* ⊙ *Apr.–Sept., Sat.–Thurs. 10–4; Oct.–Mar., weekends 10–4.*

㉚ **Pollok House.** Dating from the mid-1700s, the classic Georgian Pollok House contains the Stirling Maxwell Collection of paintings, including works by El Greco (1514–1614), Murillo (1617–82), Goya

REDISCOVERING CHARLES RENNIE MACKINTOSH

NOT SO LONG AGO, THE furniture of Glasgow-born architect Charles Rennie Mackintosh (1868–1928) was broken up for firewood. Today his major bookcases and chairs go for hundreds of thousands of pounds at auction, art books are devoted to his astonishingly elegant Arts and Crafts interiors, and artisans around the world look to his theory that "decoration should not be constructed, rather construction should be decorated" as holy law. Mackintosh's stripped-down designs slammed the door on Victorian antimacassars and floral chintz, ushering in the modern age with their deceptively stark style. Ironically, Scotland's most innovative designer had an extensive influence on European design, but only recently has he been once again acknowledged in his native country as a true original.

Mackintosh trained in architecture at the Glasgow School of Art and was apprenticed to the Glasgow firm John Hutchison at the age of 16. During his training, his exceptional talent was recognized by the award of various prizes. In 1889 he joined the Glasgow firm Honeyman and Keppie. Early influences on his work included the Pre-Raphaelites, James McNeill Whistler (1834–1903), Aubrey Beardsley (1872–98), and Japanese art, but by the 1890s a distinct Glasgow style had been developed by Mackintosh and others. The building for the *Glasgow Herald* newspaper, which he designed in 1893 (and which is now the Lighthouse Centre for Architecture, Design and the City) was soon followed by other major Glasgow buildings: Queen Margaret's Medical College; the Martyrs Public School, tearooms for Catherine Cranston (including the famous Willow Tearooms that can still be seen today); the Hill House, Helensburgh (now owned by the National Trust for Scotland); and Queen's Cross Church (completed in 1899 and now the headquarters of the Charles Rennie Mackintosh Society). The year 1897 saw work started on a new home for the Glasgow School of Art, now recognized as one of his major achievements and which still retains original fittings, furnishings, ornamentation, and documents.

Mackintosh married Margaret Macdonald in 1900, and in later years her decorative work enhanced the interiors of his buildings. Over the next few years he worked abroad as well as in Scotland, being especially successful in Germany and Austria. In 1904 he became a partner in Honeyman and Keppie and designed Scotland Street School (now the Museum of Education) in the same year. Until 1913, when he left Honeyman and Keppie and moved to England, Mackintosh's various projects included work on buildings and/or interiors over much of Scotland, but especially in the Central Belt: Comrie, Bridge of Allan, Kilmacolm, and many other places. He preferred whenever possible to include interiors—furniture and fittings—as part of his overall design (a talent demonstrated clearly at the Hill House). He believed that building design should be "a total work of art, to the wholeness of which each contrived detail contributes."

Commissions in England after 1913 included a variety of design challenges not confined to buildings, including fabrics, furniture, and even bookbindings (for the publishers Blackie and Sons). In 1923 Mackintosh settled in France but returned to London in 1927 and died there in 1928.

Glasgow must be the best place in the world to admire Mackintosh's work: in addition to the buildings mentioned above, most of which can be visited, the Hunterian Art Gallery contains magnificent reconstructions of the principal rooms at 78 Southpark Avenue, Mackintosh's Glasgow home, and original drawings, documents, and records plus the re-creation of a room at 78 Derngate, Northampton.

(1746–1828), Signorelli (circa 1445–1523), and William Blake (1757–1827). Fine 18th- and early 19th-century furniture, silver, glass, and porcelain are also on display. Now cared for by the National Trust for Scotland, the house has fine gardens and looks over the White Cart River and Pollok Park, where, amid mature trees and abundant wildlife, the city of Glasgow's own highland cattle peacefully graze. ⊠ *Pollok Ave.,* ☎ *0141/616–6410.* ☒ *Apr.–Oct., £4; Nov.–Mar., free.* ☉ *Apr.–Oct., daily 10–5; Nov.–Mar., daily 11–4.*

DINING

Until the 1980s Glaswegians were famously unfussy about whatever vittles they ate—a lot of them wound up eating fast-food rubbish, and, not surprisingly, newspaper surveys determined they had the shortest life span in the United Kingdom. Then something strange quietly occurred: Glasgow became acquainted with the concept of discerning taste buds and then eagerly welcomed one of the liveliest, and most varied, dining scenes in the country. No longer were hot curries and anything fried in batter enough. Today, gastronomes no longer need approach Glasgow with trepidation and, more important, the local life expectancy has risen by six years.

Today, the key to Glaswegian cuisine is not Glasgow. It's the flurry of foreign restaurants that abound—from late-night crepe stalls and *pakora* (Indian fried chickpea cakes) bars to elegant restaurants with worldly menus. Glasgow restaurants tend to be larger than their Edinburgh counterparts, so getting a table at the establishment of your choice shouldn't be a problem, though making reservations for a Friday or Saturday night is still advisable.

CATEGORY	COST*
££££	over £40
£££	£30–£40
££	£15–£30
£	under £15

per person for a three-course meal, including VAT and excluding drinks and service

Victorian Glasgow and Merchant City

Caribbean

£–££ ✕ **Millars.** Despite the dull name, this restaurant is an adventurous mix of Caribbean, creole, and Cajun, all overseen by the equally adventurous Cassandra Mackie, Glasgow's answer to Whoopi Goldberg. Steel bands and New Orleans jazz combos play the occasional gig, and the paintwork is as loud as any music. Specially imported ingredients like plantain, yams, and delicious chilies ensure the food is authentic, and creative recipes make sure it's as fun and colorful as the surroundings. Avocado pear with lime juice and coconut milk served with deep-fried crispy plantain is a particularly mouthwatering concoction, but you'll find all sorts of tropical tastes on the three-course menus (£15). ⊠ *515–519 Sauchiehall St.,* ☎ *0141/248–2016. AE, DC, MC, V.*

Chinese

££ ✕ **Loon Fung.** There's plenty of space in this popular Cantonese restaurant, which was once a cinema and now seats 200. The pleasant, efficient staff guides you enthusiastically through the house specials, including the famed dim sum. If you like seafood, try the deep-fried wonton with prawns, crispy stuffed crab claws, or lobster in garlic and cheese sauce. The three-course business lunch is first class and only £6.30. ⊠ *417 Sauchiehall St.,* ☎ *0141/332–1240. AE, MC, V.*

Eclectic

££–££££   ✕ **Rogano.** The very spacious art deco interior, modeled after the style of the *Queen Mary* liner—bird's-eye maple paneling, chrome trim, and dramatic ocean murals—is enough to recommend this restaurant. Portions are generous in the main dining area, where impeccably prepared specialties include roast rack of lamb and classic seafood dishes such as lobster thermidor. Downstairs in the Café Rogano diner, the brasserie-style food is more modern and imaginative; the menu, which changes monthly, might list clam chowder or Mediterranean grilled swordfish. The theater menu provides early-evening and late-night bargains, and the fixed-price lunch menu is popular upstairs. There's also an oyster bar near the entrance. Rogano is patronized by the Glasgow establishment and visiting glitterati, who appreciate, as you will, the extremely good service. ⊠ *11 Exchange Pl.,* ☎ *0141/248–4055. AE, DC, MC, V.*

££–£££   ✕ **Buttery.** The exquisite Victorian-Edwardian surroundings of dark
★   colors and wood trim here are echoed by the staff's period uniforms. The best in Scottish fish, beef, and game is on the international menu; try the fillet of veal with mustard and cheese glaze. There's also a varied vegetarian menu. Service is friendly and the ambience relaxed. ⊠ *652 Argyle St.,* ☎ *0141/221–8188. Reservations essential. AE, DC, MC, V. Closed Sun. No lunch Sat.*

££   ✕ **Drum and Monkey.** This spectacular bar-restaurant is housed in a glorious Victorian building. The food ranges from acceptable enough pub fodder to some Scottish-French delights, served up in an adjacent bistro setting. Try the roasted monkfish and leek fish cakes with wilted spinach and ginger and coriander butter sauce, or the cheese-stuffed roasted chicken with olive oil mash. ⊠ *93–95 St. Vincent St.,* ☎ *0141/ 221–6636. AE, DC, MC, V. Closed Sun. in winter.*

££   ✕ **Brasserie.** A hotel basement (☞ Lodging, *below*) fitted with wooden booths provides a quiet, relaxed environment in which to appreciate a varied British-French menu. Traditional favorites such as fish cakes with chips or seared scallops appear alongside classic French *boeuf en daube* (beef braised in herbs and a red-wine stock). For dessert try the signature lemon tart. ⊠ *Malmaison Hotel, 278 W. George St.,* ☎ *0141/572–1001. Reservations essential. AE, DC, MC, V.*

££   ✕ **Café Gandolfi.** Once a Victorian pub, this café's location and decor reflect its trendsetting aspirations. On the edge of the Merchant City, it's now a haven for the design-conscious under-30 crowd. Wooden tables and chairs carved by Scottish artist Tim Stead are so fluidly shaped it's hard to believe they're inanimate. The café opens early for breakfast, serving croissants, eggs *en cocotte* (casserole-style), and espresso. The rest of the day the menu is filled with interesting soups, salads, local specialties, and Mediterranean favorites. Don't miss the smoked venison or the finnan haddie. Homemade ice cream and good pastries ensure busy afternoons, and evenings are livened up with good beers but less compelling wines. ⊠ *64 Albion St.,* ☎ *0141/552–6813. MC, V.*

£–££   ✕ **78 St. Vincent.** In what was originally the German Embassy—with stone
★   eagles outside and elaborate plasterwork within—maroon velvet drapes and quirky ironwork are now the setting in which to enjoy contemporary Scottish, French-influenced cuisine. Try loin of lamb with a confit of garlic, vegetables, and port, or salmon and scallops with ginger and spring onions *en papillote* (baked in parchment paper). Reservations are advised. ⊠ *78 St. Vincent St.,* ☎ *0141/248–7878. AE, DC, MC, V.*

Indian

£   ✕ **Mr. Singh's.** One of Glasgow's most popular eateries serves superb Indian and international cuisine backed by three generations of family experience. The restaurant benefited from a "Millennium makeover" and is now a restful cream, blue, and beechwood haven, rather quirkily combined with Indian waiters in kilts and a menu including haggis *pakora* (deep-fried haggis parcels). A choice of meats or vegetables can be cooked in a number of deliciously different sauces: try the lamb Mazadar—hot and spicy, with Rémy Martin—or the pistachio *korma* (curried meat with onions and vegetables). ✉ *149 Elderslie St.,* ☎ *0141/ 204–0186 or 0141/221–1452. AE, DC, MC, V.*

Italian

££ ✗ **Pavarotti Trattoria.** Despite the somewhat silly name this is not a kitsch affair but a sincerely Italian joint run by the Scala family. The menu changes regularly since Federico will only purchase the freshest ingredients. Consequently, the standard meat and fish dishes are unusually succulent. The lunch and pretheater set menus—only £8.90 each—are exceptionally good values. ✉ *91 Cambridge St.,* ☎ *0141/ 332–9713. AE, DC, MC, V.*

£ ✗ **Fazzi Café Bar.** This inexpensive Italian café-bar, with red tablecloths and bentwood chairs set on a tiled floor, is a cheerful place for a quick plateful of gnocchi *alla Emiliana* (with tomato, basil, and cheese sauce), or spinach and ricotta ravioli. The delicatessen at one end sells takeout. ✉ *65–67 Cambridge St.,* ☎ *0141/332–0941. AE, DC, MC, V.*

Pan-Asian

££ ✗ **Ruby.** From a Chinese base the menu of this friendly restaurant ventures south to take in Thai and Indonesian specialties. It then mixes the three together and the resulting taste sensations attract a cultlike clientele. Feeling indecisive, or are you in a large quibbling group? Here, the wide variety offers something for everyone. You can even get local fish-and-chips, but far more tempting is the *ho mok talag* (mixed seafood in herbs and a coconut sauce) or *dading rendang* (Spice Islands beef). The menu prices can be deceptive, for while most main courses are under £10, adding side dishes, starters, and dessert means you're likely to spend more than £20 a head. ✉ *377 Sauchiehall St.,* ☎ *0141/ 331–1277. AE, DC, MC, V.*

Russian

£–££ ✗ **Café Cossachok.** Situated near the Tron theater this is a willfully arty
★ place. The menu features Petrushka blintzes, which are much like normal blintzes, and very nice. There's also trout à la Pushkin (in a thirstrousing salty sauce). The tables are hand-carved, the lighting courtesy of candles, and the decor is a sea of shawls. The Russian emigré owner pays further homage to his homeland with live music from 3 PM Sunday, and a nicely chilled variety of vodkas. With an upstairs gallery, this fun venue is fashionable among the fashionable, from actors to pop stars, so it's best to book ahead. ✉ *10 King St.,* ☎ *0141/553–0733. AE, MC, V. No lunch Sun.*

£–££ ✗ **Khublai Khan Barbecue.** This sincerely Mongolian effort is about as exotic as you can get in this cosmopolitan age. Wild boar and things you haven't heard of feature strongly, as you'll discover if you dare to try the Mongolian Feast (£15.50). The massive space is festooned with handwoven rugs and a huge mural of Mongolian warrior hordes advancing threateningly. Don't worry: the service is friendly. Children are always welcome and they seem to thrill to the majestic decor and the theme-park history. You may not want to opt for a dessert but don't pass up the unique "ristretto"—a coffee, sort of. ✉ *26 Candleriggs St.,* ☎ *0141/400–8090. MC, V. No lunch.*

Scottish

££–£££ ✗ **Yes.** The basement location belies this restaurant's style, with careful
★ lighting and mirrors setting off the dramatic red, purple, and cream color

Glasgow Dining and Lodging

Dining

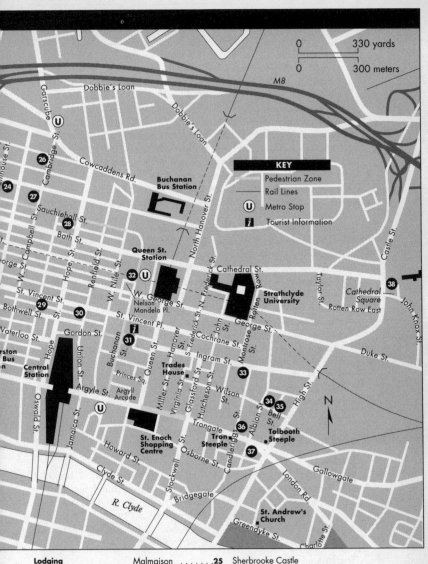

KEY

Pedestrian Zone

—— Rail Lines

Ⓤ Metro Stop

𝒊 Tourist Information

0 ___ 330 yards
0 ___ 300 meters

Lodging

Angus	**18**
Babbity Bowster's	**35**
Cathedral House	**38**
Devonshire Hotel	**1**
Glasgow Hilton	**14**
Kirklee Hotel	**4**
Malmaison	**25**
Number Thirty Six	**16**
One Devonshire Gardens	**2**
The Sandyford	**19**
Sherbrooke Castle Hotel	**13**
Town House	**3**
Victorian House	**21**
Wickets	**5**

scheme. Widely spaced tables enhance the relaxed ambience in which to enjoy contemporary Scottish cuisine. Try the "Surprise Menu": an eclectic four-course selection reflecting the best fresh produce available, which might include rack of lamb with a wild mushroom risotto, or seared chicken breast on a bed of spinach. The ground-floor café-bar serves Mediterranean-Italian specialties in flashy digs. Reservations are advised. ⊠ 22 *West Nile St.,* ☎ *0141/221–8044. AE, DC, MC, V. Closed Sun.*

£–££ ✕ **Willow Tearoom.** There are two branches of this restaurant, but this
★   one on Sauchiehall Street is the authentic one (the Buchanan Street branch is a replica). One of the landmark decors conceived by the great Charles Rennie Mackintosh, the room is kitted out with his trademark furniture, including those high-back chairs. The long lines and subtle curves create an effect that's elegance incarnate. So famous is the design that it's often forgotten that the food is jolly good, too. The St. Andrew's Platter is an exquisite selection of trout, salmon, and prawns. Scottish and Continental breakfasts are available throughout the day, and the scrambled eggs with Scottish salmon is traditional Scots food at its finest. The in-house baker guarantees fresh scones, cakes, and pastries to accompany your tea—the original and humble raison d'être of this legendary eatery. ⊠ *217 Sauchiehall St.,* ☎ *0141/332–0521. MC, V.*

£   ✕ **City Merchant.** In Glasgow a purely Scottish restaurant is almost a novelty, and few can compare with this venue. The food and decor are plain and simple, but great efforts are made to obtain the best ingredients. You can sample venison and steak that's the freshest in the land, but seafood remains the real attraction. The mussels and oysters from Loch Etive are wondrous, and the sea bass is positively renowned. Given the simple preparations, it may seem pricey (two- and three-course set menus cost £10.50 and £12.75, respectively) but if you have a penchant for fresh and honest cuisine, this place is a joy. Note that the set menus are only available between 11:45 AM and 6:30 PM. ⊠ *97-99 Candleriggs St.,* ☎ *0141/553–1577. AE, DC, MC, V.*

West End and Environs

Dutch

£–££ ✕ **Janssens Café Restaurant.** Described as "Amsterdam in Glasgow,"
★   this restaurant has spare but pleasantly relaxing surroundings in which to enjoy a Continental menu served by a friendly Dutch staff. Pita bread filled with grilled lamb or gratinéed mussels are typical of the dishes served, and there are lots of fresh salads. Reservations are advised on weekends. ⊠ *1355 Argyle St.,* ☎ *0141/334–9682. MC, V.*

Indian

£   ✕ **Ashoka West End.** This Punjabi restaurant consistently outperforms
★   its many competitors in quality, range, and taste. All portions are large enough to please the ravenous, but there's nothing heavy-handed about the cooking here: vegetable *samosas* (stuffed savory deep-fried pastries) are crisp and light, the spicing for the lamb, chicken, and prawn dishes is fragrant, and the selection of breads is superb. The eclectic decor, involving a bizarre mixture of plants, murals, rugs, and brass lamps, and inappropriate Western music simply emphasize Ashoka's idiosyncrasy. Reservations are advised on weekends. ⊠ *1284 Argyle St.,* ☎ *0800/454817. AE, MC, V. No lunch Sat.–Tues.*

Italian

£–££ ✕ **Sal e Pepe.** Behind the inconsequential facade are three floors of homey atmosphere and homey cooking, making it all seem like a very effortless little Italy. Seafood is a specialty but the half-price pizza and pasta dishes are perfect for value-conscious diners; they're offered from 3 to 6 PM Monday—Friday, when everyone else is at work. There's also a supremely filling three-course pretheater special in the evening for only £8.95. ⊠ *18 Gibson St.,* ☎ *0141/341–0999. MC, V.*

Scottish

£££ ✕ **Ubiquitous Chip.** In a pretty lane behind the Hillhead underground
★ station, this restaurant is an institution among members of Glasgow's media and thespian communities, with schmoozing galore (reservations are advised). The service is famously friendly, and the decor very outdoorsy, with a glass roof, much greenery, and a fishpond. This converted mews stable has won several awards, including one for its pioneering and delicious venison haggis. The menu has always specialized in game but Scotch-smoked salmon in Darjeeling tea is typical of the chef's clever blending of Scots fare with exotic elements. All in all, the Chip has a jovial atmosphere, suitably spacious for private chats and romantic intimacies. And the wines are excellent, especially by Glaswegian standards. There are specially priced two- or three-course meals, from £19 to £32; the Sunday special comes in at a mere £16.60 for four courses and a glass of bubbly. ⊠ *12 Aston La.,* ☎ *0141/334–5007. AE, DC, MC, V.*

££–£££ ✕ **Puppet Theater.** Down an unprepossessing side street is one of Glasgow's most delightful restaurants. Housed in a converted Edwardian mews and a striking, angled conservatory, the four dining rooms all have different moods. The contemporary Scottish menu, with a Mediterranean influence, might offer red mullet, vegetable couscous and crispy basil with pernod and fennel cream, or seared lamb cutlet with homegrown herbs, creamed vegetables, and deviled sauce. ⊠ *11 Ruthven La., off Byres Rd.,* ☎ *0141/339–8444. Reservations essential. AE, MC, V.*

££–£££ ✕ **Two Fat Ladies.** It's easy to mistake this restaurant for an all-night grocery because the kitchen can be seen through the window. The dining room has no ornamentation of any sort, just varnished wooden tables, nicotine-yellow walls, and a wooden floor. The cooking, in modern Scottish style, compensates for the austerity. Fish and shellfish predominate—fresh and prepared with imagination and skill. Try the char-grilled king scallops with fresh tomato salsa, or baked whole lemon sole with sesame seeds and teriyaki sauce. Portions are generous; the salads, colossal. ⊠ *88 Dumbarton Rd.,* ☎ *0141/339–1944. MC, V. No lunch Tues.–Thurs. Closed Sun. and Mon.*

South American

£–££ ✕ **Cottier's.** A converted Victorian church with interior decor by Glasgow artist Daniel Cottier is the unusual setting for this theater bar and restaurant (the Arts Theatre is attached). Red walls and beamed ceilings warm the downstairs bar, where the pub grub on offer has Tex-Mex flavors. In the restaurant, try the spicy lamb cooked with coconut, lime, cilantro and beans, or the tuna and snapper fillets with anchovy, chili, and citrus butter—two excellent choices from the South American dishes on the menu. Weekend reservations are advised. ⊠ *93 Hyndland St.,* ☎ *0141/357–5825. AE, MC, V.*

Vegetarian

£ ✕ **Bay Tree.** A small haven in the university area, this partially no-smoking café serves delightful vegetarian dishes. The modern paintings on the walls are often for sale. ⊠ *403 Great Western Rd.,* ☎ *0141/334–5898. No credit cards.*

LODGING

Central Glasgow never really goes to sleep, so downtown hotels will be noisier than those in the leafy and genteel West End (convenient for museums and art galleries) or southern suburbs (for the Burrell Collection). The flip side is that most downtown hotels are within walking distance of all the main sights, while you will need to make use of the (excellent) bus service from the suburbs. Breakfast will be included in the room rate for most smaller hotels and all guest houses and B&Bs. Larger hotels have adopted the custom of a room rate, with breakfast charged extra. Facilities on offer are equal to those offered with the accommodation in any other major city—as elsewhere, you pay for what you get, with room service being standard in most hotels (you may also get sports and leisure facilities in the largest), although rarer in guest houses and nonexistent in B&Bs.

CATEGORY	COST*
££££	over £150
£££	£100–£150
££	£60–£100
£	under £60

*All prices are for a standard double room, including service, breakfast, and VAT.

✎ following the text of a review is your signal that the property has a Web site, where you will find details and, usually, images; for a link, visit www.fodors.com/urls.

Medieval Glasgow and Merchant City

££££–££££ 🏨 **Glasgow Hilton.** You'll be struck by the professionalism at this typical international hotel; Glasgow friendliness permeates the very upscale image. Two themed restaurants—Cameron's, a Highland shooting lodge, and Minsky's, a New York–style deli and carvery—serve superb food, as does the Raffles bar, with its colonial Singapore theme. ⊠ *1 William St., G3 8HT,* ☎ *0141/204–5555,* 𝖥𝖠𝖷 *0141/204–5004. 319 rooms with bath. 2 restaurants, bar, beauty salon, health club, meeting rooms, free parking. AE, DC, MC, V.* ✎

£££ 🏨 **Malmaison.** In a converted church, the small, modern Malmaison prides itself on personal service and outstanding amenities: each room has robes and puffy down comforters; suites have CD players. The chic art deco decor employs bold colors—eggplant, navy, cream, red—in playful prints and geometric shapes all balanced out by traditional fabrics and furniture. The lobby's splendid staircase has a wrought-iron balustrade illustrating Napoléon's exploits (the hotel takes its name from his home). The warm Brasserie (☞ Dining, *above*) offers traditional British–French cooking. Café Mal serves savory pizzas and pasta in an airy terra-cotta-hued room with iron fixtures and a spiral staircase. ⊠ *278 W. George St., G2 4LL,* ☎ *0141/572–1000,* 𝖥𝖠𝖷 *0141/572–1002. 72 rooms with bath, 8 suites. 2 restaurants, bar, minibars, exercise room, meeting rooms. AE, DC, MC, V.* ✎

££ 🏨 **Babbity Bowster's.** There's a lively atmosphere at this intimate hotel in a restored 18th-century Robert Adam town house. Rooms have dark-wood Victorian reproductions, white-lace bedding, and floral curtains. The first-floor gallery features many works by Glaswegian artists. The restaurant's teak tables, upholstered chairs, wood floor, and gray-and-white color scheme complement the handsome hotel. ⊠ *16–18 Blackfriars St., G1 1PE,* ☎ *0141/552–5055,* 𝖥𝖠𝖷 *0141/552–7774. 6 rooms with bath. Restaurant, bar, café. AE, MC, V.*

££ 🏨 **Cathedral House.** In the heart of old Glasgow, near the cathedral, this small, friendly, freshly decorated hotel is convenient for sightseeing. The café-bar offers a fixed-price lunch, and there's also a restaurant with an à la carte menu that lists interesting South American dishes among the more usual fare. ⊠ *28–32 Cathedral Sq., G4 0XA,* ☎ *0141/552–3519,* 𝖥𝖠𝖷 *0141/552–2444. 8 rooms, 6 with bath, 2 with shower. Restaurant, bar, free parking. AE, MC, V.*

West End and Environs

££££   ⊞ **One Devonshire Gardens.** This hotel comprises a group of Victorian
★   houses on a sloping tree-lined street 10 minutes west of the city center.
       Celebrities such as Luciano Pavarotti and Elizabeth Taylor name it as
       their favorite. Each individually decorated bedroom has rich wallpaper,
       heavy drapes, and French mahogany furniture; 10 rooms have four-poster
       beds. The restaurant is equally stylish, with a menu that changes daily
       and specialties that include fillet of venison with potato and turnip gratin
       and terrine of chicken and bacon with Cumberland sauce. The wine list
       is commanding, as are the prices. ⊠ *1 Devonshire Gardens, G12 0UX,*
       ☎ *0141/339–2001,* FAX *0141/337–1663. 27 rooms, 24 with bath, 3*
       with shower. Restaurant, free parking. AE, DC, MC, V.☜

£££–££££ ⊞ **Devonshire Hotel.** The native Glasgow hospitality and friendliness con-
       trast sharply with the setting in an elegant terraced mansion and the sump-
       tuous, formal decor—elegant drapes, marbled pillars, stained glass, and
       four-poster beds. Frequented by stars when they're in town (Tina Turner,
       Whitney Houston, and Bruce Springsteen among them), the hotel strives
       for excellence in every department, including the modern British cuisine,
       for guests only, which makes the most of Scotland's fish and game. ⊠
       5 Devonshire Gardens, G12 0UX, ☎ *0141/339–7878,* FAX *0141/339–*
       3980. 14 rooms with bath or shower. Restaurant. AE, DC, MC, V.

££   ⊞ **Kirklee Hotel.** Near the university and in the West End, this B&B is
★   housed in a small and cozy Edwardian town house, replete with home-
       away-from-home comforts. A bay window overlooks a garden and the
       Victorian morning room is adorned with embroidered settees and silk-
       wash wallpapers, while engravings and a large library offer decorative
       touches that any university don would appreciate. The owners are friendly
       and helpful. ⊠ *11 Kensington Gate, G12 9LG,* ☎ *0141/334–5555,* FAX
       0141/339–3828. 9 rooms with bath and shower. AE, DC, MC, V.☜

££   ⊞ **Town House.** A B&B establishment in a handsome old terraced house
★   in a quiet cul-de-sac, the Town House thrives on repeat business. The
       owners are welcoming. The high ceilings, plasterwork, and other orig-
       inal architectural features of the house are complemented by restrained
       cream-and-pastel–stripe decor, stripped pine doors, and plain fabrics.
       There's a comfortable sitting room with books and informative leaflets.
       ⊠ *4 Hughenden Terr., G12 9XR,* ☎ *0141/357–0862,* FAX *0141/339–*
       9605. 10 rooms with shower. MC, V.

££   ⊞ **Wickets.** In the heart of Billy Connolly's neighborhood, Partick, this
       hotel dominates one of the area's few green spaces—the West of Scot-
       land cricket ground. It's a handsome white mansion house with an airy,
       Continental feel. Rooms are furnished with a cheerful bravado. Its glass-
       front restaurant looking onto an extensive garden is a rare pleasure in
       the city. The bar areas are split between the traditional and the art-
       fully Parisienne. Since cricket isn't Glasgow's premier sport, Wickets
       enjoys a tranquil, leafy setting. ⊠ *52 Fortrose St., G11 5LP,* ☎ FAX *0141/*
       334–9334. 11 rooms, 7 with bath, 4 with shower. AE, MC, V.

£–££   ⊞ **Angus.** Another privately run city-center hotel on Sauchiehall Street,
       the Angus is cozy yet spacious. Its biggest pluses are the friendly staff
       members with their eye for detail. All rooms have been tastefully deco-
       rated, creating a Victorian ambience. Note that this hotel doesn't serve
       evening meals. ⊠ *966–970 Sauchiehall St., G3 7TH,* ☎ *0141/357–5155,*
       FAX *0141/339–9469. 18 rooms with bath or shower. AE, MC, V.*☜

£–££   ⊞ **Number Thirty Six.** A Victorian terraced house in the West End, con-
       venient to the Kelvingrove and Hunterian museums and art galleries,
       this B&B serves a Continental-style breakfast in your room. The house
       is entirely no-smoking. ⊠ *36 St. Vincent Crescent, G3 8NG,* ☎ *0141/*
       248–2086, FAX *0141/221–1477. 5 rooms with bath or shower. No*
       credit cards. Closed Oct.–Mar.

£   🏠 **The Sandyford.** With a fine Victorian exterior, this hotel on the west end of famous Sauchiehall Street is convenient to all city-center facilities, including the Scottish Exhibition Centre and many art galleries. The Sandyford is more an upscale B&B than a hotel, with burgundy-and-green decor and pine furniture. No evening meals are served. ✉ *904 Sauchiehall St., G3 7TF,* ☎ *0141/334–0000,* FAX *0141/337–1812. 55 rooms with bath or shower. MC, V.*

£   🏠 **Victorian House.** This bed-and-breakfast on a quiet residential street is only a block away from the Charles Rennie Mackintosh–designed Glasgow School of Art. Although the staff is welcoming, the plain bedrooms are disappointing after the dramatic bright yellow decor of the entrance hall and reception area. No meals are served other than breakfast, but there are plenty of restaurants on nearby Sauchiehall Street. ✉ *212 Renfrew St., G3 6TX,* ☎ *0141/332–0129,* FAX *0141/353–3155. 58 rooms, 3 with bath, 47 with shower. MC, V.*

South Side

££–££££   🏠 **Sherbrooke Castle Hotel.** Come to the Sherbrooke for a flight of Gothic fantasy. Its cavernous rooms hark back to grander times when the South Side of Glasgow was home to the immensely wealthy tobacco barons, whose homes boasted turrets and towers. The spacious grounds are far from the noise and bustle of the city yet only a 10-minute drive from the city center. Like the tobacco barons, the hotel's proprietor insists on tasteful decor and good traditional cooking; the restaurant offers fine dining with entirely fresh ingredients and everything made on the premises, including the breads. The busy bar is well patronized by locals. ✉ *11 Sherbrooke Ave., Pollokshields, G41 4PG,* ☎ *0141/427–4227,* FAX *0141/427–5685. 25 rooms, 16 with bath, 9 with shower only. Restaurant, bar. AE, DC, MC, V.*

NIGHTLIFE AND THE ARTS

Held in the second half of January, **Celtic Connections** (✉ Glasgow Royal Concert Hall, 2 Sauchiehall St., G2 3NY, ☎ 0141/332–6633) is an ever-expanding annual homage to Celtic music, with musicians from Africa, France, Canada, Ireland, and Scotland playing and offering hands-on workshops on such things as harp making and -playing.

The Arts

Concerts

City Halls (✉ Candleriggs, ☎ 0141/287–4000) houses a wide variety of musical events. The **Henry Wood Hall** (✉ Claremont St., ☎ 0141/226–3868), a former church, is now used for occasional classical concerts and is the administrative base and rehearsal center for the Royal Scottish National Orchestra (RSNO). Glasgow's **Royal Concert Hall** (✉ 2 Sauchiehall St., ☎ 0141/332–6633) has 2,500 seats and is the main venue of the RSNO, which performs winter and summer. The **Scottish Exhibition and Conference Centre** (✉ Finnieston, ☎ 0141/248–3000) is a regular venue for pop concerts.

Dance and Opera

Glasgow is home to the Scottish Opera and Scottish Ballet, both of which perform at the **Theatre Royal** (✉ Hope St., ☎ 0141/332–9000). Visiting dance companies from many countries appear here also.

Film

The **Glasgow Film Theatre** (✉ 12 Rose St., ☎ 0141/332–6535) is an independent public cinema screening the best new-release films from all over the world. The **Grosvenor** (✉ West End, ☎ 0141/339–4298) and the **Odeon Film Centre** (✉ Renfield St., ☎ 0141/332–3413) show all the latest releases.

Theater

Tickets for theatrical performances can be purchased at theater box offices or at the **Ticket Center** (✉ Candleriggs, ☎ 0141/287–4000).

The **Arches** (✉ Midland St., ☎ 0141/287–4000) stages serious and controversial drama from around the world. Some of the most exciting theatrical performances take place at the internationally renowned **Citizen's Theatre** (✉ 119 Gorbals St., ☎ 0141/429–0022), where productions, and their sets, are often of hair-raising originality. Contemporary works are staged at **Cottier's Arts Theatre** (✉ 93 Hyndland St., ☎ 0141/287–4000), in a converted church. The **King's Theatre** (✉ Bath St., ☎ 0141/287–4000) puts on drama, light entertainment, variety shows, musicals, and amateur productions. The **Pavilion** (✉ 121 Renfield St., ☎ 0141/332–1846) offers family variety entertainment along with rock and pop concerts.

The **Royal Scottish Academy of Music and Drama** (✉ 100 Renfrew St., ☎ 0141/332–5057) stages a variety of international and student performances. **Theatre Royal** (✉ Hope St., ☎ 0141/332–9000) has performances of major dramas, including an occasional season of plays by international touring companies, as well as opera and ballet performances. The **Tron Theatre** (✉ 63 Trongate, ☎ 0141/552–4267) houses Scottish and international contemporary theater.

Nightlife

Consult the biweekly magazine the *List* and the *Herald* and *Evening Times* newspapers for up-to-date listings.

Bars and Pubs

Glasgow's pubs were once famous for hard drinkers who demanded few comforts. Times have changed, and many pubs have been turned into smart wine bars. For a taste of an authentic Glasgow pub with some traditional folk music occasionally thrown in, go to the Stockwell Street area and search out the **Scotia Bar** (✉ 112 Stockwell St., ☎ 0141/552–8682), the **Victoria Bar** (✉ 157–159 Bridgegate, ☎ 0141/552–6040), or **Clutha Vaults** (✉ 167 Stockwell St., ☎ 0141/552–7520).

Real ale enthusiasts should visit the **Bon Accord** (✉ 153 North St., ☎ 0141/248–4427) or the **Brewery Tap** (✉ 1055 Sauchiehall St., ☎ 0141/339–0643). If you visit only one pub in Glasgow, make it the **Horseshoe Bar** (✉ 17–21 Drury St., ☎ 0141/229–5711), which offers a sentimental, sepia-tinted glimpse of all the friendlier Glasgow myths and serves that cheerful distillation over what is purported to be the world's longest bar. Refurbishment would be a curse on its original tiling, stained glass, and deeply polished woodwork. Almost as intriguing as the decor is the clientele—a complete cross section of the city's populace. The upstairs lounge (with a bargain three-course lunch for £2.60) serves the steak pie Britain became famous for, and the waitress will ask some pretty pointed questions if you don't finish your food.

In the center of town the classic Victorian **Drum and Monkey** (✉ 93 St. Vincent St., ☎ 0141/221–6636) attracts an after-work crowd of young professionals. There's good live music in the **Halt** (✉ 160 Woodlands Rd., ☎ 0141/564–1527), which has a mixed-age clientele. **Nico's** (✉ 375 Sauchiehall St., ☎ 0141/332–5736), designed along the lines of a Paris café, is a favorite with art students and young Glaswegian professionals. In the city center, close to the River Clyde, the **Riverside Club** (✉ Fox St. off Clyde St., ☎ 0141/248–3144) features traditional *ceilidh* (a mix of country dancing, music, and song; pronounced *kay-lee*) bands on Friday and Saturday evenings; get there early—it's very popular. The best Gaelic pub is **Uisge Beatha** (⊠ 232–246 Woodlands Rd., ☎ 0141/564–1596), pronounced *oos*-ki *bee*-ha, which means "water of life" and is the origin of the word *whisky* (the term is a phonetic transliteration of the Gaelic word *uisge*). It serves Fraoch (heather beer) in season and has live music on Wednesday and Sunday.

Nightclubs

As in most of Britain's clubs, electronic music—from house to techno to drum and bass—is par for the course in dance clubs. The **Arches** (⊠ Midland St., ☎ 0141/221–4001) is one of the city's largest arts venues, for both its own and touring theater groups, but on Friday (11 PM–3 AM) and Saturday (10:30 PM–4 AM) it thumps with house and techno and welcomes big music names. **Archaos** (⊠ 25 Queen St., ☎ 0141/204–3189), Glasgow's biggest club, has three dance floors blasting house, garage, indie, R&B, soul, and hip-hop music. It's open Wednesday–Sunday 11 PM–4 AM. **The Polo Lounge** (⊠ 84 Wilson St., ☎ 0141/553–1221) is Glasgow's largest gay club, with three bars and two dance floors for 1970s, '80s, and '90s sounds—something for everyone. The festivities run Monday–Thursday 5 PM–1 AM; Friday 5 PM–3 AM; Saturday–Sunday noon–3 AM.

OUTDOOR ACTIVITIES AND SPORTS

Biking and Running

The tourist board (☞ Glasgow A to Z, *below*) can provide a list of cycle paths and of the 70 parks and gardens in Glasgow where you can jog or pedal around the pathways; many parks also have tennis courts and/or bowling greens.

Fishing

With loch, river, and sea fishing available, the area is a mecca for fishermen. Details of fishing permits and locations are available from the tourist board (☞ Glasgow A to Z, *below*).

Football

The city has been sports mad, especially for football (soccer), for more than 100 years, and the rivalry between its two main clubs, Rangers and Celtic, is legendary. Rangers wear blue, are predominantly Protestant, and play at **Ibrox** (pronounced *eye*-brox; ⊠ Edmiston Dr., ☎ 08706/001993) to the west of the city. Celtic wear green, are predominantly Roman Catholic, and play in the east at **Celtic Park** (⊠ 95 Kerrydale St., ☎ 0141/556–2611). Matches are held usually on Saturday in winter, and Glasgow has in total nine different teams playing in the Scottish Leagues. Admission prices start at about £15. Do not go looking for the family-day-out atmosphere of many American football games; soccer remains a fiercely contested game played in relatively primitive surroundings, though Ibrox is an exception to this.

Golf

Ten municipal courses are operated within Glasgow proper by the local authorities. Bookings are relatively inexpensive and should be made directly to the course 24 hours in advance to ensure prime tee times (courses open at 7 AM). A comprehensive list of contacts, facilities, and greens fees of the 30 or so other courses near the city is available from the Greater Glasgow and Clyde Valley Tourist Board (☞ Glasgow A to Z, *below*,).

Kings Park (⊠ Croftpark Ave., ☎ 0141/630–1597) 9 holes, 2,071 yards, SSS 30. **Lethamhill** (⊠ 1240 Cumbernauld Rd., ☎ 0141/770–6220, FAX 0141/770–0520) 18 holes, 5,836 yards, SSS 68. **Linn Park** (⊠ Simshill

Rd., ☎ 0141/637–5871) 18 holes, 5,132 yards, SSS 65. **Littlehill** (✉ Auchi-nairn Rd., ☎ 0141/772–1916) 18 holes, 6,240 yards, SSS 70. **Ruchill** (✉ Brassey St., ☎ 0141/946–8793) 9 holes, 2,217 yards, SSS 31.

Health Clubs

There are 19 municipal sports centers, ranging from fairly basic swimming pools to facilities for a wide range of sports. There are also many private clubs, though membership isn't usually available to visitors. The larger hotels also offer a variety of sports and leisure facilities, usually free of charge, to their guests. The best of the municipal-run sports centers are **Bellahouston Leisure Center** (✉ 31 Bellahouston Dr., ☎ 0141/427–5454), **Kelvin Hall International Sports Arena** (✉ Kelvin Hall, Argyle St., ☎ 0141/357–2525), and **Scotstoun Leisure Centre** (✉ Danes Dr., Scotstoun, ☎ 0141/959–4000). See the brochure available from the tourist board (☞ Glasgow A to Z, *below*) for details.

Sailing and Water Sports

The Firth of Clyde and Loch Lomond (each about a 30-minute drive southwest and north of Glasgow, respectively) both offer water-sports facilities for sailing, canoeing, windsurfing, and rowing, with full equipment rental. Details are available from the tourist board (☞ Glasgow A to Z, *below*).

SHOPPING

Glasgow has long been famous for its shopping, and you can cover its main shopping centers and streets at small expense by bus, *provided* you don't get off. No one has yet discovered any way of keeping shop-'til-you-droppers on the buses, however, and considering the range, value, and attractiveness of the goods in the city's boutiques, no one can blame them.

Arcades and Shopping Centers

St. Enoch's Shopping Centre (✉ 55 St. Enoch Sq., ☎ 0141/204–3900) is eye-catching if not especially pleasing. It houses various stores, but most could be found elsewhere. By far the best complex is **Princes Square** (✉ 48 Buchanan St., ☎ 0141/221–0324), with high-quality shops in an art nouveau setting, along with cafés and restaurants. Look particularly for the Scottish Craft Centre, which has an outstanding collection of work created by some of the nation's best craftspeople. The **Buchanan Galleries** (✉ 220 Buchanan St., ☎ 0141/333– 9898), at the top end of Buchanan Street next to the Royal Concert Hall, offers high-quality shopping opportunities; its magnet attraction is John Lewis (☞ *below*).

Department Stores

The main department stores are **Debenham's** (✉ 97 Argyle St., also accessed from St. Enoch Centre, ☎ 0141/221–0088), with china and crystal as well as women's and men's clothing, and **Frasers** (✉ 21–45 Buchanan St., ☎ 0141/221–3880), a Glasgow institution whose wares reflect much of Glasgow's new and traditional images—leading European designer clothes and fabrics combining with home-produced articles, such as tweeds, tartans, glass, and ceramics. The magnificent interior, set off by the grand staircase rising to various floors and balconies, is itself worth a visit.

British Home Stores (✉ 67–81 Sauchiehall St., ☎ 0141/332–0401), **C&A** (✉ 218 Sauchiehall St., ☎ 0141/333–9441), and **Marks & Spencer** (✉ 2–12 Argyle St., ☎ 0141/552–4546) are good bets. **John Lewis** (✉ Buchanan Galleries, Buchanan St., ☎ 0141/353–6677) is a favorite for its good-value mix of clothing and household items.

Shopping Districts

St. Enoch Square, which is also the main underground station, houses the St. Enoch Shopping Centre. On the main, often-crowded pedestrian area of **Argyle Street,** you'll find all the usual High Street chain stores, such as Debenham's. An interesting diversion off Argyle Street is **Argyll Arcade,** a covered street that has the largest collection of jewelers under one roof in Scotland. This L-shape arcade, built in 1904, houses several locally based jewelers and a few shops specializing in antique jewelry. The other end of the Argyll Arcade leads to **Buchanan Street,** Glasgow's premier shopping street and almost totally a pedestrian area. The usual suspects are here: Laura Ashley, Burberry's, Jaeger, and many other household names, some with premises in one of the city's newest shopping centers, the Buchanan Galleries at the top end of the street.

Merchant City, on the edge of the city center, is home to many of Glasgow's young and upwardly mobile. Shopping here is expensive, but the area is worth visiting if you're seeking the young Glasgow style. The huge **Barras** (☞ Exploring Glasgow, *above*) indoor market prides itself on selling everything "from a needle to an anchor"; stalls hawk antique (and not-so-antique) furniture, bric-a-brac, student-designed jewelry, and textiles—you name it, it's here. If you're an antiques connoisseur and art lover, a walk along **West Regent Street** is highly recommended, as there are various galleries and shops, some specializing in Scottish antiques and paintings. The area around **West End** and **Byres Road** is dominated by the university, and the shops cater to local and student needs. Take the underground system or Bus 44 or 59 to Hillhead.

Specialty Shops

Antiques and Fine Art

The **Compass Gallery** (✉ 178 W. Regent St., ☎ 0141/221–6370) usually has interesting fine art exhibitions. **Cyril Gerber Fine Art** (✉ 148 W. Regent St., ☎ 0141/221–3095 or 0141/204–0276), specialists in British paintings from 1880 to the present, will export, as will most galleries. **De Courcey's** (✉ 5–21 Cresswell La.) antiques and crafts arcade has quite a few shops to visit, and a variety of goods, including paintings and jewelry, are regularly auctioned here. De Courcey's is in one of the cobblestone lanes to the rear of Byres Road.

Books and Paper

The **Glasgow School of Art** (✉ 167 Renfrew St., ☎ 0141/353–4526) has the Mackintosh Shop, selling various books, cards, jewelry, and ceramics. Students often sell their work, if you're lucky enough to be visiting during the degree shows in June. **John Smith & Son (Glasgow) Ltd.** (✉ 57 St. Vincent St., ☎ 0141/221–7472), founded in the mid-18th century, prides itself on being a thoroughly Scottish bookstore, with a super selection of books about the country, plus a friendly café upstairs. **Papyrus** (✉ 374 Byres Rd., ☎ 0141/334–6514; ✉ 296–298 Sauchiehall St., ☎ 0141/353–2182) has a wide range of designer cards, small gifts, and a good selection of books.

Clothing Boutiques

At Princes Square there are famous designer names: **Ted Baker** (✉ Unit 19 The Glasshouse, Princes Sq., ☎ 0141/221–9664) stocks men's and women's designer wares—lots of clothing, ties, and accessories—at designer prices. Worth a special mention is the West End's **Strawberry Fields** (✉ 517 Great Western Rd., ☎ 0141/339–1121), selling a colorful array of children's wear.

Gourmet Foods

Peckham's Delicatessen (⊠ 100 Byres Rd., ☎ 0141/357–1454; ⊠ 43 Clarence Dr., ☎ 0141/357–2909; ⊠ Central Station, ☎ 0141/248–4012; ⊠ Glassford St., ☎ 0141/553–0666) is *the* place for Continental sausages, cheeses, and everything for a delicious picnic.

Home Furnishings and Textiles

Casa Fina (⊠ 1 Wilson St., ☎ 0141/552–6791) stocks stylish modern furniture and giftware. **In House** (⊠ 24–26 Wilson St., ☎ 0141/552–5902) has top-quality, contemporary designer furniture as well as glassware, china, and textiles. **Linens Fine** (⊠ The Courtyard, Princes Sq., ☎ 0141/248–7082) has a wonderful selection of embroidered and embellished bed linens and other textiles. At the **National Trust for Scotland**'s shop (⊠ Hutcheson's Hall, 158 Ingram St., ☎ 0141/552–8391) many of the items for sale, such as china, giftware, textiles, toiletries, and housewares, are designed exclusively for trust properties and are often handmade. Wander around **Stockwell Bazaar** (⊠ 67–77 Glassford St., ☎ 0141/552–5781) for a huge array of fine china and earthenware, glass, and ornaments. Items will be packed and sent overseas for you, if requested.

Scottish Specialties

Glasgow has a definite place in the history of art and design, being most famous for its association with Charles Rennie Mackintosh. For high-quality giftware in his style, **Catherine Shaw** (⊠ 24 Gordon St., ☎ 0141/204–4762; ⊠ 32 Argyll Arcade, ☎ 0141/221–9038) offers a unique selection. **Hector Russell Kiltmakers** (⊠ 110 Buchanan St., ☎ 0141/221–0217) specializes in Highland outfitting, Scottish gifts, woolens, cashmere, and ladies' fashions. **MacDonald MacKay Ltd.** (⊠ 161 Hope St., ☎ 0141/204–3930) makes, sells, and exports Highland dress and accessories for men and custom-made kilts and skirts for women.

Sports Gear

You'll find good-quality outerwear at **Tiso Sports** (⊠ 129 Buchanan St., ☎ 0141/248–4877), handy if you are planning some Highland walks.

Tobacco

Robert Graham (⊠ 71 St. Vincent St., ☎ 0141/221–6588) has a tremendous variety of tobaccos and pipes. Much of Glasgow's wealth was generated by the tobacco lords during the 17th and 18th centuries; at Graham's you'll experience a little of that colorful history.

SIDE TRIPS FROM GLASGOW: IN AND AROUND ROBERT BURNS COUNTRY

Those grand solitudes you see when flying into Glasgow Airport, that jigsaw puzzle of firths and straits and interlocking islands harbor a wide array of one-day excursion destinations. Here you can travel south to visit the fertile farmlands of Ayrshire—Robert Burns country—or west to the Firth of Clyde, or southeast to the Clyde Valley, all by car or, in a modified form, by public transportation. You may want to begin with the town of Paisley. Once a distinct burgh but now part of the Glasgow suburban area, it offers plenty of gritty character, largely because of vestiges of its industrial heritage. It was once famous for its paisley shawl manufacturing, and its museum has a fine collection of these garments. Palatial treasures are also en route—the Hamilton Mausoleum, the Marquess of Bute's Mount Stuart House on the Isle of Bute, and Culzean Castle, a favored retreat for Eisenhower and Churchill that's famous for its Robert Adam design and spectacular seaside setting.

The highlight of this region is Robert Burns country. English children learn that Burns (1759–96) is a good minor poet. But Scottish children know that he's Shakespeare, Dante, Rabelais, Mozart, and Karl Marx rolled into one. As time goes by, it seems that the Scots have it more nearly right. As poet and humanist, Burns increases in stature. When you plunge into the Burns country, don't forget that he's held in extreme reverence by Scots of all degrees. They may argue about Sir Walter Scott and Bonnie Prince Charlie; there's no disputing the merits of the poet of "Bonnie Doon." A few words of warning: call him Robert, Robin, Robbie, Rob, or Rab—but never Bobbie.

Paisley

32 The industrial prosperity of Paisley came from textiles and, in particular, from the woolen paisley shawl. The internationally recognized pattern is based on the shape of a palm shoot, an ancient Babylonian fertility symbol brought to Britain by way of Kashmir. The full story of the pattern and of the innovative weaving techniques introduced in Paisley is told in the **Paisley Museum and Art Gallery,** which has a world-famous shawl collection. ⊠ *High St.,* ☎ *0141/889–3151.* ▣ *Free.* ☉ *Tues.– Sat. 10–5, Sun. 2–5; bank holidays 10–5.*

To get an idea of the life led by textile industry workers, visit the **Sma' Shot Cottages.** Re-creations of mill workers' houses contain displays of linen, lace, and Paisley shawls. An 18th-century weaver's cottage is also open to visitors. ⊠ *11–17 George Pl.,* ☎ *0141/889–1708.* ▣ *Free.* ☉ *Apr.–Sept., Wed. and Sat. 1–5 or by appointment.*

Paisley's 12th-century Cluniac **Abbey** dominates the town center. Almost completely destroyed in 1307 and then rebuilt after the Battle of Bannockburn, the abbey is associated with Walter Fitzallan, the high steward of Scotland, who gave his name to the Stewart monarchs of Scotland. Outstanding features include the vaulted stone roof and stained glass of the choir. Paisley Abbey is today a busy parish church. Groups should call ahead. ☎ *0141/889–7654.* ▣ *Free.* ☉ *Mon.–Sat. 10–3:30, and for Sun. services (11, 12:15, and 6:30).*

Paisley A to Z

ARRIVING AND DEPARTING

By Bus: There's regular service (Bus 9) to Paisley from the **Renfield Street bus station** (☎ 0141/885–4040).

By Car: Take the M8 westbound and then the A737, which is clearly signposted to Paisley.

By Train: Service runs every 5–10 minutes throughout the day from **Glasgow Central Station** (☎ 0345/484950 for information on national train service).

VISITOR INFORMATION

The **tourist information center** is at the Town Hall (⊠ Gilmour St., ☎ 0141/889–0711, ☉ daily 9–5).

Ayrshire and the Clyde Coast

Robert Burns is Scotland's national and most well-loved poet. His birthday is celebrated with speeches and dinners, drinking and dancing (Burns Suppers) on January 25, in a way in which few other countries celebrate a poet. He was born in Alloway, beside Ayr, just an hour or so south of Glasgow, and the towns and villages where he lived and loved make an interesting day out.

On your way here, you'll travel beside the estuary and firth of the great River Clyde and be able to look across to Dumbarton and its Rock, a nostalgic farewell point for emigrants leaving Glasgow. The river is surprisingly narrow here, when you remember that the *Queen Elizabeth 2* and the other great ocean liners sailed these waters from the place of their birth. Farther along the coast, the views north and west to Loch Long, Holy Loch, and the Argyll Forest Park are outstanding on a clear day. Two high points of the trip, in addition to the Burns connections, are Mount Stuart House, on the Isle of Bute, and south of Ayr, Culzean Castle, flagship of the National Trust for Scotland.

33 Wemyss Bay

From the old Victorian village of Wemyss Bay there's a ferry service to the Isle of Bute, once a favorite holiday spot for Glaswegians. The many handsome buildings, especially the station and its covered walkway between platform and steamer pier, with its exuberant wrought ironwork, are a reminder of the Victorian era's grandeur and style and of the generations of visitors who used trains and ferries for their summer holidays. South of Wemyss Bay, you can also look across to the island of Arran, another Victorian holiday favorite, and then the island of Great Cumbrae, a weighty name for a tiny island.

34 Isle of Bute

The Isle of Bute offers a host of relaxing walks and scenic vistas. ★ **Rothesay,** a faded but appealing resort, is the main town. Bute's biggest draw is spectacular **Mount Stuart,** ancestral home of the marquesses of Bute, about 5 mi south of Rothesay. The massive Victorian Gothic palace built in red sandstone has ornate interiors, including the Marble Hall, with star-studded vault, stained glass, arcaded galleries, and magnificent tapestries woven in Edinburgh in the early 20th century. The paintings and furniture throughout the house are equally outstanding. ⊠ *Isle of Bute,* ☎ *01700/503877.* ⊃ *Joint ticket, house, and gardens, £6; gardens only, £3.50.* ⊙ *May–Sept., Mon., Wed., and Fri.– Sun., gardens: 10–5; house: guided tours only, starting at 11 then every 20 mins until last tour at 3:30.* ⊗

DINING AND LODGING

££ ✗🏠 **Ardmory House Hotel.** Set in large gardens in a peaceful residential area, this hotel evokes a modern home away from home, with Bute fabric (woven on the island) covering the chairs and a cozy bar with an open fire downstairs, and plainly furnished but comfortable bedrooms each individually decorated in muted colors. The staff is exceptionally friendly and attentive. Standard bar meals such as homemade soup, lasagna, or chili are on offer, and the restaurant serves more elaborate creations—breast of duck with spiced mandarin orange and cherry mulled-wine sauce or salmon on a nest of fettuccine vegetables with saffron butter sauce. ⊠ *Ardmory Rd., Ardbeg, Isle of Bute, PA20 0PG,* ☎ *01700/502346,* FAX *01700/505596. 5 rooms, 2 with bath, 3 with shower. Restaurant, bar. AE, DC, MC, V.*

35 Largs

At the coastal resort of Largs, the community makes the most of the town's Viking history. It was the site in 1263 of a major battle that finally broke the power of the Vikings in Scotland, and every September a commemorative Viking Festival is held. All year round, **Vikingar! the Viking Heritage Centre,** tells the story of the Viking influence in Scotland by way of film, tableaux, and displays. ⊠ *Barrfields, Greenock Rd., KA30 8QL,* ☎ *01475/689777.* ⊃ *£3.75.* ⊙ *May–Sept., daily 10:30–5:30; Oct.–Apr., daily 10:30–3:30.*

If you're in Largs on the seafront on a summer's afternoon, take time to look into the **Clark Memorial Church** (☎ 01475/675186), which has a particularly splendid array of Glaswegian Arts and Crafts stained glass of the 1890s in its windows. Among the studios involved in their de-

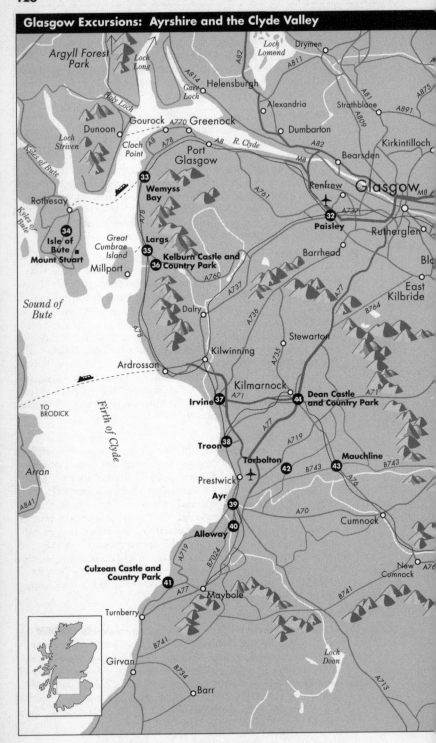

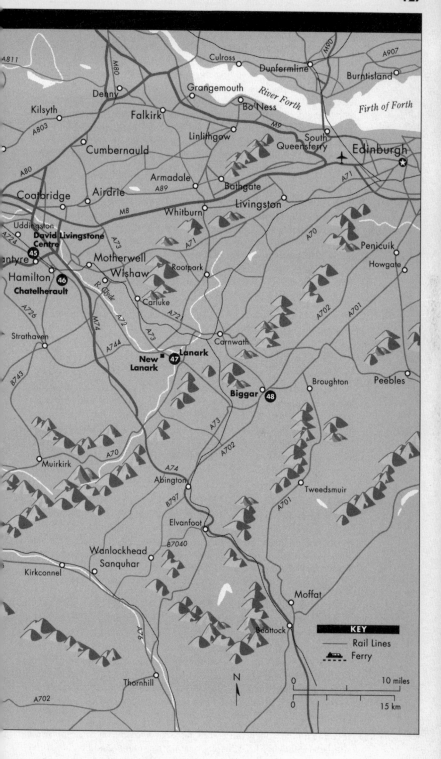

A811
M80
A907
Culross
Dunfermline
Grangemouth
Burntisland
Denny
River Forth
Bo'Ness
Firth of Forth
Kilsyth
Falkirk
A803
Linlithgow
M9
Cumbernauld
South
Queensferry
Edinburgh
A80
Armadale
Bathgate
A71
Coatbridge
Airdrie
A89
Livingston
Uddingston
M8
Whitburn
David Livingstone
Centre
A73
A71
Penicuik
antyre
45
Motherwell
Rootpark
A70
Howgate
Hamilton
46
Wishaw
Chatelherault
R. Clyde
Carluke
A72
A702
A726
Strathaven
M74
A72
A73
Carnwath
A701
A744
New
Lanark
Lanark
47
B743
Biggar
48
Broughton
Peebles
A73
Muirkirk
A70
A702
A74
Tweedsmuir
Abington
B797
A701
Elvanfoot
Wanlockhead
B7040
Kirkconnel
Sanquhar
Moffat
A76
Beattock
| KEY |
| Rail Lines |
| Ferry |
Thornhill
N
0 ——— 10 miles
A702
0 ——— 15 km

sign were those of Stephen Adam (1848–1910) and his contemporary Christopher Wall.

36 Just south of Largs is **Kelburn Castle and Country Park,** the historic estate of the earl of Glasgow. There are walks and trails through the mature woodlands, including the mazelike Secret Forest, which leads deep into the thickets. The adventure center and commando-assault course will wear out overexcited children. (They tell a tale here of rescuing an elderly lady from halfway around the assault course, who commented, "Well, I did think it was rather a *hard* nature trail." Make sure you read the signposts.) ⊠ *Fairlie, Ayrshire KA29 0BE,* ☎ *01475/568685.* ⊠ *£4.50.* ☼ *Castle: July–Sept., daily 10–6; grounds: Easter–Oct., daily, 10–6; Nov.–Easter, daily 11–5.*

37 ## Irvine

Robert Burns puts in an appearance at Irvine. The Irvine Burns Club is possibly the oldest in the world. He came here to learn to dress flax (the raw material for linen), and the heckling (flax-dressing) shed where he worked and the house where he lived are museums known as the **Glasgow Vennel Art Gallery.** ⊠ *4 and 10 Glasgow Vennel,* ☎ FAX *01294/275059.* ⊠ *Free.* ☼ *June–Sept., Mon., Tues., and Thurs.–Sat. 10–1 and 2–5; Oct.–May, Tues., Thurs.–Sat. 10–1 and 2–5.*

38 ## Troon

The small coastal town of Troon is famous for its international golf course, Royal Troon. You can easily see why golf is so popular here. At times, the whole 60-mi-long Ayrshire coast seems one endless golf course.

LODGING

£££ 🏨 **Piersland House Hotel.** This hotel is set in a late-Victorian mansion, formerly the home of a whisky magnate. All the bedrooms are individually decorated and furnished in traditional style. Oak paneling and log fires in the restaurant provide a warm backdrop for traditional Scottish cuisine, including specialties such as beef medallions in pickled walnut sauce. ⊠ *15 Craigend Rd. (just north of Ayr), KA10 6HD,* ☎ *01292/314747,* FAX *01292/315613. 28 rooms, 22 with bath, 6 with shower. Restaurant. AE, DC, MC, V.*

GOLF

Royal Troon (⊠ Troon, Ayrshire, ☎ 01292/311555), a club founded in 1878, has two 18-hole courses: the Old, or Championship (7,097 yards, SSS 74), and the Portland (6,289 yards, SSS 70). Access for visitors is limited between May and October to Monday, Tuesday, and Thursday only; a round costs £125.

SHOPPING

Many Glaswegians frequent **Regalia** (⊠ 46 Church St., ☎ 01292/312162) for its unusual collection of designer outfits for women.

39 ## Ayr

The commercial port of Ayr is Ayrshire's chief town, a peaceful and elegant place with an air of prosperity and some good shops. Robert Burns was baptized in the Auld Kirk (Old Church) here and wrote a humorous poem about the Twa Brigs (Two Bridges), which cross the river nearby. He described Ayr as a town unsurpassed "for honest men and bonny lasses."

40 If you're on the Robert Burns trail, head for **Alloway,** on B7024 in Ayr's southern suburbs. In Alloway, among the many middle-class residences, you'll find the one-room thatched **Burns Cottage,** where Scotland's national poet was born in 1759 and which his father built; a museum of Burnsiana is next door. Not many outside Scotland appreciate the depth of affection that Scotland has for Burns. To his fellow countrymen he's more than a great lyric bard; he's the champion of the underdog, the lover of noble causes, the hater of pomposity and cant, the prophet of social justice. "A man's a man for a' that"—such phrases have exalted the Scottish character, while his love songs warm the coldest Presbyterian hearts. The man in the street still quotes Burns—which is more than can be said, south of the border, for Shakespeare. January 25, Burns Night, is an anniversary of importance in Scotland. ☎ 01292/441215. ✉ £2.80 (includes admission to Burns Monument and allows discounted admission to Tam o' Shanter Experience). ⊗ Apr.–Oct., daily 9–6; Nov.–Mar., Mon.–Sat. 10–4, Sun. noon–4.

Find out all about Burns at the **Tam o' Shanter Experience.** Here you can first enjoy a 10-minute audiovisual journey through his life and times, then watch as one of Burns's most famous poems, "Tam o' Shanter," is brought to life on a three-screen theatrical set. It's down the road from Burns Cottage and around the corner from Alloway's ruined church. ☎ 01292/443700. ✉ £2.80 (includes admission to Burns Monument and allows discounted admission to Burns Cottage and museum). ⊗ Apr.–Sept., daily 9–6; Oct.–Mar., daily 9–5.

Auld Alloway Kirk is where Tam o' Shanter unluckily passed a witches' revel—with Old Nick himself playing the bagpipes—on his way home from a night of drinking. Tam, in flight from the witches, managed to cross the **Brig o' Doon** (brig is Scots for bridge) just in time. His gray mare, Meg, lost her tail to the closest witch. (Any resident of Ayr will tell you that witches cannot cross running water.) The **Burns Monument** (entrance fee included in charge for Burns Cottage and for Tam o' Shanter Experience) overlooks the Brig o' Doon.

DINING

££ ✕ **Fouter's Bistro.** Fouter's is in a long and narrow cellar, yet its white ★ walls and decorative stenciling create an airy ambience. The cuisine is also light and skillful—no heavy sauces here. Try the roast Ayrshire lamb with pan juices and red wine and mint, or sample the "Taste of Scotland" appetizer—smoked salmon, trout, and other goodies. This is modern Scottish and French cooking at its best, all in a friendly setting. ✉ 2A Academy St., ☎ 01292/261391. AE, DC, MC, V.

SHOPPING

Ayr has a good mixture of traditional and new shops. The **Diamond Factory** (✉ 27 Queen's Court, ☎ 01292/280476) is a jewelry workshop where you can watch craftsmen work. All jewelry is designed and made on the premises. Particularly coveted are the handmade Celtic wedding bands. The store will export your purchases if you don't have time to wait for the work to be completed. The **Mill Shop, Begg of Ayr** (✉ Viewfield Rd., ☎ 01292/267615) has a good selection of scarves, stoles, plaids, and travel rugs handmade on site.

★ ㊶ Culzean Castle and Country Park

The dramatic cliff-top Culzean (pronounced ku-lain) Castle and Country Park is the National Trust for Scotland's most popular property, yet it remains unspoiled. Complete with a walled garden, the neoclassical mansion was designed by Robert Adam (1728–92) in 1777. In addition to its marvelous interiors, it contains the National Guest Flat, given by the people of Scotland in appreciation of General Eisenhower's (1890–1969) services during World War II. As president he stayed here once or twice, and his relatives still do so occasionally. Between visits it's used by the National Trust for official entertaining. The rooms on the approach to this special apartment evoke the atmosphere of World War II: mementos of Glenn Miller (1904–44), Winston Churchill (1871–

1947), and other personalities of the era all help create a suitably 1940s mood. On the estate grounds, shrubberies reflect the essential mildness of this coast, though some visitors, meeting the full force of a westerly gale, might think otherwise. Culzean's perpendicular sea cliff offers views across the Firth of Clyde to Arran and the Irish coast. Not a stone's throw away, it seems, the pinnacle of Ailsa Craig rears from mid-channel. ☎ 01655/760269. 🖾 *Country park and castle, £7; country park only, £3.50.* ◷ *Castle: Apr.–Oct., daily 10:30–5:30 (last admission 5); country park: daily year-round, 9:30–sunset.*

④② Tarbolton

At Tarbolton you will find the **Bachelors' Club,** the 17th-century house where Robert Burns learned to dance, founded a debating and literary society, and became a Freemason. ☎ 01292/541940. 🖾 *£2.50.* ◷ *Easter and May–Oct., daily 1:30–5:30.*

④③ Mauchline

Mauchline has strong connections with the poet Robert Burns. There's a **Burns House** here, four of his daughters are buried in the churchyard, and **Poosie Nansie's Pub,** where he used to drink, is still serving pints today. The village is also famous for making curling stones.

Kilmarnock

This industrial town, home of Johnny Walker whisky, has more enjoyment for Burns enthusiasts: the Burns Museum and the Dick Institute. If you're looking for something a little different, go to **Dean Castle and Country Park** to enjoy a 14th-century castle with a wonderful collection of medieval arms and armor. Burns also inevitably gets a mention. 🖾 *Off Glasgow Rd.,* ☎ 01563/522702. 🖾 *Free.* ◷ *Apr.–Sept., daily noon–5; Oct.–Mar., weekends 12:15–4.*

Ayrshire and the Clyde Coast A to Z

ARRIVING AND DEPARTING

By Bus and Train: Take the bus or train to Largs for Cumbrae; Ardrossan for Arran; Ayr and Kilmarnock for the Burns Heritage Trail; and Troon, Prestwick, and Ayr to play golf. Bus companies also operate one-day guided excursions; for details contact the tourist information center in Glasgow, **Strathclyde Passenger Transport (SPT) Travel Centre** (☎ 0141/226–4826), or the **National Train Enquiry Line** (☎ 0345/484950).

By Car: Begin your trip from the Glasgow city center westbound on the M8, signposted for Glasgow Airport and Greenock. Join the A8 and follow it from Greenock to Gourock and around the coast past the Cloch Lighthouse. Head south on the A78 to the old Victorian village of Wemyss Bay and take the ferry over to Bute to see Mount Stuart (leave your car behind: a bus service takes you to the house from the ferry). Then continue down the A78 through Largs, Irvine, Troon, and so to Ayr and Alloway. Travel on to Culzean Castle, then return to Ayr and turn eastward on the B743, the Mauchline Road; but before you get here, turn left on a little road to Tarbolton. Return to the B743, visit Mauchline, and then head north on A76 to Kilmarnock. Glasgow is only a half hour away on the fast A77.

VISITOR INFORMATION

Ayr (🖾 22 The Sandgate, ☎ 01292/288688). **Irvine** (🖾 New St., ☎ 01294/313886). **Kilmarnock** (🖾 62 Bank St., ☎ 01563/539090). **Largs** (🖾 Promenade, ☎ 01475/673765). **Rothesay** (🖾 The Winter Gardens, Rothesay, Isle of Bute, ☎ 01700/502151).

Clyde Valley

The River Clyde is (or certainly was) famous for its shipbuilding and heavy industries, yet its upper reaches flow through some of Scotland's most fertile farmlands, rich with tomato crops. It's an interesting area, with ancient castles as well as museums that tell the story of manufacturing and mining prosperity.

Blantyre

45 In the not-very-pretty town of Blantyre, look for signs to the **David Livingstone Centre,** a park area around the tiny (tenement) apartment where the great explorer of Africa (1813–73) was born. Displays tell of his journeys, of his meeting with Stanley ("Dr. Livingstone, I presume"), of Africa, and of the area's industrial heritage. ☎ 01698/823140. ☒ £3. ☉ Apr.–Sept., Mon.–Sat. 10–5, Sun. 12:30–5; Oct.–Mar., Mon.–Sat. 10:30–3:30, Sun. 12:30–3:30 (call to confirm in winter).

Close to the David Livingstone Centre is **Bothwell Castle,** dating from the 13th century. Its walls are well preserved and stand above the River Clyde. ☎ 0131/668–8800. ☒ £2. ☉ Apr.–Sept., daily 9:30–6; Oct.–Mar., Mon.–Wed. and Sat. 9:30–4, Sun. 2–4, Thurs. 9:30–noon.

Hamilton

The **Hamilton Mausoleum,** in Strathclyde Country Park near the industrial town of Hamilton, was built in the 1840s as an extraordinary monument to the lavish eccentricities of the dukes of Hamilton (who **46** had more money than sense). Near Hamilton is **Chatelherault** (pronounced *shat*-lerro), a unique one-room-deep facade—part shooting lodge, part glorified dog kennel—designed in elegant Georgian style by William Adam for the dukes of Hamilton. Within Chatelherault is an exhibition describing the glories of estate life. ☎ 01698/426213. ☒ Free. ☉ Apr.–Sept., Mon.–Thurs. and Sat. 10–5, Sun. noon–5:30; Oct.–Mar., Mon.–Thurs. and Sat. 10–5, Sun. noon–5.

47 Lanark

Set in pleasing, rolling countryside, Lanark is a typical old Scottish town. It's now most often associated with its unique neighbor New Lanark, a nominated World Heritage Site that was the site of a social experiment. The River Clyde powers its way through a beautiful wooded gorge, and its waters were harnessed to drive textile mill machinery before the end of the 18th century. The owner, David Dale (1739–1806), was noted for his caring attitude to the workers, unusual for that era. Later, his son-in-law, Robert Owen (1771–1858), took these social experiments farther, founding a benevolent doctrine known as Owenism and eventually crossing the Atlantic to become involved in a similar project in Indiana, called New Harmony, which, unlike New Lanark, failed. (Robert Owen's son Robert Dale Owen, 1801–77, helped found the Smithsonian Institution.)

After many changes of fortune the mills eventually closed, but the site has been saved and has a new lease on life, with renovated housing and a hotel (☞ *below*). The refurbishment was a success, and those who bought the houses seem able to lead normal lives despite having tourists peering in all day long. One of the mills has been converted into an **interpretative center** (☎ 01555/665876, ☒ £3.75, ☉ daily 11–5), which tells the story of this brave social experiment. Upstream, the Clyde flows through some of the finest river scenery anywhere in Lowland Scotland, with woods and spectacular waterfalls.

££ ⊞ **New Lanark Mill Hotel.** Housed in a converted cotton mill at the 18th-century model village of New Lanark, this hotel is decorated in a spare, understated style that allows the impressive architecture of barrel-vaulted ceilings and elegant Georgian windows to speak for itself. Right next to the river in the heart of the village, all attractions—visitor center, shops, Falls of Clyde Wildlife Reserve—are at its doorstep. ⊠ *New Lanark ML11 9DB,* ☎ *01555/667200,* FAX *01555/667222. 38 rooms, 33 with bath and shower, 5 with shower; 8 cottages. AE, DC, MC, V.* ✍

Lanark offers an interesting selection of shops within walking distance of each other. **McKellar's the Jewellers** (⊠ 41 High St., ☎ 01555/661312) has a good range of Charles Rennie Mackintosh–inspired designs in gold and silver. **Strands** (⊠ 8 Bloomgate, ☎ 01555/665757) carries a wide variety of yarns and knitwear, including Aran designs and one-of-a-kind creations by Scottish designers.

❹❽ Biggar

A pleasant town built of stone, Biggar is a rewarding place to spend an hour or two, out of all proportion to its size. **Gladstone Court Museum** offers a fascinating portrayal of life in the town, with reconstructed Victorian shops, a bank, a phone exchange, and a school. ⊠ *Gladstone Court,* ☎ *01899/221050.* ⊡ *£2.* ⊙ *Apr.–Oct., Mon.–Sat. 10–5, Sun. 2–5.*

For Biggar's geology and prehistory, plus an interesting embroidery collection (including samplers and fine patchwork coverlets), visit the **Moat Park Heritage Centre,** also in the town center, in a former church. ⊠ *Moat Park Church, Moat Park,* ☎ *01899/221050.* ⊡ *£2.* ⊙ *Easter–mid-Oct., Mon.–Sat. 10–5, Sun. 2–5.*

The **gasworks,** built in 1839, is a fascinating reminder of the efforts once needed to produce gas for light and heat. ⊠ *Moat Park,* ☎ *01899/221050.* ⊡ *£1.* ⊙ *June–Sept., daily 2–5.*

The **Greenhill Covenanters' House** is a farmhouse with Covenanting relics, 17th-century furnishings, costume dolls, and rare farm breeds. ⊠ *Moat Park,* ☎ *01899/221050.* ⊡ *£1.* ⊙ *Easter–early Oct., daily 2–5.*

⊙ **Biggar Puppet Theatre** regularly presents performances by Purves Puppets. Before and after performances, two hands-on, half-hour tours are available, led by the puppeteers. One tour goes backstage with the puppets being demonstrated on stage; the other is of the puppet museum. The theater also has games and a picnic area. ⊠ *B7016, east of Biggar,* ☎ *01899/220631.* ⊡ *Performances £5.* ⊙ *Mon.–Sat. 10–5; Easter–Aug., Mon.–Sat. 10–5, Sun. 2–5. Call for additional opening times and details.*

At Biggar you are near the headwaters of the Clyde, on the moors in the center of southern Scotland. The Clyde flows west toward Glasgow and the Atlantic Ocean, while the Tweed, only a few miles away, flows east toward the North Sea. There are fine views around Biggar: to Culter Fell and to the Border Hills in the south.

£££–££££ ✕⊞ **Shieldhill.** This foursquare Norman manor has stood on this spot since 1199, though it was greatly enlarged in 1560. It's in an ideal location for touring the Borders—just 27 mi from Edinburgh and 31 mi from Glasgow. The rooms are named after great Scottish battles—Culloden, Glencoe, Bannockburn—and are furnished with great comfort (miles of Laura Ashley fabrics and wallpaper). ⊠ *Quothquan, near Biggar, ML12 6NA,* ☎ *01899/220035,* FAX *01899/221092. 16 rooms, 13 with bath, 3 with shower. 2 restaurants. MC, V.* ✍

Clyde Valley A to Z
ARRIVING AND DEPARTING

By Bus: Buses run between Glasgow and Hamilton. Inquire at the
Buchanan Street bus station (☎ 0141/332–7133) for details.

By Car: Take A724 east out of Glasgow, south of the river through
Rutherglen toward Hamilton. It's not a very pretty route, but in Blantyre look for signs to the David Livingstone Centre. From Blantyre take
the main road to Hamilton. Then travel on the A72 past Chatelherault toward Lanark. You pass the ruins of medieval Craignethan Castle, lots of greenhouses for tomatoes, plant nurseries, and gnarled old
orchards running down to the Clyde. Before reaching Lanark, follow
the signs down a long winding hill, to New Lanark. A72 continues south
of Lanark to join A702 near Biggar. At the end of a full day of touring you can return to Glasgow the quick way by joining the M74 from
the A744 west of Lanark (the Strathaven road). Or take a more scenic
route through Strathaven (pronounced *stra*-ven) itself, A726 to East
Kilbride, and enter Glasgow from south of the river.

By Train: Service runs from Glasgow Central Station to Hamilton and
Lanark (for details call the **National Train Enquiry Line**; ☎ 0345/
484950). There are no trains to Biggar, but there's a connecting bus
from Hamilton to Biggar.

VISITOR INFORMATION
Biggar (✉ 155 High St., ☎ 01899/221066, ✐). **Hamilton** (✉ Road
Chef Services, M74 Northbound, ☎ 01698/285590). **Lanark** (✉
Horsemarket, Ladyacre Rd., ☎ 01555/661661).

GLASGOW A TO Z

Arriving and Departing

By Bus

Glasgow's **bus station** (☎ 0141/332–7133) is at Buchanan Street. The
main intercity operators are **National Express** (☎ 0990/808080) and **Scottish Citylink** (☎ 0990/505050), which serve a wide variety of towns and
cities in Scotland, Wales, and England, including London (8½–9 hours);
there's also service to Edinburgh. Buchanan Street is close to the underground station of the same name and to the Queen Street station.

By Car

If you come to Glasgow from England and the south of Scotland, you'll
probably approach the city from the M6, M74, and A74. The city center is clearly marked from these roads. From Edinburgh the M8 leads to
the city center and is the route that cuts straight across the city center
and into which all other roads feed. From the north either the A82 from
Fort William or the A/M80 from Stirling also feed into the M8 in the Glasgow city center. From then on, you only have to know your exit: Exit 16
serves the north of the city center, Exit 17/18 leads to the northwest and
Great Western Road, and Exit 18/19 takes you to the hotels of Sauchiehall
Street, the Scottish Exhibition Centre, and the Anderston Centre.

By Plane

Glasgow Airport (☎ 0141/887–1111 information; 0141/848–4440
tourist information desk and accommodations-booking service) is
about 7 mi west of the city center on the M8 to Greenock. The airport
serves international and domestic flights, and most major European
carriers offer frequent and convenient connections (some via airports
in England) to many Continental cities. There's frequent shuttle service from London, as well as regular flights from Birmingham,

Bournemouth, Bristol, East Midlands, Leeds/Bradford, Manchester, Southampton, Isle of Man, and Jersey. There are also flights from Wales (Cardiff) and Ireland (Belfast, Dublin, and Londonderry). Local Scottish connections can be made to Aberdeen, Barra, Benbecula, Campbeltown, Inverness, Islay, Kirkwall, Shetland (Sumburgh), Stornoway, and Tiree.

Airlines operating through Glasgow Airport to Europe and the rest of the United Kingdom include **Aer Lingus** (☎ 0645/737747), **Air Malta** (☎ 0181/785–3177), **British Airways** (☎ 0345/222111), **British Midland** (☎ 0870/607–0555), **easyJet** (☎ 0870/600–0000), **Icelandair** (☎ 0171/388–5599), **KLM UK** (☎ 0870/507–4074), **Lufthansa** (☎ 0345/737747), **Manx** (☎ 0345/256256), **Sabena** (☎ 0345/581291), **SAS Wideroe** (☎ 0845/607–27727), and **Scot Airways** (☎ 0870/606–0707).

Several carriers fly from North America, including **Air Canada** (☎ 0990/247226), **American Airlines** (☎ 0345/789789), **Continental** (☎ 0800/776464), and **Icelandair** (☎ 02078/741000; service via Reykjavík).

Prestwick Airport (☎ 01292/479822), on the Ayrshire coast about 30 mi southwest of Glasgow and for some years eclipsed by Glasgow Airport, is beginning to come back into the reckoning, not least because of the activities of **Ryanair** (☎ 01292/678000), a company that has sparked a major price war on the Anglo-Scottish routes (e.g., between London and Glasgow). It offers unbeatable, no-frills, rock-bottom air fares between Prestwick and London's Stansted Airport.

BETWEEN GLASGOW AIRPORT AND CENTER CITY

Though there's a railway station about 2 mi from Glasgow Airport (✉ Paisley Gilmour St.), most people travel the short distance to the city center by bus or taxi. Journey time is about 20 minutes except at rush hour.

By Bus: Express buses run from Glasgow Airport (Bus Depot 2, outside departures lobby) to near the Central railway station, to Queen Street railway station, and to the **Buchanan Street bus station** (☎ 0141/332-7133). There's service every 15 minutes throughout the day. The fare is £3 on Scottish Citylink buses, and £2.70 on Fairline buses.

By Car: The drive from Glasgow Airport into the city center is normally quite easy, even if you are used to driving on the right. The M8 motorway runs beside the airport (Junction 29) and takes you straight into the Glasgow city center. Thereafter Glasgow's streets follow a grid pattern, at least in the city center, but a map is useful and can be supplied by the rental company.

By Limousine: Most companies that provide chauffeur-driven cars and tours will also do limousine airport transfers. Companies that are currently members of the Greater Glasgow and Clyde Valley Tourist Board are **Charlton Chauffeur Drive** (☎ 0141/445–1777), **Corporate Travel** (☎ 0141/639–8057), **Little's** (☎ 0141/883–2111), **Peter Holmes** (☎ 01389/830688), and **Robert Neil** (☎ 0141/641–2125).

By Taxi: Metered taxis are available at the terminal building. The fare should be £15–£18.

BETWEEN PRESTWICK AIRPORT AND CENTER CITY

By Bus: An hourly coach service operates to Glasgow but takes much longer than the frequent train service.

By Car: The city center is reached via the fast A77 in about 40 minutes (longer in rush hour).

By Taxi: Metered taxi cabs are available at the airport. The fare to Glasgow is about £40.

By Train: There's a rapid half-hourly train service (hourly on Sundays) direct from the terminal building.

By Train

Glasgow has two main rail stations: **Central** and **Queen Street.** Central is the arrival and departure point for trains from London's Euston station (five hours), which come via Crewe and Carlisle in England, as well as via Edinburgh from Kings Cross. It also serves other cities in the northwest of England and towns and ports in the southwest of Scotland: Kilmarnock, Dumfries, Ardrossan (for the island of Arran), Gourock (for Dunoon), Wemyss Bay (for the island of Bute, Rothesay), and Stranraer (for Ireland). The Queen Street station has connections to Edinburgh (50 minutes) and onward by the east-coast route to Aberdeen or south via Edinburgh to Newcastle, York, and London's Kings Cross. Other services from Queen Street go to Stirling, Perth, and Dundee; northward to Inverness, Kyle of Lochalsh, Wick, and Thurso; along the Clyde to Dumbarton and Balloch (for Loch Lomond); and on the scenic West Highland line to Oban, Fort William, and Mallaig. Oban and Mallaig have island ferry connections. For details contact the **National Train Enquiry Line** (☎ 0345/484950).

A regular bus service links the Queen Street and Central stations. Both are close to stations on the Glasgow underground. At Queen Street go to Buchanan Street, and at Central go to St. Enoch. Black city taxis are available at both stations.

Getting Around

The Glasgow city center—the area defined by the M8 motorway to the north and west, the River Clyde to the south, and Glasgow Cathedral to the east—is relatively compact. Glaswegians themselves walk a good deal, and the streets are designed for pedestrians (some for pedestrians only). The streets are relatively safe even at night (but you should be sensible), and good street maps are available from bookstores and the helpful tourist information center (☞ Visitor Information, *below*). Most streets follow a grid plan; if you get lost, though, just ask the locals.

To go farther afield, to the West End (the university, the Transport Museum, Kelvingrove Museum and Art Gallery, or the Hunterian Museum) or to the south (the Burrell Collection), some form of transportation is required. Glasgow is unusual among British cities in having an integrated transport network, and information about all options is available from **Strathclyde Passenger Transport (SPT) Travel Centre** (✉ St. Enoch Sq., ☎ 0141/226–4826).

By Bus

The many bus companies cooperate with the underground and ScotRail to produce the Family Day Tripper Ticket (£13), which is a great way to get around the whole area from Loch Lomond to Ayrshire. Tickets are a good value and are available from **Strathclyde Passenger Transport (SPT) Travel Centre** (✉ St. Enoch Sq., ☎ 0141/226–4826) and at main railway and bus stations.

By Car

You don't need a car in the city center, and you're probably better off without one; though most new hotels have their own lots, parking here can be trying. More convenient are the park-and-ride operations at underground stations (Kelvinbridge, Bridge Street, and Shields Road), which will bring you into the city center in a few minutes. The West End museums and galleries have their own lots, as does the Burrell. Parking wardens are constantly on patrol, and you'll be fined (upwards of £26) if you park illegally. Multistory garages are open 24 hours a day at the following locations: Anderston Centre, George Street, Waterloo Place, Mitchell Street, Cambridge Street, and Buchanan Street. Rates run between £1 and £2 per hour.

By Taxi

You'll find metered taxis (usually black and of the London sedan type) at stands all over the city center. Most have radio dispatch (Dial 0141/429–7070). Some have also been adapted to take wheelchairs. You can hail a cab on the street if its FOR HIRE sign is illuminated. A typical ride from the city center to the West End or South Side costs £5.50–£6.

By Train

The Glasgow area has an extensive network of suburban railway services. Locals still call them the Blue Trains, even though most are now painted orange. Look for signs to LOW LEVEL TRAINS at the Queen Street and Central stations. For more information and a free map, call **Strathclyde Passenger Transport (SPT) Travel Centre** (⊠ St. Enoch Sq., ☎ 0141/226–4826) or the **National Train Enquiry Line** (☎ 0345/484950). Details are also available from the tourist board (☞ Visitor Information, *below*).

By Underground

Glasgow is the only city in Scotland that has a subway, or underground, as it's called here. It was built at the end of the 19th century and takes the simple form of two circular routes, one going clockwise and the other counterclockwise. All trains eventually bring you back to where you started, and the complete circle takes 24 minutes. This extremely simple and effective system operated relatively unchanged in ancient carriages (cars) until the 1970s, when it was modernized. The tunnels are small, so the trains themselves are tiny (by London standards), and this, together with the affection in which the system is held and the bright orange paint and circular routes of the trains, gave it the nickname the Clockwork Orange.

Flat fares (80 pence) and the Discovery Ticket one-day pass (£2.50) are available. Trains run regularly from Monday through Saturday from early morning to late evening, with a limited Sunday service, and connect the city center with the West End (for the university) and the city south of the River Clyde. Look for the orange U signs marking the 15 stations. Further information is available from **Strathclyde Passenger Transport (SPT) Travel Centre** (⊠ St. Enoch Sq., ☎ 0141/226–4826).

Contacts and Resources

Car Rentals

Costs vary according to the size of the car but average about £30–£40 per day.

Avis (⊠ 161 North St., ☎ 0141/221–2827; ⊠ Glasgow Airport, ☎ 0141/887–2261 or 0141/842–7599; ⊠ Prestwick Airport, ☎ 01292/477218). **Budget Rent-a-Car** (⊠ 101 Waterloo St., ☎ 0845/606–6669; ⊠ Glasgow Airport, ☎ 0845/606–6669). **Europcar** (⊠ 38 Anderson Quay, ☎ 0141/248–8788; ⊠ Glasgow Airport, ☎ 0141/887–0414; ⊠ Prestwick Airport, ☎ 01292/678198). **Hertz** (⊠ 106 Waterloo St., ☎ 0141/248–7736; ⊠ Glasgow Airport, ☎ 0141/887–2451). **National Alamo Car Rental** (⊠ Glasgow Airport, ☎ 0141/887–7915; ⊠ Prestwick Airport, ☎ 01292/671222).

Discount Admission Tickets

The **Scottish Explorer Ticket,** available from any staffed Historic Scotland (HS) property and from many tourist information centers, allows visits to HS properties over a three-day (£10), seven-day (£15), or 14-

day (£20) period. The **Touring Ticket,** issued by the National Trust for Scotland (☎ 0131/243–9300), is also available for seven (£18) or 14 (£26) days and allows access to all National Trust for Scotland properties. It's available to overseas visitors only, and can be purchased from the National Trust for Scotland or some main tourist information centers (including Glasgow TIC) (☞ *below*).

Emergencies

Ambulance, police, fire, or coast guard: ☎ 999. (No coins are needed for emergency calls from public phones.) **Dentists: Glasgow Dental Hospital** (✉ 378 Sauchiehall St., ☎ 0141/211–9600 weekdays 9–3). **Hospitals: Glasgow Royal Infirmary** (✉ Castle St., near cathedral, ☎ 0141/211–4000). **Glasgow Western Infirmary** (✉ Dumbarton Rd., near university, ☎ 0141/211–2000); **Southern General Hospital** (✉ 1345 Govan Rd., south side of Clyde Tunnel, ☎ 0141/201–1100); and **Stobhill Hospital** (✉ 133 Balornock Rd., near Royal Infirmary and Bishopriggs, ☎ 0141/201–3000). **Pharmacies: Munro Pharmacy** (✉ 693 Great Western Rd., ☎ 0141/339–0012) is open daily 9–9. (Note that pharmacies operate on a rotating basis for late-night opening; hours are posted in storefront windows.)

Guided Tours

BOAT TOURS

Cruises are available on Loch Lomond and to the islands in the Firth of Clyde; details are available from the tourist board (☞ Visitor Information, *below*). Contact the **Waverley** paddle steamer (☎ 0141/221–8152) from June through August; **Clyde Marine Cruises** (✉ Greenock, ☎ 01475/721281) from May through September.

ORIENTATION TOURS

"Discovering Glasgow" bus tours leave daily in summer from the west side of George Square. The Greater Glasgow and Clyde Valley Tourist Board (☞ Visitor Information, *below*) can give further information and arrange reservations. Details of longer tours northward to the Highlands and islands can be obtained from the tourist board or Strathclyde Passenger Transport (SPT) Travel Centre, St. Enoch Square (☞ Getting Around, *above*).

PERSONAL GUIDES

Little's Chauffeur Drive (✉ 1282 Paisley Rd. W, Glasgow, ☎ 0141/883–2111) offers personally tailored car-and-driver tours, both locally and throughout Scotland. The **Scottish Tourist Guides Association** (☎ FAX 0131/453–1297) also offers an all-around service. Taxi firms offer city tours. If you allow the driver to follow a set route, the costs are £15 for one hour, £26 for two hours, and £34 for three hours (they take American Express, MasterCard, and Visa) for up to five people. If you wish the driver to follow your own route, the charge will be £15 an hour or the reading on the meter, whichever is greater. You can book tours in advance and be picked up and dropped off wherever you like. Contact the Glasgow-wide **TOA Taxis** (☎ 0141/429–7070 or 0141/429–4900).

SPECIAL-INTEREST

Your first contact should be the tourist board (☞ Visitor Information, *below*), where you can find out about special walks on a given day. **Classic Coaches** (☎ 0141/889–4050) operates restored coaches from the 1950s, '60s, and '70s on tours to the north and west and to the islands. The following Glasgow companies run regular bus tours around the region: **Scott Guide Tours** (☎ 0141/204–0444); **Southern Coaches** (☎ 0141/876–1147); and **Weirs Tours** (☎ 0141/944–6688).

Post Office

Although there's a **main post office** (✉ St. Vincent St., ☎ 0141/204–3688), there are many smaller post offices around the city.

Travel Agencies

American Express (⊠ 115 Hope St., ☎ 0141/221–4366). **Thomas Cook** (⊠ 15–17 Gordon St., ☎ 0141/201–7200).

Visitor Information

The **Greater Glasgow and Clyde Valley Tourist Board** (⊠ 11 George Sq., near Queen Street station, ☎ 0141/204–4400, FAX 0141/221–3524) offers information and has an accommodations-booking service; a bureau de change; a Western Union money transfer service; and a ticket office for the theater, city bus tours, guided walks, boat trips, and coach tours around Scotland. Books, maps, and souvenirs are sold. The office is open Monday–Saturday 9–6 and, July–August, Monday–Saturday 9–8 and Sunday 10–6. The tourist board's branch office at the airport is open Monday–Saturday 7:30–5, Sunday 8–3:30 (Sunday, 7:30–5 April–September).

3 THE BORDERS AND THE SOUTHWEST

DUMFRIES, GALLOWAY,
SIR WALTER SCOTT COUNTRY

One of Scotland's icon regions, the Borders is the heartland of minstrelsy, ballad, and folklore—the homeland of the tweed suit and cashmere sweater, of medieval abbeys, of the lordly Tweed and its salmon, and the native soil of Sir Walter Scott, who created so much of the aura of Scotland's historical romance. Beyond, hilly and sparsely populated, the Dumfries and Galloway region, south of Glasgow, is a riot of green pastures, brooding forests, and radiant gardens, where the palm, in places, is as much at home as the pine.

By Gilbert
Summers

Updated by
Mark Porter

I F YOU ARE COMING TO SCOTLAND from England, the Borders is the first region you're likely to encounter. Although you'll find no check-points or customs outposts, the Scottish tourist authorities firmly promulgate the message that it is indeed Scottish land you've entered. All the idiosyncrasies that distinguish Scotland—from the myriad different names for things to the seemingly unpredictable local holidays—start as soon as you reach the first Scottish signs by the main roads north.

The region embraces the whole 90-mi course of one of Scotland's greatest rivers, the Tweed, and its tributaries. By mill chimneys and peel (small fortified tower common to this region) fortresses and woodlands luxuriant with game birds and stately homes, in a series of fast-rushing torrents and dark serpentine pools, the rivers flow through the history of two nations; for at different times, the region has been in English hands, just as slices of northern England have been in Scottish hands (just to the east is that large English city, Berwick-upon-Tweed). All the main routes from London to Edinburgh traverse the Borders region, whose hinterland of undulating pastures, woods, and valleys is enclosed within three lonely groups of hills: the Cheviots, Moorfoots, and the Lammermuirs. Most of the towns are overgrown villages and often so full of history that their everyday life and provincial Victorian Gothic style may disappoint you. Innumerable hamlets dot the land, so valley slopes have quite a lived-in look; yet the total population is still relatively sparse. Sheep still outnumber human beings by 14 to 1—which is just as Sir Walter Scott would have wanted it. The Borders region's most famous resident, his pseudo-monastic, pseudo-baronial home at Abbotsford is the most visited of Scottish literary landmarks.

Although most visitors inevitably pass this way, the Borders and especially Galloway, to the west, are unfortunately often overlooked. So strong is the tartan-ribboned call of the Highlands that many visitors rush on, pause for breath at Edinburgh, then plunge northward, thus missing this scenic portion of upland Scotland. And that's a shame since the Borders and the Dumfries and Galloway regions have as broad a selection of stately homes and fortified castles as you will encounter anywhere in Scotland (with the possible exception of Grampian). Galloway, west of the town of Dumfries and the surrounding area called Dumfrieshire, has the advantage of a coastline facing south, made even more appealing by the North Atlantic Drift (Scotland's part of the Gulf Stream), which bathes the coastal lands with warmer water. With its coastal farmlands giving way to woodlands, high moors, and some craggy hills, Galloway may not be the Highlands, but it gives a convincing impression to those seeking the authentic Scotland.

Pleasures and Pastimes

Biking
In the rural farming areas and upland stretches you will have a wide choice of quiet side roads to avoid the heavy traffic on A routes, the main arteries. The Craik Forest is typical of Forestry Commission properties, with bike routes in mountains and trails in the network of forestry access roads.

Dining
The Borders is reasonably well served by hotels ranging from budget to luxury, and most good restaurants are found usually within hotels rather than as independent establishments. Despite being slightly off the beaten tourist path, the region of Dumfries and Galloway offers a

good selection of relatively inexpensive options for dining, though once again most are within hotels.

CATEGORY	COST*
££££	over £40
£££	£30–£40
££	£15–£30
£	under £15

*per person for a three-course meal, including VAT and excluding drinks and service.

Fishing

This region is a fisherman's paradise. The Solway Firth is noted for sea angling, notably at the Isle of Whithorn, Port William, Portpatrick, Stranraer, and Loch Ryan. The wide range of game-fishing opportunities extends from the expensive salmon beats of the River Tweed, sometimes known by its nickname, the Queen of Scottish Rivers, to undiscovered hill lochans (small lakes). You can buy permits at tourist offices, tackle shops, newsstands, and post offices.

Lodging

In the Borders you'll have a wide range of price categories to choose from, ranging from top-quality hotels to cozy 18th-century drovers' inns to quaint bed-and-breakfasts. Dumfries and Galloway tend to be a little cheaper, and here farmhouse B&Bs are good options. You're likely to get a hearty farm breakfast, but keep in mind that many of these B&Bs are *working* farms, where early morning activity and the presence of animals are an inescapable part of the scene.

CATEGORY	COST*
££££	over £130
£££	£100–£130
££	£60–£100
£	under £60

*Prices are for a standard double room, including service, breakfast, and VAT.

✎ following the text of a review is your signal that the property has a Web site, where you will find details and, usually, images; for a link, visit www.fodors.com/urls.

Shopping

The Borders in particular has a fairly affluent population, which is reflected in the variety of upscale shops in Peebles, for example, where there are more deluxe stores than might be expected. The Borders is well known for its knitwear industry, and mill shops are in abundance. Throughout the Borders region also look for the specialty peppermint or fruit-flavor boiled sweets (hard candies)—Jethart Snails, Hawick Balls, Berwick Cockles, and Soor Plums—which, with tablet (a solid caramel-like candy) and fudge, are available at most local confectioners.

Exploring the Borders and the Southwest

The best way to explore the region is to get off the main arterial roads—the A1, A697, A68, A7, M74/A74, and A75—for the little back roads. You may occasionally be delayed by a herd of cows on their way to the milking parlor, but this is often far more pleasant than, for example, tussling on the A75 with heavy-goods vehicles rushing to make the Irish ferries.

The Scottish Borders is largely characterized by upland moors and hills, with fertile, farmed, and forested river valleys. The textile towns of the Borders have plenty of personality—Border folk are sure of their own identity and are fiercely partisan toward their own native towns. The Southwest, often known as Dumfries and Galloway, shares the upland characteristics and, if anything, has a slightly wilder air (the highest hill in Dumfries and Galloway is the Merrick, 2,765 ft). Easygoing and peaceful, its towns are usually very attractive, with wide streets and colorful frontages.

Numbers in the text correspond to numbers in the margin and on the Borders and the Southwest maps.

Great Itineraries

To visit all the places described in the Borders would certainly take more than one day. To travel at a leisurely pace and spend time at some of the grand mansions noted, you could easily allow three days, although the total driving distance between each town is not great: In the Borders there are several points of interest quite close to one another.

Owing to the high ground and forests at the heart of Dumfries and Galloway, a linear itinerary that keeps largely to the coast might be best. Once again, distances between towns are not large, but traveling on narrow country roads can take a little longer than you might expect. If you particularly enjoy sketching or taking photographs, this is not an area to be rushed, in which case three days is the minimum time needed to sample an abbey or two and see the settings of Dumfries and Galloway towns.

IF YOU HAVE 2 DAYS

Jedburgh ① is the best orientation place to get an idea of how important the Border abbeys were. If you cross the border to the west, then head for somewhere like **Kirkcudbright** ㉜ for a flavor of Dumfries and Galloway. In short, if you only have two days, then you will have to choose between the Borders and the Southwest.

IF YOU HAVE 5 DAYS

Plan to divide your time between the Borders (three days) and Dumfries and Galloway (two days); you will have to be selective about which abbeys and stately homes to which you can make more than a quick visit. Jedburgh Abbey, in **Jedburgh** ①, is a must-see, as is Melrose Abbey, in **Melrose** ⑫. Melrose Abbey also has gardens to enjoy, several museums, and famous stately homes nearby, including **Abbotsford House** ⑬, home of Sir Walter Scott. Finish up at **Peebles** ⑳, where you should allow plenty of time to shop.

In Dumfries and Galloway, two days will give you time to visit **Sweetheart Abbey** ㉗, in New Abbey, then **Arbigland Gardens** ㉘, in Kirkbean, an excellent example of the lush gardens for which the area is famous. Try to fit in Castle Douglas and **Threave Gardens** ㉛, with the nearby gaunt Threave Castle, on a river island and reached by boat, providing a gritty contrast. **Kirkcudbright** ㉜ is also worth even a quick visit for its artistic connections.

IF YOU HAVE 10 DAYS

In five days in the Borders, such jewels as **Floors Castle** ⑤, **Mellerstain House** ⑦, and **Paxton House** ⑩ can all be enjoyed (though you may get stately home indigestion), and you will also have time to admire the views and soak up the historic atmosphere at **Smailholm Tower** ⑧ or **Dryburgh Abbey** ⑭. One of the most unlikely attractions, Robert Smail's Printing Works, at **Innerleithen** ⑲, is also one of the most historically interesting, and it is close to Traquair House, acknowledged as the oldest lived-in house in Scotland. You will also have time for an essential shopping visit to **Peebles** ⑳.

Five days in Dumfries and Galloway will also minimize the problem of choosing what to see—you'll have time for nearly everything. Still,

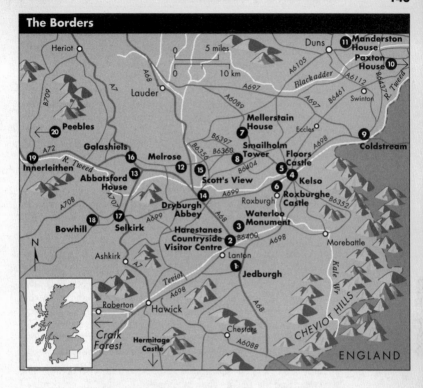

The Borders

at the top of your list should be **Threave Gardens** ㉛, Threave Castle, and **Kirkcudbright** ㉜. You should spend some time exploring the hills above Gatehouse of Fleet, with its **Cardoness Castle** ㉝ and heritage center, meander around the southern coastline, penetrate the wild and wooded **Glen Trool** ㊱, and travel deep into the Machars to **Whithorn** ㊳, a site of early religious importance. You will even be able to see **Castle Kennedy Gardens** ㊵ and the Logan Botanic Gardens to complete your Galloway gardens experience.

When to Tour the Borders and the Southwest

Because many properties are privately owned and are closed from early autumn until early April, the area is less well suited to off-season touring than some other parts of Scotland. The region does look magnificent in autumn, however, especially along the wooded river valleys of the Borders. Late spring is the time to see the rhododendrons of the gardens in Dumfries and Galloway.

THE BORDERS

Towns, Towers, and Countryside

Although the Borders has many attractions, it is most famous for being the home base for Sir Walter Scott, the early 19th-century poet, novelist, and creator of *Ivanhoe,* who single-handedly transformed Scotland's image from that of a land of brutal savages to one of romantic and stirring deeds and magnificent landscapes. One of the best ways to approach this district is to make the theme of your tour the life and works of Scott. The novels of Scott are not read much nowadays—in fact, frankly, some of them are difficult to wade through—but the mystique that he created, the aura of historical romance, has outlasted his books and is much in evidence in the ruined abbeys, historical houses, and grand vistas of the Borders.

In addition to the Scott heritage, Border folk take great pride in the region's fame as Scotland's main woolen-goods manufacturing area. To this day the residents possess a marked determination to defend their towns and communities. We can all be thankful, however, that the changing times have allowed them to reposition their priorities: Instead of guarding against southern raiders, they now concentrate on maintaining a fiercely competitive rugby team for the popular inter-town rugby matches. The Borders is a stronghold of this European counterpart to American football.

Border communities are also reestablishing their identities through the curious affairs known as the Common Ridings. Long ago it was essential that each town be able to defend its area, and over the centuries this need has become formalized in mounted gatherings to "ride the boundaries." The observance of the tradition lapsed in certain places but has now been revived. Leaders and attendants are solemnly elected each year, and Borderers who now live away from home make a point of attending their town's event. (You are welcome to watch and enjoy the excitement of clattering hooves and banners proudly displayed, but this is essentially a time for native Borderers.) The Common Ridings possess at least as much authenticity and historic significance as the concocted Highland Games, so often taken to be the essence of Scotland. The little town of Selkirk, in fact, claims its Common Riding to be the largest mounted gathering anywhere in Europe.

The Borders towns cluster around and between the two great rivers, the Tweed and the Teviot. They encompass all four of the great ruined Border abbeys. The monks in these long-abandoned religious foundations were the first to work the fleeces of their sheep flocks, thus laying the foundation for what is still the area's main manufacturing industry.

Jedburgh

❶ *50 mi south of Edinburgh, 95 mi southeast of Glasgow.*

The town of Jedburgh (*-burgh* is always pronounced *burra* in Scots) was for centuries the first major Scottish target of invading English armies. In more peaceful times it developed textile mills, most of which have since languished. The large landscaped area around the town's tourist information center was once a mill but now provides an encampment for the armies of modern tourists. The past still clings to this little town, however. The ruined abbey dominates the skyline and is compulsory visiting if you are interested in acquiring a feeling of the former role of the Border abbeys.

★ Far the most impressive of the Borders abbeys, **Jedburgh Abbey** was nearly destroyed by the English earl of Hertford's forces in 1544–45, during the destructive time known as the Rough Wooing. This was English king Henry VIII's (1491–1547) armed attempt to persuade the Scots that it was a good idea to unite the kingdoms by the marriage of his young son to the infant Mary, Queen of Scots (the Scots disagreed and sent Mary to France instead). The full story is explained in vivid detail at the **Jedburgh Abbey Visitor Centre,** which also provides information on interpreting the ruins. Ground patterns and foundations are all that remain of the once-powerful religious complex. ⊠ *High St.,* ☎ *0131/668–8800.* ☜ *£3.* ☉ *Apr.– Sept., daily 9:30–6; Oct.–Mar., Mon.–Sat. 9:30–4, Sun. 2–4.*

There is much else to see in Jedburgh, including the **Mary, Queen of Scots House.** This *bastel* (from the French *bastille*) was the fortified town house in which, some say, Mary stayed before embarking on her famous 20-mi ride to visit her wounded lover, the earl of Bothwell, at **Hermitage Castle** (☞ Off the Beaten Path, *below*). An interpretative center in the building relates the tale. ✉ *Queen St.,* ☎ *01835/863331.* ✆ *£2.* ☽ *Call for hours.*

Jedburgh Castle Jail re-creates life in a Howard Reform Prison, with prison cells to inspect. The history of the Royal Burgh of Jedburgh is told through room settings in period style, costumed figures, and audiovisuals. ✉ *Castlegate,* ☎ *01835/863254.* ✆ *£1.25.* ☽ *Mid-Mar.– mid-Nov., Mon.–Sat. 10–4:45, Sun. 1–4.*

☺ ❷ Just a few miles north of Jedburgh, the **Harestanes Countryside Visitor Centre** conveys life in the Borders. The Discovery Room has changing displays on the countryside, wildlife, and crafts, plus you'll find a wooden games and puzzles room, and a tearoom and gift shop. Outside are a play area, marked trails, and guided walks. ✉ *Monteviot, at junction of A68 and B6400,* ☎ *01835/830306.* ✆ *Free.* ☽ *Apr.–Oct., daily 10–5.*

❸ In view on the skyline is the **Waterloo Monument,** an imposing tower that is another reminder of the power of the landowning gentry: A marquis of Lothian built the monument in 1815, with the help of his tenants, in celebration of the victory of Wellington at Waterloo. If you have time, you can walk to the tower from the Harestanes Countryside Visitor Centre (one hour). ✉ *Off B6400, 5 mi north of Jedburgh.*

OFF THE
BEATEN PATH

HERMITAGE CASTLE – To appreciate the famous 20-mi ride of Mary, Queen of Scots, to visit her wounded lover, the earl of Bothwell (circa 1535–78), travel southwest from Jedburgh to this, the most complete remaining example of the bare and grim medieval border castles, full of gloom and foreboding. Restored in the early 19th century, it was built in the 14th century (replacing an earlier structure) to guard what was at the time one of the important routes from England into Scotland. The original owner, Lord Soulis, notorious for diabolical excess, was captured by the local populace, which wrapped him in lead and boiled him in a cauldron—or so the tale goes. The castle lies on an unclassified road between the A7 and B6399, about 15 mi south of Hawick, in the desolate Borders hills. ✉ *Liddesdale,* ☎ *0131/668–8800.* ✆ *£1.80.* ☽ *Apr.–Sept., daily 9:30–6.*

Dining and Lodging

£ ✕ **Cross Keys, Ancrum.** A national treasure, this traditional pub spe-
★ cializes in local produce, from fish to game. A splendid array of Scottish beers (real ale, as it is known here) are served. This is the quintessential village inn, right down to the quaint green outside the front door. ✉ *The Green, Ancrum ,* ☎ *01835/830344. DC, MC, V.*

£ ▦ **Spinney Guest House.** Made up of two unpretentiously converted and modernized farm cottages, this B&B offers the highest standards for the price. Two log cabins each sleep three, with self-catering or B&B service. ✉ *Langlee TD8 6PB,* ☎ *01835/863525,* FAX *01835/864883. 3 rooms with bath or shower, 2 log cabins. No credit cards. Closed mid-Nov.–Feb.*

Kelso

❹ *12 mi northeast of Jedburgh.*

One of the most charming Borders burghs, Kelso is often described as having a Continental flavor—some visitors think it resembles a Belgian market town. The town has a broad, paved Market Square and fine examples of Georgian and Victorian Scots town architecture.

Kelso Abbey is the least intact ruin of the four great Border abbeys— just a bleak fragment of what was once the largest of the group. On a main invasion route, the abbey was burned three times in the 1540s alone, on the last occasion by the English earl of Hertford's forces in 1545, when the garrison of 100 men and 12 monks were butchered and the structure all but destroyed. ⊠ *Bridge St.,* ☎ *0131/668–8800.* ☜ *Free.* ⊙ *Apr.–Sept., daily 9:30–6; Oct.–Mar., Mon.–Sat. 9:30–4, Sun. 2–4.*

★ **❺** On the bank of the River Tweed, just 2 mi northwest of Kelso, stands the palatial **Floors Castle,** the largest inhabited castle in Scotland. Ancestral home of the duke of Roxburghe, Floors is an architectural extravagance bristling with pepper-mill turrets and towers that stand on the "floors," or flat terrain, of the Tweed bank opposite the barely visible ruins of Roxburghe Castle. The enormous home was built by William Adam (1689–1748) in 1721 and modified in the 1840s by William Playfair (1789–1857), using mock-Tudor touches. A holly tree in the deer park marks the place where King James II (1430–60) was killed in 1460 by a cannon that "brak in the shooting." ⊠ *A6089,* ☎ *01573/223333.* ☜ *Joint ticket for castle and grounds, £5; grounds only, £3.* ⊙ *Apr.–Oct., daily 10–4.*

❻ Do not confuse the comparatively youthful Floors Castle with **Roxburghe Castle,** nearby. Only traces of rubble and earthworks remain of this ancient structure. The modern-day village of **Roxburgh** is young; the original Roxburgh, one of the oldest burghs in Scotland, has virtually disappeared, though its name lives on in the duke's title and in the name of the old county of Roxburghshire. ⊠ *Off A699, 4 mi southwest of Kelso.*

❼ If you are a devotee of ornate country houses, you are well served in the Borders. Begun in the 1720s, **Mellerstain House** was finished in the 1770s by Robert Adam (1728–92) and is considered one of his finest creations. Sumptuous plasterwork covers almost all interior surfaces, and there are outstanding examples of 18th-century furnishings. The beautiful terraced gardens are as renowned as the house. ⊠ *Off A6089, 7 mi northwest of Kelso,* ☎ *01573/410225.* ☜ *£4.50.* ⊙ *House: Easter and May–Sept., Sun.–Fri. 12:30–5; restaurant: Easter and May–Sept., Sun.–Fri. 11:30–5:30.*

★ **❽** In the hills south of Mellerstain sits a characteristic Borders structure that certainly contrasts with the luxury of Mellerstain House. **Smailholm Tower** stands uncompromisingly on top of a barren, rocky ridge. Built solely for defense, this 16th-century Border peel offers memorable views. If you let your imagination wander in this windy spot, you can almost see the flapping pennants and rising dust of an advancing raiding party and hear the anxious securing of doors and bolts. Sir Walter Scott found this an inspiring spot. His grandfather lived at nearby Sandyknowe Farm (not open to the public), and the young Scott visited the tower often during his childhood. ⊠ *Off B6404, 8 mi west of Kelso,* ☎ *0131/668–8800.* ☜ *£2.* ⊙ *Apr.–Sept., daily 9:30–6.*

Dining and Lodging

£££–££££   ✕🏠 **Edenwater House.** A former manse, this handsome and restful stone
★ house overlooking Edenwater in the hamlet of Ednam has three luxurious guest suites with ensuite bathroom facilities and superb views of the river and of the Eildon Hills. The house is filled with antiques, is tastefully decorated, and serves what connoisseurs regard as the best food in the Borders. Roast saddle of hare with foie gras, pork fillet with a ginger and honey glaze, or fillet of monkfish crusted with basil and coriander in a beurre blanc typify the refined but simple menu. The restaurant is open three nights a week for nonguests. ⊠ *Ednam, TD5 7QL,* ☎ *01573/224070,* 🖷 *01573/224070. 3 rooms with bath and shower. Restaurant, golf privileges, horseback riding, fishing. No credit cards. Closed Dec. 25–26, Jan. 1–14.*

££–£££   🏨 **Ednam House Hotel.** Some 90% of the guests are return visitors to
★   this large, appealing hotel on the banks of the River Tweed, close to
Kelso's grand abbey and old Market Square. The open fire in the hall,
sporting paintings, and cozy armchairs impart a homey feeling. The restaurant's three glass walls afford views of the garden and river; the Scottish fare here includes fresh local vegetables, salmon from the River Tweed,
Aberdeen Angus beef, and homemade ice cream and traditional puddings. ⊠ *Bridge St., TD5 7HT,* ☎ *01573/224168,* 𝙵𝙰𝚇 *01573/226319.
32 rooms with bath or shower. Restaurant, golf privileges, horseback
riding, fishing. MC, V. Closed late Dec.–early Jan.* 🍴

Coldstream

❾ *9 mi east of Kelso.*

Three miles west of Coldstream, the England–Scotland border comes
down from the hills and runs beside the Tweed for the rest of its journey to the sea. Coldstream itself, like Gretna (☞ *below*), was once a
marriage place for runaway couples from the south at a time when the
marriage laws of Scotland were more lenient than those of England (a
plaque on the former bridge tollhouse recalls this fact). It is also celebrated in military history: in 1659 General Monck raised a regiment
of foot guards here on behalf of his exiled monarch, Charles II (1630–
85). Known as the Coldstream Guards, the successors to this regiment
have become an elite corps in the British army.

The **Coldstream Museum,** in the Coldstream Guards' former headquarters, investigates the history of the community of Coldstream, past
and present. A special exhibition recalls the history of the Coldstream
Guards. ⊠ *Market Sq.,* ☎ *01890/882630.* 🎫 *£1.* ♡ *Apr.–Sept., Mon.–
Sat. 10–4, Sun. 2–4; Oct., Mon.–Sat. 1–4.*

The stretch of the Tweed near Coldstream is lined with dignified houses
and gardens. The best-known house is **The Hirsel,** where a complex of
farmyard buildings now serves as a crafts center and museum, with
interesting walks on the extensive grounds. It's a favorite spot for
bird-watchers, and superb rhododendrons bloom here in late spring.
The house itself is not open to the public. ⊠ *A697, immediately west
of Coldstream,* ☎ *01890/882834.* 🎫 *Free; parking Easter–Sept. £2,
Oct.–Easter £1.* ♡ *Grounds: daily sunrise–sunset; museum and crafts
center: weekdays 10–5, weekends noon–5.*

If you are spending a lot of time in the area, you could tour northeast from
❿ Coldstream to see more stately mansions. **Paxton House** is a comely Palladian mansion, with interiors designed by Adam and Chippendale and
Trotter furniture. The splendid Regency picture gallery is an outstation
of the National Galleries of Scotland and contains a magnificent collection of paintings. The garden is delightful, with an ice house, squirrel hide,
and a restored boathouse with a museum of salmon net fishing; a crafts
shop and a tearoom are adjacent to the house. ⊠ *Paxton, 15 mi northeast of Coldstream (take A6112 and B6461),* ☎ *01289/386291.* 🎫 *Joint
ticket for house and garden, £4.50; garden only, £2.25.* ♡ *House and garden: Apr.–Oct., daily 11–5 (last tour 4:15); tearoom: daily 10–5:30.*

⓫ **Manderston House** is a good example of the grand, no-expense-spared
Edwardian country house. The family that built it made its fortune selling herring to Russia. An original 1790s Georgian house on the site
was completely rebuilt 1903–05 to the specifications of John Kinross.
The silver-plated staircase (thought to be unique) was modeled after
the Petit Trianon at Versailles. There is also much to see downstairs in
the kitchens, and outside, among a cluster of other buildings, is the
one-of-a-kind marble dairy. The house is reached by traveling farther

northwest from Coldstream along the A6112 to Duns, then taking the A6105 east. ⊠ *2 mi east of Duns,* ☎ *01361/882636.* 🎫 *Joint ticket for house and grounds, £5.50; grounds only, £3.50.* ☉ *Mid-May–Sept., Thurs. and Sun. 2–5:30; also Bank Holiday Mon. 2–5:30.*

Dining and Lodging

££   ✕🏠 **Wheatsheaf Hotel and Restaurant.** A country inn on the main street
★   of Swinton, midway between Coldstream and Duns, the Wheatsheaf offers outstanding food in both the black-beamed bar and the restaurant. The sheer class of the Scottish cuisine, whether the meal is beef, salmon, or venison, has won widespread praise, yet neither the food nor the small but carefully chosen wine list is overpriced. If you do not want to leave after your meal, stay in one of the six country-style bedrooms. ⊠ *Wheatsheaf Hotel, Swinton TD11 3JJ,* ☎ ℻ *01890/860257. 6 rooms with bath or shower. Restaurant. MC, V. Closed last wk in Feb. and last wk in Oct.*

Melrose

⑫   *15 mi west of Coldstream.*

In the center of the handsome community of Melrose sits **Melrose Abbey,** another of the four Borders abbeys. "If thou would'st view fair Melrose aright, go visit it in the pale moonlight," wrote Scott in *The Lay of the Last Minstrel,* and so many of his fans took the advice literally that a sleepless custodian begged him to rewrite the lines. Today the abbey is still impressive: a red-sandstone shell with slender windows in the Perpendicular style and some delicate tracery and carved capitals, carefully maintained. Among the carvings high on the roof is one of a bagpipe-playing pig. An audio tour is included in the admission price. ⊠ *Main Sq.,* ☎ *0131/668–8800.* 🎫 *£3.* ☉ *Apr.–Sept., daily 9:30–6; Oct.–Mar., Mon.–Sat. 9:30–4, Sun. 2–4.*

Next to Melrose Abbey is the National Trust for Scotland's (☞ Threave Gardens, *below*) **Priorwood Gardens,** which specializes in flowers for drying. Next to the gardens is an orchard with some old apple varieties. Dried flowers are on sale in the shop. ⊠ *Main Sq.* 🎫 *£1.* ☉ *Apr.–Sept., Mon.–Sat. 10–5:30, Sun. 1:30–5:30; Oct.–Dec. 24, Mon.–Sat. 10–4, Sun. 1:30–4.*

The renovated **Melrose Station,** a poignant survivor of the old **Waverley Route,** a railroad that until 1969 ran between Edinburgh and Carlisle, is now used as offices, with a restaurant (☎ 01896/822546) on the ground floor serving morning coffee (Saturday only), light lunches, and complete evening meals. It is closed Mondays and Tuesdays; dinner is not served Wednesdays or Sundays.

The **Trimontium Exhibition,** in the Square, displays artifacts from the largest Roman settlement in Scotland, which was at nearby Newstead. Tools and weapons, a blacksmith's shop, pottery, and scale models of the fort are included in the display. A guided 5-mi, four-hour walk to the site takes place each Thursday afternoon; phone for details. ⊠ *Ormiston Institute, the Square, Melrose,* ☎ *01896/822651.* 🎫 *£1.40.* ☉ *Apr.–Oct., weekdays 10:30–4:30, weekends 10:30–12:30 and 1:30–4:30.*

Teddy Melrose, a teddy bear museum, tells the story of British teddy bears from the early 1900s. There is, of course, a bear collector's shop. ⊠ *High St.* 🎫 *£1.50.* ☉ *Daily 10–5.*

★ ⑬   Two miles west of Melrose stands **Abbotsford House,** home of Sir Walter Scott (1771–1832). In 1811, already an established writer, Scott bought a farm on this site named Cartleyhole, which was a euphemism for the real name, Clartyhole (*clarty* is Scots for "muddy" or sticky"). The name was surely not romantic enough for Scott, who renamed the property and eventually had it entirely rebuilt in the Romantic style, emulating several other Scottish properties. The result was called "the most incongruous pile that gentlemanly modernism ever devised" by John Ruskin. That was Mr. Ruskin's idiosyncratic take: most people have found this to be one of the most fetching of all Scottish abodes. A gently seedy pseudo-baronial mansion chock-full of Scottish curios, Ramsay portraits, and mounted deer heads, it is an appropriate domicile for a man of such an extraordinarily romantic imagination. It is worth visiting just to feel the atmosphere that the most successful writer of his day created and to see the condition in which he wrote, driving himself to pay off his endless debts (for more on his life and history, *see* the Close-Up box, "Sir Walter Scott: A Voice from the Borders"). To Abbotsford came most of the famous poets and thinkers of Scott's day, including Wordsworth and Washington Irving. Abbotsford is the repository for the writer's collection of Scottish memorabilia and historic artifacts. The library holds some 9,000 volumes. Scott died here in 1832. Today the house is owned by his descendants. ⊠ *B6360,* ☎ *01896/752043.* ≘ *£3.50.* ⊙ *Mar.–Oct., Mon.–Sat. 10–5, Sun. 2–5 (June–Sept., daily 10–5).*

★ ⑭ Sir Walter's final resting place and the most peaceful and secluded of the Borders abbeys, **Dryburgh Abbey** sits on gentle parkland in a loop of the Tweed. The abbey suffered from English raids until, like Melrose, it was abandoned in 1544. The style is transitional, a mingling of rounded Romanesque and pointed early English. The side chapel, where the Haig and Scott families lie buried, is lofty and pillared and detached from the main buildings. ⊠ *Off A68, 8 mi southeast of Melrose,* ☎ *0131/668–8800.* ≘ *£2.50.* ⊙ *Apr.–Sept., daily 9:30–6; Oct.–Mar., Mon.–Sat. 9:30–4, Sun. 2–4.*

★ ⑮ There is no escaping Sir Walter in this part of the country: 3 mi north of Dryburgh is **Scott's View,** possibly the most photographed rural view in the south of Scotland. (Perhaps the only view used more often to summon a particular interpretation of Scotland is Eilean Donan Castle, far to the north.) You arrive at this peerless vista by taking the B6356 north from Dryburgh. A poignant tale is told about the horses of Scott's funeral cortege: on their way to Dryburgh Abbey they stopped here out of habit as they had so often in the past. The sinuous curve of the River Tweed and the gentle landscape unfolding to the triple peaks of the Eildons and then rolling out into shadows beyond are certainly worth seeking.

OFF THE
BEATEN PATH

THIRLESTANE CASTLE – At the children's nursery in this 17th-century castle, children are allowed to play with Victorian-style toys and masks and to dress up in costumes. Thirlestane is on the A68 10 mi north of Melrose. ⊠ *Lauder,* ☎ *01578/722430.* ≘ *Joint ticket for castle and grounds, £4.50; grounds only, £1.50.* ⊙ *Easter wk, May–Oct., Sun.–Fri. 11–5 (last admission 4:15; grounds open 11–6).*

Dining and Lodging

££££   🏨 **Dryburgh Abbey Hotel.** Right next to the abbey ruins, this civilized hotel is surrounded by beautiful scenery and has a restaurant (no-smoking) specializing in traditional Scottish fare. The restrained decor and earthy, muted colors throughout create a peaceful atmosphere in keeping with the location. ⊠ *St. Boswells, TD6 0RQ,* ☎ *01835/822261,* FAX *01835/823945. 38 rooms with bath and shower. Restaurant, golf privileges. AE, MC, V.*

£££   🏨 **Burts Hotel.** Built in 1772, this quiet hotel retains a considerable amount of its period style. It has a particularly welcoming bar, with a cheerful open fire and a wide selection of fine malt whiskies, ideal for a quiet

SIR WALTER SCOTT: A VOICE FROM THE BORDERS

SIR WALTER SCOTT (1771–1832) was probably Scottish tourism's best-ever propagandist. Thanks to his fervid "Romantik" imagination, his long narrative poems—such as *The Lady of the Lake*—and a truly long string of historical novels, including *Ivanhoe*, *Waverley*, *Rob Roy*, *Redgauntlet*, and *The Heart of Midlothian*, the world fell in love with the image of heroic Scotland. Told seriously and thoroughly documented, his works lifted fiction high above the Gothic romances of his contemporaries. As part of the Romantic movement in Britain (the English poets William Wordsworth and Samuel Taylor Coleridge were his near-contemporaries) Scott wrote of Scotland as a place of Highland wilderness and clan romance, shaping outsiders' perceptions of Scotland in a way that to a certain extent survives even today.

Scott was born in College Wynd, Edinburgh. A lawyer by training, he was an assiduous collector of old ballads and tales. As a young boy recovering from illness, Scott was sent to his grandfather's farm, near Smailholm in the Borders, where he first heard the stirring tales of Border history. After qualifying as an advocate in 1792 and after his marriage in 1797 to Margaret Charlotte Charpentier, daughter of a French refugee, Scott seriously began to devote his spare time to writing. "The Lay of the Last Minstrel," a romantic poem published in 1805, brought him fame and was soon followed by further romantic verse narratives.

In 1811 Scott bought the house that was to become Abbotsford, his Borders mansion near Melrose, which he rebuilt and which gradually became a storehouse of Scottish history: Bonnie Prince Charlie's *quaich* (drinking bowl), library ceiling plaster casts from Rosslyn Chapel, Rob Roy's broadsword, and an entrance porch copied from Linlithgow Palace are examples of the wealth of artifacts he amassed, all of which can still be seen today.

Scott started on his series of Waverley novels in 1814, at first anonymously, and by 1820 had produced *Waverley*, *Guy Mannering*, *The Antiquary*, *Tales of My Landlord* (three series), and *Rob Roy*. Between 1820 and 1825 there followed an additional 11 titles, including *Ivanhoe* and *The Pirate* (which was partly written during a voyage around Scotland with lighthouse builder Robert Stevenson, grandfather of novelist Robert Louis Stevenson). Many of his verse narratives and novels focused on real-life settings, in particular the Trossachs, west of Stirling, which rapidly became and still remain extremely popular with visitors.

In 1826 Ballantyne's publishing house, in which Scott was a partner, went bankrupt, and Scott took it as a matter of honor to personally clear the debts. So until his death six years later, he produced a copious amount of work, including additional novels, a biographical *Life of Napoleon*, and translations of German works. Scott's health started to fail under the pressure of work (and those mounting bills), and he died on September 21, 1832.

Apart from his writing, Scott is also remembered as the discoverer, in 1819, of the Honours of Scotland (the crown, scepter, and sword of state of the Scottish monarchs), which had been wrapped up, dumped in the bottom of a chest in Edinburgh Castle, and forgotten since 1707, when Scotland lost its independence. Today these historic symbols of Scotland's sovereignty are on display in the castle.

Abbotsford can be visited in the summer season, and other houses associated with Scott can be seen (from the outside only) in Edinburgh: 25 George Square, which was his father's house, and 39 Castle Street. The site of his birthplace, in College Wynd, is marked with a plaque. The most obvious structure associated with Scott is the Scott Monument on Princes Street, which looks for all the world like a Gothic rocket ship with a statue of Scott and his pet dog as passengers.

dram before or after a meal in the elegant dining room, which has dark-green-striped wallpaper, high-back upholstered chairs, and white-linen tablecloths. Cannon of venison and roast duck terrine are typical entrées on the Scottish menu, which has Continental overtones. The bedrooms and public areas are individually decorated with reproduction antiques and floral pastels. Shooting and fishing can be arranged. ⊠ *Market Sq., TD6 9PN,* ☎ *01896/822285,* ꜰꜰ *01896/822870. 20 rooms, 13 with bath, 7 with shower. Restaurant. AE, DC, MC, V.*

Galashiels

⑯ *5 mi northwest of Melrose.*

A busy gray-stone Borders town, Galashiels is still active with textile mills and knitwear shops. At the **Lochcarron of Scotland Cashmere and Wool Centre** is a museum of the town's history and industry; visitors can go on a mill tour and learn about the manufacture of tartans and tweeds. ⊠ *Nether Mill,* ☎ *01896/752091.* 💷 *£2.50.* ⊙ *Oct.–May, Mon.–Sat. 9–5; June–Sept., Mon.–Sat. 9–5, Sun. noon–5. Guided tours Mon.–Thurs. 10:30, 11:30, 1:30, and 2:30; Fri. 10:30 and 11:30.*

Dating from 1583, **Old Gala House,** a short walk from the town center, is the former home of the lairds of Galashiels. It is now a museum with displays on the building's history and the town of Galashiels, as well as a contemporary art gallery and exhibition space. ⊠ *Scott Crescent,* ☎ *01750/20096.* 💷 *Free.* ⊙ *Apr.–Sept., Tues.–Sat. 10–4; Oct., Tues.–Sat. 1–4.*

Shopping

Lochcarron of Scotland Cashmere and Wool Centre (☞ *above*) has a wide selection of woolens and tweeds.

Selkirk

⑰ *7 mi south of Galashiels.*

Selkirk is a hilly outpost with a smattering of antiques shops and an assortment of bakers selling the Selkirk Bannock (fruited sweet bread-cake) and other cakes—evidence of Scotland's incurable sweet tooth. Sir Walter Scott was sheriff (judge) of Selkirkshire from 1800 until his death in 1832, and his statue stands in Market Place. **Sir Walter Scott's Courtroom,** where he presided, contains a display examining Scott's life, his writings, and his time as sheriff, and it includes an audiovisual presentation. ⊠ *Market Pl.,* ☎ *01750/20096.* 💷 *Free.* ⊙ *Apr.–Sept., Mon.–Sat. 10–4 (also Sun. 2–4 in June–Aug.); Oct., Mon.–Sat. 1–4.*

Tucked off the main square in Selkirk, **Halliwell's House Museum** was once an ironmonger's shop, now re-created downstairs. Upstairs, an exhibit tells the town's tale, with useful background information on the Common Ridings as well as an audiovisual presentation. ⊠ *Market St.,* ☎ *01750/20096.* 💷 *Free.* ⊙ *Apr.–Nov., Mon.–Sat. 10–5, Sun. 2–4 (July–Aug., Mon.–Sat. 10–6, Sun. 2–6).*

⑱ Another of the stately homes in the Borders, 19th-century **Bowhill** houses an outstanding collection of works by Gainsborough, Van Dyck, Canaletto, Reynolds, and Raeburn, as well as porcelain and period furniture. Note that the house itself is open in July only (parties however can book at other times); the grounds and playground have more friendly hours. ⊠ *Off A708, 3 mi west of Selkirk,* ☎ ꜰꜰ *01750/22204.* 💷 *Joint ticket for house and grounds/playground, £4.50; grounds/playground only, £2.* ⊙ *House: July, daily 1–4:30; grounds/playground: May–June and Aug., Sat.–Thurs. noon–5; July, daily noon–5.*

Innerleithen

⑲ *15 mi northwest of Selkirk.*

The main reason to come to the linear community of Innerleithen is **Robert Smail's Printing Works.** The fully operational, restored print shop with reconstructed waterwheel will fascinate adults and older children, who can try their hand at old-fashioned typesetting. ⊠ *7–9 High St.,* ☎ *01896/830206.* ▩ *£2.50.* ⊙ *Easter and May–Sept., Mon.–Sat. 10–1 and 2–5, Sun. 2–5; Oct., Sat. 10–1 and 2–5, Sun. 2–5 (last admission 45 mins before closing, morning and afternoon).*

★ Near the town is **Traquair House,** said to be the oldest continually occupied house in Scotland. Secret stairs, intricate embroidery, a bed used by Mary, Queen of Scots in 1566, more than 3,000 books, and a maze are just a few of the discoveries. Ale is still brewed in the 18th-century brew house here, and it's recommended! ⊠ *Traquair, near Innerleithen,* ☎ *01896/830323.* ▩ *£5.* ⊙ *Apr.–May and Sept., daily 12:30–5:30; June–Aug., daily 10:30–5:30; Oct., Fri.–Sun. 12:30–5:30 (last admission 5).*

Lodging

££££ 🛏 **Traquair House.** Stay in the private quarters at Traquair to experience the unique atmosphere of this ancient house for yourself. The Blue Room and the Pink Room, furnished with antiques and chintz-draped canopied beds, offer a most relaxing environment, as does the 18th-century Lower Drawing Room, where you can savor a glass of the house's own ale. ⊠ *Innerleithen, Peeblesshire EH44 6PW,* ☎ *01896/830323,* 🖷 *01896/830639. 2 rooms with bath and shower. MC, V. Closed Dec.–Feb.*

Shopping

The **Mill Shop** (⊠ Walkerburn, 2 mi east of Innerleithen, ☎ 01896/870619) has a large mill shop offering a wealth of styles, as well as an adjacent museum of woolen textiles.

Peebles

⑳ *6 mi west of Innerleithen.*

Thanks to its excellent though pricey shopping, Peebles gives the impression of catering primarily to leisured country gentlefolk. Architecturally the town is nothing out of the ordinary, a very pleasant Borders burgh (do not miss the splendid dolphins ornamenting the bridge crossing the River Tweed).

Lodging

££££ ✕🛏 **Cringletie House.** Surrounded by an old-fashioned walled garden
★ whose produce is used in the restaurant, this property—with turrets and crow-step gables in traditional Scottish baronial style—is personally supervised by the family of owners. From the spacious, elaborately ceilinged first-floor drawing room you can enjoy pretty views of the valley. The whole hotel was refurbished in 1998 in British country-house style. Locals also flock to the restaurant for such upscale Scottish fare as roast duckling with red-currant and cassis sauce. The afternoon tea, served in the conservatory, is especially recommended. ⊠ *Eddleston EH45 8PL,* ☎ *01721/730233,* 🖷 *01721/730244. 13 rooms. Restaurant, putting green, tennis court, croquet. AE, MC, V.* 🍽

££££ ✕🛏 **Peebles Hydro.** Not only does it have something for everyone, but
★ it has it in abundance: Archery, snooker, pony trekking, squash, a whirlpool, and a sauna are just a few of the diversions the hotel offers. The elegant Edwardian building, reminiscent of a French château, is set on 30 acres. High ceilings give the public areas an airy, spacious ambience. Bedrooms are comfortably furnished, though room sizes and decorative standards can vary. The restaurant features a Scottish menu

with local salmon, lamb, and beef. ⊠ *EH45 8LX,* ☎ *01721/720602,* ℻ *01721/722999. 137 rooms with bath or shower. Restaurant, pool, tennis court, health club, bicycles, baby-sitting, children's programs (ages infant–16), playground, laundry service. AE, DC, MC, V.* ⊗

£££ ✕🛏 **Park Hotel.** This hotel, on the banks of the River Tweed at the northern tip of the Ettrick Forest, offers comfort and tranquillity. Rooms have striped or floral wallpaper and pastel fabrics. The restaurant serves superior Scottish cuisine, many of the dishes based on local salmon and trout. ⊠ *Innerleithen Rd., EH45 8BA,* ☎ *01721/720451,* ℻ *01721/723510. 23 rooms with bath, 1 with shower. Restaurant. AE, DC, MC, V.*

£ 🛏 **Drummore.** This hillside B&B, set in an acre of wild gardens full of bird life, is well positioned both for touring the Borders and for visiting Edinburgh. The house is modern and clean, and the guest lounge has a vast picture window that overlooks the River Tweed. ⊠ *Venlaw High Rd., EH45 8RL,* ☎ *01721/720336,* ℻ *01721/723004. 2 rooms with bath or shower. MC, V. Closed Nov.–Mar.*

Outdoor Activities and Sports

BIKING

Scottish Border Trails (⊠ Drummore, Venlaw High Rd., Peebles EH45 8RL, ☎ 01721/720336) rents bicycles and also organizes cycling and walking holidays, including lodging.

Shopping

You can easily spend a day browsing on High Street and in the courts and side streets leading off it, temptations awaiting at every turn.

GIFTS

Head to Toe (⊠ 43 High St., ☎ 01721/722752) stocks natural beauty products of all descriptions and a variety of linens—from lace doilies to patchwork quilts, dried flowers, and porcelain pieces. If you need a rest after all that shopping, repair to the **Country Shop** (⊠ 56 High St., ☎ 01721/720630), a gift store with souvenirs aplenty and a coffee shop upstairs, replete with views over the town and bustling High Street.

HARDWARE

Scott's Hardware Store (⊠ 48 High St., ☎ 01721/720262) has every kind of tool, implement, fixture, fitting, and garden gadget (even mousetraps) spread in glorious array over floors, walls, and ceiling.

JEWELRY AND ANTIQUES

Among many craftspeople and jewelers on High Street is **Keith Walter** (⊠ 28 High St., ☎ 01721/720650), a gold- and silversmith who makes items on the premises and stocks jewelry made by other local designers.

The German-born and Swiss-trained watchmaker Jurgen Tubbecke also sells antiques alongside his handcrafted chronometers at **The Clockmaker** (⊠ 3 High St., ☎ 01721 723599).

GALLOWAY HIGHLANDS

Galloway is the name given to the southwest portion of Scotland, west of the main town of Dumfries. The area's terrain is diverse—from its gentle coastline and breezy uplands to areas gradually disappearing below blankets of conifers. Use caution when negotiating the A75: although this main trunk road has been improved in recent years, you are liable to find aggressive trucks bearing down on you as these commercial vehicles race for the Irish ferries at Stranraer and Cairnryan (anything as environmentally sensible as a direct east–west railway link was closed years ago). Trucks notwithstanding, once you are off the main roads, Dumfries and Galloway offer some of the most pleasant touring roads in Scotland—though the occasional herd of cows on the way to be milked is a potential hazard.

Gretna

㉑ *10 mi north of Carlisle, 87 mi south of Glasgow, 92 mi southwest of Edinburgh.*

Gretna and **Gretna Green** are, quite simply, an embarrassment to native Scots. What else can you say about a place that advertises "amusing joke weddings," as does one of the visitor centers here? These strange goings-on are tied to the reputation this community developed as a refuge for runaway couples from England, who once came north to take advantage of Scotland's less strict marriage laws. This was the first place they reached on crossing the border. At one time anyone could perform a legal marriage in Scotland. Often the village blacksmith did the honors, presumably because he was conveniently situated near the main road.

Ruthwell

21 mi west of Gretna, 83 mi south of Glasgow, 88 mi southwest of Edinburgh.

The landscape is not impressive around the flat fields of the Upper Solway Firth, but as you progress west, you'll find more of interest. In-
㉒ side **Ruthwell Parish Church** is the 8th-century **Ruthwell Cross,** a Christian sculpture admired for the quality of its carving. Considered an idolatrous monument, it was removed and demolished by Church of Scotland zealots in 1640 but was later reassembled. Near the church in Ruthwell is the **Savings Banks Museum,** which tells the story of the savings-bank movement, founded by the Reverend Dr. Henry Duncan in 1810. ⊠ *6½ mi west of Annan,* ☎ *01387/870640.* ⚏ *Free.* ☉ *Apr.–Sept., daily 10–1 and 2–5; Oct.–Mar., Tues.–Sat. 10–1 and 2–5.*

㉓ At nearby Clarencefield, **Comlongon,** a more recent mansion house, adjoins a well-preserved 15th-century border keep. You can also avail yourself of the B&B at the castle. ⊠ *B724, 8 mi west of Annan,* ☎ *01387/870283.* ⚏ *£3.* ☉ *Mar.–Nov., daily 10–1.*

★ **㉔** Built in a triangular design unique in Britain, moated **Caerlaverock Castle** stands overlooking a nature reserve on a coastal loop of the B725. This 13th-century fortress has solid-sandstone masonry and an imposing double-tower gatehouse. King Edward I of England (1239–1307) besieged the castle in 1300, when his forces occupied much of Scotland as the Wars of Independence commenced. The castle suffered many times in Anglo-Scottish skirmishes, as the video presentation attests. ⊠ *Off B725, 7 mi west of Ruthwell,* ☎ *01387/770244.* ⚏ *£2.50.* ☉ *Apr.–Sept., daily 9:30–6; Oct.–Mar., Mon.–Sat. 9:30–4, Sun. 2–4.*

㉕ The **Caerlaverock National Nature Reserve** is a treat for bird-watchers, who can observe wintering wildfowl from blinds and a visitor center. ⊠ *Off B725, east of Caerlaverock Castle,* ☎ *01387/770275.* ⚏ *Free.* ☉ *Year-round.*

Dumfries

㉖ *15 mi northwest of Ruthwell, 76 mi south of Glasgow, 81 mi southwest of Edinburgh.*

The town of Dumfries, where Scotland's national poet Robert Burns (1759–96) spent the last years of his short life, is a no-nonsense, red-sandstone community. Perhaps not so ironically, the playwright J. M. Barrie spent

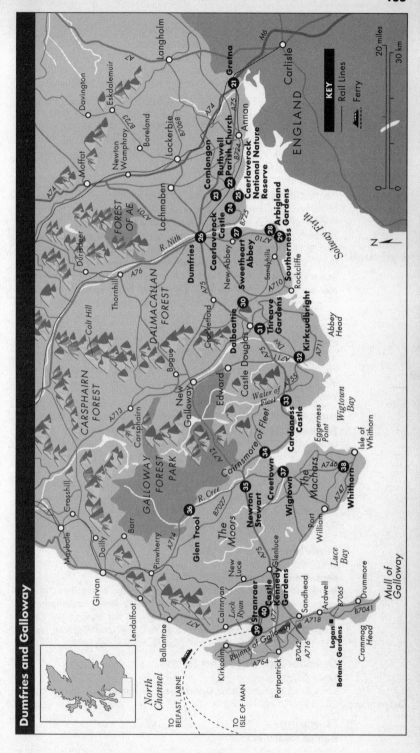

Dumfries and Galloway

20 miles
30 km

N

ENGLAND
Carlisle

Gretna
21

Comlongon
Ruthwell
Parish Church
22
23 24 25
Caerlaverock
National Nature
Reserve

Annan

Caerlaverock
Castle
26 27
Arbigland
Gardens
28 29
Southerness

Dumfries

New Abbey
Sweetheart
Abbey

Sandyhills
Rockcliffe
Abbey
Head

Solway Firth

Crocketford
Dalbeattie
30
31
Threave
Gardens
Kirkcudbright
32

Castle Douglas
Dee

A711
A745

Water of
Fleet
33
Cardoness
Castle

Eggerness
Point

Wigtown
Bay

Isle of
Whithorn

Edward

Cairnsmore of Fleet
34
Gatehouse
37
Creetown
Wigtown
The
Machars
38
Whithorn

New
Galloway

35
Newton
Stewart

Port
William

GALLOWAY
FOREST
PARK

The
Moors

R. Cree

36
Glen Trool

CARSPHAIRN
FOREST

Carsphairn

DALMACALLAN
FOREST

DALMACALLAN
FOREST

R. Nith

FOREST
OF AE

Langholm

Davington
Eskdalemuir
Boreland
Newton
Wamphray
Lockerbie

Moffat

Newton
Wamphray
Lochmaben

Thornhill

Colt Hill

Durisdeer

Bogue

Crosshill

Barr

Pinwherry

Girvan

Lendalfoot

Ballantrae

Maybole

Dailly

New
Luce
Glenluce
Stranraer
Castle
Kennedy
Gardens
39
40

Cairnryan
Loch
Ryan

Kirkcolm

Rhinns of Galloway

Portpatrick

North
Channel

TO
BELFAST, LARNE

TO
ISLE OF MAN

Sandhead
Ardwell

Luce
Bay

Drummore

Sandhead

Logan
Botanic Gardens

Crammag
Head

Mull of
Galloway

ISLE OF MAN

his childhood in Victoria Terrace here in the 1870s, and the garden of Moat Brae House is said to be the playground that inspired his boyish dreams in *Peter Pan*. The **River Nith** meanders through Dumfries, and the pedestrians-only town center makes shopping a pleasure (the A75 now bypasses the town). The town also contains Robert Burns's favorite *howff*, or pub (the Globe Inn), one of the houses he lived in, and his mausoleum.

Not surprisingly, in view of its close association to the poet, Dumfries has a **Robert Burns Centre,** housed in a sturdy former mill overlooking the river. The center has an audiovisual program and an extensive exhibit on the life of the poet. ✉ *Mill Rd.,* ☎ *01387/264808.* ✆ *Free; small charge for audiovisual show.* ☉ *Apr.–Sept., Mon.–Sat. 10–8, Sun. 2–5 (café, daily 11–4); Oct.–Mar., Tues.–Sat. 10–1 and 2–5.*

OFF THE BEATEN PATH

DRUMLANRIG CASTLE – This spectacular estate is as close as Scotland gets to the treasure houses of England—not surprisingly, since it is owned by the dukes of Buccleuch, one of the wealthiest British peerages. Ornate, square built, and romantically turreted, this pink-sandstone palace was built in 1689 by the first duke of Queensbury, who, after nearly bankrupting himself building the place, found it disappointing on his first overnight stay and never returned. Inherited by the Buccleuchs, the richly decorated rooms were soon filled with Louis XIV furniture and a valuable collection of paintings by Holbein, Rembrandt, da Vinci, Reynolds, Murillo, and many family portraits. There are also a working forge, crafts workshops, a playground, gift shop, and tearoom adorning the parklands, which offer a breathtaking setting to the house. ✉ *Near Thornhill, about 15 mi northwest of Dumfries off A76,* ☎ *01848/330248.* ✆ *Joint ticket for castle and park, £6; park only, £3.* ☉ *Castle: May–mid-Aug., Mon.–Sat. 11–5, Sun. noon–5 (last entry 4); country park, gardens, and adventure playground: May–Sept., daily 11–5.*

MUSEUM OF SCOTTISH LEAD MINING – Reached by taking the Mennock Pass through rounded moorland hills, this museum—devoted to one of Scotland's lesser-known industries—is at Wanlockhead, at Scotland's highest elevation a fairly bleak village. There are underground trips for the stouthearted. The Miners' Library not only shows how the miners educated themselves but also offers a genealogical computer database. ✉ *Goldscaur Rd., Wanlockhead, on B797 northeast of Sanquhar, 27 mi northwest of Dumfries.* ☎ *01659/74387.* ✆ *£3.95.* ☉ *Apr.–Oct., daily 10–4:30 (last guided tour at 4).*

Nightlife and the Arts

THE ARTS

Gracefield Arts Centre (✉ 28 Edinburgh Rd., ☎ 01387/262084) has public art galleries and studios with a constantly changing exhibition program. **The Dumfries and Galloway Arts Festival** is usually held at the end of May at several venues throughout the region. The **Robert Burns Centre Film Theatre** (✉ Mill Rd., ☎ 01387/264808) features special-interest, foreign, and other films not widely released.

Outdoor Activities and Sports

BIKING

Cycles can be rented from **Greirson and Graham** (✉ 10 Academy St., ☎ 01387/259483).

Shopping

GIFTS AND CRAFTS

Dumfries is the main shopping center for the region, with all the big-name chain stores as well as specialty shops. **Greyfriars Crafts** (✉ 56 Buccleuch St., ☎ 01387/264050) has mainly Scottish goods, including glass, ceramics, and jewelry.

If you are visiting Drumlanrig Castle (☞ Off the Beaten Path, *above*), do not miss the **crafts center** (☎ 01848/331555) in the stable block, chock-full of all types of crafts, including leather goods, landscape and portrait works, stainless-steel jewelry, and cutlery. The center is open May through August, daily 9 to 5; September through April, by appointment.

POSTCARDS
For a souvenir that's easier to pack, try **David Hastings** (✉ Marying, Shieldhill, Lockerbie DG11 1SG, ☎ 01387/710451; visitors by appointment), which has more than 100,000 old postcards.

New Abbey

7 mi south of Dumfries, 83 mi south of Glasgow, 88 mi southwest of Edinburgh.

27 The village of New Abbey has at its center **Sweetheart Abbey,** which provides a mellowed red and roofless backdrop to the village. It was founded in 1273 by Devorgilla Balliol in memory of her husband, John. The couple's son, also named John (1250–1315), was the puppet king installed in Scotland by Edward of England when the latter claimed sovereignty over Scotland. After John's appointment the Scots gave him a scathing nickname that would stay with him for the rest of his life: Toom Tabard (Empty Shirt). ✉ *A710 at New Abbey,* ☎ *0131/668–8800.* 🎫 *£1.20.* ☉ *Apr.–Sept., daily 9:30–6; Oct.–Mar., Mon.–Wed. and Sat. 9:30–4, Thurs. 9:30–noon, Sun. 2–4.*

Kirkbean

5 mi south of New Abbey, 88 mi south of Glasgow, 94 mi southwest of Edinburgh.

28 A little community (blink and you've missed it) set in a bright green landscape is the setting for **Arbigland Gardens;** follow signs from the village. An Arbigland local named John Paul, the son of a gardener, left Scotland and became the founder of the U.S. Navy. This seafaring son, John Paul Jones (1747–92), returned to his native coast in a series of daring raids in 1778. A museum will brief you on the history. The gardens tended by Jones's father are typical of the area: lush and sheltered, with blue water visible through the protecting trees; the walled garden dating from 1745 is currently being restored, using plantings of roses typical of the 18th century. ✉ *Off A710 by Kirkbean,* ☎ *01387/880613.* 🎫 *£2.* ☉ *Apr.–June and Sept., Tues.–Sun. 10–5; July–Aug., daily 10–5 (closed Mon. except bank holidays).*

Southerness

29 *3 mi south of Kirkbean, 91 mi south of Glasgow, 97 mi southwest of Edinburgh.*

The road to Southerness ends in a welter of recreational vehicles and trailer homes in the shadow of one of Scotland's earliest lighthouses, built in 1749 by the port authorities of Dumfries who were anxious to make the treacherous River Nith approaches safer.

En Route The road to Southerness turns west and becomes faintly Riviera-like. You can take a brisk walk from Sandyhills to Rockcliffe, two of the sleepy coastal communities overlooking the creeping tides and endless shallows of the Solway coast.

Dalbeattie

㉚   *12 mi northwest of Southerness, 89 mi south of Glasgow, 95 mi southwest of Edinburgh.*

Like the much larger Aberdeen, far to the northeast, Dalbeattie's buildings were constructed with local gray granite from the town's quarry. The predominance of granite, with its well-scrubbed gray glitter, makes Dalbeattie atypical of Galloway towns, whose housefronts are predominantly painted in pastels.

Lodging

££   **Auchenskeoch Lodge.** This quaint and informal Victorian shooting
★   lodge, now a small-scale country-house hotel, has three bedrooms and delicious food (for residents only). The antique furnishings have a comfortable, faded elegance. Many of the vegetables and herbs used in the set menu—prepared to a high standard in traditional Scottish style—are grown on the 20 acres of gardens and woodland surrounding the house. The sitting room houses crammed bookshelves and an open fire, and in the games room is a full-size billiards table. A private loch, turf and gravel maze, and croquet lawn provide outdoor entertainment. ⊠ *By Dalbeattie, DG5 4PG,* ☎ 📠 *01387/780277. 3 rooms with bath or shower. Croquet. MC, V. Closed Nov.–Easter.*

Outdoor Activities and Sports

HORSEBACK RIDING

Barend Properties Riding School and Trekking Centre (⊠ Sandyhills, by Dalbeattie, Kirkcudbright, ☎ 01387/780663) helps you to a "horse-high" view of the beautiful coast and countryside of this region.

Castle Douglas

6 mi west of Dalbeattie, 94 mi south of Glasgow, 99 mi southwest of Edinburgh.

Although it is a pleasant town with a long main street where the home bakeries vie for business, Castle Douglas's main interest is its proximity
★ **㉛** to **Threave Gardens.** As Scotland's best-known charitable conservation agency, the National Trust for Scotland cares for several garden properties. This horticultural undertaking demands the employment of many gardeners—and it is at Threave that the gardeners train, thus ensuring there is always some fresh development or experimental planting here. This gives lots of vigor and interest to the sloping parkland around the mansion house of Threave. There is a good visitor center as well. ⊠ *South of A75, 1 mi west of Castle Douglas,* ☎ *01556/502575.* 💷 *£4.40.* ☉ *Gardens: daily 9:30–sunset; walled garden and greenhouses: daily 9:30–5; visitor center, exhibition, and shop: Apr.–Oct., daily 9:30–5:30; restaurant: daily 10–5.*

Threave Castle (not to be confused with the mansion house in Threave Gardens) is a few minutes away by car and is signposted from the main road. To get there, you must leave your car in a farmyard and walk the rest of the way. Reassured by the Historic Scotland signs (because Threave is being cared for by the national government), you make your way down to the reeds by the river on an occasionally muddy path. At the edge of the river you can then ring a bell, and, rather romantically, a boatman will come to ferry you across to the great stone tower looming from a marshy island in the river. Threave was an early home of the Black Douglases, the earls of Nithsdale, and lords of Galloway. The castle was dismantled in the religious wars of the mid-17th century, though enough of it remains to have housed prisoners from the Napoleonic Wars of the 19th century. ⊠ *North of A75, 3 mi west of*

Castle Douglas, ☎ *0131/668–8800.* 🖃 *£2, includes ferry.* ☉ *Apr.–Sept., daily 9:30–6:30.*

Outdoor Activities and Sports

BIKING

You can rent cycles from **Ace Cycles** (✉ Church St., Castle Douglas, ☎ FAX 01556/504542).

WATER SPORTS

The **Galloway Sailing Centre** (✉ Loch Ken, ☎ FAX 01644/420626) rents dinghies, windsurfing equipment, and canoes. It also runs residential sailing, windsurfing, and canoeing courses.

Shopping

BOOKS

It is well worth the short drive north from Castle Douglas (A75 then B794) to visit **Benny Gillies Books, Maps and Prints** (✉ 31–33 Victoria St., Kirkpatrick Durham, ☎ 01556/650412), which stocks an outstanding selection of secondhand and antiquarian Scottish books, hand-colored antique maps, and prints featuring areas throughout Scotland.

GIFTS

The **Posthorn** (✉ 26–30 St. Andrew St., ☎ 01556/502531) consists of two shops specializing in gift items, including the figurines made by Border Fine Art.

JEWELRY

Galloway Gems (✉ 130–132 King St., ☎ 01556/503254) not only has silver jewelry but also stocks mineral specimens, polished stone slices, and art materials.

Kirkcudbright

32 *11 mi southwest of Castle Douglas, 103 mi south of Glasgow, 109 mi southwest of Edinburgh.*

Kirkcudbright is an 18th-century town of unpretentious houses, some of them color-washed in pastel shades and roofed with the blue slates of the district. For much of this century it has been known as an artists' town, and its L-shape main street is full of crafts and antiques shops. Conspicuous in the town center is **MacLellan's Castle,** the shell of a once-elaborate castellated mansion dating from the early 16th century. ✉ *Off High St.,* ☎ *0131/668–8800.* 🖃 *£1.80.* ☉ *Apr.–Sept., daily 9:30–6.*

The 18th-century **Broughton House** was once the home of the artist E. A. Hornel (he was one of the "Glasgow Boys" of the late 19th century). Many of his paintings hang in the house, which is furnished in period style and contains an extensive library specializing in local history. There is also a Japanese garden. ✉ *12 High St.,* ☎ FAX *01557/330437.* 🖃 *£3.50.* ☉ *Apr.–Oct., daily 1–5:30 (last admission 4:45).*

The delightfully old-fashioned **Stewartry Museum,** stuffed with all manner of local paraphernalia, allows you to putter and absorb as much or as little as takes your interest in the display cases. ✉ *St. Mary St.,* ☎ *01557/331643.* 🖃 *£1.50.* ☉ *Oct.–Apr., Mon.–Sat. 11–4; May, Mon.–Sat. 11–5; June and Sept., Mon.–Sat. 10–6, Sun. 2–5; July–Aug., Mon.–Sat. 10–6, Sun. 2–5.*

The **Tolbooth Arts Centre,** in the old tolbooth, gives a history of the town's artists' colony and its leaders E. A. Hornel, Jessie King, and Charles Oppenheimer, and displays some of their paintings as well as works by modern artists and craftspeople. ✉ *High St.,* ☎ *01557/331556.* 🖃 *£1.50.* ☉ *Oct.–Apr., Mon.–Sat. 11–4; May, Mon.–Sat. 11–5; June and Sept., Mon.–Sat. 11–5, Sun. 2–5; July–Aug., Mon.–Sat. 10–6, Sun. 2–5.*

Gatehouse of Fleet

9 mi west of Kirkcudbright, 108 mi southwest of Glasgow, 114 mi southwest of Edinburgh.

㉝ A peaceful, pleasant backwoods sort of place, Gatehouse of Fleet has a castle guarding its southern approach from the A75. **Cardoness Castle** is a typical Scottish tower house, severe and uncompromising. The 15th-century structure once was the home of the McCullochs of Galloway, then the Gordons. ⊠ *A75, 1 mi southwest of Gatehouse of Fleet,* ☎ *0131/668–8800.* ⚏ *£2.* ☉ *Apr.–Sept., daily 9:30–6; Oct.–Mar., Sat. 9:30–4, Sun. 2–4.*

The **Mill on the Fleet** heritage center is a converted cotton mill in which you can learn the history behind this pretty little town's involvement in this industry. Here you can see a changing program of arts and crafts exhibitions, while the tearoom serves light lunches and delicious homebaked goods. ⊠ *High St.,* ☎ *01557/814099.* ☉ *Easter–Oct., daily 10:30–4:30.*

Lodging

£££–££££ 🏨 **Cally Palace.** This hotel was once a private mansion (built in 1759). Many of the public rooms in the Georgian building retain their original grandeur, which includes elaborate plaster ceilings and marble fireplaces. The bedrooms are individually decorated and well equipped. The house is surrounded by 150 acres of gardens, loch, and parkland, including an 18-hole golf course, and has an indoor leisure center with pool, solarium, and sauna. Scottish produce stars in the restaurant in such dishes as seared medallions of Kirroughtree venison. The staff is exceptionally friendly and prepared to spoil you. ⊠ *DG7 2DL,* ☎ *01557/ 814341,* ℻ *01557/814522. 56 rooms with bath or shower. Restaurant, bar, indoor pool, hot tub, sauna, 18-hole golf course, putting green, tennis court, croquet, fishing. MC, V. Closed Jan. and Feb.*

£ 🏨 **High Auchenlarie Farmhouse.** This working beef farm, set high on a hillside overlooking Wigtown Bay, offers bed and breakfast and, for a small additional charge, evening meals. ⊠ *DG7 2HB,* ☎ *01557/840231. 3 rooms with bath or shower. No credit cards. Closed Nov.–Feb.*

Shopping

There is a well-stocked gift and crafts shop at the **Mill on the Fleet** heritage center (⊠ High St., ☎ 01557/814099). The merchandise shop at **Galloway Lodge Preserves** (⊠ 24–28 High St., ☎ ℻ 01557/814357) stocks its own marmalades and mustards, plus Scottish pottery.

En Route If you single-mindedly pursue the suggested policy of avoiding the A75, then your route will loop to the northwest. Take a right by the Anwoth Hotel, in Gatehouse of Fleet, where the signpost points to Gatehouse Station. This route will provide you with a taste of the Dumfries and Galloway hinterland. Beyond the wooded valley where the Water of Fleet runs (local rivers are often referred to as "Water of [name of river]"), dark hills and conifer plantings lend a brooding, empty air to this lonely stretch.

Creetown

㉞ *12 mi west of Gatehouse of Fleet, 95 mi southwest of Glasgow, 112 mi southwest of Edinburgh.*

The low-ground community of Creetown is noted for its **Gem Rock Museum.** The museum has an eclectic mineral collection, a dinosaur egg, and an entertaining demonstration of the various colors with which some rocks fluoresce. ⊠ *A75,* ☎ *01671/820357.* ⚏ *£2.75.* ☉ *Easter–Sept., daily 9:30–6; Oct.–Nov., daily 10–4; Dec.–Feb., week-*

Bureau de change

Cambio

外国為替

In this city, you can find money on almost any street.

NO-FEE FOREIGN EXCHANGE

The Chase Manhattan Bank has over 80 convenient locations near New York City destinations such as:

 Times Square
 Rockefeller Center
 Empire State Building
 2 World Trade Center
 United Nations Plaza

Exchange any of 75 foreign currencies

 CHASE

THE RIGHT RELATIONSHIP IS EVERYTHING.®

ends 10–4; Mar.–Easter, daily 10–4 and by appointment; last admission 30 mins before closing.

Shopping

The **Creetown Gem Rock Museum** (✉ Creetown, ☎ 01671/820357) sells extraordinary mineral and gemstone crystals—both loose and in settings—in its gift shop.

Newton Stewart

㉟ *8 mi northwest of Creetown, 89 mi southwest of Glasgow, 108 mi southwest of Edinburgh.*

The solid and bustling little town of Newton Stewart makes a good touring base for the western region of Galloway. One possible excursion to the north from Newton Stewart takes you to the **Galloway Forest Park.** Take the A714 north from town along the wooded valley of the **River Cree,** which has a nature reserve called the Wood of Cree on the far

★ **㊱** bank. After about 10 mi turn right at the signpost for **Glen Trool.** This road leads you toward the hills that have thus far been the backdrop for the woodlands. Watch for another sign for Glen Trool. Follow this little road through increasingly wild woodland scenery to its terminus at a parking lot. Only after you have left the car and climbed for a few minutes onto a heathery knoll does the full, rugged panorama become apparent. With high purple-and-green hilltops shorn rock-bare by glaciers and with a dark, winding loch and thickets of birch trees sounding with birdcalls, the setting almost looks more highland than the real Highlands, to the north. Glen Trool is one of Scotland's best-kept secrets. Note **Bruce's Stone,** just above the parking lot, marking the site where in 1307 Scotland's champion Robert the Bruce (King Robert I, 1274–1329) won his first victory in the Scottish Wars of Independence.

En Route   The **Machars** is the name given to the triangular promontory south of Newton Stewart. This is an area of gently rolling farmlands, yellow-gorse hedgerows, rich grazing for dairy cattle, and a number of stony prehistoric sites. Most of the glossy, green expanse is used for dairy farming. Fields are bordered by dry *stane dykes* (dry walling) of sharp-edge stones, and small hills and hummocks give the area its characteristic frozen-wave look, a reminder of the glacial activity that shaped the landscape.

Wigtown

㊲ *8 mi south of Newton Stewart, 96 mi southwest of Glasgow, 114 mi southwest of Edinburgh.*

The sleepy hamlet of Wigtown has a broad main street and colorful housefronts. Down by the muddy shores of Wigtown Bay there's a monument to the Wigtown Martyrs, two women who were tied to a stake and left to drown in the incoming tide during the anti-Covenant witch-hunts of 1685. Although much of Dumfries and Galloway's history is linked with Border feuds, it is associated even more with the ferocity of the so-called Killing Times, when the Covenanters were persecuted for their belief that the king should be second to the church, and not vice versa. Wigtown, like several other places in the region, is dominated by a hilltop Covenanters' Monument, a reminder of the old persecutions.

Whithorn

㊳ *11 mi south of Wigtown, 107 mi southwest of Glasgow, 125 mi southwest of Edinburgh.*

The Machars are well known for their early Christian sites. The road that is now the A746 was a pilgrims' way and a royal route that ended at **Isle of Whithorn** (which actually is not a true island), a place that early Scottish kings and barons sought to visit at least once in their lives. The pilgrimage was often prescribed as a penance, but these pleasant shores impose no penance today. The goal was St. Ninian's Chapel, the 4th-century cell of Scotland's premier saint. Some pilgrims headed for Whithorn village and others for the spit-of-sand "isle." Both places claimed to be the site of the original "Candida Casa" of the saint. As you approach Whithorn's 12th-century priory, observe the royal arms of pre-1707 Scotland—that is, Scotland before the Union with England—carved and painted above the arch of the *pend* (covered way).

The **Whithorn Dig and Visitor Centre** explains the significance of what is claimed to be the site of the earliest Christian community in Scotland. The museum includes a collection of early Christian crosses. The dig site itself is beside the shell of the priory. ⊠ *Main St., Whithorn,* ☎ *01988/500508.* ⊡ *£2.70.* ☉ *Apr.–Oct., daily 10:30–5 (last tour 4).*

Lodging

££–£££   🏠 **Corsemalzie House.** This attractive 19th-century mansion is set on 40 acres of peaceful grounds behind the fishing village of Port William, west of Whithorn. Sporting pursuits are the hotel's main draw, with shooting, sea and game fishing, and golf on tap. The restaurant features a Scottish menu with hearty venison stew or steak Auld Alliance (with red-wine sauce), and the public rooms and bedrooms are in keeping with the country-house style of the hotel. ⊠ *Corsemalzie, Port William, Newton Stewart, Wigtownshire DG8 9RL,* ☎ *01988/860254,* FAX *01988/860213. 15 rooms with bath or shower. Golf privileges, fishing. AE, MC, V. Closed late-Jan.–Feb.*

Stranraer

🌕 *34 mi northwest of Whithorn, 89 mi southwest of Glasgow via A77, 133 mi southwest of Edinburgh.*

Stranraer is the main ferry port to Northern Ireland (if you happen to make a purchase in one of its shops, you may wind up with some Irish coins in your change). It is not a very scenic place itself, but nearby is a high point of this region.

★ 🌕 Three miles east of Stranraer, **Castle Kennedy Gardens** surround the shell of the original Castle Kennedy, which was burned out in 1716. The present property owners, the earl and countess of Stair, live on the grounds, at Lochinch Castle, built in 1864 (not open to the public). Pleasure grounds dispersed throughout the property were built by the second earl of Stair in 1733. The earl was a field marshal and used his soldiers to help with the heavy work of constructing banks, ponds, and other major landscape features. When the rhododendrons are in bloom, the effect is kaleidoscopic. There is also a pleasant tearoom. ⊠ *North of A75, 3 mi east of Stranraer,* ☎ *01776/702024.* ⊡ *£3.* ☉ *Apr. (or Easter, if earlier)–Sept., daily 10–5.*

Dining

£   ✕ **Eynhallow Hotel.** A traditional pub with shining brasses, open fire, and peach-and-brown color scheme, the Eynhallow is a good bet for its home-cooked bar lunches (noon–2:30) and bar suppers (6–11). ⊠ *Eynhallow DG9 8SQ,* ☎ *01581/400256. MC, V.*

Portpatrick

8 mi southwest of Stranraer, 97 mi southwest of Glasgow, 143 mi southwest of Edinburgh.

The holiday town of Portpatrick lies across the Rhinns of Galloway from Stranraer. Once an Irish ferry port, Portpatrick's exposed harbor eventually proved too risky for larger vessels. Today the village is the starting point for Scotland's longest official long-distance footpath, the **Southern Upland Way,** which runs a switchback course for 212 mi to Cockburnspath, on the east side of the Borders. Just south of Portpatrick are the lichen-yellow ruins of 16th-century **Dunskey Castle,** accessible by a cliff-top path.

The southern half of the Rhinns of Galloway has a number of interesting places to visit, all easily reached from Portpatrick. Among them is **Ardwell House Gardens,** a pleasant retreat on a domestic scale. ⊠ *Ardwell,* ☎ *01776/860227.* ≊ *£1.50.* ⊘ *Apr.–Sept., daily 10–5.*

If you wish to visit the southern tip of the Rhinns of Galloway, called the **Mull of Galloway,** follow the B7065/B7041 until you run out of land. The cliffs and seascapes here are rugged, and there are a lighthouse and a bird reserve.

★ Spectacular for garden lovers and close to Ardwell are the **Logan Botanic Gardens,** a specialized garden of Edinburgh's **Royal Botanic Garden.** The Logan Gardens feature plants that enjoy the prevailing mild climate, especially tree ferns, cabbage palms, and other southern-hemisphere exotica. ⊠ *Off B7065 at Port Logan,* ☎ *01776/860231.* ≊ *£3.* ⊘ *Mar.–Oct., daily 9:30–6.*

THE BORDERS AND THE SOUTHWEST A TO Z

Arriving and Departing

By Bus

From the south the main bus services use the M6 or A1, with appropriate feeder services into the hinterland; contact **Scottish Citylink** (☎ 0990/505050) or **National Express** (☎ 0990/808080). There are also bus links from Edinburgh and Glasgow. Contact **First Lowland** (☎ 01896/752237) or **Stagecoach Western Scottish** (☎ 01563/525192, 01387/253496, or 01776/704484).

By Car

The main route into both the Borders and Galloway from the south is the M6, which becomes the A74. Or you can take the scenic and leisurely A7 northeastward through Hawick toward Edinburgh or the A75 and other parallel routes westward into Dumfries and Galloway and to the ferry ports of Stranraer and Cairnryan.

There are, however, a number of alternative routes: starting from the east, the A1 brings you from the English city of Newcastle to the border in about an hour. The A1 has the added attraction of Berwick-Upon-Tweed, on the English side of the border. Moving west, the A697, which leaves the A1 beside Alnwick (in England) and crosses the border at Coldstream, is a leisurely back-road option with a view of the countryside. The A68 offers probably the most scenic route to Scotland: after climbing to Carter Bar, it reveals a view of the rolling Border hills and windy skies before dropping into the ancient town of Jedburgh, with its ruined abbey.

By Ferry

P&O European Ferries runs a service from Larne, in Northern Ireland, to Cairnryan several times daily, with a crossing time of one hour. Details are available from P&O at Cairnryan (⊠ Stranraer DG9 8RF, ☎ 0870/242–4666). **Seacat** (☎ 0990/523523) operates a fast-speed catamaran service once a day, which takes only 90 minutes to cross from Belfast to Stranraer.

By Plane
The nearest Scottish airports are at Edinburgh and Glasgow (☞ Chapters 1 and 2).

By Train
The Borders are not well served by rail. You can use services from London Euston, in England, to Glasgow; these trains stop at Carlisle, just south of the border, and some stop at Lockerbie. There are also direct trains from Carlisle to Dumfries, stopping at Gretna Green. On the east coast, which offers a more regular and better service (London King's Cross to Edinburgh), many of the trains stop at Berwick-Upon-Tweed, just south of the border. For more information call the **National Train Enquiry Line** (☎ 0345/484950).

Getting Around

By Bus
Bus services in the area include **Stagecoach Western Scottish** (☎ 01563/525192, 01387/253496, or 01776/704484), which serves towns and villages in Dumfries and Galloway, and **First Lowland** (☎ 01896/752237), which offers the Reiver Rover (£28 weekly, £8 daily) and Waverley Wanderer (£33.50 weekly, £11.50 daily) flexible tickets, which provide considerable savings for travel in the Borders.

By Car
A solid network of rural roads allows you to avoid the A1 in the eastern Borders, as well as the A75, which runs along the Solway coast from east to west, linking Dumfries and Stranraer. Both roads carry heavy traffic, partly because of the poor rail connections.

By Train
There's no such thing as a rail network in the Borders. The **Scottish Borders Rail Link** is an actionable nomenclature: it's actually a bus service linking Hawick, Selkirk, and Galashiels with rail services at Carlisle. In Dumfries and Galloway you can pick up connecting trains from Carlisle to Stranraer, which also has a direct link to Ayr and Glasgow. There is also a service twice daily between Dumfries and Stranraer. (Both the Borders and the Southwest suffered badly in the shortsighted contraction of Britain's rail network in the 1960s.) Contact the **National Train Enquiry Line** (☎ 0345/484950) for further details.

Contacts and Resources

Emergencies
Ambulance, police, or fire: ☎ 999. (No coins are needed for emergency calls from public telephone booths.)

Fishing
Scottish Borders Angling Guide is the best way to find your way around the many Borders waterways. *Fishing in Dumfries and Galloway* covers the southwest. The tourist boards for Dumfries and Galloway and the Borders (☞ Visitor Information, *below*) carry these and other publications (including a comprehensive information pack). In short, finding suitable water in this area is quite easy.

Golf
There are more than 30 courses in Dumfries and Galloway and 19 in the Borders. The Freedom of the Fairways Pass (five-day pass, £75; three-day pass, £50, no play on weekends) allows play on all 19 Borders courses and is available from the Scottish Borders Tourist Board. The Gate-

way to Golf Pass (five-day pass, £95; three-day pass, £65) is accepted by most clubs in Dumfries and Galloway and is available from the Dumfries and Galloway Tourist Board. Both tourist boards (☞ Visitor Information, *below*) supply comprehensive leaflets.

Guided Tours

ORIENTATION

The bus companies mentioned above also run a variety of orientation tours in the area. In addition, tours are run by **Galloway Heritage Tours** (⊠ Rosemount Guest House, The Front, Kippford, ☎ 01556/620214).

SPECIAL-INTEREST

The area is primarily covered through Edinburgh- or Glasgow-based companies (☞ Chapters 1 and 2). **James French** (⊠ French's Garage, Coldingham, ☎ 01890/771283) runs coach tours in the summer. **Ramtrad Holidays** (⊠ 54 Edinburgh Rd., Peebles, ☎ FAX 01721/720845) offers chauffeur-driven tours tailored to customers' requirements, as well as golf and fishing packages.

Late-Night Pharmacies

All towns in the region have at least one pharmacy. Pharmacies are not found in rural areas, where general practitioners often dispense medicines. The police will provide assistance in locating a pharmacist in an emergency.

Visitor Information

Dumfries and Galloway: **Dumfries** (⊠ Whitesands, ☎ 01387/253862, FAX 01387/245555); **Stranraer** (⊠ Harbour St., ☎ 01776/702595, FAX 01776/889156). The Borders: **Jedburgh** (⊠ Murray's Green, ☎ 01835/863435, FAX 01835/864099); **Peebles** (⊠ High St., ☎ 01721/720138, FAX 01721/724401).

Seasonal information centers are at Castle Douglas, Coldstream, Eyemouth, Galashiels, Gatehouse of Fleet, Gretna Green, Hawick, Kelso, Kirkcudbright, Langholm, Melrose, Moffat, Newton Stewart, Sanquhar, and Selkirk.

4 FIFE AND ANGUS

ST. ANDREWS, DUNDEE, AND GLAMIS CASTLE

The sunniest and driest part of Scotland, Fife is famed for the ancient town of St. Andrews, home to the Old Course—but there's much more hereabouts than just a round of *gowf* at the Royal & Ancient: East Neuk villages filled with Dutch-inspired steeples, sandy beaches, and the town that gave us Robinson Crusoe lie beyond. Heading north across the Firth of Tay, Dundee—once famous for "jute, jam, and journalism"—is the gateway to the windswept glens of Angus and marvels like Glamis Castle, one of Scotland's most magnificent castles.

By Gilbert
Summers

Updated by
Beth Ingpen

THE REGIONS OF FIFE AND ANGUS sandwich Scotland's fourth-largest—and often overlooked—city, Dundee. This is typical eastern-seaboard country: open beaches, fishing villages, and breezy cliff-top walkways. Scotland's east coast has only light rainfall throughout the year; northeastern Fife, in particular, may claim the record for the most sunshine and the least rainfall in all Scotland, which all adds to the enjoyment when you're touring the East Neuk (*neuk*, pronounced nyook, is Scots for *corner*) or exploring St. Andrews's nooks and crannies.

"Farewell Scotland, I'm awa' to Fife," cried the fishwife of Newhaven, setting sail for the opposite shore of the Firth of Forth. It was all of 6 mi away, but she expressed what many Lothian people used to feel: that Fife was a foreign place. It proudly styles itself as a "kingdom," and its long history lends some substance to the boast. From earliest times its earls were first among Scottish nobility and crowned her kings. Within its confines many great monasteries were founded, and nearly every village has some remnant of history, which really began here when the Romans went home in the 4th century AD and the Picts—the word derives from the tattoos that adorned this tribe—moved in. For many, however, the most historic event in this region was the birth of golf, which, legend has it, occurred in St. Andrews, an ancient university town with romantic stone houses and seaside ruins. Here, at the Royal & Ancient Club, the ruling body of the game worldwide still has its headquarters.

Not surprisingly, fishing and seafaring have also played a role in the history of the East Neuk coastal region. At an earlier period a large population lived and worked in the small ports and harbors that form a continuous chain round Fife's coasts, which James V once called "a beggar's mantle fringed with gold." Although some fancy it a Scottish equivalent of the Italian Riviera, James V's golden fringe—today a series of waterfront villages darkened by the shrubbery of masts and rigging—is not all that golden in terms of sand or sunshine. You may think the outlook of black rocks and seaweed rather dreary, but the villages have character, with their brownstone or color-washed fronts, their rusty charm, fishy weather vanes, outside stone stairways to upper floors, with no two windows or chimney pots alike, and crude carvings of anchors and lobsters on their lintels—all crowded on steep narrow *wynds* and hugging pint-size harbors that in the golden era supported village fleets of 100 ships apiece.

North, across the Firth of Tay, lies the region of Angus, whose particular charm is its variety: in addition to its seacoast and pleasant Lowland market centers, there's also a hinterland of lonely rounded hills with long glens running into the typical Grampian Highland scenery beyond. One of Angus's interesting features, which it shares with the eastern Lowland edge of Perthshire, is its fruit-growing industry. Seen from roadside or railway, what at first sight appear to be sturdy grapevines on field-length wires turn out to be soft-fruit plants, mainly raspberries. The chief fruit-growing area is Strathmore, the broad vale between the northwesterly Grampian Mountains and the small coastal hills of the Sidlaws behind Dundee. Striking out from this valley—the heart of the Angus region—visitors can make a number of day trips to uplands or seacoast.

Pleasures and Pastimes

Dining

With its affluent population, St. Andrews supports several stylish hotel restaurants. Because it is also a university town and popular tourist destination, there are also many good-value cafés and bistro-style restaurants. Not far away at Peat Inn is a restaurant that many would claim to be one of the very best in Scotland. The coastal communities can also serve up fine seafood, in particular at Anstruther. In some of the West Fife towns, such as Kirkcaldy and Dunfermline, and in Dundee, you will find restaurants serving not only traditional Scottish fare, but also Italian, Indian, and Chinese specialties, in addition to numerous small cafés of all kinds. Bar lunches are becoming the rule in large and small hotels throughout the region, and in seaside places the "carry *oot*" (to go) meal is an old tradition.

CATEGORY	COST*
££££	over £40
£££	£30–£40
££	£15–£30
£	under £15

**per person for a three-course meal, including VAT and excluding drinks and service*

Golf

Every golfer's ambition is to play at St. Andrews, and once you are in Fife, the ambition is easily realized. Five St. Andrews courses are open to visitors (all are part of the St. Andrews Club). There are more than 40 other courses in the region. Most offer golf to the visitor by the round or by the day. Many area hotels offer golfing packages or will arrange a day of golf (☞ Chapter 11). Scotland remains a golfer's paradise; a round on a municipal course costs very little, while most clubs, apart from those pretentious places modeled on the English fashion, demand only comparatively modest greens fees.

Lodging

If you're staying in Fife, the obvious base is St. Andrews, with ample accommodations of all kinds. Other towns also offer a reasonable selection, and you will find good hotels and guest houses at Dunfermline and Kirkcaldy. Along the coastal strip and in the Howe of Fife between Strathmiglo and Cupar, there are some superior country-house hotels, many with their own restaurants.

CATEGORY	COST*
££££	over £140
£££	£110–£140
££	£65–£110
£	under £65

**All prices are for a standard double room, including service, breakfast, and VAT.*

🍃 *following the text of a review is your signal that the property has a Web site, where you will find details and, usually, images; for a link, visit www.fodors.com/urls.*

Exploring Fife and Angus

Fife lies north of the Firth of Forth, stretching far up the Forth Valley (which is west and a little north of Edinburgh), with St. Andrews on its eastern coast. Northwest of Fife, the city of Dundee and its rural hinterland, Angus, stretch still farther north and west toward the foothills of the Grampian Mountains.

Numbers in the text correspond to numbers in the margin and on the Fife Area, St. Andrews, and Angus Area maps.

Great Itineraries

This is not a huge area, so getting around is straightforward. Treat it as a series of excursions off the main north–south artery, the A90/M90, which leads from Edinburgh to Aberdeen. Fife has a pleasant but not spectacular rural hinterland—in fact, it feels a long way from the hills. Angus is different, with a strong sense of a looming massif always to the north. To explore it, take your pick of the Angus glens—especially the Glens Prosen or Clova—or, farthest north, Esk, all delightfully out of the way. They represent probably one of the most overlooked corners of Scotland.

IF YOU HAVE 2 DAYS

Two days allow you to sample the extremes of the area in every sense. Make your way to ☷ **St. Andrews** ①–⑦ to take in this most attractive of Scottish east-coast Lowland towns. Next day travel north of ☷ **Dundee** ⑱ to visit **Kirriemuir** ㉕, a typical Angus town with connections to the character of Peter Pan, and to see **Glamis** ㉗ for its castle—and perhaps to penetrate the hills via the Glens of Angus west of Kirriemuir.

IF YOU HAVE 5–6 DAYS

This allows plenty of time to spend two or three days sampling not just ☷ **St. Andrews** ①–⑦ but also the rest of the East Neuk, the easternmost corner, with its characteristic pantile-roof fishing villages—**Crail** ⑧; Anstruther, with its **Scottish Fisheries Museum** ⑨; **Pittenweem** ⑩; and, just inland, **Kellie Castle** ⑪—all strung along the south-facing coast. Also worth exploring are the inland communities of **Falkland** (its **palace** ⑬ was once a royal hunting lodge); **Cupar** ⑮, close to **Hill of Tarvit House** ⑯; and the **Fife Folk Museum** ⑰, at ☷ **Ceres** (for a real treat, have a meal and stay overnight at the Peat Inn). If you golf, then you could allocate a day on a golf course as well. Likewise, in Angus you could first travel along the breezy coast toward **Arbroath** ㉑ and **Montrose** ㉒, where the sharply contrasting Adam-designed **House of Dun** ㉓ lies within easy reach. Staying overnight near ☷ **Forfar** ㉖ would bring the inland communities of **Kirriemuir** ㉕, **Glamis** ㉗, and **Meigle** ㉘, with its outstanding collection of early medieval sculpture, within easy reach the next day.

When to Tour Fife and Angus

Spring in the Angus glens can be quite captivating, with the high tops still snow covered. Similarly, the moorland colors of autumn are appealing. (In autumn and winter, some hotels in rural Angus get busy with foreign sportsmen intent on marauding the local wildfowl.) However, it has to be said that Fife and Angus are really spring and summer destinations—unless you simply like wandering about, enjoying scenery.

ST. ANDREWS AND THE EAST NEUK VILLAGES

In its western parts, Fife still bears the scars of heavy industry, especially coal mining. Yet these signs are less evident as you move east: northeastern Fife, around the university-and-golf town of St. Andrews, seems to have played no part in the industrial revolution; the residents instead earned a livelihood from the grain fields or from the sea. Fishing has been a major industry, and in the past a string of Fife ports traded across the North Sea. Today the legacy of Dutch-influenced architecture—crow-step gables (the stepped effect on the ends of the roofs) and distinctive town houses, for example—is still plain to see and gives these East Neuk villages a distinctive charm.

St. Andrews is unlike any other Scottish town. Once Scotland's most powerful ecclesiastical center, the seat also of the country's oldest university, and then, much later, the very symbol and spiritual home of golf, the town has a comfortable, well-groomed air, sitting almost smugly apart from the rest of Scotland.

Fife Area

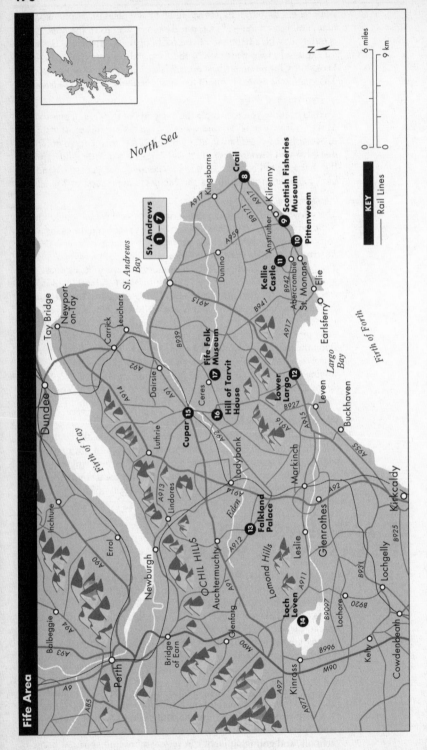

North Sea

St. Andrews Bay

Crail **8**

Kingsbarns

Kilrenny

Scottish Fisheries **9**
Museum

Anstruther

B9171

A917

Pittenweem **10**

A959

Dunino

St. Andrews **1 — 7**

Kellie **11**
Castle

B941

B942

Abercrombie

St. Monans

Elie

A915

Earlsferry

Largo
Bay

A917

Leven

Fife Folk **17**
Museum

Ceres

Lower **12**
Largo

B927

Hill of Tarvit **16**
House

Buckhaven

Cupar **15**

A916

B939

Dairsie

A91

Leuchars

Carrick

Newport-
on-Tay

Tay Bridge

Dundee

Firth of Tay

Inchture

Errol

A90

A913

Luthrie

Lindores

A914

Ladybank

Eden

Markinch

A92

Kinkcaldy

A955

OCHIL HILLS

Newburgh

A913

Bridge
of Earn

Perth

A9

A85

Balbeggie

A94

Glenfarg

Auchtermuchty

A91

A912

Falkland **13**
Palace

Lomond Hills

Leslie

Glenrothes

B931

Lochgelly

B925

A911

Loch
Leven

Loch **14**

Lochore

B9097

B920

Kinross

B996

M90

Kelty

Cowdenbeath

A977

A97

Firth of Forth

N

0 — 6 miles
0 — 9 km

St. Andrews

52 mi northeast of Edinburgh, 83 mi northeast of Glasgow.

It may have a ruined cathedral and a grand university—the oldest in Scotland—but the modern fame of St. Andrews is mainly as the home of golf. Forget that Scottish kings were crowned here, or that John Knox preached here, or that Reformation reformers were burned at the stake here. Thousands come to St. Andrews to play at the Old Course, home of the Royal & Ancient, and to follow in the footsteps of Hagen, Sarazen, Jones, and Hogan. Other visitors will tread the city streets to take in a wide array of historic sights, and, in fact, St. Andrews's layout is pure Middle Ages, with its three main streets—North, Market, and South—converging on the city's earliest religious site, near the cathedral. Like most of the town's ancient monuments, the cathedral ruins are impressive in their desolation—but this is no dusty museum-city. The streets are busy, the shops are stylish, the gray houses sparkle in the sun, and the scene is particularly brightened during the academic year by bicycling students in scarlet gowns.

Local legend has it that St. Andrews was founded by a certain St. Regulus, or Rule, who, acting under divine guidance, carried relics of St. Andrew by sea from Patras in Greece. He was shipwrecked on this Fife headland and founded a church. The holy man's name survives in the

➊ square-shape **St. Rule's Tower,** consecrated in 1126 and the oldest surviving building in St. Andrews. You can enjoy dizzying views of town from the top of the tower, accessed via a steep set of stairs. Near the

➋ tower is the city **cathedral,** today only a ruined, poignant fragment of what was formerly the largest and most magnificent church in Scotland. Work on it began in 1160, and consecration was finally celebrated in 1318, after several setbacks. The cathedral was subsequently damaged by fire and repaired, but finally fell into decay in the 16th century, during the Reformation. Only ruined gables, parts of the nave south wall, and other fragments survive. The on-site museum helps you interpret the remains and gives a sense of what the cathedral must once have been like. ⊠ *Off Pends Rd.,* ☎ *0131/668–8800.* ▭ *£2; combined admission to cathedral and castle (☞ below), £3.75.* ☉ *Apr.–Sept., daily 9:30–6; Oct.–Mar., Mon.–Sat. 9:30–4, Sun. 2–4.*

➌ Directly north of the cathedral on the shore stands **St. Andrews Castle,** which was started at the end of the 13th century. Although now a ruin, the remains include a rare example of a bottle dungeon, cold and gruesome, in which many prisoners spent their last hours. Even more atmospheric is the castle's mine and countermine. The former was a tunnel dug by besieging forces in the 16th century; the latter, a tunnel dug by castle defenders in order to meet and wage battle below ground. You can stoop and crawl into this narrow passageway—an eerie experience, despite the addition of electric light. The visitor center has a good audiovisual presentation on the castle's history. ⊠ *End of North Castle St.,* ☎ *0131/668–8800.* ▭ *£2.50; castle and cathedral, £3.75.* ☉ *Apr.–Sept., daily 9:30–6; Oct.–Mar., Mon.–Sat. 9:30–4, Sun. 2–4.*

➍ The **Royal & Ancient Golf Club of St. Andrews** on The Scores, the ruling house of golf worldwide, is the spiritual home of all who play or follow the game. Its clubhouse on the dunes—a dignified building, more like a town hall than a clubhouse and open to club members only—is adjacent to St. Andrews's famous **Old Course** (☞ Outdoor Activities and Sports, *below*). The town of St. Andrews prospers on golf, golf schools, and golf equipment (the manufacture of golf balls has been a local industry for more than 100 years), and the Old Course is associated with the greatest players of the game.

St. Andrews

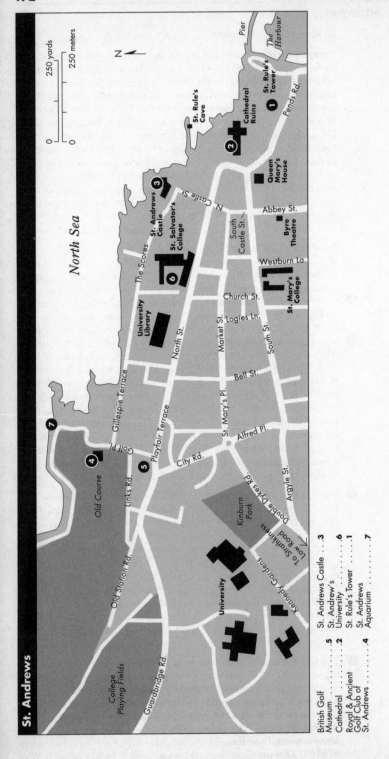

North Sea

St. Rule's Cave

Cathedral Ruins

St. Rule's Tower **1**

Pends Rd.

2

Queen Mary's House

St. Andrews Castle

3

N. Castle St.

Abbey St.

The Scores

St. Salvator's College

South Castle St.

Byre Theatre

6

Westburn La.

University Library

Church St.

St. Mary's College

North St.

Logies Ln.

Market St.

Bell St.

Gillespie Terrace

Playfair Terrace

St. Mary's Pl.

South St.

7

Golf Pl.

City Rd.

Alfred Pl.

Argyle St.

4

5

Links Rd.

Old Course

Old Station Rd.

Kinburn Park

Double Dykes Rd.

To Strathkinness Low Road

Kennedy Gardens

College Playing Fields

Guardbridge Rd.

University

Pier

The Harbour

N

250 yards

250 meters

0

As to the game and its origins on the Royal & Ancient's course, golf was perhaps originally played with a piece of driftwood, a shore pebble, and a convenient rabbit hole on the sandy, coastal turf. It has been argued that golf came to Scotland from Holland, but the historical evidence points to Scotland as the cradle, if not the birthplace, of the game. Citizens of St. Andrews were playing golf on the town links (public land) as far back as the 15th century. Rich golfers, instead of gathering on the common links, formed themselves into clubs by the 18th century. Arguably, the world's first golf club was the Honourable Company of Edinburgh Golfers (founded in Leith in 1744), which is now at Muirfield in East Lothian. The Society of St. Andrews Golfers, founded in 1754, became the Royal & Ancient Golf Club of St. Andrews in 1834.

⑤ Just opposite the Royal & Ancient Golf Club is the **British Golf Museum,** which explores the centuries-old relationship between St. Andrews and golf and displays a variety of golf memorabilia. ⊠ *Bruce Embankment,* ☎ *01334/478880.* ☞ *£3.75.* ⊙ *Mid-Apr.–mid-Oct., daily 9:30–5:30; mid-Oct.–mid-Apr., Thurs.–Mon. 11–3.*

St. Andrews is also the home of Scotland's oldest university. Founded
⑥ in 1411, **St. Andrew's University** now consists of two stately old colleges in the middle of town and some modern buildings on the outskirts. A third, weatherworn college, originally built in 1512, has become a girls' school. The handsome university buildings can be explored on guided walks, sometimes led by students in scarlet gowns. ☎ *01334/462245.* ☞ *£3.60.* ⊙ *Tours: June–Aug., Mon.–Sat. 11 and 2:30 (other times by arrangement).*

☾ ⑦ At the **St. Andrews Aquarium,** sea lions, penguins, and many other forms of marine life inhabit various aquariums and pool gardens designed to simulate their natural habitats. ⊠ *The Scores, West Sands,* ☎ *01334/474786.* ☞ *£4.35.* ⊙ *Daily 10–5.*

Only a few minutes (about 6 mi) northwest of St. Andrews's famous Old Course on the A919, **Leuchars** has a 12th-century church with some of the finest Norman architectural features to be seen anywhere in Scotland. Note in particular the blind arcading (arch shapes on the wall) and the beautifully decorated chancel and apse.

Dining and Lodging

££ ✕ **Balaka.** The handsome gray-stone premises here hide a 1-acre garden of herbs, vegetables, and flowers used in this restaurant's Bangladeshi dishes. Inside, a restrained, dusty pink decor with crisp white tablecloths and vases of roses is the setting in which the Rouf family displays its exceptional cookery prowess. Popular dishes include *Mas Bangla* (marinated Scottish salmon fried in mustard oil with garlic, scallions, and eggplant) and green herb chicken, which uses fresh coriander from the garden. ⊠ *Alexandra Place,* ☎ *01334/474825. AE, MC, V. No lunch Sun.–Thurs.*

££££ ✕⌂ **Rufflets Country House Hotel.** This creeper-covered country house just outside St. Andrews is surrounded by 10 acres of formal and informal gardens. All the rooms are handsomely decorated and comfortable, with the amenities you would expect of a top-class hotel. Dinner is served in the roomy Garden Restaurant, famous for its use of local produce to create memorable Scottish dishes. Recommended are the Tay salmon and the fillet of Aberdeen Angus beef. Lighter and less expensive bar meals are also available at lunch and in the evening. ⊠ *Strathkinness Low Rd., KY16 9TX,* ☎ *01334/472594,* 𝖥𝖠𝖷 *01334/478703. 22 rooms with bath. Restaurant, bar. AE, DC, MC, V.* ☙

£ 🏠 **Aslar Guest House.** This Victorian terraced house is central to shops, golf courses, and historic attractions such as the castle. All rooms are individually decorated—one with a four-poster bed—and have private bathrooms or shower rooms (unusual for B&Bs). ✉ *230 North St., KY16 9AF,* ☎ *01334/473460,* 🖷 *01334/477540. 5 rooms, 4 with bath, 1 with shower. MC, V.* 🐾

£ 🏠 **University of St. Andrews.** For accommodation within walking distance of all attractions, it's hard to better the university for value and convenience. Room sizes—mainly singles—vary from adequate in the new building to happily spacious in the old one. The newer rooms have private bathrooms. ✉ *79 North St., KY16 9AJ,* ☎ *01334/462000,* 🖷 *01334/462500. 153 rooms, 72 with shower. Restaurant, bar, lounge, coin laundry. MC, V. Closed early Sept.–May.* 🐾

Nightlife and the Arts

PUBS

Chariots (✉ The Scores), inside the Scores Hotel, is popular with locals in their thirties and forties.

THEATER

Byre Theatre (✉ Abbey St., ☎ 01334/476288) has a resident repertory company. A brand-new theater will be ready to open in 2001.

Outdoor Activities and Sports

GOLF

The following five 18-hole and one 9-hole St. Andrews courses (all are part of the St. Andrews Links Trust) are open to visitors. For details of availability—there is usually a waiting list which varies according to the time of year—contact the **Reservations Department** (✉ Links Management Committee, Pilmour Cottage, St. Andrews KY16 9SF, ☎ 01334/466666, 🖷 01334/477036), or phone the **Golf Line** (☎ 01334/477685) for an expert answer to all your golfing queries.

Eden Course (1914) 18 holes, 6,112 yards, par 70. **Jubilee Course** (1897) 18 holes, 6,805 yards, par 70. **New Course** (1895) 18 holes, 6,604 yards, par 71. **Old Course** (15th century) 18 holes, 6,566 yards, par 72, handicap certificate required year-round. **Strathyrum Course** (1993) 18 holes, 5,094 yards, par 69. **Balgove Course** 9 holes, 1,530 yards, par 60.

Shopping

Renton Oriental Rugs (✉ 72 South St., ☎ 01334/476334) is the best place in the region, if not in all Scotland, for Oriental rugs and carpets of all colors, patterns, and sizes—many of them antique. **The St. Andrews Pottery Shop** (✉ Church Sq. between South St. and Market St., ☎ 01334/477744) sells decorative and domestic stoneware, porcelain, ceramics, and enamel jewelry. **Bonkers** (✉ 80 Market St., ☎ 01334/473919) has a huge selection of clocks, books, cards, pottery, and gift items. **St. Andrews Fine Art** (✉ 84A Market St., ☎ 01334/474080) is the place to go for Scottish paintings from 1800 to the present (oils, watercolors, drawings, and prints).

Crail

★ ⑧ *10 mi south of St. Andrews via A917.*

The oldest, most palatial by local standards, and most aristocratic of East Neuk burghs, where fish merchants retired and built cottages, Crail is one of numerous fishing communities along the Fife coast. The town landmark is a picturesque Dutch-influenced town house, or *tolbooth,* which contains the oldest bell in Fife, cast in Holland in 1520. Full details on the heritage and former trading links of this tiny port can be found in the **Crail Museum and Heritage Center.** As you head into the East Neuk from

Crail, look about for tolbooths, market crosses, and merchant houses and their little *doocots* (dovecotes, where pigeons were kept for winter meat)—typical picturesque touches of this region. ✉ *62 Marketgate,* ☎ *01333/ 450869.* 🎟 *Free.* ⊘ *Easter wk and June–Sept., Mon.–Sat. 10–1 and 2– 5, Sun. 2–5; after Easter wk–end of May, weekends and holidays 2–5.*

Anstruther

4 mi southwest of Crail.

★ ❾ Locally called Anster, Anstruther has a picturesque waterfront (larger than Crail's), with a few shops brightly festooned with children's pails and shovels as a gesture to seaside vacationers. Facing Anstruther harbor is the **Scottish Fisheries Museum,** housed in a colorful cluster of buildings, the earliest of which dates from the 16th century. This museum illustrates the difficult life of Scottish fishermen, past and present, through documents, artifacts, ship models, paintings, and tableaux. (These displays, complete with the reek of tarred rope and net, have been known to induce nostalgic tears in not a few old deckhands.) There are also floating exhibits at the quayside. ✉ *Anstruther harbor,* ☎ *01333/310628.* 🎟 *£3.50.* ⊘ *Apr.–Oct., Mon.–Sat. 10–5:30, Sun. 11–5; Nov.–Mar., Mon.–Sat. 10–4:30, Sun. noon–4:30 (last admission 45 mins before closing).*

Dining

££ ★ **✕ The Cellar.** Specializing in fish but offering a selection of Scottish beef and lamb as well, the Cellar is devoted to serving top-quality ingredients cooked simply in modern Scottish style, preserving all the natural flavor. The crayfish-and-mussel bisque is famous, and the wine list reflects high standards. Entered through a small courtyard, the restaurant is charmingly furnished in an unpretentious, old-fashioned style. It is popular with the locals, but its fame is widespread. ✉ *24 E. Green,* ☎ *01333/310378. AE, DC, MC, V.*

Nightlife and the Arts

The **Dreel Tavern** (✉ 16 High St., ☎ 01333/310727) is a 16th-century coaching inn famous for its hand-drawn ales.

Outdoor Activities and Sports

The back roads of Fife make pleasant biking terrain. Bicycles can be rented from **East Neuk Outdoors** (✉ Cellardyke Park, ☎ 01333/ 311929), which also has archery, rappelling, and canoeing equipment and offers instruction.

Pittenweem

❿ *1½ mi southwest of Anstruther.*

The working harbor at Pittenweem is backed by many examples of East Neuk architecture. Look for the crow-step gables, the white *harling* (Scots for roughcasting, the rough mortar finish on walls), and the red pantiles (S-shape in profile). The *weem* part of the town's name comes from the Gaelic *uaime,* or cave. This town's particular cave is **St. Fillan's Cave,** which contains the shrine of St. Fillan, a 6th-century hermit who lived inside it. It's up a close (alleyway) behind the waterfront. ✉ *Cove Wynd, near harbor,* ☎ *01333/311495 (Gingerbread Horse Craft Shop holds the key).* 🎟 *50p.* ⊘ *Mon.–Tues. and Thurs.–Sat. 10–5, Sun. noon–5.*

⓫ For a break from this nautical atmosphere, follow B942 inland to **Kellie Castle.** Dating from the 16th and 17th centuries and restored in Victorian times, the castle stands among the grain fields and woodlands of northeastern Fife. The castle is surrounded by 4 acres of pretty gardens. ✉ *B9171, 3 mi northwest of Pittenweem,* ☎ *01333/720271.* 🎟 *£1; combined ticket to castle and gardens, £4.* ⊘ *Castle: Easter and*

May–Sept., daily 1:30–5:30; Oct., weekends 1:30–5:30 (last admission 4:45); garden and grounds: daily 9:30–sunset.

Lower Largo

⑫ *10 mi west of Pittenweem.*

The main claim to fame of Lower Largo is that it was the birthplace of Alexander Selkirk (1676–1721), the Scottish sailor who was the inspiration for Daniel Defoe's (1660–1731) *Robinson Crusoe* (1719). Once a juvenile delinquent, he grew up to terrorize the region and then departed to sail the sea. In 1704, having quarreled with his captain, Selkirk was put ashore on the isle of Juan Fernandez off the coast of Chile. Four years later a British privateer picked him up; his rescuers found him dressed in goatskins and surrounded by tame goats. Piratical adventures on the way home earned him a fortune, and he returned to Largo so richly dressed his mother didn't recognize him. His story inspired Defoe, and his statue can be seen above the doorway of the house on Main Street where he was born.

Shopping

At nearby Upper Largo, in a converted barn, **Scotland's Larder** (✉ Upper Largo, ☎ 01333/360414) is a shop (and restaurant) that sells a huge assortment of Scottish preserves, baked goods, and seasonal produce—anything from shortbread to smoked salmon, Dundee cakes to oysters. It also offers tastings, talks, and cooking demonstrations, all of which show off the savory foods of Scotland.

Falkland

★ *14 mi northwest of Lower Largo.*

One of the loveliest communities in all Fife, Falkland is a royal burgh of twisting streets and crooked stone houses. The town is dominated ★ **⑬** by **Falkland Palace,** a former hunting lodge of the Stuart monarchs and one of the earliest examples in Britain of the French Renaissance style. Overlooking the main street is the palace's most impressive feature—the range of walls and chambers on its south side, all rich with Renaissance buttresses and stone medallions, built for King James V (1512–42) in the 1530s by French masons. He died here, and the palace was a favorite resort of his daughter, Mary, Queen of Scots (1542–87). Behind the palace are gardens that contain a most unusual survivor: a royal tennis court (not at all like its modern counterpart) built in 1539 and still in use, although James's zoo of lions and performing seals has vanished. In the beautiful gardens, overlooked by the palace turret windows, you may easily imagine yourself back at the solemn hour when James on his deathbed pronounced the doom of the house of Stuart: "It cam' wi' a lass and it'll gang wi a lass." ✉ *Falkland,* ☎ *01337/857397.* 🎫 *£5; gardens only, £2.50.* ⊙ *Easter, May, and Sept.–Oct., Mon.–Sat. 11–5:30, Sun. 1:30–5:30; June–Aug., Mon.–Sat 10–5:30, Sun. 1:30–5:30 (last admission to palace 4:30, to garden 5).*

Loch Leven

⑭ *10 mi southwest of Falkland via A911.*

Scotland's largest Lowland loch, Loch Leven is famed for its fighting trout. The area is also noted for its bird life, particularly its wintering wildfowl. Mary, Queen of Scots, was forced to sign the deed of abdication in her island prison in the loch. On the southern shore overlooking the loch, **Vane Farm Nature Reserve,** a visitor center run by the Royal Society for the Protection of Birds, provides information about

Loch Leven's ecology. ✉ *Vane Farm, Rte. B9097, just off M90 and B996,* ☎ *01577/862355.* 🎫 *£3.* ⊙ *Apr.–Dec., daily 10–5; Jan.–Mar., daily 10–4.*

Cupar

🟊 *21 mi northwest of Loch Leven via M90 and A91.*

🟊 Cupar is a busy market town with a variety of shops. On rising ground near the town is the National Trust for Scotland's **Hill of Tarvit House.** A 17th-century mansion, the house was altered in the high-Edwardian style in the late 1890s and early 1900s by the Scottish architect Sir Robert Lorimer (1864–1929). Inside the house are fine collections of antique furniture, Chinese porcelain, bronzes, tapestries, and Dutch paintings. There is also a tearoom. ✉ *2 mi south of Cupar off A916,* ☎ *01334/ 653127.* 🎫 *£4; gardens only, £1.* ⊙ *House: Easter, May–June, and Sept., daily 1:30–5:30; July–Aug., daily 11–5:30; Oct., weekends 1:30–5:30 (last admission 4:45); tearoom: 11–5:30; garden and grounds: Apr.– Sept., daily 9:30–9; Oct.–Mar., daily 9:30–4:30.*

Just outside Cupar, at the **Scottish Deer Centre,** red deer can be seen at close quarters on ranger-guided tours. There are also nature trails, a winery, falconry displays, an adventure playground (a wood and tire fortress not suited for young children), five shops, and a coffee bar. ✉ *A91, near Rankelour Farm,* ☎ *01337/810391.* 🎫 *£3.95.* ⊙ *Easter– Oct., daily 10–6; Nov.–Easter, daily 10–5.*

OFF THE
BEATEN PATH

DAIRSIE BRIDGE – A few minutes east of Cupar at Dairsie, an unclassified road goes off to the right from the A91 and soon runs by the River Eden. The Dairsie Bridge, which goes over the river, is 450 years old and has three arches. Above the trees rises the spire of Dairsie Church, dating from the 17th century, and the stark ruin of Dairsie Castle, often overlooked, stands gloomily over the river nearby. With wild-rose hedges, grazing cattle, and pheasants calling from the woody thickets, this is the very essence of rural Lowland Fife, yet it's only about 15 minutes from the Old Course.

Outdoor Activities and Sports
Cupar Sports Centre (✉ Carselogie Rd., ☎ 01334/412290) has a swimming pool, sports hall, fitness rooms, squash, and steam bath.

Shopping
Margaret Urquhart (✉ 13–17 Lady Wynd, ☎ 01334/652205) attracts customers from as far away as Edinburgh and Glasgow and stocks a wide range of British and international designer-clothing labels.

Ceres

3 mi southeast of Cupar via A916 and B939, 9 mi southwest of St. Andrews.

🟊 To learn more about the history and culture of rural Fife, visit the **Fife Folk Museum** at Ceres. The life of local rural communities is reflected in artifacts and documents, all housed in suitably authentic buildings that include a former weigh house and adjoining weavers' cottages. ✉ *Town center,* ☎ *01334/828180.* 🎫 *£2.50.* ⊙ *Easter and May–early Oct., daily 2–5.*

Dining and Lodging
££££ ✕🏨 **Peat Inn.** This popular inn and modern Scottish-style eatery is best
★ known for its outstanding restaurant, generally considered one of the finest in Scotland. Mouthwatering entrées, such as herb salad with prawns, scallops, roast peppers, and olives, or medallions of monkfish and lobster with artichoke hearts and mushrooms in a lobster sauce, jus-

tify the high prices. Of course, book well in advance. In a detached building there are eight comfortable suites. ✉ *Jct. B940 and B941, 6 mi southwest of St. Andrews, KY15 5LH,* ☎ *01334/840206,* FAX *01334/840530. 8 suites. Restaurant, bar. AE, DC, MC, V. Closed Sun. and Mon.*

DUNDEE AND ANGUS

The industrial city of Dundee, famed historically for its economic reliance on "jute, jam, and journalism," contrasts dramatically with the farmlands and glens of its rural hinterland and the coastal links northward. Peaceful back roads in this area are uncluttered; the main road from Perth/Dundee to Aberdeen—the A90—requires special care, with its mix of fast cars, lorries, and unexpectedly slow farm traffic.

Dundee

⑱ *14 mi northwest of St. Andrews, 58 mi north of Edinburgh, 79 mi northeast of Glasgow.*

Modern highways now enter Dundee, which is more than many guidebooks used to do, for it was once a center of industry, not sightseeing. Dundee's urban renewal program—its determination to shake off its grimy industrial past—was motivated in part by the arrival of the **RRS (Royal Research Ship)** *Discovery,* the vessel used by Captain Robert Scott (1868–1912) on his polar explorations. The steamer was originally built and launched in Dundee; now it's a permanent tourist exhibit. An onboard exhibition allows visitors to sample life as it was aboard the intrepid *Discovery,* while the *Polarama* exhibition lets you experience life in Antarctica hands-on and heads-in—feel the temperature and the wind chill as if you were there! ✉ *Discovery Point, Discovery Quay,* ☎ *01382/201245.* ✆ *£5.* ☉ *Apr.–Oct., Mon.–Sat. 10–5, Sun. 11–5; Nov.–Mar., Mon.–Sat. 10–4, Sun. 11–4.*

At Victoria Dock, the frigate **Unicorn**, a 46-gun wooden warship, lies berthed. The *Unicorn* has the distinction of being the oldest British-built warship afloat (it is also the fourth oldest in the world), having been launched at Chatham, England, in 1824. On board, you can clamber right down into the hold, or discuss the models and displays about the Royal navy's history with the enthusiastic staff. ✉ *Victoria Dock (just east of Tay Rd. bridge),* ☎ *01382/200900 or 01382/200893.* ✆ *£3.50.* ☉ *Mid-Mar.–Oct., daily 10–5; Nov.–mid-Mar., weekdays 10–4 (but best to call ahead in winter; last admission 30 mins before closing).*

On dry land, in a former jute mill, the **Verdant Works** houses a multifaceted exhibition on the story of jute and Dundee's historical involvement in the jute trade. Restored machinery, audiovisuals, and tableaux all re-create vividly the hard, noisy life of the jute worker. ✉ *W. Hendersons Wynd,* ☎ *01382/225282.* ✆ *£5.* ☉ *Apr.–Oct., Mon.– Sat. 10–5, Sun. 11–5; Nov.–Mar., Mon.–Sat. 10–4, Sun. 11–4.*

Dundee's principal museum and art gallery is the **McManus Galleries,** which has displays on a range of subjects, including local history, trade, and industry. ✉ *Albert Sq.,* ☎ *01382/432084.* ✆ *Free.* ☉ *Mon.–Wed. and Fri.–Sat. 10–5, Thurs. 10–7, Sun. 12:30–4.*

The city's most exciting new artistic venue, the **Dundee Contemporary Arts** opened in March 1999 in a superbly innovative building designed by architect Richard Murphy. Its galleries specialize in the best works of both Scottish and international artists. Creative facilities include a print studio and a visual research center linked to the University of Dundee; the presence of working artists encourages many "meet the artist" events year-round. There are also two cinemas and a café. ✉ *152*

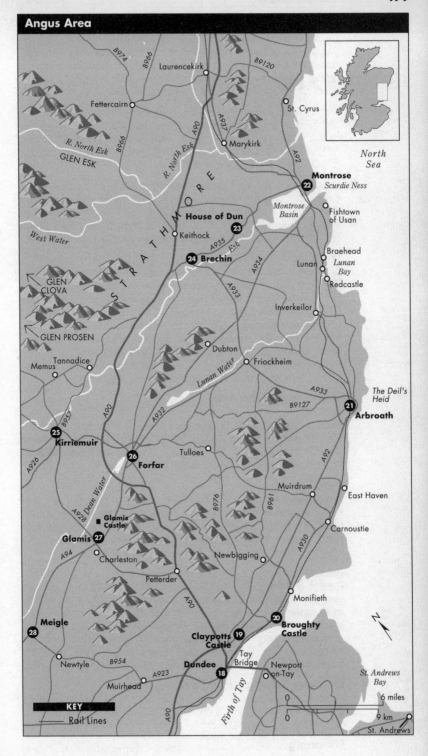

Angus Area

Nethergate, ☎ *01382/432290.* 🎫 *Free.* ⊘ *Tues.–Sat. 10:30–midnight, Sun. 10:30 AM–11 PM (gallery and print studio hrs are shorter; call first).*

The **University Botanic Gardens** are a well-landscaped collection of native and exotic plants. Also on the premises are tropical and temperate greenhouses and a visitor center. ⊠ *Riverside Dr.,* ☎ *01382/566939.* 🎫 *£1.50.* ⊘ *Mar.–Oct., daily 10–4:30; Nov.–Feb., daily 10–3:30.*

In the eastern suburbs of Dundee, away from the surviving Victorian **⑲** architecture of the city center, are two castles of interest. **Claypotts Castle** is a well-preserved 16th-century tower house laid out in a Z plan. ⊠ *South of A92 (3 mi east of city center),* ☎ *0131/668–8800.* 🎫 *£1.50.* ⊘ *July–Sept., weekends 9:30–6:30.*

⑳ Built to guard the Tay estuary, **Broughty Castle** is now a museum focusing on fishing, ferries, and the history of the town's whaling industry. There is also a display of arms and armor. ⊠ *Broughty Ferry (4 mi east of city center),* ☎ *01382/436916.* 🎫 *Free.* ⊘ *Apr.–Sept., Mon.– Sat. 11–5, Sun. 12:30–4; Oct.–Mar., Tues.–Sat. 11–5, Sun. 12:30–4.*

Lodging

££££ 🏨 **Kinnaird.** A luxurious country house set in extensive grounds above the Tay Valley northwest of Dundee, Kinnaird has elegant, individually decorated bedrooms with king-size beds and antique furniture. Reception rooms welcome you with open fires and fresh flowers. Two dining rooms offering imaginative Scottish cuisine round out the memorable experience. The management does not allow families with children younger than 12. ⊠ *Kinnaird Estate, PH8 0LB,* ☎ *01796/ 482440,* FAX *01796/482289. 9 rooms with bath and shower. 2 restaurants, tennis court, bowling, croquet, fishing. MC, V.* ✍

Nightlife and the Arts

DISCOS

Dundee has several discos: **Enigma** (⊠ 4–6 S. Ward Rd., ☎ 01382/ 200066), **Fat Sam's Disco** (⊠ 31 S. Ward Rd., ☎ 01382/228181), **Mardi Gras** (⊠ 21 S. Ward Rd., ☎ 01382/205551), and **Oasis Night Club** (⊠ St. Andrews La., ☎ 01382/221061).

MUSIC

Bonar Hall (⊠ Park Pl., ☎ 01382/345466) hosts classical, jazz, and rock concerts, as well as chamber music. **Caird Hall** (⊠ City Sq., ☎ 01382/434940) is one of Scotland's finest concert halls, staging a wide range of music. **West Port Bar** (⊠ Henderson's Wynd, ☎ 01382/ 200993) offers folk music on Mondays.

THEATER

Dundee Repertory Theatre (⊠ Tay Sq., ☎ 01382/223530) is in an award-winning complex that includes an exhibition gallery and is home to a resident theater group as well as a dance company. Both offer diverse programs. **Little Theatre** (⊠ Victoria Rd., ☎ 01382/225835) presents a wide variety of performances, especially modern theatrical works by local and visiting groups. **Whitehall Theatre** (⊠ Bellfield St., ☎ 01382/ 322684) offers a variety of musical entertainment, including light opera.

Outdoor Activities and Sports

Dundee Olympia Leisure Centre (⊠ Earl Grey Pl., ☎ 01382/434888) has four swimming pools, a diving pool, sauna, water slides, exercise equipment, and a restaurant.

Shopping

COFFEE AND TEA

J. Allan Braithwaite (⊠ 6 Castle St., ☎ 01382/322693) offers 13 freshly roasted coffees and more than 30 blended teas, including mango and apricot. (Remember that such specialty teas can usually be taken home without import restriction if you purchase them as gifts.)

SHOPPING MALL

The modern covered shopping mall in Dundee, the **Wellgate Shopping Centre** (⊠ Off Panmure St., ☎ 01382/225454), is the place to visit if you're looking for the major retail chains.

Arbroath

㉑ *15 mi north of Dundee via A92.*

You'll find traditional boatbuilding in the holiday resort and fishing town of Arbroath. It also has several small curers and processors, with shops offering the town's most famous delicacy, "Arbroath smokies"—whole haddock gutted and lightly smoked.

Arbroath Abbey, founded in 1178, in the town center, is unmistakable and seems to straddle whole streets, as if the town were simply ignoring the red-stone ruin in its midst. Surviving today are remains of the church, as well as one of the most complete examples in existence of an abbot's residence. From here in 1320 a passionate plea was sent by King Robert the Bruce (1274–1329) and the Scottish Church to Pope John XXII (circa 1245–1334) in far-off Rome. The pope had until then sided with the English kings, who adamantly refused to acknowledge Scottish independence. The Declaration of Arbroath stated firmly, "For as long as but a hundred of us remain alive, never will we on any conditions be brought under English rule. It is in truth not for glory, nor riches, nor honours that we are fighting, but for freedom—for that alone, which no honest man gives up but with life itself." Some historians describe this plea (originally drafted in Latin) as the single most important document in Scottish history. The pope advised English king Edward II (1284–1327) to make peace, but warfare was to break out along the border from time to time for the next 200 years. ⊠ *Arbroath town center,* ☎ *0131/668–8800.* 🎟 *£2.* ⊙ *Apr.–Sept., daily 9:30–6; Oct.–Mar., Mon.–Sat. 9:30–4, Sun. 2–4.*

Arbroath was the shore base for the construction of the Bell Rock lighthouse on a treacherous, barely exposed offshore rock in the early 19th century. A signal tower was built to facilitate communication between the mainland and the builders working offshore. In the tower now is the **Signal Tower Museum,** which tells the story of the lighthouse, built by Robert Stevenson (1772–1850) in 1811. (The name Stevenson is strongly associated with the building of lighthouses throughout Scotland, though the most famous son of that family is remembered for another talent. In fact, Robert Louis Stevenson [1850–94] gravely disappointed his family by choosing to become a writer instead of an engineer.) The museum also houses a collection of items related to the history of the town, its folk life, and the local fishing industry. ⊠ *Ladyloan (west of harbor),* ☎ *01241/875598.* 🎟 *Free.* ⊙ *Sept.–June, Mon.–Sat. 10–5; July–Aug., Mon.–Sat. 10–5, Sun. 2–5.*

Nightlife and the Arts

For a good pint, seek out the **Foundry Bar** (⊠ E. Mary St., ☎ 01241/872524), a spartan bar frequented by locals and enlivened by impromptu music sessions on Wednesdays and Fridays—customers often bring along their fiddles and accordions, and all join in.

Montrose

 14 mi north of Arbroath via A92.

A handsome, unpretentious town with a museum and a selection of shops, Montrose is also noted for its beach. Behind Montrose the

River Esk forms a wide estuary known as the Montrose Basin. The **Scottish Wildlife Trust** (✉ Montrose Basin, ☎ 01674/676336) operates a nature reserve here, with a good number of geese, ducks, and swans.

★ ㉓   The National Trust for Scotland's leading attraction in this area is the **House of Dun,** which overlooks the Montrose Basin. This 1730s mansion, built by architect William Adam (1689–1748), is particularly noted for its ornate plasterwork. ✉ *A935 (4 mi west of Montrose),* ☎ *01674/810264.* ✇ *House and garden, £4; garden only, £1.* ☉ *House: Easter and May–Sept., daily 1:30–5:30; Oct., weekends 1:30–5:30 (last admission 5); restaurant: 11–closing; garden and grounds: daily 9:30–sunset.*

Brechin

㉔   *10 mi southwest of Montrose.*

The small market town of Brechin, in Strathmore, has a cathedral that was founded about 1200 and contains an interesting selection of antiquities. The town's 10th-century **Round Tower** is one of only two on mainland Scotland (they are more frequently found in Ireland). It was originally built for the local Culdee monks.

Nightlife and the Arts

Flicks (✉ 79–81 High St., ☎ 01356/624313) has a mix of live bands and DJs and attracts young people (who must be at least 18) from a wide area.

En Route   You can rejoin the hurly-burly of the A90 for the return journey south; the more pleasant route, however, leads southwesterly on minor roads (there are several options) that go along the face of the Grampians, following the fault line that here separates Highland and Lowland. The **Glens of Angus** extend north from various points on Route A90. Known individually as the glens of Isla, Prosen, Clova, and Esk, these long valleys run into the high hills of the Grampians and offer a choice of clearly marked walking routes (those in Glen Clova are especially appealing).

Kirriemuir

㉕   *15 mi southeast of Brechin.*

Kirriemuir stands at the heart of Angus's red-sandstone countryside and was the birthplace of the writer and dramatist Sir James Barrie (1860–1937), best known abroad as the author of *Peter Pan.* **Barrie's birthplace,** now in the care of the National Trust for Scotland, has upper floors furnished as they might have been in Barrie's time, with manuscripts and personal mementos displayed. The outside washhouse is said to have been Barrie's first theater. Next door, at 11 Brechin Road, is an exhibition called *The Genius of J. M. Barrie,* which gives literary and theatrical information on the author. ✉ *9 Brechin Rd.,* ☎ *01575/572646 or 01575/572353.* ✇ *£2.50.* ☉ *Apr.–Sept., Mon.–Sat. 11–5:30, Sun. 1:30–5:30; Oct., Sat. 11–5:30, Sun. 1:30–5:30 (last admission 5).*

Dining

£   ✕ **Drovers Inn.** Set in the heart of the Angus farmlands, the Drovers
★   is a rare find in Scotland, with more the feeling of an English country pub rather than a Scottish inn. Plain but friendly surroundings, decorated with old farm implements and historic photographs, are the setting for simple bar food, homemade pies, and nourishing soups, as well as a restaurant serving a Scottish menu of venison, *cloutie* (fruit pudding boiled or steamed in a cloth) dumplings, and other delights. It's popular with locals; on weekends it's best to make reservations, even for bar meals. ✉ *Memus, near Kirriemuir,* ☎ *01307/860322. MC, V.*

Forfar

㉖ *7 mi east of Kirriemuir.*

Forfar goes about its business of being the center of a farming hinterland without being preoccupied with tourism. This means it is an everyday, friendly, and pleasant-enough Scottish town, bypassed by the A90 on its way north.

Dining and Lodging

££ ✕▣ **Royal Hotel.** In the center of Forfar, this former coaching inn has been fully modernized and is a welcoming base for exploring or golfing. Bedrooms are well equipped, though some in the most modern part of the hotel are rather small. All are decorated in a green-and-peach color scheme, with stained-wood finishes and floral fabrics. The public rooms have retained their 19th-century charm. The leisure complex has a pool, gym, and roof garden. The restaurant turns out well-cooked standard international fare—fish-and-chips, lasagna—served by a friendly staff. ⊠ *Castle St., DD8 3AE,* ☎ ‌FAX‌ *01307/462691. 19 rooms with bath or shower. Restaurant, indoor pool, sauna, exercise room. AE, DC, MC, V.*

£ ▣ **Redroofs.** This former cottage hospital, now a hospitable private
★ home, offers superb bed-and-breakfast accommodations in spacious surroundings set among trees. Guests can also use a characterful sitting room decorated with curios collected by the owners on their travels. Evening meals can be provided by prior arrangement. ⊠ *Balgavies, DD8 2UE,* ☎ ‌FAX‌ *01307/830268. 3 rooms with shower. No credit cards.*

Glamis

★ **㉗** *5 mi southwest of Forfar, 6 mi south of Kirriemuir via A928.*

Set in pleasantly rolling countryside is the village of Glamis (pronounced Glahms), which features a village green, a line of cottages, a folk museum, and Glamis Castle. The latter is the second most visited residence in Scotland, after Balmoral Castle. The **Angus Folk Museum** is made up of a row of 19th-century cottages with unusual stone-slab roofs; exhibits focus on the crafts and tools of domestic and agricultural life in the region during the past 200 years. ⊠ *Off A94,* ☎ *01307/840288.* ▦ *£2.50.* ◷ *Apr.–June and Sept., daily 11–5; July–Aug., daily 10–5; Oct., weekends 11–5 (last admission 4:30).*

One of Scotland's best-known and most spectacularly beautiful cas-
★ tles, **Glamis Castle** connects Britain's royalty through 10 centuries, from Macbeth ("thane of Glamis") to the present Queen's sister, Princess Margaret, who was born there in 1930—the first royal princess born in Scotland in 300 years—because the castle was the ancestral home of her mother, the current Queen Mother. The property of the earls of Strathmore and Kinghorne since 1372, the castle was largely reconstructed in the late 17th century; the original keep, which is much older, is still intact. One of the most famous rooms in the castle is Duncan's Hall, the legendary setting for Shakespeare's *Macbeth*. Guided tours offer visitors a look at fine collections of china, tapestries, and furniture. Other visitor facilities include shops, a produce stall, and a licensed restaurant. ⊠ *A94, 1 mi north of Glamis,* ☎ *01307/840393.* ▦ *Castle and grounds, £6; grounds only, £3.* ◷ *Apr.–June and Sept.–Oct., daily 10:30–5:30; July–Aug. (last tour 4:45), daily 10–5:30 (last tour 4:45); early Nov., daily 10:30–4 (last tour 3:15).*

Meigle

 7 mi southwest of Glamis, 15 mi west of Dundee.

The **local museum** at Meigle, in the wide swath of Strathmore, has a magnificent collection of some 25 sculptured monuments from the Celtic Christian period (8th to 10th centuries), nearly all of which were found in or around the local churchyard. This is one of the most notable collections of medieval work in Western Europe. ⊠ *A94,* ☎ *0131/ 668-8800.* 🖾 *£1.80.* ☉ *Apr.–Sept., daily 9:30–6.*

FIFE AND ANGUS A TO Z

Arriving and Departing

By Bus

From Edinburgh's St. Andrew Square bus station and Glasgow's Buchanan Street bus station, services run into Fife and Angus. There is hourly service to Dundee from both Glasgow and Edinburgh, operated by **Scottish Citylink** (☎ 0990/505050). **Stagecoach Fife Buses** (☎ 01592/261461) serves Fife and St. Andrews.

By Car

The M90 motorway from Edinburgh takes you to within a half hour of St. Andrews and Dundee. Travelers coming from Fife can use the A91 and the A914 and then cross the Tay Bridge to reach Dundee, though the quickest way is to use the M90/A90. Travel time from Edinburgh to Dundee is about one hour, from Edinburgh to St. Andrews, 1½ hours.

By Plane

Glasgow Airport (☞ Chapter 2), 50 mi west of Edinburgh, is now a major point of entry for international flights. Passengers landing in Glasgow have easy access to Edinburgh and Fife and Angus. **Edinburgh Airport** (☞ Chapter 1), 7 mi west of downtown Edinburgh, offers connections throughout the United Kingdom, as well as with a number of cities on the Continent.

By Train

ScotRail stops at Kirkcaldy, Markinch (for Glenrothes), Cupar, Leuchars (for St. Andrews), Dundee, Arbroath, and Montrose. For details of the various services, call the **National Train Enquiry Line** (☎ 0345/484950).

Getting Around

By Bus

A local network provides service from St. Andrews and Dundee to many of the smaller towns throughout Fife and Dundee. The fare for the Kirkcaldy–St. Andrews run is £3.95; St. Andrews–Dundee, £2.40; Perth–Montrose, £6.80. For information about routes and fares call **Stagecoach Fife Buses** (☎ 01592/261461), **Scottish Citylink** (☎ 0990/505050), or **Strathtay Scottish** (☎ 01382/228345).

By Car

Fife is an easy area to get around and presents no major obstacles. Most of the roads are quiet and uncongested. The most interesting sights are in the east, which is served by a network of cross-country roads. Angus is likewise an easy region to explore because it's serviced by a fast main road—the A90—which travels through the middle of the Strathmore valley and then on to Aberdeen; another, gentler road—the A92—that runs to the east near the coast; and a network of rural roads between the Grampians and Route A90.

By Train
For the main towns with stations in this area, *see* Arriving and Departing, *above*.

Contacts and Resources

Car Rentals
Arnold Clark (✉ E. Dock St., Dundee, ☎ 01382/225382). **Avis** (c/o DIS, ✉ Old Glamis Rd., Dundee, ☎ 01382/832264). **Hertz** (✉ 18 Marketgate, Dundee, ☎ 01382/223711).

Doctors and Dentists
Consult your hotel, a tourist information center, or the yellow pages of the telephone directory for listings of local doctors and dentists. Late-night pharmacies are not found outside the larger cities. In St. Andrews, Dundee, and other larger centers, pharmacies use a rotating system for off-hours and Sunday prescription service.

Emergencies
Ambulance, fire, police: ☎ 999. (No coins are needed for emergency calls made from public phone booths.)

Guided Tours

ORIENTATION

Travel Greyhound (✉ Commercial St., Dundee, ☎ 01382/340006 or 01382/340007) offers a variety of general orientation tours of the main cities and the region from late July to early August. **Fisher Tours** (✉ West Port, Dundee, ☎ 01382/227290) has tours all year both within and outside the region; one of their most popular is the "Lochs and Glens" tour.

SPECIAL-INTEREST

Links Golf Tours (✉ 7 Pilmour Links, St. Andrews, ☎ 01334/478639, FAX 01334/474086) offers tours tailored to individual requirements.

Visitor Information
Arbroath (✉ Market Pl., ☎ 01241/872609). **Dundee** (✉ 7–21 Castle St., ☎ 01382/527527, ✍). **Kirkcaldy** (✉ 19 Whytescauseway, ☎ 01592/267775). **St. Andrews** (✉ 70 Market St., ☎ 01334/472021). Smaller tourist information centers operate seasonally in the following towns: Anstruther, Brechin, Carnoustie, Crail, Cupar, Forfar, Kirriemuir, and Montrose.

5 THE CENTRAL HIGHLANDS

STIRLING, LOCH LOMOND AND
THE TROSSACHS, PERTHSHIRE

Memories of Rob Roy McGregor, Robert
the Bruce, and that braveheart, William
Wallace, abound in the Central Highlands.
Here, in Scotland's wasp waist, Perth and
Stirling are the main gateways to rugged
and spectacular wild country, including the
fabled Trossachs, where deep, wandering
lochs—including Loch Lomond—shimmer
under hills cloaked in the browns and
purples of bracken and heather. No matter
if "ye'll take the high road and I'l tak' the
low road"—this region is a must for many.

By Gilbert
Summers

Updated by
Beth Ingpen

TAND ON STIRLING CASTLE ROCK TO SURVEY the whole Central
Highland region, and you will see Scotland coast to coast. This is
where Scotland draws in her waist, from the Clyde in the west to
the Forth in the east. You can judge just how near the area is to the well-
populated Midland Valley by looking out from the ramparts of Edinburgh
Castle: the Highland hills—which meander around the Trossachs region
and above Callander—are clearly visible. Similarly, the high-tower blocks
of some of Glasgow's peripheral housing developments are noticeable from
many of the countryside's higher peaks, notably Ben Lomond. Today the
old county seats of Perth and Stirling still play important roles as the primary administrative centers of the counties of Perthshire and Stirlingshire,
respectively, which make up the Central Highlands. Geographically, it is
no surprise that this region is a favorite vacation getaway for Edinburghers and Glaswegians, and this has been the case for centuries.

As early as 1794 the local minister in Callander, on the very edge of
the Highlands, wrote: "The Trossachs are often visited by persons of
taste, who are desirous of seeing nature in her rudest and unpolished
state." What these early visitors came to see was a series of lochs and
hills, whose crags and slopes were hung harmoniously with shaggy birch,
oak, and pinewoods. The tops of the hills are high but not too sav-
age—real wilderness would have been too much for these fledgling nature lovers. The Romantic poets, especially William Wordsworth
(1770–1850), sang the praises of such locales. Though Wordsworth is
more closely associated with the Lake District in England, his travels
through Scotland and the Trossachs inspired several of his poems. But
it was Sir Walter Scott (1771–1832) who definitively put this area on
the tourist map by setting his 1810 dramatic verse narrative, *Lady of
the Lake,* in the landscape of the Trossachs. Scott's verse was an immediate and huge success, and visitors flooded in to trace the events
of the poem across the region. The poem is still the most comprehensive guide to the area since it mentions every little bridge and farmhouse. Various engineering schemes of the Glasgow Water Department,
however, have rendered some of the topography out of date.

Just as the Trossachs have long attracted those with discriminating
tastes, so has Loch Lomond. This is Scotland's largest loch in terms of
surface area. The hard rocks to the north confine it to a long thin rib-
bon, and the more yielding Lowlands allow it to spread out and assume
a softer, wider form. Here the Lowlands' fields and lush hedgerows quickly
give way to dark woods and crags—just a half hour's drive north from
the center of Glasgow. The song, "The Banks of Loch Lomond," said
to have been written by a Jacobite prisoner incarcerated in Carlisle, England, captures beautifully a particular style of Scottish sentimentality,
resulting in the popularity of the "bonnie, bonnie banks" around the
world, especially wherever Scots are to be found.

Scots, in particular, prize the sights of this region, for they are some of
the most hallowed in their history. "Scots Wha He Wi' Wallace Bled,"
a rousing pipe-band tune generally regarded as the Scottish national
anthem, is played much about here. It deals with William Wallace who,
like Robert the Bruce, waged war against England in the 13th and 14th
centuries. At Stirling Bridge and Bannockburn, respectively, the most
notable battles of Wallace and Bruce were fought. In nearby Callander, Rob Roy MacGregor, the Scottish Robin Hood, lived (and looted
and terrorized) his way into the storybooks.

Within the region, the physical contrast between Lowland and Highland is quite pronounced because of the Highland boundary fault. This

geological divide also marked the boundary between Scotland's two languages and cultures, Gaelic and Scots, with the Gaels ensconced northwest behind the mountain barrier. In the Central Highlands the fault runs through Loch Lomond, close to Callander, to the northeast above Perth, and into the old county of Angus. Remember that even though the Central Highlands are easily accessible, there is still much high, rough country in the region. Ben Lawers, near Killin, is the ninth-highest peak in Scotland, and the moor of Rannoch is as bleak and empty a stretch as can be seen anywhere in the northlands. But if the glens and lochs prove to be too lonely or intimidating, it's only a short journey to the softer and less harsh Lowlands.

Pleasures and Pastimes

Biking

The big attraction for cyclists is the dedicated Glasgow–Killin cycleway. This route runs along former railroad track beds, as well as otherwise private and minor roads, to reach well into the Central Highlands by way of the Trossachs and Callander. Away from the cycleway, the main roads can be busy with holiday traffic.

Dining

Central Highlands restaurants have been continually improving for the past several years. Regional country delicacies—loch trout, river salmon, mutton, and venison—are now found regularly on even modest menus. The urban areas south and southwest of Stirling, in contrast, lack refinement in matters of eating and drinking. Here you will find simple pubs, often crowded and noisy, but serving substantial food at lunchtime (eaten balanced on your knee, perhaps, or at a shared table). Three sturdy courses at one of these pubs will cost you about £10.

CATEGORY	COST*
££££	over £40
£££	£30–£40
££	£15–£30
£	under £15

per person for a three-course meal, including VAT and excluding drinks and service

Fishing

There are several fishing options in the area, including coarse and game fishing, loch and river fishing, and sea angling. There are statutory fishing seasons for salmon and sea trout (January 15–October 15 on the Tay River system). Coarse fishing for grayling, pike, perch, and roach on the Earn River system is reserved February–October. In some cases, Sunday fishing is illegal. Tourist information centers have publications, updated annually, that show the best locations.

Golf

There are many excellent courses in the region (☞ Chapter 11). Tourist information centers can supply details of local courses.

Hiking

Hill walking and "Munro-bagging" (climbing all the mountains more than 3,000 ft high so-called in honor of the mountaineer who first listed them) are popular, so even in the wilder parts of the Highlands, you will find locals able to give advice on routes. For high-level routes, it is essential to be properly supplied with boots and safety equipment. Tourist information centers carry information on a variety of local routes. The publications *Walk Loch Lomond and the Trossachs* and *Walk Perthshire* are invaluable for hikers and trekkers and are available at bookstores or tourist information centers.

Lodging

In Stirling and Callander, as well as in the small towns and villages throughout the region, you will find a selection of tourist accommodations out of all proportion to the size of the communities (industrial towns are the exceptions). Standards of less expensive establishments have improved in recent years and are still improving. The grand hotels, though few, were brought into existence by the carriage trade of the 19th century, when travel in Scotland was the fashion. The level of service at these places has, by and large, not slipped; you will also find many country hotels that are a match for the grand hotels in comfort.

CATEGORY	COST*
££££	over £140
£££	£110–£140
££	£65–£110
£	under £65

Prices are for a standard double room, including service, breakfast, and VAT.

✎ *following the text of a review is your signal that the property has a Web site, where you will find details and, usually, images; for a link, visit www.fodors.com/urls.*

Exploring the Central Highlands

The main towns of Stirling and Perth serve as roadway hubs for the area, making both places natural starting points for Highland tours. Stirling itself is worth covering in some detail on foot. The successive waves of development of this important town can easily be traced—from castle and Old Town architecture to Victorian developments and urban and industrial sprawl.

The Trossachs are a short distance from Stirling, all easily covered in a loop. You can get to Loch Lomond from either Glasgow or Stirling, and there are two other routes to take. The main road up the west bank (A82) is not recommended for leisurely touring. Do use this road, however, if you are on your way to Oban, Kintyre, or Argyll. Loch Lomond is best seen from one of two cul-de-sac roads: by way of Drymen at the south end, up to Rowardennan, or if you are pressed for time, west from Aberfoyle to reach Loch Lomond near its northern end, at Inversnaid. Visitors should note that in the Trossachs, the road that some maps show going all the way around Loch Katrine is a private road belonging to the Strathclyde Water Board and is open only to walkers and cyclists.

Getting around Perthshire is made interesting by the series of looped tours accessible from the A9, a fast main artery. Exercise caution while driving the A9 itself, however: there have been many auto accidents in this area. Although the entire route can be completed in a single day, travelers with some time on their hands who seek a little spontaneity can choose from a variety of accommodations in villages along the way.

Numbers in the text correspond to numbers in the margin and on the Central Highlands and Stirling maps.

Great Itineraries

This is excellent touring country. The glens, in some places, run parallel to the lochs, including those along Lochs Earn, Tay, and Rannoch, making for satisfying loops and round-trips.

IF YOU HAVE 2 DAYS

There's enough to see in 🗺 **Stirling** ①–⑱ to take up at least a day. The second day, cover the **Trossachs** loop, which includes **Loch Venachar** ㉔, Loch Achray, and **Loch Katrine** ㉕, and the historic towns of **Dunblane** ⑲, **Doune** ⑳, **Callander** ㉑, and **Aberfoyle** ㉖.

The Central Highlands

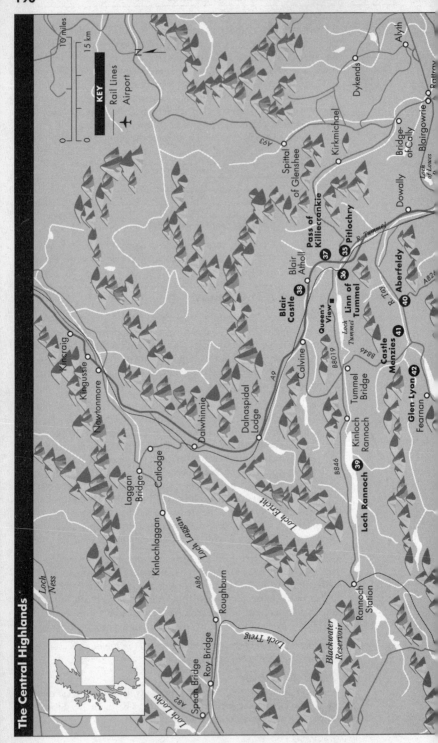

KEY

Rail Lines

✈ Airport

10 miles

15 km

N

Loch Ness

Kincraig

Kingussie

Newtonmore

Laggan
Bridge

Catlodge

Kinlochlaggan

Loch Laggan

A86

Roughburn

Spean Bridge

Roy Bridge

A82

Loch Lochy

Loch Treig

Blackwater
Reservoir

Rannoch
Station

Loch Rannoch

Loch Ericht

Dalwhinnie

Dalnaspidal
Lodge

A9

Calvine

Kinloch
Rannoch

Tummel
Bridge

B846

B8019

39

Queen's View

Loch
Tummel

Linn of
Tummel

Castle
Menzies

Glen Lyon

Fearnan

Blair
Castle

Blair
Atholl

38

37

Pass of
Killiecrankie

35

Pitlochry

R. Tummel

36

26

R. Tay

40

41

42

Aberfeldy

A826

Spittal
of Glenshee

A93

Kirkmichael

Dowally

Dykends

Alyth

Bridge
of Cally

Blairgowrie

Rattray

Loch
o Lowes

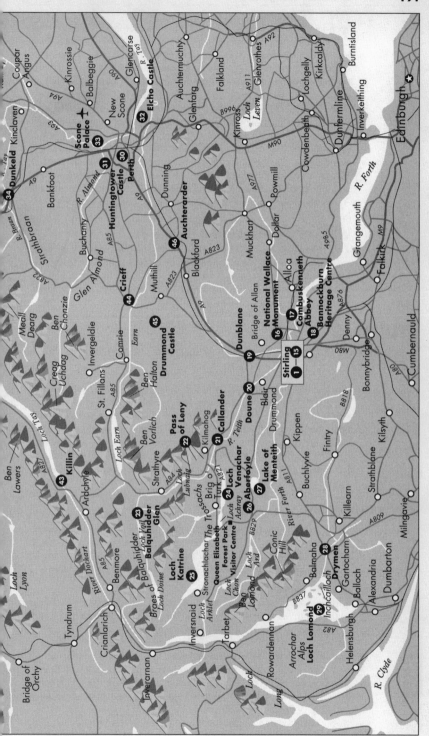

IF YOU HAVE 6 DAYS
Spend a day in ⊞ **Stirling** ①–⑱. (Don't overlook the Mill Trail country, east of Stirling, if you are shopping for Scottish woolens.) Then visit **Dunblane** ⑲ and **Doune** ⑳, staying overnight at ⊞ **Callander** ㉑ to explore the fine country northward toward **Balquhidder Glen** ㉓. Spend a day in the **Trossachs** around ⊞ **Loch Venachar** ㉔ and **Loch Katrine** ㉕, and take a boat ride to see the landscape at its best. The next day travel to **Drymen** ㉘ for a morning around **Loch Lomond** ㉙ before driving into Perthshire. Spend a night at ⊞ **Auchterarder** ㊻ with its antiques shops, or travel straight to ⊞ **Perth** ㉚, where you should base yourself for two or three days while exploring Perthshire. Go west for **Crieff** ㊹ and **Drummond Castle** ㊺ or north for Highland resort towns such as **Dunkeld** ㉞, with its cathedral; **Pitlochry** ㉟, close to the historic **Pass of Killiecrankie** ㊲ and impressive **Blair Castle** ㊳; and **Aberfeldy** ㊵. Between Pitlochry and Aberfeldy, make time for the bleak landscapes of **Loch Rannoch** ㊴—a great contrast to the generally pastoral Perthshire countryside.

When to Tour the Central Highlands

The Trossachs and Loch Lomond can get quite busy and crowded in high summer, so the area would also be a good choice for off-season touring. You're near enough to the Lowland edge to take advantage of any good weather in winter in order to enjoy the dramatic Highland light; fall colors are also spectacular.

STIRLING

26 mi northeast of Glasgow, 36 mi northwest of Edinburgh.

In some ways, Stirling is a little Edinburgh with similar "crag-and-tail" foundations and a royal half mile. Its castle, built on a steep-sided plug of rock, dominates the landscape, and its esplanade offers views of the surrounding valley plain of the River Forth. Stirling's strategic position, commanding the lowest bridge on the Forth, was appreciated by the Stuart kings, and they spent a lot of time at its castle—a fact which, together with the relics of freedom fighters in the neighborhood, has led some Scottish nationalists to declare that Stirling, not Edinburgh, should really be the capital city.

Exploring Stirling

The historic part of town is tightly nestled around the castle—everything is within easy walking distance. You can either taxi or walk (if you're feeling energetic) out to Bannockburn Heritage Centre or the National Wallace Monument, which are on the town's outskirts.

A Good Tour

Stirling is one of Britain's great historic towns. An impressive proportion of the old town walls remain and can be seen from Dumbarton Road, as soon as you step outside the tourist information center. If you're an art lover you'll want to make a foray west along Dumbarton Road to visit the **Smith Art Gallery and Museum** ①. Back near the information center, on Corn Exchange Road, there is a modern statue of Robert MacGregor (1671–1734), better known as Rob Roy, notorious cattle dealer and drover, part-time thief and outlaw, Jacobite (most of the time), and hero of Sir Walter Scott's namesake novel (1818). In 1995 Hollywood paid homage to this local folk legend with the film *Rob Roy*, starring actor Liam Neeson. Rob is practically inescapable if you visit Callander and the Trossachs, where he had his home.

Near Rob Roy's statue, a gentle but relentless uphill path known as the **Back Walk** ② eventually leads to the town's most famous and

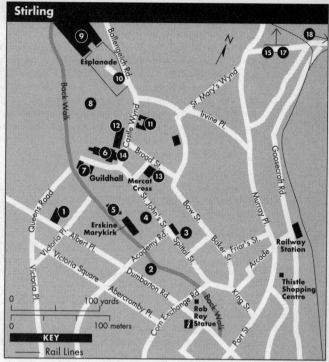

worthwhile sight—Stirling Castle. On Academy Road is the Old High School, built in 1854 on the site of the former Greyfriars Monastery and now the Stirling Highland Hotel (☞ Dining and Lodging, *below*). Two fine examples of Scottish domestic architecture, now used for private housing, stand near the junction of Academy Road and Spittal Street: **Darrow House** ③ and **Spittal House.**

Another typical town house stands on St. John's Street, uphill from Darrow House and sometimes known as **Bothwell Ha** ④. The former military detention barracks behind Bothwell Ha is now known as the **Old Town Jail** ⑤, with exhibits describing life in a 19th-century Scottish prison. Adjacent to the Old Town Jail is Erskine Marykirk, a neoclassical church built in 1824 that now houses a youth hostel (☞ Dining and Lodging, *below*). At the top of St. John's Street is the medieval **Church of the Holy Rude** ⑥. The nearby **Guildhall** ⑦ was built as almshouses in 1639. Within the **cemetery** ⑧, beyond the Church of the Holy Rude, are some unusual monuments.

You're almost at the castle, to which you have been making your way uphill since the start of the walk: at this point, you'll appreciate the strategic position of **Stirling Castle** ⑨. The **Royal Burgh of Stirling Visitor Centre** ⑩ stands beside the Stirling Castle Esplanade. After exploring the castle, walk downhill toward the heart of the old town of Stirling, recently the subject of a massive renovation program. Along Castle Wynd is a series of interesting buildings, the most important of which is **Argyll's Lodging** ⑪, now fully restored after a considerable period of neglect. The long and ornate facade of the distinctively Renaissance **Mar's Wark** ⑫ extends along the street frontage opposite Argyll's Lodging.

When you stand in front of Mar's Wark and look downhill, you gaze into the heart of the old town. One of its most notable structures is the **Tolbooth** ⑬ on Broad Street. The Mercat Cross, where proclamations were made, stands nearby, as does the **Mar Place House** ⑭, a restored Georgian town house. Continue downhill to the more modern part of Stirling, with its variety of shopping, or walk a few minutes down from the castle (via Barn Road, Castlehill, and Lower Bridge Street) to see the medieval **Old Stirling Bridge** ⑮. Drive north–northeast down Causewayhead Road from the castle to get to the Gothic pencil that is the **National Wallace Monument** ⑯, commemorating Scotland's great freedom fighter. Due east of the castle and most easily reached from the monument are the ruins of **Cambuskenneth Abbey** ⑰, in an idyllic riverside setting. The historic battle site of **Bannockburn Heritage Centre** ⑱—rather incongruously set in the middle of a housing development—is south of town, off Glasgow Road (A80).

TIMING

Stirling is a compact town, and this tour, though it has many sights to admire, can be done at speed in a day or in a more leisurely fashion over two days.

Sights to See

⑪ **Argyll's Lodging.** A nobleman's town house built in three phases from the 16th century onward, this building is actually older than the name it bears—that of Archibald, the ninth earl of Argyll (1629–85), who bought it in 1666. It was for many years a military hospital, then a youth hostel. It has now been refurbished to show how the nobility lived in 17th-century Stirling. Specially commissioned reproduction furniture and fittings are based on the original inventory of the house's contents at that time. ⊠ *Castle Wynd*, ☎ *0131/668–8800.* ☞ *£6, including admission to Stirling Castle.* ☉ *Apr.–Sept., daily 9:30–5:15; Oct.–Mar., daily 9:30–4:15.*

❷ **Back Walk.** The Back Walk will take you along the outside of the city's walls, past a watchtower and the grimly named Hangman's entry, carved out of the great whinstone boulders that once marked the outer defenses of the town. One of several access areas is off Dumbarton Road, opposite the tourist information center. ⊠ *Runs from Dumbarton Rd. to Castle Rock.*

★ ⑱ **Bannockburn Heritage Centre.** In 1298, the year after William Wallace's victory, Robert the Bruce (1274–1329) materialized as the nation's champion, and the final bloody phase of the Wars of Independence began. Bruce's rise resulted from the uncertainties and timidity of the great lords of Scotland (ever unsure of which way to jump and whether to bow to England's demands). This tale is recounted at the Bannockburn Heritage Centre, hidden among the sprawl of housing and commercial development on the southern edge of Stirling. This was the site of the famed Battle of Bannockburn in 1314. In Bruce's day the Forth had a shelved and partly wooded floodplain. So he cunningly chose this site, noting the boggy ground on the lower reaches in which the heavy horses of the English would founder. The atmosphere has been re-created within the center by means of an audiovisual presentation, models and costumed figures, and an arresting mural depicting the battle in detail (look closely for some particularly unsavory goings-on). ⊠ *Off M80*, ☎ *01786/812664.* ☞ *£2.50.* ☉ *Mar. and Nov.–Dec. 23, daily 11–4:30; Apr.–Oct., daily 10–5:30.* ❧

❹ **Bothwell Ha.** Said to have been owned by the earl of Bothwell, the third husband of Mary, Queen of Scots (1542–87), this hall (*ha* is Scots for *hall*) dates to the 16th century. ⊠ *St. John's St. Closed to the public.*

⑰ **Cambuskenneth Abbey.** On the south side of the Abbey Craig, the scanty remains of this 13th-century abbey lie in a sweeping bend of the River Forth, with the dramatic outline of Stirling Castle as a backdrop. Important meetings of the Scottish Parliament were once held here, and King Edward I (1239–1307) of England visited in 1304. The abbey was looted and damaged during the Scots Wars of Independence (1307–14). The reconstructed tomb of King James III (1452–88) can be seen near the outline of the high altar. ⊠ *Ladysneuk Rd.,* ☎ *0131/668–8800.* 🖃 *Free.* ⊙ *Daily 9–6.*

⑧ Cemetery. Among the most notable of the many unusual monuments in the cemetery near the Church of the Holy Rude is the **Star Pyramid** of 1858. Also be sure to look for the macabre, glass-walled **Martyrs Monument,** erected in memory of two Wigtownshire girls who were drowned in 1685 for their Covenanting faith. The castle dominates the foreground, and from **Ladies' Rock,** a high perch within the cemetery, there are excellent views of the looming fortress. ⊠ *Top of St. John's St.*

⑥ Church of the Holy Rude. The nave of this handsome church survives from the 15th century, and a portion of the original medieval timber roof can also be seen. This is the only Scottish church still in use to have witnessed the coronation of a Scottish monarch—James VI (1566–1625) in 1567. ⊠ *St. John's St.*

③ Darrow House. Dating from the 17th century, this house displays the characteristic crow-step gables, dormer windows, and projecting turnpike stair of the period. ⊠ *Spittal St.*

⑦ Guildhall. Built as Cowane's Hospital in 1639 for *decayed breithers* (unsuccessful merchants), this building has above its entrance a small, cheery statue of the founder himself, John Cowane, which is said to come alive on Hogmanay Night (December 31) to walk the streets with the locals and join in their New Year's revelry. ⊠ *St. John's St. View from outside only.*

⑭ Mar Place House. This handsome Georgian building was saved from dereliction and painstakingly restored through the town council's ongoing Old Town renovation program. It now houses a restaurant. ⊠ *Mar Pl.*

⑫ Mar's Wark. These distinctive windowless and roofless ruins are the stark remains of a Renaissance palace built in 1570 by Lord Erskine (died 1572), earl of Mar and Stirling Castle governor. Its name means "Mar's work," or building. Look for the armorial carved panels, the gargoyles, and the turrets flanking a railed-off *pend* (archway). During the 1745 Jacobite rebellion, Mar's Wark was laid siege to and severely damaged, but its admirably worn shell survives. ⊠ *Castle Wynd,* ☎ *0131/668–8800. View from outside only.*

⑯ National Wallace Monument. It was near Old Stirling Bridge that the Scottish freedom fighter William Wallace (1270–1305) and a ragged army of Scots won a major victory in 1297. The 1995 movie *Braveheart,* directed by and starring Mel Gibson, was based on Wallace's life, and attendance here has soared as a result of the film. A more accurate version is told in an exhibition and audiovisual presentation at this pencil-thin museum on the Abbey Craig. Up close, this Victorian shrine to William Wallace, built between 1856 and 1869, becomes less slim and soaring, revealing itself to be a substantial square tower with a creepy spiral stairway. To reach the monument, follow the Bridge of Allan signs (A9) northward, crossing the River Forth by Robert Stephenson's (1772–1850) New Bridge of 1832, next to the historic old one. The National Wallace Monument is signposted at the next traffic circle. ⊠ *Abbey Craig,* ☎ *01786/ 472140.* 🖃 *£3.30.* ⊙ *Mar.–May and Oct., daily 10–5; June and Sept., daily 10–6; July–Aug., daily 9:30–6:30; Nov.–Feb. daily 10:30–4.*

⑮ Old Stirling Bridge. North of Stirling Castle, on the edge of town, this narrow, humped, 15th-century bridge is now only for pedestrian use. ⊠ *Off Drip Rd. (A84).*

⑤ Old Town Jail. The original town jail, now restored, has living exhibitions about life in a 19th-century Scottish prison. Furnished cells, models, and staff—appropriately dressed as prisoners, wardens, and prison reformers—bring the past vividly to life. ⌂ *Access from St. John's St.,* ☎ *01786/450050.* ⌂ *£3.30.* ☉ *Apr.–Sept., daily 9:30–5:30; Oct.–Mar., daily 9:30–4 (last admission 30 mins before closing).*

⑩ Royal Burgh of Stirling Visitor Centre. Standing at the foot of the Castle Esplanade, this visitor center houses a shop and exhibition hall with an audiovisual presentation on the town and surrounding area. ⌂ ☎ *01786/462517.* ⌂ *Free.* ☉ *Apr.–June and Sept.–Oct., daily 9:30–6; July–Aug., daily 9–6:30; Nov.–Mar., daily 9:30–5.*

① Smith Art Gallery and Museum. Founded in 1874 with the bequest of a local collector, this is a good example of a community art gallery that offers a varied exhibition program of paintings and sculpture. ⌂ *Albert Pl., Dumbarton Rd.,* ☎ *01786/471917.* ⌂ *Free.* ☉ *Tues.–Sat. 10:30–5, Sun. 2–5.*

★ **⑨ Stirling Castle.** Its magnificent strategic position made Stirling Castle the grandest prize in the Scots Wars of Independence in the late 13th and early 14th centuries. The Battle of Bannockburn in 1314 was fought within sight of its walls, and the victory by Robert the Bruce yielded both the castle and freedom from English subjugation for almost four centuries.

The daughter of King Robert I (Robert the Bruce), Marjory, married Walter, the high steward of Scotland. Their descendants included the Stewart dynasty of Scottish monarchs (Mary, Queen of Scots, was a Stewart, though she preferred the French spelling, *Stuart*). The Stewarts were mainly responsible for many of the works that survive within the castle walls today. They made Stirling Castle their court and power base, creating fine Renaissance-style buildings that were not completely obliterated, despite subsequent reconstruction for military purposes.

The castle is entered through its outer defenses, which consist of a great curtain wall and batteries that date from 1708, built to bulwark earlier defenses by the main gatehouse. From this lower square the most conspicuous feature is the **palace,** built by King James V (1512–42) between 1538 and 1542. The decorative figures festooning the ornately worked outer walls of this edifice show the influence of French masons. Overlooking the upper courtyard is the **Great Hall,** built by King James IV (1473–1513) in 1503. Before the Union of Parliaments in 1707, when the Scottish aristocracy sold out to England, this building had been used as one of the seats of the Scottish Parliament. After 1707 it sank into decline, becoming a riding school, then a barracks. It has been restored to its original splendor.

Among the later works built for regiments stationed here, the **King's Old Building** stands out; it is a 19th-century baronial revival on the site of an earlier building. The oldest building on the site is the **Mint,** or **Coonzie Hoose,** perhaps dating from as far back as the 14th century. Below is an arched passageway leading to the westernmost section of the ramparts, the **Nether Bailey.** You'll have the distinct feeling here of being in the bow of a warship sailing up the *carselands* (valley plain) of the Forth Valley, which fans out before the great superstructure of the castle. Among the gun platforms and the crenellations of the ramparts, you may find yourself pondering the strategic significance of Stirling. To the south lies the hump of the Touch and the Gargunnock hills (part of the Campsie Fells), which diverted potential direct routes from Glasgow and the south. For centuries all roads into the Highlands across the narrow waist of Scotland led to Stirling. If you look carefully northward, you can still see the Old Stirling Bridge (☞ *above*), once the lowest and most convenient place to cross the river. For all these geographic reasons, the castle was perhaps the single most important fortress in Scotland. ⊠ *Castlehill,* ☎ *0131/668–8800.* ⚑ *£6, including admission to Argyll's Lodging.* ☉ *Apr.–Sept., daily 9:30– 5:15; Oct.–Mar., daily 9:30–4:15.* ✑

⑬ Tolbooth. Built in 1705, the Tolbooth has a traditional Scottish steeple and gilded weathercock. For centuries the Burgh Court handed down sentences here. ⊠ *Broad St.*

Dining and Lodging

£££–££££ ✕🏠 **Stirling Highland Hotel.** The attractive building this hotel occupies was once the Old High School, and many original architectural features have been retained. Furnishings are old-fashioned, with solid wood, tartan, florals, and low-key, neutral color schemes. The hotel has two restaurants: the Italian Rizzio's and the traditional Scottish Scholars, with outstanding seafood. ⊠ *Spittal St., FK8 1DU,* ☎ *01786/475444,* ᴵᴬˣ *01786/ 462929. 94 rooms with bath. 2 restaurants, bar. AE, DC, MC, V.* ✑

££ ✕🏠 **Park Hotel.** This elegant 18th-century establishment is run by a French family. The decor is all fanlights, antique furniture, and candles; the menu in the Heritage Restaurant features French classics such as *filet au poivre* (pepper beef steak) and *magret de canard* (duck breast). ⊠ *32 Park Terr.,* ☎ *01786/473660. 10 rooms with bath or shower. Restaurant. MC, V.*

£ ✕🏠 **Cross Keys Hotel.** A stone-walled dining room adds atmosphere to the restaurant's varied, traditionally Scottish menu in this cozy inn; if you decide to stay the night, there are two comfortable bedrooms to choose from. ⊠ *Main St., Kippen (A811, west of Stirling),* ☎ *01786/870293. 2 rooms with bath. Restaurant. MC, V.*

££ 🏠 **Terraces Hotel.** This central hotel with plenty of parking is a good base for exploring Stirling and the region. A comfortable Georgian town house, it is comparatively small, with friendly and attentive service. ⊠ *4 Melville Terr., FK8 2ND,* ☎ *01786/472268,* ᴵᴬˣ *01786/450314. 17 rooms with bath or shower. Restaurant. AE, DC, MC, V.*

£–££ 🏠 **Castlecroft.** Tucked beneath Stirling Castle, with fine views over the ★ plain of the River Forth toward the Highland hills, this warm and comfortable modern house is very central for sightseeing in the Old Town. ⊠ *Ballengeich Rd., FK8 1TN,* ☎ *01786/474933.* ᴵᴬˣ *01786/466716. 6 rooms with shower. MC, V.*

£ 🏠 **Lochend Farm.** Extensive views, wholesome farm cooking, and a pleasantly relaxing pace are the hallmarks of this peaceful working farm. Only 5 mi from the M9/M80, southwest of Stirling, it also makes a good touring base. The traditionally furnished (and very comfortable) bedrooms have washbasins and share a bathroom. ⊠ *Carronbridge, Denny, Stirlingshire FK6 5JJ,* ☎ *01324/822778. 2 rooms without bath. No credit cards.*

£ 🏠 **Stirling Youth Hostel.** Built within the shell of a former church, the hostel offers high-grade four- and six-bed rooms (and a few doubles) with in-room bath facilities. Use of the television room, the dining room, and the self-service, fully equipped kitchen is included in the bargain price of £12.25 (£13.25 in July and August) per person, including breakfast. ⊠ *Erskine Marykirk, St. John's St., FK8 1DU,* ☎ *01786/473442,* ᴵᴬˣ *01786/445715. 129 beds. MC, V.*

£ 🏠 **West Plean.** This handsome house is part of a working farm, with a walled garden and woodland walks. Well-prepared food and spacious rooms make this bed-and-breakfast an excellent bargain. ⊠ *Denny Rd., FK7 8HA,* ☎ *01786/812208,* ᴵᴬˣ *01786/480550. 3 rooms with bath or shower. No credit cards.*

Nightlife and the Arts

The **Macrobert Arts Centre** (⊠ Stirling University, ☎ 01786/461081) has a theater, art gallery, and studio with programs that range from films to pantomime.

Shopping

Though in a nondescript 1970s building, the downtown Thistle Shopping Centre nevertheless has a good variety of stores.

Books
In the Old Town, **McCutcheons** (⊠ 51 Baker St., ☎ 01786/461771) will keep lovers of antiquarian books happy for an hour or two with its huge range of titles, including books on every aspect of Scotland.

Ceramics
South of Stirling, at Larbert, don't miss **Barbara Davidson's pottery studio** (⊠ Muirhall Farm, ☎ 01324/554430), run by one of the best-known potters in Scotland, in an 18th-century farm setting. It's open Monday–Saturday 10–5 and Sunday noon–5. In July and August you can even try throwing your own pot for a small fee.

Knitwear
East of Stirling is **Mill Trail** country, along the foot of the Ochil Hills. A leaflet from any local tourist information center will lead you to the delights of a real mill shop and low mill prices—even on cashmere— at Tillicoultry, Alva, and Alloa.

Scottish Specialties
R. R. Henderson Ltd. (⊠ 6–8 Friars St., ☎ 01786/473681) is a Highland outfitters, selling tartans, woolens, and accessories and offering a made-to-measure kilt service.

THE TROSSACHS AND LOCH LOMOND

Immortalized by Wordsworth and Sir Walter Scott, the Trossachs (the name means "bristly country") may contain some of Scotland's loveliest forest, hills, and glens. The area has a very peculiar charm: it combines the wildness of the Highlands with the prolific vegetation of an old Lowland forest. The Trossachs' open ground is a dense mat of bracken and heather and its woodland is of silver birch, dwarf oak, and hazels—trees that fasten their roots into every crevice of the rocks and stop short on the very brink of the lochs. The most colorful season is fall, particularly October—a lovely time when visitors have departed and the hares, deer, and game birds have taken over. Even in rainy weather the Trossachs of "darksome glens and gleaming lochs" are memorable: the water filtering through the rocks comes out so pure and clear that the lochs are like sheets of crystal glass.

Inspired by the views of mountainous terrain seen from the ramparts of Stirling Castle, you can use this northward route to explore areas west and north to the Highland line. Distances are not great if you go by car. If you travel the classic Trossachs loop, you will share the route with plenty of day-trippers.

Dunblane

★ ⑲ *7 mi north of Stirling.*

The oldest part of Dunblane—with its twisting streets and lovely town houses—huddles around the square where the partly restored ruins of **Dunblane Cathedral** stand. King David built the existing structure in the

13th century on the site of St. Blane's tiny 8th-century cell. It is contemporary with the Border abbeys (☞ Chapter 3), but more mixed in its architecture—part early English and part Norman. Dunblane ceased to be a cathedral, as did most others in Scotland, at the time of the Reformation, in the mid-16th century. ☎ *0131/668–8800.* 🖃 *Free.* ☉ *Apr.–Sept., daily 9:30–6; Oct.–Mar., Mon.–Sat. 9:30–4, Sun. 2–4; and for services.*

Dining and Lodging

££££ ✕🏨 **Cromlix House Hotel.** This Victorian hunting lodge's period atmosphere is enhanced by cherished furniture and paintings, the original conservatory, and a library. The restaurant offers country-house decor and a choice of two elegant dining rooms. Specialties include game and lamb from the hotel estate. Try the delicious confit of guinea fowl as a starter, followed by beef with pickled walnuts. ✉ *Kinbuck, on B8033, 3 mi northeast of Dunblane, 10 mi northeast of Stirling, FK15 9JT,* ☎ *01786/822125,* ᖴᴬˣ *01786/825450. 6 rooms with bath, 8 suites. Restaurant, tennis court, fishing, library. AE, DC, MC, V. Closed Jan.* ✎

Doune

★ ⑳ *5 mi west of Dunblane.*

The Highland-edge community of Doune was once a center for pistol making. No self-respecting Highland chief's attire was complete without a prestigious and ornate pair of pistols. Today Doune is more widely known as the site of one of the best-preserved medieval castles in Scotland. **Doune Castle** looks like an early castle is supposed to look: grim and high-walled, with echoing, drafty stone vaults. Construction of the fortress began in the early 15th century on a now-peaceful riverside tract. The best place to photograph this squat, great-walled fort is from the bridge, a little way upstream, west on A84. The castle is signposted to the left as you enter the town from the Dunblane road. ✉ *Off A84,* ☎ *0131/668–8800.* 🖃 *£2.50.* ☉ *Apr.–Sept., daily 9:30–6; Oct.–Mar., Mon.–Wed. and Sat. 9:30–4, Thurs. 9:30–noon, Sun. 2–4.* ✎

Callander

㉑ *8 mi northwest of Doune.*

A traditional Highland-edge resort, Callander bustles throughout the year—even during off-peak times—simply because it is a gateway to the Highland scenery that's within easy reach of Edinburgh and Glasgow. As a result, there is plenty of window-shopping here, plus nightlife in pubs and a good choice of accommodations.

Callander's **Rob Roy and Trossachs Visitor Centre** provides another encounter with the overly romanticized "tartan Robin Hood," Rob Roy MacGregor. A man of great physical strength and courageous energy, MacGregor is known as a defender of the downtrodden and scourge of authorities. He was, in fact, a medieval throwback, a cattle thief, an embezzler of lairds' rents, and the operator of a vicious protection racket among poor farmers. You can learn more about his high jinks from the high-tech account—replete with displays and tableaux—in the modern visitor center. ✉ *Ancaster Sq.,* ☎ *01877/330342.* 🖃 *£2.95.* ☉ *Mar.–May and Oct.–Dec., daily 10–5; June and Sept., daily 9:30–6; July–Aug., daily 9–7.*

A walk is signposted from the east end of the main street to the **Bracklinn Falls,** over whose lip Sir Walter Scott once rode a pony to win a bet. Another walk goes through the woods up to the **Callander Crags,** with views of the Lowlands as far as the Pentland Hills behind Edinburgh (this walk is for the fit and well-shod only).

Callander is the gateway to the Trossachs, but since it is on the main road, the A84, it also attracts overnight visitors on their way to Oban, Fort William, and beyond. All this traffic enters the proper Highlands just north of Callander, where the slopes squeeze both the road and rocky river into the narrow **Pass of Leny.** An abandoned railway—now a pleasant walking or bicycling path—also goes through the pass, past Ben Ledi Mountain and Loch Lubnaig.

A 20-minute drive from Callander, through the Pass of Leny and beyond Strathyre, is **Balquhidder Glen** (pronounced *bal*-whidd-*er*), a typical Highland glen that runs westward. The glen has characteristics seen throughout the north: a flat-bottomed U-shape profile, formed by prehistoric glaciers; extensive Forestry-Commission plantings replacing much of the natural woodlands above; a sprinkling of farms; and farther up the glen, new hill roads bulldozed into the slopes to provide access for shepherds and foresters. You'll notice the boarded-up look of some of the area's houses, many of which are second homes for affluent residents of the south. The glen is also where Loch Voil and Loch Doune spread out, adding to the stunning vistas. This area is often known as the Braes (Slopes) of Balquhidder and was once the home of the MacLarens and the MacGregors. **Rob Roy MacGregor's grave** is signposted beside Balquhidder village. The site of his house, now a private farm, is beyond the parking lot at the end of the road up the glen. The glen has no through road, though there is a right-of-way (on foot) from the churchyard where Rob Roy is buried, through the plantings in Kirkton Glen and then on to open windy grasslands and a blue *lochan* (little lake). This path eventually drops into the next valley, Glen Dochart, and rejoins the A84.

Dining and Lodging

£   ✗ **Pip's Coffee House.** Just off the main street, this cheerful little place offers light meals, soups, and salads, as well as Scottish home baking. There is also a small picture gallery with plenty of Scottish material to browse through. ⊠ *Ancaster Sq.,* ☎ *01877/330470. Closed Wed. Oct.–Mar. No credit cards.*

£££–££££ ✗⊞ **Roman Camp.** This former hunting lodge, dating from 1625, has ★ 20 acres of gardens with river frontage, yet is within easy walking distance of Callander's town center. The sitting rooms and the library, with their numerous antiques, are more reminiscent of a stately family home than a hotel. The restaurant has high standards, with a good reputation for its salmon, trout, and other seafood, which are all cooked in an imaginative, modern Scottish style. ⊠ *Callander, Perthshire FK17 8BG,* ☎ *01877/330003,* 𝖥𝖠𝖷 *01877/331533. 14 rooms with bath or shower. Restaurant, fishing, library. AE, DC, MC, V.* ✆

Outdoor Activities and Sports

BIKING

You can rent bicycles from two outlets in Callander. **Wheels/Trossachs Backpackers** (⊠ Invertrossachs Rd., ☎ 01877/331100) is a friendly firm, which can also help with route planning, and offers hostel accommodations, organized walks, and canoe trips. **Mounter Bikes** (⊠ Ancaster La., ☎ 01877/331052) rents out and repairs mountain bikes and stocks spare parts.

GOLF

The **golf course** at Callander (⊠ Aveland Rd., ☎ 01877/330090) was designed by Tom Morris and has a scenic, upland feel, with fine views and a tricky moorland layout. The course is 18 holes, 5,151 yards, par 66.

Shopping

A vast selection of woolens is on display at three mill shops in and near Callander. All the stores, which are part of the Edinburgh Woollen Mill

Group, offer overseas mailing and tax-free shopping: **Kilmahog Woollen Mill** (☎ 01877/330268), **Trossachs Woollen Mill** (✉ North of town at Trossachs Turning, ☎ 01877/330178), and **Callander Woollen Mill** (✉ Main St., ☎ 01877/330273).

The Trossachs

10 mi west of Callander.

With its harmonious scenery of hill, loch, and wooded slopes, the Trossachs region has been a tourist mecca since the late 18th century, at the dawn of the age of the Romantic poets. Influenced by the writings of Sir Walter Scott, early visitors who strayed into the Highlands from the central belt of Scotland admired this as the first "wild" part of Scotland they encountered. The Trossachs represent the very essence of what the Highlands are supposed to be: birch wood and pine forests; vistas down lochs where the woods creep right to the water's edge; and in the background, peaks that rise high enough to be called mountains, though they're not as high as those to the north and west. The Trossachs are almost a Scottish visual cliché. They're popular right through the year, drawing not only first-time visitors from all around the world, but also Scots out for a Sunday drive.

㉔ The A821 runs west together with the first and gentlest of the Trossachs lochs, **Loch Venachar.** The sturdy gray-stone building, with a small dam at the Callander end, controls the water that feeds into the River Teith (and, hence, into the Forth) to compensate for the Victorians having tinkered with the water supply. Within a few minutes the road becomes muffled in woodlands and twists gradually down to **Brig o' Turk.** (*Turk* is Gaelic for the Scots *tuirc,* meaning wild boar, a species that has been extinct in this region since about the 16th century.)

West of Brig o' Turk stretches **Loch Achray,** dutifully fulfilling expectations of what a verdant Trossachs loch should be: small, green, reedy meadows backed by dark plantations, rhododendron thickets, and lumpy, thickly covered hills. The parking lot by Loch Achray is where to begin the ascent of steep, heathery **Ben An** where you'll enjoy some of the best Trossachs' views. The climb requires a couple of hours and good lungs.

★ ㉕ At the end of Loch Achray, a side road turns right into a narrow pass, leading to **Loch Katrine,** the heart of the Trossachs. During the time of Sir Walter Scott, the road here was narrow and almost hidden by the overhanging crags and mossy oaks and birches. Today it ends at a slightly anticlimactic parking lot with a shop, café, and visitor center. To see the finest of the Trossachs lochs properly, you must—even for just a few minutes—go westward on foot; the road beyond the parking lot (open only to Strathclyde Water Board vehicles) is well paved and level. Loch Katrine's water is taken by aqueduct and tunnel to Glasgow—a Victorian feat of engineering that has ensured the purity of the supply to Scotland's largest city for more than 100 years. Not readily visible from the parking lot, the steamer SS *Sir Walter Scott* embarks on cruises of Loch Katrine every summer. Take the cruise if time permits, as the shores of Katrine remain undeveloped and scenic. This loch is the setting of Scott's narrative poem, *Lady of the Lake,* and Ellen's Isle is named after his heroine. ✉ *Trossachs Pier,* ☎ *01877/376316.* ☞ *£5.50 (£6 in high season).* ☉ *Cruises Apr.–late Oct., Sun.–Fri. 11, 1:45, and 3:15; Sat. 1:45 and 3:15.*

Dining and Lodging

££ ✕ **Byre Inn.** Adjoining Dundarroch Country House (☞ *below*), this is a well-run pub and restaurant just beyond Brig o' Turk, with dark beams and loosely defined Victorian decor, as well as attentive, friendly service. It's a lunchtime haven, particularly on a wet day in the wood-

HOLLYWOOD COMES IN FOR THE KILT

THE RECENT SUCCESS OF MOVIES such as *Rob Roy* and, to an even greater extent, *Braveheart* has virtually created a new genre—the so-called kilt movie. In 1996 Scotland became hot, with Scotland's scenery a greater-than-ever attraction to Hollywood. So what if big chunks of *Braveheart* were actually filmed in Ireland?

Not that there is anything new about Scotland as a dramatic backdrop. In 1922 a silent film described at the time as "the first Scottish epic" featured the character of Rob Roy and a cast of 2,000. It was shot partly around Loch Lomond, onetime homeland of the real-life Rob Roy MacGregor (1671–1734). As defender of the downtrodden and scourge of the authorities, MacGregor was known as a tartan Robin Hood. In 1953 Rob Roy's adventures again made it to the screen, in Walt Disney's *The Sword and the Rose*, starring Richard Todd. Locations for this version of the much-revered Highland outlaw's story included Aberfoyle, the southern gateway to the Trossachs.

The 1995 *Rob Roy*, starring Liam Neeson, was shot at and around Glen Nevis and Glencoe, both near Fort William; the gardens of Drummond Castle, near Crieff; and Crichton Castle, near Edinburgh. Another 1995 release, and winner of the Academy Award for that year's Best Picture, Mel Gibson's blockbuster *Braveheart* is the story of Scotland's first freedom fighter, Sir William Wallace (1270–1305). It also uses the spectacular craggy scenery of Glen Nevis, a spot well worth a visit if you find yourself in Fort William; it offers a big change from the many woolen shops.

The Prime of Miss Jean Brodie (1969), based on the Muriel Spark novel, starred Dame Maggie Smith in the title role. She won an Academy Award for Best Actress for her performance as an eccentric teacher who reigns over an Edinburgh girls' school. (Pauline Kael praised her for being "very funny—snobbish, full of affectations, and with a jumble shop of a mind.") Filmed in a variety of locations around Edinburgh (as well as in London), it's a Scottish classic. Even Greyfriars Bobby—the Skye terrier who watched over his master's grave at Greyfriars for 14 years, beginning in 1858, and who was made a citizen of Edinburgh to save him from being destroyed as a stray—had his moment on the silver screen, in the eponymous 1961 Walt Disney film.

Mel Gibson's *Hamlet* (1990) was filmed at Dunnottar Castle, at Stonehaven in the east. Looking farther back, *Highlander* (1986), with Christopher Lambert and Sean Connery, also used the spectacular crags of Glencoe, along with the prototypical Scottish castle Eilean Donan—almost a visual cliché in Scottish terms. Starring Peter Riegert and Burt Lancaster, *Local Hero* (1983) put together the best of east- and west-coast Scotland. In the movie the village of Pennan, an hour's drive north of Aberdeen, which huddles below spectacular cliffs, became Ferness, the village threatened by oil development. The village phone box (telephone booth), which played an important part in the film's story, has been carefully preserved. (And, yes, you can see the Aurora Borealis [the Northern Lights] from it—sometimes.) In fact, the phone box has become something of a local landmark, and lots of visitors still travel there especially to see it.

Trainspotting (1996), based on the novel of the same name by Irvine Welsh, is a flip commentary on heroin addicts in an economically depressed Edinburgh. Although it was produced in Britain, it found a large North American audience. *Small Faces* (1995), written and directed by Gillies MacKinnon, tells the harrowing story of gangland violence in Glasgow in 1968. It looks like Scotland will remain fertile ground for moviemakers for some time to come.

lands, but also offers a full evening menu. Savory Scottish offerings include roasted venison. Call ahead in winter, when hours are limited. ✉ *Brig o' Turk,* ☎ *01877/376292. MC, V.*

££ ⌂ **Dundarroch Country House.** This Victorian country house, set on 14 acres, offers first-class accommodations furnished with antiques, paintings, and tapestries in a warm, relaxing atmosphere. The mountain views from the guest rooms are stunning. ✉ *Brig o' Turk, Trossachs, Perthshire FK17 8HT,* ☎ *01877/376200,* 𝖥𝖠𝖷 *01877/376202. 3 rooms with bath or shower. No credit cards. Closed Nov.–Mar.*

Outdoor Activities and Sports

The **Highland Boundary Fault Walk** (✉ Forest Enterprise, Aberfoyle, Stirlingshire FK8 3UX, ☎ 01877/382383) runs along the Highland boundary fault edge, offering superb views of both the Highlands and Lowlands, 6 mi south of the Trossachs on A821.

En Route For more exquisite nature-viewing after your visit to Loch Katrine, go back through the pass to the main A821 and turn right, heading south to higher moorland blanketed with conifer plantations (some of which have near-mature timber planted about 60 years ago by the Forestry Commission). The conifers hem in the views of Ben Ledi and Ben Venue, which can be seen over the spiky green waves of trees as the road snakes around heathery knolls and hummocks. There is another viewing area at the highest point here in a small parking lot on the right. Soon the road swoops off the Highland edge and leads downhill. Near the start of the descent, the **Queen Elizabeth Forest Park Visitor Centre** can be seen on the left. The center features displays on the life of the forest, a summer-only café, some fine views over the Lowlands to the south, and a network of footpaths. The Trossachs end here.

Aberfoyle

❷❻ *11 mi south of Loch Katrine, in the Trossachs.*

You are unlikely to want to linger in the small resort town of Aberfoyle, with its range of souvenir shops, unless you have children with ☺ you. The **Scottish Wool Centre** tells the story of Scottish wool "from the sheep's back to your back." The Sheep Amphitheatre has live specimens of the main breeds, and in the Textile Display Area you can try spinning and weaving. There are also a Kids' Farm (with lambs and kids) and Sheepdog Training Display (weekends in summer only). The shop stocks a huge selection of woolen garments and knitwear. Live sheep shows (three each day) are held in summer. ✉ *Off Main St., Aberfoyle, Stirlingshire,* ☎ *01877/382850.* 🎟 *£3.* ☉ *Apr.–Sept., daily 9:30–6; Oct.–Dec. and Feb.–Mar., daily 10–5; Jan., daily 10–4.*

❷❼ A short distance to the east of Aberfoyle is the **Lake of Menteith.** The tiny island of **Inchmahome** on the loch was a place of refuge in 1547 for the young Mary, Queen of Scots.

From Aberfoyle you can take a trip to see the more enclosed northern portion of **Loch Lomond** (☞ Loch Lomond, *below*). During the off-season the route has an untamed and windswept air when it extends beyond the shelter of trees. Take the B829 (signposted INVERSNAID and STRONACHLACHAR), which runs west from Aberfoyle and offers outstanding views of **Ben Lomond**, especially in the vicinity of **Loch Ard.** The next loch, where the road narrows and bends, is **Loch Chon,** which appears dark and forbidding. Its ominous reputation is further enhanced by the local legend: the presence of a dog-headed monster prone to swallowing passersby. Beyond Loch Chon, the road climbs gently from the plantings to open moor with a breathtaking vista over **Loch Arklet** to the **Arrochar Alps,** the name given to the high hills west of Loch Lomond. Hidden from sight in a deep trench, Loch Arklet is dammed to feed Loch Katrine. Go left at the road junction (a right will take you to the town of Stronachlachar) and take the open road along Loch Arklet. These deserted green hills were once the rallying grounds of the Clan Gregor. Near the dam on Loch Arklet, on your right, **Garrison Cottage** recalls the days when the government had to billet troops here to keep the MacGregors in order. From Loch Arklet the road zigzags down to **Inversnaid**, where you will see a hotel, house, and parking lot, with Loch Lomond stretching out of sight above and below. The only return to Aberfoyle is by retracing the same route.

Outdoor Activities and Sports

BIKING

Rent bicycles from **Trossachs Cycle Hire** (✉ Trossachs Holiday Park, ☎ 01877/382614).

WALKING

The long-distance walkers' route, the **West Highland Way**, which runs 95 mi from Glasgow to Fort William, follows the bank of Loch Lomond at Inversnaid. Take a brief stroll up the path, particularly if you are visiting during the spring, when the oak-tree canopy is filled with birdsong. You may get an inkling why Scots get so romantic about their bonnie, bonnie banks.

Drymen

28 *11 mi southwest of Aberfoyle.*

Drymen is a respectable and cozy town in the Lowland fields, with shops, tea shops, and pubs catering to the well-to-do Scots who have moved here from Glasgow.

For the most outstanding Loch Lomond view from the south end, drive west from Drymen and take just a few minutes to clamber up bracken-covered **Duncryne Hill**. At dusk you may be rewarded by a spectacular sunset. You can't miss this distinctive dumpling-shape hill, south of Gartocharn on the Drymen–Balloch road, the A811.

Shopping

The Rowan Gallery (✉ 36 Main St., ☎ FAX 01360/660996) shows original paintings and prints, specializing in Scottish scenes, but also has a fine selection of crafts, cards, gifts, and jewelry.

Loch Lomond

29 *3 mi west of Drymen via B837, signposted ROWARDENNAN and BALMAHA; 14 mi west of Aberfoyle.*

At the little settlement of **Balmaha**, the versatile recreational role filled by Loch Lomond is clear: cruising craft are at the ready, hikers appear out of woodlands on the West Highland Way, and day-trippers stroll at the loch's edge. The heavily wooded offshore islands look alluringly close. One of the best ways to explore them is by taking a cruise or renting a boat (☞ Guided Tours, *below*). The island of **Inchcailloch** (*inch* is *innis*, Gaelic for island), just offshore, can be explored in an hour or two. Pleasant pathways thread through oak woods planted in the 18th century, when the bark was used by the tanning industry.

Behind Balmaha is **Conic Hill**, a wavy ridge of bald, heathery domes above the pine trees. You can note from your map how Inchcailloch and the other islands line up with it. This geographic line is indicative of the Highland Boundary Fault, which runs through Loch Lomond and the hill.

If you want to take in even more of Loch Lomond, take the road (a cul-de-sac) northwest to **Rowardennan.** The loch is seldom more than a narrow field's length away. Where the drivable road ends, in a parking lot crunchy with pinecones, you can ramble along one of the marked lochside footpaths or make your way toward not-so-nearby Ben Lomond.

Dining and Lodging

££££ ✕🏨 **Cameron House.** This luxury hotel offers a mix of top-quality hotel
★ and country-club facilities on the shores of Loch Lomond. Bedrooms are decorated in modern pastel shades with high-quality reproductions of antique furniture. The outstanding restaurants, with rich Victorian decor, serve excellent Scottish-French cuisine. There's also a nautical-style diner called Breakers. ✉ *Loch Lomond, Alexandria, Dumbartonshire G83 8QZ,* ☎ *01389/755565,* FAX *01389/759522. 96 rooms with bath. 3 restaurants, bar, 2 pools, golf privileges, health club, squash, fishing. AE, DC, MC, V.*

Outdoor Activities and Sports

MacFarlane and Son (✉ Boatyard, Balmaha, Loch Lomond, ☎ 01360/870214) runs cruises on Loch Lomond. They also run a mail boat to the islands that takes passengers; it operates July–August, Monday–Saturday at 11:30; April–June and September–October, Monday, Thursday, and Saturday at 11:30; and November–March, Monday and Thursday at 10:50. You can even rent a rowboat or a small powerboat from MacFarlane's if you prefer to do your own exploration. From Tarbet, on the western shore, **Cruise Loch Lomond** (✉ Boatyard, Tarbet, ☎ 01301/702356) runs tours all year.

Shopping

Thistle Bagpipe Works (✉ Luss, Dunbartonshire G83 8NX, ☎ FAX 01436/860250), on the western shore of Loch Lomond, will let you commission your own made-to-order set of bagpipes. You can also order a complete Highland outfit, including kilt and jacket.

PERTHSHIRE

Although Perth has an ancient history, it has been rebuilt and recast innumerable times, and sadly, no trace remains of the pre-Reformation monasteries that once dominated the skyline. In fact, modern Perth has swept much of its colorful history under a grid of bustling shopping streets. The town serves a wide rural hinterland and has a well-off air, making it one of Scotland's most interesting shopping towns, aside from Edinburgh and Glasgow.

Perth's rural hinterland is grand in several senses. On the Highland edge, prosperous-looking farms are scattered across heavily wooded countryside, and even larger properties are screened by trees and parkland. All this changes as the mountain barrier is penetrated, giving rise to grouse moors and deer forest (in this case, *forest* has the Scots meaning of, paradoxically, *open hill*). Parts of Perthshire are quite remote without ever losing their cozy feel.

Perth

❸ *36 mi northeast of Stirling, 43 mi north of Edinburgh, 61 mi northeast of Glasgow.*

Perth has long been a focal point in Scottish history, and several critical events took place here, including the assassination of King James I of Scotland (1394–1437) and John Knox's (1513–72) preaching in St. John's Kirk in 1559. Later, the 17th-century religious wars in Scotland saw the town occupied, first by the marquis of Montrose (1612–

50), then later by Oliver Cromwell's (1599–1658) forces. Perth was also occupied by the Jacobites in the 1715 and 1745 rebellions. Perth's attractions—with the exception of the shops—are scattered and take time to reach on foot. Some, in fact, are far enough away to necessitate the use of a car, bus, or taxi.

St. John's Kirk, dating from the 15th century, escaped the worst excesses of the Reformation mob and is now restored. ⊠ *St. John St.,* ☎ *01738/626159.* ☉ *Weekdays 10–2 and 2–4, and for Sun. services.*

The **Perth Art Gallery and Museum** has a wide-ranging collection of natural history, local history, and archaeology, plus a rotating exhibit program. ⊠ *George St.,* ☎ *01738/632488.* ☞ *Free.* ☉ *Mon.–Sat. 10–5.*

On the North Inch of Perth, look for **Balhousie Castle** and the **Regimental Museum of the Black Watch.** Some will tell you the Black Watch was a Scottish regiment whose name is a reference to the color of its tartan. An equally plausible explanation, however, is that the regiment was established to keep an undercover watch on rebellious Jacobites. *Black* is the Gaelic word *dubh,* meaning, in this case, "hidden" or "covert," used in the same sense as the word *blackmail.* ⊠ *Facing North Inch Park (entrance from Hay St.),* ☎ *0131/310–8530.* ☞ *Free.* ☉ *May–Sept., Mon.–Sat. 10–4:30; Oct.–Apr., weekdays 10–3:30. Closed last Sat. in June.*

The nearby Round House is home to the **Fergusson Gallery,** displaying a selection of 6,000 works—paintings, drawings, and prints—by the Scottish artist J. D. Fergusson (1874–1961). ⊠ *Marshall Pl.,* ☎ *01738/441944.* ☞ *Free.* ☉ *Mon.–Sat. 10–5.*

Off the A9 west of town is **Caithness Glass,** where from the viewing gallery, you can watch glassworkers creating silky-smooth bowls, vases, and other glassware. There are also a small museum, restaurant, and shop. ⊠ *Inveralmond, Perth,* ☎ *01738/637373.* ☞ *Free.* ☉ *Factory: weekdays 9–4:30; shop: Easter–mid-Oct., Mon.–Sat. 9–5, Sun. 10–5; mid-Oct.–Easter, Mon.–Sat. 9–5, Sun. noon–5.*

❸❶ A modest selection of castles is within easy reach of Perth. **Huntingtower Castle,** a curious double tower that dates from the 15th century, is associated with an attempt to wrest power from the young James VI in 1582. Some early painted ceilings survive, offering the vaguest hint of the sumptuous interiors, once found in many such ancient castles, that are now reduced to bare and drafty rooms. ⊠ *Off A85,* ☎ *0131/668–8800.* ☞ *£2.* ☉ *Apr.–Sept., daily 9:30–6; Oct.–Mar., Mon.–Wed. and Sat. 9:30–4, Thurs. 9–noon, Sun. 2–4.*

❸❷ **Elcho Castle** is a fortified mansion on the east side of Perth. It is the abandoned 15th-century seat of the earls of Wemyss, and all that remains is a shell. ⊠ *On River Tay,* ☎ *0131/668–8800.* ☞ *£1.80.* ☉ *Apr.–Sept., daily 9:30–6.*

★ ☺ **❸❸** **Scone Palace** is much more cheerful and vibrant than Perth's other castles. The palace is the current residence of the earl of Mansfield but is open to visitors. Although it incorporates various earlier works, the palace today has mainly a 19th-century theme, featuring mock castellations that were fashionable at the time. There is plenty to see if you have an interest in the acquisitions of an aristocratic Scottish family: magnificent porcelain, furniture, ivory, clocks, and 16th-century needlework. A coffee shop, restaurant, gift shop, and play area are on site, and the extensive grounds have a pine plantation.

The palace has its own mausoleum nearby, on the site of a long-gone abbey on **Moot Hill,** the ancient coronation place of the Scottish kings.

To be crowned, they sat on the Stone of Scone, which was seized in 1296 by Edward I of England (1239–1307), Scotland's greatest enemy, and placed in the coronation chair at Westminster Abbey, in London. It was returned to Scotland in November 1996 and is now on view in Edinburgh Castle. Some Scots hint darkly that Edward was fooled by a substitution and that the real stone is hidden, waiting for Scotland to regain its independence. ⊠ *Braemar Rd.,* ☎ *01738/552308.* 🎫 *£5.60.* ☉ *Easter–Oct., daily 9:30–5:15 (last admission 4:45).*

� Near Perth, **Fairways Horse Sanctuary** is a charity caring for Clydesdale horses, once the mainstay of horse-powered agriculture and transport in Scotland. You can tour the center's stables and exercise fields, and there are occasional special days with children's activities. The Sanctuary has a café and souvenir shop with appropriate horsey offerings. ⊠ *Glencarse Village,* ☎ *01738/860888.* 🎫 *£3.* ☉ *Daily 10–5.*

Dining and Lodging

£££ ✕🖫 **Parklands.** A stylish Georgian town house overlooking lush woodland, this top-quality hotel is perhaps best known for its cuisine, featuring Scottish fish, game, and beef. The restrained decor and modern furniture are in keeping with the subdued but elegant ambience. ⊠ *2 St. Leonard's Bank, PH2 8EB,* ☎ *01738/622451,* 📠 *01738/622046. 14 rooms with bath or shower. Restaurant. AE, DC, MC, V.*

££ ✕🖫 **Sunbank House Hotel.** You'll find this early Victorian gray-stone
★ mansion in a fine residential area near Perth's Branklyn Gardens. A lesson in traditional style, it offers solid, unpretentious comforts along with great views over the River Tay and the city. The restaurant specializes in locally raised meats and game, imaginatively prepared Continental style with some Scottish overtones. ⊠ *50 Dundee Rd., PH2 7BA,* ☎ *01738/624882,* 📠 *01738/442515. 10 rooms with bath or shower. Restaurant. MC, V.*

Nightlife and the Arts

The Victorian **Perth Repertory Theatre** (⊠ High St., ☎ 01738/621031) offers a variety of plays and musicals. In the summer it is the main venue for the Perth Festival of the Arts. The **Perth City Hall** (☎ 01738/ 624055) is the main venue for musical performances of all types.

Shopping

CLOTHING

A comprehensive selection of sheepskins, leather jackets, and hand-knit Aran sweaters is sold at **C & C Proudfoot** (⊠ 104 South St., ☎ 01738/ 632483).

GLASS AND CHINA

Perth is an especially popular hunting ground for china and glass: **Watson of Perth** (⊠ 163–167 High St., ☎ 01738/639861) has sold exquisite bone china and cut crystal since 1900 and can pack your purchase safely for shipment overseas. At **Caithness Glass** (⊠ Inveralmond, off A9 at northern town boundary, ☎ 01738/637373), you can buy all types of glassware in the factory shop.

JEWELRY AND ANTIQUES

Perth proffers an unusual buy: Scottish freshwater pearls from the River Tay, in delicate settings, some of which take their theme from Scottish flowers. The Romans coveted these pearls. If you do, too, then you can make your choice at **Cairncross Ltd., Goldsmiths** (⊠ 18 St. John's St., ☎ 01738/624367), where you can also admire a display of some of the more unusual shapes and colors of pearls. Antique jewelry and silver (including Scottish items) can be found at **Timothy Hardie** (⊠ 25 St. John's St., ☎ 01738/633127). **Whispers of the Past** (⊠ 15 George St., ☎ 01738/635472) has a collection of jewelry, linens, and other items.

SCOTTISH SPECIALTIES

The Mill Shop (⊠ Lower City Mills, W. Mill St., ☎ 01738/627958) sells high-quality Scottish gifts, foods, and meal products produced at this working Victorian mill. In the same building is Perth's tourist information center, where you can buy ties and scarves in Perthshire's own tartan.

Dunkeld

㉞ *14 mi north of Perth.*

At Dunkeld, Thomas Telford's sturdy river bridge of 1809 carries the road into town. In Dunkeld you will find that the National Trust for Scotland not only cares for grand mansions and wildlands but also actively restores smaller properties. Its Little Houses project can be seen in the square off the main street, opposite the fish-and-chips shop. The houses on the square had all been rebuilt after the 1689 defeat of the Jacobite army here, which occurred after its early victory in the Battle of Killiecrankie (☞ *below*).

The ospreys that frequent Speyside's Loch Garten in summer get so much attention from conservation societies that they sometimes overshadow those to be found at **Loch of Lowes,** a Scottish Wildlife Trust reserve near Dunkeld. Here the domestic routines of the osprey, one of Scotland's conservation success stories, can be observed in relative comfort. ⊠ *Off A923 northeast of Dunkeld,* ☎ *01350/727337.* ☉ *Apr.–Sept., daily 10–5.*

Shopping

Dunkeld Antiques (⊠ Tay Terr., ☎ 01350/728832), facing the river as you cross the bridge, stocks everything from large items of furniture to ornaments, jewelry, books, and prints. At the **Highland Horn and Deerskin Centre** (⊠ City Hall, Atholl St., ☎ 01350/727569), you can purchase stag antlers and cow horns shaped into walking sticks, cutlery, and tableware. Deerskin shoes and moccasins, a range of small leather goods made from deerskin, and a specialty malt-whisky collection of more than 200 different malts are also sold. The center has a worldwide postal service and a tax-free shop.

Pitlochry

㉟ *15 mi north of Dunkeld.*

A typical central Highland resort, always full of leisurely hustle and bustle, Pitlochry has wall-to-wall souvenir and gift shops, large hotels recalling the days when this area was even more laid-back, and a mountainous golf course. Most Scottish dams have salmon passes or ladders of some kind, enabling the fish to swim upstream to their spawning grounds. In Pitlochry, the **Pitlochry Dam and Fish Ladder,** just behind the main street, leads into a glass-paneled pipe that allows the fish to observe the visitors.

For those with a whisky-tasting bent, Pitlochry also is home to **Edradour Distillery,** which claims to be the smallest single-malt distillery in Scotland (but then, so do others). ⊠ *2½ mi east of Pitlochry,* ☎ *01796/472095.* 🎫 *Free.* ☉ *Tour and tastings: Mar.–Oct., Mon.–Sat. 9:30–5, Sun. noon–5; Nov.–Dec., Mon.–Sat. 10–3; shop only: Nov.–Feb., Mon.–Sat. 10:30–4.*

㊱ The **Linn of Tummel,** a series of marked walks along the river and through tall, mature woodlands, is a little north of Pitlochry. Above the Linn, the new A9 is raised on stilts and gives an exciting view of the valley.

★ **㊲** The **Pass of Killiecrankie,** set among the oak woods and rocky river just north of the Linn of Tummel, was a key strategic point in the Central Highlands: a famous battle was won here in the Jacobite rebellion of 1689. The National Trust for Scotland's **visitor center** at Killiecrankie explains the significance of this battle, which was the first attempt to restore the Stewart monarchy. The battle was noted for the death of the central Jacobite leader, John Graham of Claverhouse (1649–89), also known as Bonnie Dundee, who was hit by a stray bullet; the rebellion fizzled after that.&del; ⊠ *Signposted off A9,* ☎ ℻ *01796/ 473233.* ⊡ *£1.* ☉ *Apr.–Oct., daily 10–5:30.*

★ ❸❽ Only a few minutes farther north from the Pass of Killiecrankie sits **Blair Castle.** Thanks to its historic contents and its war-torn past, this castle is one of Scotland's most highly rated sites. Turreted and painted white, Blair Castle was home to successive dukes of Atholl and their families, the Murrays, until the death of the 10th duke. Its ownership and care have now passed to a charitable trust. One of the many fascinating details in the interior is a preserved piece of the floor still bearing marks of the red-hot shot fired through the roof during the 1745 Jacobite rebellion—the last occasion in Scottish history that a castle was besieged. The castle holds not only military artifacts—historically, the duke was allowed to keep a private army, the Atholl Highlanders—but also a fine collection of furniture and paintings. Outside, a Victorian walled garden has been restored, and there are extensive parklands backed by high, rounded hills. ⊠ *From Pitlochry, take the A9 to Blair Atholl and follow signs,* ☎ *01796/481207.* ⊡ *Castle and grounds: £6; grounds only: £2.* ☉ *Apr.–late Oct., daily 10–6 (last admission 5).* ⊛

❸❾ Also easily reached from Pitlochry is **Loch Rannoch,** which, with its shoreline of birch trees framed by dark pines, is the quintessential Highland loch. To reach this atmospheric locale, take B8019 at the Linn of Tummel north of Pitlochry; a the Tummel Bridge, pick up B846, which travels along the shores of the loch. Fans of Robert Louis Stevenson (1850–94), especially of *Kidnapped* (1886), will not want to miss the last, lonely section of road. Stevenson describes the setting: "The mist rose and died away, and showed us that country lying as waste as the sea; only the moorfowl and the peewees crying upon it, and far over to the east a herd of deer, moving like dots. Much of it was red with heather, much of the rest broken up with bogs and hags and peaty pools . . ." Apart from the blocks of alien conifer plantings in certain places, little here has changed. To reach this atmospheric locale, take the B8019 at the Linn of Tummel north of Pitlochry, then the B846 at Tummel Bridge. The road ends at Rannoch, where you meet the West Highland railroad line on its way across Rannoch Moor to Fort William.

Nightlife and the Arts

Pitlochry Festival Theatre (⊠ Pitlochry, ☎ 01796/484626 box office, ☎ 01796/484600 general enquiries) presents six plays each season and features eight Sunday concerts. The theater is open all year.

Aberfeldy

❹❽ *15 mi southwest of Pitlochry.*

Aberfeldy is a sleepy town popular as a tourist base. Aberfeldy Bridge (1733), with five arches and a humpback, was designed by William Adam (1689–1748). West of Aberfeldy, on the opposite bank of the River Tay, stands **Castle Menzies.** This 16th-century fortified tower house is now the setting for the **Clan Menzies' Museum,** which has many relics of the clan's history. ☎ *01887/820982.* ⊡ *£3.* ☉ *Apr.–mid-Oct., Mon.–Sat. 10:30–5, Sun. 2–5 (last admission 4:30).*

❹❷ **Glen Lyon** is one of central Scotland's most attractive glens; it has a rushing river, forests, high hills on both sides, prehistoric sites (complete with legendary tales), and the typical *big hoose* (big house) hidden on private grounds. There is even a dam at the head of the loch, a reminder that little of Scotland's scenic beauty is unadulterated. You can reach the glen by a high road from Loch Tay: take the A827 to Fearnan, then turn north to Fortingall. The Fortingall yew, in the churchyard near the Fortingall Hotel, wearily rests its great limbs on the ground. This tree is thought to be more than 3,000 years old. Legend has it that Pontius Pilate was born beside it, during the time his father was serving as a Roman legionnaire in Scotland. After viewing the yew, turn west into Glen Lyon.

Outdoor Activities and Sports

Loch Tay Boating Centre (⊠ Carlin and Brett, Pier Rd., Kenmore, ☎ 01887/830291) has cabin cruisers, fishing boats, and canoes from April through October.

En Route   Between Aberfeldy and Killin, take the north-bank road by Loch Tay, the A827, which offers fine views west along Loch Tay toward Ben More and Stobinian and north to Ben Lawers.

Killin

43   *24 mi southwest of Aberfeldy, 39 mi north of Stirling, 45 mi west of Perth.*

A village with an almost alpine flavor, known for its modest but surprisingly diverse selection of crafts and woolen wares, Killin is also noted for its scenery. The **Falls of Dochart,** white-water rapids overlooked by a pine-clad islet, are at the west end of the village. By the Falls of Dochart you will find the **Breadalbane Folklore Centre,** with its descriptions of the area's heritage and folk tales. The most curious of these are the "Healing Stones of St. Fillan"—water-worn stones that have been looked after lovingly for centuries for their supposed curative powers. ⊠ Killin, ☎ 01567/820254. ☜ £1.50. ☼ Mar.–June and Sept.–Oct., daily 10–5; July–Aug., daily 9:30–6:30; Nov.–Dec. and Feb., weekends 10–4 (call to confirm hrs in winter).

Across the River Dochart and near the golf course sit the ruins of **Finlarig Castle,** built by Black Duncan of the Cowl, a notorious Campbell laird. The castle can be visited at any time.

Lodging

£–££   🏠 **Lodge House.** Few other guest houses in Scotland can match the mountain views from this 100-year-old property; it's certainly worth the short drive (about 15 mi) west from Killin to Crianlarich. Informal and cozy, the guest house is successful thanks to what the Scots call good "crack"—conviviality, in this case between host and guests. The food (for resident guests only) is good Scots fare: haggis, salmon, and oatcakes. The bedrooms are plain and unfussy, but more than adequate. You may wish to walk along the riverbank after dinner, or have a wee dram in the tiny bar instead. ⊠ *Lodge House, Crianlarich, Perthshire FK20 8RU,* ☎ *01838/300276. 6 rooms with bath or shower. MC, V.* ❧

Outdoor Activities and Sports

If you want to explore the north end of the Glasgow–Killin cycleway, rent a bicycle from **Killin Outdoor Centre and Mountain Shop** (⊠ Main St., ☎ 01567/820652, ℻ 01567/820116). For more ambitious explorers, this company also rents canoes, crampons, skis, and ice axes.

En Route   Southwest of Killin the A827 joins the main A85. By turning south over the watershed, you will see fine views of the hill ridges behind Killin. The road leads into Glen Ogle, "amid the wildest and finest scenery we had yet seen . . . putting one in mind of prints of the Khyber Pass," as Queen Victoria (1819–1901) recorded in her diary when she passed this way in 1842.

Crieff

44 *25 mi southwest of Killin.*

The hilly town of Crieff offers walks with Highland views from **Knock Hill** above the town. Tours of the **Glenturret Distillery** can be undertaken if you have not already discovered the delights of whisky distilling. There are also two restaurants offering Taste of Scotland menus, an audiovisual presentation entitled *The Water of Life*, and the *Spirit of the Glen* exhibition. The distillery is signposted on the west side of the town. ☎ *01764/656565.* ☑ *£3.50; free in Jan.* ☼ *Jan., weekdays 11:30–4 (last tour 2:30); Feb., Mon.–Sat. 11:30–4, Sun. noon–4 (last tour 2:30); Mar.–Dec., Mon.–Sat. 9:30–6, Sun. noon–6 (last tour 4:30).*

Just south of Crieff is a paperweight manufacturer, part of a complex called the **Crieff Visitors Centre.** Adjacent to the complex is a small pottery factory, a restaurant, and a shop, where you can purchase Thistle hand-painted pottery and intricate millefiori, among other things. ☒ *A822, south of Crieff,* ☎ *01764/654014.* ☑ *Free.* ☼ *Daily 9–5 (restricted hrs during winter; call ahead).*

45 **Drummond Castle,** southwest of the town, has an unusual formal Italian garden. ☒ *Off Crieff–Muthill road,* ☎ *01764/681257.* ☑ *Gardens £3.* ☼ *Easter weekend and May–Oct., daily 2–6 (last admission 5).*

Shopping

Crieff is a center for china and glassware. **Stuart Crystal** (☒ Muthill Rd., ☎ 01764/654004), a factory shop, sells not only its own Stuart crystal but also Waterford and Wedgwood wares. Also visit the **Crieff Visitors Centre** (☞ *above*).

Auchterarder

46 *11 mi southeast of Crieff.*

Famous for the **Gleneagles Hotel** (☞ Dining and Lodging, *below*), Auchterarder also has a flock of antiques shops.

Dining and Lodging

££££ ✕🏨 **Auchterarder House Hotel.** This secluded and richly furnished
★ Victorian country mansion has a plush, exuberantly styled dining room filled with glittering glassware; it's an appropriate setting for the unusual and creative presentation of many locally produced foods. ☒ *On B8062 at Auchterarder, 15 mi southwest of Perth, PH3 1DZ,* ☎ *01764/663646,* 🅵🅰🆇 *01764/662939. 15 rooms with bath. Restaurant, golf privileges, croquet. AE, DC, MC, V.* ☙

££££ ✕🏨 **Gleneagles Hotel.** One of Britain's most famous hotels, Gleneagles is the very essence of modern grandeur. Like a vast, secret palace, it stands hidden in breathtaking countryside amid world-famous golf courses. Recreation facilities are nearly endless, and there are three restaurants: the Strathearn, for à la carte and table d'hôte; the Clubhouse Grill (at the 18th hole of the King's Course), for à la carte; and the Club Restaurant, by the swimming pool. All this, plus a shopping arcade, Champneys Health Spa, the Gleneagles Equestrian Centre, the British School of Falconry, the Golf Academy, and the Off-Road at Gleneagles driving school, make a stay here a luxurious and unforgettable experience. ☒ *Auchterarder, near Perth, PH3 1NF,* ☎ *01764/662231,* 🅵🅰🆇 *01764/662134. 229 rooms with bath. 3 restaurants, sauna, golf privileges, tennis court, exercise room. AE, DC, MC, V.* ☙

THE CENTRAL HIGHLANDS A TO Z

Arriving and Departing

By Bus

A good network of buses connects with the central belt via Edinburgh and Glasgow. Express services also link the larger towns in the Central Highlands with all main towns and cities in England. For more information contact **Scottish Citylink** (☎ 0990/505050) or **National Express** (☎ 0990/808080).

By Car

"You'll find easy access to the area from the central belt of Scotland via the motorway network. The M9 runs within sight of the walls of Stirling Castle, and Perth can be reached via the M90 over the Forth Bridge.

By Plane

Perth and Stirling can be reached easily from the **Edinburgh** and **Glasgow** airports (☞ Chapters 1 and 2) by train, car, or bus.

By Train

The Central Highlands are linked to Edinburgh and Glasgow by rail, with through routes to England (some direct-service routes from London take fewer than five hours). A variety of Savers ticket options are available, although in some cases on the ScotRail system, the discount fares must be purchased before your arrival in the United Kingdom. Contact the **National Train Enquiry Line** (☎ 0345/484950) for details.

Getting Around

By Bus

The following companies organize reliable service on a number of convenient routes: **Scottish Citylink** (⊠ Leonard St. bus station, Perth, ☎ 01738/626848), **First Edinburgh Bus Services** (⊠ Goosecroft Rd. bus station, Stirling, ☎ 01786/446474), and **Stagecoach** (⊠ Ruthvenfield Rd., Inveralmond Industrial Estate, Perth, ☎ 01738/629339).

By Car

There is an adequate network of roads, and the area's proximity to the central belt speeds road communications. The Scottish Tourist Board's touring map is useful.

By Train

The **West Highland Line** runs through the western portion of the area. Services also run to Stirling, Dunblane, Perth, and Gleneagles; destinations on the Inverness–Perth line include Dunkeld, Pitlochry, and Blair Atholl. Contact the **National Train Enquiry Line** (☎ 0345/484950) for details.

Contacts and Resources

Car Rental

Arnold Clark (⊠ St. Leonard's Bank, Perth, ☎ 01738/638511). **Avis** (⊠ 54–56 Victoria St., Perth, ☎ 01738/442646). **Europcar** (⊠ 26 Glasgow Rd., Perth, ☎ 01738/636888).

Doctors and Dentists

Local practitioners will usually treat visitors. Information is available from tourist information centers, or from your hotel receptionist or bed-and-breakfast host. Late-night pharmacies are found only in the larger towns and cities. In an emergency the police will help you find a pharmacist.

Emergencies

Ambulance, fire, or police: ☎ 999. (No coins are needed for emergency calls from phone booths.)

Perth Royal Infirmary (✉ Taymount Terr., Perth, ☎ 01738/623311). **Stirling Royal Infirmary** (✉ Livilands Gate, Stirling, ☎ 01786/434000). **Vale of Leven Hospital** (✉ Main St., Alexandria, ☎ 01389/754121).

Guided Tours

ORIENTATION

The bus companies listed in Getting Around by Bus (☞ *above*) offer a number of general orientation tours. Inquire at the nearest tourist information center, where tour reservations can usually be booked.

SPECIAL-INTEREST

There are many taxi and chauffeur companies offering tailor-made tours by the day or week; the nearest tourist visitor center is your best source for detailed, up-to-date information. Don't miss the opportunity to take a boat trip on a loch, especially in the Trossachs (Loch Katrine) and Loch Lomond; consult a visitor center for details.

Visitor Information

Aberfeldy (✉ The Square, ☎ 01887/820276); **Alva** (✉ Mill Trail Visitor Centre, West Stirling St., ☎ 01259/769696); **Auchterarder** (✉ 90 High St., ☎ 01764/663450); **Blairgowrie** (✉ 26 Wellmeadow, ☎ 01250/872960); **Crieff** (✉ Town Hall, High St., ☎ 01764/652578); **Drymen** (✉ The Square, ☎ 01360/660068); **Kinross** (✉ Service Area Junction 6 M90, ☎ 01577/863680); **Perth** (✉ Lower City Mills, W. Mill St., ☎ 01738/450600); **Pitlochry** (✉ 22 Atholl Rd., ☎ 01796/472215); **Stirling** (✉ 41 Dumbarton Rd., ☎ 01786/475019; ✉ Royal Burgh of Stirling Visitor Centre, ☎ 01786/479901).

Seasonal tourist information centers are also open (generally April–October) in the following towns: Aberfoyle, Balloch, Callander, Dumbarton, Dunblane, Dunkeld, Helensburgh, Killin, Pirnhall, Tarbert, Tarbet, and Tyndrum. All are clearly marked with the standard i sign in white on a blue background.

6 ABERDEEN AND THE NORTHEAST

Here, in this granite shoulder of Grampian, are Royal Deeside, the countryside that Queen Victoria made her own; the Castle Country route, where fortresses stand hard against the hills; and the Whisky Trail, where peaty streams embrace the country's greatest concentration of distilleries. The region's gateway is Aberdeen, constructed of granite and now aglitter with new wealth and new blood drawn together by North Sea oil.

By Gilbert
Summers

Updated by
Beth Ingpen

BECAUSE OF ITS ISOLATION, the granite city of Aberdeen has historically been a fairly autonomous place. Even now it's perceived by many U.K. inhabitants as lying almost out of reach in the northeast. In reality, it's only 90 minutes' flying time from London or a little more than two hours by car from Edinburgh. Its magnificent, confident 18th- and early 19th-century city center amply rewards exploration, and there are also many surviving buildings from earlier centuries for you to seek out. Yet even if Aberdeen vanished from the map, an extensive portion of the northeast would still remain at the top of many travelers' wish lists, studded as it is with some of Scotland's most enduring travel icons.

Some credit Sir Walter Scott with having opened up Scotland for tourism through his poems and novels. Others say General Wade did it when he built the Highland roads. But it was probably Queen Victoria who gave Scottish tourism its real momentum when, in 1842, she first came to Scotland and when, in 1847—on orders of a doctor, who thought the relatively dry climate of upper Deeside would suit her—she bought Balmoral. At first sight she described it as "a pretty little castle in the old Scottish style." The pretty little castle was knocked down to make room for a much grander house in full-flown Scottish baronial style, designed, in fact, by her husband, Prince Albert. Before long the entire Deeside and the region north were dotted with handsome country houses and mock-baronial châteaux, as the ambitious rich thought it wise to stake a claim in the neighborhood. The locals, bless 'em, took it all in stride. Until this day, the hundreds who line the road when the queen and her family arrive for services at the family's parish church at Crathie are invariably visitors to the Deeside—one of Balmoral's great attractions for the monarch has always been the villagers' respect for royal privacy.

Balmoral is merely the most famous castle in the area. Nowhere else in Scotland is there such an eclectic selection of these residences, offering you an opportunity to touch the fabric of Scotland's story. There are so many that in one part of the region a Castle Trail has been established, leading you to such fortresses as the ruined medieval Kildrummy Castle, which once controlled the strategic routes through the valley of the River Don. Later work, such as Craigievar, a narrow-turreted structure resembling an illustration from a fairy-tale book, reflects the changing times of the 17th century, when defense became less of a priority. Later still, grand mansions, such as Haddo House, with its symmetrical facade and elegant interiors, surrender any defensive need entirely and instead make statements about their owner's status.

South of Elgin and Banff, where the peaty streams jostle for elbow room on their race down from the Grampian heights to the sea, the glens embrace Scotland's greatest concentration of malt whisky distilleries. With so many in Morayshire, where the distilling is centered in the valley of the River Spey and its tributaries, there's now a Whisky Trail. Just as the Gironde in France has famous vineyards clustered around it, the Spey has famous single-malt distilleries. Instead of Lafite-Rothschild, Pétrus, and Haut-Brion, there's Glenfiddich, Glen Grant, Tamdhu, or Tamnavulin. As well as being sweeter and less peaty than some of the island malts, eastern or Speyside malts generally have names that are easier to pronounce.

The northeast's chief attraction lies in the gradual transition from high mountain plateau—by a series of gentle steps through hill, forest, and farmland—to the Moray Firth and North Sea coast where the word *unadulterated* is redefined. Here you'll find some of the United Kingdom's most perfect wild shorelines, both sandy and sheer cliff. The Grampian Mountains to the west contain some of the highest ground in the nation, in the area of the Cairngorms. But the Grampian hills also have shaped the character of the folk who live in the northeast. In earlier times the massif made communication with the south somewhat difficult. As a result, native northeasterners still speak the richest Lowland Scottish (*not* Gaelic, which is an entirely different language).

Pleasures and Pastimes

Biking

Northeast Scotland is superb biking country, with networks of minor roads and farm roads crisscrossing rolling fields. You can also ride along former railway track beds that have been converted to bicycle and pedestrian pathways. The Buchan line, from Aberdeen to Fraserburgh and Peterhead, is a good route.

Dining

Partly in response to the demands of spendthrift oilmen, the number of restaurants in Aberdeen has grown during the past several years, and the quality of the food has improved. Elsewhere in the region you're never far from a good pub lunch or a hotel high tea or dinner.

CATEGORY	COST*
££££	over £40
£££	£30–£40
££	£15–£30
£	under £15

per person for a three-course meal, including VAT and excluding drinks and service

Fishing

With major rivers such as the Dee, Don, Deveron, and Ythan, as well as popular smaller rivers like the Ugie, plus loch and estuary fishing, this is one of Scotland's leading game-fishing areas. You can obtain details of beats, boats, and permit prices from local tourist information centers. Some hotels offer fishing packages or at the least can organize permits. Prices vary widely, depending on the fish and individual river beat.

Golf

The Northeast has more than 50 golf clubs, some of which have championship courses (☞ Chapter 11). Tourist information centers can supply leaflets appropriate to their area. All towns and many villages have their 9- and 18-hole municipal links, at which you pay £5–£10 per round. The more prestigious clubs charge up to £60 a day and expect you to book by letter or to bring a letter of recommendation from a member.

Lodging

The northeast has some splendid country hotels with log fires and rich furnishings, where you can also be sure of eating well if you have time for a leisurely meal. Many Aberdeen hotels offer competitive rates on weekends.

CATEGORY	COST*
££££	over £140
£££	£110–£140
££	£65–£110
£	under £65

All prices are for a standard double room, including service, breakfast, and VAT.

🕿 *following the text of a review is your signal that the property has a Web site, where you will find details and, usually, images; for a link, visit www.fodors.com/urls.*

Skiing

The main ski area is at **Glenshee** (☎ 013397/41320), just south of Braemar, though the season can be brief here. Visitors accustomed to long alpine runs and extensive choices will find the runs here short, unlike the lift lines. **The Lecht** (☎ 01975/651440) lies at even lower altitude and is mainly suitable for beginners. The area at **Cairngorm** (☎ 01479/861261), by Aviemore, is another ski option (☞ Chapter 8). There's an artificial "dry" slope at **Alford** (☎ 019755/63024).

Exploring Aberdeen and the Northeast

Once you have spent time in Aberdeen, you may be inclined to venture west into Deeside, with its royal connections and looming mountain backdrop, and then pass over the hills into the Castle Country to the north. You might head farther west to touch on Speyside and the Whisky Trail, before meandering back east and south along the pristine coastline at Scotland's northeasternmost tip.

Union Street is the center of Aberdeen, and traffic from the north and northwest is signposted through the city and beyond to its east end and the harbor. Traffic from the south is signposted around Anderson Drive, from where all the main routes into the Grampian hinterland are also signposted (e.g., the Deeside and Donside routes, the main Inverness A96, and the coastal routes to the north). Outside Aberdeen, the Castle and Whisky trails are generally well marked.

Numbers in the text correspond to numbers in the margin and on the Royal Deeside, Aberdeen, and the Northeast maps.

Great Itineraries

Although the Grampian area isn't huge, it has a great variety of terrains. To get a real flavor of this most authentic of Scottish regions, sample both the coastline and the mountains.

IF YOU HAVE 2 DAYS

Setting out from **Aberdeen** ①–⑳, follow in the footsteps of Queen Victoria and tour the castles and glens of Royal Deeside. Head for **Crathes Castle** ㉓ and **Banchory** ㉑, with its largely unchanged Victorian High Street. After lunch, follow the river upstream to Aboyne, turning north on B9094, then left onto B9119 for 6 mi for a panorama (signposted on B9119) known as the Queen's View, a bit north of Dinnet—this is one of the northeast's most spectacular vistas, stretching across the Howe of Cromar to Lochnagar. Then continue on B9119, dropping gently downhill through the birch woods to A93 and ⌖ **Ballater** ㉗ to the west. The next morning visit Her Majesty's **Balmoral Castle** ㉙ (note that it's only open for three months in the summer) if royal residences are high on your list—explore the ballroom and grounds, take a pony ride, and then treat yourself to a walk in nearby Glen Muick. Here you'll find the famous climb of Lochnagar, so beloved by Victoria. Head for ⌖ **Braemar** ㉚. The next morning set off for Castle Country and some serious castle hopping—**Corgarff Castle** ㉜, **Kildrummy Castle** ㉝, **Craigievar Castle** ㉟, and **Castle Fraser** ㊱—then return to Aberdeen.

IF YOU HAVE 4 DAYS

Downtown ⌖ **Aberdeen's** ①–⑳ silver granite certainly deserves a little time. Then travel into Speyside for its distilleries: **Dufftown** ㊲, and north via **Craigellachie** ㊳ and **Aberlour** ㊴ to ⌖ **Elgin** ㊵. Spend a morning exploring Elgin before moving east along the coast to stay overnight in ⌖ **Fordyce** ㊼ or ⌖ **Banff** ㊽. Visit the magnificent Duff House gallery in Banff, before returning to Aberdeen. If you have time on the last day, see a castle or two: **Drum** ㉒ or **Crathes** ㉓ on Deeside; **Haddo House** ㊶ or **Fyvie Castle** ㊷ northwest of **Ellon** ㊾; or loop northwest-

Royal Deeside

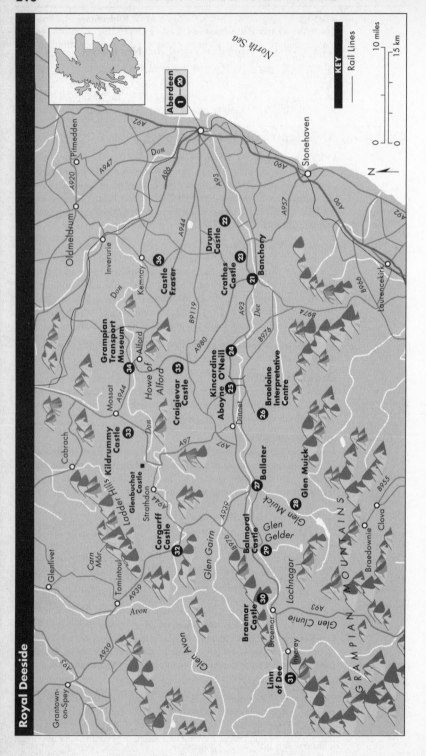

Aberdeen ① — ⑳

North Sea

KEY
— Rail Lines

10 miles

15 km

ward for **Corgarff** ㉜, the ruined castle at **Kildrummy** ㉝, fairy-tale **Craigievar** ㉟, or **Castle Fraser** ㊱.

When to Tour Aberdeen and the Northeast

Because the National Trust for Scotland tends to close its properties in winter, many of the northeast's castles are not suitable for off-season travel, though you can always see them from the outside. Duff House, Macduff Marine Aquarium, and some of the distilleries are open much of the year, but May and June are probably the best times to visit.

ABERDEEN, THE SILVER CITY

In the 18th century local granite quarrying produced a durable silver stone that would be used boldly in the glittering blocks, spires, columns, and parapets of Victorian-era Aberdonian structures. The city remains one of the United Kingdom's most distinctive, although some would say it depends on the weather and the brightness of the day. The mica chips embedded in the rock look like a million mirrors in the sunshine. In rain and heavy clouds, however, their sparkle is snuffed out.

The North Sea has always been important to Aberdeen: in the 1850s the city was famed for its sleek, fast clippers that sailed to India for cargoes of tea. In the late 1960s the course of Aberdeen's history was unequivocally altered when oil and gas were discovered off shore. The city seemed destined to become an oil-rich Klondike, and throughout the 1970s it was overcome by new shops, new office blocks, new hotels, new industries, and new attitudes. Fortunately, the vision of a race of tartan sheikhs in Scotland has now evaporated: some innate local caution has helped the city to retain a sense of perspective.

Exploring Aberdeen

Aberdeen centers on Union Street, whose role as the main shopping area has been diluted by the arrival of three large malls nearby. Still, there are many fine survivors of the Victorian and Edwardian streetscape. Old Aberdeen is very much a separate area of the city, north of the modern center and clustered around St. Machar's Cathedral and the many fine buildings of the University of Aberdeen.

A Good Tour

Start your walk at the east end of **Union Street** ①. Here within the original old town is the Castlegate. The actual castle once stood somewhere behind the Salvation Army Citadel (1896), an imposing baronial granite tower whose design was inspired by Balmoral Castle. On the north side of Castle Street stands the 17th-century **Tolbooth** ②, a reminder of Aberdeen's earliest days. The impressive **Mercat Cross** ③ stands just beyond King Street. Turn north down Broad Street to reach **Marischal College** ④, whose sparkling granite frontage dominates the top end of the street.

A survivor from an earlier Aberdeen can be found opposite Marischal College, beyond the concrete supports of St. Nicholas House (of which the tourist information center is a part): **Provost Skene's House** ⑤ was once part of a closely packed area of town houses and is now a museum portraying civic life. Just around the corner in Upperkirkgate, at the lowest point, are two modern shopping malls—the St. Nicholas Centre on the left, the Bon-Accord Centre on the right. Until recent years George Street, at the foot of the hill here, was a bustling shopping thoroughfare. But not even Aberdeen, in its far northern perch, exempted itself from the British trend toward chain-store anonymity. If you do enter the portals of the Bon-Accord Centre, you'll eventually emerge at the truncated George Street.

Upperkirkgate becomes Schoolhill, where there's a complex of silver-tone buildings in front of which stands a statue of General Charles Gordon (1833–85), the military hero of Khartoum (1885). Interestingly, he is not the Gordon recalled in **Robert Gordon's University** ⑥, behind the statue. The university's next-door neighbor is **Aberdeen Art Gallery** ⑦, which plays an active role in the city's cultural life and is a popular rendezvous for locals.

A library, church, and nearby theater on **Rosemount Viaduct** ⑧ are collectively known by all Aberdonians as Education, Salvation, and Damnation: the silvery and handsome Central Library, St. Mark's Church, and the restored Edwardian His Majesty's Theatre. If you're taking photographs, you can choose an angle that includes the statue of Scotland's first freedom fighter, Sir William Wallace (1270–1305), in the foreground pointing majestically to Damnation. **The Millennium Village** ⑨, great for kids, is off Rosemount Viaduct on Rosemount Place.

Union Terrace ⑩, a 19th-century development, runs back toward Union Street. Smug cats decorate **Union Bridge** ⑪, where Union Terrace meets Union Street. Here you can turn left across the bridge and follow Union to **St. Nicholas Kirk** ⑫. It's set in a peaceful green churchyard that's screened by a colonnaded facade (1829) and is popular with office workers at lunchtime in summer.

You're now almost back at your starting point. Turn right, opposite Broad Street, and head down Ship Row to enjoy the Aberdeen Maritime Museum, housed partly in **Provost Ross's House** ⑬ (1593) and partly in a magnificent modern glass extension. Below Ship Row is the harbor, which contains some fine 18th- and 19th-century architecture. Explore it if time permits and you don't mind the traffic. An essential place to visit if you have children with you is **Satrosphere** ⑭, a hands-on exhibition of science and technology. It's up off the west end of Union Street but worth the 15-minute walk.

For the second part of your city walk hop on a bus traveling north from a stop near Marischal College, or up King Street, off the Castlegate, to reach **Old Aberdeen. College Bounds** ⑮ has handsome 18th- and 19th-century houses, cobbled streets, and paved sidewalks. **King's College** ⑯ was founded in 1494 and is now part of the University of Aberdeen. This area has some fine Georgian houses, including the **Town House** ⑰. Behind it the modern intrusion of St. Machar's Drive destroys some of the ambience, but you can savor the old-town atmosphere again on a stroll along the Chanonry, past the elegant structures that once housed officials connected with the cathedral nearby. Today they're home mainly to university staff.

North on the Chanonry is **St. Machar's Cathedral** ⑱. Though built in AD 580, nothing remains of the original foundation; much of what you see is from the 15th and 16th centuries. Beyond St. Machar's lies **Seaton Park** ⑲, full of daffodils in spring. Until the early 19th century the only way north out of Aberdeen was over the River Don on the **Brig o'Balgownie** ⑳ (constructed in 1314), at the far end of Seaton Park—a 15-minute walk.

TIMING

You can devote a day to each half of this walk, or you can spend a long morning in the center of Aberdeen, then take a bus out to Old Aberdeen after a late lunch, and do the tour in a (long) day.

Sights to See

❼ **Aberdeen Art Gallery.** This popular gallery, in which locals take great pride and pleasure, houses a wide-ranging collection—from 18th-cen-

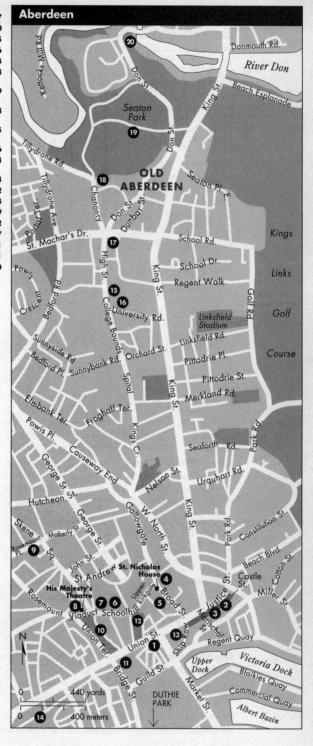

Aberdeen

tury art to contemporary work—of paintings, prints and drawings, sculpture, porcelain, costumes, and much else. It also hosts frequent temporary exhibitions. ⊠ *Schoolhill,* ☎ *01224/523700.* ☞ *Free.* ⊙ *Mon.–Sat. 10–5, Sun. 2–5.*

㉑ Brig o'Balgownie. Until 1827 the only way out of Aberdeen going north was over the River Don on this single-arch bridge. It dates from 1314 and is thought to have been built by Richard Cementarius, Aberdeen's first provost. ⊠ *Seaton Park.*

⑮ College Bounds. Handsome 18th- and 19th-century houses line this cobbled street, which has paved sidewalks. ⊠ *Old Aberdeen.*

★ **⑯ King's College.** Founded in 1494, King's College is now part of the University of Aberdeen. Its chapel, which was built around 1500, has an unmistakable flying (or crown) spire. That it has survived at all was due to the zeal of the principal, who defended his church against the destructive fanaticism that swept through Scotland during the Reformation, when the building was less than a century old. Today the renovated chapel plays an important role in university life. The tall oak screen that separates the nave from the choir, the ribbed wooden ceiling, and the stalls constitute the finest medieval wood carvings found anywhere in Scotland. The **King's College Centre** will tell you more about the university. ⊠ *High St.,* ☎ *01224/273702.* ⊙ *Mon.–Sat. 10–5, Sun. noon–5.*

★ **❹ Marischal College.** Founded in 1593 by the earl Marischal as a Protestant alternative to the Catholic King's College in Old Aberdeen, the two colleges combined to form Aberdeen University in 1860. (The earls Marischal held hereditary office as keepers of the king's mares.) The original university buildings on this site have undergone extensive renovations, and the present facade was built in 1891. The spectacularly ornate work is set off by the gilded flags, and this turn-of-the-last-century creation is still the world's second-largest granite building. Only the Escorial, in Madrid, is larger. The main part of the building, no longer needed by the university, is at present the subject of various plans, one of which is to turn it into a hotel. The **Marischal Museum**'s two main galleries house the *Encyclopaedia of the North East,* an A-to-Z look at the northeast's heritage, and *Collecting the World,* the worldwide ethnographic collections of 19th-century northeast travelers. ⊠ *Broad St.,* ☎ *01224/274301.* ☞ *Free.* ⊙ *Museum weekdays 10–5, Sun. 2–5.*

❸ Mercat Cross. Built in 1686 and restored in 1820, the Mercat Cross, always the symbolic center of a Scottish medieval burgh, stands just beyond King Street. Along its parapet are 12 portrait panels of the Stewart monarchs.

🦢 **❾ The Millennium Village.** This houses an interactive heritage museum and learning center, based on life in a 2,000-year-old village and today's developing world. The center has costumes, spinning and weaving, mosaic making, puppet plays, and jigsaw puzzles. ⊠ *Rosemount Pl.,* ☎ *01224/648041.* ☞ *£3.* ⊙ *Mon., Wed., Fri., Sat. 10–noon; Sun. 2:30–4:30.*

Old Aberdeen. Once an independent burgh, near the River Don, but swallowed up by the expanding main city before the end of the 19th century, Old Aberdeen still retains a certain degree of character and integrity. ⊠ *Between King's College and St. Machar's Cathedral.*

★ 🦢 **⑬ Provost Ross's House.** Dating from 1593, with a striking modern extension, this houses the **Aberdeen Maritime Museum.** Displays here tell the story of the city's involvement with the sea, from early inshore fisheries by way of tea clippers to the North Sea oil boom. It's a fascinating place for grade-schoolers, with its ship models, paintings, and equipment associated with the fishing, shipbuilding, and North Sea oil and gas industries. ☒ *Ship Row,* ☎ *01224/337701.* 🎫 *£3.50.* ☉ *Mon.–Sat. 10–5, Sun. noon–3.* 🐾

❺ Provost Skene's House. *Provost* is Scottish for mayor, and this former mayor's domestic dwelling was once part of a closely packed area of town houses. Steeply gabled and built of rubble, it survives in part from 1545. It is now a museum portraying civic life, with rooms restored and furnished in period style and a painted chapel. ☒ *Guestrow off Broad St.,* ☎ *01224/641086.* 🎫 *£2.50.* ☉ *Mon.–Sat. 10–5, Sun. 1–4.*

❻ Robert Gordon's University. Built in 1731, this was originally called Robert Gordon's Hospital and was used to educate poor boys. It later became an independent school and then an institute of technology, before gaining university status in 1992. ☒ *Schoolhill.* ☉ *View from outside only.*

❽ Rosemount Viaduct. Three buildings on this bridge are collectively known by all Aberdonians as Education, Salvation, and Damnation. Silvery and handsome, the **Central Library** and **St. Mark's Church** date from the last decade of the 19th century, and **His Majesty's Theatre** (1904–08) has been restored inside to its full Edwardian splendor (☞ Nightlife and the Arts, *below*).

❿ St. Machar's Cathedral. Founded in AD 580, this cathedral has nothing of its original structure. It's said that St. Machar was sent by St. Columba to build a church on a grassy platform near the sea, where a river flowed in the shape of a shepherd's crook. This spot fit the bill. Much of the existing building dates from the 15th and 16th centuries. The central tower collapsed in 1688, reducing the building to half its original length. The twin octagonal spires on the western towers date from the first half of the 16th century. The nave is thought to have been rebuilt in red sandstone in 1370, but the final renovation was completed in granite by the middle of the 15th century. Along with the nave ceiling, the twin spires were finished in time to take a battering in the Reformation, when the barons of the Mearns stripped the lead off the roof of St. Machar's and stole the bells. The cathedral suffered further mistreatment—including the removal of stone by Oliver Cromwell's (1599–1658) English garrison in the 1650s—until a 19th-century scheme fully restored the church. ☒ *Chanonry,* ☎ *01224/485988.* ☉ *Daily 9–5.*

⓬ St. Nicholas Kirk. The original burgh church, the Mither Kirk, as this edifice is known, is curiously not within the bounds of the early town settlement; that was located to the east, near the end of present-day Union Street. During the 12th century the port of Aberdeen flourished, and there wasn't room for the church within the settlement. Its earliest features are its pillars—supporting a tower built much later—and its clerestory windows: both date from the 12th century. St. Nicholas was divided into east and west kirks at the Reformation, followed by a substantial amount of renovation from 1741 on. Some early memorials and other works have survived. ☒ *Union St.* ☉ *Weekdays 10–1, Sun. for services.*

🌙 ⓮ Satrosphere. The hands-on exhibits here make science and technology come alive. Children (and adults) of even the most unscientific bent will love it. ☒ *19 Justice Mill La.,* ☎ *01224/213232.* 🎫 *£4.50.* ☉ *Apr.– early Oct., Mon.–Sat. 10–5, Sun. 1:30–5; mid-Oct.–Mar., Mon. and Wed.–Fri. 10–4, Sat. 10–5, Sun. 1:30–5.*

⓳ Seaton Park. With its spring daffodils, tall trees, and herbaceous, boldly colored borders, this park is typical of Aberdeen's exceptionally high standards of civic horticulture. The city is a frequent prizewinner in the annual Britain in Bloom contest. ☒ *Don St., Old Aberdeen.*

❷ Tolbooth. The city was governed from this building for 200 years. It was also the burgh court and jail: narrow, winding stairs lead to dank stone cells where prisoners once despaired ("Jacobite prisoner" William Baird now reenacts his tale of woe for museum goers). Many other exhibits show the evolution of the city's government and the development of its take on crime and punishment since medieval times. ⊠ *Castle St.,* ☎ *01224/621167.* 🎫 *£2.50.* ⊙ *Apr.–Sept., Tues.–Sat. 10–5, Sun. 2–5.*

⑰ Town House. This Georgian work, plain and handsome, uses parts of an earlier building from 1720. ⊠ *High St., Old Aberdeen.*

⑪ Union Bridge. Built in the early 19th century, as was much of Union Street, this bridge has a gentle rise—or descent, if you're traveling east—and the street is carried on a series of blind arches. The north side of Union Bridge is the most obvious reminder of the artificial raising of the grand thoroughfare's levels (despite appearances, you'll discover you're not at ground level). Much of the original work remains. ⊠ *Union St.*

❶ Union Street. This great thoroughfare is to Aberdeen what Princes Street is to Edinburgh: the central pivot of the city plan and the product of a wave of enthusiasm to rebuild the city in a contemporary style in the early 19th century.

⑩ Union Terrace. In the 19th-century development of Union Terrace stands a statue of Robert Burns (1759–96) addressing a daisy. Behind Burns are the **Union Terrace Gardens,** faintly echoing Edinburgh's Princes Street Gardens in the sense that both separate the older part of the city, to the east, from the 19th-century development to the west. Most of the buildings around the grand-looking Caledonian Hotel are late Victorian.

OFF THE
BEATEN PATH
DUTHIE PARK AND WINTER GARDENS – A great place to feed the ducks, Duthie Park also has a boating pond and trampolines, carved wooden animals, and playgrounds. In the very attractive (and warm!) Winter Gardens are fish in ponds, free-flying birds, turtles, and terrapins among the luxuriant foliage and flowers. The park lies close beside Aberdeen's other river, the Dee. ⊠ *Polmuir Rd., Riverside Dr., about 1 mi south from city center.* 🎫 *Free.* ⊙ *Entertainment in summer only, gardens daily 10–dusk.*

Dining and Lodging

££££ ✕ **Silver Darling.** Situated right on the quayside, the Silver Darling is
★ one of Aberdeen's most acclaimed restaurants. It specializes, as its name suggests, in fish. The style is French provincial, and an indoor barbecue guarantees flavorful grilled fish and shellfish. ⊠ *Pocra Quay, Footdee,* ☎ *01224/576229. Reservations essential. AE, MC, V. Closed Sun. No lunch Sat.*

££–£££ ✕ **Gerard's Brasserie.** On a side street moments from the upscale west end of Union Street, Gerard's is a long-established part of the Aberdeen dining scene. Satisfying classic French cuisine is ably prepared with local produce—fish and red meats in particular. Try the seafood thermidor, with king prawns, scallops, and monkfish, served with creole rice. The relaxed, softly lit setting includes a flagstone-floor garden room, with greenery and tile or marble tables. Note that the fixed-price lunch here is a really good value. ⊠ *50 Chapel St.,* ☎ *01224/639500. AE, DC, MC, V.*

££££ 🏨 **Marcliffe at Pitfodels.** The spacious, old country-house hotel in the
★ West End benefits from the skills and experience of leading Scottish hotelier Stewart Spence. The combination of old and new in the individually decorated rooms is impressive—some have reproduction antique furnishings, others are more modern. There are two restaurants: an informal conservatory dining area and the Invery, offering international fare with a Scottish flavor. ⊠ *N. Deeside Rd., Pitfodels, AB15 9YA,* ☎ *01224/861000,* ℻ *01224/868860. 42 rooms with bath. 2 restaurants. AE, DC, MC, V.*

When it Comes to Getting Local Currency at an ATM, Same Thing.

Whether you're in Yosemite or Yemen, using your Visa® card or ATM card with the PLUS symbol is the easiest and most convenient way to get local currency. For example, let's say you're in France. When you make a withdrawal, using your secured PIN, it's dispensed in francs, but is debited from your account in U.S. dollars. This makes it easy to take advantage of favorable exchange rates. And if you need help finding one of Visa's 627,000 ATMs in 127 countries worldwide, visit **visa.com/pd/atm**. We'll make finding an ATM as easy as finding the Eiffel Tower, the Pyramids or even the Grand Canyon.

It's Everywhere You Want To Be.

SEE THE WORLD
IN FULL COLOR

Fodor's Exploring Guides bring all the great sights vividly to life with hundreds of photographs, fascinating historical background, and colorful anecdotes. Detailed maps and practical information keep you headed in the right direction.

Pair a **Fodor's** Exploring Guide with your trusted Gold Guide for a complete planning package.

££–££££ ⊡ **Thistle Aberdeen Caledonian Hotel.** Well situated and offering pleasant views over city gardens, one of the city's larger hotels is generally considered to be one of the best. Rooms are decorated in traditional style, and the pleasant restaurant serves tasty dishes from a menu best described as eclectic Scottish. ⊠ *Union Terr., AB10 1WE,* ☎ *01224/640233,* FAX *01224/641627. 80 rooms, 77 with bath, 3 with shower. 2 restaurants, bar, coffee shop. AE, DC, MC, V.*

££ ⊡ **Atholl Hotel.** All turrets and gables, the granite Atholl is set in a leafy residential area to the west of the city. Rooms are done in rich, dark colors; if space is more important than a view, opt for a room on the first floor. The restaurant prepares such traditional Scottish dishes as lamb cutlets and roasted rib of beef. ⊠ *54 Kings Gate, AB15 4YN,* ☎ *01224/323505,* FAX *01224/321555. 35 rooms with bath or shower. Restaurant. AE, DC, MC, V.* ✎

££ ⊡ **Craighaar Hotel.** Perhaps because it's convenient to the airport, the Craighaar is popular with businesspeople. But what makes it stand out is the service—this is the kind of place where staff members remember your name. Guest rooms are cheerful, with bright floral prints. The gallery suites—split-level rooms—are outstanding. The comfortable restaurant serves cuisine with a Scottish slant: Orkney oysters, smoked trout, crab claws, and char-grilled steaks. ⊠ *Waterton Rd., Buckburn, AB21 9HS,* ☎ *01224/712275,* FAX *01224/716362. 55 rooms with bath or shower. Restaurant, bar. AE, DC, MC, V. No lunch Sat.* ✎

££ ⊡ **Palm Court.** This sister hotel to the Craighaar (☞ *above*) offers the same high standards of accommodation and service. Rooms, though not especially spacious, are well equipped and attractively furnished with warm, floral color schemes. Traditional Scottish meals are served in the Conservatory, where your attention may well be distracted from a plate of fresh salmon or roasted chicken by the wealth of intriguing decorative artifacts surrounding you. ⊠ *81 Seafield Rd., AB15 7YU,* ☎ *01224/310351,* FAX *01224/312707. 24 rooms with bath and shower. Restaurant, bar. AE, DC, MC, V.*

Nightlife and the Arts

In part because of the oil-industry boom, Aberdeen has a fairly lively nightlife scene, though much of it revolves around pubs and hotels; theaters, concert halls, arts centers, and cinemas are also well represented. The principal newspapers—the *Press and Journal* and the *Evening Express*—and *Aberdeen Leopard* magazine can fill you in on what's going on anywhere in the northeast. Aberdeen's tourist information center (☞ Visitor Information *in* Aberdeen and the Northeast A to Z, *below*) has a monthly publication with an events calendar as well as contact phone numbers.

Nightlife

CASINO

If you're interested in trying your luck at the gaming tables, you can place bets at the **Ladbrokes Casino** (⊠ 59 Summer St., ☎ 01224/645273). Membership is granted within 24 hours' notice.

DISCOS

Most clubs don't allow jeans or athletic shoes, and it's best to check beforehand that a particular disco is not closed for a private function. **Cotton Club** (⊠ 491 Union St., ☎ 01224/581858). **De Niro's** (⊠ 120 Union St., ☎ 01224/640641). **Franklyn's** (⊠ Justice Mill La., ☎ 01224/212817). **G's Nightclub** (⊠ 70–78 Chapel St., ☎ 01224/642112). **Hotel Metro** (⊠ 17 Market St., ☎ 01224/583275). **The Ministry** (⊠ 16 Dee St., ☎ 01224/211661). **The Palace Nightclub** (⊠ Bridge Pl., ☎ 01224/581135).

MUSIC CLUBS

The **Lemon Tree** (⊠ 5 W. North St., ☎ 01224/642230), with a wide-ranging music program, is the main rock venue and stages frequent jazz events. There's jazz on Saturday night (except in January) at the **Masada Continental Lounge** (⊠ Rosemount Viaduct, ☎ 01224/641587).

The Arts

ARTS CENTERS

Aberdeen Arts Centre (⊠ 33 King St., ☎ 01224/635208) hosts experimental plays, poetry readings, exhibitions by local and Scottish artists, and many other arts presentations. At **Haddo House** (⊠ Off B9005 near Methlick, ☎ 01651/851770), 20 mi north of Aberdeen, the Haddo House Arts Trust runs a wide-ranging program of events, from opera and ballet to Shakespeare, Scots-language plays, and puppetry. The **Lemon Tree** (⊠ 5 W. North St., ☎ 01224/642230) features an innovative and international program of dance, stand-up comedy, folk, jazz, rock and roll, and art exhibitions.

CONCERT HALL

The **Music Hall** (⊠ Union St., ☎ 01224/641122) presents seasonal programs of concerts by the Scottish National Orchestra, the Scottish Chamber Orchestra, and other major groups. Its wide-ranging program of events also includes folk concerts, crafts fairs, and exhibitions.

DANCE

Aberdeen Arts Centre (⊠ 33 King St., ☎ 01224/635208) and **His Majesty's Theatre** (⊠ Rosemount Viaduct, ☎ 01224/637788) are regular venues for dance companies.

FESTIVALS

August sees the world-renowned **Aberdeen International Youth Festival** (box office, ⊠ Music Hall, Union St., ☎ 01224/641122), which attracts youth orchestras, choirs, dance troupes, and theater companies from many countries. During the festival some companies take their productions to other venues in the northeast. The October **Aberdeen Alternative Festival** (☎ 01224/635822) offers an eclectic mix of arts events at venues throughout the city.

FILM

The following cinemas show general-release films. **Odeon** (⊠ Justice Mill La., ☎ 01224/584531). **Virgin Multiplex** (⊠ Queen's Links, ☎ 01224/572228).

OPERA

Both **Haddo House Arts Trust** (⊠ Off B9005 near Methlick, ☎ 01651/851770) and **His Majesty's Theatre** (⊠ Rosemount Viaduct, ☎ 01224/637788) present operatic performances throughout the year.

THEATER

At **His Majesty's Theatre** (⊠ Rosemount Viaduct, ☎ 01224/637788), shows are presented throughout the year, many of them in advance of their official opening in London's West End.

Outdoor Activities and Sports

Biking

The tourist information center can provide a leaflet with suggestions for cycle tours. The average rate for a mountain bike is £12–£14 a day. You can rent bicycles at **Alpine Bikes** (⊠ 70 Holburn St., ☎ 01224/211455) and **Outdoor Gear** (⊠ 88 Fonthill Rd., ☎ FAX 01224/573952).

Golf

The following courses in and around Aberdeen are open to visitors: **Auchmill** (☎ 01224/714577): 18 holes, 5,123 yards, SSS 67. **Balgownie, Royal Aberdeen Golf Club** (☎ 01224/702571): 18 holes, 6,372 yards, SSS 70 (☞ Chapter 11). **Balnagask** (⊠ St. Fitticks Rd., ☎ 01224/876407): 18 holes, 6,065 yards, SSS 69. **Hazlehead** (☎ 01224/321830): course 1, 18 holes, 6,211 yards, SSS 70; course 2, 18 holes, 5,742 yards, SSS 67; course 3, 9 holes, 2,770 yards, SSS 35. **Kings Links** (☎ 01224/632269): 18 holes, 6,384 yards, SSS 71. **Murcar** (⊠ Bridge of Don, ☎ 01224/704354): 18 holes, 6,241 yards, SSS 71. **Westhill** (☎ 01224/742567): 18 holes, 5,849 yards, SSS 69.

Shopping

Department Stores

You'll find most of the large national department stores in the Bon Accord, St. Nicholas, and Trinity shopping malls or along Union Street.

The spacious **John Lewis** store (⊠ George St., reached via Bon Accord Centre, ☎ 01224/625000; closed Mon.) closely resembles a double-decker sandwich with its filling illuminated. It has a good-value, wide-ranging stock of clothing, household items, giftware, and much more. **Esslemont & Macintosh** (⊠ 26 Union St., ☎ 01224/647331) is a long-established Aberdeen store. The favorite haunt of well-off ladies who lunch, it has an excellent stock of upscale clothing and accessories, cosmetics, and furniture.

Specialty Shops

There are still clusters of small specialty shops in the **Chapel Street–Thistle Street** area at the west end of **Union Street** and on the latter's north side.

ANTIQUES

Colin Wood (⊠ 25 Rose St., ☎ 01224/643019) is the place to go for antiques, maps, and prints.

BOOKS

At the **Aberdeen Family History Society Shop** (⊠ 164 King St., ☎ 01224/646323) you can browse through a huge range of publications related to local history and genealogical research. For a small fee, the Aberdeen & North East Family History Society will undertake some research on your behalf.

GIFTS

Nova (⊠ 20 Chapel St., ☎ 01224/641270), where the locals go for gifts, stocks major U.K. brand names, such as Liberty of London, Dartington Glass, and Crabtree and Evelyn, as well as a wide range of Scottish silver jewelry.

TOYS

The **Early Learning Centre** (⊠ Bon-Accord Centre, George St., ☎ 01224/624188) specializes in toys with educational value. The **Toy Bazaar** (⊠ 45 Schoolhill, ☎ 01224/640021) stocks a range of toys for children preschool age and up.

ROYAL DEESIDE AND CASTLE COUNTRY

Deeside, the valley running west from Aberdeen down which the River Dee flows, earned its "royal" appellation when discovered by Queen Victoria. To this day, where royalty goes, lesser aristocracy and freshly minted millionaires follow. It's still the aspiration of many to own a grand shooting estate in Deeside. In a sense this yearning is understandable since piney hill slope, purple moor, and blue river intermingle tastefully here. Royal Deeside's gradual scenic change adds a growing sense of excitement as you travel deeper into the Grampians.

There are castles along the Dee as well as to the north in Castle Country, a region that also illustrates the gradual geological change in the northeast: uplands lapped by a tide of farms. All the Donside and Deeside castles are picturesquely sited, with most fitted out with tall slender turrets, winding stairs, and crooked chambers that are the epitome of Scottish baronial. All have tales of ghosts and bloodshed, siege and torture. Many were tidied up and "domesticated" during the 19th century. Although best toured by car, much of this area is accessible either by public transportation or on tours from Aberdeen.

Banchory

㉑ *19 mi west of Aberdeen via A93.*

Banchory is an immaculate place with a pinkish tinge to its granite. It's usually bustling with ice-cream-eating strollers, out on a day trip from Aberdeen. If you visit in autumn and have time to spare, drive out to the **Brig o'Feuch** (pronounced fyooch, the *ch* as in loch). Here, salmon leap in season, and the fall colors and foaming waters make for an attractive scene.

㉒ Just east of town are two castles to explore. **Drum Castle** is a foursquare tower that dates from the 13th century, with later additions. Note the tower's rounded corners, said to make battering-ram attacks more difficult. Nearby, fragments of the ancient Forest of Drum still stand, dating from the days when Scotland was covered by great woodlands of oak and pine. ⊠ *Off A93, 10 mi west of Aberdeen,* ☎ *01330/811204.* *Castle and garden: £5; grounds and garden: £2.* ☉ *Castle: Easter, May and Sept., daily 1:30–5:30 (last admission 4:45); June–Aug., daily 11–5:30; Oct., weekends 1:30–5:30; garden of historic roses: Easter and May–Sept., daily 10–6; Oct., weekends 10–6; grounds: daily 9:30–dusk.*

㉓ **Crathes Castle** was once home of the Burnett family. Keepers of the Forest of Drum for generations, the family acquired lands here by marriage and later built a new castle, completed in 1596. Crathes is in the care of the National Trust for Scotland; the trust also looks after the grand gardens, with their calculated symmetry and clipped yew hedges. Sample the tasty home baking in the tearoom. ⊠ *Off A93, 3½ mi east of Banchory,* ☎ *01330/844525.* *Castle: £2.10; grounds or garden: £2; grounds and garden: £4; castle, grounds, and garden: £5.* ☉ *Castle: Apr.–Sept., daily 10:30–5:30 (last admission 4:45); Oct., daily 10:30–4:30; garden and grounds: daily 9–dusk.*

Dining and Lodging

£££–££££   ✕🏠 **Banchory Lodge.** With the River Dee running past at the bottom of the garden just a few yards away, tranquil Banchory Lodge is an ideal spot for anglers. This 17th-century country house has retained its period charm. Rooms are individually decorated, though all have bold color schemes and tartan or floral fabrics. The restaurant has high standards for its Scottish cuisine with French overtones; try the fillet of salmon, roasted duckling, or guinea fowl with wild berries. ⊠ *Banchory, Kincardineshire AB31 5HS,* ☎ *01330/822625,* 🅵🅰🆇 *01330/825019. 22 rooms with bath. Restaurant, fishing. AE, DC, MC, V.*

Kincardine O'Neill

㉔ *9 mi west of Banchory.*

The ruined kirk in the little village of Kincardine O'Neill was built in 1233 and once sheltered travelers: it was the last hospice before the

Mounth, the name given to the massif that shuts off the south side of the Dee Valley. Beyond Banchory (and the B974), no motor roads run south until you reach Braemar (A93), though the Mounth is crossed by a network of tracks once used by Scottish soldiers, invading armies (including the Romans), and cattle drovers. Photography buffs won't want to miss the bridge at Potarch, just to the east.

Aboyne

㉕ *5 mi west of Kincardine O'Neill.*

Aboyne is a pleasant, well-laid-out town, with a village green (unusual for Scotland) that's the setting for an annual Highland Games. However, there is not a lot to detain the visitor here, except a good coffee shop.

㉖ The **Braeloine Interpretative Centre,** in Glen Tanar beyond Aboyne, has a natural history display, café, picnic area, and walks. ⊠ *Glen Tanar (cross River Dee, take right on B976, and left into the glen),* ☎ *013398/86072.* ☉ *Apr.–Sept., Wed.–Mon. 10–5; Oct.–Mar., Thurs.–Mon. 10–5.*

Dining

£ ✕ **At the Sign of the Blackfaced Sheep.** Filled rolls, soups, salads and delicious home-baked goods are served here, but another good reason to visit is the range of upscale gifts and paintings that you can buy in this coffee and crafts shop. ⊠ *Ballater Rd., Aboyne AB34 5HT,* ☎ *013398/87311. MC, V.*

En Route   Look for a large granite boulder next to the A93 on which is carved YOU ARE NOW ENTERING THE HIGHLANDS. You may find this piece of information superfluous, given the quality of the scenery.

Ballater

㉗ *12 mi west of Aboyne, 43 mi west of Aberdeen.*

The handsome holiday resort of Ballater, once noted for the curative properties of its local well, has profited from the proximity of the royals, nearby at Balmoral (☞ *below*). You might be amused by the array of BY ROYAL APPOINTMENT signs proudly hanging from many of its various shops (even monarchs need bakers and butchers). Take time to stroll around this well-laid-out community. Note that the railway station now houses the tourist information center and a display on the glories of the Great North of Scotland branch line, closed in the 1960s along with so many others in this country.

★ **㉘** As long as you have your own car, you can capture the feel of the eastern Highlands yet still be close to town. Start your expedition into **Glen Muick** (Gaelic for pig, pronounced mick) by crossing the River Dee and turning upriver on the south side, shortly after the road forks, into this fine glen. The native red deer are quite common throughout the Scottish Highlands, but the flat valley floor here is one of the very best places to see them. Beyond the lower glen, the prospect opens to reveal not only grazing herds but also fine views of the battlement of cliffs edging the mountain called Lochnagar.

㉙ The enormous parking lot is indicative of the popularity of **Balmoral Castle,** one of Queen Elizabeth II's favorite family retreats. Balmoral is a Victorian fantasy, designed, in fact, for Queen Victoria (1819–1901) by her consort, Prince Albert (1819–61) in 1855. "It seems like a dream to be here in our dear Highland Home again," Queen Victoria wrote. "Every year my heart becomes more fixed in this dear Paradise." Balmoral's visiting hours depend on whether the royals are in residence. In truth, there are more interesting and historic buildings to explore, as the only part of the castle on view is the ballroom, with an exhibition of royal artifacts. The Carriage Hall has displays of commemorative china, carriages, and native wildlife. Perhaps it's just as well that most of the house is closed to the public, for Balmoral suffers from a bad rash of tartanitis. Thanks to Victoria and Albert, stags' heads abounded, the bagpipes wailed incessantly, and the garish Stuart tartan was used for every item of furnishings, from carpets to chair covers. A more somber Duff tartan, black and green to blend with the environment, was later adopted, and from the brief glimpse you may get of Balmoral's interior, it's clear that royal taste is now more restrained. Queen Elizabeth II, however, follows her predecessors' routine in spending a holiday of about six weeks on Deeside, usually from mid-August to the end of September. During this time call to determine if Balmoral is open to visitors before setting out.

Victoria loved Balmoral more for its setting than its house, so be sure to take in its pleasant gardens. Year by year, Victoria and Albert added to the estate, taking over neighboring houses, securing the forest and moorland around it, and developing the deerstalking and the grouse shooting. In consequence, Balmoral is now a large property, as the grounds run 12 mi along the Deeside road. Its privacy is protected by belts of pinewood, and the only view of the castle from the A93 is a partial one, from a point near Inver, 2 mi west of the gates. But there's an excellent bird's-eye view of it from an old military road, now the A939, which climbs out of Crathie, northbound for Cockbridge and the Don Valley. This view embraces the summit of Lochnagar (3,786 ft) in whose *corries* (hollows) the snow lies year-round. Around and about Balmoral are some notable spots—Cairn O'Mount, Cambus O'May, and the Cairngorms from the Linn of Dee—and some of them may be seen on pony-trekking expeditions, available on the Balmoral stalking ponies around the grounds and estate. Note that when the royals are in residence, even the grounds are closed to the public. ⊠ *A93, 7 mi west of Ballater,* ☎ *013397/42334.* ⊡ *£4.* ☉ *Mid-Apr.–July, daily 10–5 (last admission 4).*

Dining and Lodging

££££   ✕⊞ **Hilton Craigendarroch Hotel.** This magnificent country-house hotel, just outside Ballater on a hillside overlooking the River Dee, really does manage to keep everyone happy. You're cosseted in luxurious surroundings with many facilities. An even better value are the pine lodges set among the trees around the hotel. These self-catering cottages are geared for families and fitted with every kind of labor-saving appliance. There's also a solid choice of on-site restaurants, including the top-quality Oaks, for modern Scottish à la carte cuisine, and the Clubhouse poolside brasserie. ⊠ *Ballater AB35 5XA,* ☎ *013397/55858,* ⅢX *013397/55447. 45 rooms with bath, 6 suites. 2 restaurants, 2 indoor pools, wading pool, beauty salon, hot tub, sauna, tennis court, exercise room, squash. AE, DC, MC, V.*

£££   ✕⊞ **Balgonie Country House.** A tranquil Edwardian country house on 3 acres of gardens overlooking Ballater's golf course, Balgonie delivers top-quality food and accommodations at real value-for-money prices. Bedrooms are all individually decorated in soft greens, blues, or pinks, with either antique furniture or, in the attic rooms, specially designed modern Swedish-style furniture. The dining room is a peaceful setting for a four-course meal of dishes cooked in classic French style. ⊠ *Braemar Pl., Ballater AB35 5NQ,* ☎ ⅢX *013397/55482. 9 rooms, 7 with bath, 2 with shower. AE, DC, MC, V. Closed Jan.–Feb.*

££–£££   ✕⊞ **Darroch Learg Hotel.** Amid tall trees on a hillside, the Darroch Learg is everything a Victorian Scottish country house should be. Most guest rooms are decorated with mahogany furniture and designer fabrics in rich colors. The Scottish cuisine in the conservatory restaurant is sophisticated but also substantial, with the rich flavors of local beef and fish. ⊠ *Braemar Rd., Ballater, Aberdeenshire AB35 5UX,* ☎ *013397/ 55443,* FAX *013397/55252. 18 rooms with bath or shower. Restaurant. AE, DC, MC, V.*

Shopping

At either of **Countrywear**'s three shops (⊠ 15, 24 and 35 Bridge St., ☎ 013397/55453), you'll find everything you need for Highland country living, including fishing tackle, shooting accessories, cashmere, tweeds, children's clothes, and that flexible garment popular in Scotland between seasons: the body warmer.

For a low-cost gift you could always see what's being boiled up at **Dee Valley Confectioners** (⊠ Station Sq., ☎ 013397/55499). For Scottish designer knitwear, head to **Goodbrand Knitwear** (⊠ 1 Braemar Rd., ☎ 013397/55947). The **McEwan Gallery** (⊠ On A939, 1 mi west of Ballater, ☎ 013397/55429) displays a good range of fine paintings, watercolors, prints, and books (many with a Scottish or golf theme) in an unusual house built by the Swiss artist Rudolphe Christen in 1902.

En Route   Continuing west into Highland scenery, further pine-framed glimpses appear of the "steep frowning glories of dark Lochnagar," as it was described by the poet Lord Byron (1788–1824). Lochnagar (3,786 ft) was made known to an audience wider than hill walkers by the Prince of Wales, who published a children's story, *The Old Man of Lochnagar.*

Braemar

17 mi west of Ballater, 60 mi west of Aberdeen, 51 mi north of Perth via A93.

The village of Braemar is associated with the Braemar Highland Gathering, held every September. Although there are many such gatherings celebrated throughout Scotland, this one is distinguished by the presence of the royal family. You can find out more about the event at the **Braemar Highland Heritage Centre,** in a converted stable block in the middle of town. It tells the history of the village with displays and a film, and it also has a gift shop. ⊠ *The Mews, Mar Rd.,* ☎ *013397/ 41944.* ⊡ *Free.* ☉ *Daily 9–5 (extended hrs in summer).*

③⓪ Braemar is dominated by **Braemar Castle** on its outskirts. The castle dates from the 17th century, although its defensive walls, designed in the shape of a pointed star, came later. At Braemar (the *braes,* or slopes, of the district of Mar) the standard, or rebel flag, was first raised at the start of the spectacularly unsuccessful Jacobite Rebellion of 1715. Thirty years later, during the last rebellion, Braemar Castle was strengthened and garrisoned by Hanoverian (government) troops. ⊠ *Braemar,* ☎ *013397/41219; 013397/41224 off-season.* ⊡ *£3.* ☉ *Apr.– June and Sept.–Oct., Sat.–Thurs. 10–6; July–Aug., daily 10–6.*

Although the main A93 slinks off to the south from Braemar, a little unmarked road will take you farther west into the hilly heartlands. In fact, even if you do not have your own car, you can still explore this area by catching the post bus that leaves from the Braemar post office once a day. The road offers you delectable views over the winding River Dee and the blue hills before passing through the tiny hamlet of Inverey and

★ ③① crossing a bridge at the **Linn of Dee.** *Linn* is a Scots word meaning "rocky narrows," and the river's rocky gash here is deep and roaring. Park beyond the bridge and walk back to admire the sylvan setting.

Dining and Lodging

£££   ✕⊡ **Invercauld Arms.** This handsome stone Victorian hotel in the center of Braemar makes a good base for exploring Royal Deeside. The entrance lounge, with plush sofas and elegant velvet chairs, leads to beautifully restored public rooms—with attractive plasterwork and prints—and to comfortable guest rooms with floral drapes and reproduction antique furniture. The restaurant serves an international cuisine with Scottish overtones. Dishes might include Aberdeen Angus steak with tomato and wild mushroom sauce or chicken with bean sprouts and water chestnuts in oyster sauce. ⊠ *Braemar AB35 5YR,* ☎ *013397/41605,* ℻ *013397/41428. 68 rooms with bath and shower. Restaurant, bar. AE, DC, MC, V.* ✍

Outdoor Activities and Sports

Braemar has a tricky golf course laden with foaming waters. Erratic duffers take note: The compassionate course managers have installed, near the water, poles with little nets on the end for those occasional shots that may go awry.

En Route   From Braemar retrace the A93 as far as Balmoral. From Balmoral look for a narrow road going north, signposted B976. Be careful on the first twisting mile through the trees. You'll soon emerge from scattered pines into the open moor in upland Aberdeenshire. Behind is the massif of Lochnagar again, and to the west are snow-tipped domes of the big Cairngorms. Roll down to a bridge and go left on the A939, which comes in from Ballater. Another high moor section follows: as the road leaves the scattered buildings by the bridge, see if you can spot the roadside inscription to the company of soldiers who built the A939 in the 18th century.

Corgarff Castle

③② *23 mi northeast of Braemar, 14 mi northwest of Ballater.*

Eighteenth-century soldiers paved a military highway, now the A939, north from Ballater to Corgarff Castle, a lonely tower house with another star-shape defensive wall—a curious replica of Braemar Castle (☞ *above*). Corgarff was built as a hunting seat for the earls of Mar in the 16th century. After an eventful history that included the wife of a later laird being burned alive in a family dispute, the castle ended its career as a garrison for Hanoverian troops. The troops were responsible for preventing illegal whisky distilling. ⊠ *Signposted off A939,* ☎ *0131/668–8800.* 💷 *£2.50.* 🕙 *Apr.–Sept., daily 9:30–6; Oct.–Mar., Sat. 9:30–4, Sun. 2–4.*

En Route   If you return east from Corgarff Castle to the A939/A944 junction and make a left onto the A944, the thorough castle signposting indicates you are on the **Castle Trail.** The A944 meanders along the River Don to the village of Strathdon, where a great mound by the roadside—on the left—turns out to be a *motte,* or the base of a wooden castle, built in the late 12th century. Although it takes considerable imagination to become enthusiastic about a great grass-covered heap, surviving mottes have contributed greatly to the understanding of the history of Scottish castles. The A944 then joins the A97 (go left), and just a few minutes later a sign points to Glenbuchat Castle, a plain Z-plan tower house.

Kildrummy

18 mi northeast of Corgarff, 23 mi north of Ballater, 22 mi north of Aboyne.

★ ③③ **Kildrummy Castle** is significant because of its age (13th century) and because it has ties to the mainstream medieval traditions of European castle building. It shares features with Harlech and Caernarfon, in Wales, as well as with Château de Coucy, near Laon, France. Kildrummy underwent several expansions at the hands of England's King Edward I (1239–1307); the castle was back in Scottish hands in 1306, when it was besieged by King Edward I's son. The defenders were betrayed by a certain Osbarn the Smith, who was promised a large amount of gold by the English forces. They gave it to him after the castle fell, pouring it molten down his throat, or so the ghoulish story goes. Kildrummy's prominence ended after the collapse of the 1715 Jacobite uprising. It had been the rebel headquarters and was consequently dismantled. ☎ *0131/668–8800.* ⌨ *£2.* ○ *Apr.–Sept., daily 9:30–6.* ❧

Kildrummy Castle Gardens, behind the castle—with a separate entrance from the main road—are built in what was the original quarry for the castle. This sheltered bowl within the woodlands has a broad range of shrubs and alpine plants and a notable water garden. If the weather is pleasant, it makes for a nice place to pause and plan the next stage of your journey. ✉ *A97,* ☎ *019755/71203 or 019755/71277.* ⌨ *£2.* ○ *Apr.–Oct., daily 10–5 (call to confirm opening times late in season).*

Dining and Lodging

££££ ✕▥ **Kildrummy Castle Hotel.** A grand late-Victorian country house, this
★ hotel offers a peaceful setting, attentive service, and sporting opportunities. Oak paneling, beautiful plasterwork, and gentle color schemes create a serene environment, enhanced by the views of Kildrummy Castle Gardens next door. The award-winning Scottish cuisine features local game as well as seafood. ✉ *Kildrummy, by Alford, Aberdeenshire AB33 8RA,* ☎ *019755/71288,* ⅲ *019755/71345. 16 rooms with bath or shower. Restaurant, golf privileges, fishing. AE, MC, V.*

Alford

9 mi east of Kildrummy, 28 mi west of Aberdeen.

A plain and sturdy settlement in the Howe (Hollow) of Alford, this town gives those visitors who have grown somewhat weary of castle hopping a
㉞ break: it has a museum instead. The **Grampian Transport Museum** specializes in road-based means of locomotion, backed up by a library and archives. One of its more unusual exhibits is the *Craigievar Express,* a steam-driven creation invented by the local postman to deliver mail more efficiently. ✉ *Alford,* ☎ *019755/62292.* ⌨ *£3.75.* ○ *Apr.–Oct., daily 10–5.*

★ ㉟ Near Alford, the **Craigievar Castle,** is much as the stonemasons left it in 1626, with its pepper-pot turrets and towers. It was built in relatively peaceful times by William Forbes, a successful merchant in trade with the Baltic Sea ports (hence he was also known as Danzig Willie). Centuries of care and wise stewardship have ensured that the experience proffered you today is as authentic as possible. ✉ *5 mi south of Alford on A980,* ☎ *013398/83635.* ⌨ *£6, grounds only: £1.* ○ *Castle: May–Sept., daily 1:30–5:30 (last admission 4:45); grounds: daily 9:30–sunset.* ❧

㊱ The massive **Castle Fraser,** southeast of Alford, is the largest of the castles of Mar. Although it shows a variety of styles reflecting the taste of its owners from the 15th through the 19th centuries, its design is typical of the cavalcade of castles that exist here in the northeast—and for good reason, as this—along with many other of the region's castles, including Midmar, Craigievar, Crathes, and Glenbuchat—was designed by a family of master masons called Bell. Castle Fraser has the further advantages of a walled garden, picnic area, and tearoom. ✉ *8 mi southeast of Alford off A944,* ☎ *01330/833463.* ⌨ *£5.* ○ *Castle: Easter–May and Sept., daily 1:30–5:30; June–Aug., daily 11–5:30; Oct., weekends 1:30–5:30 (last admission 4:45); gardens: daily 9:30–6; grounds: daily 9:30–sunset.*

THE NORTHEAST

This route starts inland, traveling toward Speyside—the valley, or strath, of the River Spey—famed for its whisky distilleries, which it promotes in yet another signposted trail. Distilling scotch is not an intrinsically spectacular process. It involves pure water, malted barley, and sometimes peat smoke, then a lot of bubbling and fermentation, all of which cause a range of odd smells. The result is a prestigious product with a fascinating range of flavors that you either enjoy immensely or not at all.

Instead of assiduously following the Whisky Trail, just dip into it and blend it with some other aspects of the lower end of Speyside—the county of Moray. Whisky notwithstanding, Moray's scenic qualities, low rainfall, and other reassuring weather statistics are also worth remembering. The suggested route then allows you to sample the northeastern seaboard, including some of the best but least-known coastal scenery in Scotland.

Dufftown

★ ③⑦ *54 mi from Aberdeen via A96 and A920 (turn west at Huntly).*

On one of the Spey tributaries, Dufftown was planned in 1817 by the earl of Fife. One of the most famous malt whiskies of all is distilled at **Glenfiddich Distillery.** The independent company of William Grant and Sons Limited was the first to realize the tourist potential of the distilling process. It subsequently built an entertaining visitor center in addition to offering tours. In short, if you do intend to visit a distillery, it may as well be Glenfiddich. The audiovisual show and displays are as worthwhile as the tour, and the traditional stone-walled premises with the typical pagoda-roof malting buildings have a pleasant period ambience. You don't have to like whisky to come away feeling you've learned something about a leading Scottish export. ⊠ *North of Dufftown on A941,* ☎ *01340/820373.* ☒ *Free.* ⊙ *Easter–mid-Oct., weekdays 9:30–4:30, Sat. 9:30–4:30, Sun. noon–4:30; mid-Oct.– Easter, weekdays 9:30–4:30.*

On a mound just above the Glenfiddich Distillery is a grim, gray, and squat curtain-walled castle, **Balvenie.** This fortress, which dates from the 13th century, once commanded the glens and passes toward Speyside and Elgin. ⊠ *Dufftown,* ☎ *0131/668–8800.* ☒ *£1.20.* ⊙ *Apr.– Sept., daily 9:30–6.*

In the center of Dufftown, the conspicuous battlemented **clock tower**— the centerpiece of the planned town and a former jail—houses a local museum open in summer. **Mortlach Church,** set in a hollow by the Dullan Water, is thought to be one of Scotland's oldest Christian sites, perhaps founded by St. Moluag, a contemporary of St. Columba, as early as AD 566. Note the weathered Pictish cross in the churchyard and the even older stone under cover in the vestibule, with a strange Pictish elephant-like beast carved on it. Though much of the church was rebuilt after 1876, some early work survives, including three lancet windows from the 13th century and a leper's squint (a hole extended to the outside of the church so that lepers could hear the service but be kept away from the rest of the congregation).

Craigellachie

③⑧ *4 mi northwest of Dufftown via A941.*

Renowned as an angling resort, Craigellachie, like so many Speyside settlements, is sometimes enveloped in the malty reek of the local industry. As you arrive in the village, you'll notice the huge **Cooperage,**

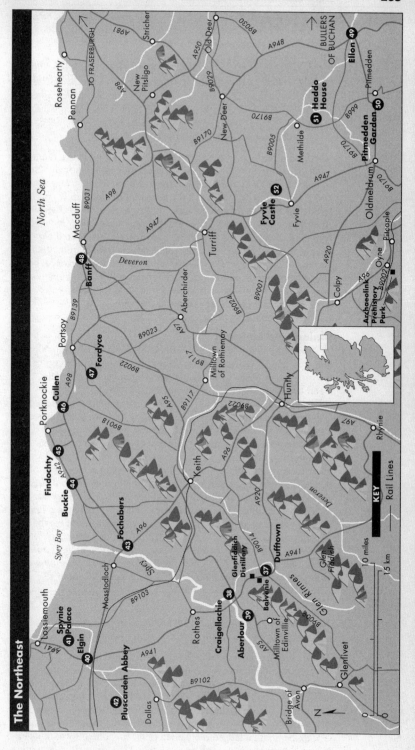

The Northeast

where you can watch craftsman make and repair barrels. ✉ *Dufftown Rd.,* ☎ *01340/871108.* 🎫 *£2.95.* ⊗ *July–Sept., Mon.–Fri. 9:30–5, Sat. 10–4:30; Oct.–June, Mon.–Fri. 9:30–5.*

The Spey itself is crossed by a handsome suspension bridge, designed by Thomas Telford (1757–1834) in 1814 and now bypassed by the modern road.

Aberlour

③⑨   *2 mi southwest of Craigellachie via A95.*

Aberlour, often listed as Charlestown of Aberlour on maps, is another handsome little burgh, essentially Victorian in style, though actually founded in 1812 by the local landowner. Glenfarclas, Cragganmore, and Aberlour are the names of the noted local whiskies. If you're interested in something nonalcoholic, take a look at the **Village Store.** After the owners retired in 1978, the shop was locked away intact, complete with stock. In the late 1980s new owners discovered they had bought a time capsule—a range of products dating from the early decades of the present century—as well as all the paraphernalia, books and ledgers, and notes of a country business. Part of the premises is now a gift shop, but the remainder is preserved for you to enjoy, with stock of a bygone era on the shelves. ✉ *76 High St.,* ☎ *01340/871243.* 🎫 *Free.* ⊗ *Feb.–Dec., Mon.–Sat. 10–5, Sun. 1:30–5.*

Dining and Lodging

£   ✕ **Old Pantry.** This corner restaurant, overlooking Aberlour's pleasant, tree-shaded central square, serves everything from a cup of coffee with a sticky cake to a four-course spread of soup, roast meat, and traditional pudding. ✉ *The Square,* ☎ *01340/871617. MC, V.*

££–£££   ✕🏠 **Minmore House.** Former home of George Smith, founder of the
★   Glenlivet Distillery, Minmore, a 25-minute drive from Aberlour, retains a strong private-house feel. Faded chintz in the drawing room (where afternoon tea is served) and a paneled library (now housing a bar with nearly 100 malt whiskies) are complemented by very comfortable guest rooms (one, allegedly, with a ghost) with an eclectic mix of antiques. The restaurant serves exceptional modern Scottish dishes, including Highland lamb with a mint-and-honey glaze. The Speyside Way long-distance footpath passes below the house, and the area is famous for bird-watching—you might sight buzzards, peregrines, or maybe even a golden eagle. Take the A95 south from Aberlour, then turn left on the B9008 at Bridge of Avon. ✉ *Glenlivet, Ballindalloch, Banffshire AB37 9DB,* ☎ *01807/590378,* 📠 *01807/590472. 10 rooms with bath or shower. Restaurant, bar. MC, V. Closed Nov.–Mar.* 🐾

Elgin

④⓪   *16 mi north of Aberlour via A941, 69 mi northwest of Aberdeen, 41 mi east of Inverness via A96.*

As the center of the fertile Laigh (low-lying lands) of Moray, Elgin has been of local importance for centuries. Like Aberdeen, it's self-supporting and previously remote, sheltered by great hills to the south and lying between two major rivers, the Spey and the Findhorn. Beginning in the 13th century, Elgin became an important religious center, a cathedral city with a walled town growing up around the cathedral and adjacent to the original settlement. Left in peace for at least some of its history, Elgin prospered, and by the early 18th century it became a mini-Edinburgh of the north and a place where country gentlemen spent their winters. It even echoed Edinburgh in carrying out wide-scale reconstruction in the early part of the 18th century: much of the old town was swept away in a wave of rebuilding, giving Elgin the fine neoclassical buildings that survive today.

The town's old street plan survived almost intact until the late 20th century, when it succumbed to the modern madness of demolishing great swaths of buildings for the sake of better traffic flow: Elgin suffered from its position on the Aberdeen–Inverness main road. However, the central main-street plan and some of the older little streets and *wynds* (alleyways) remain. You'll also see Elgin's past in the arcaded shop fronts—some of which date from the late-17th century—on the main shopping street.

At the center of Elgin, the most conspicuous structure is **St. Giles Church,** which divides High Street. The grand foursquare building built in 1828 exhibits the Greek revival style: note the columns, the pilasters, and the top of the spire, surmounted by a representation of the Lysicrates Monument. Past the arcaded shops at the east end of High Street, you can see the **Little Cross** (17th century), which marked the boundary between the town and the cathedral grounds. Near the Little Cross, the **Elgin Museum** (☉ summer months only) has an especially interesting collection of dinosaur relics.

★ Cooper Park, a short distance to the southeast across the modern bypass road, is home to a magnificent ruin, the **Elgin Cathedral,** consecrated in 1224. Its eventful story included devastation by fire: a 1390 act of retaliation by Alexander Stewart (circa 1343–1405), the Wolf of Badenoch. The illegitimate-son-turned-bandit of King David II (1324–71) had sought revenge for his excommunication by the bishop of Moray. The cathedral was rebuilt but finally fell into disuse after the Reformation in 1560. By 1567 the highest authority in the land, the regent earl of Moray, had stripped the lead from the roof to pay for his army. Thus ended the career of the religious seat known as the Lamp of the North. Some traces of the cathedral settlement survive— the gateway Pann's Port and the Bishop's Palace—although they've been drastically altered. ☎ *0131/668–8800.* ☞ *£2.50; combined admission with Spynie Palace £3.* ☉ *Apr.–Oct., daily 9:30–6; Nov.–Mar., Mon.– Wed. and Sat. 9:30–4, Thurs. 9:30–noon, Sun. 2–4.* ♺

㊶ Just northwest of Elgin is **Spynie Palace,** the large 15th-century former headquarters of the bishops of Moray. It has now fallen into ruin, though the top of the tower has good views over the Laigh of Moray. Find it by turning right off the main A941 Elgin–Lossiemouth road. ☎ *0131/668–8800.* ☞ *£1.80; combined admission with Elgin Cathedral £3.* ☉ *Apr.–Oct., daily 9:30–6; Nov.–Mar., Sat. 9:30–4, Sun. 2–4.*

Given the general destruction caused by the 16th-century upheaval of the Reformation, abbeys in Scotland tend to be ruinous and deserted, ㊷ but at **Pluscarden Abbey** the monks' way of life continues. Originally a 13th-century foundation, the religious community abandoned their abbey after the Reformation. The third marquis of Bute bought the remains in 1897 and initiated a restoration program that continues today. Monks from an abbey near Gloucester, England, returned here in 1948, and the abbey is now an active community. ✉ *6 mi southwest of Elgin, off B9010.* ☞ *Free.* ☉ *Daily 5 AM–8:30 PM.*

Dining and Lodging

£££–££££ ✕▥ **Mansion House Hotel.** This Scottish baronial mansion complete with tower is set on the River Lossie. The rooms are individually decorated; all are pleasant and comfortable. The restaurant's Scottish cuisine includes a fine breast of pheasant with port sauce; vegetarians are also well catered to. ✉ *The Haugh, IV30 1AW,* ☎ *01343/548811,* ℻ *01343/547916. 23 rooms with bath. Restaurant, bar, indoor pool, beauty salon, sauna, exercise room. AE, DC, MC, V.*

Shopping

In addition to the usual range of High Street stores, you can duck into **Gordon and MacPhail** (✉ 58 South St., ☎ 01343/545110), an outstanding delicatessen and wine merchant that also stocks a breathtaking range of scarce malt whiskies. This is a good place to shop for gifts for those foodies among your friends. **Johnstons of Elgin** (✉ Newmill, ☎ 01343/554099) is a woolen mill with a worldwide reputation for its luxury fabrics, including cashmere. The bold color range is particularly appealing.

Fochabers

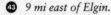 *9 mi east of Elgin.*

Just before reaching Fochabers, you'll see the works of a major local employer, Baxters of Fochabers, a family-run firm with an international reputation for fine foods. From Tokyo to New York, upmarket stores stock their soups, jams, chutneys, and other gourmet products—all of which are made here, close to the River Spey. The **Baxters Visitors Centre** offers a video, "Baxters Experience," which presents the history of the business; interactive exhibits and cooking demonstrations; a re-creation of the Baxters' first grocery shop; a shop that stocks Baxters' goods (among other products); the Best of Scotland shop (specializing in Scottish goods); Baxters at Home for fashion items; a store that sells quality cooking utensils; and two restaurants offering an assortment of delectables. ✉ *1 mi west of Fochabers,* ☎ *01343/820666.* ▣ *Free; small charge for cooking demonstrations and other special features.* ✆ *Apr.–Oct., daily 9–6; Nov.–Dec., daily 9–5; Jan.–Mar., daily 10–5 (check ahead to ensure all areas are operating in these winter months).*

Once over the Spey Bridge, you'll find that Fochabers itself has a symmetrical village green. Perhaps this pleasing, mellow ambience attracts the antiques dealers to Fochabers, their wares ranging from near-junk to designer pieces. Through one of the antiques shops, you can enter the **Fochabers Folk Museum,** a converted church that has a fine display of items relating to past life in the village and surrounding rural area, ranging from carts and carriages to interesting farm implements and Victorian toys. ☎ *01343/821204.* ▣ *Free.* ✆ *Winter, daily 9:30–1 and 2–5; summer, daily 9:30–1 and 2–6.*

One of the village's lesser known treasures is the **Gordon Chapel** (✉ Duke St., just off the Square), which has an exceptional set of stained-glass windows by pre-Raphaelite artist Sir Edward Burne-Jones.

Consider diverting onto the road that runs south directly opposite the Fochabers Folk Museum. Leaving the houses behind for well-hedged country lanes, you will discover a Forestry Commission sign to the **Earth Pillars.** These curious eroded sandstone pillars are framed by tall-trunked pines and overlook a wide prospect of the lower Spey Valley.

Shopping

This is the place for antiques hunters, with several antiques shops all within a few yards of each other on the main street. **Antiques (Fochabers)** (✉ Hadlow House, The Square, ☎ 01343/820838) for kitchenware and furniture. Take a break from all the white elephants by stopping into **Balance Natural Health** (✉ 59 High St., ☎ 01343/821443), which stocks homeopathic remedies, potpourris, and the like. If you're interested in local artwork, **Just Art** (✉ 64 High St., ☎ 01343/820500) is a fine gallery with high-quality ceramics and paintings. **Pringle Antiques** (✉ High St., ☎ 01343/820362) is a good place to shop for small furniture, pottery, glassware, and jewelry. At the **Quaich** (✉ 85 High St., ☎ 01343/820981), you can stock up on gifts, then sit with a cup of tea and a home-baked snack.

Buckie

44 *8 mi east of Fochabers via A98 and A942.*

The fishing port of Buckie and its satellite villages are gray and worka-day, with plenty of Victorian architecture added to the original fisher-men's cottages, which sit almost on the sea. The **Buckie Heritage Maritime Museum,** housed in premises designed to be reminiscent of an old fishing drifter (a fishing vessel with sails), is a hands-on visitor center that tells the story of the herring industry and of Buckie's de-velopment as a port. Upstairs, you enter a 1920s quayside scene, with a replica steam drifter that you can board and barrels you can pack with herring. ⊠ *Freuchny Rd. off Commercial Rd.,* ☎ *01542/834646.* ⊡ *£2.75.* ☉ *Apr.–Oct., Mon.–Sat. 10–5, Sun. noon–5.*

The **Peter Anson Gallery** shows a selection of watercolor works also related to the development of the fishing industry. The gallery is housed in a room accessed through the library. ⊠ *Cluny Pl.,* ☎ *01542/832121.* ⊡ *Free.* ☉ *Weekdays 10–8, Sat. 10–noon.*

Dining

£££–££££ ★ ✕ **Old Monastery.** On a broad, wooded slope set back from the coast near Buckie, with westward views as far as the hills of Wester Ross, the Old Monastery was once a Victorian religious establishment. This theme carries through to the restrained decor of the Cloisters Bar and the Chapel Restaurant, with its hand stenciling. The local specialties—the freshest fish, venison, and Aberdeen Angus beef—make up the Scottish menu. There's a no-smoking dining room. ⊠ *Drybridge, Buckie,* ☎ *01542/ 832660,* ℻ *01542/839437. AE, MC, V. Closed Sun., Mon., 3 wks in Jan.*

En Route Heading east are a string of salty little fishing villages. They paint a colorful scene with their gabled houses and fishing nets set out to dry amid the rocky shoreline.

Findochty

45 *2 mi east of Buckie on A942.*

The residents of Findochty are known for their fastidiousness and cre-ativity in painting their houses, taking the fine art of house painting to a new level. Some residents even paint the mortar between the stonework a different color from the exterior. The harbor here has a faint echo of the Mediterranean about it.

Cullen

★ **46** *3 mi east of Findochty.*

Look for some wonderfully painted homes at Cullen, in the old fish-ermen's town below the railway viaduct. But the real attractions of this little resort are its white-sand beach and the fine view west toward the aptly named Bowfiddle Rock. A stroll along the beach reveals the shape of the fishing settlement below and the planned town above. Cullen and its shops are far enough away from major town superstores to sur-vive on local, intermittent trade; most unusual for a town of its size, Cullen has a full range of specialty shops—antiques and gift stores, butch-ers, an ironmonger, a baker, a haberdasher, and a locally famous ice cream shop among them—as well as several hotels and cafés.

Dining and Lodging

££ ✕🏨 **Seafield Arms Hotel.** A former coaching inn built in 1822, this hotel has high standards in every area: service, decor, and food. Deep, rich colors prevail, and comfort and friendliness are the keynotes. The restaurant, with its deep blue walls and tartan carpet, offers an extensive

Scotland Scene Ltd. (☎ 01309/676563) offers chauffeur-driven limousines to take you on tailor-made tours. The **Scottish Tourist Guides Association** (✉ Wendy Simpson, Howemill Cottage, Craigievar, Aberdeenshire AB33 8JD, ☎ FAX 019755/81335) can supply experienced personal guides, including foreign-language-speaking guides if necessary.

The **Scottish Tourist Guides Association** (☞ *above*) conducts an "Old Aberdeen" walk from mid-May through August on Wednesday evening and Sunday afternoon.

Late-Night Pharmacies

Notices on pharmacy doors will guide you to the nearest open pharmacy at any given time. The police can provide assistance in an emergency. **Anderson Pharmacy** (✉ 34 Holburn St., ☎ 01224/587148) and **Boots the Chemists Ltd.** (✉ Bon Accord Centre, George St., ☎ 01224/626080), both in Aberdeen, keep longer hours than most. There's an in-store pharmacist at **Safeway Food Store** (✉ 215 King St., Aberdeen, ☎ 01224/624398).

Visitor Information

Aberdeen (✉ St. Nicholas House, Broad St., ☎ 01224/632727); this tourist information center has a currency exchange and supplies information on all of Scotland's Northeast. **Braemar** (✉ The Mews, Mar Rd., ☎ 013397/41600). **Elgin** (✉ 17 High St., ☎ 01343/542666).

In summer, also look for tourist information centers in Alford, Ballater, Banchory, Banff, Crathie, Dufftown, Forres, Fraserburgh, Huntly, Inverurie, Stonehaven, and Tomintoul.

7 ARGYLL AND THE ISLES

With long sea lochs carved into its hilly, wooded interior, and its mossy terrain richly nourished by rainy Atlantic weather, Argyll is a beguiling interplay of water and land. The Kintyre Peninsula is a wonderland of sea views and ancient monuments, while the neighboring isles are at once microcosms of Scotland and distinct communities. Arran has long been the Scots' outdoor playground; scenic Islay is synonymous with whisky; Iona was an early Christian sanctuary; and Tobermory, a town of brightly painted houses on the Isle of Mull, has a Mediterranean feel.

By Gilbert
Summers

Updated by
Beth Ingpen

DIVIDED IN TWO by the long peninsula of Kintyre, western Scotland is characterized by a complicated, splintered seaboard. The west is an aesthetic delight, though it does catch those moist (yes, that's a euphemism) Atlantic weather systems. But the occasional wet foray is small price to pay for the glittering freshness of oak woods and bracken-covered hillsides, and for the bright interplay of sea, loch, and rugged green peninsula. Only a few decades ago the Clyde estuary was a coastal playground for people living in Glasgow and along Clydeside: their annual holiday was a steamer trip to any one of a number of Clyde resorts, known as going *doon the watter* (down the water, the estuary of the Clyde).

Some impressive castles gaze out over this luxuriant landscape. Ruined Dunstaffnage and Kilchurn castles once guarded the western seaboard; turreted Inveraray Castle and magnificent Brodick, on the Isle of Arran, now guard their own historic interiors, with antiques and portraits galore. The Kilmartin area has a wealth of stone circles, carved stones, and burial mounds from the Bronze Age and earlier, taking imaginative travelers thousands of years back in time. Gardens are another Argyll specialty thanks to the temperate west-coast climate—Crarae Gardens, south of Inveraray, invites you down winding paths through plantings of magnolias and azaleas that reach their colorful peaks in late spring. The Brodick Castle Garden also has fine azalea plantings, and Ardkinglas Woodland Garden adds an outstanding conifer collection.

Kintyre separates the islands of the Firth of Clyde (including Arran) from the islands of the Inner Hebrides. These isles are essentially microcosms of Scotland: each has its jagged cliffs or tongues of rock, its smiling sands and fertile pastures, its grim and ghostly fortress, and its tale of clan outrage or mythical beast. The pace of life is gentle out here, and the roads narrow and tortuous—not designed for heavy vehicles (beware pilgrim buses to Iona in summer, as they can cause major delays on the south-side routes). Arran is the place for hill walking on Goat Fell, the mountain that gives the island its distinctive profile. On Islay you can hunt down peaty, iodine-scented malt whisky: each of the island's distilleries makes a subtly different malt, and the process of choosing your favorite makes for a pleasant evening in the island's friendly pubs and hotels. Mull and Iona (just off Mull's western tip) are different again: Mull has yet more castles; a short stretch of narrow-gauge railway; the pretty port of Tobermory, with its brightly painted houses; and some demanding walks along the rocky coastline of the Burg. Iona is famous as an early seat of Christianity in Scotland, and was the burial place of Scottish kings in the Dark Ages. You could spend all your time in this region touring these larger islands, but keep in mind that plenty of small islands are just as rich. Coming from the mainland, you can't avoid Oban, an important ferry port with a main road leading south into Kintyre.

Pleasures and Pastimes

Biking

As both a vacation destination and a ferry gateway, Oban gets a lot of bike traffic. The main routes into and out of town are busy, and there are few side roads. Arran is popular for cycling, with a large number of bike-rental shops; but many roads here have one lane only, so wear high-visibility clothing, especially in the busy summer months—and, above all, bring rain gear.

Dining

This part of Scotland is not a great gastronomic center, but it does have some restaurants of distinction, and local ingredients are high in quality: the fish, fresh from the sparkling lochs and sea, could hardly be better. Beef, lamb, and game are also common. In rural districts, it's prudent to choose a hotel or guest house that serves a decent evening meal as well as breakfast.

CATEGORY	COST*
££££	over £40
£££	£30–£40
££	£15–£30
£	under £15

*per person for a three-course meal, including VAT and excluding drinks and service

Fishing
Local fishing literature, available in tourist offices, identifies at least 50 loch and river sites for game fishing and at least 20 coastal settlements suited to sea angling.

Golf
This area has about two dozen golf courses, notably some fine coastal links. Machrihanish, near Campbeltown, is the best known.

Lodging
Accommodations in Argyll and the isles range from châteaulike hotels to modest inns. Many traditional provincial hotels and small coastal resorts have been equipped with all modern conveniences yet retain their personalized service and historic charm. Apart from these, however, your choices are limited; the best overnight option is usually a simple guest house offering bed, breakfast, and an evening meal.

CATEGORY	COST*
££££	over £140
£££	£110–£140
££	£65–£110
£	under £65

*All prices are for standard double room, including service, breakfast, and VAT.

✎ following the text of a review is your signal that the property has a Web site, where you will find details and, usually, images; for a link, visit www.fodors.com/urls.

Exploring Argyll and the Isles

Loch Fyne tends to get in the way of a breezy mainland tour: it's a long haul around the end of this fjordlike sea loch to Inveraray. Ferry services allow all kinds of interisland tours, and can shorten mainland trips as well.

Numbers in the text correspond to numbers in the margin and on the Argyll and the Isles map.

Great Itineraries
You could easily spend a week exploring the islands alone, so consider spending at least a few nights in this region.

IF YOU HAVE 2 DAYS
From Glasgow, make your way to **Inveraray** ④ via Loch Lomond (A82) and the Rest and Be Thankful pass (A83). Continue south via the **Crarae Gardens** ⑥, then south to Lochgilphead, where you take A816 north to the **Crinan Canal** ⑧. Continue north on A816 and stay overnight in 🏨 **Oban** ①. The next day, follow the A85 east to see **Dunstaffnage Castle** ② and **Kilchurn Castle** ③, before returning to the Loch Lomond/Glasgow area.

Argyll and the Isles

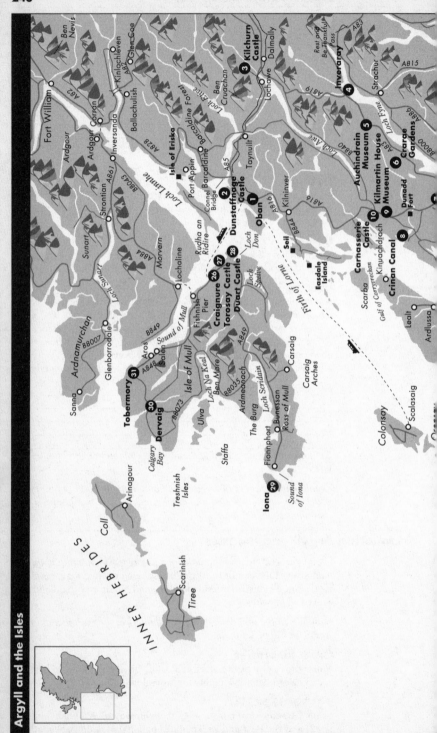

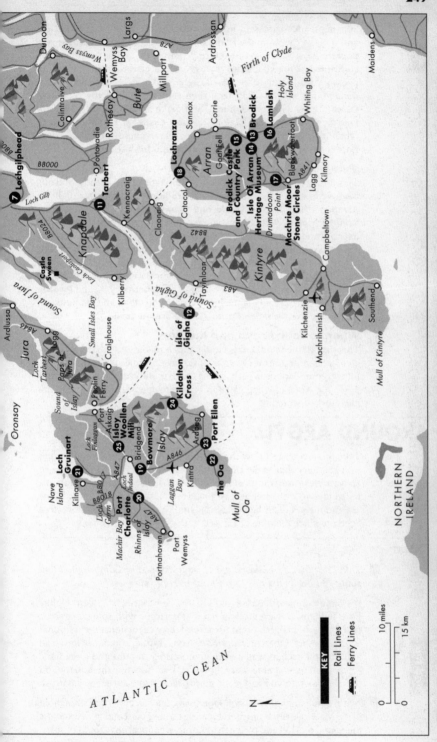

ATLANTIC OCEAN

NORTHERN IRELAND

Firth of Clyde

KEY
Rail Lines
Ferry Lines

0   10 miles
0   15 km

N

Largs
Dunoon
Wemyss Bay
Colintraive
Bute
Rothesay
Portavadie
Tarbert
Millport
Ardrossan
Maidens

Lochgilphead
Loch Gilp
B8000
Knapdale
Castle Sween
Loch Caolisport
B8024

Ardlussa
A846
Oronsay
Jura
Loch Tarbert
Paps of Jura
Craighouse
Feolin Ferry
Sound of Islay
Port Askaig

Kilberry
Kennacraig
Claonaig
Sannox
Corrie
Goatfell
Arran
Lochranza
Brodick
Lamlash
Holy Island
Whiting Bay
Blackwaterfoot
Lagg
Kilmory
A841
B842
Catacol
Tayinloon
Sound of Gigha
Isle of Gigha
Kintyre
A83
Campbeltown
Kilchenzie
Machrihanish
Southend
Mull of Kintyre

Nave Island
Kilnave
Loch Gorm
Machir Bay
Port Charlotte
Rhinns of Islay
A847
Portnahaven
Port Wemyss
B8018
Loch Indaal
Loch Finlaggan
Islay Woollen Mill
Bridgend
Bowmore
A846
Laggan Bay
Kintra
The Oa
Mull of Oa
Port Ellen
Ardbeg
Kildalton Cross
Islay

Loch Gruinart
Small Isles Bay

Drumadoon Point
Machrie Moor Stone Circles

7 Lochgilphead
11 Tarbert
12 Isle of Gigha
13 Brodick
14 Isle Of Arran Heritage Museum
15 Brodick Castle and Country Park
16 Lamlash
17 Machrie Moor Stone Circles
18 Lochranza
19 Bowmore
20 Port Charlotte
21 Loch Gruinart
22 The Oa
23 Port Ellen
24 Kildalton Cross
25 Islay Woollen Mill

IF YOU HAVE 4 DAYS

Starting from Ardrossan, in Ayrshire, take the ferry to ⛴ **Brodick** ⑬ and stay overnight on the island of Arran, visiting **Brodick Castle and Country Park** ⑮. Cross to Kintyre Peninsula by taking the ferry from **Lochranza** ⑱ for Claonaig; then cross the peninsula itself to Kennacraig. Head south to the Isle of Gigha, and its **Achamore House Gardens** ⑫, for a lovely day trip; then return north to the ⛴ **Crinan Canal** ⑧ area. Go up to **Oban** ① and make an excursion to Mull for **Iona** ㉙, ⛴ **Tobermory** ㉛, and **Torosay Castle** ㉗. Finally, return to Oban *or* leave Mull via Fishnish Pier, where you can take a ferry to Lochaline and travel north on the mainland from there.

IF YOU HAVE 7 DAYS

This noncircular route provides a good flavor of the islands. Starting from Ardrossan, take the ferry to ⛴ **Brodick** ⑬ and stay overnight on Arran, visiting **Brodick Castle and Country Park** ⑮. Take the ferry from **Lochranza** ⑱ to Claonaig, cross the Kintyre Peninsula to Kennacraig, and continue west to the island of ⛴ **Islay** ⑲–㉕, staying two nights to sample its wildlife preserves, coastal scenery, and malt whisky. Return to the mainland to explore the area around Knapdale, staying at ⛴ **Lochgilphead** ⑦ for at least one night. Go north to ⛴ **Oban** ① and take the ferry to Mull to see **Iona** ㉙, ⛴ **Tobermory** ㉛, and **Torosay Castle** ㉗, staying two nights. Finally, return to Oban and head east on A85 to see **Dunstaffnage Castle** ② and **Kilchurn Castle** ③.

When to Tour Argyll and the Isles

This part of the mainland is close enough to Glasgow that it's convenient year-round. You can take advantage of quiet roads and plentiful accommodations in early spring and late autumn. Avoid the islands in winter, when howling gales and frigid temperatures may prove unpleasantly distracting.

AROUND ARGYLL

Take time to get to know the mixture of topographical grandeur and lush greenery that make this part of Argyll special. Oban, the major ferry gateway and transport hub, is likely to figure in your explorations; try to take to the water at least once, even if your time is limited. The sea and the sea lochs have played a vital role in the history of western Scotland since the time of the war galleys of the clans.

Oban

❶ *96 mi northwest of Glasgow, 125 mi northwest of Edinburgh, 50 mi south of Fort William, 118 mi southwest of Inverness.*

It's almost impossible to avoid Oban when touring the west. Unlike Fort William, however, Oban has a waterfront with some character, and serves as a launch point for several ferry excursions. A traditional Scottish resort, Oban offers *ceilidhs* (song, music, and dance festivals) and tartan kitsch as well as late-night revelry in pubs and hotel bars. There is an inescapable sense, however, that just over the horizon, on the islands or down Kintyre, lie more peaceful and authentic environs.

❷ North of Oban stands **Dunstaffnage Castle,** once an important stronghold of the MacDougalls. From the ramparts, you have outstanding views across the **Sound of Mull** and the **Firth of Lorne,** a nautical crossroads of sorts, once watched over by Dunstaffnage Castle and commanded by the galleys (*birlinn* in Gaelic) of the Lords of the Isles. ✉ *Just off A85,* ☎ *0131/ 668–8800.* 🎫 *£2.* ◷ *Apr.–Sept., daily 9:30–6; Oct.–Nov., Mon.–Sat. 9:30– 4, Sun. 2–4; Dec.–Mar., Mon.–Wed. and Sat. 9:30–4, Sun. 2–4.*

From Dunstaffnage Castle you should be able to see **Connel Bridge,** less than a mile to the east. This elegant structure once carried a branch railway along the coast, but it has since surrendered to the all-conquering automobile. Below the bridge, in the shadow of the girders, the **Falls of Lora** foam, given the right tidal conditions. Upstream is fjordlike **Loch Etive** (with cruises from Oban); the water leaving this deep, narrow loch foams and fights with the incoming tides, creating turbulence and curious cascades under the bridge.

Dining and Lodging

££££ ✕ ⌂ **Isle of Eriska.** Embodying top quality, with prices to match, this hotel sits on its own island 10 mi north of Oban, accessible by a short bridge from the mainland. A rather severe, baronial-style granite facade belies the luxurious welcome within, the spacious rooms with every detail carefully chosen for your comfort. The restaurant serves sublime, innovative Scottish cuisine made with local ingredients: try the scallop and zucchini timbale with lobsters, artichoke, and champagne butter sauce. Take a stroll to catch sight of seals and otters offshore, or herons and badgers on the grounds. ⊠ *Ledaig, by Oban, Argyll PA37 1SD,* ☎ *01631/720371,* FAX *01631/720531. 17 rooms with bath or shower. Restaurant, pool, 6-hole golf course, tennis court, health club. AE, MC, V. Closed Jan.* ✍

££ ⌂ **Manor House Hotel.** Once the home of the duke of Argyll, this 1780 stone house on the shore just outside Oban has wonderful sea views. The public areas are furnished with antiques, the bedrooms with reproductions; and bedcovers and curtains are floral, in country-house style. The restaurant serves Scottish and French dishes, including lots of local seafood and game in season, complemented by a carefully chosen wine list. The house is walking distance from downtown Oban and the bus, train, and ferry terminals. ⊠ *Gallanach Rd., Oban, Argyll PA34 4LS,* ☎ *01631/562087,* FAX *01631/563053. 11 rooms with bath. Restaurant. AE, MC, V. Closed Mon., Tues. Nov.–Feb.*

£ ⌂ **Dungrianach.** Aptly named with a word meaning "the sunny house
★ on the hill," this B&B is set in woodland with superb views of the ocean and islands; yet it's only a few minutes' walk from Oban's ferry piers and town center. Both rooms in this late Victorian house have private bathrooms and are decorated with antique and reproduction furniture. ⊠ *Pulpit Hill, Oban, Argyll PA34 4LX,* ☎ FAX *01631/562840. 2 rooms with shower. No credit cards. Closed Oct.–Mar.* ✍

£ ⌂ **Kilchrenan House.** A fully refurbished Victorian house just a few minutes' walk from the town center, this is a high-grade bed-and-breakfast. Guest rooms look out to the sea and the islands. ⊠ *Corran Esplanade, Oban, Argyll PA34 5AQ,* ☎ FAX *01631/562663. 10 rooms, 7 with bath, 3 with shower. MC, V. Closed Nov.–Mar.*

£ ⌂ **Ronebhal Guest House.** You can see Loch Etive and the mountains beyond from this stone house east of Oban, set back within its own grounds. It offers B&B in spacious surroundings. ⊠ *Connel, Argyll PA37 1PJ,* ☎ FAX *01631/710310. 6 rooms with shower. MC, V. Closed Dec., Jan.* ✍

Nightlife and the Arts

The **Highland Theatre** (⊠ George St., ☎ 01631/562444) shows feature films and has a separate theater for plays.

Outdoor Activities and Sports

Rent bicycles from **Oban Cycles** (⊠ 9 Craigard Rd., ☎ 01631/566996).

Shopping

The factory store **Caithness Glass Oban** (⊠ Railway Pier, ☎ FAX 01631/563386) is a good place to buy a memento of Scotland. The paperweights with swirling colored patterns are particularly lovely.

OFF THE
BEATEN PATH

OBAN SEAL AND MARINE CENTRE – Kids (as well as adults) will love
this outstanding display of marine life, including shoals of herring, sharks,
rays, catfish, and seals. There's even a children's adventure playground,
and of course a gift shop. The restaurant serves morning coffee with
homemade scones, a full lunch menu (which might include homemade
soup, fish pie, or baked potatoes with various fillings), and afternoon
teas. Drive north from Oban on A828. ⊠ *Barcaldine, Connel, Argyll,*
☎ *01631/720386.* ⊡ *£6.50.* ☉ *Jan.–mid-Feb., weekends 10–4; mid
to end Feb., daily 10–4; first 2 wks Mar., weekends 10–4; mid-Mar.–
June and Sept.–Dec., daily 10–5; July–Aug., daily 9–6.*

Lochawe

18 mi east of Oban.

Lochawe is a loch-side community squeezed between the broad shoulder of Ben Cruachan and Loch Awe itself. The road gets busy in peak
season, filled with people trying to park by Lochawe Station. Cruises on
Loch Awe and to Kilchurn Castle start here on the **Lady Rowena Steam
Launch,** an Edwardian peat-fired steamboat. You can reserve on the spot
or in advance. ⊠ *Lochawe Station,* ☎ *01838/200440.* ⊡ *£4.50, including
admission to castle.* ☉ *May–Sept., departures daily 10–5 on the hr.*

★ ❸ Near Lochawe is **Kilchurn Castle,** a ruined fortress at the east end of
Loch Awe. The castle was built in the 15th century by Sir Colin Campbell (d. 1493) of Glenorchy (the Campbells had their original power
base in this area), and rebuilt in the 17th century. You'll see fine
panoramas from the airy vantage points amid the towers. You can drive
to the castle, but there is no safe parking, and the route across the fields
is boggy. We recommend parking at Lochawe Station and taking the
steam launch, a five-minute ride (☞ *above*). ⊠ *1 mi northeast of
Lochawe,* ☎ *0131/668–8800.* ⊡ *£1.* ☉ *Apr.–Sept., daily 9:30–6;
Oct.–Mar., Mon.–Sat. 9:30–4, Sun. 2–4.* ✎

Near Dalmally, just east of Lochawe, the **Duncan Ban Macintyre Monument** was erected in honor of this Gaelic poet (1724–1812), sometimes referred to as the Robert Burns of the Highlands. The view from
here is one of the finest in Argyll, taking in Ben Cruachan and the other
peaks nearby, as well as Loch Awe and its scattering of islands. To find
the monument from Dalmally, follow an old road running southwest
toward the banks of Loch Awe—you'll see the round, granite structure from the road's highest point, often called Monument Hill.

En Route   The A819 south to Lochawe and Inveraray initially runs alongside Loch
Awe, the longest loch in Scotland, but soon leaves these pleasant banks
to turn east and join the A83, which carries traffic from Glasgow and
Loch Lomond by way of the high Rest and Be Thankful pass. (Many
travelers come up Loch Lomond and head west by the A83.) The Rest
and Be Thankful is perhaps the road's most scenic point—aptly named,
it's a quasi-alpine pass among high green slopes and gray rocks. For
information on Loch Lomond, *see* Chapter 5.

Inveraray

★ ❹ *21 mi south of Lochawe, 61 mi north of Glasgow, 29 mi west of Loch
Lomond.*

On the approaches to Inveraray, note the ornate 18th-century bridge-
work that carries the road along the loch side. This is your first sign
that Inveraray is not just a jumbled assembly of houses; much of it was,
in fact, designed as a planned town for the third duke of Argyll in the
mid-18th century. The current seat of the Campbell duke is **Inveraray**

Castle, a smart, grayish-green turreted stone house with a self-satisfied air, visible through trees from the town itself. Like the well disciplined town, the castle was built around 1743; tours of the interior convey the history of this powerful family. ☎ 01499/302203. ⌨ £4.50. ☉ July–Aug., Mon.–Sat. 10–5:45, Sun. 1–5:45; Apr.–June and Sept.–mid-Oct., Mon.–Thurs. and Sat. 10–1 and 2–5:45, Sun. 1–5:45.

The **Inveraray Jail** is one of the latest generation of visitor centers. The old town jail and courtroom now house realistic courtroom scenes, period cells, and other paraphernalia that give you a glimpse of life behind bars in Victorian times—and today. The site includes a Scottish crafts shop. ⊠ Inveraray, ☎ 01499/302381. ⌨ £3.80. ☉ Apr.–Oct., daily 9:30–6; Nov.–Mar., daily 10–5 (last admission 1 hr before closing).

The 1911 lightship **Arctic Penguin** is a rare example of a riveted iron vessel. It now houses exhibits and displays on the maritime heritage of the River Clyde and Scotland's west coast. ☎ 01499/302213. ⌨ £3. ☉ Apr.–Oct., daily 10–6; Nov.–Mar., daily 10–5.

Ardkinglas Woodland Garden is home to one of Britain's finest collections of conifers, set off by rhododendron blossoms in early summer. You'll find it around the head of Loch Fyne, about 4 mi east of Inveraray. ⊠ Cairndow, ☎ 01499/600263. ⌨ £2. ☉ Daily.

At **Loch Fyne Oysters** you can purchase these delicious shellfish to go (or order them to be shipped), or sit down and consume a dozen with a glass of white wine. ⊠ Clachan Farm, Cairndow, Argyll, ☎ 01499/600236.

★ ❺ Step back into the 18th century at the **Auchindrain Museum.** Once a communal tenancy farm, this 18th-century cooperative venture has been restored. The old bracken-thatched and iron-roof buildings give you a feel for early farming life in the Highlands, and the interpretation center explains it. A83, 5 mi south of Inveraray, ☎ 01499/500235. ⌨ £3. ☉ Apr.–Sept., daily 10–5.

★ ❻ Well worth a visit for plant lovers are the **Crarae Gardens,** where magnolias and azaleas flourish in the moist and lush atmosphere. ⊠ Off A83, about 10 mi southwest of Inveraray, ☎ 01546/886614 or 01546/886388. ⌨ £3.50. ☉ Gardens: daily 9–6 (reduced to daylight hrs in winter); visitor center: Easter–Oct., seasonal hrs (call ahead).

Dining and Lodging

£££ ✕☷ **Creggans Inn.** This traditional inn overlooking Loch Fyne from its eastern shore, 21 mi east and south of Inveraray, dates from the 17th century. At mealtimes you can take an appetizing lunch or supper in the bar, or sit down to a more formal dinner in the cozy dining room—the menu features local produce and seafood, including Loch Fyne oysters. Guest rooms vary in size from large to rather small, but each one is individually decorated in traditional style. The staff is friendly and hospitable. ⊠ Strachur, Argyll PA27 8BX, ☎ 01369/860279, ☒ 01369/860637. 17 rooms, 15 with bath, 2 with shower. Restaurant. AE, DC, MC, V. ⊛

Lochgilphead

❼ 26 mi south of Inveraray.

The largest town in this region, Lochgilphead looks best when the tide is in, as Loch Gilp (really a bite out of Loch Fyne) reveals a muddy shoreline at low tide. With a series of well-kept, colorful buildings along ❽ its main street, this neat little town is worth a look. The **Crinan Canal** was opened in 1801 to enable fishing vessels to reach the Hebridean fishing grounds without making the long haul south around the Kintyre Peninsula. At its west end, the canal drops to the sea in a series of lochs. This area gets busy at times, with yachting enthusiasts strolling around and taking coffee in the shop beside the Crinan Hotel. To reach Crinan, take the A816 Oban road north from Lochgilphead for about a mile, then turn left.

❾ For an exceptional encounter with early Scottish history, visit the **Kilmartin House Museum** at Kilmartin, north of Crinan on the A816. Housed in a former manse, this award-winning museum explores the stone circles and avenues, burial mounds, and carved stones dating from the Bronze Age and earlier that are scattered thickly around this neighborhood. Nearby **Dunadd Fort**, a rocky hump rising out of the level ground between Crinan and Kilmartin, was once the capital of the early kingdom of Dalriada, founded by the first wave of Scots who migrated from Ireland around AD 500. Clamber up the rock to see a basin, a footprint, and an outline of a boar carved on the smooth upper face of the knoll. *At Kilmartin, on A816,* ☎ *01546/510278.* 🖃 *£3.90.* ☉ *Daily 10–5:30.*

❿ The tower house called **Carnasserie Castle** has the distinction of having belonged to the writer of the first book printed in Gaelic. The writer, John Carswell, bishop of the isles, translated a text by the Scottish reformer John Knox into Gaelic and published it in 1567. *Off A816, 9 mi north of Lochgilphead,* ☎ *0131/668–8800.* 🖃 *Free.* ☉ *Daily.*

Dining and Lodging

£££   ✕🛏 **Crinan Hotel.** This turn-of-the-20th-century property overlooks
★   the picturesque Crinan Canal and the Sound of Jura. One of the owners, the friendly and helpful Frances Macdonald, is also an artist, and her talents are evident in the hotel's interior design. Two restaurants serve Scottish cuisine and the freshest local seafood: the Westward Room serves dinner in a luxurious country-mansion setting that surrounds you with antiques and floral arrangements, and the rooftop Loch 16 has a nautical theme, with superb sunsets to accompany the award-winning seafood. ⊠ *Near Lochgilphead, PA31 8SR,* ☎ *01546/830261,* FAX *01546/830292. 22 rooms with bath and shower. 2 restaurants, coffee shop, boating, fishing. AE, MC, V.* 🍴

Outdoor Activities and Sports

From **Castle Riding Centre and Argyll Trail Riding** (⊠ Brenfield, Ardrishaig, Argyll, ☎ 01546/603274), south of Lochgilphead, highly qualified trail guides lead riders along routes throughout Argyll.

Shopping

At the **Highbank Porcelain Pottery** (⊠ Highbank Industrial Estate, Lochgilphead, ☎ 01546/602044), you can watch slip casting, hand painting, and firing on a £2 tour of the workshop. A shop sells the results (including reasonably priced seconds), and throws in ceramic giftware from other potteries.

OFF THE   **CASTLE SWEEN –** The oldest stone castle on the Scottish mainland, dating
BEATEN PATH   from the 12th century, sits on a rocky bit of coast about 15 mi southwest of Lochgilphead. You can reach it by an unclassified road from Crinan that grants outstanding views of the Paps of Jura (the mountains on Jura), across the sound. There are some temptingly deserted white-sand beaches here.

Kintyre Peninsula

52 mi (to Campbeltown) south of Lochgilphead.

Tarbert, a name that appears throughout the Highlands, is the Gaelic word for "place of portage," and a glance at the map tells you why it was given to this little town with a workaday waterfront: Tarbert sits on the narrow neck of land between East and West Loch Tarbert, where, long ago, boats were actually carried across the land to avoid looping all the way around the peninsula. The **Tairbeart Heritage Centre,** a two-minute drive south of the village, will tell you more about area history. ✉ *Tarbert, Argyll PA29 6SX,* ☎ *01880/820190.* ☒ *Free.* ☉ *Mid-Mar.–Dec., daily 10–sunset.*

The **Isle of Gigha** is a delectable Hebridean island, barely 5 mi long, sheltered in a frost-free, sea-warmed climate between Kintyre and Islay. The island was long favored by Scottish and English aristocrats as a summer destination; one relic of their posh legacy are the **Achamore House Gardens,** which, taking their cue from the climate, produce lush shrubberies with spectacular azalea displays in late spring. For a nimble day trip, take the 20-minute ferry to Gigha from Tayinloan and walk right over to the gardens. ☎ *01583/505267.* ☒ *Gardens: £2; ferry: £4.15 per person plus £16 per car.* ☉ *Gardens: daily dawn–dusk; ferry: May–mid Oct., daily 9–6, hourly; mid-Oct.–Apr., daily 9:15–4:30, hourly.*

ARRAN

Many Scots, especially those from Glasgow and the west, are well disposed toward Arran, as it reminds them of unhurried childhood holidays. Today the Scottish masses go to Spain, but, like other parts of the Clyde, the island of Arran has long been associated with the healthy outdoor life.

To get to Arran, take the ferry from Ardrossan. You'll see a number of fellow travelers wearing hiking boots: they're ready for the delights of Goat Fell, the impressive peak (2,868 ft) that gives Arran one of the most distinctive profiles of any island in Scotland. As the ferry approaches Brodick, you'll see Goat Fell's cone, its satellites forming an eye-catching backdrop to the northwest. Arran's southern half is less mountainous; the Highland Boundary Fault crosses just to the north of Brodick Bay. Exploring the island is easy, as the A841 road neatly circles it.

Brodick

⑬ *1 hr by ferry from Ardrossan.*

The largest township on Arran, Brodick is really just a village, its frontage set spaciously back from a promenade and beach. In nearby **Glen Rosa,** you can stroll through a long glen that offers a glimpse of the wild ridges that beckon so many outdoors enthusiasts; to get here, pass the Isle of Arran Heritage Museum and find the junction where the String Road cuts across the island. Drive a short way up the String Road and turn right at the signpost into the glen. The road soon becomes undrivable; park the car and wander on foot.

⑭ Brodick is home to the **Isle of Arran Heritage Museum,** which documents the life of the island from ancient times to the present. A number of buildings, including a cottage and *smiddy* (blacksmith's workshop), have period furnishings as well as displays on prehistoric life, geology, farming, fishing, and other aspects of the island's social history. ✉ *Rosaburn, Brodick,* ☎ *01770/302636.* ☒ *£2.* ☉ *Apr.–Oct., Mon.–Sat. 10–5, Sun. 11–4.*

★ ⑮ Arran's biggest cultural draw is **Brodick Castle and Country Park,** on the north side of Brodick Bay, its red sandstone cosseted by trees and parkland. Once the seat of the dukes of Hamilton, it's now under the auspices of the National Trust for Scotland. A number of rooms are open to the public—the castle's furniture, paintings, silver, and sporting trophies are opulent in their own right—but the real attraction is the garden, where brilliantly colored rhododendrons bloom, particularly in late spring and early summer. There are many unusual varieties here, though the ordinary yellow variety is unmatched for its scent: your first encounter with these is like hitting a wall of perfume. Save time to visit the Servants' Hall, where an excellent restaurant serves morning coffee (with hot scones—try the date-and-walnut variety), a full lunch menu that changes daily, and afternoon teas with home-baked goods, including bread. Eat on the terrace if the weather's fine, with chaffinches clamoring for crumbs. ⊠ *Just under a mile north of Brodick Pier,* ☎ *01770/ 302202.* ⊡ *£6; gardens only, £2.50.* ☉ *Castle: Apr.–June and Sept.– Oct., daily 11–4:30 (last admission 4); July–Aug., daily 11–5 (last admission 4:30); garden and country park: daily 9:30–dusk.* ☜

Dining and Lodging

£££–££££ ✕🖼 **Kilmichael Country House Hotel.** Built by the Fullerton family on
★ land granted to them by Robert the Bruce, this 300-year-old mansion sits at the head of Glen Cloy, just outside Brodick. Now an outstanding small hotel, it's decorated in light, sunny colors and furnished with Georgian oak antiques and Sanderson fabrics. At one end of the blue-and-yellow sitting room, in what was once a private chapel, a stained-glass window shows the Fullerton family crest. Cuisine in the restaurant is exceptional, a marriage of fresh Scottish produce an international flair: recent dishes include fresh beetroot ravioli filled with four Italian cheeses and seasoned with balsamic dressing; chestnut and roasted-garlic soup; turban of sea bass with tiger prawns, lemongrass, and ginger butter; and rack of Scottish lamb on red cabbage with rosemary and red-currant sauce. Children under 12 are not allowed, and guests may not smoke except in one sitting room. ⊠ *Brodick, Isle of Arran, KA27 8BY,* ☎ *01770/302219,* 🖷 *01770/302068. 3 rooms with bath and shower, 4 suites. Restaurant. MC, V. Closed Nov.–Mar.*

Outdoor Activities and Sports

BIKING

Rent bikes from **Brodick Boat and Cycle Hire** (⊠ The Beach, ☎ 01770/ 302009) or **Brodick Cycles** (⊠ Opposite Village Hall, ☎ 01770/ 302460).

HORSEBACK RIDING

Explore Arran on horseback with the **Brodick Riding Centre** (☎ 01770/ 302800).

Shopping

Arran's shops are well stocked with island-produced goods. The **Duchess Court Shops** (⊠ The Home Farm, ☎ 01770/302831) include **Bear Necessities,** with everything bearly; the **Nature Shop,** with nature-oriented books and gifts; the **Home Farm Kitchen Shop** for locally made mustards and other preserves, along with kitchenware; and the **Island Cheese Company,** with such Arran specialties as blue cheese and a wide selection of other handmade British cheeses. Also within the Home Farm is a small restaurant.

Lamlash

 4 mi south of Brodick.

With views offshore to steeply flanked Holy Island, Lamlash has a breezy, seaside-holiday atmosphere. To reach the highest point accessible by car, go through the village and turn right beside the bridge onto Ross Road, which climbs steeply from a thickly planted valley, **Glen Scorrodale,** and yields fine views of Lamlash Bay. From Lamlash you can explore the southern part of Arran: 10 mi southwest is the little community of **Lagg,** sitting peacefully by the banks of the Kilmory Water, while **Whiting Bay** has a waterfront string of hotels and well-kept property.

Outdoor Activities and Sports

Rent bikes, rent a boat, or arrange a ferry to Holy Island with **Whiting Bay Cycle Hire** (⊠ Elim, Silverhill, Whiting Bay, ☎ 01770/700382), open May–September.

Shopping

Patterson Arran Ltd. (⊠ The Old Mill, Lamlash, ☎ 01770/600606) is famous for its mustards, preserves, and marmalades.

Machrie

11 mi north of Lagg.

⑰ Near the scattered homesteads of Machrie (which has a popular beach), a HISTORIC SCOTLAND sign points to the **Machrie Moor Stone Circles,** about a mile farther along. A well-surfaced track takes you to a grassy moor by a ruined farm, where you'll see small, rounded granite-boulder circles and much taller, eerie, red-sandstone monoliths. Out on the bare moor, the lost and lonely stones are very evocative, well worth even a walk to see if you like the feeling of solitude. The Machrie area is littered with these sites: chambered cairns, hut circles, and standing stones dating from the Bronze Age.

Outdoor Activities and Sports

Even novices can enjoy a guided ride on a mount from **Cairnhouse Riding Centre** (⊠ Blackwaterfoot, ☎ 01770/860466).

Shopping

The **Old Byre Showroom** (⊠ Auchencar Farm, ☎ 01770/840227) sells sheepskin goods, locally hand-knit "jumpers" (sweaters), designer knitwear, leather goods, and rugs.

En Route Continuing to Blackwaterfoot, you can return to Brodick via the String Road: turn left by the Kinloch Hotel, up the hill. As you drive, there are more fine views of the granite complexities of Arran's hills: gray notched ridges beyond brown moors and, past the watershed, a vista of Brodick Bay. From this high point the road rolls down to Brodick.

Lochranza

⑱ *8 mi north of Corrie.*

North of Brodick is Lochranza, a crafts community sheltered by the Bay of Loch Ranza, which spills in shallows up the flat-bottom glacial glen. The village is set off by a picturesque ruin, **Lochranza Castle,** set on a low sand spit. This is said to have been the landing place of Robert the Bruce when he returned from Rathlin Island in 1307 to start the campaign that won Scotland's independence. ☎ *0131/668–8800.* ⊠ *Free.* ☉ *Weekdays 9–5.*

En Route South of Lochranza, there are fine views across the Kilbrannan Sound to the long rolling horizon of Kintyre.

ISLAY

Islay has a character distinct from that of the rest of the Hebrides. In contrast to areas where most residents live on crofts (generally worked by someone who has another job, i.e., fisherman, teacher, postman), Islay's western half in particular has large, self-sustaining farms. Many of the island's best beaches, wildlife preserves, and historical sites are also on its western half, while the southeast is mainly an extension of Jura's inhospitable quartzite hills. A number of distilleries—source of the island's delectable malt whiskies—provide jobs for the locals. Islay is particularly known for its wildlife, especially its birds, including the rare chough (a crow with red legs and beak) and, in winter, its barnacle geese.

Bowmore

⑲ *11 mi north of Port Ellen.*

Compact Bowmore is about the same size (population 1,000) as Port Ellen, but it works slightly better as a base for touring. Sharing its name with the whisky made in the distillery by the shore (founded 1779), Bowmore is a tidy town, its grid pattern having been laid out in 1768 by the local landowner Daniel Campbell, of Shawfield. Main Street stretches from the pier head to the commanding parish church, built in 1767 in an unusual circular design—so the devil could not hide in a corner.

Dining and Lodging

£–££ ✕🏠 **Harbour Inn.** The cheerfully noisy bar is frequented by locals and off-duty distillery workers, who are happy to rub elbows with travelers and exchange island gossip. The superb restaurant serves morning coffee, lunch, and dinner, and both the bistro-style lunch menu and the "modern Scottish" dinner menu are also available at the bar. Both menus feature local lobster, crab, prawns, and island lamb and beef. Each of the seven guest rooms is decorated with a different theme—Victorian Garden, Seaside, Tartan, Captain's Cabin. ⊠ *Main St., Bowmore,* ☎ *01496/810330,* FAX *01496/810990. 7 rooms with shower. Restaurant. AE, MC, V.* ⊛

Shopping

Islay's sheer number of distilleries will spoil you for choice. Characterized by a peaty taste, Islay's malt whiskies are available in local pubs, off-license shops, and distillery shops. Though not all have shops, most distilleries welcome visitors by appointment; some charge a small fee for a tour, which you can redeem against a purchase of whisky.

Distilleries: **Bowmore** (⊠ School St., Bowmore, ☎ 01496/810671). **Bunnahabhain** (⊠ Port Askaig, ☎ 01496/840646). **Caol Ila** (⊠ Port Askaig, ☎ 01496/840207). **Lagavoulin** (⊠ Port Ellen, ☎ 01496/302400). **Laphroaig** (⊠ Port Ellen, ☎ 01496/302418).

En Route Traveling north out of Bowmore (past a sign for Bridgend), the road skirts the sand flats at the head of Loch Indaal. To reach Port Charlotte, follow the loch shores all the way past Bruichladdich, which, like Bowmore, produces a malt whisky with the same name.

Port Charlotte

⑳ *11 mi west of Bowmore via A846/A847.*

Above the road on the right in a converted *kirk* (church), is the **Museum of Islay Life,** a haphazard but authentic and informative display of times past. ☎ 01496/850358. 💷 £2. ⊙ Apr.–Oct., Mon.–Sat. 10–5, Sun. 2–5.

South of Port Charlotte, a loop road lets you explore the wild landscapes of the **Rhinns of Islay.** At the south end of the Rhinns are the scattered cottages of **Portnahaven** and its twin, **Port Wemyss.** Take the A847 to the villages, then return by the bleak, unclassified road that loops north and east, passing by the recumbent stone circle at Coultoon and the chapel at Kilchiaran.

En Route For a glimpse of Islay's peerless western seascapes, turn left onto the B8018 north of Bruichladdich. After about 2 mi, turn left again onto a little road that meanders past Loch Gorm and ends near Machir Bay, with its superb (and usually deserted) sandy beach. Soon after you turn around to go back, turn right to see the derelict kirk of Kilchoman. The kirkyard holds some interesting grave slabs and two late-medieval stone crosses from the Iona school of carving (as opposed to the Kintyre school). From Kilchoman, turn right and then left to circle Loch Gorm, pausing as the road all but touches the coast at Saligo. It's worth a stroll (beyond the former wartime camp) to absorb the fine sea views, especially if westerly breezes are piling high breakers onto the rocky ridges. Heading east from here, turn right at the B8018, then left on the B8017, and take a left at Aoradh Farm onto the minor road that runs north along the west side of Loch Gruinart.

Loch Gruinart

㉑ *7 mi northeast of Port Charlotte, 8 mi north of Bowmore.*

You're bound to feel magnetically pulled toward the long reaches of Loch Gruinart. Dunes flank its outlet to the sea, and pale beaches rise from the falling tides. Traveling north up the loch's western shore, the road soon brings you to **Cill Naoimh** (Kilnave). The ruined chapel here carries a dark tale of a group of Maclean clansmen defeated in a nearby battle with the Macdonalds in 1598: the Macleans sought sanctuary in the chapel, but their pursuers set its roof aflame, and the clansmen perished within. There's a weathered 8th-century carved cross in the graveyard.

If you're into wide skies, crashing waves, and lonely stretches of coast, the best view of Loch Gruinart is to the north up its eastern shore. From the far dunes of the headland, held together with marram grass, you can see the islands of **Colonsay** and **Oronsay** across Hebridean waters, on which plumes and fans of white spray rise from hidden reefs. The priory on the island of Oronsay, with its famous carved cross, is barely distinguishable. To witness this peerless scenery, return to the B8017 from Kilnave, cross the flats at the head of the loch, then turn left up its eastern shore. Park in front of the gate, where the road deteriorates, and continue on foot.

The Oa

㉒ *13 mi south of Bowmore.*

The southern Oa peninsula is a region of caves that's rich in smuggling lore. At its tip, the Mull of Oa, is a monument recalling the 650 men who lost their lives in 1918 when the troopships *Tuscania* and *Otranto* went down nearby. To get here, drive south on the A846: before you reach Port Ellen, go straight ahead; when the A846 turns to a minor road to Imeraval, make a right at the junction, then a left.

Port Ellen

㉓ *11 mi south of Bowmore.*

The sturdy community of Port Ellen was founded in the 1820s, and much of its architecture dates from the 19th century. It has a harbor, a few shops, and some inns, but not enough commercial development to mortgage its personality.

The road east from Port Ellen passes communities bearing names—such as Lagavulin—that will be familiar to the malt-whisky connoisseur. The whisky of the **Laphroaig Distillery,** which offers tours, is one of the most distinctive local whiskies, with a tangy, peaty, seaweed-and-iodine flavor. The distillery is a little less than a mile along the road to Ardbeg. ☎ *01496/302418.* 🎫 *Free.* ☉ *Tours by appointment.*

Northeast of Port Ellen is one of the highlights of Scotland's Celtic heritage. After passing through a pleasantly rolling, partly wooded landscape, take a narrow road (it's signposted KILDALTON CROSS) from Ardbeg. This leads to a ruined chapel with surrounding kirkyard, in which stands the

★ ㉔ finest carved cross anywhere in Scotland: the 8th-century **Kildalton Cross.** Carved from a single slab of epidiorite rock, the ringed cross is encrusted on both sides with elaborate designs in the style of the Iona school. The surrounding grave slabs date as far back as the 12th and 13th centuries.

Outdoor Activities and Sports
Ballivicar Pony Trekking (⊠ Ballivicar Farm, Port Ellen, ☎ 01496/ 302251) leads trips on nearby beaches and into the surrounding countryside.

Bridgend

3 mi north of Bowmore via A846 (follow signs for Port Askaig).

Bridgend itself is a tiny community beside the main road, but hardly

★ ㉕ a mile beyond is a sign for the **Islay Woollen Mill.** Set in a wooded hollow by the river, the mill has a fascinating array of working machinery; the proud owner will take you around.

Shopping
The shop at the **Islay Woollen Mill** sells high-quality products that were woven on site. Beyond the usual tweed lengths, there is a distinctive range of hats, caps, and clothing made from the mill's own cloth. All of the tartans and tweeds worn in the film *Braveheart* originated here. ☎ *01496/810563.* ⊠ *Free.* ⊙ *Mon.–Sat. 10–5.*

Port Askaig

3 mi northeast of Loch Finlaggan via A846.

Serving as the ferry port for Jura, Port Askaig is nothing more than a cluster of cottages by the pier. Uphill, just outside the village, a side road travels along the coast, giving impressive views of Jura on the way. At road's end, the **Bunnahabhain Distillery** (☎ 01496/840646) sits on the shore. You need a reservation to visit.

Dining and Lodging
££ ✕▣ **Port Askaig Hotel.** This modernized roadside drovers' inn overlooks the Sound of Islay and the island of Jura and is convenient to the ferry terminal. The grounds extend to the shore. Accommodations are comfortable without being luxurious, and the traditional Scottish food is well prepared using homegrown produce. ⊠ *Port Askaig, Isle of Islay, Argyll PA46 7RD,* ☎ *01496/840245,* ℻ *01496/840295. 8 rooms, 6 with bath. Restaurant, 2 bars. MC, V.* ⊛

IONA AND THE ISLE OF MULL

Though Mull certainly has an indigenous population, the island is often called the Officers' Mess for its popularity with retired military personnel. Make your way across the Ross of Mull to the island of Iona, cradle of Scottish Christianity and ancient burial site of the kings of Scotland.

Craignure

㉖ *40-min ferry crossing from Oban, 15-min ferry crossing to Fishnish (5 mi northwest of Craignure) from Lochaline.*

Little more than a pier and some houses, Craignure is close to Mull's two best-known castles, Torosay and Duart. Reservations for the year-round ferry trip from Oban to Craignure are advisable in summer. The ferry from Lochaline to Fishnish, just northwest of here, runs only in summer and takes no reservations.

★ ㉗ A trip to **Torosay Castle** includes the novelty of steam-and-diesel service on a narrow-gauge railway, which takes 20 minutes to run from the pier at Craignure to the grounds of Torosay (about half a mile). Scottish Baronial in style, the turreted castle has a friendly air. Between Easter and mid-October, you have the run of much of the house, which is full of intrigue and humor by way of idiosyncratic information boards and informal family albums. The main feature of the castle's gardens—a gentle blend of formal and informal elements—is its Italian statue walk. ⊠ *Off the A849, about 1 mi southeast of Craignure,* ☎ *01680/812421.* ☜ *Castle and gardens: £4.50; train: £2.30.* ☺ *Castle: Easter–mid-Oct., daily 10:30–5:30 (last admission 5); gardens: Easter–mid-Oct., daily 9–7; mid-Oct.–Easter, daily dawn–dusk.* ☜

㉘ Enthusiastic hikers can take a long walk along the shore from Torosay to **Duart Castle.** The less-energetic can drive the 3 mi from Craignure. This ancient Maclean seat was ruined by the Campbells in 1691, but was purchased and restored by Sir Fitzroy Maclean in 1911. Inside, one display depicts the wreck of the *Swan,* a Cromwellian vessel sunk offshore in the mid-17th century and recently excavated by marine archaeologists. To reach Duart by car, take the A849 and turn left around the shore of Duart Bay. ⊠ *3 mi southeast of Craignure,* ☎ *01680/ 812309.* ☜ *£3.50.* ☺ *May–mid-Oct., daily 10:30–6.*

Lodging

£ ㊅ **Inverlussa.** Idyllically set beside a stream near Loch Spelve, this warm, friendly, modern guest house makes a good base of exploration. Pine furniture, tranquil green, blue, or cream color schemes in the guest rooms, and an open fire in the lounge create a relaxing environment, and you have your pick of several nearby restaurants and pubs for evening meals. ⊠ *By Craignure, Argyll PA65 6BD,* ☎ FAX *01680/812436. 3 rooms, 1 with shower. No credit cards. Closed Nov.–Mar.*

En Route Between Craignure and Fionnphort, the double-lane road narrows as it heads southwest, touched by sea inlets at Lochs Don and Spelve. Inland, vivid grass and high rock faces in Glen More make gray and green the prevalent hues. These stepped-rock faces, the by-product of ancient lava flows, reach their highest point in Ben More, the only island *munro* outside Skye (a munro is a Scottish mountain more than 3,000 ft high). Its high, bald slopes are prominent by the time you reach the road junction at the head of Loch Scridain. Stay on the A849 for a pleasant drive the length of the Ross of Mull, a wide promontory with scattered settlements. There are good views to the right of the dramatic cliff ramparts of Ardmeanach, the stubbier promontory to the north: the National Trust for Scotland cares for the rugged stretch of coast, known as The Burg and home to a 40-million-year-old fossil tree (at the end of a long walk from the B8035, signposted west off the A849). The A849 continues through the village of Bunessan and eventually ends in a long parking lot opposite the houses of Fionnphort.

Fionnphort

36 mi west of Craignure.

The vast parking space at the small village of Fionnphort is a testament to the popularity of the nearby island of Iona, which does not allow cars. Ferry service is frequent in the summer.

Iona

★ ㉙ *5 mins by ferry from Fionnphort.*

No less a travel writer than Dr. Johnson wrote, "We were now treading that illustrious Island which was once the luminary of the Caledonian regions . . ." The fiery and argumentative Irish monk Columba chose Iona for the site of a monastery in 563 because it was the first landing place from which he could *not* see Ireland. Christianity had been brought to Scotland (Galloway) by St. Ninian in 397, but until St. Columba's church was founded, the word had not spread widely among the ancient northerners, the Picts. Iona was the burial place of the kings of Scotland until the 11th century, so many Dark Age kings, 48 of them Scottish, are interred here, not to mention princes and bishops. Many carved slabs also commemorate clan chiefs.

Columba's monastery survived repeated Norse sackings but finally fell into disuse around the time of the Reformation. Restoration work began at the turn of the 20th century, and in 1938 the **Iona Community** was founded. Today the restored buildings, including the abbey, serve as a spiritual center under the jurisdiction of the Church of Scotland. The ambience of the complex is a curious amalgam of the ancient and the earnest. Beyond the ancient cloisters, the island's most delightful aspect is its almost mystical tranquility—enhanced by the fact that most visitors make only the short walk from the ferry pier to the abbey (by way of the nunnery), rather than press on to the island's farther reaches. ☎ *01681/700404.* ☼ *Abbey gift shop and bookstore: Apr.–Oct., Mon.–Sat. 10–5, Sun. noon–4; abbey coffeehouse and Iona Community shop: Apr.–Oct., Mon.–Thurs. and Sat. 11–4:30, Fri. and Sun. noon–4:30.*

Shopping

Iona has a few pleasant surprises for shoppers, the biggest of which is the **Old Printing Press Bookshop** (✉ Beside St. Columba Hotel), an excellent antiquarian and secondhand bookstore. The **abbey** shop (☎ 01681/700404), across the road from the abbey itself, has a nice selection of Celtic-inspired gift items.

En Route   Back on Mull, turn west onto the B8035 at Loch Scridain: the road rises away from the loch to the conifer plantations and green slopes of Gleann Seilisdeir. The main road through the glen breaches the stepped cliffs and drops to the shore, granting inspiring views of the island of Ulva guarding Loch na Keal. This stretch of the B8035 feels remote, with splinters of rock from the heights strewn across in places. High ledges eventually give way to vistas of the screes of Ben More. Continue to skirt the coast on the B8073 and you'll take in a succession of fine coastal views with Ulva in the foreground. Beyond Calgary Bay the landscape is gentler, as you approach the village of Dervaig.

Dervaig

㉚ *60 mi north of Fionnphort, 27 mi northwest of Craignure.*

Just before the village of Dervaig, you'll see signs for the **Old Byre Heritage Centre.** An audiovisual presentation on the history of Mull plays hourly on the half hour; there's also a crafts shop. The restaurant's wholesome fare is a boon to weary travelers, particularly the thick, hearty homemade soups. ✉ *Dervaig PA75 6QR,* ☎ *01688/400229.* ▦ *£3.* ☼ *Easter–Oct., daily 10:30–6:30 (last admission 6).*

With 43 seats, the aptly named **Mull Little Theatre** (☞ *below*) has the not-insignificant distinction of being the smallest professional theater in the United Kingdom.

Dining and Lodging

£££–££££ ✕🏠 **Druimard Country House.** From this handsome Victorian house on the village outskirts, you have both loch and glen views over the River Bellart. The room rate includes dinner, and the elegant restaurant has an original menu (with several vegetarian options); two popular dishes are roast loin of venison on a bed of red cabbage with game sauce, and medallions of local monkfish topped with Provençal bread crumbs and served on a pool of two pepper sauces. The guest rooms, furnished with antique Victorian oak and mahogany furniture, are individually decorated with floral wallpaper and fabrics. ⊠ *Dervaig, Isle of Mull, Argyll PA75 6QW,* ☏ 📠 *01688/400345. 7 rooms with bath or shower. Restaurant. MC, V. Closed Nov.–Mar.*

Nightlife and the Arts

The **Mull Little Theatre** (☏ 01688/400267) stages a varied program of plays throughout the summer.

Tobermory

㉛   *5 mi east of Dervaig.*

Founded as a fishing station, Tobermory gradually declined, hastened by the arrival of railroad service in Oban. Still, the brightly painted crescent of 18th-century buildings around the harbor—now a popular mooring for yachtsmen—gives Tobermory a Mediterranean look.

Dining and Lodging

££–£££ ✕🏠 **Western Isles Hotel.** Set high above town, many of the spacious rooms in this traditional resort hotel have superb views, and each is individually decorated with floral fabrics, grand bed canopies, and touches of tartan. The terra-cotta lounge and airy conservatory bar are comfortable and relaxing. The restaurant serves a "Taste of Scotland" menu with local fish, seafood, game, and lamb, and you can take bar meals in the conservatory. ⊠ *Tobermory, Argyll PA75 6PR,* ☏ *01688/302012,* 📠 *01688/302297. 24 rooms with bath, 1 suite. Restaurant, bar. AE, MC, V.* ✍

Outdoor Activities and Sports

Rent cycles from **On Yer Bike** (⊠ Salen, Aros, ☏ 01680/300501).

En Route To reach the ferry, drive south from Tobermory on the A848, which yields pleasant, if unspectacular, views across to Morvern, on the mainland. On the coast just beyond Aros, across the river flats, stands the ruined 13th-century **Aros Castle.** The road continues through Salen to Fishnish, for the ferry to Lochaline, and then Craignure, for the ferry to Oban.

ARGYLL AND THE ISLES A TO Z

Arriving and Departing

By Bus

Scottish Citylink (☏ 0990/505050) runs daily bus service from Glasgow's Buchanan Street station to the mid-Argyll region and Kintyre.

By Car and Ferry

The A85 takes you to Oban, the main ferry terminal for Mull. The A83 rounds Loch Fyne and heads down Kintyre to Kennacraig, the ferry terminal for Islay. Farther down the A83 is Tayinloan, the ferry port for Gigha. You can reach Brodick on Arran by ferry from Ardrossan, on the Clyde coast (A8/A78 from Glasgow), or, in summer, you can travel to Lochranza from Claonaig on the Kintyre Peninsula. All ferries take cars as well as pedestrians. For schedules and reservations, contact **Cale-**

donian MacBrayne (CalMac; main office, ⊠ Ferry Terminal, Gourock, ☎ 01475/650100 for schedules, 08705/650000 for reservations).

By Plane
The nearest full-service airport is in Glasgow, but there are two small airports in this region: **British Airways Express** (☎ 0345/222111) flies from Glasgow to **Campbeltown** (on the Kintyre Peninsula) and the island of Islay.

By Train
Oban and Ardrossan are the main rail stations. For information, call the **National Train Enquiry Line** (☎ 0345/484950). All trains connect with ferries.

Getting Around

By Bus
Companies serving this area: **B. Mundell Ltd.** (⊠ Islay, ☎ 01496/840273). **Bowman's Coaches** (⊠ Mull, ☎ 01680/812313). **C. MacLean** (⊠ Jura, ☎ 01496/820314). **Oban & District Buses** (⊠ Oban and Lorne, ☎ 01631/562856). **Stagecoach Western Buses** (⊠ Arran, ☎ 01770/302000). **West Coast Motor Service** (⊠ Mid-Argyll and Kintyre, ☎ 01586/552319).

By Car and Ferry
Negotiating this area is easy except in July and August, when the roads around Oban may be congested. There are some single-lane roads, especially on the east side of the Kintyre Peninsula and on the islands. Car-ferry services to and from the main islands are operated by **Caledonian MacBrayne** (CalMac; main office, ⊠ Ferry Terminal, Gourock; ☎ 01475/650100 for schedules, 08705/650000 for reservations). An Island Hopscotch ticket reduces the cost of island-hopping. **Serco Denholm Ltd.** (☎ 01475/731540) operates the Islay–Jura ferry.

By Train
Aside from the main line to Oban—with stops at Dalmally, Loch Awe, Falls of Cruachan (on request), Taynuilt, and Connel Ferry—there is no train service to this part of Scotland. A narrow-gauge railway takes ferry passengers from the pier head at Craignure (Mull) to **Torosay Castle,** a distance of about half a mile.

Contacts and Resources

Doctors and Dentists
If you need medical or dental care, inquire at your hotel, the local tourist office, or the police station, or look under "Doctors" or "Dentists" in the local Yellow Pages.

Emergencies
For **police, fire assistance,** or an **ambulance,** dial ☎ 999 from any phone (toll-free). **Lorne and Islands District General Hospital** (⊠ Glengallen Rd., Oban, ☎ 01631/567500) has an emergency room.

Guided Tours
ORIENTATION
Many of the bus companies listed in Getting Around by Bus (☞ *above*) offer general sightseeing tours. **Bowman's Coaches** (⊠ Mull, ☎ 01680/812313) offers trips from Oban to Mull, Staffa, and Iona between March and October.

SPECIAL-INTEREST
Gordon Grant Marine (⊠ Staffa Ferries, Iona, ☎ 01681/700338) leads a "Three Isle" ferry excursion to Mull, Iona, and Staffa, and leaves

Mull on other trips to Treshnish Isles and Staffa. From Oban, boat trips are available from **Loch Etive Cruises** (✉ Taynuilt, ☎ 01866/822430; or call Oban tourist office). **Sea Life Surveys** (✉ Torrbreac, Dervaig, Mull, PA75 6QL, ☎ 01688/400223) offers four- and six-hour whale-watching and wildlife day trips from Tobermory. **Turas Mara** (✉ Penmore Mill, Dervaig, Mull, ☎ FAX 01688/400242) runs daily excursions from Oban and Mull to Staffa, Iona, and the Treshnish Isles.

Visitor Information

Bowmore, Islay (✉ The Square, ☎ 01496/810254). **Brodick, Arran** (✉ The Pier, ☎ 01770/302140, FAX 01770/302395). **Campbeltown** (✉ Mackinnon House, The Pier, ☎ 01586/552056). **Craignure, Mull** (✉ The Pierhead, ☎ 01680/812377). **Dunoon** (✉ 7 Alexandra Parade, ☎ 01369/703785, FAX 01369/706085). **Inveraray** (✉ Front St., ☎ 01499/302063). **Lochgilphead** (☎ 01546/602344), April–October only. **Oban** (✉ Albany St., ☎ 01631/563122, FAX 01631/564273). **Tarbert** (☎ 01880/820429), April–October only. **Tobermory, Mull** (☎ 01688/302182).

8 AROUND THE GREAT GLEN

INVERNESS, LOCH NESS,
CAWDOR CASTLE, FORT WILLIAM

Sooner or later, all feet march in the direction of mythical Brigadoon, toward those splendid heath-clad mountain slopes and shimmering lochs so typical of the southern Highlands. Here, where the Great Glen runs from Inverness to Fort William—two of the Highlands' best areas for lodging and shopping—is Ben Nevis, Britain's highest peak, and here, too, is Loch Ness, supposedly home to Nessie, everyone's favorite monster and charter member of the local chamber of commerce.

By Gilbert
Summers

Updated by
Beth Ingpen

THE ANCIENT RIFT VALLEY of the Great Glen is a dramatic feature on the map of Scotland, giving the impression that the top half of the country has slid southwest. Geologists confirm that this actually occurred, after matching granite from Strontian, in Morvern, west of Fort William, with the same type of rock found at Foyers, on the east side of Loch Ness, some 65 mi away. The Great Glen, with its sense of openness, lacks the grandeur of Glencoe or the mountains of the Torridons, but the highest mountain in the United Kingdom, Ben Nevis (4,406 ft), looms over its southern portals, and spectacular scenery lies within a short distance of the main glen. A map of Scotland gives a hint of the grandeur and beauty to be found here: fingers of inland lochs, craggy and steep-sided mountains, rugged promontories, and deep inlets. But the map does not give an inkling of the brilliant purple and emerald moorland, the forests, and the astonishingly varied wildlife (mountain hares, red deer, golden eagles, ospreys); or the courtesy of the soft-spoken inhabitants; or the depth of ancestral memory and clan mythology. All these are delights that await the visitor who ventures out of the main cities, Inverness and Fort William.

Though it's the capital of the Highlands, Inverness has the flavor of a Lowland town, its winds blowing in a sea-salt air from the Moray Firth. Inverness is also home to one of the world's most famous monster myths: in 1933, during a quiet news week for the local paper, the editor decided to run a story about a strange sighting of something splashing about in Loch Ness. Close to 70 years later the story lives on, and the dubious Loch Ness phenomenon continues to keep cameras trained on the deep waters, which have an ominous tendency to create mirages in still conditions. The loch also has the greatest volume of water of any Scottish loch.

Fort William, without a monster on its doorstep, makes do with Ben Nevis and the Road to the Isles, a title sometimes applied to the breathtakingly scenic route to Mallaig. This is best seen by rail, since the road to Mallaig is still partially narrow, winding, and single track in places, and to meet an oncoming coach can be alarming—especially if you are distracted by the view. On the way, road and rail routes pass Loch Morar, the country's deepest body of water, which lays claim to its own monster, Morag. Away from the Great Glen to the north lie the heartlands of Scotland, a bare backbone of remote mountains.

The great hills that loom to the south can be seen clearly on either side of Strathspey, the broad valley of the River Spey, an area also commonly known as Speyside. This is one of Scotland's main whisky-distilling areas, with the industry's distinctive kilns, bonded stores, and pungent reek to be found all across the countryside. Speyside malt whiskies are generally sweeter in taste, with much less of the peaty, iodine-like tang of the western, island malts, which you may have encountered on Islay.

Impressive and historic castles are also on the agenda in the Great Glen, perhaps one of the best known of which is Urquhart Castle, a favorite haunt of Nessie-watchers because of its location halfway down Loch Ness. It was once a great royal base and dates to the 13th and 14th centuries, though it's largely in ruins. To the east are two top-of-the-list castles that are still inhabited: Cawdor Castle, with its happy marriage of different furnishings—modern and ancient, mellow and brightly colored—and Brodie Castle, with its magnificent library and a collection of paintings that extend well into the 20th century.

Pleasures and Pastimes

Biking

The Great Glen itself has a very busy main road, not recommended for cyclists, along the west bank of Loch Ness via Drumnadrochit. The B862/B852, which runs by the east side of Loch Ness, has less traffic and is a better bet for cyclists. There is now a dedicated cycle path running from Fort William to Inverness: local tourist information centers can provide details. To the east, there is a good network of back roads around Inverness and toward Nairn. The A9, however, on either side of Aviemore, is not recommended for cyclists.

Dining

There are some fine places with superb cuisine in this area, with a wealth of country-house hotels from which to choose, as well as an excellent seafood restaurant in Fort William.

CATEGORY	COST*
££££	over £40
£££	£30–£40
££	£15–£30
£	under £15

per person for a three-course meal, including VAT and excluding drinks and service

Fishing

The Great Glen is laced with rivers and lochs where you can fly-fish for salmon and trout. The fishing seasons are as follows: salmon, from early February through September or early October (depending on the area); brown trout, from March 15 to September 30; sea trout, from May through September or early October; rainbow trout, no statutory-close season. Sea angling from shore or boat is also possible. Tourist centers (☞ Visitor Information *in* Around the Great Glen A to Z, *below*) can provide information on locations, permits, and fishing rights (which differ from those in England and Wales).

Lodging

The main centers, Inverness, Fort William, and Aviemore, have plenty of accommodations in all price ranges. Since this is such an old and established vacation area, there are few places where you'd have trouble finding a room for a night. However, the area is quite busy in peak season.

CATEGORY	COST*
££££	over £140
£££	£110–£140
££	£65–£110
£	under £65

Prices are for a standard double room, including service, breakfast, and VAT.

✎ *following the text of a review is your signal that the property has a Web site, where you will find details and, usually, images; for a link, visit www.fodors.com/urls.*

Walking

The Great Glen area is renowned for its hill-walking opportunities, but if you head for the hills, you should be fit and properly outfitted. Remember that on Ben Nevis, a popular route even for inexperienced hikers, it can snow on the summit plateau at any time of the year—Ben Nevis is a large and often dangerous mountain.

Exploring the Great Glen

The first possible route centers on Inverness, moving east into Speyside, then west down the Great Glen. The second route, originating in Fort William, takes in the special qualities of the birch-knoll and blue-island West Highland views. There are many romantic and historic associations with this area. It was here that the rash adventurer Prince Charles Edward Stuart (1720–88) arrived for the final Jacobite Rebellion, of 1745–46, and it was from here that he departed after the last battle.

Numbers in the text correspond to numbers in the margin and on the Around the Great Glen map.

Great Itineraries

The road between Fort William and Mallaig, though narrow and winding, is one of the classic routes of Scottish touring and is popularly known as the Road to the Isles. Similarly, the Great Glen road is a vital coast-to-coast link. The fact that it passes by a loch with a "monstrous" reputation is just a happy coincidence.

IF YOU HAVE 2 DAYS

Both ⊞ **Inverness** ① and ⊞ **Fort William** ㉔ have a choice of loops running from them. Base yourself anywhere around Fort William so that you can take in the spectacular scenery of **Glencoe** ㉒ and Glen Nevis and also get at least a glimpse of the western seaboard toward **Mallaig** ㉗.

IF YOU HAVE 4 DAYS

Spend two days at one of two bases at each end of the Great Glen, say, ⊞ **Inverness** ① or ⊞ **Nairn** ④, at the north end, and ⊞ **Fort William** ㉔ or ⊞ **Ballachulish** ㉓, at the south end. This will give you adequate time to see this chunk of Scotland. On the first day travel to Nairn from Inverness, and from Nairn go southward via **Cawdor Castle** ⑥ and/or **Brodie Castle** ⑦ to **Grantown-on-Spey** ⑧. Then follow the Spey as far as you like via **Boat of Garten** ⑨, with its ospreys in spring and early summer; **Aviemore** ⑫ and its mountain scenery; and **Kingussie** ⑮, where the Highland Folk Museum does a good job of explaining what life was really like before modern domestic and agricultural equipment made things easy. The next day explore **Loch Ness** ⑲, traveling down the eastern bank as far as **Fort Augustus** ⑱ and returning up the western bank via **Drumnadrochit** ⑳; if you have time on a long summer evening, divert northward at Drumnadrochit to discover the beautiful glens Affric and Cannich, before returning to Inverness. On the third day travel to ⊞ **Fort William** ㉔, taking in the **Caledonian Canal** ⑰. Spend a day doing the suggested loop to **Mallaig** ㉗ and go back through **Glenfinnan** ㉘ to Fort William, or go straight to **Arisaig** ㉖ and take an unforgettable day cruise among the Small Isles.

IF YOU HAVE 7 DAYS

Seven days will give you plenty of time to visit all the highlights of the Great Glen area. Base yourself at ⊞ **Inverness** ① or ⊞ **Nairn** ④ for two nights, then spend a night at ⊞ **Kingussie** ⑮ and a night at ⊞ **Drumnadrochit** ⑳. Moving west to the Fort William area, either stay in ⊞ **Fort William** ㉔ itself, or go farther west and spend two nights in the excellent accommodations of ⊞ **Arisaig** ㉖ for two nights. Either base will allow for exploration of the suggested circular route, a day at sea among the Small Isles, and a half day or day amid the grandeur of **Glencoe** ㉒ or Glen Nevis, behind Fort William. You may also want to make excursions farther north and west.

When to Tour the Great Glen

This is a spring and autumn kind of area—summer contends with pesky midges, and winter brings raw chill. However, in summer, if the weather

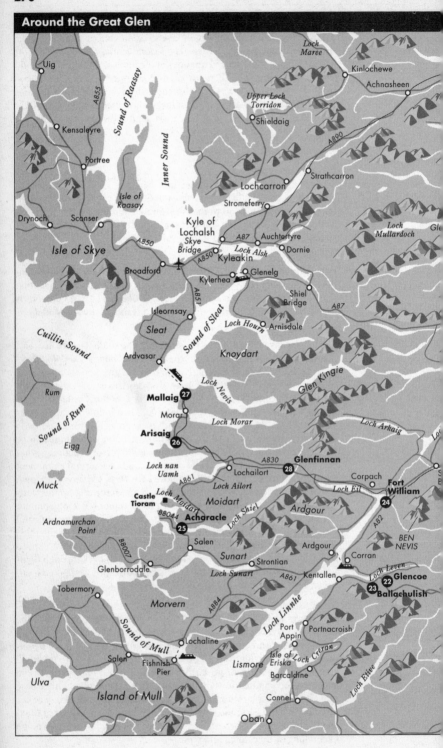

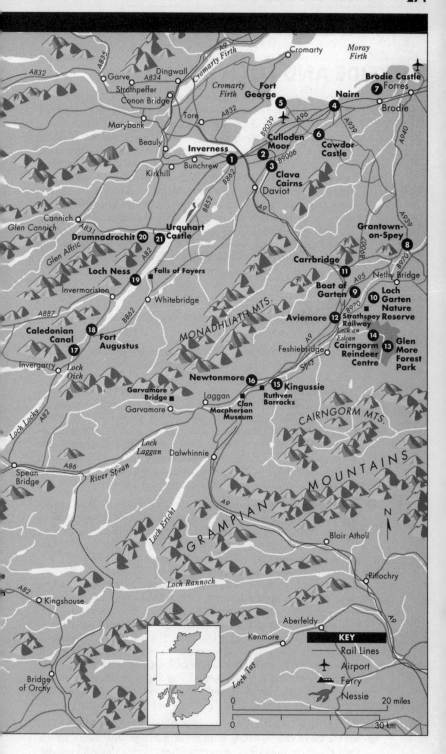

A832 Garve Dingwall
A835
Strathpeffer
Conon Bridge
A834
Cromarty
Cromarty Firth
Cromarty Firth
Fort George
Nairn
Brodie Castle **7** Forres
Brodie
Moray Firth
Marybank
Tore A832
Beauly
Inverness **1**
Bunchrew
Kirkhill
B862
B852
Culloden Moor **6**
Culloden Moor
Clava Cairns
Daviot
A9
Cawdor Castle
A939
A940
Cannich
Glen Cannich
A831
Urquhart Castle
Drumnadrochit **20** **21**
Glen Affric
A82
Grantown-on-Spey **8**
B9007
Carrbridge **11**
A95 Nethy Bridge
B970
Loch Ness **19**
Falls of Foyers
Invermoriston
A887
Whitebridge
MONADHLIATH MTS.
Boat of Garten **9**
Loch Garten Nature Reserve **10**
Aviemore **12** Strathspey Railway
Loch an Eilean
Cairngorm Reindeer Centre **14**
Glen More Forest Park **13**
Caledonian Canal **18**
Fort Augustus
17
B862
Feshiebridge
Spey
A9
Invergarry
Loch Oich
A82
Newtonmore **16**
Kingussie **15**
Ruthven Barracks
Clan Macpherson Museum
CAIRNGORM MTS.
Loch Lochy
Garvamore Bridge
Laggan
Garvamore
A86
Loch Laggan
Dalwhinnie
Spean Bridge
River Spean
Loch Ericht
Loch Rannoch
G R A M P I A N   M O U N T A I N S
A9
Blair Atholl
Kingshouse
Pitlochry
A9
Bridge of Orchy
Aberfeldy
Kenmore
Loch Tay

KEY
— Rail Lines
✈ Airport
⛴ Ferry
🦕 Nessie

0   20 miles
0   30 km

is settled, it can be very pleasant in the far west, perhaps on the Road to the Isles, toward Mallaig. Early spring is a good time to sample Scottish skiing at Nevis Range or Glencoe.

SPEYSIDE AND LOCH NESS

Because Jacobite tales are interwoven with landmarks throughout this entire area, you should first learn something about this thorny but colorful period of Scottish history in which the Jacobites tried to restore the exiled Stuarts to the British monarchy. One of the best places to do this is at Culloden, just east of Inverness, where a major battle ended in final, catastrophic defeat for the Jacobites. Inverness itself is not really a town in which to linger, unless you need to do some shopping. Other areas to concentrate on are the inner Moray Firth moving down into Speyside, before moving west into the Great Glen. Loch Ness is just one of the attractions hereabouts. In the Great Glen and Speyside, the best sights are often hidden from the main road, an excellent reason to favor peaceful rural byways and to avoid as far as possible the busy A82 (down Loch Ness's western shore), as well as the A96 and A9, which carry much of the eastern traffic in the area.

Inverness

❶ *176 mi north of Glasgow, 109 mi northwest of Aberdeen, 161 mi northwest of Edinburgh.*

Inverness seems designed for the tourist, with its banks, souvenirs, high-quality woolens, and well-equipped visitor center. Compared with other Scottish towns, however, Inverness has less to offer visitors who have a keen interest in Scottish history. Throughout its past, Inverness was burned and ravaged by one or another of the restive Highland clans competing for dominance in the region. Thus, a decorative wall panel here and a fragment of tower there are all that remain amid the modern shopping facilities and 19th-century downtown developments. One of Inverness's few historic landmarks is the **castle** (the local Sheriff Court), nestled above the river. The present structure is Victorian, built after a former fort was blown up by the Jacobites in the 1745 campaign.

❷ **Culloden Moor** was the scene of the last battle fought on British soil—to this day considered one of the most infamous and tragic in all of warfare. Here, on a cold April day in 1746, the outnumbered Jacobite forces of Bonnie Prince Charlie were destroyed by the superior firepower of George II's army. The victorious commander, the duke of Cumberland (George II's son), earned the name of "Butcher" Cumberland for the bloody reprisals carried out by his men on Highland families, Jacobite or not, caught in the vicinity; in the battle itself, the duke's army—greatly outnumbering the Scots—decimated more than 1,000 soldiers. The National Trust for Scotland has re-created a slightly eerie version of the battlefield as it looked in 1746. The uneasy silence of the open moor almost drowns out the merry clatter from the visitor center's coffee shop and the tinkle of cash registers. ✉ *5 mi east of Inverness via B9006,* ☎ *01463/790607.* 🎟 *£3.50.* ☉ *Site: daily; visitor center: Apr.–Oct., daily 9–6; Nov.–Dec. and Feb.–Mar., daily 10–4 (last entry 30 mins before closing).*

❸ Not far from Culloden, on a narrow road southeast of the battlefield, are the **Clava Cairns,** dating from the Bronze Age. In a cluster among the trees, these stones and monuments form a large ring with passage graves, which consist of a central chamber below a cairn, reached via a tunnel. Placards explain the graves' significance.

Dining and Lodging

££££ ✕🏨 **Dunain Park Hotel.** You'll receive individual attention in this 18th-century mansion set amid 6 acres of wooded gardens. An open fire awaits you in the living room, a good place to sip a drink and browse through books and magazines. Antiques and traditional decor make the bedrooms equally cozy and attractive. The restaurant offers French-influenced Scottish dishes—Shetland salmon baked in sea salt or medallions of venison rolled in oatmeal with a claret and crème de cassis sauce—served on bone china with crystal glasses. ⊠ *Dunain, 2½ mi southwest of Inverness on A82, IV3 8JN,* ☎ *01463/230512,* FAX *01463/224532. 13 rooms with bath and shower. Restaurant, indoor pool, sauna. AE, MC, V.* ⊛

££–££££ ✕🏨 **Kingsmills Hotel.** About 1 mi from the center of Inverness sits Kingsmills, a rambling mansion set among 4 acres of gardens on the edge of a golf course. It's a great place for families: children under 14 stay for free, and the heated indoor pool and extensive leisure facilities, including privileges at the golf course next door, offer plenty to do. The bedrooms are particularly spacious, comfortable, and well equipped. The restaurant serves well-prepared and reliable steaks, seafood tagliatelle, and game pâté. ⊠ *Culcabock Rd., IV2 3LP,* ☎ *01463/237166,* FAX *01463/225208. 82 rooms with bath. Restaurant, indoor pool, 3-hole golf course, health club. AE, DC, MC, V.* ⊛

££ 🏨 **Ballifeary House.** This well-maintained Victorian bed-and-breakfast is within easy reach of downtown Inverness. The particularly helpful proprietors offer high standards of comfort and service. Rooms are individually decorated with modern furnishings, and the downstairs has reproduction antiques. ⊠ *10 Ballifeary Rd., IV3 5PJ,* ☎ *01463/ 235572,* FAX *01463/717583. 5 rooms with bath or shower. Dining room. MC, V. Closed Nov.–Mar.* ⊛

£–££ 🏨 **Clach Mhuilinn.** This modern family home is set in a pretty garden ★ and has good parking facilities. It offers a B&B of a very high standard. ⊠ *7 Harris Rd., IV2 3LS,* ☎ *01463/237059,* FAX *01463/242092. 2 rooms with shower. MC, V. Closed Dec.–Feb.*

£ 🏨 **Atholdene House.** A family-run 19th-century stone villa serves as a B&B with a friendly welcome and modernized accommodations. The bus and railway stations are a short walk away. ⊠ *20 Southside Rd., IV2 3BG,* ☎ *01463/233565,* FAX *01463/729101. 9 rooms, 7 with shower. MC, V.* ⊛

£ 🏨 **Daviot Mains Farm.** This establishment built in Highland-lodge ★ style, 5 mi south of Inverness on the A9, provides the perfect setting for home comforts and traditional Scottish cooking (for guests only); lucky ones may find wild salmon on the menu in the dining room. ⊠ *Daviot Mains IV1 5ER,* ☎ *01463/772215,* FAX *01463/772099. 6 rooms with bath or shower. MC, V.* ⊛

Nightlife and the Arts

BARS AND LOUNGES

Inverness has an array of bars and lounges. **Gunsmith's** (⊠ Union St., ☎ 01463/710519) is a traditional pub offering bar meals. **DJ's Café Bar** (⊠ High St.) serves everything from breakfast to late-night cocktails.

CABARET

June through September, **Scottish Showtime** (⊠ Spectrum Community Centre, Faraline Park Bus Station; ☎ 01349/830930 for details from organizers) offers Scottish cabaret of the tartan-clad dancer and bagpipe/accordion variety.

THEATER

Eden Court Theatre (⊠ Bishops Rd., ☎ 01463/234234) offers not only drama but also a program of music, film, and light entertainment, plus an art gallery.

Outdoor Activities and Sports

Inverness Golf Club (☎ FAX 01463/239882) welcomes visitors. **Torvean Golf Course** (☎ 01463/711434) is open to visitors paying a greens fee.

Shopping

Although Inverness has the usual indoor shopping mall with High Street names and department stores—including Marks and Spencer—the most interesting goods are to be found in the specialty outlets in and around town.

FINE ART AND ARTS AND CRAFTS

For contemporary art there's **art.tm** (⊠ 20 Bank St., ☎ 01463/712240), formerly the Printermakers' Workshop, which doubled in size in 1998 and now aims to present the best of contemporary arts and crafts. **The Riverside Gallery** (⊠ 11 Bank St., ☎ 01463/224781) sells paintings and prints of Scottish landscapes, natural history, and sporting themes.

SCOTTISH SPECIALTIES

Highland Aromatics (⊠ Drumchardine, Kirkhill, ☎ 01463/831625), in a converted church, makes sweet-smelling soaps, perfumes, colognes, and other toiletries with the scents of the Highlands. **Highland Wineries** (⊠ Moniack Castle, Kirkhill, ☎ 01463/831283) creates wines from Scottish ingredients, such as birch sap, and also makes jams, marmalade, and other preserves.

Duncan Chisholm and Sons (⊠ 49 Castle St., ☎ 01463/234599) specializes in Highland dress, tartans, and Scottish crafts. Mail-order and made-to-measure services are available. **Hector Russell Kiltmakers** (⊠ 4–9 Huntly St., ☎ 01463/222781) explains the history of the kilt, shows them being made, and then gives you the opportunity to buy from a huge selection or have a kilt made to measure. The firm offers overseas mail order. **James Pringle Ltd.** (⊠ Holm Woollen Mills, Dores Rd., ☎ 01463/223311) has a shop stocked with a vast selection of cashmere, lamb's-wool, and Shetland knitwear, tartans, and tweeds, plus a weaving exhibit.

Nairn

❹ *17 mi east of Inverness via B9006/B9091, 92 mi west of Aberdeen.*

Although Nairn has the air of a Lowland town, it is actually part of the Highlands. A once-prosperous fishing village, Nairn has something of a split personality. King James VI (1566–1625) once boasted of a town so large the residents in either end spoke different languages. This was a reference to Nairn, whose fisherfolk, living by the sea, spoke Lowland Scots, while its uptown farmers and crofters spoke Gaelic.

The fishing boats have since moved to larger ports, but Nairn's historic flavor has been preserved at the **Nairn Museum** in Viewfield House, a handsome Georgian building in the center of town. Exhibits emphasize artifacts, photographs, and model boats relating to Nairn's fishing past. A genealogy service is also offered. A library in the same building has a strong local-history section. ⊠ *Viewfield House, King St.,* ☎ *01667/456791.* ☜ *£1.50.* ☉ *1st Mon. after Easter–Sept., Mon.–Sat. 10–4:30.*

Two contrasting defensive structures lie within easy reach of Nairn. As a direct result of the battle at Culloden, the nervous government in London ordered the construction of a large fort on a promontory reaching
★ **❺** into the Moray Firth: **Fort George** was started in 1748 and completed some 20 years later. It survives today as perhaps the best-preserved 18th-century military fortification in Europe. A visitor center and a number of tableaux at the fort portray the 18th-century Scottish soldier's way of life, as does the **Regimental Museum of the Queen's Own Highlanders.** To reach the fort, take the B9092 north from A96 west of Nairn. ⊠

Ardersier, ☎ *0131/668–8800.* 🎫 *Fort: Apr.–Sept. £4, Oct.–Mar. £3.50; museum: free.* ⊙ *Apr.–Sept., daily 9:30–6; Oct.–Mar., Mon.–Sat. 9:30–4, Sun. 2–4 (last admission 45 mins before closing).* 🐾

★ ❻ Southwest of Nairn is **Cawdor Castle.** Shakespeare's (1564–1616) Macbeth was Thane of Cawdor, but the sense of history that exists within these turreted walls is more than fictional. Cawdor is a lived-in castle, not an abandoned, decaying structure. The earliest part of the castle is the 14th-century central tower; the rooms contain family portraits, tapestries, fine furniture, and paraphernalia reflecting 600 years of history. Outside the castle walls are sheltered gardens and woodland walks. ⊠ *Cawdor, off B9090, 5 mi southwest of Nairn,* ☎ *01667/404615.* 🎫 *Castle: £5.60; garden and grounds: £2.90.* ⊙ *May–mid-Oct., daily 10–5.*

★ ❼ East of Nairn at Brodie is **Brodie Castle,** in the care of the National Trust for Scotland. The original medieval castle was rebuilt and extended in the 17th and 19th centuries. Fine examples of late-17th-century plasterwork are preserved in the Dining Room and Blue Sitting Room; an impressive library and a superb collection of pictures extend into the 20th century. ⊠ *Brodie, by Nairn,* ☎ *01309/641371.* 🎫 *£5.* ⊙ *Castle: Apr.–Sept., Mon.–Sat. 11–5:30, Sun. 1:30–5:30; Oct., Sat. 11–5:30, Sun. 1:30–5:30 (last admission 4:30); grounds: daily 9:30–sunset.* 🐾

Dining and Lodging

£££ ✕🏨 **Clifton House.** Original works of art cover the walls of this unique
★ hotel, antique furniture graces its rooms, and antique silver gleams in the dining room. The hotel is also licensed as a theater, and each year (September through April) you can enjoy excellent theatrical and musical performances. The restaurant is famous for its classic Scottish cuisine—the lamb cutlets and the duck *à l'orange* (sautéed with oranges and orange liqueur) are particularly good—and the wine list is probably the longest in the area. ⊠ *Viewfield St., IV12 4HW,* ☎ *01667/453119,* FAX *01667/452836. 12 rooms with bath. 2 restaurants. AE, DC, MC, V. Closed Dec.–Jan.*

££ 🏨 **Carnach House Hotel.** An overnight at this elegant stone mansion on 7 acres of lawns and woodland is an experience, thanks to the pleasant setting, nice rooms, good food, and caring service—it's a fun stay at a reasonable price. ⊠ *Delnies, IV12 5NT,* ☎ *01667/452094,* FAX *01667/452994. 8 rooms with bath or shower. Restaurant, bar. AE, MC, V.*

Nightlife and the Arts

Clifton House (☞ Dining and Lodging, *above*), at Nairn, runs a program of concerts, recitals, and plays from September through April.

Outdoor Activities and Sports

GOLF

Nairn's courses, which welcome visitors, are highly regarded by golfers: indeed, the Walker Cup was held here in September 1999. They're very popular, so be sure to book far in advance at the **Nairn Dunbar Golf Club** (☎ 01667/452741) and **Nairn Golf Club** (☎ 01667/453208). For additional information on golfing, *see* Chapter 11.

Shopping

Don't miss **Nairn Antiques** (⊠ St. Ninian Pl., near the traffic circle, ☎ 01667/453303) for a wide selection of antique jewelry, glassware, furniture, pottery, prints, and some unusual giftware. Visit **Brodie Country Fare** (⊠ Brodie, east of Nairn, ☎ 01309/641555) only if you are feeling flush: you may covet the unusual knitwear, quality designer clothing and shoes, gifts, and toys, but they are *not* cheap. You'll also find a food store and delicatessen stocking only the highest quality produce (rather like a miniature Harrods food hall, or Fortnum and Mason).

Finally, there is an excellent and inexpensive restaurant. Not surprisingly, this establishment is extremely popular with the locals.

Grantown-on-Spey

8 *24 mi south of Nairn via A939.*

The sturdy settlement of Grantown-on-Spey, set amid tall pines that flank the River Spey, is a classic Scottish planned town. This means it is a community that was planned and laid out by the local landowner, in this case Sir James Grant in 1776. It has handsome buildings in silver granite and some good shopping for Scottish gifts.

Shopping
Speyside Heather Centre (⊠ Skye of Curr, ☎ 01479/851359) has 200–300 varieties of heather for sale. The company can supply heather plants by mail-order (United Kingdom only). A crafts shop, floral-art sundries, an antiques shop, and a tearoom can also be found here. **Ewe and Me** (⊠ 82 High St., ☎ 01479/872911) is a well-stocked, high-quality gift shop.

Boat of Garten

9 *11 mi southwest of Grantown via B970.*

In the peaceful village of Boat of Garten, the scent of pine trees mingles with an equally evocative smell: this is the terminus of the **Speyside Railway,** and the oily scent of smoke and steam hang faintly in the air near the authentically preserved train station. From here you can take a 5-mi train trip to Aviemore, offering a chance to wallow in nostalgia and enjoy superb views of the high and often white domes of the Cairngorm Mountains.

10 The **Loch Garten Nature Reserve,** administered by the Royal Society for the Protection of Birds (RSPB), is about 1 mi east of Boat of Garten. This sanctuary achieved fame when the osprey, a bird that was facing extinction in the early part of the 20th century, returned to breed here. Instead of cordoning off the nest site, conservation officials encouraged visitors by constructing a blind for bird-watching. Now thousands of bird lovers visit annually to get a glimpse of the domestic arrangements of this fish-eating bird, which has since bred in many other parts of the Highlands. ☎ 01479/831694 or 01463/715000. ⊡ £2.50. ☉ *Osprey observation post: Apr.–mid-Sept., daily 10–6; other areas of reserve: year-round daily.*

11 In **Carrbridge,** just north of Boat of Garten, is the **Landmark Highland Heritage and Adventure Park,** an early pioneer in the move toward more sophisticated visitor attractions. It has a display on forestry with a working steam-powered sawmill and a Clydesdale horse to haul the logs; a forestry workshop, where you can try out forest skills such as cross-cut sawing; a bookstore; and a restaurant. Outdoors you'll find nature trails; a treetop trail; and a giant, climbable fire tower. Diversions for children include a Wild Forest Maze, terrifying Wild Water coasters (incredibly steep water slides—kids love them), and an adventure playground. Reach Carrbridge on the quiet B9153—keep off the A9. ⊠ *Carrbridge,* ☎ 01479/841613. ⊡ *£3.75–£6.90.* ☉ *Apr.–mid-July, daily 10–6; mid-July–Aug., daily 10–7; Sept.–Oct., daily 9:30–5:30; Nov.–Mar., daily 10–5 (last admission 1 hr before closing).*

Aviemore

12 *6 mi southwest of Boat of Garten via B970.*

Once a quiet junction on the Highland Railway, Aviemore now has all the brashness and concrete boxiness of a year-round holiday resort, although upgrading plans seem to be perennially on the drawing board. The Aviemore area is a versatile walking base, but you must be dressed properly and carry emergency safety gear for high-level excursions onto the near-arctic plateau. Visitors interested in skiing and rugged hiking can follow the B970 from Aviemore, in the **Glen More Forest Park,** past Loch Morlich to the high parking lots on the exposed shoulders of the **Cairngorm Mountains.** A funicular railway is currently under construction, due to be completed in winter 2002, but for now, you can take chairlifts during and after the ski season for higher, more extensive views of the broad valley of the Spey. Be forewarned: it can get very cold above 3,000 ft, and weather conditions can change rapidly, even in the middle of summer. ⊠ *Off B9152,* ☎ *01479/861261.* ⊠ *£6 for chairlift.* ⊙ *Daily, weather permitting.*

On the high slopes of the Cairngorms, you may see the reindeer herd that was introduced here in the 1950s. You can inquire at the **Cairngorm Reindeer Centre,** by Loch Morlich, about accompanying the herders on their daily rounds. The reindeer are surprisingly docile creatures and seem to enjoy human company. Be sure to wear waterproof gear as conditions can be wet and muddy. ⊠ *Loch Morlich, Glen More Forest Park,* ☎ FAX *01479/861228.* ⊠ *Reindeer Centre: £5; paddocks: £1.50.* ⊙ *Reindeer Centre: daily 10–5 (or dusk); rounds (subject to weather conditions): Apr.–Sept., daily at 11 and 2:30; Oct.–Mar., daily at 11. Paddocks closed Jan.–Easter.*

★ The place that best sums up Speyside's piney ambience is probably **Loch an Eilean** (signs guide you to it from Aviemore). A converted cottage beside Loch an Eilean, which is on the **Rothiemurchus Estate** (☎ 01479/ 810858), houses a visitor center (the area is a National Nature Reserve). The estate also offers several diversions, including fly-fishing for salmon and trout, guided walks, safari tours, off-road driving, clay-pigeon shooting, and farm-shop tastings of estate-produced beef, venison, and trout.

Kingussie

⑮ *13 mi southwest of Aviemore, via A9 and A86.*

The village of Kingussie (pronounced Kin-*yoo*-see) is of interest primarily for its **Highland Folk Museum.** The interior exhibits are housed in what was an 18th-century shooting lodge, its paneled and varnished ambience still apparent. Displays include 18th-century furniture, clothing, and implements. Outside, various types of Highland buildings have been reconstructed. In summer local weavers and other artisans demonstrate Highland crafts. You can wander around the grounds freely or see the highlights of the museum on a guided tour. The museum also maintains a Victorian schoolhouse in nearby Newtownmore. ⊠ *Kingussie,* ☎ *01540/661307.* ⊠ *£4.* ⊙ *Apr. and Sept.–Oct., weekdays 10:30–4:30; May–Aug., weekdays 10:30–5:30, weekends 1–5; Nov.– Mar., weekdays, guided tours only, at 11 and 1.*

Ruthven Barracks, which from a distance looks like a ruined castle on a mound, is redolent with tales of the '45 (as the last Jacobite Rebellion is often called). The defeated Jacobite forces rallied here after the battle at Culloden, but then abandoned and blew up the government outpost they had earlier captured. You'll see it as you approach Kingussie. ⊠ *B970, ½ mi south of Kingussie,* ☎ *0131/668–8800.* ⊠ *Free.* ⊙ *At all times.*

The rounded **Monadhliath Mountains** (*monadhliath* is Gaelic for "gray moors") loom northward over Kingussie and Strathspey (the valley of the River Spey), separating Speyside from the Great Glen. The Monadhliath are less often explored by hikers than the Cairngorms, which form Speyside's south side.

Dining and Lodging

££££   ✕🍴 **The Cross.** Meals are superb and the wine list extensive. This is
  ★   an award-winning "restaurant with rooms," in the French style. Din-
        ner, which could be fillet of local venison with port and red currants
        or scallop mousse with a prawn and basil sauce, is included in the price
        of your room. Bedrooms—all with king-size beds—are individually dec-
        orated and may have a balcony, canopy bed, or an antique dressing
        table. ✉ *Tweed Mill Brae, Inverness-shire PH21 1TC,* ☎ *01540/
        661166,* 🇫🇦🇽 *01540/661080. 9 rooms with bath. Restaurant. MC, V.
        Closed Dec.–Feb. No dinner Tues.*

£–££   ✕🍴 **Osprey Hotel.** This friendly hotel is an ideal base for skiing and
        hiking. Rooms have old or antique furniture and floral wallpaper. An
        impressive wine list complements the much praised cuisine, which might
        include breast of duck with grape and red wine sauce or monkfish with
        Bloody Mary sauce. ✉ *Ruthven Rd., Inverness-shire PH21 1EN,* ☎
        🇫🇦🇽 *01540/661510. 8 rooms with bath. Restaurant. AE, DC, MC, V.* 🐾

Newtonmore

   ⓰ *3 mi southwest of Kingussie.*

        Newtonmore is home to the **Clan Macpherson Museum,** one of many
        clan museums scattered throughout the old homelands. On display are
        a number of interesting artifacts associated with the '45 Rebellion, as
        well as those of clan chiefs of the even more distant past. ✉ *Newton-
        more,* ☎ *01540/673332.* 🎫 *Donation suggested.* ☉ *Apr.–Oct., Mon.–
        Sat. 10–5, Sun. 2:30–5; by appointment rest of yr.*

En Route A few miles southwest of Newtonmore on the A86 at Laggan Bridge, where
        the main road crosses the River Spey, an unnamed road runs west up the
        glen to Garvamore. If you're not pressed for time, it's worth taking this
        road to view the **Garvamore Bridge** (about 6 mi north of the junction, at
        the south side of Corrieyairack Pass). This dual-arched bridge was built
        in 1735 by General Wade (1673–1748), who had been ordered to improve
        Scotland's roads by a British government concerned that its troops would
        not be able to travel the Highlands quickly enough to quell an uprising.

        A stretch of the A86, quite narrow in some places, hugs the western shore
        of Loch Laggan. It offers superb views of the mountainous heartlands to
        the north, where high peaks loom, and to the south, over the silvery spine
        of hills known as the Grey Corries, culminating with views of Ben Nevis.

Caledonian Canal

   ⓱ *37 mi west of Newtonmore.*

        Traveling north up the Great Glen takes you parallel to Loch Lochy
        (on the eastern shore) and over the Caledonian Canal at Laggan Locks.
        From this beautiful spot, which offers stunning vistas of lochs, moun-
        tains, and glens in all directions, you can look back on the impressive
        profile of Ben Nevis. The canal, which links the lochs of the Great Glen—
        Loch Lochy, Loch Oich, and Loch Ness—owes its origins to a combi-
        nation of military as well as political pressures that emerged at the time
        of the Napoleonic Wars with France: for the most part, the British needed
        a better and faster way to get naval vessels from one side of Scotland
        to the other. The great Scottish engineer Thomas Telford (1757–1834)
        surveyed the route in 1803. The canal, which took 19 years to com-
        plete, has 29 locks and 42 gates. Telford ingeniously took advantage
        of the three lochs that lie in the Great Glen, which have a combined
        length of 45 mi, so that only 22 mi of canal had to be constructed to
        connect the lochs and complete the waterway from coast to coast.

Dining and Lodging

££–£££ ✕🏨 **Glengarry Castle Hotel.** This rambling, pleasantly old-fashioned mansion makes a good touring base; Invergarry is just south of Loch Ness and within easy reach of the Great Glen's best sights. Rooms have traditional Victorian decor; some have superb views over Loch Oich. The food is traditional Scottish fare. Try the poached salmon with hollandaise or the loin of lamb with rosemary. The grounds include the ruins of Glengarry Castle, a seat of the MacDonnell clan. The hotel entrance is south of the A82–A87 road junction. ✉ *Invergarry, Invernessshire PH35 4HW,* ☎ *01809/501254,* 🖷 *01809/501207. 26 rooms with bath. Restaurant, tennis court, fishing. MC, V. Closed Nov.–Mar.* 🐾

Fort Augustus and Loch Ness

53 mi north of Laggan.

The best place to see the lochs of the Caledonian Canal in action is at **⑱ Fort Augustus,** at the southern tip of Loch Ness. In the village center, considerable canal activity takes place at a series of lochs that rise from Loch Ness. Fort Augustus itself was captured by the Jacobite clans during the 1745 Rebellion. Later the fort was rebuilt as a Benedictine abbey, but monks no longer live here.

From the B862, just east of Fort Augustus, you'll get your first good long **⑲** view of the formidable and famous **Loch Ness,** which has a greater volume of water than any other Scottish loch, a maximum depth of more than 800 ft, and its own monster—at least according to popular myth. Early travelers who passed this way included English lexicographer Dr. Samuel Johnson (1709–84) and his guide and biographer, James Boswell (1740–95), who were on their way to the Hebrides in 1783. They remarked at the time about the condition of the population and the squalor of their homes. Another early travel writer and naturalist, Thomas Pennant (1726–98), noted that the loch kept the locality frost-free in winter. Even General Wade came here, his troops blasting and digging a road up much of the eastern shore. None of these observant early travelers ever made mention of a monster. Clearly, they had not read the local guidebooks.

En Route A more leisurely alternative to the fast-moving traffic on the busy A82 to Inverness, and one that combines monster-watching with peaceful road touring, is to take the B862 from Fort Augustus and follow the east bank of Loch Ness; join the B852 just beyond Whitebridge and take the opportunity to view the waterfalls at Foyers. The B862 runs around the end of Loch Ness, then climbs into moorland and forestry plantation. Fine views of Fort Augustus can be seen by climbing a few yards up and to the right, onto the moor; here you'll be able to see above the conifer spikes. The half-hidden track beside the road is a remnant of the military road built by General Wade. Loch Ness quickly drops out of sight but is soon replaced by the peaceful, reedy Loch Tarff.

Drumnadrochit

⑳ *21 mi north of Fort Augustus via A82.*

If you're in search of the infamous beast Nessie, head to Drumnadrochit: here you'll find the **Official Loch Ness Monster Exhibition Centre,** which presents the facts and the fakes, the photographs, the unexplained sonar contacts, and the sincere testimony of eyewitnesses. You'll have to make up your own mind on Nessie. All that's really known is that Loch Ness's huge volume of water has a warming effect on the local weather, making the lake conducive to mirages in still, warm conditions. These are often the circumstances in which the "monster" appears, and you may draw your own conclusions. Whether or not the *bestia aquatilis* lurks in the depths—more than ever in doubt since 1994, when the man who took one of the most convincing photos of Nessie confessed on his deathbed that it was a fake—plenty of camera-toting, sonar-wielding, and submarine-traveling scientists and curiosity seekers haunt the lake, gazing hopefully lochward. ⊠ *Drumnadrochit,* ☎ *01456/450573 or 01456/450218.* ✆ *£5.95.* ⊙ *Mar., daily 9:30–5; day after Easter–May, daily 9:30–5:30; June and Sept., daily 9:30–6:30; July–Aug., daily 9–8:30; Oct., daily 9:30–6; Nov.–Feb., daily 10–4 (last admission 45 mins before closing).*

㉑ **Urquhart Castle,** near Drumnadrochit, is a favorite Loch Ness monster–watching spot. This weary fortress stands on a promontory overlooking the loch, as it has since the Middle Ages. Because of its central and strategic position in the Great Glen line of communication, the castle has a complex history involving military offense and defense, as well as its own destruction and renovation. The castle was begun in the 13th century and was destroyed before the end of the 17th century to prevent its use by the Jacobites. The ruins of what was one of the largest castles in Scotland were then plundered for building material. Today swarms of bus tours pass through after investigating the Loch Ness phenomenon. ⊠ *2 mi southeast of Drumnadrochit on A82,* ☎ *0131/668–8800.* ✆ *£3.80.* ⊙ *Apr.–Sept., daily 9:30–6; Oct.–Mar., daily 9:30–4 (last admission 45 mins before closing).*

Dining and Lodging

££–£££   ✕🏨 **Polmaily House.** This country house amid lovely parkland is on
    ★   the northern edge of Loch Ness; sailing on the loch is even possible. Books, log fires, and a helpful staff contribute to an atmosphere that is warmer and more personal than that found at grander, more expensive hotels, and families are sincerely welcomed. The restaurant is noted for its traditional British cuisine using fresh Highland produce. Tay salmon in pastry with dill sauce, roast rack of lamb with rosemary, and cold smoked venison with melon are examples of some flavorful dishes. ⊠ *Drumnadrochit IV63 6XT,* ☎ *01456/450343,* 🅵🅰🆇 *01456/450813. 9 rooms with bath, 5 family suites. Restaurant, indoor pool, tennis court, croquet, horseback riding, boating, fishing. MC, V.* ◈

TOWARD THE SMALL ISLES

Fort William has enough points of interest—a museum, exhibits, and shopping—to compensate for its less-than-picturesque setting. The town's primary purpose is to serve the west Highland hinterland; its role as a tourist stop is secondary. Because this is a relatively wet part of Scotland and because Fort William itself can always be explored if it rains, strike west toward the coast if the weather looks clear: on a sunny day the Small Isles—Rum, Eigg, Canna, and Muck—look as blue as the sea and sky together. From here you can also visit Skye via the ferry at Mallaig, or take a day cruise from Arisaig to the Small Isles for a glimpse of traffic-free island life. South of Fort William, Ballachulish and Glencoe are within easy striking distance.

Glencoe

㉒ *92 mi north of Glasgow, 44 mi northwest of Edinburgh.*

Glencoe, where great craggy buttresses loom darkly over the road, has a special place in the folk memory of Scotland: it was the site of an infamous massacre in 1692, still remembered in the Highlands for the treachery with which soldiers of the Campbell clan, acting as a government militia, treated their hosts, the MacDonalds. According to Highland code, in his own home a clansman should give shelter even to his sworn enemy. In the face of bitter weather, the Campbells were accepted as guests by the MacDonalds. Apparently acting on orders from the British government, the Campbells turned on their hosts, committing murder "under trust." The National Trust for Scotland's **visitor center** at Glencoe (at the west end of the glen) tells the story of the massacre and also offers excellent displays on local geology. ☎ 01855/ 811307. 🎫 50p. ☯ Mar.–Apr. and Sept.–Oct., daily 10–5; May–Aug., daily 9:30–5:30 (last admission 30 mins before closing).

Outdoor Activities and Sports

The **Glencoe ski development** (☎ 01855/851226), at the east end of the glen, once had a formidable reputation in Scotland: because of its frequent combination of severe weather and icy runs, as well as fairly primitive facilities, it was believed if you could ski here, you could ski anywhere. Things have improved in recent years. Although the black runs are still very challenging, there are now extensive, well-maintained beginner and intermediate runs on the lower plateau. There's also a good restaurant.

Ballachulish

㉓ 1 mi west of Glencoe, 15 mi south of Fort William, 39 mi north of Oban.

Ballachulish, once a slate-quarrying community, acts as gateway to the western approaches to Glencoe. There is a Glencoe village as well.

Dining and Lodging

£££–££££ ✕🏨 **Airds Hotel.** This former ferry inn, dating from the 17th century, has some of the finest views in all of Scotland. Set in a peaceful village midway between Ballachulish and Oban, the long, white building, backed by trees, has a congenial feel to it. Quilted bedspreads and family mementos make you feel right at home. Shooting and fishing trips can be arranged. The restaurant serves Scottish cuisine, including venison and grouse. ⊠ Port Appin, Argyll PA38 4DF, ☎ 01631/730236, 🆖 01631/730535. 12 rooms with bath. Restaurant. MC, V. ⊛

£££ ✕🏨 **Holly Tree Hotel.** Railway buffs should enjoy this converted Edwardian railway station, complete with some of its original fixtures and fittings. The spacious restaurant is on the carefully extended former platform. You may see seals in Loch Linnhe from your dinner table, along with memorable sunsets over the Ardgour Mountains. The menu emphasizes fresh, locally raised pigeon, venison, lamb, scallops, and salmon. Bedrooms, though on the small side, are modern and well equipped. ⊠ Kentallen, on A828, south of Ballachulish, ☎ 01631/740292, 🆖 01631/ 740345. 10 rooms with bath or shower. Restaurant. MC, V.

££–£££ ✕🏨 **Isles of Glencoe Hotel.** An excellent base for families, this hotel
★ has its own leisure facilities including a toy corner. Everything from food to staff attitude makes children welcome, but adults won't feel neglected. The decor is modern, with streamlined, fitted furniture in the bedrooms and plenty of original landscape paintings. Though neither original nor inventive, the cuisine—a choice of well-cooked beef, chicken, fish, and game dishes—is satisfying after a hard day's sightseeing. In keeping with its youth-friendly atmosphere, there is also a separate children's menu. ⊠ Ballachulish PA39 4HL, ☎ 01855/ 821582, 🆖 01855/821463. 59 rooms with bath. Restaurant, pool, sauna, playground. MC, V. ⊛

Fort William

㉔ 15 mi north of Ballachulish, 69 mi southwest of Inverness, 108 mi northwest of Glasgow, 138 mi northwest of Edinburgh.

As its name suggests, Fort William originated as a military outpost, first established by Oliver Cromwell's (1599–1658) General Monk in

1655 and refortified by George I (1660–1727) in 1715 to help combat an outbreak by the turbulent Jacobite clans. It remains the southern gateway to the Great Glen and the far west, and it is a bustling, tourist-oriented place. The **West Highland Museum,** in the town center, explores the history of Prince Charles Edward Stuart and the '45 Rebellion. Included in the museum's folk exhibits are a costume and tartan display and a famous collection of Jacobite relics. ⊠ *Cameron Sq.,* ☏ *01397/702169.* ⚏ *£2.* ☉ *June and Sept., Mon.–Sat. 10–5; July–Aug., Mon.–Sat. 10–5 and Sun. 2–5; Oct.–May, Mon.–Sat. 10–4.*

Britain's highest mountain, the 4,406-ft **Ben Nevis,** looms over Fort William less than 4 mi from Loch Linnhe, an inlet of the sea. A trek to its summit is a rewarding experience, but you should be fit and well prepared—food and water, compass, first-aid kit, whistle, hat, gloves, and warm clothing (yes, even in summer) for starters—as the unpredictable weather can make it a hazardous hike.

A huge collection of gemstones, crystals, and fossils, including a 26-pound uncut emerald, are displayed at **Treasures of the Earth,** in a converted church near Fort William. ⊠ *A830, Corpach,* ☏ *01397/772283.* ⚏ *£3.* ☉ *July–Sept., daily 9:30–7; Oct.–Dec. and Feb.–June, daily 10–5; Jan., by appointment.*

Dining and Lodging

£–££ ✗ **Crannog Scottish Seafoods.** Set conspicuously on a small pier pro-
★ jecting over the waters of Loch Linnhe, the Crannog has transformed Fort William dining. The sight of a fishing boat drawing up to the pier to take its catch straight to the kitchen says it all about the freshness of the seafood. The chef's deft touch ensures the fresh flavors are not overwhelmed. Window seats afford views of the sun setting behind the steep hills on the far side of the loch. Pine predominates in fixtures and fittings. ⊠ *Town Pier,* ☏ *01397/705589. MC, V.*

££££ ✗🏨 **Inverlochy Castle.** A red-granite Victorian castle, Inverlochy stands on 50 acres of woodlands in the shadow of Ben Nevis, with striking Highland landscape on every side. Dating from 1863, the hotel retains all the splendor of its period, with a fine fresco ceiling, crystal chandeliers, a handsome staircase in the Great Hall, paintings and hunting trophies everywhere, and plush, comfortable bedrooms. The restaurant is exceptional—a lovely room with wonderful cuisine. Many specialties use local ingredients, such as roast saddle of roe deer or wood-pigeon consommé, with orange soufflé as the final touch. ⊠ *Torlundy (3 mi northeast of Fort William on A82), PH33 6SN,* ☏ *01397/702177,* ℻ *01397/702953. 17 rooms with bath. Restaurant, tennis court, croquet, fishing, billiards. AE, MC, V. Closed Jan.–Feb.* ⚏

££ 🏨 **Ashburn House.** A Victorian house with its own grounds, but only a five-minute walk from downtown, offers luxury at B&B prices. Chintz-draped bedrooms in shades of pink and blue are complemented by the conservatory lounge with stunning loch views, along with a delightful Victorian-corniced dining room in which to enjoy a breakfast that includes home-baked oven scones. This is a no-smoking establishment. ⊠ *Achintore Rd., PH33 6RQ,* ☏ *01397/706000,* ℻ *01397/702024. 7 rooms with bath or shower. AE, MC, V. Closed Dec.* ⚏

££ 🏨 **Crolinnhe.** An elegant Victorian house with colorful gardens, over-
★ looking Loch Linnhe yet only a 10-minute walk from town, Crolinnhe is an exceptionally comfortable B&B. Antique and high-quality reproduction furniture is set off by pastel walls and bold-tone curtains, with each bedroom individually decorated. The breakfasts are among the best you will taste in any establishment in any price range in Scotland. ⊠ *Grange Rd., PH33 6JF,* ☏ *01397/702709,* ℻ *01397/700506. 3 rooms with bath or shower. No credit cards. Closed Nov.–Mar.*

Outdoor Activities and Sports

BIKING

Bicycles can be rented from **Off Beat Bikes** (⊠ 117 High St., ☎ 01397/704008).

GOLF

The 18-hole golf course (6,217 yards, par 72) at **Fort William** (☎ 01397/704464) welcomes visitors.

HIKING

This area, especially around Glen Nevis, Glencoe, and Ben Nevis, is very popular with hikers, but you should try it only if fit and properly outfitted. The tourist information center (☞ Visitor Information *in* Around the Great Glen A to Z, *below*) can offer guidance on low-level routes. Several excellent guides are available locally; they can and should be consulted for high-altitude routes. Keep in mind that **Ben Nevis** is a large and dangerous mountain, where snow can fall on the summit plateau any time of the year.

SKIING

Nevis Range (☎ 01397/705825), the newest of Scotland's ski areas, is a fashionable and modern development on the flanks of Aonach Mor, offering good and varied skiing, as well as superb views of Ben Nevis. There are runs for all ability levels and a gondola system, unique in Scotland.

Shopping

The majority of shops here are along High Street, which in summer attracts ever-present, bustling crowds intent on stocking up for excursions to the west. The **Ben Nevis Woollen Mill** (⊠ Belford Rd., ☎ 01397/704244), at the north end of town, is a major supplier of tartans, woolens, and tweeds and has a restaurant. **The Granite House** (⊠ High St., ☎ 01397/703651) stocks Scottish contemporary jewelry, china and crystal giftware, wildlife sculptures, folk music CDs, unusual ethnic clothing, musical instruments, toys and collectibles, and cards.

The **Scottish Crafts and Whisky Centre** (⊠ 135–139 High St., ☎ 01397/704406) has the usual range of souvenirs, but it also sells homemade chocolates and a vast range of malt whiskies, including miniatures and limited-edition bottlings. **Treasures of the Earth** (⊠ Corpach, ☎ 01397/772283) has a shop that stocks an Aladdin's Cave assortment of gemstone jewelry, crystal ornaments, mineral specimens, polished stones, fossils, and books on related subjects. It's a treasure trove of unusual gifts.

En Route   Travel down the east side of Loch Linnhe to Corran, where a frequent ferry shuttles cars and foot passengers across the loch to Ardgour. (You can avoid the ferry by driving around the head of Loch Eil, but it's not a particularly scenic route.) From Ardgour the two-lane A861 runs south along Loch Linnhe before heading into Glen Sanda, crossing the watershed, and running down to the long shores of **Loch Sunart.** This is a typical western Highlands sea loch: orange kelp marks the tide lines, and herons stand muffled and miserable, wondering if it's worth risking a free meal at the local fish farm. As for the fish farms themselves, you'll become accustomed to their floats and cages turning up in the foreground of every sea-loch view. The farms were originally hailed as the savior of the Highland economy because of the number of jobs they created, but questions are now being raised about their environmental impact, at the same time as the market for their product is threatened by Scandinavian imports.

At the little village of Salen, either turn north immediately or divert to the westernmost point of mainland Scotland, at **Ardnamurchan Point,** reached along a narrow road with blind curves, in part through thickets of rhododendrons. The Ardnamurchan Peninsula is a must-see if you love unspoiled coastal scenery. Here you'll find small farming communities and vacation homes.

Acharacle

★ ㉕ *3 mi north of Salen.*

On the way north to Acharacle (pronounced ach-*ar*-ra-kle with a Scots *ch*), you'll pass through deep-green plantations and moorland lily ponds. This spread-out settlement, backed by the hills of Moidart, lies at the shallow and reedy west end of **Loch Shiel;** the north end is more dramatic and sits deep within the rugged hills.

En Route   Traveling between Acharacle and Arisaig, you'll reach the upper sandy shores of Loch Moidart by climbing on the A861 over a high moorland pass. On the next ascent, from Loch Moidart, you'll be greeted by stunning sea views. You can reach the sea coast by the mouth of **Loch Ailort** (pronounced *eye*-ort), and there are plenty of places to pull off among the boulders and birch scrub and sort out the view of the islands. In the distance you'll be able to spot Eigg, a low island marked by the dramatic black peak of An Sgurr. Beyond Eigg is the larger Rum, with its range of hills and the Norse-named, cloud-capped Rum Coullin looming over the island. Loch Ailort itself is another picturesque inlet, now cluttered with the garish floats of fish cages. You'll meet the main road again at the junction with the A830, the main route from Fort William to Mallaig. Turn left here. The breathtaking seaward views should continue to distract you from the road beside **Loch nan Uamh** (from Gaelic, meaning "cave" and pronounced oo-am). This loch is associated with Prince Charles Edward Stuart's nine-month stay on the mainland, during which he gathered a small army, marched as far south as Derby in England, alarmed the king, retreated to unavoidable defeat at Culloden in the spring, and then spent a few months as a fugitive in the Highlands. A cairn by the shore marks the spot where the prince was picked up by a French ship; he never returned to Scotland.

Arisaig

㉖ *27 mi north of Acharacle.*

Considering its small size, Arisaig, gateway to the Small Isles, offers a surprising choice of high-quality options for dining and lodging. To the north of Arisaig, the road cuts across a headland to reach a stretch of coastline where silver sands glitter with the mica in the local rock; clear water, blue sky, and white sand lend a tropical flavor to the beaches—when the sun is shining.

From Arisaig try to visit at least a couple of the **Small Isles: Rum, Eigg, Muck,** and **Canna.** Contact **Murdo Grant** (⊠ Arisaig Marine, Arisaig, Inverness-shire PH39 4NH, ☎ 01687/450224), who runs a service from the harbor at Arisaig. The MV *Shearwater,* a former naval inshore minesweeper, delivers supplies and mail as well as visitors to the diminutive island communities. What sets Grant's operation apart from the tourism-oriented excursions is that it offers visitors a glimpse of island life from a working vessel going about its summer routine.

Dining and Lodging

££££   ✕⌂ **Arisaig House Hotel.** This secluded and grand Victorian mansion offers tranquillity and some marvelous scenery, including views of Loch nan Uamh. The bedrooms are plush and restful, with soft pastels, original moldings, and antique furniture. The cuisine showcases fresh local produce, such as seafood or venison cooked in the modern British style: try the poached fillet of turbot, with crushed potatoes and chilled oyster cream, or the roast loin of spring lamb, with potato and herb *galette* (round, flat cake), broad beans, and a rosemary jus. A nine-hole golf course is at Traigh, 6 mi to the north. ⊠ *Beasdale, by Arisaig (13 mi south of Mallaig on A830, west of Glenfinnan), PH39 4NR,* ☎ *01687/ 450622,* FAX *01687/450626. 10 rooms with bath or shower, 2 suites. Restaurant, croquet, billiards, library. MC, V. Closed Nov.–Easter.* ⊛

££ ✕▥ **Arisaig Hotel.** An old coaching inn close to the water, with magnificent views of the Small Isles, this hotel offers a slightly more modest environment than Arisaig House (☞ *above*). The inn has retained its provinciality with simple decor and home cooking. High-quality local ingredients are used here to good advantage; lobster, langoustines, and crayfish are specialties, as are "proper" puddings, such as fruit crumbles. ⊠ *Arisaig PH39 4NH,* ☎ *01687/450210,* FAX *01687/450310. 13 rooms with bath or shower. Restaurant, recreation room. MC, V.* ⊛

££ ✕▥ **Old Library Lodge and Restaurant.** A barn on the waterfront has been converted into a guest house and a fine restaurant with reasonable prices. Local produce is prepared in a French-bistro style and served in a whitewashed, airy dining room. The bedrooms are very comfortable, with flowery duvets and cozy armchairs. ⊠ *Arisaig PH39 4NH,* ☎ *01687/450651,* FAX *01687/450219. 6 rooms with bath or shower. Restaurant. AE, MC, V. Closed Nov.–Mar.* ⊛

Outdoor Activities and Sports

Bespoke Highland Tours (⊠ The Bothy, Camusdarach, by Arisaig, ☎ 01687/450272) rents bicycles and arranges cycling and trekking tours of the Great Glen and the western Highlands and islands.

Mallaig

❷⑦ *8 mi north of Arisaig, 44 mi northwest of Fort William.*

After the approach along the coast, the workaday fishing port of Mallaig itself is anticlimactic. It has a few shops, and there is some bustle by the quayside when fishing boats unload or the Skye ferry departs: this is the departure point for the southern ferry connection to the Isle of Skye (☞ Chapter 9), the largest island of the Inner Hebrides. Mallaig is also the starting point for day cruises up the Sound of Sleat, which separates Skye from the mainland. The sound offers views into the rugged Knoydart region and its long, fjordlike sea lochs, Lochs Nevis and Hourn. The area to the immediate north and west beyond Loch Nevis, one of the most remote in Scotland, is often referred to as the Rough Bounds of Knoydart. For cruises, which operate all year, contact **Bruce Watt Sea Cruises** (⊠ Western Isles Guest House, PH41 4QG, ☎ 01687/ 462320).

The **Heritage Centre** of Mallaig has exhibits, films, photographs, and models on all aspects of the local history. ⊠ *Station Rd.,* ☎ *01687/ 462085. Call for admission and hrs of operation.*

Beside the harbor, **Mallaig Marine World** shows you what goes on beneath the surface of the Sound of Sleat: live fish and shellfish and a display on the local fishing traditions are among the attractions here. ⊠ *The Harbour,* ☎ *01687/462292.* 🎫 *£2.75.* ☉ *Daily 9:30–5:30 (longer hrs in summer; call to confirm hrs in winter).*

A small, unnamed side road just south of Mallaig leads east to an even smaller road that will bring you to **Loch Morar,** the deepest of all the Scottish lochs (more than 1,000 ft); the next deepest point is miles out into the Atlantic, beyond the continental shelf. The loch is said to have its own resident monster, Morag, who undoubtedly gets less recognition than its famous cousin Nessie. Apart from this short public road, the area around the loch is all but roadless.

Glenfinnan

㉘ *26 mi southeast of Mallaig.*

Glenfinnan, perhaps the most visitor-oriented stop on the route between Mallaig and Fort William, has much to offer if you're interested in Scottish history. Here the National Trust for Scotland has capitalized on the romance surrounding the story of the Jacobites and their intention of returning a Stuart monarch and the Roman Catholic religion to a country that had become staunchly Protestant. In Glenfinnan in 1745, the sometimes-reluctant clans joined forces and rallied to Prince Charles Edward Stuart's cause.

The raising of the prince's standard is commemorated by the **Glenfinnan Monument** (an unusual tower on the banks of Loch Shiel), and the story of his campaign is told in the nearby visitor center. Note that the figure at the top of the monument is of a Highlander, not the prince. The view down Loch Shiel from the Glenfinnan Monument is one of the most photographed views in Scotland. ⊠ *A830,* ☎ *01397/722250.* 🖼 *£1.50.* ⊙ *Visitor center: Apr.–mid-May and Sept.–Oct., daily 10–5; mid-May–Aug., daily 9:30–6.*

As impressive as the Glenfinnan Monument (especially if you've tired of the Jacobite "Will He No Come Back Again" sentiment) is the curving railway viaduct that stretches across the green slopes behind the monument. The **Glenfinnan Viaduct,** 21 spans and 1,248 ft long, was in its time the wonder of the Highlands. The railway's contractor, Robert MacAlpine, known as Concrete Bob by the locals, pioneered the use of mass concrete for viaducts and bridges when his company built the Mallaig extension, which opened in 1901.

The train is the most relaxing way to take in the landscape of birch- and bracken-covered wild slopes; **rail services** (☎ 0345/484950) run all year on the stretch of line between Fort William and Mallaig, with the possibility of steam engines operating in summer.

AROUND THE GREAT GLEN A TO Z

Arriving and Departing

By Bus
There is a long-distance **Scottish Citylink** (☎ 0990/505050) service from Glasgow to Fort William. Inverness is also well served from the central belt of Scotland; for information call the **Inverness coach station** (☎ 01463/233371).

By Car
The fast A9 brings you to Inverness in roughly three hours from Glasgow or Edinburgh, even if you take your time.

By Plane
Inverness Airport (⊠ Dalcross, ☎ 01463/232471) has flights from London, Edinburgh, and Glasgow, and a wide range of internal flights covering the Highlands and islands. Flights are operated by **British Airways** (☎ 0345/222111), **Servisair** (☎ 01667/464040), and **easyJet** (☎ 0870/600–0000). Fort William has bus and train connections with Glasgow, so **Glasgow Airport** (☎ 0141/887–1111) can be an appropriate access point (☞ Chapter 2).

By Train

The area is well served by trains. There are connections from London to Inverness and Fort William (including overnight sleeper service), as well as reliable links from Glasgow and Edinburgh. For information call the **National Train Enquiry Line** (☎ 0345/484950).

Getting Around

By Bus

There is limited service available in the Great Glen area and some local service running from Fort William. **Highland Country Buses** (☎ 01397/702373) operates buses down the Great Glen, around Fort William and also a service from Fort William south to Oban. A number of post-bus services will help get you to the more remote corners of the area. A timetable is available from the **Royal Mail** (✉ 7 Strothers La., Inverness IV1 1AA, ☎ 01463/256273).

By Car

As in all areas of rural Scotland, a car is a great asset for exploring the Great Glen and Speyside, especially since the best of the area is away from the main roads. You can use the main A82 from Inverness to Fort William to explore this area, or use the smaller A862/A852 roads (former military roads) to explore the much quieter east side of Loch Ness. The same applies to Speyside, where a variety of options open up away from the A9, especially through the pinewoods by Coylumbridge and Feshiebridge, east of the main road. Mallaig, west of Fort William, has improving road connections, but the road is still narrow and winding in many places, and rail remains the most enjoyable way to experience the rugged hills and loch scenery between these two places. In Morvern, the area across Loch Linnhe southwest of Fort William, you may encounter single-lane roads, which require slower speeds and concentration.

By Train

Though the Great Glen has no rail connection (in Victorian times Fort William and Inverness had different lines built by companies that could not agree), this area has the **West Highland line,** which links Fort William to Mallaig; a trip on this scenic line is highly recommended (steam trains are an occasional bonus in the summer months). There is also train service between Glasgow (Queen Street) and Inverness, via Aviemore, which gives access to the heart of Speyside. For information call the **National Train Enquiry Line** (☎ 0345/484950).

Contacts and Resources

Car Rentals

Avis (✉ Dalcross Airport, Inverness, ☎ 01667/464070). **Budget Rentacar** (✉ Railway Terr., Inverness, ☎ 0541/565656). **Europcar Ltd.** (✉ Friar's Bridge Service Station, Telford St., Inverness, ☎ 01463/235337). **Hertz** (✉ Dalcross Airport, Inverness, ☎ 01667/462652).

Emergencies

Ambulance, police, fire, or coast guard: ☎ 999. (No coins are needed for emergency calls from phone booths.)

Belford Hospital (✉ Belford Rd., Fort William, ☎ 01397/702481). **Raigmore Hospital** (✉ Old Perth Rd., Inverness, ☎ 01463/704000). **Town and County Hospital** (✉ Cawdor Rd., Nairn, ☎ 01667/452101).

Guided Tours

ORIENTATION

From Fort William, **ScotRail** (☎ 0141/335–4612) runs services on the outstandingly beautiful West Highland Line to Mallaig. **Caledonian**

MacBrayne (☎ 01475/650100) runs scheduled service and cruises to Skye, the Small Isles, and Mull from Mallaig. **Arisaig Marine** (☎ 01687/450224) operates highly recommended Hebridean day cruises on the MV *Shearwater* to the Small Isles at Easter and daily from May through September, when charter trips also go to Skye. Also available for charter from Arisaig Marine is a fast twin-engine motor yacht, which can take up to 12 passengers for go-where-you-please cruises around the Small Isles and farther afield.

SPECIAL-INTEREST

From Inverness, **Highland Insight Tours and Travel** (☎ 01463/831403) offers personalized touring holidays and full-day or half-day tours that cater to any interest. **James Johnson** (☎ 01463/790179) is based in Inverness but will drive you anywhere; he has a particularly good knowledge of the Highlands and islands, including the Outer Isles. **Jacobite Cruises Ltd.** (☎ 01463/233999) runs morning and afternoon cruises on Loch Ness to Urquhart Castle and boat and coach excursions to the Monster Exhibition in Drumnadrochit.

Macaulay Charters (☎ 01463/717337) provides trips by boat from Inverness, offering you the chance to see dolphins in their breeding area. An unusual option from Inverness is a day trip to Orkney (☞ Chapter 10): **John o'Groats Ferries** (☎ 01955/611353) offers day tours from Inverness to Orkney, daily from June through August.

Late-Night Pharmacies

Pharmacies are not common away from the larger towns, and doctors often dispense medicines in very rural areas. In an emergency, the police will assist you in locating a pharmacist. In Inverness, **Kinmylies Pharmacy** (⊠ 1 Charleston Ct., Kinmylies, ☎ 01463/221094) is open weekdays until 6 and Saturdays until 5:30. The pharmacy at the **Scottish Co-Op** superstore (⊠ Milton of Inshes, Perth Rd., outside Inverness, ☎ 01463/712188) is open Monday–Wednesday 9–8, Thursday and Friday 9–9, Saturday 9–6, and Sunday 10–6. In Fort William, **Boots the Chemist** (⊠ High St., ☎ 01397/705143) is open weekdays 8:45–6, Saturday 8:45–5:30. For Sunday openings, consult a doctor (☞ Emergencies, *above*).

Visitor Information

Aviemore (⊠ Grampian Rd., ☎ 01479/810363). **Fort William** (⊠ Cameron Centre, Cameron Sq., ☎ 01397/703781). **Inverness** (⊠ Castle Wynd, ☎ 01463/234353).

Other tourist information centers, open seasonally, include those at Ballachulish, Fort Augustus, Grantown-on-Spey, Kingussie, Mallaig, Nairn, and Strontian.

9 THE NORTHERN HIGHLANDS

SUTHERLAND, ISLE OF SKYE, OUTER HEBRIDES

If you haven't visited the "real" Highlands, you haven't seen Scotland. In this region is concentrated much of the romance of "Caledonia stern and wild"—the glamour of the clans, the red deer and golden eagles, the Celtic mists and legends, and a mixture of splendor and tranquillity found hardly anywhere else in the world. Here is Eilean Donan—the most romantic of all Scottish castles—the land's end at John o'Groats, and Skye, the mysterious island immortalized by the exploits of Bonnie Prince Charlie.

By Gilbert
Summers

Updated by
Beth Ingpen

T HE OLD COUNTIES OF ROSS AND CROMARTY (sometimes called Easter and Wester Ross), Sutherland, and Caithness constitute the most northern portion of mainland Scotland. The population is sparse, mountains and moorland limit the choice of touring routes, and distances are less important than whether the winding, hilly roads you sometimes encounter are two lanes or one: do not underestimate driving times, especially when driving on minor roads or on the islands. On a map, this area may seem far from major urban centers, but it is easy to get to. Inverness has an airport with direct links to London, Edinburgh, Glasgow, and even Amsterdam, and you can reach destinations such as the fishing town of Ullapool in an hour by car from Inverness. In fact, much of the western seaboard is easily accessible from the Northern Highlands.

And accessible it should be, for this area contains some of Scotland's most intriguing scenery. Much of Sutherland and Wester Ross, for example, is comprised of a rocky platform of Lewisian gneiss, certainly the oldest rocks in Britain, scoured and hollowed by glacial action into numerous lochs. On top of this rolling wet moorland landscape sit strangely shaped quartzite-capped sandstone mountains, eroded and pinnacled. Take a walk here, and the Ice Age doesn't seem so far away. One of the region's leitmotivs is the sea lochs that thrust salty fingers into the loneliest landscapes in Scotland, carrying the Atlantic's salty tang among the moors and deep forests. Strange, solitary peaks rear up out of the heather, and if you're lucky, you may sight a golden eagle soaring overhead in search of grouse.

Many place-names in this region reflect its early links with Scandinavia. Sutherland, the most northern portion of mainland Scotland, was once the southernmost land belonging to the Vikings. Scotland's most northern point, Cape Wrath, got its name from the Viking word *hvarth* (turning point), and Laxford, Suilven, and dozens of other names in the area have Norse rather than Gaelic derivations.

The islands of Skye and especially the Outer Hebrides, which are now often referred to as the Western Isles, are the stronghold of the Gaelic language. Skye, famous for its misty mountains, called the Cuillins, has a surprisingly wide variety of landscape considering its relatively small size. The south of the island is generally flatter; its coastline is the place to hunt out hidden beaches, perhaps overlooked by a ruined castle, and its interior moorlands are dotted with lochans. As you travel northward, however, the landscape becomes increasingly mountainous, with green pastures surrounding the scattered crofting (farming) communities and sea inlets strewn with jewel-like islets, miniature versions of Skye itself. Both sides of the island have their own distinctive character, and both offer much to enjoy, so don't hurry north from the Mallaig-Armadale ferry terminal or the new bridge to Skye. Instead, take time to divert down side roads for an exhilarating autumn trip through the glowing gold, silver, russet, and copper of southern Skye—birch, bracken, heather, and peat bog all playing their part in nature's rich tapestry. Leave plenty of time for some excellent shopping, then travel on northward to explore Trotternish (Flora Macdonald's home base), Waternish (with some excellent restaurants), Dunvegan (with castle and more good restaurants), or Glendale, its winding road threaded with craft and heritage sites in profusion.

Pleasures and Pastimes

Biking
The landscapes are great, but the open and rugged terrain has not favored the development of a network of rural back roads. Be prepared

to meet holiday traffic at peak season, especially on the mainland. Some side roads (and even some main roads, especially on the islands) are single track and narrow, meaning there will be traffic coming the other way between passing places. High-visibility clothing is advised.

Dining

Restaurant options are more limited here than in other parts of Scotland; the exception is Skye, which has several restaurants of very high standard. Reliable country houses and inns serving hearty, traditional Highland fare can be found throughout the region.

CATEGORY	COST*
££££	over £40
£££	£30–£40
££	£15–£30
£	under £15

*per person for a three-course meal, including VAT and excluding drinks and service

Fishing

The possibilities for fishing are endless here, as a glance at the loch-covered map of Sutherland suggests. Trout-fishing permits for several hill lochans are available at local post offices, shops, and hotels. Inquire at your lodging or at the nearest tourist information center.

Lodging

This region of Scotland has some good modern hotels and charming inns but not many establishments in the more expensive categories, except in the more popular areas such as Skye. You will often find that the most enjoyable accommodations are low-cost guest houses (often family run) offering a bed and breakfast. Dining rooms of country-house lodgings frequently reach the standard of top-quality restaurants.

CATEGORY	COST*
££££	over £140
£££	£110–£140
££	£65–£110
£	under £65

*All prices are for a standard double room, including service, breakfast, and VAT.

✑ following the text of a review is your signal that the property has a Web site, where you will find details and, usually, images; for a link, visit www.fodors.com/urls.

Exploring the Northern Highlands

From Inverness (☞ Chapter 8), the gateway to the Northern Highlands, roads fan out like the spokes of a wheel to join the coastal route around the rim of mainland Scotland. Many roads here are single track, and you pause at passing places to allow ongoing traffic to pass. There are simply no roads into the wilder areas, and few roads at all—so you are bound to be sharing the roads with heavy trucks and buses. Ferry services are generally very reliable, weather permitting.

Numbers in the text correspond to numbers in the margin and on the Northern Highlands and Skye and the Outer Hebrides maps.

Great Itineraries

The quality of the northern light and the sheer ambience of the landscapes add to the touring adventure. Above all, don't rush things. And take a good look at how multiple-journey ferry tickets—the Island Hopscotch, for example—can help you stay flexible (☞ Getting Around by Car and Ferry *in* The Northern Highlands A to Z, *below*).

IF YOU HAVE 2 DAYS

If you only have two days, head to the fabled isle of **Skye,** whose mists shroud so many legends. Stay in towns that feature remarkable hotels, such as **Broadford** ⑱ or **Armadale** ⑲, then tour the spectacular countryside, including the celebrated Cuillin ridges near **Glen Brittle** ㉕. Be sure to detour to see Scotland's most romantic castle, **Eilean Donan** ⑰, on your way back to the mainland.

IF YOU HAVE 5 DAYS

If the weather looks settled, then head for Skye, basing yourself at 🏨 **Portree** ⑳. You could then hop over from Uig, in the north of Skye, to 🏨 **Tarbert** ㉛, in the Western Isles, for **Calanais (Callanish) Standing Stones** ㉚, the **Arnol Black House** ㉙, and some deserted beaches, returning to 🏨 **Ullapool** ③, in the north, and traveling to Inverness via **Strathpeffer** ①. Otherwise, stick to the mainland and do the entire loop of the north of Scotland, staying overnight at 🏨 **Ullapool** ③, 🏨 **Scourie** ⑥, 🏨 **Thurso** ⑨, 🏨 **Wick** ⑪, or 🏨 **Dornoch** ⑮.

IF YOU HAVE 8 DAYS

Tackle the coastal loop of the north of Scotland counterclockwise, taking the ferry at 🏨 **Ullapool** ③ for 🏨 **Stornoway** ㉗ and the Western Isles, and returning to the mainland via the ferry from 🏨 **Tarbert** ㉛ to Uig on Skye, then go over the Skye Bridge.

When to Tour the Northern Highlands

The Northern Highlands and islands are really best seen in late spring, summer, and early autumn. The earlier in the spring or later in the autumn you go, the greater the chances of your encountering the elements in their extreme form, and the fewer visitor attractions and accommodations you will find open; even tourist-friendly Skye closes down almost completely by the end of October. As a final deciding factor, you may not want to take a western sea passage in a gale, a frequent occurrence in the winter months.

THE NORTHERN LANDSCAPES

Wester Ross and Sutherland

The northern landscapes offer some of the most distinctive mountain profiles in all of Scotland, although the coastal rim roads are more interesting than the cross-country routes. In recent years an influx of newcomers from other parts of the United Kingdom has led to improvements in lodging and dining options.

The essence of Caithness, the area at the top of Scotland, is space, big skies, and distant blue hills beyond endless rolling moors (although "tax-break" conifer planting has begun to encroach on the views in some areas). There is a surprising amount to see and do on the east coast beyond Inverness—so make sure you allow enough time to see the visitor centers and croft houses open to view.

Strathpeffer

❶ *19 mi northwest of Inverness via A9, A835, and A834.*

At the former Victorian spa town of Strathpeffer you can take a walk to admire Victorian "holiday houses" and a Pictish stone carved with a lifelike eagle, or enjoy a toy museum in the former railway station. Not far from Strathpeffer are the tumbling **Falls of Rogie** (signposted off the A835), where an interestingly bouncy suspension bridge presents you with a fine view of the splashing waters below.

Lodging

£ ▣ **Craigvar.** Host Margaret Scott is a delight and keeps plenty of tourist leaflets to keep you busy. The rooms at this Georgian bed-and-breakfast are prettily decorated; the so-called Beige Room is actually white and cream, with a swag of dried hydrangea above the bed. Idiosyncratic pictures—from 18th-century portraits to Japanese-style still lifes—hang on the walls. The Blue Room has a four-poster bed and Victorian bath. ✉ *The Square, Strathpeffer, Ross-shire IV14 9DL,* ☎ *01997/421622,* FAX *01997/421796. 3 rooms, 1 with bath, 2 with shower. MC, V.*

Corrieshalloch Gorge

★ ❷ *39 mi west of Strathpeffer.*

For a thrilling touch of vertigo, the Corrieshalloch Gorge is not to be missed. A burn draining the high moors plunges 150 ft into a 200-ft-deep, thickly wooded gorge. There is a suspension-bridge viewpoint and a heady atmosphere of romantic grandeur, like an old Scottish print come to life.

OFF THE BEATEN PATH

INVEREWE GARDENS – The reputation of the gardens at Inverewe has grown steadily, despite their remote location. The main attraction lies in the contrast between the bleak coastal headlands and thin-soiled moors and the lush plantings of the gardens behind the dense shelterbelts. Here you find proof of the efficiency of the warm North Atlantic Drift, part of the Gulf Stream, which takes the edge off winter frosts. Note that although Inverewe is sometimes described as subtropical, this is an inaccuracy that truly irritates the head gardener. Don't expect coconuts and palm trees here. Do expect rhododendrons from the Himalayas and such Southern Hemisphere species as Tasmanian eucalyptus trees. *Off A832 roughly 25 mi west of Corrieshalloch Gorge,* ☎ *01445/781200.* ▨ *£5.* ◷ *Mid-Mar.–Oct. daily 9:30–9; Nov.– mid-Mar. daily 9:30–5; guided walks with gardener Apr.–Sept. weekdays at 1:30.*

Ullapool

❸ *5 mi west of Corrieshalloch Gorge, 238 mi north of Glasgow.*

Set by the shores of salty **Loch Broom,** Ullapool was founded in 1788 as a fishing station to exploit the local herring stocks. Ullapool has a cosmopolitan air and comes alive when the Lewis ferry docks and departs.

Dining and Lodging

£–££££ ✕▣ **Ceilidh Place.** This hostelry is extremely comfortable and about as far away in style as you can get from a major chain hotel. You can while away the hours on deep, luxurious sofas in the first-floor sitting room—which overlooks the bay—and borrow one of the many books scattered throughout. Rooms have cream bedspreads and rich, warm color schemes. The inn's restaurant specializes in seafood and vegetarian food (try the monkfish and prawn brochettes or pasta with zucchini and mushrooms in creamy garlic sauce). *Ceilidhs* and other musical events are held frequently; chamber music, folk music, and opera all find a place here. An inexpensive alternative, but with access to the hotel's facilities, is the bunkhouse across the road. ✉ *W. Argyle St., Ullapool IV26 2TY,* ☎ *01854/612103,* FAX *01854/612886. 26 rooms, 10 with bath or shower. Restaurant. AE, DC, MC, V.*

En Route Drive north of Ullapool, and you'll enter into a different kind of landscape. Here you won't find the broad flanks of great hills that hem you

The Northern Highlands and Skye

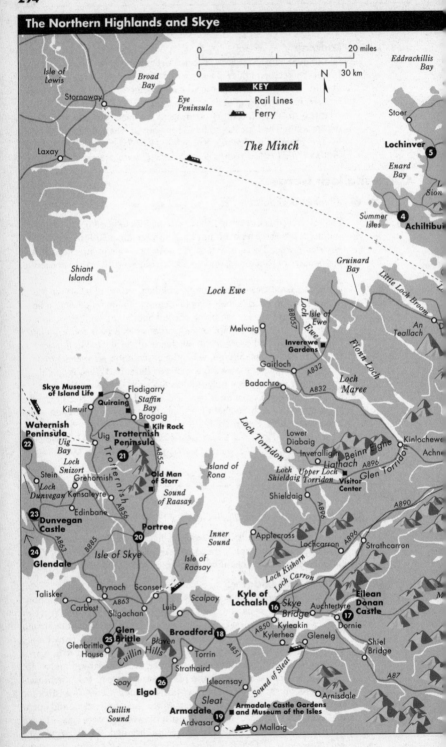

KEY
— Rail Lines
⛴ Ferry

0 ——— 20 miles
0 ——— 30 km

N

Isle of Lewis

Stornoway

Broad Bay

Eye Peninsula

Eddrachillis Bay

Stoer

Lochinver 5

Laxay

The Minch

Enard Bay

L Sion

Summer Isles

Achiltibu 4

Shiant Islands

Loch Ewe

Gruinard Bay

Little Loch Broom

Lo

An Teallach

Melvaig

B8057

Loch Ewe

Isle of Ewe

Inverewe Gardens ■

Gairloch

A832

Loch Maree

Fionn Loch

Badachro

A832

Kinlochewe

Achne

Skye Museum of Island Life ●

Flodigarry

Quiraing ●

Staffin Bay

Brogaig

Kilmuir

Kilt Rock ■

Lower Diabaig

Beinn Eighe

Loch Torridon

Inveralligin

Liathach

A896

Waternish Peninsula 22

Uig

Trotternish Peninsula

21

Uig Bay

Loch Snizort

Loch Shieldaig

Upper Loch Torridon

Visitor Center ■

Glen Torridon

A890

Stein

Grehornish

Old Man of Storr ■

Island of Rona

Shieldaig

A896

Loch Dunvegan

Kensaleyre

Sound of Raasay

Edinbane

Dunvegan Castle 23

Isle of Skye

Portree

20

Inner Sound

Applecross

Lochcarron

A896

Strathcarron

Isle of Raasay

Glendale 24

B885

Talisker

Drynoch

Sconser

Loch Kishorn

Loch Carron

Eilean Donan Castle

A863

A863

Scalpay

Kyle of Lochalsh 16

Skye Bridge

Auchtertyre

17

Carbost

Sligachan

Luib

A850

Kyleakin

Dornie

Glen Brittle 25

Broadford 18

Kylerhea

Glenelg

Shiel Bridge

Glenbrittle House

Blaven

Cuillin Hills

Torrin

A851

Sound of Sleat

A87

Soay

Strathaird

Elgol 26

Isleornsay

Arnisdale

Cuillin Sound

Sleat

Armadale 19

Armadale Castle Gardens and Museum of the Isles ■

Ardvasar

Mallaig

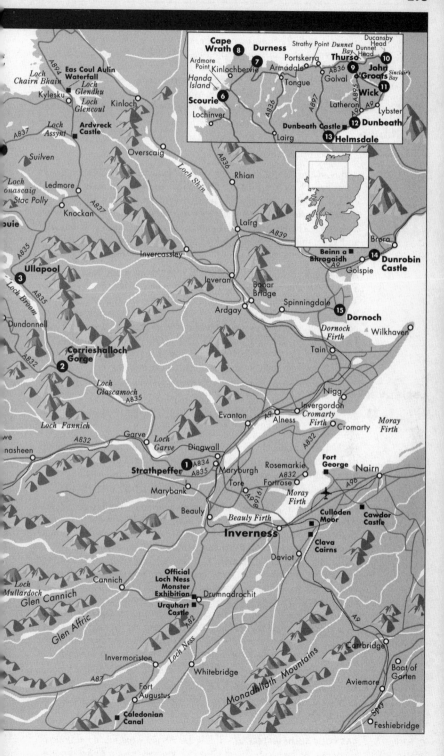

Cape Wrath 8
Durness 7
Strathy Point
Dunnet Bay
Ducansby Head
Portskerra
Thurso
Dunnet Head
Ardmore Point
Kinlochbervie
Armadale
A836
John O'Groats 10
Handa Island
Tongue
Golval
A895
Wick 11
Sinclair's Bay
Scourie 6
A836
A897
Latheron
Lybster
Lochinver
A9
Dunbeath Castle
Dunbeath 12
Lairg
Helmsdale 13

Loch Chairn Bhain
A894
Eas Coul Aulin Waterfall
Loch Glendhu
Kylesku
Loch Glencoul
Kinloch
Ardvreck Castle
Overscaig
A837
Suilven
Loch Assynt
Rhian
Ledmore
Loch onascaig
Stac Polly
Knockan
A837
Loch Shin
Lairg
A839
ouie
A835
Invercassley
Brora
Ullapool 3
Inveran
Beinn a Bhragaidh
Dunrobin Castle 14
Loch Broom
A835
Ardgay
Bonar Bridge
Golspie
Dundonnell
A832
Spinningdale
Dornoch 15
Corrieshalloch Gorge
Dornoch Firth
Wilkhaven
2
Loch Glascamoch
A835
Tain
Loch Fannich
Nigg
Invergordon
Cromarty Firth
Moray Firth
we
A832
Garve
Evanton
Alness
Cromarty
nasheen
A832
Loch Garve
Dingwall
Strathpeffer 1
A834
Maryburgh
Rosemarkie
Fort George
Nairn
A835
Tore
A832
Fortrose
A96
Marybank
A9
Moray Firth
Beauly
Beauly Firth
Culloden Moor
Cawdor Castle
Inverness
Clava Cairns
Daviot
Loch Mulardoch
Cannich
Glen Cannich
Official Loch Ness Monster Exhibition
Drumnadrochit
Glen Affric
Urquhart Castle
A82
Carrbridge
Boat of Garten
Invermoriston
Loch Ness
Whitebridge
Monadhliath Mountains
Aviemore
A87
Fort Augustus
Spey
Caledonian Canal
Feshiebridge

in, as you would in Great Glen or Glen Coe. Instead, in Wester Ross the mountains rear out of the hummocky terrain and seem to shift their position, hiding behind one another in a slightly bewitching way. Even their names seem different from those of the *bens* (mountain peaks or high hills) elsewhere: Cul Mor, Cul Beag, Stac Polly, Canisp, Suilven. Some owe their origins to Norse words rather than to undiluted Gaelic—a reminder that Vikings used to sail this northern seaboard. Much of this area lies within the Inverpolly National Nature Reserve.

Achiltibuie

④ *25 mi northwest of Ullapool.*

A spread-out line of crofts, many now owned by newcomers, marks the approach to Achiltibuie. Offshore are the **Summer Isles,** romantic enough in theory, but in reality bleak and austere. In Achiltibuie there's a **smokehouse** that serves succulent smoked cuts of venison and other delicacies. The **Hydroponicum** hydroponically produces luscious fruit and vegetables year-round, which would otherwise be impossible in the harsh winter climate.

En Route   A single-lane unclassified road winds north from Achiltibuie, through a wild though harmonious landscape of bracken and birch trees, heather and humped-hill horizons, with outstanding sea views on the second half of the route. Don't fall victim to the breathtaking landscape views, however: the road has several blind curves that demand extreme care. Just before Inverkirkaig is a parking lot next to the River Kirkaig, and a short stroll away is Achins Book and Craft Shop (☞ Shopping *in* Lochinver, *below*)—perhaps Scotland's most remote bookstore.

Lochinver

⑤ *18 mi north of Achiltibuie via unclassified road, 38 mi north of Ullapool via A835/A837.*

Lochinver is a charming community with a few dining and lodging options. Behind the town the mountain Suilven rises abruptly. This unusual monolith is best seen from across the water, however. Take the cul-de-sac, **Baddidarroch Road,** for the finest photo opportunity.

Bold souls spending time at Lochinver may enjoy the interesting single-lane B869 **Drumbeg loop** to the north of Lochinver—it has several challenging hairpin turns along with breathtaking views. (The junction is just north of the River Inver bridge on the outskirts of the village, signposted as STOER and CLASHNESSIE.) Just beyond the scattered community of Stoer, a road leads west to **Stoer Point Lighthouse.** If you're an energetic walker, you can hike across the short turf and heather along the cliff top for fine views east toward the profiles of the northwest mountains. There is also a red-sandstone sea stack: the **Old Man of Stoer.** This makes a pleasant excursion on a long summer evening. If you stay on the Drumbeg section, there is a particularly tricky hairpin turn in a steep dip, which may force you to take your eyes off the fine view of Quinag, yet another of Sutherland's shapely mountains.

Beside Loch Assynt, on the road east from Lochinver, stand the abandoned ruins of **Ardvreck Castle.** This was a clan MacLeod stronghold, built in the 15th century.

OFF THE
BEATEN PATH

EAS COUL AULIN WATERFALL – This is the longest waterfall in the United Kingdom. At the head of Loch Glencoul, the falls have a 685-ft drop. A rugged hike leads to the falls; in summer, cruises offer a less taxing alternative. The falls are located 3 mi southeast of the Kylesku Bridge off the

A894; contact the tourist information center in Ullapool or Lochinver for more information.

Shopping

Highland Stoneware (⊠ Baddidarroch, Lochinver, ☎ 01571/844376) manufactures tableware and decorative items with hand-painted designs of Highland wildflowers, animals, and landscapes. In the showroom you can browse and purchase wares.

At Inverkirkaig, just south of Lochinver, don't miss **Achins Book and Craft Shop** (⊠ Inverkirkaig, ☎ 01571/844262). It's a great place for Scottish books on natural history, hill walking, fishing, and crafts. It also has a well-chosen variety of craft items for sale—knitwear, tweeds, and pottery—along with artwork and traditional music. The shop is open daily 9:30–6 (phone ahead for winter opening hours), and its pleasant coffee shop is open from Easter through October, daily 10–5.

Scourie

❻ *28 mi north of Lochinver.*

Scourie is a small settlement catering to visitors—fishermen especially—with a choice of local accommodations. It also makes a good base for a trip to the bird sanctuary on the island of Handa.

Dining and Lodging

££ ✕🛏 **Eddrachilles Hotel.** This long-established, traditional inn has one of the best views of any hotel in Scotland—across the islands of Eddrachillis Bay (which can be explored by boat from the hotel). The hotel sits on 320 acres of private moorland and is just south of the Handa Island bird sanctuary. The bedrooms are modern and comfortable, each outfitted with tea- and coffeemaking facilities. The chef uses local produce to prepare meals in straightforward Scottish style, with the emphasis on fish and game; try the saddle of venison or the poached salmon. ⊠ *Badcall Bay, Scourie IV27 4TH,* ☎ *01971/502080,* 🖷 *01971/502477. 11 rooms with bath or shower. Restaurant, bar. MC, V. Closed Nov.–Feb.* ✿

En Route From Scourie northward, the A894/A838 traverses the most northerly landscapes, with the empty quarter below Cape Wrath on its west side. You can sample this route by hiking to Sandwood Bay, at the end of the B801, beyond the fishing port of Kinlochbervie. Sandwood has rock stacks and a white beach—and its own ghost, said to frequent a cottage (or *bothy*) near the shore; so this is a truly haunting area in all senses of the word.

Durness

❼ *55 mi north of Lochinver.*

The sudden patches of green at Durness, on the north coast, are caused by the richer limestone outcrops among the acid moorlands. The limestone's most spectacular feature is **Smoo Cave,** a cave system hollowed out of the limestone by water action. Boat tours run daily from April through September (reservations are advised since there's a limit of six per 20-minute tour). The seasonal tourist information center (⊠ Sango, ☎ 01971/511259) has complete information.

If you have made it this far north, you will probably want to go all the way to **❽ Cape Wrath,** at the northwest tip of Scotland. You can't drive your own vehicle, though, as a small boat (May–September) ferries only people across the Kyle of Durness, a sea inlet, from Keoldale; a minibus will then take you to the lighthouse. The highest mainland cliffs in Scotland lie between the Kyle and Cape Wrath—the 800-ft **Cleit Dubh.** The name is Gaelic for "black cleft" and comes from the Old Norse *klettr* (crag).

En Route   The north-coast road along the top of Scotland is both attractive and severe. It runs, for example, round the head of Loch Eriboll, which was a World War II convoy assembly point and was usually referred to as "Loch 'orrible" by the crews. Yet it has its own desolate charm. There are little beaches and settlements to explore along this road, and the landscape gradually softens as you journey east.

Thurso

❾ *74 mi east of Durness.*

The town of Thurso is hard to categorize. Quite substantial for a community so far north, since the 1950s its development has been related to the atomic reactor (Britain's first) along the coast at Dounreay—presumably situated there to be as far as possible from the seat of government, in London. There is not much to see in the town itself, though there are fine beaches, particularly to the east, at Dunnet Bay. Many people make the trip to the northernmost point of mainland Britain, which is at **Dunnet Head,** with its fine views to Orkney.

Lodging

£££–£££   🏠 **Forss Country House Hotel.** Surrounded by woodland, this house dating from 1810 is 4 mi west of Thurso. Despite its stark, gray exterior, it offers a welcoming environment as a base for fishing (guide service and instruction provided) or touring. Restrained decor with plain, soft-tone walls and spare, dark-wood antique and reproduction furniture, along with log fires and sturdy Scottish cuisine, make for a charming place to stay. ⊠ *Forss, about 4 mi west of Thurso, KW14 7XY,* ☎ *01847/861201,* FAX *01847/861301. 10 rooms, 9 with bath, 1 with shower. Restaurant, golf privileges, fishing. AE, MC, V.*

£   🏠 **Murray House.** This Victorian town house in the center of Thurso is a B&B of a very high standard, and it's convenient to the Orkney ferry. ⊠ *1 Campbell St., Thurso KW14 7HD,* ☎ *01847/895759. 4 rooms with shower. No credit cards.*

Outdoor Activities and Sports

Bikes can be hired from **Wheels Cycle Shop** (⊠ 35 High St., Thurso, ☎ FAX 01847/896124), whose staff is also happy to advise on routes.

John o'Groats

❿ *21 mi east of Thurso via A836.*

The windswept little outpost of John o'Groats is usually taken to be the most northern community in the Scottish mainland, though that is not strictly accurate, as an exploration of the little network of roads between Dunnet Head and John o'Groats will confirm. However, John o'Groats has some high-quality crafts shops and should be visited if you have the time. Go east to **Duncansby Head** for spectacular views of cliffs and sea stacks by the lighthouse—and puffins, too, if you know where to look.

Nightlife and the Arts

The **Lyth Arts Centre,** between Wick and John o'Groats, is set in an old country school. From April through November each year, it hosts frequent performances by professional touring music and theater companies (it forms part of the circuit of British Arts Centres). In July and August there are also local and touring exhibitions of contemporary fine art. ⊠ *Lyth, 4 mi off A9,* ☎ *01955/641270.* 🎟 *Performances: £9; concessions: £6; exhibitions: £2.* ☉ *Exhibitions: July–Aug., daily 2–4 (call ahead to confirm); performances: Apr.–Nov., daily 8 PM.*

Outdoor Activities and Sports

Wildlife cruises are operated from John o'Groats Harbor by **John o'-Groats Ferries.** The 1½-hour trip takes passengers into the Pentland Firth, to Duncansby Stacks, and to the island of Stroma, and offers spectacular cliff scenery and bird life. ☎ *01955/611353.* 🎫 *£12.* ☉ *Cruise: mid-June–Aug., daily 2:30 PM.*

Wick

⓫ *17 mi south of John o'Groats, 22 mi southeast of Thurso via A882.*

Wick is a substantial town that was built on its fishing industry. To learn how this town grew, visit the **Wick Heritage Centre**—it's run by local people in part for the local community, and they're real enthusiasts. ✉ *18 Bank Row,* ☎ *01955/605393 or 01955/603385.* 🎫 *£2.* ☉ *June–Sept., Mon.–Sat. 10–5 (last admission 3:45).*

The gaunt, bleak ruins of **Castle Sinclair** and **Castle Girnigoe** teeter on a cliff top to the north of Wick. The **Northlands Viking Centre,** which highlights the role of Scandinavian settlers in this area, has models of the Viking settlement at Freswick and of a Viking long ship, as well as artifacts such as coins. ✉ *The Old School, Auckengill,* ☎ *01955/ 607771.* 🎫 *£1.40.* ☉ *June–Sept., daily 10–4.*

Lodging

£ 🏠 **Greenvoe.** This B&B is a well-appointed modern house, fresh and beautifully maintained, with unfussy, functional, and comfortable bedrooms. A delicious, generous breakfast is included in the room rate, and late-night snacks are a hospitable touch. Smoking is prohibited. ✉ *George St., Wick, Caithness KW1 4DE,* ☎ *01955/603942. 3 rooms with shared bath. No credit cards. Closed last 2 wks Dec.*

Shopping

Perhaps the best-known purveyor of crafts in the area is **Caithness Glass** (✉ Airport Industrial Site, Wick Airport, ☎ 01955/602286). Producing a distinctive style of glassware and paperweights (most of the better gift shops stock Caithness Glass), the factory has tours of the glassblowing workshops and a shop stocking the full product range.

Dunbeath

⓬ *21 mi south of Wick.*

As the moors of Caithness roll down to the sea at Dunbeath, you find the **Dunbeath Heritage Centre,** an old school that the local community, interested in recording their past, turned into a museum. It displays photographs and domestic and crofting artifacts that relay the history of the area from the Bronze Age to the oil age, and is particularly helpful to those researching family histories. ✉ *Dunbeath,* ☎ *01593/ 731233.* 🎫 *£1.50.* ☉ *Apr.–Sept., daily 10–5.*

It's appropriate that the **Laidhay Croft Museum,** just north of Dunbeath, feels more like a private home than a museum. It was built around 1842, comprises a longhouse and barn—animals and people lived under the same long roof—and is furnished as it would have been during its working life. ✉ *Dunbeath,* ☎ *01593/731244.* 🎫 *£1.* ☉ *Easter–Oct., daily 10–6.*

Helmsdale

⓭ *15 mi south of Dunbeath.*

At Helmsdale, the **Timespan Heritage Centre,** a thought-provoking mix of displays, artifacts, and audiovisual materials, portrays the history of the area, from the Stone Age to the 1869 gold rush in the Strath of

Kildonan. The complex also includes a café and an art gallery, with exhibitions that change monthly and cover the whole breadth of the arts. ⊠ *Helmsdale,* ☎ *01431/821327.* 🖾 *£3.50.* ☉ *Apr.–June and Sept.–Oct., Mon.–Sat. 9:30–5, Sun. 2–5 (last admission 1 hr before closing); July–Aug., Mon.–Sat. 9:30–6, Sun. 2–6.*

Golspie

18 mi south of Helmsdale.

⑭ Golspie is a little coastal town with a number of shops and accommodations, though it has the air of a place that visitors merely pass through. The Scottish home of the dukes of Sutherland is **Dunrobin Castle,** an ancient seat developed by the first duke into a 19th-century flamboyant white-turreted behemoth. Trains so fascinated the duke that he built his own railroad in the park and staffed it with his servants. This duke, who also owned one of the largest palaces in London, had more than a touch of Marie Antoinette in him; for instance, he was in good part responsible for the Sutherland Clearances of 1810–20, which devastated this region in the 19th century. Thousands of native Gaels were shamefully evicted from settlements in the interior and forced to emigrate or settle at sites on the coast. Traveling south on the A9, you'll see the controversial statue of the duke, in which he looks like some Eastern Bloc despot, on Beinn a Bragaidh (Ben Braggie), the hilltop to the west. Many people strongly feel that it should be removed, as the "improvement" policies of the duke were ultimately responsible for the brutality associated with the Clearances. ⊠ *Golspie (on the A9),* ☎ *01408/633177.* 🖾 *£5.50.* ☉ *Apr.–May and Oct., Mon.–Sat. 10:30–4:30, Sun. noon–4:30; June and Sept., Mon.–Sat. 10:30–5:30, Sun. noon–5:30; July –Aug., daily 10:30–5:30 (last entry 30 mins before closing).*

Shopping

The **Orcadian Stone Company** (⊠ Main St., Golspie, ☎ 01408/633483) makes stone products (including giftware made from local Caithness slate), jewelry, incised plaques, and prepared mineral specimens. There is also a geological exhibition.

Dornoch

⑮ *10 mi south of Golspie.*

A town of sandstone, tiny, rose-filled gardens, and a 13th-century cathedral with stunning traditional and modern stained-glass windows, Dornoch is also noted for its golf. You may hear it called the St. Andrews of the North, but due to the town's location so far north, the courses here are delightfully uncrowded. Royal Dornoch is the pearl in its crown, praised by the world's top golfers.

Dining and Lodging

££ ✕🏨 **Dornoch Castle Hotel.** A genuine late-15th-century castle, once the
★ palace of the bishops of Caithness and set right in the center of Dornoch, this hotel is a delightful blend of the very old and the more modern (there are rooms in the 1974 wing). The lounge is a relaxing Adamesque room of soft green and cream, and the bedrooms wear pastel stripes and floral fabrics. This is not a luxury hotel, but it's clean and comfortable, with friendly staff and satisfying, well-cooked Scottish food: try the crisp-battered cod fillet with seasonal vegetables. ⊠ *Dornoch, Sutherland, IV25 3SD,* ☎ *01862/810216,* ℻ *01862/810981. 17 rooms with bath or shower. AE, MC, V. Closed Nov.–mid-Mar.*

£–££ 🏨 **Highfield.** In its own grounds on the edge of town, the no-smoking Highfield delivers deluxe B&B accommodations in a modern family home. ⊠ *Evelix Rd., Dornoch IV25 3HR,* ☎ ℻ *01862/810909. 3 rooms with bath and shower. No credit cards.*

Outdoor Activities and Sports

Were it not for its northern location, **Royal Dornoch** (☎ 01862/810219) would undoubtedly be a candidate for the British Open Championship. It's a superb, breezy, and challenging links course, offering 18 holes, par 70. For more information *see* Chapter 11.

SKYE, THE MISTY ISLAND

Skye ranks near the top of most visitors' priority lists: The romance of Prince Charles Edward Stuart (1720–88), known as Bonnie Prince Charlie, combined with the misty Cuillin Hills and their proximity to the mainland all contribute to its popularity. Today the island remains fey, mysterious, and mountainous, an island of sunsets that linger brilliantly until late at night and of beautiful, soft mists. Much photographed are the really old crofts, one or two still inhabited, with their thick stone walls and thatch roofs. Much written about is the story known as the Adventure—the sad history of the "prince in the heather" and pretender to the British throne, Bonnie Prince Charlie. After the disastrous Battle of Culloden he wandered over the Highlands, a passive object, handed like a bale of contraband from one smuggler to another, numbed with constant applications of whisky—the beginnings of the alcoholism that finally killed him. He then escaped to the isles of Harris and South Uist, where he met Flora Macdonald, the woman who took him, disguised as her maid, "over the sea to Skye" and then back to the mainland. His Scottish exploits were the stuff that myths are made of. *Will ye no' come back again . . . Speed, bonnie boat . . . Charlie is my darling . . .* the tunes and lyrics of Lady Nairn, jaunty or mournful, composed long after the events, are as good an epitaph as any adventurer could wish for.

To reach Skye these days, you can cross over the bridge spanning the narrow channel of Kyle Akin, between Kyle of Lochalsh and Kyleakin, or take the (more romantic) ferry options between Mallaig and Armadale or between Glenelg and Kylerea. You can tour comfortably around the island in two or three days. Orientation is easy: follow the only roads around the loops on the northern part of the island and enjoy the road running the length of the Sleat Peninsula in southern Skye, taking the loop roads that exit to the north and south as you please. There are some stretches of single-lane road, but none poses a problem.

Kyle of Lochalsh

⑯ *55 mi west of Inverness, 120 mi northwest of Glasgow.*

This little town is the mainland gateway to Skye. Time used to mean nothing in this part of Scotland—so many other things were of greater importance. But the area has seen great changes in recent years, as the Skye Bridge has transformed not only travel to Skye but the very seascape itself. The most noticeable visitor attraction, though (in fact, almost a cliché), is still the castle, slightly east of the town. At Dornie, guarding the confluence of lochs Long, Alsh, and Duich, stands that most picturesque of all Scottish castles, **Eilean Donan Castle,** perched on a little islet connected to the mainland by a stone-arched bridge. Dating from the 14th century, this romantic icon has all the massive stone walls, timber ceilings, and winding stairs that anyone could ask for. Empty and neglected for years after being bombarded by frigates of the Royal Navy during an abortive Spanish-Jacobite landing in 1719, it was almost entirely rebuilt from a ruin in the early 20th century. Now the hero of travel brochures, Eilean Donan has been fea-

★ ⑰

tured in many Hollywood movies and TV series. ⊠ *Dornie,* ☎ FAX *01599/ 555202.* ⊠ *£3.75.* ⊘ *Apr.–Oct., daily 9–6.*

Broadford

🔞 *8 mi west of Kyle of Lochalsh via Skye Bridge.*

One of the larger of Skye's settlements, Broadford lies along the shore of Broadford Bay, which has on occasion welcomed whales to its sheltered waters. Other unusual wildlife can be seen and handled at the **Serpentarium** (⊠ The Old Mill, Harrapool, ☎ 01471/822209), in the town center, where snakes, frogs, lizards, and tortoises are on show. An unlikely but worthwhile stop-off is **Sutherlands** (⊠ Broadford IV49 9AN, ☎ 01471/822225), where the Esso gas station offers a lot more than gasoline: 24-hour car rental (with pickup service at Armadale Pier or Kyle of Lochalsh), a bureau de change, a launderette, a well-stocked gift and book shop, and a wide variety of fresh foods and ready-made snacks.

Lodging

£ 🏠 **Ptarmigan.** This top-of-the-range no-smoking bed-and-breakfast es-
★ tablishment is run by the Macphies, a couple who know Skye inside out and can help with planning your route (whether driving or hiking), birdwatching, crafts shopping, or anything else. The three bedrooms, all with sea views, have modern dark-wood furnishings, neutral wall coverings, and sophisticated green-and-purple tartan drapes, while the cozy sitting room, lined with large-scale maps of the island, has a window looking right onto the water's edge, ideal for spotting birds, otters, and the occasional whale. There is a separate cottage also, which has cooking facilities. ⊠ *Broadford, Isle of Skye, IV49 9AQ,* ☎ *01471/822744,* FAX *01471/822745. 3 rooms with shower, 1 cottage. AE, MC, V.* ⊗

Outdoor Activities and Sports
Broadford Bicycle Hire (⊠ Fairwinds, Elgol Rd., Broadford, ☎ 01471/ 822270) rents bicycles year-round.

Shopping
Craft Encounters (⊠ Broadford, ☎ 01471/822754) stocks an array of Skye crafts, including pottery and jewelry.

Armadale

🔞 *43 mi south of Portree, 5 mi (ferry crossing) west of Mallaig.*

Sleat is the name given to the southernmost part of Skye, where rolling interior moorlands, scattered with rivers and lochans, give way to enchanting hidden coves and scattered waterside communities. Sleat well rewards a day or two spent exploring its side roads and its many craft outlets. For most visitors, Armadale is the first town to visit.

At Armadale the popular **Armadale Castle Gardens and the Museum of the Isles** (which includes the Clan Donald Centre) tell the story of the Macdonalds and their proud title: the Lords of the Isles, with the help of an excellent audiovisual presentation. In the 15th century they were powerful enough to threaten the authority of the Stuart monarchs of Scotland. There is a major exhibition here in a restored part of the castle, as well as extensive gardens and nature trails, a large and well-chosen selection in the gift shop, and a restaurant. There is also a choice of high-quality accommodation in cottages with kitchen facilities on the grounds. ⊠ *Armadale, ½ mi north of Armadale Pier,* ☎ *01471/844305 or 01471/844227.* ⊠ *£3.85.* ⊘ *Clan Donald Centre: Apr.–Oct., daily 9:30–5:30 (last entry 5); gardens: year-round.*

Dining and Lodging

££££–££££   ✗🏠 **Kinloch Lodge.** Just a few miles up the road from Armadale, this hotel offers elegant comfort on the edge of the world. Run by Lord and Lady Macdonald with flair and considerable professionalism, Kinloch Lodge is a supremely comfortable country house, with warm, restful lounges with antiques, chintz fabrics, bookcases, and family photographs. Snug bedrooms are individually decorated with quilted bedspreads and pastel wallpaper. Lady Macdonald is now offering cooking demonstrations and short courses (very popular, so advance booking is essential). Dinner is served at 8 PM in the handsome dining room, and you choose from the small menu that changes daily and features such savory dishes as smoked Achiltibuie chicken and melon with curried mayonnaise; roast pork stuffed with spinach, shallots, and Parmesan cheese in vermouth gravy; and for dessert, dark chocolate nemesis. ⊠ *Sleat, Isle of Skye, IV43 8QY,* ☎ *01471/833214,* FAX *01471/833277. 14 rooms with bath. Restaurant, fishing, helipad. AE, MC, V.* ◈

£££   ✗🏠 **Hotel Eilean Iarmain.** The Isle Ornsay Hotel (as it is also more pronounceably known) sits beside the shore and is an enchanting, old-world haven of wood paneling, chintz, antiques, and soft country-house-style color schemes. All 12 rooms—six in the main hotel and six in the neighboring Garden House—as well as the four suites in the old stable block are individually decorated, giving each a distinctive character. Try the Tower Room, with its nooks and crannies, or the room in which the canopy bed came from Armadale Castle. The menu in the dining room changes daily but might include such dishes as seared venison with juniper and rowan or steamed mussels with cream and whisky. ⊠ *Isleornsay, Sleat, Isle of Skye, IV43 8QR,* ☎ *01471/833332,* FAX *01471/ 833275. 12 rooms with bath, 4 suites. Fishing, helipad. AE, MC, V.*

££   ✗🏠 **Ardvasar Hotel.** This 19th-century roadside inn offers accommodations in pine-furnished rooms and a bar where you will meet all the locals (beware: it often gets smoky). The restaurant serves competently cooked familiar fare, such as steaks and roasts. ⊠ *Ardvasar, Isle of Skye, IV45 8RS,* ☎ *01471/844223,* FAX *01471/844495. 10 rooms with bath. Bar. AE, DC, MC, V.*

Outdoor Activities and Sports

The Skye Ferry Filling Station (⊠ Ardvasar, ☎ 01471/844249) rents bicycles in summer.

Shopping

Enjoying spacious new premises that replaced the old overgrown shed, **Ragamuffin** (⊠ Armadale Pier, ☎ 01471/844217) specializes in designer knitwear and clothing. Once inside, you'll find a huge array of styles, and the friendly staff will be happy to make you a cup of coffee while you browse, then mail your purchases back home for you. **Skye Batiks** (⊠ Armadale, ☎ 01471/844396), just up the road from the pier, stocks unusual Celtic-influenced batik clothing, cushion covers, and wall hangings; chunky, handwoven cotton smocks, jackets, and skirts; silver jewelry; wood carvings; and much more (they also have a shop at the Green, in Portree). **Harlequin Knitwear** (⊠ Duisdale, Sleat, ☎ 01471/833321) sells colorful wool sweaters created by local designer Chryssy Gibbs. She works from her home, which is up a rather bumpy, steep track; but it's worth the trek because once you arrive (and after being greeted by the family cats), you will find distinctive sweaters (with descriptive names such as Stained Glass, Mosaic, and Tudor) of Shetland wool, mohair, or chenille, in colors that reflect the tones of the Skye landscape.

Portree

⓴ *43 mi north of Armadale.*

The population center of the island, Portree is not overburdened by historical features, but it's a pleasant center clustered around a small and sheltered bay, and it makes a good touring base. On the outskirts of town is **Tigh na Coille: The Aros Experience** (⊠ Viewfield Rd., Portree IV51 9EU, ☎ 01478/613649), where the story of Skye, told via tableaux and a taped guide (daily for £3.50), continues where the Armadale Castle audiovisual tour left off; together the two provide an excellent account of Skye's often turbulent history over the centuries. You'll also find a gift shop, restaurant, and cinema (which also hosts musical events), and forest walks can be enjoyed in the surrounding woodlands: discover the link between the Gaelic alphabet and tree names.

Dining and Lodging

£££ ✕🏨 **Cuillin Hills Hotel.** Set just outside Portree, this gabled hotel has many rooms with outstanding views over Portree Bay toward the Cuillin Hills. Bedrooms are individually decorated in bold floral patterns, and there is a choice of public rooms. The seafood dishes in the restaurant are especially tasty: try the local prawns, lobster, or scallops, or the glazed ham carved from the bone. ⊠ *Portree, Isle of Skye,* ☎ *01478/612003,* 🆏 *01478/613092. 30 rooms with bath or shower. Restaurant, bar. AE, MC, V.* 🍽

££ ✕🏨 **Rosedale Hotel.** Right on the harbor, the Rosedale offers modern accommodations and delicious Scottish cooking within converted 19th-century buildings. The menu might include breast of duck with cranberries and parsnip puree or pasta rolls with smoked haddock and lemon butter. ⊠ *Beaumont Crescent, Portree, Isle of Skye, IV51 9DB,* ☎ *01478/613131,* 🆏 *01478/612531. 23 rooms with bath or shower. MC, V. Closed Nov.–Mar.* 🍽

Shopping

Skye Original Prints (⊠ Portree, Isle of Skye, ☎ 01478/612544) stocks original prints by local artist Tom Mackenzie. **Skye Batiks** (⊠ The Green, Portree, Isle of Skye, ☎ 01478/613331; ⊠ Armadale, ☎ 01471/844396) is the second outlet of this unique company, whose batik wall hangings and clothing and handwoven cotton smocks you may have seen at Armadale. **Croft Comforts Antiques** (⊠ 2 Wentworth St., Portree, Isle of Skye, IV51 9EJ, ☎ 🆏 01478/613762) has an enviable selection of silver, porcelain, and pottery, as well as larger items; in addition, it provides a mine of information about Skye: just ask for David or Fiona Middleton's advice on places to eat, attractions to visit, or hidden coves to enjoy, and you won't be disappointed.

Trotternish Peninsula

㉑ *16 mi north of Portree via A855.*

As the road goes north from Portree, cliffs rise to the left. They are actually the edge of an ancient lava flow, set back from the road, and running for miles as your rugged companion. In some places the hardened lava has created spectacular features, including a curious pinnacle called the **Old Man of Storr.** The A855 travels past neat white croft houses and forestry plantings to **Kilt Rock.** Everyone on the Skye tour circuit stops here to peep over the cliffs (there is a safe viewing platform) for a look at the geology of the cliff edge: bands of two types (and colors) of rock create a folded, pleated effect, just like a kilt.

The spectacular **Quiraing** dominates the horizon 5 mi past Kilt Rock. For a closer view of the strange pinnacles and rock forms, make a left onto a small road at Brogaig by Staffin Bay. There is a parking lot near the point where this road breaches the ever-present cliff line, though you will have to be physically fit to walk back toward the Quiraing itself, where the rock formations and cliffs are most dramatic. The trail is on uneven, stony ground, and it's a steep scramble up to the rock formations. In ages past stolen cattle were hidden deep within the Quiraing's rocky jaws.

The main A855 reaches around the top end of Trotternish, to the **Skye Museum of Island Life** at Kilmuir, where you can see the old farming ways brought to life. Included in the displays and exhibits are documents and photographs, reconstructed interiors, and implements. Flora Macdonald, helpmate of Bonnie Prince Charlie, is buried nearby. ⊠ *Kilmuir, Isle of Skye,* ☎ FAX *01470/552206.* ⚏ *£1.75.* ☉ *Easter–Oct., Mon.–Sat. 9:30–5:30.*

Dining and Lodging

££–£££ ✕⛨ **Flodigarry Country House Hotel.** Close links with Flora Macdonald, Prince Charles Edward Stuart's helpmate, are not the least of the attractions at this country-house hotel, which is well placed for exploring the north and west of Skye. Yes, you can actually have a room in Flora's own cottage, adjacent to the hotel, where six of her children were born. The main hotel is a bit grander but just as comfortable, and excellent seafood is a feature of the restaurant's menu. ⊠ *Staffin, Isle of Skye, IV51 9HZ,* ☎ *01470/552203,* FAX *01470/552301. 19 rooms with bath or shower. Bar. MC, V.* ⚑

Waternish Peninsula

㉒ *20 mi northwest of Portree via A850.*

The northwest corner of Skye has scattered crofting communities, magnificent coastal views, and two good restaurants, well worth the trip in themselves. In the Hallin area, look westward for an islet-scattered sea loch with miniature cliffs rising from the water—and looking like miniature models of full-size islands—while just above the village of Stein, notice on the left side of the road a restored and inhabited "black house" (a thatch cottage blackened over time because a hole in its roof stood in for a chimney), today a rare sight on Skye and, in any event, now painted white.

At **Edinbane Pottery,** in southern Waternish, where stoneware pottery is fired in a wood-fired kiln, you can visit the workshops to watch the potters, then buy from the showroom. ⊠ *Edinbane, Isle of Skye,* ☎ *01470/ 582234.* ☉ *Easter–Oct., daily 9–6; Nov.–Easter, Mon.–Fri. 9–6.*

Dining and Lodging

££ ✕ **Loch Bay Seafood Restaurant.** Down on the waterfront at Stein is a
★ distinctive black-and-white-painted restaurant known as the place where the island's top chefs eat on their nights off. The atmosphere is laid back, the fish and seafood freshly caught and simply prepared; top-quality ingredients are allowed to speak for themselves without being overwhelmed with extraneous sauces. ⊠ *Stein, Isle of Skye, IV55 8GA,* ☎ *01470/ 592235. MC, V. Closed late Oct.–wk before Easter, and weekends.*

££ ✕⛨ **Greshornish House.** A MacLeod (of Dunvegan Castle) house until 1959, Greshornish now offers spacious, if rather eclectically furnished, public rooms and a variety of bedrooms of all shapes and sizes. However, the best reason to come here is the restaurant, where mahogany tables are laid with damask, crystal, and candelabra. The menu offers, for example, scallops poached in white wine with flakes of smoked haddock and cream, freshly caught local lobster or king prawns with salad and mayonnaise, or Skye lamb cutlets with heather honey and ginger, served with wild Skye berries. ⊠ *Greshornish, Isle of Skye, IV51 9PN,* ☎ *01470/582266,* 𝔽𝔸𝕏 *01470/582345. AE, MC, V.*

Dunvegan Castle

㉓ *22 mi west of Portree.*

In a commanding position above a sea loch, Dunvegan Castle has been the seat of the chiefs of Clan MacLeod for more than 700 years. Though greatly changed over the centuries, a gloomy ambience prevails, and there's plenty of family history on display, notably the Fairy Flag—a silk banner, thought to be originally from Rhodes or Syria and believed to have magically saved the clan from danger. The banner's powers are said to suffice for only one more use. Also make time to visit the gardens, with water garden and falls, fern house, a walled garden, and viewing points. ⊠ *Dunvegan,* ☎ *01470/521206.* 🖾 *Garden only: £3.80; castle and garden: £5.50; boat trips to see the seals £4.* ☉ *Mid-Mar.–Oct., daily 10–5:30 (last admission 5); Nov.–mid-Mar., daily 11–4 (last entry 3:30).*

Dining and Lodging

£ ✕🏨 **Roskill House.** A white 19th-century croft house (which once housed the local post office in the dining room), Roskill is more home-away-from-home in atmosphere than a country-house-style hotel. Bedrooms have been recently redecorated in bolder colors; the lounge has books and games; and the dining room, with a publike feel—stone walls, dark stick-back chairs, and scarlet carpet—has old favorites on the menu, such as Lancashire hot pot, pork Haslet with bacon, onion and mustard sauce, and raspberry trifle. ⊠ *Roskhill by Dunvegan, Isle of Skye, IV55 8ZD,* ☎ *01470/521317,* 𝔽𝔸𝕏 *01470/521761. 4 rooms, 2 with shower, 1 with bath and shower (ground floor), 1 with private hall bath. AE, MC, V.*

Glendale

㉔ *2 mi south of Dunvegan.*

The Glendale Visitor Route is a signed driving trail through the westernmost area of northwest Skye and leads past a variety of craft outlets, museums, and other attractions for visitors. **Skye Silver** (⊠ The Old School, Colbost, Glendale, ☎ 01470/511263), west of Dunvegan, designs gold and silver jewelry with a Celtic theme and also has more unusual pieces that reflect the natural forms of the seashore and countryside: silver-coral earrings, silver-leaf pendants, and starfish and cockleshell earrings are just a few of these landscape-inspired designs.

The **Toy Museum** (⊠ Glendale, ☎ 01470/511240), open Monday–Saturday 10–6, is a trip back to childhood, with bears, dolls, trains, puzzles and games, books, and puppets. Admission is £2.50. **Borreraig Park** (⊠ Borreraig Park, by Dunvegan, ☎ 01470/511311) has a fascinating museum of island life (rightly described by the owner as "a unique gallimaufry for your delight and edification") that includes a detailed series of panels on the making of bagpipes and on the history of the MacCrimmons, hereditary pipers to the Clan MacLeod. It also has a superb gift shop that stocks island-made sweaters (the exact sheep can be named), wool, walnut knitting needles, bagpipes, Celtic silver and gold jewelry, and CDs of traditional music. You won't see many of the items elsewhere on Skye.

Dining and Lodging

££££ ✕🏨 **Three Chimneys Restaurant with Rooms.** Another of Skye's top-notch restaurants, Shirley Spear's shore-side cottage might be small on space, but it's big on flavor: fresh local seafood, beef, lamb and game are transformed into dishes such as prawn and lobster bisque, or red-deer scallops with pear-and-potato *dauphinoise*; Skye soft fruits (raspberries, strawberries, blackcurrants) may follow. Adjacent to the restaurant are luxury accommodations in a courtyard wing, with magnificent sea views from all the rooms. ⊠ *Colbost, by Dunvegan, Isle of Skye, IV55 8ZT,* ☎ *01470/511258,* 𝖥𝖠𝖷 *01470/511358. 6 rooms with bath. MC, V. Closed for lunch Sun.* ✍

Glen Brittle

★ ㉕ *28 mi southeast of Glendale.*

You can enjoy spectacular mountain scenery in Glen Brittle, with some fine views of the Cuillin ridges, though it is not a place for the ordinary walker (there are many dangerous ridges and steep faces). Glen Brittle extends off the A863/B8009 on the west side of the island. Having explored Glen Brittle, go farther west on the B8009; then take the next left turn (signed TALISKER), at Carbost, which will take you 4 mi across moorland to Talisker House, one of the best places to stay on Skye.

Lodging

££ 🏨 **Talisker House.** Dating from the 1720s, this beautiful small coun-
★ try house set beneath the great rocky peak of Preshal Mhor looks down over Talisker Bay, where sea eagles skim the cliff tops. Bedrooms are spaciously elegant, with antiques and chintz; the drawing room has a grand piano and open fire; the menu (dinner is for residents only) is a treat of homemade practically everything: breads, preserves, puddings, soups, muesli, with fine local seafood and game. ⊠ *Talisker, Isle of Skye, IV47 8SF,* ☎ *01478/640245,* 𝖥𝖠𝖷 *01478/640214. 4 rooms, 2 with bath and 2 with shower. MC, V. Closed Nov.–mid-Mar.* ✍

Elgol

㉖ *12 mi southeast of Glen Brittle.*

The B8083 leads from **Broadford** to one of the finest views in Scotland. This road passes through **Strath Suardal** and little **Loch Cill Chriosd** (Kilchrist) by a ruined church. If there are cattle wading in the loch and the light is soft—typical of Skye—then this place takes on the air of a romantic oil painting. Skye marble, with its attractive green veining, was produced from the marble quarry at **Torrin.**

You can appreciate breathtaking views of **Blaven mountain** as the A881 continues to **Elgol,** a gathering of crofts along this road that descends to a pier. Admire the heart-stopping profile of the Cuillin peaks from the shore, or, at a point about halfway down the hill, you can find the path that goes toward them across the rough grasslands.

For even better views, take a boat trip on the **Bella Jane** (⊠ Elgol Jetty, ☎ 0800/731–3089) from Elgol jetty toward Loch Coruisk; you'll be able to land and walk up to the loch itself, as well as see seals during your boat trip. The boat excursion is offered from April through October, daily, with advance booking (ticket price is £12.50) essential.

OUTER HEBRIDES (WESTERN ISLES)

The Outer Hebrides—the Western Isles in common parlance—stretch about 130 mi from end to end and lie about 50 mi from the Scottish mainland. This splintered archipelago extends from the Butt of Lewis in the north to the 600-ft Barra Head on Berneray in the south, whose lighthouse has the greatest arc of visibility in the world. The Isle of Lewis and Harris is the northernmost and largest of the group. The island's only major town, Stornoway, is on a nearly landlocked harbor on the east coast of Lewis; it's probably the most convenient starting point for a driving tour of the islands if you're approaching the Western Isles from the Northern Highlands.

Just south of the Sound of Harris is North Uist, rich in monoliths, chambered cairns, and other reminders of a prehistoric past. Though it is one of the smaller islands in the chain, Benbecula, sandwiched between North and South Uist and sometimes referred to as the Hill of the Fords, is in fact less bare and neglected looking than its bigger neighbors to the north. South Uist, once a refuge of the old Catholic faith, is dotted with ruined forts and chapels; in summer its wild gardens burst with alpine and rock plants. Eriskay and a scattering of islets almost block the 6-mi strait between South Uist and Barra, the southernmost major formation in the Outer Hebrides, an isle you can walk across in an hour.

Harris tweed is available at many outlets on the islands, including some of the weavers' homes; keep an eye out for signs directing you to weavers' workshops. Sundays on the islands are strictly observed days of rest, and nearly all shops and visitor attractions are closed.

Stornoway

㉗ *2½-hr ferry trip from Ullapool.*

The port capital for the Outer Hebrides is Stornoway on Lewis. In the Town Hall, the **An Lanntair Gallery** has exhibitions of contemporary and traditional art that change monthly, as well as a coffee and gift shop and frequent traditional Gaelic musical and theatrical events. ⊠ *Town Hall, S. Beach St., Stornoway,* ☎ *01851/703307.* ⌂ *Free.* ☉ *Mon.–Sat. 10–5:30.*

Lodging

£ ⊞ **Ravenswood.** On a quiet residential street just a few minutes' walk from the harbor and town center, the house dates from the turn of the century. A stay reveals high-quality B&B accommodations, with a residents' lounge and attractive gardens. ⊠ *12 Matheson Rd., Stornoway, Lewis, HS87 2LR,* ☎ *01851/702673. 3 rooms, 2 with bath or shower. No credit cards.*

Outdoor Activities and Sports

Hire bicycles from **Alex Dan Cycle Centre** (⊠ 67 Kenneth St., Stornoway, ☎ 01851/704025).

En Route The best road to use to explore the territory north of Stornoway is the A857, which runs first across the island to the northwest and then to the northeast all the way to Port of Ness (about 30 mi).

Port of Ness

30 mi north of Stornoway.

The stark, windswept community of Port of Ness cradles a small harbor squeezed in among the rocks and overlooked by **Harbour View,** a small gallery and café. At the northernmost point of Lewis stands the **㉘ Butt of Lewis Lighthouse,** designed by David and Thomas Stevenson (of the prominent engineering family, whose best-known member was actually not an engineer at all: the novelist Robert Louis Stevenson [1850–94]). The lighthouse was first lit in 1862. The adjacent cliffs provide a good vantage point for viewing seabirds, whales, and porpoises. The lighthouse is just a few minutes northwest of Port of Ness along the B8014.

Shopping

At **Borgh Pottery** (⊠ Fivepenny House, Borve, on the road to Ness, ☎ 01851/850345) you can buy attractive hand-thrown studio pottery made on the premises, including lamps, vases, mugs, and dishes.

Arnol

21 mi southwest of Port of Ness, 16 mi northwest of Stornoway.

㉙ In the small community of Arnol, look for signs off the A858 for the **Arnol Black House,** a well-preserved example of an increasingly rare type of traditional Hebridean home. Once common throughout the islands (as recently as 50 years ago), these dwellings were built without mortar and thatched on a timber framework without eaves. Other characteristic features include an open central peat hearth and the absence of a chimney—hence the sooty atmosphere and the designation *black*. On display inside are many of the house's original furnishings. To reach Arnol from Port of Ness, go back south on the A857 and pick up the A858 at Barvas. ⊠ *Arnol,* ☎ *0131/668–8800.* ⧄ *£2.50.* ☉ *Apr.–Sept., Mon.–Sat. 9:30–6; Oct.–Mar., Mon.–Thurs. and Sat. 9:30–4.*

En Route Shawbost is home of the rather dusty but illuminating **Shawbost School Museum** (⊠ Shawbost, ☎ 01851/710213), which survives from the Highland Village Competition in 1970, during which school pupils gathered artifacts and contributed to displays aimed at illustrating a past way of life in Lewis. The museum is open April–November, Monday–Saturday, 10–5, with admission by donation. The scattered community of Carloway, on the other hand, is dominated by **Dun Carloway** (open at all times), one of the best-preserved Iron Age *brochs* (circular stone towers) in Scotland. The mysterious circular defensive tower of the Dun Carloway broch was built about 2,000 years ago, possibly as protection against seaborne raiders. The interpretative center explains more about the broch and its setting. Up a side road north from Carloway at **Garenin,** an old black-house village is gradually being brought back to life.

Calanais

22 mi southeast of Arnol.

★ ㉚ At Calanais (Callanish) are the **Calanais Standing Stones,** lines of megaliths reminiscent of those in Stonehenge, in England. Probably positioned in several stages between 3000 and 1500 BC, this grouping consists of an avenue of 19 monoliths extending northward from a circle of 13 stones, with other rows leading south, east, and west. It's believed they may have been used for astronomical observations. The site is accessible at any time. The **visitor center** (☎ 01851/621422) has an exhibition on the stones, a shop, and a tearoom. The restored black house next to the gate leading to the stones houses the **Callanish Stones Tearoom** (☎ 01851/621373), a more interesting atmosphere in which to take refreshment or browse among the crafts on display.

Tarbert

㉛ *47 mi south of Calanais.*

Tarbert is the main port of Harris, with one or two shops and accommodations. About 10 mi northwest of Tarbert on the B887 stands **Amhuinnsuidhe Castle** (the name is almost impossible for foreigners to pronounce—try avun-*shooee*), a turreted structure built in the 1860s by the earls of Dunmore as a base for fishing and hunting in the North Harris deer forest. **Traigh Luskentyre,** roughly 5 mi southwest of Tarbert, is a spectacular example of Harris's tidy selection of beaches—2 mi of yellow sands adjacent to **Traigh Seilebost** beach, with superb views northward to the hills of the Forest of Harris.

Lodging

£££ 🏰 **Ardvourlie Castle.** A former Victorian hunting lodge, Ardvourlie is
★ set in splendid isolation amid the dramatic mountain scenery of Harris, an ideal habitat for hill walking. The decor is bold, idiosyncratic,
and entirely in keeping with the High Victorian atmosphere of the castle. The country-house hospitality is complemented by the well-stocked
library and roaring fires. The cooking (for guests only) is along traditional lines and of a high standard, favoring fresh local produce and,
often, wild game. ⊠ *Isle of Harris, 15 mi north of Tarbert, signed off
the A859, HS3 3AB,* ☎ *01859/502307,* 🆙 *01859/502348. 4 rooms,
3 with bath, 1 with shower. Restaurant, library. No credit cards.*

Northton

16 mi south of Tarbert.

This little community has two attractions: The **McGillivray Centre** (☎
01859/502011) focuses on the life and work of William McGillivray,
a noted naturalist with strong links to Harris. **Co Leis Thu?** (⊠ The Old
Schoolhouse, Northton HS3 3JA, ☎ 🆙 01859/520258) is a family-
history resource center with a genealogical research service, publications (which can be purchased on-line), and exhibitions.

Rodel

20 mi south of Tarbert.

At the southernmost point of Harris is the community of Rodel. Here
③② you'll find **St. Clement's Church,** a cruciform church standing on a hillock.
It was built around 1500 and contains the magnificently sculptured
tomb (1528) of the church's builder, Alasdair Crotach, MacLeod chief
of Dunvegan Castle. An arched recess contains sculpted panels showing, among other scenes, St. Michael and Satan weighing souls. There
are also other effigies and carvings within this building, the most impressive pre-Reformation church in the Outer Hebrides.

North Uist

8 mi south of Rodel via ferry from Leverburgh, Harris.

③③ At **Newtonferry (Port nan Long),** by Otternish and the ferry pier for
the Leverburgh (Harris) ferry service, stand the remains of what was
reputed to be the last inhabited broch in North Uist, **Dun an Sticar.**
This defensive tower, reached by a causeway over the loch, was home
to Hugh Macdonald, a descendant of MacDonald of Sleat, until 1602.

You can see the ruins of **Trinity Temple (Teampull na Trionaid),** a medieval college and monastery said to have been founded in the 13th
century by Beathag, daughter of Somerled, the progenitor of the Clan
Donald, 8 mi southwest of Lochmaddy, off the A865.

The **Barpa Langass Chambered Cairn,** dating from the 3rd millennium
BC, is the only chambered cairn in the Western Isles known to have retained its inner chamber fully intact. It sits very close to the A867 on
the stretch between Lochmaddy and Clachan.

The **Balranald Nature Reserve** (⊠ Visitor Centre at Goular, ☎ 01870/
620369 or 01463/715000), administered by the Royal Society for the
Protection of Birds (RSPB), is home to large numbers of waders and
seabirds, including red-necked phalaropes, living in a varied habitat
of loch, marsh, *machair* (grasslands just behind the beach), and sandy
and rocky shore. The reserve can be viewed anytime (guided walks by
an RSPB warden April–September), but visitors are asked to keep to

the paths during breeding season (March–July) so as not to disturb the birds. It is on the west side of North Uist, about 3 mi northwest of Bayhead, which you can reach via A865.

Outdoor Activities and Sports

Uist Outdoor Centre (⊠ Lochmaddy, North Uist, ☎ 01876/500480) offers a wide range of activities, from rock climbing to diving, from walking to offshore island trips and sea-kayaking expeditions.

South Uist

34 mi south of Newtonferry via Grimsay, Benbecula, and 3 causeways.

You can travel the length of South Uist along Route A865, making short treks off this main road on your way to Lochboisdale, on the southeast coast of the island. At Lochboisdale you can get ferries to Barra, the southernmost principal island of the Outer Hebrides, or to Oban, on the mainland.

About 5 mi south of the causeway from Benbecula, atop Reuval Hill, stands the 125-ft-high statue of the Madonna and Child known as **Our Lady of the Isles.** The work of sculptor Hew Lorimer, the statue was erected in 1957 by the local Catholic community. A few miles south of Reuval Hill, to the west of A865, you will come to the **Loch Druidibeg National Nature Reserve.** One of only two remaining British native— that is, nonmigrating—populations of greylag geese make their home here in a fresh and brackish loch environment (stop at the warden's office for information about access).

A few miles south of Howmore, just west of A865, stand the ruins of **Ormaclete Castle,** built in 1708 for the chief of the Clan Ranald but accidentally destroyed by fire in 1715 on the eve of the Battle of Sheriffmuir, during which the chief was killed.

Kildonan Museum and Heritage Centre (⊠ Kildonan, ☎ 01878/710343) focuses on local history, archaeology, and culture and has a crafts shop and tearoom. At Gearraidh Bhailteas (just west of A865 near Milton), you can see the ruins of **Flora Macdonald's birthplace.** South Uist's most famous daughter, Flora helped the Young Pretender, Prince Charles Edward Stuart, avoid capture and was feted as a heroine afterward.

Shopping

Hebridean Jewelry (⊠ Garrieganichy, Lochdar, ☎ 01870/610288) makes decorative jewelry and framed pictures; the owners also run a crafts shop.

THE NORTHERN HIGHLANDS A TO Z

Arriving and Departing

By Bus

Scottish Citylink (☎ 0990/505050) and **National Express** (☎ 0990/808080) run buses from England to Inverness, Ullapool, Thurso, Scrabster, and Wick. There are also coach connections between the ferry ports of Tarbert and Stornoway; consult the local tourist information center for details.

By Car and Ferry

The fastest route to this area is the A9 to the gateway town of Inverness. The ferry services—run by **Caledonian MacBrayne,** called CalMac—link the Outer Hebrides (☞ Getting Around by Car and Ferry, *below*). Ferries run from Ullapool to Stornoway (☎ 01854/612358), from Oban to Castlebay and Lochboisdale (☎ 01631/566688), and from Uig, on the Isle of Skye, to Tarbert and Lochmaddy (☎ 01470/542219). Causeways link North Uist, Benbecula, and South Uist.

By Plane

The main airports for the Northern Highlands are **Inverness** and **Wick** (both on the mainland). There is direct air service from Edinburgh and Glasgow to Inverness and from Edinburgh to Wick. Contact **British Airways** (☎ 0345/222111). You can fly from London's Luton Airport to Inverness on one of the daily **easyJet** (☎ 0990/292929) flights. **Gill Air** (☎ 0191/214–6666) operates the Aberdeen–Wick service (weekdays). There are island flight connections to Stornoway (Lewis) and to Barra and Benbecula, in the Outer Hebrides; contact British Airways for details.

By Train

Main railway stations in the area include Oban (for Barra and the Uists) and Kyle of Lochalsh (for Skye), on the west coast, or Inverness (for points north to Thurso and Wick). There is direct service from London to Inverness and connecting service from Edinburgh and Glasgow. For information contact the **National Train Enquiry Line** (☎ 0345/484950).

Getting Around

It is in the Highlands and islands that the **Freedom of Scotland Travelpass** really becomes useful, saving you money on ferries, trains, and some buses (☞ Smart Travel Tips A to Z).

By Bus

Highland Country Buses (in the mainland and Skye, ☎ 01463/233371) provides bus service in the Highlands area. On the Outer Hebrides a number of small operators run regular routes to most towns and villages. The **post-bus** service—which also delivers mail—becomes increasingly important in remote areas; it supplements the regular bus service, which runs only a few times per week because of the small population in the region. A full timetable of services for the Northern Highlands (and the rest of Scotland) is available from the **Royal Mail** (✉ 7 Strothers La., Inverness IV1 1AA, ☎ 01463/256273).

By Car and Ferry

Note that in this sparsely populated area, distances between gas stations can be considerable. Although getting around is easy, even on single-lane roads, the choice of routes is restricted by the rugged terrain. Because of the infrequent bus services and sparse railway stations, a car is definitely the best way to explore this region.

The **Island Hopscotch** planned-route ticket and the **Island Rover** pass, both offered by CalMac, give considerable reductions on interisland ferry fares; for details contact **Caledonian MacBrayne** (✉ Ferry Terminal, Gourock PA19 1QP, ☎ 01475/650100).

An important caveat for visitors driving in this area: the twisting, winding single-lane roads here demand a degree of driving dexterity. Local rules of the road require that when two cars meet, whichever driver reaches a passing place first must stop in it or opposite it and allow the oncoming car to continue. Small cars tend to yield to large commercial vehicles. Never park in passing places, and remember that these sections of the road can also allow traffic behind you to pass; don't hold up a vehicle trying to pass you—tempers can flare over such discourtesies.

By Plane

British Regional Airways/Loganair (☎ 0345/222111) operates flights between the islands of Barra, Benbecula, and Stornoway in the Outer Hebrides (weekdays only).

By Train

Stations on the northern lines (Inverness to Thurso/Wick and Inverness to Kyle of Lochalsh) include Beauly, Muir of Ord, and Dingwall; on the Thurso/Wick line, Alness, Invergordon, Fearn, Tain, Ardgay, Culrain, Invershin, Lairg, Rogart, Golspie, Brora, Helmsdale, Kildonan, Kinbrace, Forsinard, Altnabreac, Scotscalder, and Georgemas Junction; and on the Kyle line, Garve, Lochluichart, Achanalt, Achnasheen, Achnashellach, Strathcarron, Attadale, Stromeferry, Duncraig, Plockton, and Duirinish.

Contacts and Resources

Car Rentals

Europcar Ltd. (⊠ Telford St., Inverness, ☎ 01463/235337). **Hertz** (⊠ Dalcross Airport, Inverness, ☎ 01667/462652).

Emergencies

Ambulance, fire, or police: ☎ 999. (No coins are needed for emergency calls from public phone booths.)

Guided Tours

ORIENTATION

From Inverness, **Spa Coach Tours** (⊠ Strathpeffer, ☎ 01997/421311) offers tours during the summer season.

SPECIAL-INTEREST

From Inverness, **Highland Insight Tours and Travel** (☎ 01463/831533) offers personalized touring holidays and full-day or half-day tours that cater to any interest. **James Johnson** (☎ FAX 01463/790179) will drive you anywhere, and knows a lot about the Highlands and islands, including the Outer Hebrides. **Puffin Express** (☎ 01463/717181, FAX 01463/717188) runs rather more unusual "Wildlife and Stone Age" day tours from Inverness between Easter and September (in the winter, the owner goes wolf-watching in Poland).

A number of small firms run boat cruises along the spectacular west-coast seaboard. On Skye there is also a broad selection of mountain guides. Contact the local tourist information center for details about local operators (☞ Visitor Information, *below*). **Dunvegan Sea Cruises,** at Dunvegan Castle, Skye (☎ 01470/521206), runs a boat trip to the nearby seal colony (£4). Wildlife cruises are operated from John o'-Groats harbor by **John o'Groats Ferries** (☎ 01955/611353), daily from mid-June through August. The trip takes passengers into the Pentland Firth, to Duncansby Stacks and the island of Stroma, and it offers spectacular cliff scenery and bird life. The same company runs day tours to Orkney from Inverness (with a guided tour of the islands), daily June through early September.

Raasay Outdoor Centre (⊠ Raasay House, Isle of Raasay reached by ferry from Sconser, Isle of Skye, ☎ 01478/660266) organizes a variety of residential or day courses in kayaking, sailing, windsurfing, climbing, abseiling (rappelling), archery, walking, and navigation skills.

Late-Night Pharmacies

These are not found in rural areas. Pharmacies in the main towns—Thurso, Wick, Stornoway—keep normal shop hours. In an emergency the police will provide assistance in locating a pharmacist. General practitioners may also dispense medicines.

Visitor Information

Dornoch (⊠ The Square, Dornoch IV25 3SD, ☎ 01862/810400). **North Kessock** (⊠ North Kessock IV1 1XB, ☎ 01463/731505). **Portree,** Isle of Skye (⊠ Bayfield House, Bayfield Rd., Portree, Isle of Skye, IV51

9EL, ☎ 01478/612137). **Stornoway,** Isle of Lewis and Harris (✉ 26 Cromwell St., ☎ 01851/702941). **Ullapool** (✉ Argyll St., Ullapool IV26 2UB, ☎ 01854/612135). **Wick** (✉ Whitechapel Rd. off High St., Wick KW1 4EA, ☎ 01955/602596).

Seasonal tourist information centers are at Bettyhill, Broadford (Skye), Castlebay (Barra, Outer Hebrides), Durness, Gairloch, Helmsdale, John o'Groats, Kyle of Lochalsh, Lairg, Lochboisdale (South Uist, Outer Hebrides), Lochcarron, Lochinver, Lochmaddy (North Uist, Outer Hebrides), Shiel Bridge, Strathpeffer, Thurso, and Uig.

10 THE NORTHERN ISLES

ORKNEY, SHETLAND

The wind and frequent mists, the austere
exposure, and the proximity to the sea make
the northern islands a challenge as much as
an adventure. Orkney—a cluster of almost
70 islands, 20 of which are inhabited—has
the greatest concentration of prehistoric sites
in all Scotland. Shetland's islands, with their
epic cliffs, dramatic fissurelike sea inlets,
and barren moors in the interior, do not
feel "British" at all.

By Gilbert
Summers

Updated by
Beth Ingpen

BOTH ORKNEY AND SHETLAND possess a Scandinavian heritage that gives their collective 200 islets an ambience different from any other region of Scotland. For mainland Scots, visiting this archipelago is a little like traveling abroad without having to worry about a different language or currency. Bound by the sea, both Orkney and Shetland are essentially bleak and austere, with awe-inspiring seascapes and genuinely warm, friendly people. Neither has yet been overrun by tourism.

An Orcadian has been defined as a farmer with a boat, while a Shetlander has been called a fisherman with a croft (small farm), a contrast in definitions that sums up the differences between Orkney and Shetland themselves. Orkney is the greener archipelago and is rich with artifacts—stone circles, burial chambers, ancient settlements, and fortifications that emphasize many centuries of continuous settlement. Shetland, with its ocean views and sparse landscapes—trees are a rarity because of ever-present wind—is endowed with a more remote atmosphere than neighboring Orkney. However, don't let Shetland's desolate countryside fool you—it has a wealth of historic interest and is far from being a backwater island. Oil money from its mineral resources and from its position as a crossroads in the northern seas for centuries have helped make Shetland a cosmopolitan place.

Pleasures and Pastimes

Boating
There are good anchorages among Orkney's many islands. Contact the tourist information centers for details. There are also sailboats available on Shetland. Details may be obtained from the Lerwick Boating Club, which can be contacted through the tourist information center.

Dining
Seafood is first class and so is Orkney's malt whisky. At its best, dining in the islands is as good as anywhere else, but vegetable gardeners do face some extra challenges from the northerly latitude. Look out for Orkney *bere bannocks* (bere is a kind of primitive barley, bannock a kind of oatcake), Orkney-brewed ales, and local cheeses.

CATEGORY	COST*
££££	over £40
£££	£30–£40
££	£15–£30
£	under £15

per person for a three-course meal, including VAT and excluding drinks and service

Diving
Orkney, especially the former wartime anchorage of Scapa Flow on Hoy, claims to have the best dive sites in Britain. Part of the attraction is some remains of the German navy that were scuttled here in 1919. Many boat-rental companies offer diving charters (contact the tourist information centers). Shetland also has exceptional underwater visibility, perfect for viewing the treasure wrecks and abundant marine life.

Festivals
Shetland has quite a strong cultural identity, thanks to its Scandinavian heritage. There are, for instance, books of local dialect verse, a whole folklore contained in knitting patterns, and a strong tradition of fiddle playing. In the middle of the long winter, at the end of January, the Shetlanders celebrate their Viking culture with the Up-Helly-

Aa Festival, which involves much merrymaking, dressing up, and the burning of a replica of a Viking long ship. The Shetland Folk Festival, held in April, and October's Shetland Accordion and Fiddle Festival both attract large numbers of visitors. Orkney's St. Magnus Festival, a musical celebration, is based in Kirkwall and usually held the third week in June. Orkney also has a jazz festival in April and an annual folk festival at the end of May.

Fishing

Sea angling is such a popular sport in Orkney that the local tourist board advises fishermen to book early. There are at least seven companies offering sea-angling boat rentals, with fishing rods available in most cases. Loch angling in Orkney is also popular; Loch of Harray and Loch of Stenness are the best-known spots. Contact the Orkney Tourist Board for information. Shetland, also renowned for sea angling, holds several competitions throughout the year. Contact the Shetland Association of Sea Anglers via the tourist information center.

Lodging

The Northern Isles' exoticism does not translate as "primitive": at its best, accommodations are about as good as anywhere else in Scotland.

CATEGORY	COST*
££££	over £110
£££	£80–£110
££	£45–£80
£	under £45

*All prices are for a standard double room, including service, breakfast, and VAT.

🐝 following the text of a review is your signal that the property has a Web site, where you will find details and, usually, images; for a link, visit www.fodors.com/urls.

Orkney Discount Ticket

Visitors to Orkney should take advantage of a joint entry ticket to all of Historic Scotland's Orkney sights. The ticket, available at all the sites themselves, costs only £10 (£9 in October and November) and is valid until all the sites have been visited. There is a generic telephone and fax number (☞ individual sites, below), which is operated daily 9–5, for all information relating to Orkney's Historic Scotland sites, so be sure to be specific when calling for information.

Exploring the Northern Isles

Both island groupings need at least a couple of days if you are to do more than just scratch the surface of learning their respective characteristics. The extra effort required to get there means Shetland certainly deserves four or five days: the Northern Isles in any case generate their own laid-back approach to life, and once there, you will not want to hurry around.

Numbers in the text correspond to numbers in the margin and on the Shetland Islands and the Orkney Islands maps.

Great Itineraries

Getting around is quite straightforward—the roads are good on both Shetland and Orkney. A fast and frequent interisland passenger and car ferry service makes island hopping perfectly practical. Only at peak season are reservations advisable.

IF YOU HAVE 1 DAY
Launch yourself from Inverness (☞ Arriving and Departing by Bus, *below*) on a day trip to Orkney—though it will be a long one—by bus

and ferry, to see some of Orkney's top historic sites. Shetland is not practicable for such a short length of time.

IF YOU HAVE 4 DAYS

You could get a good flavor of Orkney and take in the main sights—St. Magnus Cathedral and Earl Patrick's Palace and the Bishop's Palace on ⊞ **Kirkwall** ⑳—then go out to **Skara Brae** ⑯, **Maes Howe** ⑮, and the **Ring of Brogar** ⑭ (you could probably get to one of the other islands as well). You could also see a bit of Shetland in this length of time, provided you get a good night's sleep on the direct Orkney–Shetland ferry, leaving you a full day as soon as you arrive to take in the south of the island: **Shetland Croft House Museum** ④, **Jarlshof** ⑤, Sumburgh Head, **St. Ninian's Isle** ⑥, and so on. Staying overnight in ⊞ **Lerwick** ①, on your fourth day you could make a quick exploration of Lerwick itself and **Scalloway** ⑦, then make a trip up to **Esha Ness** to get the flavor of the north of Mainland. In theory, in this length of time it is possible to get out to the very end of Scotland at Muckle Flugga, but Shetland is such an extraordinary place that it merits more time.

IF YOU HAVE 8 DAYS

This is enough time in the Northern Isles for you to see all the main sights on Orkney and then catch a midweek ferry to Shetland, with enough time to get to the far north of Shetland as well.

When to Tour the Northern Isles

Go in the early summer when the bird colonies are at their most spectacular and the long northern daylight hours give you plenty of sightseeing time.

AROUND SHETLAND

The Shetland coastline is an incredible 900 mi because of all the indentations, and there isn't a point on the island farther than 3 mi from the sea. Settlements away from Lerwick, the primary town, are small and scattered—ask the friendly locals for directions.

Lerwick

❶ *14 hrs by ferry from Aberdeen.*

You would be remiss if you failed to explore some of Lerwick's nearby diversions before venturing beyond it. **Fort Charlotte** is a 17th-century Cromwellian stronghold, built to protect the Sound of Bressay. ☎ *0131/ 668–8800.* ⊡ *Free.* ⊙ *Apr.–Sept., daily 9:30–6; Oct.–Mar., Mon.–Sat. 9:30–4, Sun. 2–4.*

The **Shetland Museum** in Lerwick gives an interesting account of the development of the town, with displays on archaeology, art and textiles, shipping, and folk life. ⊠ *Lower Hillhead,* ☎ *01595/695057.* ⊡ *Free.* ⊙ *Mon., Wed., and Fri. 10–7; Tues., Thurs., and Sat. 10–5.*

❷ **Clickhimin Broch** (a *broch* is a circular stone structure), on the site of what was originally an Iron Age fortification, can be your introduction to these mysterious Pictish structures, possibly intended as a place of retreat and protection in the event of attack. South of the broch are vivid views of the cliffs at the south end of the island of Bressay, which shelters Lerwick Harbor. ⊠ *1 mi south of Lerwick,* ☎ *0131/668–8800.* ⊡ *Free.* ⊙ *Apr.–Sept., daily 9:30–6; Oct.–Mar., Mon.–Sat. 9:30–4, Sun. 2–4.*

Dining and Lodging

£££ ✕⊞ **Shetland Hotel.** Modern and well appointed (a result of the oil boom in the area and the needs of high-flying oil executives), the Shetland is directly opposite the ferry terminal in Lerwick. The hotel is done

The Shetland Islands

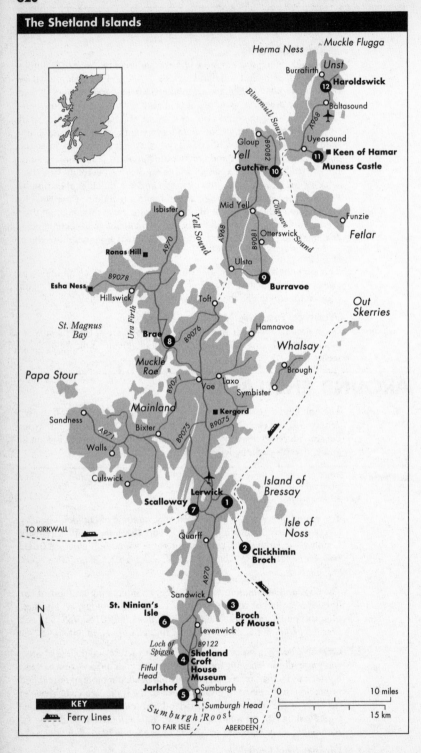

Muckle Flugga

Herma Ness

Burrafirth Unst

12 **Haroldswick**

Baltasound

Bluemull Sound

A968

Uyeasound

Gloup

B9082

Yell **11** ■ **Keen of Hamar**

Gutcher **10** **Muness Castle**

Mid Yell

Colgrave Sound

Isbister

A970

A968

B9081

Otterswick

Funzie

Ronas Hill

Yell Sound

Ulsta

Fetlar

B9078

Ura Firth

Esha Ness ■

Hillswick

9 **Burravoe**

Toft

Out Skerries

St. Magnus Bay

Hamnavoe

Brae **8** B9076

Whalsay

Muckle Roe

Brough

Papa Stour

B9071

Voe Laxo

Symbister

Mainland

■ **Kergord**

Sandness

A971

Bixter B9075 B9075

Walls

Culswick

Scalloway

Lerwick **1**

Island of Bressay

TO KIRKWALL

Quarff

Isle of Noss

2 **Clickhimin Broch**

A970

Sandwick

3 **Broch of Mousa**

St. Ninian's Isle

6

Levenwick

Loch of Spiggie

B9122

4 **Shetland Croft House Museum**

Fitful Head

Jarlshof **5**

Sumburgh

N

Sumburgh Head

Sumburgh Roost

TO FAIR ISLE

TO ABERDEEN

0 10 miles

0 15 km

KEY

⛴ Ferry Lines

up in an attractive blend of burgundy and blue color schemes. The food is rich and filling, with sometimes wildly clashing flavors. One entrée consists of saddle of Shetland lamb filled with haggis forcemeat stuffing, sliced and served with a rich Orkney malt whisky and rosemary jus—enough of a meal to sink the Shetland ferry! ⊠ *Holmsgarth Rd., Lerwick ZE1 0PW,* ☎ *01595/695515,* FAX *01595/695828. 64 rooms with bath. 2 restaurants, 2 bars. AE, DC, MC, V.* 🍽

Outdoor Activities and Sports

Bicycles can be rented from **Eric Brown Cycles** (⊠ Grantfield Garage, North Rd., Lerwick, ☎ 01595/692709).

Shopping

There are many places for knitwear and woolen goods in Lerwick. **The Spider's Web** (⊠ 41 Commercial St., ☎ 01595/693299), open by appointment only, sells hand-spun and hand-knit goods in neutral earth tones, as well as pottery made in Shetland. **Anderson & Co.** (⊠ The Shetland Warehouse, 60–62 Commercial St., ☎ 01595/693714) sells handmade knitwear and has a small stock of machine-made items and tourist souvenirs. **Millers** (⊠ 116 Commercial St., Lerwick, ☎ 01595/692517) stocks machine-made knitwear in Shetland and Argyle patterns, Aran sweaters, and capes, rugs, and scarves made elsewhere in Scotland.

J. G. Rae Limited (⊠ 92 Commercial St., ☎ 01595/693686) stocks Shetland silvercraft and gold and silver jewelry with Norse and Celtic motifs. **Hjaltasteyn** (⊠ 161 Commercial St., Lerwick, ☎ 01595/696224) handcrafts gems and jewelry in gold, silver, and enamels. **Shetland Jewelry** (⊠ Sound Side, Weisdale, ☎ 01595/830275) makes jewelry and cutlery, which are also stocked at J. G. Rae (☞ *above*).

Sandwick

14 mi south of Lerwick via A970.

★ ❸ The community of Sandwick is the departure point for the ferry to the tiny isle of Mousa where you can see the **Broch of Mousa,** the most fully extant of all the broch towers remaining in Scotland. ⊠ *Mousa,* ☎ *0131/668–8800, 01950/431367 for the ferry.* 🖾 *Broch free, ferry £7.* ⊙ *Broch: year-round; ferry: May–Sept., Mon.–Thurs. and Sat. 2, Fri. and Sun. 12:30 and 2.*

Shopping

Lawrence J. Smith Ltd. (⊠ Hoswick, ☎ 01950/431215) sells Shetland knitwear—both handmade and machine-made—at all prices and for all ages and in a wide range of colors.

Voe

7 mi south of Sandwick.

★ ❹ The scattered village of Voe (one of several with this name on Shetland; *voe* means "coastal inlet") is the home of the **Shetland Croft House Museum.** This traditionally constructed 19th-century thatched house contains a broad range of artifacts that depict the former way of life of the rural Shetlander, which the museum attendant will be delighted to discuss with you. ⊠ *Voe, Dunrossness, unclassified road east of A970,* ☎ *01595/695057.* 🖾 *£2.* ⊙ *May–Sept., daily 10–1 and 2–5.*

Sumburgh

4 mi south of Voe.

★ ❺ The big attraction at Sumburgh is **Jarlshof,** a centuries-old site that includes the extensive remains of Norse buildings, as well as prehistoric wheelhouses and earth houses representing thousands of years of continuous settlement. The site also includes a 17th-century laird's (landowner's) house built on the ruins of a medieval farmstead. Recent excavations at nearby Old Scatness, under the auspices of the Shetland Amenity Trust, have uncovered a broch and an Iron Age village with one building still in possession of its roof. ⊠ *Sumburgh Head,* ☎ *0131/668–8800.* 🖃 *£2.50.* ⊘ *Apr.–Sept., daily 9:30–6.* ✍

St. Ninian's Isle

❻ *8 mi north of Sumburgh via A970 and B9122 (turn left at Skelberry).*

It was on St. Ninian's Isle—actually a tombolo, a spit of sand that moors an island to the mainland—that archaeologists in the 1950s uncovered the St. Ninian treasure, a collection of 28 silver objects from the 8th century. This Celtic silver is now in the Museum of Scotland in Edinburgh (☞ Chapter 1), though good replicas are on view in the Shetland Museum in Lerwick (☞ *above*).

Scalloway

❼ *21 mi north of St. Ninian's Isle, 6 mi west of Lerwick.*

On the west coast of Mainland Island is Scalloway. Look for the information board just off the main road (A970), which overlooks the settlement and its castle. **Scalloway Castle** was built in 1600 by the Earl Patrick, who coerced the locals to build it for him. He was executed in 1615 for his cruelty and misdeeds, and the castle was never used again. ⊠ *Scalloway,* ☎ *0131/668–8800.* 🖃 *Free.* ⊘ *Apr.–Sept., daily 9:30–6; Oct.–Mar., Mon.–Sat. 9:30–4, Sun. 2–4.*

OFF THE
BEATEN PATH
Take the B9075 east off the A970, at the head of a narrow sea inlet. This leads into the unexpectedly green **Kergord Valley,** noted for its woodland. This would be unremarkable farther south, but here it is a novelty.

Shopping

The **Shetland Woollen Company** (⊠ Castle St., ☎ 01595/880243) is one of many purveyors with a selection of Shetland knitwear.

Brae

❽ *24 mi north of Scalloway.*

Brae is the home of the Busta House Hotel (☞ Lodging, *below*), probably the best hotel on the island. Beyond Brae the main road meanders past **Mavis Grind,** a strip of land so narrow you can throw a stone—if you are strong—from the Atlantic, in one inlet, to the North Sea, in another.

OFF THE
BEATEN PATH
ESHA NESS AND RONAS HILL – For outstanding views of the rugged, forbidding cliffs around Esha Ness, drive north, then turn left onto the B9078. On the way, look for the sandstone stacks in the bay that resemble a Viking galley under sail. After viewing the cliffs at Esha Ness, return to join the A970 at Hillswick and follow an ancillary road from the head of Ura Firth. This road provides vistas of rounded, bare Ronas Hill, the highest hill in Shetland. Though only 1,468 ft high, it is noted for its arctic-alpine flora growing at low levels.

Dining and Lodging

£££ ✕🏠 **Busta House.** Busta House dates in part from the 16th century and
★   is surrounded by terraced grounds. Bedrooms are well furnished in traditional style—floral chintzes and antique furniture—and the 16th-cen-

tury Long Room is a delightful place to sample the hotel's selection of malt whiskies while sitting beside a peat fire. On the Taste of Scotland menu, Shetland salmon and lamb are usually available. ✉ *Brae, Shetland, ZE2 9QN,* ☎ *01806/522506,* ᴍ *01806/522588. 20 rooms with bath or shower. Restaurant, bar. AE, DC, MC, V.* 🐢

Yell

11 mi northeast of Brae, 31 mi north of Lerwick via A970, A968, or B9076, and ferry from Toft.

9 After crossing to Ulsta, on the island of Yell, take the B9081 east to **Burravoe.** There's not a lot to say about the blanket bog that cloaks two-thirds of Yell, but the **Old Haa** (hall) of Burravoe, the oldest building on the island, is architecturally interesting—it was formerly a merchant's house—and has a museum upstairs. One of the displays tells the story of the wrecking of the German sail ship, the *Bohus,* in 1924. A copy of the ship's figurehead is displayed outside the Old Haa itself; the original is at the shipwreck site, overlooking Otterswick along the coast on the B9081. The Old Haa serves light meals with home-baked buns, cakes, and other goodies; has a crafts shop; and acts as a kind of unofficial information point. The staff is friendly and gives advice to sightseers. ☎ *01957/722339.* 🎫 *Free.* 🕐 *Late Apr.–Sept., Tues.–Thurs. and Sat. 10–4, Sun. 2–5.*

10 Travel to the main A968 at Mid Yell to reach **Gutcher,** the ferry pier.

Unst

49 mi north of Lerwick via ferry from Gutcher.

The ferry crosses the Bluemull Sound to Unst, the northernmost inhabited island in Scotland. Because of its strategic location—it protrudes well into the northern seas—Unst is inhabited by the military.

11 From the A968 turn right on the B9084 to find **Muness Castle,** Scotland's northernmost castle (admission is free; ask for the key keeper), built just before the end of the 16th century. If lucky, you'll be pleasantly surprised to find some photogenic Shetland ponies in the field nearby. Just to the north of Muness Castle is the **Keen of Hamar** national nature reserve.

12 In the far north of Unst is **Haroldswick,** with its post office (proud of its status as the most northerly one) and heritage center. If you take the B9086 at Haroldswick, you will go around the head of **Burra Firth** (a sea inlet) and eventually reach a parking lot. From there a path goes north across moorland and up a gentle hill. Bleak and open, this is bird-watchers' territory and is replete with diving skuas—single-minded sky pirates that attack anything that strays near their nest sites. Gannets, puffins, and other seabirds nest in spectacular profusion by the cliffs on the left as you look out to sea. You should keep to the path; this is a national nature reserve.

At the top of the hills, amid the windy grasslands, you can see **Muckle Flugga** to the north, a series of tilting offshore rocks; the largest of these sea-battered protrusions has a lighthouse. This is the northernmost point in Scotland—the sea rolls out on three sides, and no land lies beyond.

AROUND ORKNEY

Most of Orkney's many prehistoric sites are open to view, offering an insight into the life of bygone eras. At Maes Howe, for example, visitors will discover that graffiti is not solely an expression of today's youths: the Vikings left their marks here in the 12th century.

Stromness

⑬ *1¼ hrs north of Thurso via ferry from Scrabster.*

You will find two points of interest in Stromness as soon as you arrive. The **Pier Arts Centre** is a former Stromness merchant's house (circa 1800) and has adjoining buildings that now serve as a gallery with a permanent collection of 20th-century paintings and sculptures. ⊠ *Victoria St.,* ☎ *01856/850209.* ▦ *Free.* ☉ *Tues.–Sat. 10:30–5.*

The **Stromness Museum** has a varied collection of natural-history material on view, including preserved birds and Orkney shells. The museum also displays exhibits on fishing, shipping, whaling, and the Hudson Bay Company, as well as ship models and a feature on the German fleet that was scuttled on Scapa Flow in 1919. ⊠ *Alfred St.,* ☎ *01856/850025.* ▦ *£2.* ☉ *May–Sept., daily 10–5; Oct.–Apr., Mon.–Sat. 10:30–12:30 and 1:30–5.*

★ ⑭ The **Ring of Brogar** is a magnificent circle of 36 stones (originally 60) surrounded by a deep ditch. When the fog descends over the stones— a frequent occurrence—their looming shapes seem to come alive. Though their original use is uncertain, it is not hard to imagine strange rituals taking place here in the misty past. The stones stand between Loch of Harray and Loch of Stenness, 5 mi northeast of Stromness. ☎ *0131/668–8800.* ▦ *Free.* ☉ *Year-round.* ⊜

★ ⑮ The huge burial mound of **Maes Howe** (circa 2500 BC) measures 115 ft in diameter and contains an enormous burial chamber. It was raided by Vikings in the 12th century, and Norse crusaders found shelter here, leaving a rich collection of runic inscriptions. Maes Howe is 1 mi farther on the A965 from the Ring of Brogar. ☎ *0131/668–8800.* ▦ *£2.50; joint Historic Scotland's Orkney entry ticket, £10.* ☉ *Apr.–Sept., daily 9:30–6; Oct.–Mar., Mon.–Sat. 9:30–4, Sun. 2–4.* ⊜

★ ⑯ At the Neolithic village of **Skara Brae** you will find houses, joined by covered passages, with stone beds, fireplaces, and cupboards that have survived since the village was first occupied around 3000 BC. The site was preserved in sand until it was uncovered in 1850, and it can be found 8 mi north of Stromness off the A967/B9056. ☎ *0131/668–8800.* ▦ *£4.50 (£3.50 in winter); joint Historic Scotland's Orkney entry ticket, £10.* ☉ *Apr.–Sept., daily 9:30–6; Oct.–Mar., Mon.–Sat. 9:30–4, Sun. 2–4.* ⊜

⑰ The **Marwick Head Nature Reserve,** with its spectacular seabird cliffs, is tended by the Royal Society for the Protection of Birds. The **Kitchener Memorial,** which recalls the 1916 sinking of the cruiser HMS *Hampshire* with Lord Kitchener aboard, can also be seen in the reserve, on a cliff-top site. The reserve lies to the north of Skara Brae, up the B9056; access to the reserve is along a path north from Marwick Bay. ☎ *01856/791298.* ▦ *Free.* ☉ *Year-round.*

Nightlife and the Arts

The Pier Arts Centre (⊠ Victoria St., ☎ 01856/850209) focuses on artistic life in Stromness, with an eclectic display of paintings and sculptures and changing exhibitions, often by local artists.

Birsay

12 mi north of Stromness, 25 mi northwest of Kirkwall.

⑱ At Birsay is **Earl's Palace,** the impressive remains of a 16th-century palace built by the earls of Orkney. The **Brough of Birsay** and the remains of a Romanesque church and a Norse settlement stand close to Birsay on

The Orkney Islands

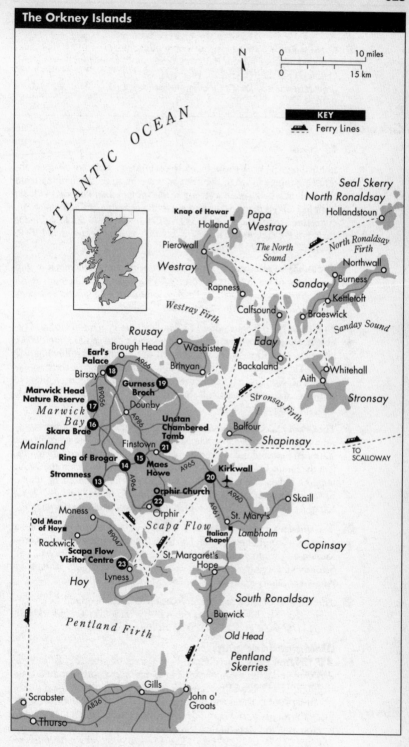

N

0 — 10 miles
0 — 15 km

KEY
⛴ Ferry Lines

ATLANTIC OCEAN

Seal Skerry
North Ronaldsay
Hollandstoun

Knap of Howar
Holland
Papa
Westray

Pierowall
The North
Sound
North Ronaldsay
Firth

Westray
Northwall
Burness
Sanday
Kettletoft

Rapness
Calfsound
Braeswick

Westray Firth
Sanday Sound

Rousay
Wasbister
Eday
Aith
Whitehall

Brough Head
Brinyan
Backaland
Stronsay

Earl's
Palace
Birsay **18**
A966

Gurness
Broch **19**
Marwick Head
Nature Reserve **17**
B9056
Dounby
Balfour
Shapinsay

Marwick
Bay **16**
A986
Unstan
Chambered
Tomb

Skara Brae
Finstown
21
Stronsay Firth

Mainland
Ring of Brogar
15
14
Maes
Howe
A965
Kirkwall
TO
SCALLOWAY

Stromness
13
A964
20

Orphir Church
Skaill

Moness
22
Orphir
St. Mary's

Old Man
of Hoy
B9047
Scapa Flow
Lambholm
Copinsay

Rackwick
Italian
Chapel

Scapa Flow
Visitor Centre
23
Lyness
St. Margaret's
Hope

Hoy
South Ronaldsay

Pentland Firth
Burwick
Old Head

Pentland
Skerries

Scrabster
Gills
John o'
Groats
Thurso
A836

an island accessible only at low tide. To ensure you won't be swept away, check the tide tables before setting out.

⑲ Gurness Broch is an Iron Age tower standing more than 10 ft high, surrounded by stone huts. It is off the A966, about 8 mi from Birsay along Orkney's northern coast. ⊠ *Aikerness,* ☎ *0131/668–8800.* 🎫 *£2.50; joint Historic Scotland's Orkney entry ticket, £10.* ⊙ *Apr.–Sept., daily 9:30–6.* 🐾

Kirkwall

⑳ *16 mi east of Stromness.*

In bustling Kirkwall, the main town on Orkney, there are plenty of interesting things to see in the narrow, winding streets, extending from the harbor, which retain a strong medieval feel. **Earl Patrick's Palace,** built in 1607, is perhaps the best surviving example of Renaissance architecture in Scotland. ⊠ *Kirkwall,* ☎ *0131/668–8800.* 🎫 *£2 (includes Bishop's Palace); joint Historic Scotland's Orkney entry ticket, £10.* ⊙ *Apr.–Sept., daily 9:30–6.*

The **Bishop's Palace** nearby dates from the 13th century, though its round tower was added in the 16th century. ⊠ *Kirkwall,* ☎ *0131/668–8800.* 🎫 *£2 (includes Earl Patrick's Palace); joint Historic Scotland's Orkney entry ticket, £10.* ⊙ *Apr.–Sept., daily 9:30–6.*

★ Founded by Jarl Rognvald in 1137 and dedicated to his uncle St. Magnus, **St. Magnus Cathedral** in Kirkwall was built between 1137 and 1200; however, additional work was carried out during the following 300 years. The cathedral is still in use and contains some of the best examples of Norman architecture in Scotland. The ornamentation on some of the tombstones is particularly striking. ⊙ *Mon.–Sat. 9–1 and 2–5, Sun. for services and 2–6.*

The **Orkney Wireless Museum** in Kirkwall tells the story of wartime communications at Scapa Flow. Thousands of service men and women were stationed here and used the equipment displayed in the museum to protect the Home Fleet. The museum also contains many handsome 1930s wireless radios and examples of the handicrafts produced by Italian prisoners-of-war. ⊠ *Kiln Corner, Junction Rd.,* ☎ *01856/874272.* 🎫 *£2.* ⊙ *Apr.–Sept.; check with tourist information center for opening hrs.*

㉑ The **Unstan Chambered Tomb** is a 5,000-year-old cairn containing a chambered tomb. Pottery that has been found within the tomb is now known as Unstan ware. The tomb is midway between Kirkwall and Stromness, roughly 3½ mi from each. ☎ *0131/668–8800.* 🎫 *Free.* ⊙ *Apr.–Sept., daily 9:30–6; Oct.–Mar., Mon.–Sat. 9:30–4, Sun. 2–4.*

㉒ The remains of the 12th-century **Orphir Church,** Scotland's only circular medieval church, lie near the A964, 8 mi southwest of Kirkwall. ☎ *0131/668–8800.* 🎫 *Free.* ⊙ *At all times.*

Dining and Lodging

££ ✕🏨 **Foveran Hotel.** Surrounded by 34 acres of grounds just outside Kirkwall and overlooking Scapa Flow, this warm hotel has an attractive light-wood, Scandinavian-style dining room and an open fire in its sitting room. The menu features Taste of Scotland, and the homemade soups, pâtés, and seafood have helped secure the restaurant's reputation as a very dependable place to eat. ⊠ *St. Ola, Kirkwall KW15 1SF,* ☎ *01856/872389,* 📠 *01856/876430. 8 rooms with bath or shower. Restaurant, 2 lounges. MC, V. Closed Jan.*

£   🏨 **Polrudden Guest House.** Quietly situated yet close to the town center and public parks, this modern guest house offers a high standard of lodging for the price. Multicolored matching curtains and quilt covers complement the cream-color rooms and pine furnishings. ⊠ *Pickaquoy Rd., KW15 1UH,* ☎ *01856/874761,* ℻ *01856/870950. 7 rooms with shower. MC, V.*

Nightlife and the Arts

Orkney's cultural highlight is the **St. Magnus Festival** (☎ 01856/ 872669 for details), a festival of music based in Kirkwall and usually held the third week in June. Orkney also has an annual folk festival at the end of May.

Outdoor Activities and Sports

Bicycles can be rented from **Bobby's Cycle Centre** (⊠ Tankerness La., Kirkwall, ☎ ℻ 01856/873097).

Shopping

Kirkwall is the main shopping hub. Do not miss **Ola Gorrie at the Longship** (⊠ 7–9 Broad St., ☎ 01856/873251), which crafts gold and silver jewelry with Celtic and Norse themes, including a delightful representation of a dragon, originally drawn on the wall of the burial chamber at Maes Howe. **Ortak Jewelry** (⊠ 10 Albert St., ☎ 01856/ 873536) stocks a potpourri of gifts: Celtic-theme jewelry, crystal, barometers, and many other craft items, many made locally. At **Judith Glue** (⊠ 25 Broad St., ☎ 01856/874225) you can purchase designer knitwear with traditional patterns, as well as Orkney-made crafts.

Hoy

14 mi southwest of Kirkwall, 6 mi south of Stromness via ferry.

The **㉓ Scapa Flow Visitor Centre,** on Hoy, has a growing collection of material portraying the strategic role of the sheltered anchorage of Scapa Flow (said to be Britain's best diving site) in two world wars. ⊠ *Lyness, off the B9047,* ☎ *01856/791300.* ⊡ *£2.* ☉ *Nov.–Mar., weekdays 9–4; Apr.–Oct., weekdays 9–4, Sat. 9–3:30, Sun. 9–6.*

THE NORTHERN ISLES A TO Z

Arriving and Departing

By Bus

Aberdeen and Thurso have reliable bus links to and from and all over Scotland: **Scottish Citylink** (☎ 0990/505050) and **National Express** (☎ 0990/808080). **John o'Groats Ferries** (☎ 01955/611353) operates the Orkney Bus, a direct express coach from Inverness to Kirkwall (via ferry) that runs daily from May to early September. The same company offers a day tour from Inverness to Orkney daily from June through August.

By Car and Ferry

To get to Lerwick, Shetland, take the ferry from the port in Aberdeen. To reach Stromness, Orkney, take the passenger and car ferry from the port in Scrabster. Contact **P&O Ferries** (⊠ Orkney and Shetland Services, Box 5, Jamieson's Quay, Aberdeen AB11 5NP, ☎ 01224/572615) for reservations. As an alternative, take the ferry from John o'Groats to Burwick, Orkney, operated by **John o'Groats Ferries,** with up to eight sailings daily from May through September (☎ 01955/611353).

By Plane

British Airways (☎ 0345/222111) provides regular service to Lerwick (Shetland) and Kirkwall (Orkney) from Edinburgh, Glasgow, Aberdeen, and Inverness.

By Train

There are no trains on Orkney or Shetland, although Aberdeen (which has a ferry to Shetland) is well served by train, and Thurso is the terminus of the far-north line. For information contact the **National Train Enquiry Line** (☎ 0345/484950). From Thurso a bus connects to Scrabster for Orkney.

Getting Around

By Bus

The main bus services on Orkney are operated by **James D. Peace & Co.** (☎ 01856/872866), **Causeway Coaches** (☎ 01856/831444), and **Orkney Coaches** (☎ 01856/870555); on Shetland, by **Shalder Coaches** (☎ 01595/880217) and **J. Leask** (☎ 01595/693162).

By Car and Ferry

Because of the oil wealth, the roads on Shetland are in very good shape. Both Orkney and Shetland are part of a network of islands with interconnecting ferries that are heavily subsidized. Book ferry tickets in advance. In Shetland, for **ferry information,** contact the tourist information center (☞ Visitor Information, *below*) or ☎ 01957/722259 or 01957/722268 if you are visiting during peak season. Shetland visitors who want to get to Orkney can do so by way of ferry from Lerwick on Shetland to Stromness, in Orkney (☞ P&O Ferries, *above*).

In Orkney, for details of ferry services operated interisland, call **Orkney Ferries** (☎ 01856/872044). Orkney also has causeways connecting some of the islands, but in some cases using these roads will take you on fairly roundabout routes.

By Plane

Note that because of the isolation of Orkney and Shetland there is a network of interisland flights. Tourist information centers (☞ Visitor Information, *below*) will provide details, or call **British Airways Express/Loganair** (☎ 0345/222111, 01856/872494 in Orkney) for interisland flights.

Contacts and Resources

Car Rentals

Although Shetland has a number of car-rental firms, you can take your car from Aberdeen by sea. Generally, for fewer than five days, it's cheaper to rent a car in Shetland. Most rental companies are based in Lerwick; they include **Star Rent-a-Car** (✉ 22 Commercial Rd., Lerwick, ☎ 01595/692075) and **Bolts Car and Minibus Hire** (✉ 26 North Rd., Lerwick, ☎ 01595/693636). On Orkney try **James D. Peace & Co.** (✉ Junction Rd., Kirkwall, ☎ 01856/872866).

Discount Pass

A joint entry ticket to all of **Historic Scotland's Orkney** sites is available from the sites themselves. The ticket lasts until you've seen all the sites and costs £10 (£9 in October and November).

Diving

Selkie Charters (✉ Voe, ☎ 01806/588297), operated by Colin and Linda Ruthven, provides boat rentals and information.

Doctors and Dentists

Most general practitioners will see visitor patients by appointment or immediately in case of emergency. Your hotel or local tourist information center can advise you accordingly. You can also consult the Yellow Pages of the telephone directory, under "Doctor" or "Dentist."

Emergencies

Ambulance, fire, or police: ☎ 999. (No coins are needed for emergency calls from public phone booths.)

Gilbert Bain Hospital (✉ South Rd., Lerwick, Shetland, ☎ 01595/695678). **Balfour Hospital** (✉ New Staffa Rd., Kirkwall, Orkney, ☎ 01856/885400).

Guided Tours

ORIENTATION

General tours are offered in Orkney by **Orkney Coaches** (☎ 01856/870555). The tour companies that service Shetland are **J. Leask** (☎ 01595/693162) and **Shalder Coaches** (☎ 01595/880217).

SPECIAL-INTEREST

All the companies that offer orientation tours run special-interest tours to specific places of interest on the islands, as well. Most can also tailor tours to your interests. Michael Hartley, an accredited tour guide in Orkney, runs **Wildabout** (☎ 01856/851011); phone for details on minibus tours that combine sightseeing of archaeological sites and the folklore, flora, and fauna of the islands. In Shetland several companies tour the spectacular Noss Bird Sanctuary—a national nature reserve—in the summer, weather permitting. The tourist information center can provide details and take reservations.

Visitor Information

Kirkwall, Orkney (✉ 6 Broad St., ☎ 01856/872856, ✆). **Stromness, Orkney** (✉ Ferry Terminal Bldg., ☎ 01856/850716). **Lerwick, Shetland** (✉ Market Cross, ☎ 01595/693434).

11 SCOTLAND: THE HOME OF GOLF

GOLFING THROUGHOUT THE COUNTRY

By John
Hutchinson

Updated by
Beth Ingpen

HERE ARE MORE THAN 400 GOLF COURSES in Scotland and only 5 million residents, so the country has probably the highest ratio of courses to people anywhere in the world. Some of these courses are renowned venues for major championships, and if you're a golfer coming to Scotland, you'll probably want to play the "famous names" sometime in your career. Telling your friends in the clubhouse back home that you got a birdie at the Road Hole on the Old Course in St. Andrews, where Lyle, Faldo, and Jacklin have played, somehow conveys more prestige than an excellent round at a delightful but obscure course.

So, by all means, play the championship courses and get your prestige, but remember they *are* championship courses and therefore difficult; you may enjoy the game itself much more at a less challenging, albeit less known, course. Remember, too, that everyone else wants to play them, so booking can be a problem, particularly at peak times during the summer. Book early, or if you're staying in a hotel attached to a course, get them to book for you.

There has always been considerable debate as to who invented golf, but there's no doubt that its development into one of the most popular games in the world stems from Scotland. Like many other games that involve hitting a ball with a stick, golf evolved in the countries that border the North Sea during the Middle Ages and gradually took on its present form in the last 200 years.

The first written reference to golf, variously spelled as "gowf" or "goff," was as long ago as 1457, when James II (1430–60) of Scotland declared that both golf and football should be "utterly cryit doune and nocht usit" (publicly criticized and prohibited) because they were distracting his subjects from their archery practice. Mary, Queen of Scots (1542–87), it seems, was fond of golf. When in Edinburgh in 1567, she played on Leith Links and on Bruntsfield Links, perhaps the oldest course in the world and where the game is still played. When in Fife, she played at Falkland, near the palace, and at St. Andrews itself.

Golf must surely rank as one of Scotland's earliest cultural exports. In 1603, when James VI (1566–1625) of Scotland also became James I of England, he moved his court to London. With him went his golf-loving friends, and they set up a course on Blackheath Common, then on the outskirts of London.

Golf clubs (i.e., organizations) as we know them today first arose in the middle of the 18th century. Written evidence attests to the founding of the Honourable Company of Edinburgh Golfers, now residing at Muirfield, in 1744, and to the Royal & Ancient at St. Andrews, which began in 1754. From then on, clubs sprang up all over Scotland: Royal Aberdeen (1780), Crail Golfing Society (1786), Dunbar (1794), and the Royal Perth Golfing Society (1824).

By the early 19th century, clubs had been set up in England, and the game was being carried all over the world by enthusiastic Scots. These golf missionaries spread their knowledge not only of the sport, but also of the courses. Large parts of the Scottish coast are natural golf courses; indeed, the origins of bunkers and the word *links* (courses) are found in the sand dunes of Scotland's shores. In countries where such natural terrain didn't exist, courses had to be designed and created. Willie

Park of Musselburgh (who laid out Sunningdale), James Braid, and C. K. Hutchison (whose crowning glory is at Gleneagles Hotel) are some of the best known of Scotland's golf-course architects.

Golf has always had a peculiar classlessness in Scotland. It's a game for everyone, and for centuries Scottish towns and cities have maintained golf courses for the enjoyment of their citizens. The snobbishness and exclusivity of golf clubs in some parts of the world have few echoes here. Admittedly, there are at least a few clubs that have always been noted for their exclusive air, and newer golf courses are emerging as part of exclusive leisure complexes. These are exceptions to the long tradition of recreation for all. Golf here is usually a democratic game, played by ordinary folk as well as the rich and carefree.

Many of the important changes in the design and construction of balls and clubs were pioneered by the professional players who lived and worked around the town courses and who made the balls and clubs themselves. The original balls, called *featheries,* were leather bags stuffed with boiled feathers. Often they only lasted one round. When, in 1848, the gutta-percha ball, called a *guttie,* was introduced, there was considerable friction, particularly in St. Andrews, between the makers of the two rival types of ball. The gutta-percha proved superior and was in general use until the invention of the rubber-core ball in 1901.

Clubs were traditionally made of wood: shafts were of ash, later hickory, and heads were of thorn or some other hardwood like apple or pear. Heads were spliced, then bound to the shaft with twine. Players generally managed with far fewer clubs than today. About 1628 the marquis of Montrose, a golf enthusiast, had a set of clubs made for him in St. Andrews that illustrates the range of clubs used in Stuart times: "Bonker clubis, a irone club, and twa play clubs."

Caddies—the word comes from the French *cadet* (young boy) and was used, particularly in Edinburgh, to refer to anyone who ran messages—carried the players' clubs around, usually under the arm. Golf carts didn't come into fashion in Britain until the 1950s, and some people still considered them to be potentially injurious to the national health and moral fiber.

The technology of golf may change, but its addictive qualities are timeless. Toward the end of the 18th century, an Edinburgh golfer named Alexander McKellar regularly played golf all day and refused to stop even when it grew dark. One night his wife carried his dinner and nightcap onto Bruntsfield Links, where he was playing, in an attempt to shame him into changing his ways. She failed.

And the addiction continues.

Where to Play

There are courses everywhere in Scotland except for the far northern Highlands and some of the islands. Most courses welcome visitors with a minimum of formalities, and some at surprisingly low cost. (Off-season, a few clubs still use the "honest box," into which you drop your fees!)

Just three pieces of advice, particularly for North Americans: 1) In Scotland the game is usually played fairly quickly, so don't dawdle if others are waiting; 2) caddy carts are hand-pulled carts for your clubs; driven golf carts are rarely available in Scotland (most courses charge from

£1.30 to £2 per round for use of caddy carts); and 3) when they say "rough," they really mean "rough."

Unless specified otherwise below, course playing hours are generally 9 AM to sundown, which in June can be as late as 10 PM. For a complete list of courses, contact local tourist offices, and for more regional information, *see* Outdoor Activities and Sports *in* individual chapters.

The Stewartry

At the very southern border, the Stewartry is a delightful part of Scotland set in the rich farmlands around Dumfries, a golfing vacation area since Victorian times. Powfoot and Southerness are enjoyable links courses along the shores of the Solway Firth, and inland, Dumfries and Moffat have long-established courses that provide superb golf in a clean, invigorating environment. There are also several fine nine-hole courses in the area.

Southerness. The first to be designed in Scotland after World War II (Mackenzie Ross, 1947), Southerness is a long course, played over extensive links with fine views southward over the Solway Firth. The greens are hard and fast, and the frequent winds make for some testing golf. ☎ 01387/880677. *18 holes. Yardage 6,566. Par 70.* ▨ *Weekdays £32 daily; weekends £45 daily.* ☉ *Daily (limited on Tues.). Reservations essential. Caddy carts, catering.*

Ayrshire and the Clyde Coast

Just an hour south of Glasgow by car or train, Ayrshire and the Clyde Coast have been a holiday area for Glaswegians for generations. Few golfers need an introduction to the names of Turnberry, Royal Troon, Prestwick, or Western Gailes—all challenging links courses along this coast. There are at least 20 other courses in the area within an hour's drive. Remember, too, that at major areas, such as Turnberry, Troon, and Ayr, there are several different courses to play from the same base.

Girvan. This is an old, established course with play along a narrow coastal strip and a more lush inland section next to the Water of Girvan—a river that constitutes a particular hazard at the 15th, unless you are a big hitter. This is a scenic course, with good views of Ailsa Craig and the Clyde Estuary. ☎ 01465/714346. *18 holes. Yardage 4,590. Par 64.* ▨ *Weekdays £13 per round, £20 daily; weekends £14.50 per round, £26 daily.* ☉ *Daily. Caddy carts, catering.*

Glasgow

As Scotland's industrial and commercial hub, Glasgow is well known for its shopping, nightlife, art galleries, theaters, and restaurants. Less well known are the parks and gardens, affectionately called the "dear green places," that breathe life into the city. Most of the old golf courses have now moved out to the suburbs, but you can tee off from at least 30 different courses less than an hour from the city center. And remember: in addition to these, all the Ayrshire courses are just down the road.

Douglas Park. North of the city near Milngavie (pronounced mul-*gai*), Douglas Park is a long, attractive course set among birch and pine trees with masses of rhododendrons blooming in early summer. The Campsie Fells form a pleasing backdrop. ☎ 0141/942–2220. *18 holes. Yardage 5,959. Par 69.* ▨ *£14 per round, £24 daily.* ☉ *Daily after 3 PM. Caddy carts.*

Killermont and Gailes, The Glasgow Golf Club. Originally the club played on Glasgow Green in the heart of the ancient city center, but as the pressure for space grew, it moved north to the leafy suburb of Bearsden, on the road to Loch Lomond. The Killermont course was laid out by Tom Morris (1904) in beautiful parkland with ancient trees, fine greens, and an elegant clubhouse. Visitors are offered the facilities of the club's other course at Gailes, near Irvine on the Firth of Clyde. The Glasgow Club's Tennant Cup (June) is the oldest open amateur tournament in the world. *Gailes:* ☎ *0141/942–2011. 18 holes. Yardage 6,520. Par 71. ✉ Weekdays £42 per round, £50 daily; weekends: £55 per round. ☉ Weekdays 9–sundown, weekends after 2:30. Reservations essential. Practice area, caddy carts, catering.*

East Lothian

The sand dunes that stretch eastward from Edinburgh along the southern shore of the Firth of Forth made an ideal location for some of the world's earliest golf courses. Muirfield is perhaps the most famous course in the area, but around it are more than a dozen others, at Gullane, North Berwick, Dunbar, and Aberlady and, nearer Edinburgh, at Longniddry, Prestonpans, and Musselburgh. All are links courses, many with views to the islands of the Firth of Forth and northward to Fife. If you weary of the East Lothian courses, you'll find that just 20 mi or so to the west are nearly 30 more within the city of Edinburgh.

Dunbar. This ancient golfing site by the sea even has a lighthouse at the ninth hole. It's a good choice for a typical east-coast links course in a seaside town but within easy reach of Edinburgh. ☎ *01368/862086. 18 holes. Yardage 6,426. Par 71. ✉ Weekdays £28 per round, £35 daily; weekends £35 per round, £45 daily. ☉ Fri.–Wed. after 9:30. Reservations essential. Practice area, caddies (by reservation), catering.*

Edinburgh

Edinburgh is best known as Scotland's capital and home to the Edinburgh International Festival, the largest of its kind in the world. The city also has nearly 30 golf courses within its boundaries. Most are parkland courses, though along the shores of the Firth of Forth they take on the characteristics of traditional links. Some are used by private clubs and offer visitors limited access; others that belong to the city are more accessible and have much lower fees. Golf historians should also visit and play on Bruntsfield Links, where the game has been enjoyed for more than 450 years.

Barnton, Royal Burgess Golfing Society. One of the world's oldest golf clubs (1735), its members originally played on Bruntsfield Links; now they and their guests play on elegantly manicured parkland in the city's northwestern suburbs. It's a long course with fine greens. ☎ *0131/339–2075. 18 holes. Yardage 6,111. Par 68. ✉ Weekdays £40 per round, £50 daily. ☉ Weekdays. Reservations essential. Caddy carts, golf carts (£5 per round), catering.*

Braids. Two courses built by the city as urban development nearly 90 years ago forced golfers out of the center: Braids Number 1 and Braids Number 2 (no connection with James Braid) are beautifully laid out over a rugged range of small hills in the southern suburbs. The views to the south and the Pentland Hills and north toward the Edinburgh skyline are worth a visit in themselves. ☎ *0131/447–6666. 18 holes. No. 1: Yardage 5,412. Par 70; No. 2: Yardage 3,900. Par 65. ✉ Weekdays £8.80 per round, weekends £9.65 per round. ☉ Daily. Reservations essential. Caddy carts.*

Fife

Few would dispute the claim of St. Andrews to be the home of golf, holding as it does the Royal & Ancient, the organization that governs the sport worldwide. Golf has been played here since the game's inception, and to play in Fife is for most golfers a cherished ambition. St. Andrews itself has a wide range of full 18-hole courses in addition to the famous Old Course. Along the north shores of the Firth of Forth is a string of ancient villages, each with its harbor, ancient red-roof buildings, and golf course. In all, there are about 30 courses in the area.

Ladybank. Fife is known for its choice of coastal courses, but this one offers an interesting inland contrast: although Ladybank is laid out on fairly level ground (Tom Morris, 1876), the fir woods, birches, and heathery rough give it a Highland flavor among the gentle Lowland fields. Qualifying rounds of the British Open are played here when the main championship is played at St. Andrews. ☎ 01337/830814. *18 holes. Yardage 6,580. Par 71.* ✉ *May–Oct.: weekdays £30 per round, £40 daily; weekends £35 per round. Nov.–Apr.: weekdays £20 per round, £30 daily; weekends £25 per round.* ☉ *Daily. Reservations essential. Practice area, caddy carts, golf carts (£18 per round), catering.*

Leven. Another fine Fife course used as a British Open qualifier, this one, a links course, feels like the more famous St. Andrews, with hummocky terrain and a tang of salt in the air. The 1st and 18th share the same fairway, and the 18th green has a burn running by it. ☎ 01333/428859. *18 holes. Yardage 6,436. Par 71.* ✉ *Weekdays £28 per round, £40 daily; Sun. £30 per round, £40 daily.* ☉ *Sun.–Fri. Reservations essential. Catering.*

Perthshire

Perthshire has a variety of attractive country courses developed specifically for visiting golfers. Gleneagles Hotel is, with its outstanding facilities, the most famous of these golf resorts. But several courses in the area, set on the edges of beautiful Highland scenery, will delight any golfer. Crieff, Taymouth, and other courses are in the mountains; Blairgowrie and Perth are amid the rich farmlands nearer the sea.

Callander. Callander was designed by Tom Morris (1913) and has a scenic upland feel in a town well prepared for visitors. Pine and birch woods and hilly fairways offer fine views, especially toward Ben Ledi, and the tricky moorland layout demands accurate hitting off the tee. ☎ 01877/330090. *18 holes. Yardage 5,151. Par 66.* ✉ *Weekdays £18 per round, £26 daily; weekends £26 per round, £31 daily.* ☉ *Daily. Practice area, caddy carts, catering.*

Killin. A scenic course, Killin is typically Highland, with a roaring river, woodland birdsong, and a backdrop of high green hills. There are a few surprises, including two blind shots to reach the green at the fourth. The attractive village of Killin has an almost alpine feel, especially in spring, when the hilltops may still be white. ☎ 01567/820312. *9 holes. Yardage 2,508. Par 65.* ✉ *£12 per round, £15 daily.* ☉ *Apr.–Oct., daily. Caddy carts, club rental, catering.*

Rosemount, Blairgowrie Golf Club. Well known to native golfers looking for a challenge, Rosemount's 18 (James Braid, 1934) are laid out on rolling land in the pine, birch, and fir woods, which bring a wild air to the scene. You may encounter a browsing roe deer if you stray too far. There are, however, wide fairways and at least some large greens (and two other courses to play if you can't manage a game at Rosemount itself). A handicap certificate is required to play here. ☎ 01250/872622. *18 holes. Yardage 6,588. Par 72.* ✉ *Weekdays £50 per round (Rosemount), £60 daily; weekends*

£55 per round (Rosemount). ☉ Daily (some restrictions). Practice area, caddies, golf carts (£17), trolleys (£2.50), catering.

Angus

East of Perthshire, north of the city of Dundee, lies a string of demanding courses along the shores of the North Sea and inland into the foothills of the Grampian Mountains. The most famous course in Angus is probably Carnoustie, one of several British Open Championship venues in Scotland, but there are many more along the same stretch of coast from Dundee northward as far as Stonehaven. Golfers who excel in windy conditions will particularly enjoy the sea breezes blowing eastward from the sea. Inland Edzell, Forfar, Brechin, and Kirriemuir all have courses nestling in the Strathmore farmlands.

Carnoustie. The venue for the British Open Championship in 1999, the extensive coastal links around Carnoustie have been played since at least 1527. Open winners here have included Armour, Hogan, Cotton, Player, and Watson. Carnoustie was also once a training ground for coaches, many of whom went to the United States. The choice municipal course here is full of historical snippets and local color, as well as being tough and interesting. ☎ 01241/853789. 18 holes. Yardage 6,941. Par 72. ▣ £70 per round. ☉ Weekdays 9–sundown, Sat. after 2, Sun. after 12:30. Reservations essential. Caddies, caddy carts, catering.

Aberdeenshire

Aberdeen, Scotland's third-largest city, is known for its sparkling granite buildings and the amazing displays of roses each summer. It also offers a good range of courses. Aberdeen itself has six courses, and to the north, as far as Fraserburgh and Peterhead, there are five others, including the popular Cruden Bay. Royal Deeside has three, and in the rich farmlands to the north are three more with at least six nine-hole courses.

Balgownie, Royal Aberdeen Golf Club. This old club (1780) is the archetypal Scottish links course: long and testing over uneven ground, with the frequently added hazard of a sea breeze. Prickly gorse is inclined to close in and form an additional hurdle. The two courses are tucked behind the rough, grassy sand dunes, and there are surprisingly few views of the sea. One historical note: in 1783 this club originated the five-minute-search rule for a lost ball. ☎ 01224/702571. 18 holes. Yardage 6,204. Par 70. ▣ Weekdays £55 per round, £75 daily; weekends £65 per round. ☉ Tee-off weekdays 10–11:30 and 2–4; Sat. after 3:30. Handicap limit 24; handicap certificate or letter of introduction required from visitor's home club. Reservations essential. Practice area, caddies, caddy carts, catering.

Ballater. This club has a holiday atmosphere and a course laid out along the sandy flats of the River Dee, surrounded by the mountains of Royal Deeside. Originally opened in 1906, the club makes maximum use of the fine setting between river and woods and is ideal for a relaxing round of golf. The variety of shops and pleasant walks in nearby Ballater makes this a good place for nongolfing partners. ☎ 013397/55567. 18 holes. Yardage 6,112. Par 70. ▣ Weekdays £18 per round, £27 daily; weekends £21 per round, £31 daily. ☉ Daily. Reservations advised. Practice area, caddy cars, golf carts (£15 per round), catering.

Cruden Bay. Another east-coast Lowland course sheltered behind extensive sand hills, this one offers a typical Scottish golf experience. Runnels and valleys, among other hazards, on the challenging fairways ensure plenty of excitement, and some of the holes are rated among the country's finest. Like Gleneagles and Turnberry, this course owes its origins to an association with the grand railway hotels that were built in the heyday of steam. Unlike the other two, however, Cruden Bay's railway hotel and the railway itself have gone, but the course remains in fine shape. ☎ 01779/812285. *18 holes. Yardage 6,395. Par 70. ✉ Weekdays £45 per round, £60 daily; weekends £55 per round (restricted access). ⊙ Daily. Reservations essential. Practice area, covered driving range, caddy carts, catering.*

Speyside

Set on the main A9 road an hour south of Inverness amid the Cairngorm Mountains, the valley of the River Spey is one of Scotland's most attractive all-year sports centers, with winter skiing and, in summer, sailing and canoeing, pony trekking, fishing, and some fine golf. The area's main courses are Newtonmore, Grantown-on-Spey, and Boat of Garten, all fine inland courses with wonderful views of the surrounding mountains and challenging golf provided by the springy turf and the heather. For a change of pace, the links courses along the coastline of the Moray Firth, with their seaside attractions, are only an hour's drive away.

Boat of Garten. Possibly one of Scotland's greatest "undiscovered" courses celebrated its centennial in 1998. Boat of Garten was redesigned and extended by famous golf architect James Braid in 1932, and each of its 18 holes is individual: some cut through birch wood and heathery rough; most have long views to the Cairngorms and a strong Highland ambience. An unusual feature is the preserved steam railway that runs along part of the course. The occasional puffing locomotive can hardly be considered a hazard. ☎ 01479/831282. *18 holes. Yardage 5,866. Par 69. ✉ Weekdays £23 per round, £28 daily; weekends £28 per round, £33 daily. ⊙ Daily. Starting sheet used. Reservations essential. Caddies on request, caddy carts, catering.*

Moray Coast

No one can say that the Lowlands have a monopoly on Scotland's fine seaside golf courses. The Moray Coast, stretching eastward from Inverness, has some spectacular sand dunes that have been adapted to create stimulating and exciting links courses. The two courses at Nairn have long been known to golfers both famous and unknown. Charlie Chaplin regularly played here. But in addition there are a dozen courses looking out over the sea from Inverness as far along as Fraserburgh, Banff, and Macduff and several inland amid the fertile Moray farmland.

Banff, Duff House Royal Golf Club. Although within moments of the sea, this club is a blend of a coastal course with a parkland setting. Only minutes from Banff center, it lies within the parkland grounds of Duff House, a country-house art gallery in an Adam mansion. The club has inherited the ancient traditions of seaside play (golf records here go back to the 17th century). Mature trees and gentle slopes create a pleasant playing atmosphere. ☎ 01261/812075. *18 holes. Yardage 6,161. Par 68. ✉ Weekdays £18 per round, £24 daily; weekends £25 per round, £30 daily (all fees halved Oct.–Mar.). ⊙ Daily. Reservations essential. Practice area, caddy carts, catering.*

Fraserburgh. This northeast fishing town has extensive links and dunes that seem to have grown up around the course rather than the other way around. Be prepared for a hill climb and a tough finish. ☎ 01346/518287. *18 holes (9 additional for warm-up). Yardage 6,200. Par 70.*

⌨ *Weekdays £14 per round, £17 daily; weekends £20 per round, £25 daily. ☉ Daily. Practice area, catering.*

Lossiemouth, Moray Golf Club. Discover the mild airs of what's called the Moray Riviera, as Tom Morris did in 1889 when he was inspired by the lie of the natural links. There are two courses plus a six-hole minicourse. There's lots of atmosphere here, with golfing memorabilia in the clubhouse, as well as the tale of the pre–World War I British prime minister Asquith, who took a vacation in this out-of-the-way spot yet still managed to be attacked by a crowd of militant suffragettes at the 17th. All other hazards on these testing courses are entirely natural, with the 18th hole providing a memorable finish. ☎ 01343/813330. *18 holes each. Yardage 6,667. Par 71.* ⌨ *Old Course: weekdays £30 per round, £45 daily; weekends £40 per round, £60 daily. New Course: weekdays £20 per round, £30 daily; weekends £25 per round, £35 daily. Joint ticket (1 round on each course) £40 weekdays, £50 weekends. ☉ Daily. Practice area, caddy carts, catering.*

Nairn. Widely regarded in golfing circles as a truly great course, Nairn dates from 1887 and is the regular home of Scotland's Northern Open. Huge greens, aggressive gorse, a beach hazard for five of the holes, a steady prevailing wind, and distracting views across the Moray Firth to the northern hills make play here unforgettable. ☎ 01667/453208. *18 holes. Yardage 6,745. Par 72.* ⌨ *Weekdays £60 per round, weekends £65 per round. ☉ Daily. Reservations essential. Practice area, caddies available on request, caddy carts, catering.*

Dornoch Firth

North of Inverness, the east coast is deeply indented with firths (the word is linked to the Norwegian *fjord*) that border some excellent, relatively unknown golf courses. Royal Dornoch has recently been "discovered" by international golf writers, but knowledgeable golfers have been making the northern pilgrimage for well over 100 years. There are half a dozen enjoyable links courses around Dornoch, and inland, another Victorian golfing holiday center, Strathpeffer, preserves much of the atmosphere those gentlemen of a past age set out to achieve.

Royal Dornoch. This course, laid out by Tom Morris in 1886 on a sort of coastal shelf behind the shore, has matured to become one of the world's finest. Its location in the north of Scotland, though less than an hour's drive from Inverness Airport, means it's far from overrun even in peak season. It may not have the fame of a Gleneagles or a St. Andrews, but if time permits, Dornoch is memorable. The little town of Dornoch, behind the course, is sleepy and timeless. ☎ 01862/810219. *18 holes. Yardage 6,514. Par 70.* ⌨ *Weekdays £57 per round, £144 for 3 days; Sun. £67 per round. ☉ Sun.–Fri., and occasional Sat. Handicap limit: men 24, women 39. Reservations essential. Practice area, caddies, caddy carts, catering.*

Argyll

The lochs and glens of Argyll in the west of Scotland have provided the scenic backdrop for family outings for generations. Wherever Scots take their holidays, golf courses are soon developed, so the string of courses north from the Mull of Kintyre all offer golf in a relaxed atmosphere, with sea, beach, and hills not far away.

Machrihanish, by Campbeltown. This is a course that many enthusiasts discuss in hushed tones—it's a kind of out-of-the-way golfers' Shangri-la. It was laid out in 1876 by Tom Morris on the links around the sandy Machrihanish Bay. The drive off the first tee is across the beach to reach the green—an intimidating start to a memorable series of individual holes. If you're short on time, consider flying from Glasgow to nearby Campbeltown, the last town on the long peninsula of Kintyre. ☎ 01586/810277. 18 holes. Yardage 6,225. Par 70. ✉ Weekdays and Sun. £28 per round, £45 daily; Sat. £35 per round, £55 daily; £120 weekly. ☉ Daily. Reservations essential. Practice area, caddy carts, catering.

12 BACKGROUND AND ESSENTIALS

Portraits of Scotland

Scotland at a Glance: A Chronology

Smart Travel Tips A to Z

BEYOND THE
TARTAN PLAID

On some old recordings of Scottish songs still in circulation, you may run across "Roamin' in the Gloamin' " or "I Love a Lassie" or one of the other comic ditties of Harry Lauder, a star of the music halls of the 1920s. With his garish kilt, short crooked walking stick, rich rolling *R*s, and *pawky* (cheerfully impudent) humor—chiefly based on the alleged meanness of the Scots—he impressed a Scottish character on the world. But his was, needless to say, a false impression and one the Scots have been trying to stamp out ever since.

How, then, do you characterize the Scots? Temperamentally, they're a mass of contradictions. They've been likened, not to a Scotch egg, but to a soft-boiled egg: a dour hard shell, a mushy middle. The Scots laugh and weep with almost Latin facility, but to strangers they're reserved, noncommittal, and in no hurry to make an impression. Historically, fortitude and resilience have been their hallmarks, and there are streaks of both resignation and pitiless ferocity in their makeup, warring with sentimentality and love of family. Very Scottish was the instant reaction of an elderly woman of Edinburgh 200 years ago, when news arrived of the defeat in Mysore in India and of the Scottish soldiers being fettered in irons, two by two: "God help the puir chiel that's chained tae oor Davie."

The Scots are in general suspicious of the go-getter. "Whiz kid" is a term of contempt. But they're by no means plodders, though it's true they're determined and thorough, respecting success only when it has been a few hundred years in the making. Praise of some bright ambitious youngster is quenched with the sneer: "Him? Ah kent [knew] his faither."

Yet this is the nation that built commerce throughout the British Empire, opened wild territories, and was responsible for much of humankind's scientific and technological advancement; a nation boastful about things it's not too good at and shamefacedly modest about genuine achievements. Consider the following extract from a handout about the Edinburgh School of Medicine: "If one excepts a few discoveries such as that of 'fixed air' by Black, of the diverse functions of the nerve-roots by Bell, of the anaesthetic properties of chloroform by Simpson, of the invention of certain powerful drugs by Christison, and of the importance of antiseptic procedures by Lister, the influence of Edinburgh medicine has been of a steady constructive rather than a revolutionary type."

Among things that strike most newcomers to Scotland are the generosity of the Scots; their obsession with respectability; their satisfaction with themselves and their desire to stay as they are; and, above all, their passionate love of Scotland. An obstinate refusal to go along with English ideas has led to accusations that the nation has a head-in-the-sand attitude toward progress. But the Scots have their own ideas of progress, and they jealously guard the institutions that remain unique to them.

At the start of the new millennium, Scotland can once again celebrate its nationhood via its own parliament, elected for the first time in May 1999 and due to move into its own specially built premises at the foot of the Royal Mile in early 2002. The return of a parliament to Scottish soil, albeit one with limited powers, has generated a new surge of pride in national identity, and over the next few years it will be interesting to see how the Scottish Parliament develops its role.

When it comes to education, Scotland has a proud record. The nation had four universities—St. Andrews,

Aberdeen, Glasgow, and Edinburgh—when England had only two: Oxford and Cambridge. The *lad o' pairts* (man of talents)—the poor child of a feckless father and a fiercely self-sacrificing mother, sternly tutored by the village *dominie* (schoolmaster) and turned loose at the age of 13 with so firm a base of learning that he rose to the top of his profession—is a phenomenon of Scottish social history. The sacrifices that boys made as a matter of course to further their education are an old Scottish tradition. "Meal Monday," the midsemester holiday at a Scottish university, is a survivor of the long weekend that once enabled students to return to their distant homes—on foot—and replenish the sack of "meal" (oatmeal) that was their only subsistence.

It's a British cliché that an English education teaches you to think and a Scottish education stuffs your head with information. The average Scot does appear to be better informed than his English neighbor and to discuss facts rather than ideas. Scots pride themselves on their international outlook and on being better linguists than the English. The Scots get on well with foreigners, and they offer strangers a kindly welcome and a civility not often found in the modern world.

Just as the Scots have their own traditions in education, so is their legal system distinct from England's. In England the police both investigate crime and prosecute suspects. In Scotland there's a public prosecutor directly responsible to the lord advocate (equivalent to England's attorney general), who is himself accountable to parliament.

For the most part, however, you'll notice few practical differences except in terminology. The barrister in England becomes an advocate in Scotland. Law-office nameplates designate their occupants "S. S. C." (solicitor to the supreme court) or "W. S." (writer to the signet); cases for prosecution go before the "procurator fiscal" and are tried by the "sheriff" or "sheriff-substitute." The terms are different in England, and procedures are slightly different, too, for Scotland is one of

the few countries that still bases its legal system on the old Roman law.

Crimes with picturesque names from ancient times remain on the statute book: *hamesucken,* for example, means assaulting a person in his home. In criminal cases Scotland adds to "guilty" and "not guilty" a third verdict: "not proven." This, say the cynics, signifies "Don't do it again."

The Presbyterian Church of Scotland—the Kirk—is entirely independent of the Church of England. Until the 20th century it was a power in the land and did much to shape Scottish character. There are still those who can remember when the minister visited houses like an inquisitor and put members of the families through their catechism, punishing or reprimanding those who weren't word perfect. On Sunday mornings the elders patrolled the streets, ordering people into church and rebuking those who sat at home in their gardens.

Religion in Scotland, as elsewhere, has lost much of its grip. But the Kirk remains influential in rural districts, where Kirk officials are pillars of local society. Ministers and their wives are seen in all their somber glory in Edinburgh in springtime, when the General Assembly of the Kirk takes place, and, for a week or more Scottish newspapers devote several column inches daily to the deliberations.

The Episcopal Church of Scotland has bishops, as its name implies (unlike the Kirk, where the ministers are all equal), and a more colorful ritual. Considered genteel, Episcopalianism in Scotland has been described rather sourly by the Scottish novelist Lewis Grassie Gibbon as "more a matter of social status than theological conviction . . . a grateful bourgeois acknowledgment of anglicisation."

Of the various nonconformist offshoots of the established Kirk, the Free Kirk of Scotland is the largest. It remains faithful to the monolithic unity of its forefathers, promoting the grim discipline that John Knox promoted long ago. The Free Kirk is strong in parts of the Outer Hebrides—Lewis, Harris, and North Uist. On Sunday in these areas no buses run, all the shops are shut, and there's a general atmosphere of a people cowering under the wrath of God. Among the fishing communities, especially those of the northeast from Buckie to Peterhead, evangelical movements, such as the Close Brethren and Jehovah's Witnesses, have made impressive inroads.

Other than religion, Scotland on the whole is mercifully free of the class consciousness and social elitism that so often amuse or disgust foreign residents in England. But its turbulent history has left Scotland a legacy of sectarian bigotry comparable to that of Northern Ireland. Scotland's large minority population of Roman Catholics is still to some extent underprivileged. Catholics tend to stick together, Protestants to mix only with Protestants. Even the two most famous soccer teams in Scotland—Rangers and Celtic—are notorious for their sectarian bias.

Finally, a word is needed on the vexed subject of nomenclature. A "scotchman" is not a native of Scotland but a nautical device for "scotching," or clamping, a running rope. Though you may find some rather more conservative people refer to themselves as Scotchmen and consider themselves Scotch, most prefer Scot or Scotsman and call themselves Scottish or Scots.

You may include the Scots in the broader term British, but they dislike the word "Brits," and nothing infuriates them more than being called English. Nonetheless, there are a lot of Anglo-Scots, that is, people of Scottish birth who live in England or are the offspring of marriages between Scottish and English people. The term Anglo-Scots is not to be confused with Sassenachs, the Gaelic word for Saxon, which is applied facetiously or disdainfully to all the English. But at the same time, English people who live in Scotland remain English to their dying day, and their children after them. Similarly, the designation of North Britain for Scotland, which crept in during Victorian times, has now crept out again. It survives only in the names of a few north British hotels. Scots feel it denies their national identity, and there are some who, on receiving a letter with "N. B." or "North Britain" in the address, will cross it out and return the envelope to the sender.

ROBERT BURNS, SCOTLAND'S ETERNAL LAUREATE

Before I visited Scotland, I had only a foggy notion of who Robert Burns was. When I traveled to Edinburgh one summer for the arts festival, I discovered him everywhere. His rakish dark eyes and bold features peered skeptically from portraits and monuments and even biscuit tins; phrases from his poems popped up in advertising jingles and newspaper headlines and in the names of tea shops and bed-and-breakfasts.

On subsequent trips, I discovered that Scotland's map is covered with places that claim an association with Burns: not just his own homes—and there are plenty, since he was constantly on the move (leaving behind him a trail of debts and lovelorn lasses)—but pubs where he drank, landscapes he praised, cemeteries where his lovers and enemies are buried. It's like the proliferation of historic homes in the eastern United States that claim "Washington slept here."

Ayrshire is officially Burns country, from the thatch cottage in Alloway, near Ayr, where Burns was born in

1759, to Dumfries, where Burns was buried in St. Michael's churchyard in 1796 (the same day his youngest son was born). Tarbolton was the village where young Burns enjoyed late evenings drinking with the Bachelor's Club and where he fell in love with Mary Campbell, the subject of some of his finest love lyrics ("Ye banks and braes and streams around/The castle o'Montgomery!/Green be your woods, and fair your flowers,/Your waters never drumlie./There Simmer first unfald her robes,/And there the langest tarry;/For there I took the last fareweel/O' my sweet Highland Mary"). At the Burns farm in Mossgiel, visitors can see the field where he ploughed up the "Wee, sleekit, cowrin, tim'rous beastie" eulogized in "To A Mouse." Klimarnock, with its Burns monument and museum, was where his first book of poetry, *Poems Chiefly in the Scottish Dialect,* was printed in 1786. Mauchline was where Burns and his wife, Jean Armour, married and had their first home together, and its churchyard's graves are covered with names from his poems. Moffat, Lochlea, Kirkoswald, and many other Ayrshire towns all have some kind of connection to Burns, often of a purely imaginative provenance: Grey Mare's Tail, near Moffatt in Galloway, is simply a magnificent cascade that has been named after the tail of Tam O'Shanter's horse, Meg, who was pursued by a horde of witches in one of Burns's most famous comic ballads.

Even the Highlands boasts Burns associations: "Wherever I wander, wherever I rove/The hills of the Highlands forever I love." Burns traveled there in 1787, following what was probably a fairly typical tourist's itinerary. He began in Stirling, where he visited the battlefield of Bannockburn, then up the north road to Inverness, with side trips to Culloden Moor and to Cawdor. From there he went east along the Moray Firth, down to Peterhead, and along the coast to Aberdeen, Dundee, and Perth, where he took side trips to Scone Palace and Ossian's grave at Crieff.

Traveling through Scotland, you get the impression that Robert Burns is as important a poet as Shakespeare or Milton or Keats or any of those English scribblers. Burns didn't just spring out of nowhere, of course. He was one of the many fruits of the Scottish Enlightenment, that glorious era of the 18th century when Scotland, seeking its own identity after being swallowed up in a political union with England, suddenly produced an astonishing crop of scientists, philosophers, and writers. Scotland's literary history up to that point boasted only the 15th century's so-called Scottish Chaucerians—William Dunbar and Robert Henryson—and Gavin Douglas, who translated the *Aeneid* into Scots (the dialect of the Lowlands) in 1513. The earliest lights of the 18th-century Scottish literary renaissance had to prove themselves by writing in English and hobnobbing in London, as did Edinburgh-born James Thomson, who published the first book of the immensely popular poem *The Seasons* in 1726, and James Boswell, whose *Journal of a Tour of the Hebrides,* documenting his travels with the sage Samuel Johnson, appeared in 1785. In midcentury, two somewhat more homegrown talents, Allan Ramsay and Robert Fergusson, brought forth poetry written in a literary mixture of Scots and English. Meanwhile, Invernesshire's James Macpherson published several volumes of Gaelic epic poems supposedly written by Ossian, the son of the ancient Scottish hero, Fingal, which Macpherson said he had simply translated into modern English. This turned into a scandal, however, when Macpherson, encouraged by his success, kept "discovering" more lost poems—whose authentic manuscripts he couldn't produce.

Although this hoax tarnished Scotland's reputation in London, Edinburgh was still a flourishing cultural capital in 1786, when the first edition of Robert Burns's poetry appeared. Intellectuals and wealthy patrons of the arts in Edinburgh were quick to seize upon this Ayrshire farmer's son, praising his portraits of rural Scotland and extolling the vigor and grace of his use of Scots dialect. To boot, Burns came equipped with good looks, a way with the ladies, dangerously radical political views, and a taste for hard liquor. Though not conventionally handsome, with his stocky build, thick features, and thin, dark hair, he managed to cut quite a figure at fashionable Edinburgh soirees between 1786 and 1788, after the phenomenal success of his first volume. Perhaps it helped that everyone, expecting to meet a clownish Ayrshire farmer with clods of mud still sticking to his boots, found instead a literate, intelligent fellow in genteel dark jacket, light-colored waistcoat, and modestly ruffled lined shirt.

Yet while Edinburgh's elite pursued this new prodigy, Burns himself seemed uncomfortable with all the lionizing, asserting himself with forthright honesty that all too often bordered on rudeness. He became increasingly restless as his stay in the capital dragged on (and his debts piled up and his love affairs grew more entangled). One senses in his letters a note of relief upon his return to Ayrshire and to the uncertain prospect of life as a farmer—and, after the failure of his crops, as an excise collector. Centuries later, these are the images that live on: Burns riding about the countryside, singing to himself as he molded random bits of song into polished poems, or hunkering down with a congenial group of local wits at a country pub.

Neither of Scotland's other two great literary figures, Sir Walter Scott (1771–1832) or Robert Louis Stevenson (1850–94), have remained as firmly lodged in the hearts of their countrymen as Burns has. Scott, who celebrated Scotland in both poetry (*The Lay of the Last Minstrel, Marmion,* and *The Lady of the Lake*) and novels (*Ivanhoe, The Heart of Midlothian,* and *Waverly*), was enormously popular throughout the 19th century, and his career was longer and his output greater than Burns's. Stevenson, although born in Edinburgh, was never associated as closely with Scotland as Burns and Scott were, since frail health, poverty, and a roaming spirit conspired to make him live abroad from the age of 23 on. Except for a handful of Scottish historical novels—*The Master of Ballantrae, Kidnapped, David Balfour,* and *Weir of Hermiston*—Stevenson's best-known works (*Dr. Jekyll and Mr. Hyde, Treasure Island*) are not even set in Scotland.

Of course, Robert Burns has never really faded from the general public's literary consciousness. For instance, just about every song that we associate with Scotland turns out to have lyrics by Burns: "My Love Is Like a Red, Red Rose," "Auld Lang Syne," "Flow Gently, Sweet Afton," "Green Grow the Rushes," "My Heart's in the Highlands," "The Banks O'Doon." *Bartlett's Quotations* devotes several pages to Burns, listing such well-known phrases as "the best-laid schemes of mice and men," "man's inhumanity to man," "death's untimely frost," "a man's a man for all that," "nursing her wrath to keep it warm," and "nae man can tether time or tide."

The main barrier for modern readers may be the unfamiliar Scots dialect in Burns's poems. But if you read the verses out loud—the best way to enjoy those lilting stanzas anyway—many of the oddly spelled Scots words are perfectly easy to understand. After all, Burns was not writing in some kind of primitive, substandard rural slang. He was following a very specific literary style, following the precedent of Allan Ramsay and Robert Fergusson. Despite his rural upbringing, Burns had enough education to write perfectly standard English, as shown by all his personal correspondence and a good number of his poems (though, tellingly, these are usually not his most successful verses). Burns himself, teetering precariously between social classes, probably shifted in conversation from correct English, which he would have spoken at dinner parties thrown by his wealthy Edinburgh patrons, to broad Scots dialect, which he would have used when he took his farm produce to market or set about wooing local peasant girls. (Scots was the everyday speech of Lowland Scotland, as opposed to the Highlands' Gaelic dialect, and therefore it is also sometimes called lowlands, or Lallans.) In his poems, he inserted dialect where any good poet uses his or her most unusual vocabulary—as intensifying adjectives, line endings, and rhymes. The result is an extraordinarily effective poetic language, with a wide range of emotion and humor.

There are other reasons, apart from the quality of his verse, why Robert Burns has become enshrined as Scotland's national bard and why his birthday, January 25, is still celebrated with formal dinners (called Burns Suppers) around the globe. People who knew him wrote invariably of his personal magnetism—his dark, flashing eyes; his lively wit; his zest for living—and what has survived of his correspondence suggests that he must have been one of those people you can't help being fond of. He also embodies something that is very near and dear to the Scottish national character: he had a common touch. He felt at home with the ordinary village life; loved bawdiness and roistering; and was deeply suspicious of authority, especially as it was invested in the Scottish kirk, with all its dour piety. Instinctively he was a hardy partisan of individual liberty, though his political convictions were inconsistent: he also nursed a sentimental fondness for Scottish royalty, especially the romantic figure of Mary Queen of Scots. Sentimentality, indeed, was curiously mixed with cynicism in his emotional makeup. Burns was as capable a writer of achingly romantic love poetry as he was of bawdy verses about lust. And while poems such as "The Cotter's Saturday Night" mawkishly extol the virtues of humble poverty, Burns laments how hard it is to eke out a living in the poignant last stanza of "To A Mouse": "Still thou are blest, compar'd wi' me;/The present only toucheth thee,/But och! I backward cast me e'e,/On prospects drear!/An' forward, tho' I canna see,/I guess an' fear!"

There's no question that Burns enjoyed a good carouse as well as the next Scotsman—after all, this is the man who wrote, in "Scotch Drink," "O Whiskey! soul o' plays and pranks!/Accept a bardie's gratefu' thanks!/When wanting thee, what tuneless cranks/Are my poor verses!" But he was probably only a social drinker. His death was most likely a result of bacterial endocarditis, brought on by rheumatic fever, although he didn't help matters any by going out one night to a local tavern, getting roaring drunk, and passing out in the January cold on his way home. Never really robust, he had been subject to periods of weakness and depression ever since he was a teenager working long, hard days on his father's farm.

Another indelible part of the Burns myth is the image of him as a great womanizer; seducing well-born ladies, making peasant girls swoon wherever he went, and scattering bastard bairns around the countryside. It's true that his first children with Jean Armour were born out of wedlock, and one of his finest poems is written to the child he fathered with Elizabeth Paton ("Welcome! my bonie, sweet, wee dochter,/Tho' ye come here a wee unsought for;/And tho' your comin' I hae fought for,/Baith kirk and queir;/Yet, by my faith, ye're no unwrought for;/Thast I shall swear!"). But Burns was no mere rake—he was usually romantically in love with whatever girl he was chasing, and when it came down to it, he was a loyal (if not entirely faithful) husband to Jean. She herself seemed resigned to his ardent nature, saying philosophically, "Our Robbie should ha' had twa wives."

—Holly Hughes

SCOTLAND AT A GLANCE: A CHRONOLOGY

ca. 3000 BC Neolithic migration from Mediterranean: "chambered cairn" people in north, "beaker people" in southeast.

ca. 300 BC Iron Age: infusion of Celtic peoples from the south and from Ireland; "Gallic forts," "brochs" built.

79–89 Julius Agricola (AD 40–93), Roman governor of Britain, invades Scotland; Scots tribes defeated at Mons Graupius (Grampians): "They make a desert and call it peace." Roman forts built at Inchtuthil and Ardoch.

142 Emperor Antoninus Pius orders Antonine Wall built between the Firths of Forth and Clyde.

185 Antonine Wall abandoned.

367 Massive invasion of Britain by Picts, Scots, Saxons, and Franks.

392 Ninian's mission to Picts: first Christian chapel at Whitehorn.

400–1000 Era of the Four Peoples: redheaded Picts in the north, Gaelic-speaking Scots and Britons in the west and south, Germanic Angles in the east. Origins of Arthurian legend (Arthur's Seat, Ben Arthur). Picts, with bloodline through mothers, eventually dominate.

563 Columba (ca. 521–97) establishes monastery at Iona.

780–1065 Scandinavian invasions; Hebrides remain Norse until 1263, Orkney and Shetland until 1472.

1005–34 Malcolm II (ca. 953–1034) unifies Scotland and (temporarily) repels the English.

1040 Malcolm's heir, Duncan (ca. 1080–1153), is slain by his rival, Macbeth (d. 1057), whose wife has a claim to the throne.

House of Canmore

1057 Malcolm III (ca. 1031–93), known as Canmore (Big Head), murders Macbeth and assumes the throne.

1093 Death of Malcolm's queen, St. Margaret (1046–93), founder of modern Edinburgh.

1124–53 David I (ca. 1082–1153), *soir sanct* (sore saint), builds the abbeys of Jedburgh (1118), Kelso (1128), Melrose (1136), and Dryburgh (1150) and brings Norman culture to Scotland.

1290 The first of many attempts to unite Scotland peacefully with England fails when the Scots queen Margaret, the Maid of Norway, dies on the way to her wedding to Edward (1284–1327), son of Edward I (1239–1307) of England. The Scots naively ask Edward I (subsequently known as the Hammer of the Scots) to arbitrate between the remaining 13 claimants to the throne. Edward's choice, John Balliol (1250–1325), is known as Toom Tabard (Empty Coat).

1295 Under continued threat from England, Scotland signs its first treaty of the "auld alliance" with France. Wine trade flourishes.

1297 Revolutionary William Wallace (1270–1305), immortalized by Burns, leads the Scots against the English.

1305 Wallace captured by the English and executed.

1306–29 Reign of Robert the Bruce (1274–1329), King Robert I. Defeats Edward II (1284–1327) at Bannockburn, 1314; Treaty of Northampton, 1328, recognizes Scottish sovereignty.

1368 Edinburgh Castle rebuilt.

House of Stewart

1371 Robert II (1316–90), son of Robert the Bruce's (1274–1329) daughter Marjorie and Walter the Steward, is crowned. Struggle (dramatized in Scott's novels) between the crown and the barony ensues for the next century, punctuated by sporadic warfare with England.

1411 Founding of University of St. Andrews.

1451 University of Glasgow founded.

1488–1515 Reign of James IV (1473–1513). The Renaissance reaches Scotland. The Golden Age of Scots poetry includes Robert Henryson (ca. 1425–1508), William Dunbar (ca. 1460–1530), Gavin Douglas (1474–1522), and the king himself.

1495 University of Aberdeen founded.

1507 Andrew Myllar and Walter Chapman set up first Scots printing press in Edinburgh.

1513 At war against the English, James is slain at Flodden.

1542 Henry VIII (1491–1547) defeats James V (1512–42) at Solway Moss; the dying James, hearing of the birth of his daughter, Mary, declares: "It came with a lass [Marjorie Bruce] and it will pass with a lass."

1542–67 Reign of Mary, Queen of Scots (1542–87). Romantic, Catholic, and with an excellent claim to the English throne, Mary proved to be no match for her barons, John Knox (1513–72), or her cousin, Elizabeth (1533–1603) of England.

1560 Mary returns to Scotland from her childhood in France, at the same time that Catholicism is abolished in favor of Knox's Calvinism.

1565 Mary marries Lord Darnley (1545–67), a Catholic.

1567 Darnley is murdered at Kirk o' Field; Mary marries one of the conspirators, the earl of Bothwell (ca. 1535–78). Driven from Scotland, she appeals to Elizabeth, who imprisons her. Mary's son, James (1566–1625), is crowned James VI of Scotland.

1582 University of Edinburgh is founded.

1587 Elizabeth orders the execution of Mary.

1603 Elizabeth dies without issue; James VI is crowned James I of England. Parliaments remain separate for another century.

1638 National Covenant challenges Charles I's personal rule.

1639-41 Crisis. The Scots and then the English Parliaments revolt against Charles I (1600-49).

1643 Solemn League and Covenant establishes Presbyterianism as the Church of Scotland (the Kirk). Civil War in England.

1649 Charles I beheaded. Oliver Cromwell (1599-1658) made Protector.

1650-52 Cromwell roots out Scots royalists.

1658 First Edinburgh–London coach: the journey took two weeks.

1660 Restoration of Charles II (1630-85). Episcopalianism reestablished in Scotland; Covenanters persecuted.

1688-89 Glorious Revolution; James VII and II (1633-1701; the first title is Scottish, the second English), a Catholic, deposed in favor of his daughter Mary and her husband, William of Orange. Supporters of James (known as Jacobites) defeated at Killiecrankie. Presbyterianism reestablished.

1692 Highlanders who refuse oath to William and Mary massacred at Glencoe.

1698-1700 Attempted Scottish colony at Darien fails.

1707 Union of English and Scots parliaments under Queen Anne (1665-1714); deprived of French wine trade, Scots turn to whisky.

House of Hanover

1714 Queen Anne dies; George I (1660-1727) of Hanover, descended from a daughter of James VI and I, crowned.

1715 First Jacobite Rebellion. Earl of Mar defeated.

1730-90 Scottish Enlightenment. The Edinburgh Medical School is the best in Europe; David Hume (1711-76) and Adam Smith (1723-90) redefine philosophy and economics. In the arts, Allan Ramsay the elder (1686-1758) and Robert Burns (1759-96) refine Scottish poetry; Allan Ramsay the younger (1713-84) and Henry Raeburn (1756-1823) rank among the finest painters of the era. Edinburgh's New Town, begun in the 1770s by the brothers Adam (Robert, 1728-92; brother James, 1730-94; father William 1689-1748), provides a fitting setting.

1745-46 Last Jacobite Rebellion. Bonnie Prince Charlie (1720-88), grandson of James VII and II, is defeated at Culloden; wearing of the kilt is forbidden until 1782. James Watt (1736-1819) of Glasgow is granted a patent for his steam engine.

1771 Birth of Walter Scott (1771-1832), Romantic novelist.

1778 First cotton mill, at Rothesay.

1788 Death of Bonnie Prince Charlie.

1790 Forth and Clyde Canal opened.

1800–50 Highland Clearances: overpopulation, increased rents, and conversion of farms to sheep pasture lead to mass migration, sometimes forced, to North America and elsewhere. Meanwhile, the lowlands industrialize; Catholic Irish immigrate to factories of southwest.

1828 Execution of Burke and Hare, who sold their murder victims to an Edinburgh anatomist, a lucrative trade.

1832 Parliamentary Reform Act expands the franchise, redistributes seats.

1837 Victoria (1819–1901) accedes to the British throne.

1842 Edinburgh–Glasgow railroad opened.

1846 Edinburgh–London railroad opened.

1848 Queen Victoria buys estate at Balmoral as her Scottish residence. Andrew Carnegie emigrates from Dunfermline to Pittsburgh.

1884–85 Gladstone's Reform Act establishes manhood suffrage. Office of Secretary for Scotland authorized.

1886 Scottish Home Rule Association founded.

1901 Death of Queen Victoria.

House of Windsor

1928 Equal Franchise Act gives the vote to women. Scottish Office established as governmental department in Edinburgh. Scottish National Party founded.

1931 Depression hits industrialized Scotland severely.

1945 Two Scottish Nationalists elected to parliament.

1959 Finnart Oil Terminal, Chapelcross Nuclear Power Station, and Dounreay Fast Breeder Reactor opened.

1964 Forth Road Bridge opened.

1970 British Petroleum strikes oil in the North Sea; revives economy of northeast.

1973 Britain becomes a member of the European Economic Community (known as the Common Market).

1974 Eleven Scottish Nationalists elected as members of parliament. Old counties reorganized and renamed as new regions.

1979 Referendum on devolution—the creation of a separate Scotland: 33% for, 31% against; 36% don't vote.

1981 Europe's largest oil terminal opens at Sullom Voe, Shetland.

1988 Revival of Scots nationalism under banner of "Scotland in Europe," anticipating 1992 economic union.

1992 Increasing attention focused on Scotland's dissatisfaction with rule from London, England. Poll shows 50% of Scots want independence.

1995 In the face of a Tory government increasingly looking like a lame duck and divided on the issue of Europe, Scotland continues to argue its own way forward. The Labour Party promises a Scottish parliament but wants to keep Scotland within the United Kingdom; the Scottish National Party still wants independence and sees Labour's Scottish parliament as a stepping-stone to full autonomy.

1997   The Labour Party wins the general election in May. A referendum held in Scotland votes in favor of the establishment of a Scottish parliament (with restricted powers) by 2000.

2000   At the start of the new millennium, Scotland celebrates its new parliament, elected in May 1999—the first to serve on Scottish soil in more than two centuries. The parliament will move into its own government building, currently under construction at the foot of the Royal Mile in Edinburgh, in early 2002.

Scotland

ORKNEY ISLANDS

The North Sound
Westray
Sanday
Whitehall
Stronsay
Rousay
Gurness Broch
Shapinsay
Birsay
Finstown
Kirkwall
Mainland
St. Mary's
South Ronaldsay
Stromness
Rackwick
Hoy
Old Head
John o' Groats
Pentland Firth
Thurso

South Ronaldsay

Fraserburgh
Peterhead
A90
Aberdeen
Stonehaven
Ellon
A920
A92
Banff
Macduff
A97
A944
A93
Buckie
A91
A920
Huntly
A96
A98
Keith
A95
Banchory
A93
A96
Elgin
Forres
A938
GRAMPIAN MOUNTAINS

Pentland Firth
John o' Groats
A882
Wick
A836
Latheron
A9
Thurso
Golval
A836
Tongue
A897
Moray Firth
Cape Wrath
A838
Dornoch Firth
Tain
Cromarty
Nairn
Inverness
Aviemore
A9
Durness
A838
Lairg
A837
Dornoch
Tore
Kingussie
A836
Ledmore Junction
Bonar Bridge
B9176
A9
Kinlochbervie
A838
A837
Ullapool
A835
Dingwall
Loch Ness
Laggan
A86
Scourie
A835
A832
Achnasheen
A832
Cannich
A831
Invermoriston
Invergarry
Fort William
Lochinver
Loide
A835
Kinlochewe
A890
A87
Spean Bridge
A830
Poolewe
Shieldaig
Lochcarron
Kyle of Lochalsh
A830
Glenfinnan
A861
Inner Sound
Broadford
Ardvasar
A851
Mallaig

Port of Ness
A857
Stornoway
The Minch
Uig
A855
Portree
Isle of Skye
Rhum
INNER HEBRIDES
OUTER HEBRIDES
A858
A859
Tarbert
Isle of Lewis
Rodel
The Little Minch
Dunvegan
North Channel
Harris
Lochmaddy
North Uist
A865
South Uist
Daliburgh
Barra

N

North Sea

ENGLAND

The Cheviot Hills

Alnwick
Hexham
Berwick
North Berwick
Dunbar
Duns
Coldstream
Kelso
Jedburgh
Hawick
Carlisle
Annan
Lockerbie
Moffat
Dumfries
Castle Douglas
Solway Firth
A711
A710
A712
A75
A76
A74
M74
A701
A708
A7
A72
A68
A698
A1107
A1
A6091
A709
A7

Montrose
Brechin
Arbroath
Forfar
St. Andrews
Cupar
Dundee
Glenrothes
Kirkcaldy
Firth of Tay
Firth of Forth
Perth
Blairgowrie
Pitlochry
Crieff
Kinross
Dunfermline
EDINBURGH
Livingston
Dalkeith
Peebles
Biggar
Motherwell
Hamilton
Stirling
Falkirk
Airdrie
Glasgow
East Kilbride
Paisley
Helensburgh
Greenock
Gourock
Largs
Ardrossan
Irvine
Kilmarnock
Prestwick
Ayr
Girvan
Newton Stewart
Stranraer
Portpatrick
Drummore
Lace Bay

SOUTHERN UPLANDS

A70
A71
A73
A713
A76
A77
A78
A736
A716
A747
A714
A9
A91
A90
A92
A94
A924
A928
A926
A85
A84
A811
A82
A827
A80
A8
A9
M90

Duror
Oban
Mull
Lochaline
Tobermory
Bunessan
Coll
Tiree
Loch Linnhe
Firth of Lorn
Ardujaine
Inveraray
Lochgilphead
Tarbert
Criamlarich
Colonsay
Port Askaig
Islay
Jura
Kintyre
Campbeltown
Brodick
Arran
Rothesay
Firth of Clyde
North Channel
A82
A85
A83
A816
A819
A815
A846
A841
A884

ATLANTIC OCEAN

NORTHERN IRELAND

20 mi
0
0
32 km

SHETLAND ISLANDS

Herma Ness
Baltasound
Unst
Fetlar
Yell
Hamnavoe
Whalsay
Ulsta
Toft
Voe
Brae
Mainland
Lerwick
Hillswick
St. Magnus Bay
Walls
Scalloway
Sandwick
Sumburgh
Sumburgh Roost

Great Britain

N

SHETLAND ISLANDS
Unst
Yell
Mainland
Lewick

ORKNEY ISLANDS
Mainland
Kirkwall
Hoy

North Sea

ORKNEY ISLANDS
John O'Groats
Thurso
Wick
Dornoch
A9
A836
A9
A98
Banff
A96
Peterhead
A90
Aberdeen
A96
Inverness
A93
Montrose
A90
Aviemore
Braemar
A93
Dundee
Firth of Tay
Perth
M90
St. Andrew's
Firth of Forth
A838
A837
A890
Ullapool
Kyle of Lochalsh
A87
Loch Ness
A82
Fort William
A85
Oban
Callander
Stirling
A82
Dunfermline
Edinburgh
A80
M8
Berwick-on-Tweed
A68
Newcastle
Sunderland
Middlesbrough
Whitby
Durham
Carlisle
M
Keswick
Lanark
Glasgow
M74
Kilmarnock
Ayr
Dumfries
Kirkcudbright
A75
Stranraer
A7
Greenock
Arran
Campbeltown
S C O T L A N D
Portree
Skye
Mull
Coll
Tiree
Islay
INNER HEBRIDES
Stornoway
Lewis
Harris
North Uist
South Uist
OUTER HEBRIDES
Bangor
Belfast
Portadown
Londonderry
NORTHERN IRELAND

ATLANTIC OCEAN

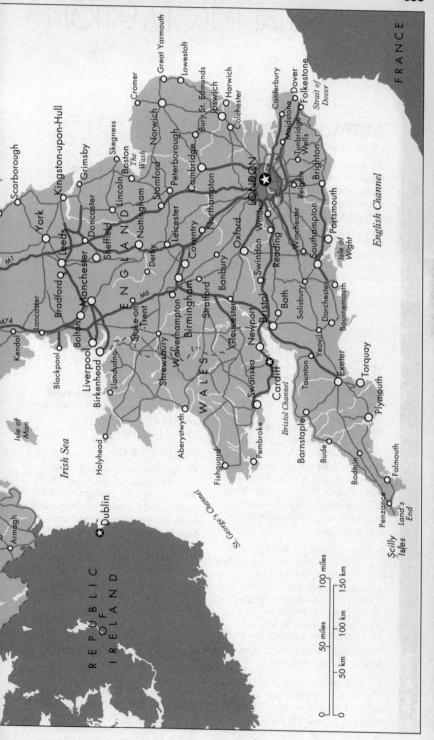

ESSENTIAL INFORMATION

AIR TRAVEL

BOOKING

When you book **look for nonstop flights** and **remember that "direct" flights stop at least once.** Try to avoid connecting flights, which require a change of plane.

CARRIERS

Although a small country, Scotland has a significant air network. Contact British Airways or British Airways Express for details of flights from London's Heathrow airport or on those from Glasgow, Edinburgh, Aberdeen, and Inverness to the farthest corners of the Scottish mainland and to the islands. KLM UK flies from London Stansted and London City; Ryanair flies from London Stansted (to Prestwick, south of Glasgow); British Midland has service from Heathrow; and easyJet flies between Glasgow, Edinburgh, Aberdeen, and Inverness (plus to and from Belfast and London Luton). **Check out discounts and passes:** For example, British Airways has in the past offered a Highland Rover Pass, which gave substantial savings on a total of five flights around Scotland in the winter season.

➤ MAJOR AIRLINES: **British Airways** (☎ 800/247–9297). Via other carriers from London and/or Manchester: **American Airlines** (☎ 800/433–7300). **Continental** (☎ 800/525–0280). **Delta** (☎ 800/221–1212). **Northwest Airlines** (☎ 800/447–4747). **TWA** (☎ 800/892–4141). **United** (☎ 800/241–6522). **Virgin Atlantic** (☎ 800/862–8621).

➤ FROM LONDON TO EDINBURGH AND GLASGOW: **British Airways** (☎ 0345/222111). **KLM UK** (☎ 0990/074074). **Ryanair** (☎ 01292/678000). **British Midland** (☎ 0345/554554). **easyJet** (☎ 0870/6000–000).

➤ WITHIN SCOTLAND: **British Airways Express** (☎ 0345/222111). **easyJet** (☎ 0870/6000–000).

CHECK-IN & BOARDING

Assuming that not everyone with a ticket will show up, airlines routinely overbook planes. When everyone does, airlines ask for volunteers to give up their seats. In return, these volunteers usually get a certificate for a free flight and are rebooked on the next flight out. If there are not enough volunteers, the airline must choose who will be denied boarding. The first to get bumped are passengers who checked in late and those flying on discounted tickets, so **get to the gate and check in as early as possible,** especially during peak periods.

Always **bring a government-issued photo I.D. to the airport.** You may be asked to show it before you are allowed to check in.

CUTTING COSTS

The least expensive airfares to Scotland must usually be purchased in advance and are nonrefundable. It's smart to **call a number of airlines, and when you are quoted a good price, book it on the spot**—the same fare may not be available the next day. Always **check different routings** and look into using different airports. Travel agents, especially low-fare specialists (☞ Discounts & Deals, *below*), are helpful.

Consolidators are another good source. They buy tickets for scheduled international flights at reduced rates from the airlines, then sell them at prices that beat the best fare available directly from the airlines, usually without restrictions. Sometimes you can even get your money back if you need to return the ticket. Carefully read the fine print detailing penalties for changes and cancellations, and

confirm your consolidator reservation
with the airline.

When you **fly as a courier,** you trade
your checked-luggage space for a
ticket deeply subsidized by a courier
service. There are restrictions on
when you can book and how long
you can stay.

At certain (less popular) times of year,
airlines may offer travel passes covering a certain number of flights within
Scotland, which offer considerable
savings over the cost of the flights
booked individually. Inquire before
your arrival in Scotland as to what is
available.

If you intend to fly to Scotland from
London, **take advantage of the current
fare wars** on internal routes—notably
between London's four airports and
Glasgow/Edinburgh. Among the
cheapest are Ryanair between London
Stansted (with its excellent rail links
from London's Liverpool Street Station) and Glasgow Prestwick, and
easyJet, offering bargain fares from
London Luton (with good rail links
from central London) to Glasgow,
Edinburgh, Aberdeen, and Inverness.
Even British Airways now offers
competitive fares on some flights.

➤ CONSOLIDATORS: **Cheap Tickets**
(☎ 800/377–1000). **Discount Airline
Ticket Service** (☎ 800/576–1600).
Unitravel (☎ 800/325–2222). **Up &
Away Travel** (☎ 212/889–2345).
World Travel Network (☎ 800/409–
6753).

ENJOYING THE FLIGHT

For more legroom, **request an emer-
gency-aisle seat.** Don't sit in the row
in front of the emergency aisle or in
front of a bulkhead, where seats may
not recline. If you have dietary con-
cerns, **ask for special meals when
booking.** These can be vegetarian, low-
cholesterol, or kosher, for example. On
long flights, try to maintain a normal
routine, to help fight jet lag. At night,
get some sleep. By day, **eat light meals,
drink water** (not alcohol), and **move
around the cabin** to stretch your legs.

FLYING TIMES

Flying time is 6½ hours from New
York, 7½ hours from Chicago, and 10
hours from Los Angeles.

HOW TO COMPLAIN

If your baggage goes astray or your
flight goes awry, complain right away.
Most carriers require that you **file a
claim immediately.**

➤ AIRLINE COMPLAINTS: U.S. Department of Transportation **Aviation Consumer Protection Division** (✉ C-75,
Room 4107, Washington, DC 20590,
☎ 202/366–2220, airconsumer@ost.
dot.gov, www.dot.gov/airconsumer).
**Federal Aviation Administration Con-
sumer Hotline** (☎ 800/322–7873).

AIRPORTS

The major gateway to Scotland is
Glasgow Airport, about 7 mi outside
of Glasgow. Edinburgh Airport, 7 mi
from the city, doesn't serve transatlantic flights, but does offer connections for dozens of European cities
and hourly flights to London Gatwick
and Heathrow.

➤ AIRPORT INFORMATION: **Edinburgh
Airport** (☎ 0131/333–1000). **Glasgow Airport** (☎ 0141/887–1111).

DUTY-FREE SHOPPING

On July 1, 1999, duty-free sales were
abolished in European Union countries, including Great Britain. The
decision to end such sales was one of
the numerous measures enacted by
the EU to create a border-free area.

TRANSFERS

Lothian Regional Transport runs
buses between Edinburgh Airport's
main terminal building and Waverley
Bridge, in the city center and within
easy reach of several hotels. The buses
run every 15 minutes daily in summer,
with slightly reduced frequency off-
season. The trip takes about 30
minutes (about 45 minutes during
rush hour). Single fare is £3.30.

Express buses run from Glasgow
Airport to near the Glasgow Central
railway station and to the Glasgow
Buchanan Street bus station. There's
service every 15 minutes throughout
the day (every 30 minutes in winter).
The fare is about £3.

➤ TAXIS & SHUTTLES: **Glasgow
Buchanan Street bus station** (☎ 0141/
332–7133). **Glasgow Central railway
station** (☎ 0345/484950). **Lothian**

Regional Transport (☎ 0131/555–6363) and **Britannia Shuttle and City Tours** (☎ 0131/556–2244).

BIKE TRAVEL

Because Scotland's main roads are continually being upgraded, it's easier than ever for bicyclists to access the network of quieter rural roads in such areas as Dumfries and Galloway, the Borders, and much of eastern Scotland, especially Grampian. Still, care must be taken in getting from some town centers to rural riding areas, so if in doubt, ask a local. In a few areas of the Highlands, notably in northwestern Scotland, the rugged terrain and limited population have resulted in the lack of side roads, making it more difficult—sometimes impossible—to plan a minor-road route in these areas.

The best months for cycling in Scotland are May, June, and September, when the roads are often quieter and the weather is usually better. Winds are predominantly from the southwest, so plan your route accordingly.

A variety of agencies are now promoting "safe routes" for recreational cyclists. These routes are signposted, and the agencies have produced maps or leaflets showing where they run. Perhaps best known is the Glasgow–Loch Lomond–Killin Cycleway, which makes use of former railway track beds, forest trails, quiet rural side roads, and some main roads. The Glasgow to Irvine Cycle Route runs south and west of Glasgow and links with the Johnstone and Greenock Railway Path. In Edinburgh there is the Innocent Railway Path from Holyrood Path to St. Leonards. Contact the relevant tourist board for more information.

The Scottish Tourist Board's (☞ Visitor Information, *below*) free brochure, "Cycling in Scotland," has some suggested routes and practical advice. The Ordnance Survey Landranger series of maps, which shows gradient, is invaluable for cyclists.

BIKES IN FLIGHT

Most airlines accommodate bikes as luggage, provided they are dismantled and boxed. For bike boxes, often free at bike shops, you'll pay about $5 from airlines (at least $100 for bike bags). International travelers can sometimes substitute a bike for a piece of checked luggage at no charge; otherwise, the cost is about $100. Domestic and Canadian airlines charge $25–$50.

BIKES ON BUSES

Although some rural bus services will transport cycles if space is available, **don't count on getting your bike on a bus.** Be sure to check well in advance with the appropriate bus company.

BIKES ON FERRIES

You can take bicycles on car and passenger ferries in Scotland, and it's not generally necessary to book in advance. The three main ferry service operators (☞ Boat & Ferry Travel, *below*) are Caledonian MacBrayne, which charges £1–£4 per journey for accompanied bicycles on some routes (on many routes, bicycles are carried free); Western Ferries, which carries accompanied bicycles free; and P&O Ferries, which charges £3–£5 single to £6–£10 return fare in addition to the cost of a passenger ticket. **Check cycles on car ferries early so that they can be loaded through the car entrance.**

BIKES ON TRAINS

ScotRail strongly advises that you **make a train reservation for you and your bike at least a month in advance.** On several trains, reservations are compulsory. A leaflet containing the latest information is available through ScotRail and can be picked up at most manned train stations within Scotland.

BIKING OFF-ROAD

People in Scotland were cycling off-road long before the mountain bike was invented. Sometimes they cycled over rights of way in the Highlands; sometimes they biked cross-country to shorten the time taken to climb less accessible high hills. The growing popularity of mountain biking, however, has forced the Scots to focus on the suitability and availability of routes.

Scotland's legal position on off-road cycling is complex. Cycling is covered by road traffic laws because a bike is classified as a vehicle. In a strict legal sense, cycling off-road is only possible on specifically designated cycle tracks, routes that have a common-law right of way for cycles, or routes that have the consent of the landowner. Legally, cyclists aren't allowed on pedestrian rights of way, but many landowners don't mind if cyclists use them. Nevertheless, it is best for off-road cyclists to seek local advice when planning routes.

BIKING ORGANIZATIONS

Cyclists' Touring Club actively campaigns for better cyclist facilities throughout the United Kingdom. It publishes a members magazine, route maps, and guides. Sustrans Ltd. is a nonprofit organization dedicated to providing environmentally friendly routes for cyclists, notably in and around cities.

➤ BIKE MAPS AND INFORMATION: **Cyclists' Touring Club** (✉ National Headquarters, Cotterell House, 69 Meadrow, Godalming, Surrey GU7 3HS, England, ☎ 01483/417217, FAX 01483/426994). **Sustrans Ltd.** (✉ 3 Coates Pl., Edinburgh EH3 7AA, ☎ 0131/623–7600, FAX 0131/623–7761).

BIKING TOURS

Bespoke Highland Tours arranges treks throughout the Highlands and the islands for cyclists and walkers of all abilities. Scottish Border Trails runs off-road mountain bike treks in the Borders and vehicle-supported road tours on which your luggage is ferried between stops. Wildcat Bike Tours sells guided, vehicle-supported tours throughout Scotland for novices and experts.

➤ BIKE TOUR OPERATORS: **Bespoke Highland Tours** (✉ The Bothy, Camusdarach, Arisaig, Inverness-shire PH39 4NT, ☎ FAX 0141/334–9017). **Scottish Border Trails** (✉ Drummore, Venlaw High Rd., Peebles EH45 8RL, ☎ 01721/720336, FAX 01721/723004). **Wildcat Bike Tours** (✉ Unit 102, John Player Building, Stirling Enterprise Park, Stirling FK7 7RP, ☎ FAX 01786/464333).

BOAT & FERRY TRAVEL

With so many islands, plus the great Firth of Clyde waterway, ferry services in Scotland are of paramount importance. Most of these now transport vehicles as well as foot passengers, although a number of the smaller ones are passengers only.

The main operator is Caledonian MacBrayne Ltd., known generally as Calmac. Services extend from the Firth of Clyde, where there is an extremely extensive network, right up to the northwest of Scotland and all of the Hebrides. Calmac offers an Island Rover runabout ticket, which is ideal for touring holidays in the islands, as well as an island-hopping scheme called Island Hopscotch.

The Dunoon–Gourock route on the Clyde is served by Western Ferries, while the Islay–Jura service is operated by SercoDenholm.

P&O Ferries operates a car ferry for Orkney between Scrabster (near Thurso) or Aberdeen and Stromness (on the main island of Orkney, called Mainland) and for Shetland between Aberdeen and Lerwick. The main ferries, the *St. Clair* and the *St. Sunniva*, have cabin accommodations and sail five times a week in each direction.

FARES & SCHEDULES

➤ BOAT & FERRY INFORMATION: **Caledonian MacBrayne** (✉ The Ferry Terminal, Gourock, ☎ 01475/650100; 08705/650000 for reservations, FAX 01475/637607; 01475/635235 for reservations). **P&O Ferries** (✉ Orkney and Shetland Services, Box 5, Jamieson's Quay, Aberdeen AB11 5NP, ☎ 01224/572615, FAX 01224/574411, www.poscottishferries.co.uk). **SercoDenholm** (☎ 01475/731540). **Western Ferries** (☎ 01369/704452, FAX 01369/706020).

BUS TRAVEL

The country's bus network is extensive. Bus service is comprehensive in cities, less so in country districts. **Remember that express service links main cities and towns,** connecting, for example, Glasgow and Edinburgh to Inverness, Aberdeen, Perth, Skye, Ayr, Dumfries, and Carlisle; or Inverness with Aberdeen, Wick, Thurso, and Fort William. These express services are very fast, and fares are quite reasonable. For town, suburban, or short-distance journeys, you normally buy your ticket on the bus, from a pay box or the driver. Sometimes you need exact change. For longer journeys—for example, Glasgow–Inverness—it's usual to reserve a seat and pay at the bus station booking office.

➤ BUS INFORMATION: **Edinburgh and Scotland Information Centre** (✉ 3 Princes St., Edinburgh EH2 2QP, ☎ 0131/473–3800, ℻ 0131/473–3881). **Travel Center** (✉ Buchanan Street Bus Station, Glasgow G2 3NP, ☎ 0141/332–7133).

CUTTING COSTS

On bus routes, Tourist Trail Pass offers complete freedom of travel on any National Express or Scottish Citylink services throughout the mainland United Kingdom. Four different permutations give up to 15 days of travel in 30 consecutive days. It's available from Scottish Citylink offices, most bus stations, and any National Express appointed agent.

➤ DISCOUNT-PASS INFORMATION: **National Express** (✉ Buchanan Street Bus Station, Killermont St., Glasgow G2 3NP, ☎ 0990/808080). **Scottish Citylink** (☎ 0990/505050).

FROM ENGLAND

Coaches (as long-distance and touring buses are usually called) usually provide the cheapest way to travel between England and Scotland; fares may be as little as one-third of the rail fares for comparable trips (though rail companies are now offering more competitive fares on some routes). About 20 companies operate service between major cities, including National Express (single class only). Journey time between London and Glasgow or Edinburgh is 8 to 8¼ hours. The main London terminal is Victoria Coach Station, but some Scottish companies use Gloucester Road Coach Station in west London, near the Penta Hotel. Many people travel to Scotland by coach; in summer a reservation three or four days ahead is advisable. Fares are about £32 round-trip, and credit cards are accepted.

➤ BUS LINES: **National Express** (✉ Buchanan Street Bus Station, Killermont St., Glasgow G2 3NP, ☎ 0990/808080).

BUSINESS HOURS

BANKS & OFFICES

Banks are open weekdays 9:30–3:30, some days to 4:45. Some banks have extended hours on Thursday evenings, and a few are open on Saturday mornings. Some also close for an hour at lunchtime. The major airports operate 24-hour banking services seven days a week.

GAS STATIONS

Service stations are located at regular intervals on motorways and are usually open 24 hours a day, though stations elsewhere usually close from 9 PM to 7 AM; in rural areas many close at 6 PM and all day on Sunday.

MUSEUMS & SIGHTS

Most museums in cities and larger towns are open seven days, although some may be closed on Sunday mornings. In smaller villages, museums are often open when there are visitors around—even late on summer evenings—but closed in poor weather when visitors are unlikely; there's often a contact phone number on the door.

PHARMACIES

Pharmacies (often called "chemists" in Scotland) usually open 9–5 or 5:30 Monday–Saturday, though most large towns and cities have either a large supermarket open extended hours, with a pharmacy on the premises, or have a rotation system for pharmacists on call (there will be a note displayed in the pharmacy's window with the number to call). In rural areas, doctors often dispense medicines themselves. In an emergency, the police should be able to locate a chemist.

SHOPS

Usual business hours are Monday–Saturday 9–5 or 5:30. Outside the main centers, most shops observe an early closing day once a week, often Wednesday or Thursday—they close at 1 PM and do not reopen until the following morning. In small villages, many also close for lunch. Department stores in large cities and many supermarkets even in smaller towns stay open for late-night shopping (usually until 7:30 or 8) one or more days a week. Apart from some newsstands and small food stores, many shops are closed on Sunday except in larger towns and cities, where main shopping malls may be open.

CAMERAS & PHOTOGRAPHY

➤ PHOTO HELP: **Kodak Information Center** (☎ 800/242–2424). *Kodak Guide to Shooting Great Travel Pictures,* available in bookstores or from Fodor's Travel Publications (☎ 800/533–6478; $16.50 plus $5.50 shipping).

EQUIPMENT PRECAUTIONS

Always **keep your film and tape out of the sun.** Carry an extra supply of batteries, and **be prepared to turn on your camera or camcorder** to prove to security personnel that the device is real. Always **ask for hand inspection of film,** which becomes clouded after repeated exposure to airport X-ray machines, and **keep videotapes away from metal detectors.**

VIDEOS

Remember that most video cartridges sold in the United Kingdom do not interface with American video players, as they have alternative video systems. Before purchasing any videos in the United Kingdom ask a staff member at the store about this concern. Happily, many attractions that have videos also market versions specially made for the American/overseas market.

CAR RENTAL

If you're traveling to more than one country, make sure your rental contract permits you to take the car across borders and that the insurance policy covers you in every country you visit. Remember that unlike cars in the United States or the rest of Europe, British cars have the steering wheel on the right. Therefore, you may want to leave your rented car in Britain and pick up a left-side drive when you cross the Channel.

Rates in Glasgow begin at £35 a day and £170 a week for an economy car with a manual transmission, and unlimited mileage. This does not include tax on car rentals, which is 17.5%.

➤ MAJOR AGENCIES: **Alamo** (☎ 800/522–9696; 020/8750–2800 in the U.K.). **Avis** (☎ 800/331–1084; 800/879–2847 in Canada; 02/9353–9000 in Australia; 09/525–1982 in New Zealand). **Budget** (☎ 800/527–0700; 0144/227–6266 in the U.K.). **Dollar** (☎ 800/800–6000; 01923/811000 in the U.K. where it is known as Europcar; 02/9223–1444 in Australia). **Hertz** (☎ 800/654–3001; 800/263–0600 in Canada; 020/8897–2072 in the U.K.; 02/9669–2444 in Australia; 03/358–6777 in New Zealand). **National InterRent** (☎ 800/227–3876; joined with Dollar in the U.K., ☞ *above*).

CUTTING COSTS

To get the best deal, **book through a travel agent who will shop around.** Do **look into wholesalers,** companies that do not own fleets but rent in bulk from those that do and often offer better rates than traditional car-rental operations. Payment must be made before you leave home.

➤ WHOLESALERS: **Auto Europe** (☎ 207/842–2000 or 800/223–5555, FAX 800–235–6321, www.autoeurope. com). **DER Travel Services** (✉ 9501 W. Devon Ave., Rosemont, IL 60018, ☎ 800/782–2424, FAX 800/282–7474 for information; 800/860–9944 for brochures, www.dertravel.com). **Kemwel Holiday Autos** (☎ 800/678–0678, FAX 914/825–3160, www. kemwel.com).

INSURANCE

When driving a rented car you are generally responsible for any damage to or loss of the vehicle. Before you rent see what coverage your personal auto-insurance policy and credit cards already provide.

Collision policies that car-rental companies sell for European rentals usually do not include stolen-vehicle coverage. Before you buy it, check your existing policies—you may already be covered.

REQUIREMENTS & RESTRICTIONS

In Scotland your own driver's license is acceptable. An International Driver's Permit is a good idea; it's available from the American or Canadian automobile association, and, in the United Kingdom, from the Automobile Association or Royal Automobile Club. These international permits are universally recognized, and having one in your wallet may save you a problem with the local authorities.

SURCHARGES

Before you pick up a car in one city and leave it in another, **ask about drop-off charges or one-way service fees,** which can be substantial. Note, too, that some rental agencies charge extra if you return the car before the time specified in your contract. To avoid a hefty refueling fee, **fill the tank just before you turn in the car,** but be aware that gas stations near the rental outlet may overcharge.

CAR TRAVEL

AUTO CLUBS

➤ IN AUSTRALIA: **Australian Automobile Association** (☎ 02/6247–7311).

➤ IN CANADA: **Canadian Automobile Association** (CAA, ☎ 613/247–0117).

➤ IN NEW ZEALAND: **New Zealand Automobile Association** (☎ 09/377–4660).

➤ IN THE U.K.: **Automobile Association** (AA, ☎ 08705/500–600). **Royal Automobile Club** (RAC; ☎ 08705/722–722 for membership; 0345/121–345 for insurance).

➤ IN THE U.S.: **American Automobile Association** (☎ 800/564–6222).

EMERGENCY SERVICES

For aid if your car breaks down, contact the 24-hour rescue numbers of either the Automobile Association or the Royal Automobile Club (☞ *above*).

GASOLINE

Though costs have been remarkably stable in recent years, **expect to pay a good deal more for gasoline than in the United States,** about £3.41 a gallon (75p a liter) for unleaded—up to 10p a gallon higher in remote rural locations. Remember, too, that the British Imperial gallon is about 20% more in volume than the U.S. gallon. A British gallon is approximately 4.5 liters; pumps dispense in liters, not gallons. Most gas stations stock unleaded, super unleaded, and LRP (replacing 4-star) plus diesel; most also accept major credit cards.

ROAD CONDITIONS

A good network of superhighways, known as motorways, and divided highways, known as dual carriageways, extends throughout Britain, though in the remoter areas of Scotland where the motorway hasn't penetrated, travel is noticeably slower. Motorways shown with the prefix "M" are mainly two or three lanes in each direction, without any right-hand turns. These are the roads to use to cover long distances, though inevitably you'll see less of the countryside. Service areas are at most about an hour apart. Dual carriageways, usually shown on a map as a thick red line (often with a black line in the center) and the prefix "A" followed by a number perhaps with a bracket "T" (for example, A304[T]), are similar to motorways, except that right turns are sometimes permitted, and you'll find both traffic lights and traffic circles on them.

The vast network of other main roads, which typical maps show as either single red "A" roads, or narrower brown "B" roads, also numbered, are for the most part the old coach and turnpike roads built originally for horses and carriages. Travel along these roads is slower than on motorways because passing is more difficult. On the other hand, you'll see much more of Scotland.

Minor roads (shown as yellow or white on most maps, unlettered and unnumbered) are the ancient lanes and byways of Britain, roads that are not only living history but a superb way of discovering the real Scotland. You have to drive along them slowly and carefully. On single-track roads, found in the north and west of Scotland, there isn't room for two vehicles to pass, and you must use a passing place if you meet an oncoming car or tractor, or if a car behind wishes to overtake. Never hold up traffic on single-track roads; it's considered extremely bad manners.

ROAD MAPS

The best general purpose touring map is the Scottish Tourist Board's Touring Map of Scotland (5 mi to the inch), widely available in bookshops, tourist information centers, or direct from the Scottish Tourist Board (☞ Visitor Information, *below*). Any bookshop in the main cities will usually sell a good range of maps. For walking or getting to know a smaller area, the readily available Ordnance Survey Landranger series (1:50,000) can't be beaten.

RULES OF THE ROAD

The most noticeable difference for the visitor is that when in Britain, you drive on the left and steer the car on the right. **Give yourself time to adjust to driving on the left**—especially if you pick up your car at the airport and are still suffering from jet lag.

One of the most complicated questions facing visitors to Britain is that of speed limits. In urban areas, except for certain freeways, it's generally 30 mi per hour (mph), but it is 40 mph on some main roads, as indicated by circular red signs. In rural areas the official limit is 60 mph on ordinary roads and 70 mph on divided highways and motorways—and traffic police can be hard on speeders, especially in urban areas. In other respects procedures are similar to those in the United States.

CHILDREN IN SCOTLAND

If you are renting a car, don't forget to **arrange for a car seat** when you reserve.

FLYING

If your children are two or older, **ask about children's airfares.** As a general rule, infants under two not occupying a seat fly at greatly reduced fares or even for free. When booking, **confirm carry-on allowances** if you're traveling with infants. In general, for babies charged 10% of the adult fare you are allowed one carry-on bag and a collapsible stroller; if the flight is full, the stroller may have to be checked or you may be limited to less.

Experts agree that it's a good idea to use safety seats aloft for children weighing less than 40 pounds. Airlines set their own policies: U.S. carriers usually require that the child be ticketed, even if he or she is young

enough to ride free, since the seats must be strapped into regular seats. Do **check your airline's policy about using safety seats during takeoff and landing.** And since safety seats are not allowed just everywhere in the plane, get your seat assignments early.

When reserving, **request children's meals or a freestanding bassinet** if you need them. But note that bulkhead seats, where you must sit to use the bassinet, may lack an overhead bin or storage space on the floor.

LODGING

The Scottish Tourist Board's two *Where to Stay* accommodation guides, *Hotels & Guest Houses* and *Bed & Breakfast,* indicate establishments that welcome children and have facilities for them, such as cots and high chairs. **Mention the age of your children when booking**—some of the more upscale country house hotels, in particular, don't allow children under a certain age (e.g., 12) to stay. On the other hand, you may well find that as soon as you arrive at your hotel or guest house, the children are warmly welcomed and a box of toys appears. Many tourist information centers have leaflets on activities for children in the surrounding area.

Although there's no general policy regarding hotel rates for children in Scotland, many hotels allow children under 14 to stay for free in their parents' room: inquire at time of booking. Many also have adjoining family rooms.

SIGHTS & ATTRACTIONS

Places that are especially appealing to children are indicated by a rubber duckie icon in the margin.

CONSUMER PROTECTION

Whenever shopping or buying travel services in Scotland, **pay with a major credit card** so you can cancel payment or get reimbursed if there's a problem. If you're doing business with a particular company for the first time, **contact your local Better Business Bureau and the attorney general's offices** in your own state and the company's home state, as well. Have any complaints been filed? Finally, if you're buying a package or tour, always **consider travel insurance** that includes default coverage (☞ Insurance, *below*).

➤ BBBs: **Council of Better Business Bureaus** (⊠ 4200 Wilson Blvd., Suite 800, Arlington, VA 22203, ☎ 703/276–0100, FAX 703/525–8277, www.bbb.org).

CRUISE TRAVEL

Many of the crossings from North America to Europe are repositioning sailings for ships that cruise the Caribbean in winter and European waters in summer. Sometimes rates are reduced, and fly/cruise packages are usually available. Check the travel pages of your Sunday newspaper or contact a travel agent for lines and sailing dates. To get the best deal on a cruise, **consult a cruise-only travel agency.**

The Scottish Tourist Board's free brochure, "Sail Scotland," includes details of many charter firms operating among the islands. The National Trust for Scotland runs a regular cruise program with lectures on natural history. The destination changes each year, but may well include the West Coast or Northern Isles the year you wish to visit. Hebridean Island Cruises offers 4-, 6-, 7-, or 14-night luxury cruises aboard the MV *Hebridean Princess* around the Scottish islands, including all the Western Isles.

➤ CRUISE LINES: **Hebridean Island Cruises Ltd.** (⊠ Griffin House, Broughton Hall, Skipton, North Yorkshire BD23 3AN, ☎ 01756/701338, FAX 01756/704794). **National Trust for Scotland** (⊠ Cruise Manager, National Trust for Scotland, 5 Charlotte Sq., Edinburgh EH2 4DU, ☎ 0131/243–9300).

CUSTOMS & DUTIES

When shopping, **keep receipts** for all purchases. Upon reentering the country, **be ready to show customs officials what you've bought.** If you feel a duty is incorrect or object to the way your clearance was handled, note the inspector's badge number and ask to see a supervisor. If the problem isn't resolved, write to the appropriate authorities, beginning with the port director at your point of entry.

IN SCOTLAND

Entering the United Kingdom from outside Europe, a traveler 17 or over can take in (1) 200 cigarettes or 100 cigarillos or 50 cigars or 250 grams of tobacco; (2) one liter of alcohol over 22% volume or two liters of fortified wine, sparkling wine or other liqueurs; (3) two liters of still table wine; (4) 60 ml of perfume and 250 ml of toilet water; (5) other goods to a value of £145 (no pooling of exemptions is allowed).

➤ INFORMATION: **HM Customs and Excise** (⊠ Dorset House, Stamford St., Bromley, Kent BR1 1XX, ☎ 020/7202–4227).

IN AUSTRALIA

Australian residents who are 18 or older may bring home $A400 worth of souvenirs and gifts (including jewelry), 250 cigarettes or 250 grams of tobacco, and 1,125 ml of alcohol (including wine, beer, and spirits). Residents under 18 may bring back $A200 worth of goods. Prohibited items include meat products. Seeds, plants, and fruits need to be declared upon arrival.

➤ INFORMATION: **Australian Customs Service** (Regional Director, ⊠ Box 8, Sydney, NSW 2001, ☎ 02/9213–2000, FAX 02/9213–4000).

IN CANADA

Canadian residents who have been out of Canada for at least 7 days may bring home C$500 worth of goods duty-free. If you've been away less than 7 days but more than 48 hours, the duty-free allowance drops to C$200; if your trip lasts 24–48 hours, the allowance is C$50. You may not pool allowances with family members. Goods claimed under the C$500 exemption may follow you by mail; those claimed under the lesser exemptions must accompany you. Alcohol and tobacco products may be included in the 7-day and 48-hour exemptions but not in the 24-hour exemption. If you meet the age requirements of the province or territory through which you reenter Canada, you may bring in, duty-free, 1.14 liters (40 imperial ounces) of wine or liquor *or* 24 12-ounce cans or bottles of beer or ale. If you are 16 or older you may bring in, duty-free,

200 cigarettes and 50 cigars. Check ahead of time with Revenue Canada or the Department of Agriculture for policies regarding meat products, seeds, plants, and fruits.

You may send an unlimited number of gifts worth up to C$60 each duty-free to Canada. Label the package UNSOLICITED GIFT—VALUE UNDER $60. Alcohol and tobacco are excluded.

➤ INFORMATION: **Revenue Canada** (✉ 2265 St. Laurent Blvd. S, Ottawa, Ontario K1G 4K3, ☎ 613/993–0534; 800/461–9999 in Canada, FAX 613/957–8911, www.ccra-adrc.gc.ca).

IN NEW ZEALAND

Homeward-bound residents 17 or older may bring back $700 worth of souvenirs and gifts. Your duty-free allowance also includes 4.5 liters of wine or beer; one 1,125-ml bottle of spirits; and either 200 cigarettes, 250 grams of tobacco, 50 cigars, or a combination of the three up to 250 grams. Prohibited items include meat products, seeds, plants, and fruits.

➤ INFORMATION: **New Zealand Customs** (Custom House, ✉ 50 Anzac Ave., Box 29, Auckland, New Zealand, ☎ 09/359–6655, FAX 09/359–6732).

IN THE U.S.

U.S. residents who have been out of the country for at least 48 hours (and who have not used the $400 allowance or any part of it in the past 30 days) may bring home $400 worth of foreign goods duty-free.

U.S. residents 21 and older may bring back 1 liter of alcohol duty-free. In addition, regardless of your age, you are allowed 200 cigarettes and 100 non-Cuban cigars. Antiques, which the U.S. Customs Service defines as objects more than 100 years old, enter duty-free, as do original works of art done entirely by hand, including paintings, drawings, and sculptures.

You may also send packages home duty-free: up to $200 worth of goods for personal use, with a limit of one parcel per addressee per day (except alcohol or tobacco products or perfume worth more than $5); label the package PERSONAL USE and attach a list of its contents and their retail value. Do not label the package UNSOLICITED GIFT or your duty-free exemption will drop to $100. Mailed items do not affect your duty-free allowance on your return.

➤ INFORMATION: **U.S. Customs Service** (✉ 1300 Pennsylvania Ave. NW, Washington, DC 20229, www.customs.gov; inquiries ☎ 202/354–1000; complaints c/o ✉ Office of Regulations and Rulings; registration of equipment c/o ✉ Resource Management, ☎ 202/927–0540).

DINING

The restaurants we review in this book are the cream of the crop in each price category. Properties indicated by an ✕🏠 are lodging establishments whose restaurant warrants a special trip.

MEALS & SPECIALTIES

The best Scottish restaurants are noted for the freshest seafood, excellent red meats and game, and the use of traditional ingredients such as oatmeal and wild berries in new, imaginative ways. City Scots usually take their midday meals in a pub, wine bar, bistro, or department-store restaurant (which might not serve alcohol and which might ban smoking). When traveling, the Scot generally eats inexpensively and quickly at a country pub or village tearoom. Places like Glasgow, Edinburgh, and Aberdeen, of course, offer restaurants of cosmopolitan character and various price levels; of these, the more notable tend to open only in the evening.

Some restaurants offer a Taste of Scotland menu. Initiated by the Scottish Tourist Board but now run independently, the Taste of Scotland scheme has helped to preserve some of the Scots language, especially the names for a variety of traditional dishes. Most smaller towns and many villages have at least one restaurant where—certainly if a local is in charge—the service is a reminder of a Highland tradition that ensured that no stranger could travel through the country without receiving a welcome.

To start the day with a full stomach, try a traditional Scottish breakfast, which consists of bacon and fried eggs served with sausage, fried mushrooms and tomatoes, and usually fried bread or potato scones. Most places also serve kippers (smoked herring). All this is in addition to juice, porridge, cereal, and toast and other bread products.

MEALTIMES

In a country so involved in the tourism industry, "all-day" meal places are becoming widespread. The normal lunch period, however, is 12:30–2:30. A few places offer "high tea"—one hot dish and masses of cakes, bread and butter, and jam, served with tea only, around 5:30–6:30. Unless otherwise noted, the restaurants listed in this guide are open daily for lunch and dinner.

PAYING

Many restaurants exclude service charges from the printed menu (which the law obliges them to display outside), then add 10%–15% to the check, or else stamp SERVICE NOT INCLUDED along the bottom, in which case you should add the 10%–15% yourself. Just **don't pay twice for service**—unscrupulous restaurateurs have been known to add service, but leave the total on the credit-card slip blank. Also note that when "pubbing," most pubs do not have any waitstaff and you're expected to go to the bar and order a beverage and your meal—this can be particularly disconcerting when you are seated in a "restaurant" upstairs, but still expected to go downstairs and get your own drinks and food.

RESERVATIONS & DRESS

Reservations are always a good idea: we mention them only when they're essential or not accepted. Book as far ahead as you can, and reconfirm as soon as you arrive. We mention dress only when men are required to wear a jacket or a jacket and tie.

WINE, BEER & SPIRITS

Whether you join in a lively political discussion in a bar in Glasgow or enjoy folk music and dancing in a rural pub in the Highlands, you'll find that a public house is the perfect site to experience the Scottish spirit and, of course, to enjoy a pint or a wee dram. Most bars sell two kinds of beer—lager and ale. Lager (try Tennent's or McEwan's), most familiar to American drinkers, is light colored, heavily carbonated, and served cold. Ale (try McEwan 80 Shilling and Caledonian 80) is dark, semicarbonated, and served just below room temperature. An increasing number of pubs, especially in the major cities, also offer a small selection of "real ales"—hand-drawn beers produced by smaller breweries, which in their range of flavors are a revelation compared to the usual pub beers. All pubs also carry any number of single-malt and blended whiskies.

If you want to do more than just sample Scottish whisky (here, most definitely spelled without an *e*) at the local pub, consider taking a distillery tour. Many have elaborate visitor facilities and attempt to inject some excitement into a process that's visually undramatic but nevertheless requires skill, method, and large-scale investment. A typical visit includes some kind of audiovisual presentation and a tour, and then a dram is usually offered. No tour of Speyside or Islay is complete without taking in a distillery.

DISABILITIES & ACCESSIBILITY

In Scotland, many hotels offer facilities for wheelchair users, and special carriages are beginning to appear on intercity and long-distance trains. However, since much of Scotland's beauty is found in hidden hills and corners "off the beaten track," renting a car is probably a better option.

The biggest organization in Britain is the Royal Association for Disability and Rehabilitation (RADAR), command central for travel information and advice on accommodations through the British Isles and Europe.

➤ LOCAL RESOURCES: RADAR (✉ 12 City Forum, 250 City Rd., London EC1, ☎ 020/7250–3222).

LODGING

When discussing accessibility with an operator or reservations agent, **ask hard questions.** Are there any stairs, inside *or* out? Are there grab bars

Terms and Conditions of Sale

1. Tickets cannot be resold, exchanged or refunded after purchase. Resale, exchange or any alteration or defacing of a ticket will render it void. Tickets may be transferred to third parties by way of a gift.

2. Lost tickets will not be replaced.

3. Ticket holders will be admitted upon presentation of their ticket on the day stated on the ticket. Royal Collection Enterprises Ltd. reserves the right in its sole and absolute discretion to refuse admission to any person without giving any reason. RCEL may require that any visitor whose behaviour is in any way disruptive should forthwith leave the Palace of Holyroodhouse.

4. For safety reasons, visitors and their belongings may be subject to security checks. Visitors' belongings must not be left unattended.

5. All children under the age of 12 must be accompanied by a ticket holding adult.

6. No photography, filming, smoking, eating or drinking is permitted within the Palace.

7. Except in the case of death or personal injury caused by negligence, RCEL excludes liability to the fullest extent permitted by law for any loss or damage suffered by a ticket holder or occurring to any items belonging to the ticket holder and will not be liable for any loss or expense due to circumstances beyond RCEL's control.

Terms and Conditions of Sale

1. Tickets cannot be resold, exchanged or refunded after purchase. Resale, exchange or any alteration or defacing of a ticket will render it void. Tickets may be transferred to third parties by way of a gift.

2. Lost tickets will not be replaced.

3. Ticket holders will be admitted upon presentation of their ticket on the day stated on the ticket. Royal Collection Enterprises Ltd. reserves the right in its sole absolute discretion to refuse admission person without giving any reason. RCEL may require that any visitor whose behaviour is in any way disruptive should forthwith leave the Palace of Holyroodhouse.

4. For safety reasons, visitors and their belongings may be subject to security checks. Visitors' belongings must not be left unattended.

5. All children under the age of 12 must be accompanied by a ticket holding adult.

6. No photography, filming, smoking, eating or drinking is permitted within the Palace.

7. Except in the case of death or personal injury caused by negligence, RCEL excludes liability to the fullest extent permitted by law for any loss or damage suffered by a ticket holder or occurring to any items belonging to the ticket holder and will not be liable for any loss or expense due to circumstances beyond RCEL's control.

THE PALACE OF
HOLYROODHOUSE
16/04/01   15:44
100   523222   69022

ADULT
(Admission)

£ 6.50

PLEASE RETAIN YOUR
TICKET
ENQ: 0131 556 7371

THE PALACE OF
HOLYROODHOUSE
16/04/01   15:44
100   523223   69022

ADULT
(Admission)

£ 6.50

PLEASE RETAIN YOUR
TICKET
ENQ: 0131 556 7371

next to the toilet *and* in the shower/tub? How wide is the doorway to the room? To the bathroom? For the most extensive facilities meeting the latest legal specifications, **opt for newer accommodations.**

TRANSPORTATION

Hertz (☞ Car Rental, *above*) can provide hand controls for its cars at its rental offices in Glasgow and Edinburgh. With advance notice, ScotRail staff will assist passengers with disabilities; inquire at any Scot-Rail area office.

➤ COMPLAINTS: **Disability Rights Section** (✉ U.S. Department of Justice, Civil Rights Division, Box 66738, Washington, DC 20035-6738, ☎ 202/514–0301 or 800/514–0301; TTY 202/514–0301 or 800/514–0301, ℻ 202/307–1198) for general complaints). **Aviation Consumer Protection Division** (☞ Air Travel, *above*) for airline-related problems. **Civil Rights Office** (✉ U.S. Department of Transportation, Departmental Office of Civil Rights, S-30, 400 7th St. SW, Room 10215, Washington, DC 20590, ☎ 202/366–4648, ℻ 202/366–9371) for problems with surface transportation.

TRAVEL AGENCIES

In the United States, the Americans with Disabilities Act requires that travel firms serve the needs of all travelers. Some agencies specialize in working with people with disabilities.

➤ TRAVELERS WITH MOBILITY PROBLEMS: **Access Adventures** (✉ 206 Chestnut Ridge Rd., Rochester, NY 14624, ☎ 716/889–9096, dltravel@prodigy.net), run by a former physical-rehabilitation counselor. **CareVacations** (✉ 5-5110 50th Ave., Leduc, Alberta T9E 6V4, ☎ 780/986–6404 or 877/478–7827, ℻ 780/986–8332, www.carevacations.com), for group tours and cruise vacations. **Flying Wheels Travel** (✉ 143 W. Bridge St., Box 382, Owatonna, MN 55060, ☎ 507/451–5005 or 800/535–6790, ℻ 507/451–1685, thq@ll.net, www.flyingwheels.com).

DISCOUNTS & DEALS

Be a smart shopper and **compare all your options** before making decisions. A plane ticket bought with a promotional coupon from travel clubs, coupon books, and direct-mail offers may not be cheaper than the least expensive fare from a discount ticket agency. And always keep in mind that what you get is just as important as what you save.

DISCOUNT RESERVATIONS

To save money, **look into discount reservations services** with toll-free numbers, which use their buying power to get a better price on hotels, airline tickets, even car rentals. When booking a room, always **call the hotel's local toll-free number** (if one is available) rather than the central reservations number—you'll often get a better price. Always ask about special packages or corporate rates.

When shopping for the best deal on hotels and car rentals, **look for guaranteed exchange rates,** which protect you against a falling dollar. With your rate locked in, you won't pay more, even if the price goes up in the local currency.

➤ AIRLINE TICKETS: ☎ 800/FLY–4–LESS. ☎ 800/FLY–ASAP.

➤ HOTEL ROOMS: **Steigenberger Reservation Service** (☎ 800/223–5652, www.srs-worldhotels.com). **Travel Interlink** (☎ 800/888–5898, www.travelinterlink.com).

PACKAGE DEALS

Don't confuse packages and guided tours. When you buy a package, you travel on your own, just as though you had planned the trip yourself. Fly/drive packages, which combine airfare and car rental, are often a good deal.

ELECTRICITY

To use your U.S.-purchased electric-powered equipment, **bring a converter and adapter.** The electrical current in Scotland is 220 volts, 50 cycles alternating current (AC); wall outlets take plugs with two round oversize prongs and plugs with three prongs.

If your appliances are dual-voltage, you'll need only an adapter. Don't use

110-volt outlets marked FOR SHAVERS ONLY for high-wattage appliances such as hair dryers. Most laptops operate equally well on 110 and 220 volts and so require only an adapter.

EMBASSIES

➤ AUSTRALIA: **Australia House** (✉ Strand, London, WC2, ☎ 020/7379–4334).

➤ CANADA: **MacDonald House** (✉ 1 Grosvenor Sq., London, W1, ☎ 020/7258–6600).

➤ NEW ZEALAND: **New Zealand House** (✉ 80 Haymarket, London, SW1, ☎ 020/7930–8422).

➤ UNITED STATES: **U.S. Embassy** (✉ 24 Grosvenor Sq., London, W1, ☎ 020/7499–9000); for passports, go to the **U.S. Passport Unit** (✉ 55 Upper Brook St., London, W1, ☎ 020/7499–9000).

EMERGENCIES

To contact the police, fire brigade, ambulance service, or coast guard, **dial 999 from any phone.** No coins are needed for emergency calls from public phone boxes.

GAY & LESBIAN TRAVEL

Outside the main cities, at least a sector of Scottish society is a little Calvinistic and not given to much in the way of open expression of heterosexuality, let alone anything else. In short, Scotland isn't San Francisco. However, most Scots also have an attitude of "live and let live," so it's unlikely you'll encounter problems or any real hostility.

➤ GAY- & LESBIAN-FRIENDLY TRAVEL AGENCIES: **Different Roads Travel** (✉ 8383 Wilshire Blvd., Suite 902, Beverly Hills, CA 90211, ☎ 323/651–5557 or 800/429–8747, FAX 323/651–3678, leigh@west.tzell.com). **Kennedy Travel** (✉ 314 Jericho Tpk., Floral Park, NY 11001, ☎ 516/352–4888 or 800/237–7433, FAX 516/354–8849, main@kennedytravel.com, www.kennedytravel.com). **Now Voyager** (✉ 4406 18th St., San Francisco, CA 94114, ☎ 415/626–1169 or 800/255–6951, FAX 415/626–8626, www.nowvoyager.com). **Skylink Travel and Tour** (✉ 1006 Mendocino Ave., Santa Rosa, CA 95401, ☎ 707/

546–9888 or 800/225–5759, FAX 707/546–9891, skylinktvl@aol.com, www.skylinktravel.com), serving lesbian travelers.

HEALTH

No particular shots are necessary for visiting Scotland from the United States. If you are traveling in the Highlands and islands in summer, **pack some midge repellent and antihistamine cream** to reduce swelling: the Highland midge is a force to be reckoned with.

MEDICAL PLANS

No one plans to get sick while traveling, but it happens, so **consider signing up with a medical-assistance company.** Members get doctor referrals, emergency evacuation or repatriation, hot lines for medical consultation, cash for emergencies, and other assistance.

➤ MEDICAL-ASSISTANCE COMPANIES: **International SOS Assistance** (✉ 8 Neshaminy Interplex, Suite 207, Trevose, PA 19053, ☎ 215/245–4707 or 800/523–6586, FAX 215/244–9617, www.internationalsos.com; ✉ 12 Chemin Riantbosson, 1217 Meyrin 1, Geneva, Switzerland, ☎ 4122/785–6464, FAX 4122/785–6424, www.internationalsos.com; ✉ 331 N. Bridge Rd., 17-00, Odeon Towers, Singapore 188720, ☎ 65/338–7800, FAX 65/338–7611, www.internationalsos.com).

HOLIDAYS

December 31–January 1 (Hogmanay and Ne'er Day); April 13 (Good Friday), April 16 (Easter Monday), May 7 (May Day); August 6 (Summer Bank Holiday); December 25–26. Note also that Scottish towns and villages set their own local holidays, on five or six Mondays in spring and summer, varying from town to town.

INSURANCE

The most useful travel insurance plan is a comprehensive policy that includes coverage for trip cancellation and interruption, default, trip delay, and medical expenses (with a waiver for preexisting conditions).

Without insurance you will lose all or most of your money if you cancel your trip, regardless of the reason. Default insurance covers you if your tour operator, airline, or cruise line goes out of business. Trip-delay covers expenses that arise because of bad weather or mechanical delays. Study the fine print when comparing policies.

If you're traveling internationally, a key component of travel insurance is coverage for medical bills incurred if you get sick on the road. Such expenses are not generally covered by Medicare or private policies. U.K. residents can buy a travel insurance policy valid for most vacations taken during the year in which it's purchased (but check preexisting-condition coverage).

Always **buy travel policies directly from the insurance company**; if you buy them from a cruise line, airline, or tour operator that goes out of business you probably will not be covered for the agency or operator's default, a major risk. Before making any purchase, **review your existing health and home-owner's policies** to find what they cover away from home.

➤ TRAVEL INSURERS: In the U.S.: **Access America** (✉ 6600 W. Broad St., Richmond, VA 23230, ☎ 804/285–3300 or 800/284–8300, FAX 804/673–1583, www.previewtravel.com), **Travel Guard International** (✉ 1145 Clark St., Stevens Point, WI 54481, ☎ 715/345–0505 or 800/826–1300, FAX 800/955–8785, www.noelgroup.com). In Canada: **Voyager Insurance** (✉ 44 Peel Center Dr., Brampton, Ontario L6T 4M8, ☎ 905/791–8700; 800/668–4342 in Canada).

➤ INSURANCE INFORMATION: In the U.K.: **Association of British Insurers** (✉ 51–55 Gresham St., London EC2V 7HQ, ☎ 020/7600–3333, FAX 020/7696–8999, info@abi.org.uk, www.abi.org.uk). In Australia: **Insurance Council of Australia** (☎ 03/9614–1077, FAX 03/9614–7924).

LANGUAGE

"Much," said Doctor Johnson, "may be made of a Scotchman if he be caught young." This quote sums up—even today—the attitude of some English people to the Scots language. They simply assume that their English is superior. Since they speak the language of Parliament and much of the media, their arrogance is understandable. The Scots have long been made to feel uncomfortable about their mother tongue and have only themselves to blame, being until recently actively encouraged—at school, for example—to ape the dialect of the Thames Valley ("Standard English") in order to "get on" in life.

The Scots language (that is, Lowland Scots, not Gaelic) was a northern form of Middle English and in its day was the language used in the court and in literature. It borrowed from Scandinavian, Dutch, French, and Gaelic. After a series of historical body blows—such as the decamping of the Scottish Court to England after 1603 and the printing of the King James Bible in English but not in Scots—it declined as a literary or official language. It survives, in various forms, virtually as an underground language spoken at home, in shops, on the playground, the farm, or the quayside among ordinary folk, especially in its heartland, in northeast Scotland. (There they describe Scots who use the brayed diphthongs of the English Thames Valley as speaking with a *bool in the mou*—marble in the mouth!)

Plenty of Scots speak English with only an accent and virtually all will "modulate" either unconsciously or out of politeness into understandable English when conversing with a nondialect speaker. As for Gaelic, that belongs to a different Celtic culture and, though threatened, hangs on in spite of the Highlands depopulation.

LODGING

The Scottish Tourist Board publishes two *Where to Stay* guides updated annually, *Hotels & Guest Houses* (£8.99) and *Bed & Breakfast* (£5.99), which give detailed information of facilities provided, and classify and grade the accommodation (☞ Hotels, *below*). The various area tourist boards also publish separate accommodation listings for their areas, annually, which can be obtained either from the Scottish Tourist Board or from the individual area tourist authority.

The lodgings we list are the cream of the crop in each price category. We always list the facilities that are available—but we don't specify whether they cost extra: when pricing accommodations, always ask what's included and what costs extra. Properties indicated by a ✕⊡ are lodging establishments whose restaurant warrants a special trip.

Assume that hotels operate on the European Plan (EP, with no meals). More and more hotels are now including a breakfast within the basic room rate; check if this is the case at your hotel when making reservations.

APARTMENT & VILLA RENTALS

➤ INTERNATIONAL AGENTS: **At Home Abroad** (✉ 405 E. 56th St., Suite 6H, New York, NY 10022, ☎ 212/421–9165, 𝔽𝔸𝕏 212/752–1591, athomabrod@aol.com, www.member. aol.com/athomabrod/index.html). **Hideaways International** (✉ 767 Islington St., Portsmouth, NH 03801, ☎ 603/430–4433 or 800/843–4433, 𝔽𝔸𝕏 603/430–4444, info@hideaways. com, www.hideaways.com; membership $99). **Hometours International** (✉ Box 11503, Knoxville, TN 37939, ☎ 865/690–8484 or 800/ 367–4668, hometours@aol.com, www.thor.he.net/åhometour/). **Interhome** (✉ 1990 N.E. 163rd St., Suite 110, N. Miami Beach, FL 33162, ☎ 305/940–2299 or 800/882–6864, 𝔽𝔸𝕏 305/940–2911, interhomeu@aol.com, www.interhome.com). **Villas and Apartments Abroad** (✉ 1270 Ave. of the Americas, 15th floor, New York, NY 10020, ☎ 212/897–5045 or 800/ 433–3020, 𝔽𝔸𝕏 212/897–5039, vaa@ altour.com, www.vaanyc.com). **Villas International** (✉ 950 Northgate Dr., Suite 206, San Rafael, CA 94903, ☎ 415/499–9490 or 800/221–2260, 𝔽𝔸𝕏 415/499–9491, villas@best.com, www.villasintl.com).

B&BS

These are a special British tradition, and the backbone of budget travel. They are usually in a family home, few have private bathrooms, and most offer only breakfast. Guest houses are a slightly larger, somewhat more luxurious version. The first of a new breed of upscale B&Bs, more along the line of American B&Bs,

have been spotted in the capital. All provide a glimpse of everyday British life. The Automobile Association grades hotels and B&Bs and publishes guides (The AA Bed and Breakfast Guide, £8.99) and have information on inspected accommodation on the Net (www.theaa.co.uk/hotels).

CAMPING

Camping is an economical option for budget travelers. Consult *Forestry Commission Camping and Caravan Sites* (free from the Forestry Commission), or the Scottish Tourist Board publication, *Caravan & Camping Parks* (£3.99 or £4.50 including postage and packing). For help planning a bicycle camping trip, contact the Camping and Caravanning Club.

➤ CONTACTS: **Camping and Caravanning Club** (✉ Greenfields House, Westwood Way, Coventry CV4 8JH, ☎ 024/7669–4995, www. campingandcaravanningclub.co.uk). **Forestry Commission** (✉ 231 Corstorphine Rd., Edinburgh EH12 7AT, Scotland, ☎ 0131/334–0303).

FARMHOUSE & CROFTING HOLIDAYS

A popular option for families with children is a farmhouse holiday, combining the freedom of bed-and-breakfast accommodations with the hospitality of Scottish family life. Information is available from the British Tourist Authority or the Scottish Tourist Board (☞ Visitor Information, *below*), from Scottish Farmhouse Holidays and from the Farm Holiday Bureau.

➤ CONTACTS: **Farm Holiday Bureau** (✉ National Agricultural Centre, Stoneleigh, Warwickshire, England CV8 2LZ, ☎ 024/7669–6909). **Scottish Farmhouse Holidays** (✉ 10 Drumtenant, Ladybank, Fife KY15 7UG, Scotland, ☎ 01337/830451, www.ourworld.compuserve.com\ homepages\scotfarmhols).

HOME EXCHANGES

If you would like to exchange your home for someone else's, **join a home-exchange organization,** which will send you its updated listings of available exchanges for a year and will include your own listing in at least one of them. It's up to you to make specific arrangements.

➤ EXCHANGE CLUBS: **HomeLink International** (✉ Box 650, Key West, FL 33041, ☎ 305/294–7766 or 800/ 638–3841, FAX 305/294–1448, usa@ homelink.org, www.homelink.org; $98 per year).

HOSTELS

No matter what your age, you can **save on lodging costs by staying at hostels.** In some 5,000 locations in more than 70 countries around the world, Hostelling International (HI), the umbrella group for a number of national youth-hostel associations, offers single-sex, dorm-style beds and, at many hostels, rooms for couples and family accommodations. Membership in any HI national hostel association, open to travelers of all ages, allows you to stay in HI-affiliated hostels at member rates; one-year membership is about $25 for adults (C$26.75 in Canada, £9.30 in the United Kingdom, $30 in Australia, and $30 in New Zealand); hostels run about $10–$25 per night. Members have priority if the hostel is full; they're also eligible for discounts around the world, even on rail and bus travel in some countries.

➤ ORGANIZATIONS: **Hostelling International—American Youth Hostels** (✉ 733 15th St. NW, Suite 840, Washington, DC 20005, ☎ 202/783–6161, FAX 202/783–6171, www. hiayh.org). **Hostelling International—Canada** (✉ 400–205 Catherine St., Ottawa, Ontario K2P 1C3, ☎ 613/ 237–7884, FAX 613/237–7868, www.hostellingintl.ca). **Independent Backpackers' Hostels Scotland** (✉ Croft Bunkhouse and Bothy, 7 Portnalong, Isle of Skye IV47 8SL, ☎ FAX 01478/640254). **Scottish Youth Hostels Association** (✉ 7 Glebe Crescent, Stirling FK8 2JA, ☎ 01786/ 891400, FAX 01786/891333). **Youth Hostel Association of England and Wales** (✉ Trevelyan House, 8 St. Stephen's Hill, St. Albans, Hertfordshire AL1 2DY, ☎ 01727/855215 or 01727/845047, FAX 01727/844126, www.yha.uk). **Australian Youth Hostel Association** (✉ 10 Mallett St., Camperdown, NSW 2050, ☎ 02/ 9565–1699, FAX 02/9565–1325, www.

yha.com.au). **Youth Hostels Association of New Zealand** (✉ Box 436, Christchurch, New Zealand, ☎ 03/ 379–9970, FAX 03/365–4476, www. yha.org.nz).

HOTELS

Hotels in the larger cities are generally of good quality. Glasgow and Edinburgh have a number of superior establishments, as well as an extensive range of good hotels in all other price categories.

If you are touring around, you are not likely to be stranded: In recent years, even in the height of the season—July and August—hotel occupancy has run at about 80%. On the other hand, if you arrive in Edinburgh at festival time or some place where a big Highland Gathering or golf tournament is in progress, your choice of accommodations will be extremely limited, and your best bet will be to try for a room in a nearby village. To secure your first choice, **reserve in advance,** either through a travel agent at home, directly with the facility, or through local Information Centers (☞ individual city or regional chapters), making use of their "Book-a-Bed-Ahead" services. Telephone bookings made from home should be confirmed by letter, and country hotels expect you to turn up by about 6 PM.

Scotland, like the rest of the United Kingdom, runs a national star (1 star to 5 stars) "Grading Scheme" to take some of the guesswork out of booking accommodations. When you're considering a hotel, guest house, or bed-and-breakfast, make sure that you pay close attention to its grading. The awards are part of the accommodations listing in the *Where to Stay* guides distributed at most tourist information centers. Not all establishments participate, but the scheme is becoming popular. All hotels listed have private bath unless otherwise noted.

➤ RECOMMENDED HOTELS: **Scotland's Hotels of Distinction** (✉ Central Reservations Office, Box 14724, St. Andrews KY16 8WA, ☎ 01333/ 360888, FAX 01333/360809).

➤ TOLL-FREE NUMBERS: **Best Western** (☎ 800/528–1234, www.bestwestern.com). **Choice** (☎ 800/221–2222, www.hotelchoice.com). **Hilton** (☎ 800/445–8667, www.hiltons.com). **Holiday Inn** (☎ 800/465–4329, www.holiday-inn.com). **Inter-Continental** (☎ 800/327–0200, www.inter-conti.com). **Sheraton** (☎ 800/325–3535, www.sheraton.com). **Westin Hotels & Resorts** (☎ 800/228–3000, www.starwood.com).

MAIL & SHIPPING

POSTAL RATES

Airmail letters to the United States and Canada cost 43p, postcards 37p, aerograms 38p. Letters and postcards to Europe under 20 grams cost 30p. Within the United Kingdom first-class letters cost 26p, second-class letters and postcards 19p.

RECEIVING MAIL

If you're uncertain where you'll be staying, you can **arrange to have your mail sent to American Express.** The service is free to cardholders; all others pay a small fee. You can also collect letters at any post office by addressing them to Poste Restante at the post office you nominate. In Edinburgh, a convenient central office is St. James Centre Post Office, St. James Centre, Edinburgh, EH1 3SR, Scotland.

MEDIA

NEWSPAPERS & MAGAZINES

Scotland's major newspapers include the *Scotsman*—a conservative sheet which also self-styles itself as the journal of record—and the *Glasgow Herald,* along with the tabloid *Daily Record.* The leader in terms of circulation, if not downright regional Scottish style, is the Aberdeen-based *Press and Journal* (an apocryphal tale relates that the P&J headlined the *Titanic* sinking as "North-East Man Drowns at Sea"). The *Sunday Post* is the country's leading Sunday paper, conservative in bent, while *Scotland on Sunday* competes directly with London's *Sunday Times* for clout north of the border, and the *Sunday Herald,* an offshoot of the *Glasgow Herald*, is another major title. There are also many regional publications in Scotland; the *List,* a twice-monthly

magazine with listings comparable to London's *Time Out,* covers the Glasgow and Edinburgh scenes. Many Scottish newsstands also feature editions of the leading London newspapers, such as the *London Times,* the *Evening Standard,* the *Independent,* and the *Guardian,* while the *Sunday Telegraph* usually has the biggest Scotland coverage.

For magazines, the selection is smaller and less sophisticated in purview. *Heritage Scotland* covers the historic preservation beat as a publication of the National Trust. *Scottish Homes and Interiors* is devoted to home design and style, while the *Scottish Field* covers matters dealing with the countryside. More regional in focus are the *People's Friend,* a Dundee-based publication that can be likened to a downmarket *Readers' Digest,* while the *Leopard* covers the northeast regions around Aberdeen. For more regional coverage, check out the glossy *Scottish Life.*

RADIO & TELEVISION

The Scotland offshoot of the British Broadcasting Corporation, BBC Scotland, is based in Glasgow and offers a wide variety of Scotland-based TV programming. BBC Scotland usually feeds their programs into the various BBC channels, including BBC1 and BBC2, with the latter considered the more eclectic and artsy, with a higher proportion of alternative humor, drama, and documentaries. Channel 3 is used by independent channels, which can change from region to region in Scotland: Grampian, the Borders, and Scottish are three channels that are regional in focus, with Grampian beamed into the north and west of Scotland and Scottish into the southern regions. Scottish TV ranges from award-winning weekly shows like *The Bill* to enormous coverage of Scottish soccer and rugby matches. Originating in England, Channel 4 is a mixture of mainstream and off-the-wall, while Channel 5 has a higher proportion of sport and films. Rupert Murdoch's satellite dishes have sprung up like an alien culture on the British skyline—his Sky cable channel, along with myriad other cable channels, has increased the daily diet now available from dawn to dusk and through till dawn again.

Radio has seen a similar explosion for every taste, from 24-hour classics on Classic FM (100–102MHz) to rock (Branson's Virgin at 105.8MHz). BBC Radio Scotland is a leading radio station, tops for local news and useful as it provides Scottish (rather than English) weather information. Originating from England—and therefore not always received in regions throughout Scotland—the BBC channels include Channel 1 (FM97.6) for the young and hip; 2 (FM88) for middle-of-the-roadsters; 3 (FM90.2) for classics, jazz, and arts; 4 (FM92.4) for news, current affairs, drama, and documentary; and 5 Live (MW693 kHz) for sports and news coverage with listener phone-ins.

MONEY MATTERS

A man's haircut will cost £4 and up; a woman's anywhere from £10 to £20. It costs about £1.50 to have a shirt laundered, from £5 to dry-clean a dress, and from £8 to dry-clean a man's suit. A local newspaper will cost you about 35p and a national daily, 45p. A pint of beer is around £1.60, and a serving of whisky about the same. A cup of coffee will run from 50p to £1, depending on where you drink it; a ham sandwich, £2; lunch in a pub, £4 and up (plus your drink).

A theater seat will cost from £5 to £30 in Edinburgh and Glasgow, less elsewhere. Nightclubs will take all they can get from you. For dining and lodging costs, *see* each chapter under that heading.

Prices throughout this guide are given for adults. Substantially reduced fees are almost always available for children, students, and senior citizens.

For information on taxes, *see* Taxes, *below.*

ATM LOCATIONS

Cirrus (☎ 800/424–7787, www. mastercard.com/atm). **Plus** (☎ 800/ 843–7587, www.visa.com/pd/atm/ main.html).

CREDIT CARDS

Throughout this guide, the following abbreviations are used: **AE,** American

Express; **DC,** Diner's Club; **MC,** MasterCard; and **V,** Visa.

➤ REPORTING LOST CARDS: **American Express** (☎ 312/935–3600; 910/668–5309 in U.S. collect). **Diners Club** (☎ 303/779–1504 in U.S. collect). **MasterCard** (☎ 800/964–767 toll-free; 314/542–7111 in U.S. collect). **Visa** (☎ 800/985082 toll-free; 410/581–3836 in U.S. collect).

CURRENCY

Britain's currency is the pound sterling, which is divided into 100 pence (100p). Notes are issued in the values of £50, £20, £10, and £5. Coins are issued to the values of £1, 50p, 20p, 10p, 5p, 2p, and 1p. Scottish coins are the same as English ones, but Scottish notes are issued by three banks: the Bank of Scotland, the Royal Bank of Scotland, and the Clydesdale Bank. They have the same face values as English notes, and English notes are interchangeable with them in Scotland.

At press time (summer 2000), the exchange rate for the pound sterling was 61p to the U.S. dollar and 40p to the Canadian dollar.

CURRENCY EXCHANGE

For the most favorable rates, **change money through banks.** Although ATM transaction fees may be higher abroad than at home, ATM rates are excellent because they are based on wholesale rates offered only by major banks. You won't do as well at exchange booths in airports or rail and bus stations, in hotels, in restaurants, or in stores. To avoid lines at airport exchange booths, **get a bit of local currency before you leave home.**

Note that with the coming of the Euro, central banks of each of the 11 Euro zone countries are obliged to exchange currencies of each nation into their own denominations. So if you arrive in any major city within the Euro zone, you can go to a central bank branch to change francs, lire, and so on, into the currency of the land for free (but not vice-versa: If you are in France, then what you get is francs, in Italy you get lire, and so on).

➤ EXCHANGE SERVICES: **International Currency Express** (☎ 888/278–6628 for orders, www.foreignmoney.com). **Thomas Cook Currency Services** (☎ 800/287–7362 for telephone orders and retail locations, www.us.thomas-cook.com).

TRAVELER'S CHECKS

Do you need traveler's checks? It depends on where you're headed. If you're going to rural areas and small towns, go with cash; traveler's checks are best used in cities. Lost or stolen checks can usually be replaced within 24 hours. To ensure a speedy refund, buy your own traveler's checks—don't let someone else pay for them: irregularities like this can cause delays. The person who bought the checks should make the call to request a refund.

PACKING

Travel light. Porters are more or less wholly extinct these days (and very expensive where you can find them).

In Scotland casual clothes are de rigueur, and very few hotels or restaurants insist on jackets and ties for men in the evenings. If you plan to attend some gala occasion, you may need evening wear. For summer, lightweight clothing is usually adequate, except in the evenings, when you'll need a jacket, sweater, or cardigan. A waterproof coat or parka is essential. Drip-dry and crease-resistant fabrics are a good bet, since only the most prestigious hotels have speedy laundering or dry-cleaning service.

Many visitors to Scotland appear to think it necessary to adopt a Scottish costume. It's not. Scots themselves do not wear tartan ties or Balmoral "bunnets" (caps), and only an enthusiastic minority prefer the kilt for everyday wear.

In your carry-on luggage, **pack an extra pair of eyeglasses or contact lenses** and **enough of any medication you take** to last the entire trip. You may also ask your doctor to write a spare prescription using the drug's generic name, since brand names may vary from country to country. In luggage to be checked, **never pack prescription drugs or valuables.** To avoid customs delays, carry medications in their original packaging. And

don't forget to carry with you the addresses of offices that handle refunds of lost traveler's checks.

CHECKING LUGGAGE

How many carry-on bags you can bring with you is up to the airline. Most allow two, but not always, so make sure that everything you carry aboard will fit under your seat or in the overhead bin, and get to the gate early. Note that if you have a seat at the back of the plane, you'll probably board first, while the overhead bins are still empty.

If you are flying internationally, note that baggage allowances may be determined not by piece but by weight—generally 88 pounds (40 kilograms) in first class, 66 pounds (30 kilograms) in business class, and 44 pounds (20 kilograms) in economy.

Airline liability for baggage is limited to $1,250 per person on flights within the United States. On international flights it amounts to $9.07 per pound or $20 per kilogram for checked baggage (roughly $640 per 70-pound bag) and $400 per passenger for unchecked baggage. You can buy additional coverage at check-in for about $10 per $1,000 of coverage, but it excludes a rather extensive list of items, shown on your airline ticket.

Before departure, **itemize your bags' contents** and their worth, and label the bags with your name, address, and phone number. (If you use your home address, cover it so potential thieves can't see it readily.) Inside each bag, **pack a copy of your itinerary.** At check-in, **make sure that each bag is correctly tagged** with the destination airport's three-letter code. If your bags arrive damaged or fail to arrive at all, file a written report with the airline before leaving the airport.

PASSPORTS & VISAS

When traveling internationally, **carry your passport even if you don't need one** (it's always the best form of I.D.) and **make two photocopies of the data page** (one for someone at home and another for you, carried separately from your passport). If you lose your passport, promptly call the nearest embassy or consulate and the local police.

ENTERING SCOTLAND

U.S., Canadian, New Zealand, and Australian citizens, even infants, need only a valid passport to enter Great Britain for stays of up to 90 days.

PASSPORT OFFICES

The best time to apply for a passport or to renew is in fall and winter. Before any trip, check your passport's expiration date, and, if necessary, renew it as soon as possible.

➤ AUSTRALIAN CITIZENS: **Australian Passport Office** (☎ 131–232, www.dfat.gov.au/passports).

➤ CANADIAN CITIZENS: **Passport Office** (☎ 819/994–3500 or 800/ 567–6868, www.dfait-maeci.gc.ca/passport).

➤ NEW ZEALAND CITIZENS: **New Zealand Passport Office** (☎ 04/494– 0700, www.passports.govt.nz).

➤ U.S. CITIZENS: **National Passport Information Center** (☎ 900/225– 5674; calls are 35¢ per minute for automated service, $1.05 per minute for operator service).

REST ROOMS

Most cities, towns, and villages have public rest rooms, indicated by signposts to WC, TOILETS, or PUBLIC CONVENIENCES. They vary hugely in cleanliness, from sweet-smelling with floral arrangements, to stinking with litter and worse on the floors. You'll often have to pay a small amount (usually 20 pence) to enter public conveniences; a request for payment usually indicates a high standard of cleanliness. Petrol stations also usually offer rest rooms (to which the above comments also apply). In towns and cities, department stores, hotels and restaurants, and pubs are usually your best bet for at least reasonable standards of hygiene.

SAFETY

WOMEN IN SCOTLAND

Scotland in general is a safe country to travel in, but normal rules of common sense apply—weirdos are found all over the world these days. Don't walk on your own late at night in major cities. Note that single rooms may be hard to find in hotels and guest houses, and proprietors may not be willing to rent out a double room at single rate if it's early enough in the day to hope for a couple to book it. Booking accommodation in advance is a good idea, especially if you're traveling in rural areas.

SENIOR-CITIZEN TRAVEL

Scotland offers a wide variety of discounts and travel bargains for anyone over 60. **Look into the Senior Citizen Railcard;** it's available in all major railway stations and offers one-third off most rail fares. Travelers over 50 are eligible for the Vantage 50 Card (£8), which provides up to 30% off all long-distance National Express or Scottish Citylink coach fares in Britain.

Many hotels advertise off-season discounts for senior citizens, and some offer year-round savings. Budget-minded seniors may also **consider overnight accommodations at a university or college residence hall** (☞ Students in Scotland, *below*).

For discounted admission to hundreds of museums, historic buildings, and attractions throughout Britain, senior citizens need show only their passport as proof of age. Reduced-rate tickets to theater and ballet are also available.

To qualify for age-related discounts, **mention your senior-citizen status up front** when booking hotel reservations (not when checking out) and before you're seated in restaurants (not when paying the bill). When renting a car, ask about promotional car-rental discounts, which can be cheaper than senior-citizen rates.

➤ EDUCATIONAL PROGRAMS: **Elderhostel** (⊠ 75 Federal St., 3rd floor, Boston, MA 02110, ☎ 877/426– 8056, FAX 877/426–2166, www.elder-hostel.org). **Interhostel** (⊠ University of New Hampshire, 6 Garrison Ave., Durham, NH 03824, ☎ 603/862– 1147 or 800/733–9753, FAX 603/862– 1113, www.learn.unh.edu).

SIGHTSEEING GUIDES

The **Scottish Tourist Guides Association** has members throughout Scotland who are fully qualified professional tourist guides able to offer walking tours in the major cities, half- or full-day tours or extended tours throughout Scotland, driver-guiding, and special study tours. Many of the guides have at least one second language other than English. Fees are negotiable with individual guides, a list of whom can be obtained from the address below.

➤ TOURIST GUIDES ASSOCIATION: **Scottish Tourist Guides Association** (✉ Kate Anderson, STGA, 2/4 Dumbryden Gardens, Edinburgh EH14 2NG, ☎ FAX 0131/453–1297).

STUDENTS IN SCOTLAND

A Student Coach Card from National Express, available to full-time students aged 17 and older, provides one-third off all long-distance coach fares in Britain; contact any National Express agent in Britain with evidence of student status. Those 16–25 are eligible for the same reduction via the National Express Young Person's Coach Card. Both passes cost £8.

➤ I.D.s & SERVICES: **Council Travel** (CIEE; ✉ 205 E. 42nd St., 14th floor, New York, NY 10017, ☎ 212/822–2700 or 888/268–6245, FAX 212/822–2699, info@councilexchanges.org, www.councilexchanges.org) for mail orders only, in the United States. **Travel Cuts** (✉ 187 College St., Toronto, Ontario M5T 1P7, ☎ 416/979–2406 or 800/667–2887, www.travelcuts.com) in Canada.

UNIVERSITY HOUSING

Many universities and colleges throughout Britain open their halls of residence to visitors during vacation periods—that is, from mid-March to mid-April, from July to September, and during the Christmas holidays. Campus accommodations—usually single rooms with access to lounges, libraries, and sports facilities—include breakfast and generally cost about $30 per night. Locations vary from city centers to bucolic lakeside parks.

➤ INFORMATION: **Scottish Universities Accommodation Consortium Campus Hotels** (✉ Box 808, Riccarton, Edinburgh EH14 4AS, ☎ 0131/449–4034, FAX 0131/451–3199). **British Universities Accommodation Consortium** (✉ Box 1730, University Park, Nottingham NG7 2RD, England, ☎ 0115/950–4571, FAX 0115/942–2505).

TAXES

VALUE-ADDED TAX

The British sales tax, VAT (Value Added Tax), is 17.5%. The tax is almost always included in quoted prices in shops, hotels, and restaurants. Global Refund is a VAT refund service that makes getting your money back hassle-free. The service is available Europe-wide at 130,000 affiliated stores. In participating stores, **ask for the Global Refund form** (called a Shopping Cheque). Have it stamped like any customs form by customs officials when you leave the European Union. Then take the form to one of the more than 700 Global Refund counters—conveniently located at every major airport and border crossing—and your money will be refunded on the spot in the form of cash, check, or a refund to your credit-card account (minus a small percentage for processing).

Further details on how to get a VAT refund and a list of stores offering tax-free shopping are available from the British Tourist Authority (☞ Visitor Information, *below*).

➤ V.A.T. REFUNDS: **Global Refund** (✉ 707 Summer St., Stamford, CT 06901, ☎ 800/566–9828, FAX 203/674–8709, taxfree@us.globalrefund.com, www.globalrefund.com).

TAXIS

In Edinburgh, Glasgow, and the larger cities, taxis with their "Taxi" sign illuminated can be hailed on the street, or booked by phone (expect a charge). Elsewhere, most communities of any size at all have a taxi service; your hotel or landlady will be able to supply telephone numbers. Very often you will find an advertisement for the local taxi service in public phone booths.

TELEPHONES

Bear in mind that hotels usually levy a hefty (up to 300%) surcharge on calls; it's better to **use pay phones or a calling card.**

AREA & COUNTRY CODES

The country code for Great Britain is 44. When dialing a Scottish or British number from abroad, drop the initial

0 from the local area code. For instance, if you were calling Edinburgh Castle from New York City to ask about opening hours, you would first dial 011 (the international code), 44 (the Great Britain country code), 131 (the Edinburgh city code), then 668–8800 (the number proper). Note the big news on the English front: London has undergone a major area code change. In April 1999, the two city area codes of 0171 and 0181 were changed to a single code, 020, with the 7 or 8 then added to the seven-digit London phone number, bringing it up to eight digits. In Scotland, cellular phone numbers, the 0800 toll-free code and local-rate 0345 numbers do not have a 1 after the initial 0, nor do a range of premium-rate numbers, for example 0891, and special-rate numbers, for example 08705.

DIRECTORY & OPERATOR ASSISTANCE

To call the operator, dial 100; directory inquiries (information), 192; international directory inquiries, 153.

INTERNATIONAL CALLS

To make international calls *from* Scotland, you must use the international access code 00 + the country code + area code + number. For the international operator, credit card, or collect calls, dial 155. The country code is 1 for the United States and Canada, 61 for Australia, and 64 for New Zealand.

LONG-DISTANCE CALLS

For long-distance calls within Britain, dial the area code (which usually begins with 01), followed by the telephone number. The area code prefix is only used when you are dialing from outside the city. In provincial areas, the dialing codes for nearby towns are often posted in the booth.

LONG-DISTANCE SERVICES

AT&T, MCI, and Sprint access codes make calling long distance relatively convenient, but you may find the local access number blocked in many hotel rooms. First ask the hotel operator to connect you. If the hotel operator balks, ask for an international operator, or dial the international operator yourself. One way to improve your odds of getting connected to your long-distance carrier is to travel with more than one company's calling card (a hotel may block Sprint, for example, but not MCI). If all else fails, call from a pay phone.

➤ ACCESS CODES: **AT&T Direct** (In the U.K., there are AT&T access numbers to dial the U.S. using three different phone types— ☎ 0500/890011 Cable & Wireless; 0800/890011 British Telecom; 0800/0130011 AT&T; 800/435–0812 for other areas). **MCI WorldPhone** (In the U.K., dial ☎ 0800/890222 to dial the U.S via MCI; 800/444–4141 for other areas). **Sprint Global One** (In the U.K., there are Sprint access numbers to dial the U.S. using two different phone types— ☎ 0500/890877 Cable & Wireless; 0800/890877 British Telecom; 800/877–4646 for other areas).

PUBLIC PHONES

There are three types of public pay phones: those that accept only coins, those that accept only phone cards, and those that take British Telecom (BT) phone cards and credit cards. For coin-only phones, insert coins *before* dialing (minimum charge is 10p). Sometimes phones have a "press on answer" (POA) button, which you press when the caller answers.

For phone card telephones, buy BT (British Telecom) cards from shops, post offices, or newsstands. They are ideal for longer calls, are composed of units of 10p, and come in values of £3, £5, £10 and more. An indicator panel on the phone shows the number of units you've used; at the end of your call the card is returned.

TIME

England sets its clocks by Greenwich Mean Time, five hours ahead of the U.S. East Coast. British summer time (GMT plus one hour) requires an additional adjustment from about the end of March to the end of October.

TIPPING

Some restaurants and most hotels add a service charge of 10%–15% to the bill. In this case you aren't expected to tip. If no service charge is indicated, add 10% to your total bill, but always check first. Taxi drivers should also get 10%, hairdressers and barbers 10%–15%. You are not expected to tip theater or movie theater ushers, elevator operators, or bartenders in pubs.

TOURS & PACKAGES

Because everything is prearranged on a prepackaged tour or independent vacation—you'll spend less time planning—and often get it all at a good price.

BOOKING WITH AN AGENT

Travel agents are excellent resources. But it's a good idea to collect brochures from several agencies as some agents' suggestions may be influenced by relationships with tour and package firms that reward them for volume sales. If you have a special interest, **find an agent with expertise in that area**; ASTA (☞ Travel Agencies, *below*) has a database of specialists worldwide.

Make sure your travel agent knows the accommodations and other services of the place they're recommending. Ask about the hotel's location, room size, beds, and whether it has a pool, room service, or programs for children, if you care about these. Has your agent been there in person or sent others whom you can contact?

Do some homework on your own, too: local tourism boards can provide information about lesser-known and small-niche operators, some of which may sell only direct.

BUYER BEWARE

Each year consumers are stranded or lose their money when tour operators—even large ones with excellent reputations—go out of business. So **check out the operator.** Ask several travel agents about its reputation, and try to **book with a company that has a consumer-protection program.** (Look for information in the company's brochure.) In the United States, members of the National Tour Association and the United States Tour Operators Association are required to set aside funds to cover

your payments and travel arrangements in the event that the company defaults. It's also a good idea to choose a company that participates in the American Society of Travel Agents' Tour Operator Program (TOP); ASTA will act as mediator in any disputes between you and your tour operator.

Remember that the more your package or tour includes the better you can predict the ultimate cost of your vacation. Make sure you know exactly what is covered, and **beware of hidden costs.** Are taxes, tips, and transfers included? Entertainment and excursions? These can add up.

➤ TOUR-OPERATOR RECOMMENDATIONS: **American Society of Travel Agents** (☞ Travel Agencies, *below*). **National Tour Association** (NTA; ✉ 546 E. Main St., Lexington, KY 40508, ☎ 606/226–4444 or 800/ 682–8886, www.ntaonline.com). **United States Tour Operators Association** (USTOA; ✉ 342 Madison Ave., Suite 1522, New York, NY 10173, ☎ 212/599–6599 or 800/468–7862, FAX 212/599–6744, ustoa@aol.com, www.ustoa.com).

TRAIN TRAVEL

Scotland has a rail network extending all the way to Thurso and Wick, the most northerly stations in the British Isles. Lowland services, most of which originate in Glasgow or Edinburgh, are generally fast and reliable. A shuttle makes the 50-minute trip between the cities every half hour. (For information about Edinburgh's and Glasgow's train stations, *see* Chapters 1 and 2, respectively.) Some lines in Scotland—all suburban services and lines north and west of Inverness—operate on one class only (standard). Long-distance services carry buffet and refreshment cars. One word of caution: There are very few trains in the Highlands on Sundays.

The British rail system has been totally privatized over the past 10 years. Although the standard of service hasn't yet reached expectations, service doesn't radically differ from the days when a national system was in place. For train information, prices, and schedules throughout Britain contact the National Rail Enquiries.

CLASSES

Most trains offer first-class and standard-class coaches. First-class coaches are always less crowded; although they have wider seats and are often cleaner and less well-worn than standard-class cars, they're a lot more expensive. However, on weekends you can often upgrade from standard to first class for a small fee (often £5)— ask at the time of booking.

CUTTING COSTS

If you plan to travel by train in Scotland, **consider purchasing a BritRail Pass,** which also allows travel in England and Wales. Remember that EurailPasses aren't honored in Great Britain, and be aware that if you don't plan to cover many miles, you may come out ahead by buying individual tickets. The cost of a BritRail adult pass for 8 days is $265 standard and $400 first-class; for 15 days, $400 standard and $600 first-class; for 22 days, $505 and $760; and for a month, $600 and $900. The Youth Pass, for those ages 16–25, provides unlimited second-class travel and costs $215 for 8 days, $280 for 15 days, $355 for 22 days, and $420 for one month. The Senior Pass, for passengers over 60, is first-class only and costs $340 for 8 days, $510 for 15 days, $645 for 22 days, and $765 for one month. (These are U.S. dollar figures; Canadian prices will be a bit higher.)

If you want the flexibility of a car combined with the speed and comfort of the train, try BritRail/Drive (from $473 for one adult, with a $166 supplement for additional adults and $72.50 for children 5–15); this gives you a three-day BritRail Flexipass and three vouchers valid for Hertz car rental from more than 100 locations throughout Great Britain. A six-day rail pass with seven days of car rental is also available (from $958 car and driver, with $241 adult supplement, $105 children, with a current "free child per adult" deal for children under five traveling gratis). Prices listed are for compact, automatic transmission cars, with first-class seats; other options—manual transmission, larger cars, and so on, are available at different prices. If you call your travel agency or Hertz's international desk, the car of your choice will be waiting for you at the station as you alight from your train.

The Freedom of Scotland Travelpass allows transportation on all Caledonian MacBrayne and Strathclyde ferries and discounts on some P&O ferry routes to the islands. You can travel any 4 days in an 8-day period ($125); 8 days in a 15-day period ($189); and 12 days in a 15-day period ($215).

Although some passes may be purchased in Scotland, **you must purchase many passes stateside;** they're sold by travel agents as well as BritRail or Rail Europe.

Many travelers assume that rail passes guarantee them seats on the trains they wish to ride. Not so. You need to **book seats ahead even if you are using a rail pass;** seat reservations are required on some European trains, particularly high-speed trains, and are a good idea on trains that may be crowded—particularly in summer on popular routes. You will also need a reservation if you purchase overnight sleeping accommodations.

FARES & SCHEDULES

Train fares vary according to class of ticket purchased and distance traveled, and you can pay with credit cards. The fare system is complex. Before you buy your ticket, be sure to stop at the Information Office/Travel Centre and request the lowest fare to your destination and information about any special offers. Note that your ticket does *not* guarantee you a seat. For that you need a seat reservation, which if made at the time of ticket purchase is usually included in the ticket price, or if booked separately, must be paid for at a cost of £1 *per train* on your itinerary (that is, £2 if you need to book seats on two trains). You can opt to sit facing toward or away from the engine, and in a smoking or nonsmoking compartment.

FROM ENGLAND

There are two main rail routes to Scotland from the south of England. The first, the west coast main line, runs from London Euston to Glasgow Central; it takes 5½ hours to make the 400-mi trip to central Scotland, and service is frequent and reliable, with one train every two hours on average. Useful for daytime travel to the Scottish Highlands, and equipped with an excellent restaurant car, is the direct train to Stirling and Aviemore, terminating at Inverness. For a restful route to the Scottish Highlands, take the overnight sleeper service, with air-conditioned, soundproof sleeping carriages. It runs from London Euston, departing in late evening, to Perth, Stirling, Aviemore, and Inverness, where it arrives the following morning.

The second route is the east coast main line from London King's Cross to Edinburgh; it provides the quickest trip to the Scottish capital, and between 8 AM and 6 PM there are 16 trains to Edinburgh, three of them through to Aberdeen. Limited-stop expresses like the *Flying Scotsman* make the 393-mi London to Edinburgh journey in around four hours. Connecting services to most parts of Scotland—particularly the Western Highlands—are often better from Edinburgh than from Glasgow.

Trains from elsewhere in England are good: There is regular service from Birmingham, Manchester, Liverpool, and Bristol to Glasgow and Edinburgh. From Harwich (the port of call for ships from Holland, Germany, and Denmark), you can travel to Glasgow via Manchester. But it is faster to change at Peterborough for the east coast main line to Edinburgh. Reservations for all sleeper services are essential.

SCENIC ROUTES

Although many routes in Scotland run through extremely attractive countryside, several stand out: from Glasgow to Oban via Loch Lomond; to Fort William and Mallaig via Rannoch (ferry connection to Skye); from Edinburgh to Inverness via the Forth Bridge and Perth; from Inverness to Kyle of Lochalsh and to Wick; and from Inverness to Aberdeen.

A luxury private train, the *Royal Scotsman,* does scenic tours, partly under steam power, with banquets en route. This is a luxury experience: Some evenings require formal wear (black tie for men, evening dresses for women). Only 36 people are carried per trip. For trips within Scotland, there is a choice of a two-night (£1,390) or four-night (£2,450) tour.

➤ TRAIN INFORMATION: **BritRail Travel** (✉ 226 Westchester Ave., White Plains, NY 10604, ☎ 888/ 274–8724 or 800/677–8585; ✉ 2087 Dundas St. E., Suite 105, Mississauga, Ontario l4X 1M2, ☎ 905/ 602–4195 or 800/361–7245) recently merged with **National Rail Enquiries** ☎ 020/7928–5151; 0345/484950; or 0161/236–3522 outside the U.K.). **Rail Europe** (✉ 226 Westchester Ave., White Plains, NY 10604, ☎ 800/848–7245).

➤ TRAIN TOURS: Book Royal Scotsman tours through **Abercrombie & Kent** (✉ Sloane Square House, Holbein Pl., London SW1W 8NS, ☎ 020/7730–9600, FAX 020/7730–9376, www.abercrombiekent.co.uk; or ✉ 1420 Kensington Rd., Oak Brook, IL 60521, ☎ 312/954–2944 or 800/ 323–7308).

TRAVEL AGENCIES

A good travel agent puts your needs first. Look for an agency that has been in business at least five years, emphasizes customer service, and has someone on staff who specializes in your destination. In addition, **make sure the agency belongs to a professional trade organization.** The American Society of Travel Agents (ASTA), with 27,000 agents in some 170 countries, is the largest and most influential in the field. Operating under the motto "Integrity in Travel," it maintains and enforces a strict code of ethics and will step in to help mediate any agent-client disputes if necessary. ASTA also maintains a Web site that includes a directory of agents. (If a travel agency is also acting as your tour operator, *see* Buyer Beware *in* Tours & Packages, *above.*)

➤ LOCAL AGENT REFERRALS: **American Society of Travel Agents (ASTA;**

☎ 800/965–2782 24-hr hot line, FAX 703/684–8319, www.astanet.com). **Association of British Travel Agents** (✉ 68–71 Newman St., London W1P 4AH, ☎ 020/7637–2444, FAX 020/ 7637–0713, abta.co.uk, www. abtanet.com). **Association of Canadian Travel Agents** (✉ 1729 Bank St., Suite 201, Ottawa, Ontario K1V 7Z5, ☎ 613/521–0474, FAX 613/521–0805, acta.ntl@sympatico.ca). **Australian Federation of Travel Agents** (✉ Level 3, 309 Pitt St., Sydney 2000, ☎ 02/9264–3299, FAX 02/9264–1085, www.afta.com.au). **Travel Agents' Association of New Zealand** (✉ Box 1888, Wellington 10033, ☎ 04/499–0104, FAX 04/499–0827, taanz@tias-net.co.nz).

VISITOR INFORMATION

For general information about Scotland, contact the British and Scottish tourism offices.

➤ BRITISH TOURIST AUTHORITY: **British Tourist Authority (BTA)** U.S.: (✉ 551 5th Ave., 7th floor, New York, NY 10176, ☎ 212/986–2200 or 800/462–2748; ✉ 625 N. Michigan Ave., Suite 1510, Chicago, IL 60611 [personal callers only]). Canada: (✉ 5915 Airport Rd., Suite 120, Mississauga, Ontario L4V 1T1, ☎ 905/405–1840 or 800/847–4885). U.K.: **British Visitor Centre** (✉ 1 Piccadilly Circus, SW1Y 4PQ) for travel, hotel, and entertainment information; also ✉ Thames Tower, Black's Rd., London W6 9EL; mail inquiries only.

➤ SCOTTISH TOURIST BOARD: U.K.: ✉ 23 Ravelston Terr., Edinburgh EH4 3EU, ☎ 0131/332–2433, FAX 0131/315–4545; ✉ 19 Cockspur St., London SW1Y 5BL, ☎ 020/7930–8661, FAX 020/7930–1817.

➤ U.S. GOVERNMENT ADVISORIES: **U.S. Department of State** (✉ Overseas Citizens Services Office, Room 4811 N.S., 2201 C St. NW, Washington, DC 20520, ☎ 202/647–5225 for interactive hot line, 301/946–4400 for computer bulletin board, FAX 202/647–3000 for interactive hot line); enclose a self-addressed, stamped, business-size envelope.

WEB SITES

Do check out the World Wide Web when you're planning. You'll find everything from current weather forecasts to virtual tours of famous cities. Fodor's Web site, www.fodors. com, is a great place to start your on-line travels. When you see a ☜ in this book, go to www.fodors.com/urls for an up-to-date link to that destination's site. For more specific information on Scotland, visit: www.holiday. scotland.net, the Scottish Tourist Board's Web site. For stately homes, try the National Trust for Scotland's site: www.nts.org..

WHEN TO GO

The Scottish climate has been much maligned (sometimes with justification). You can be unlucky: You may spend a summer week in Scotland and experience nothing but low clouds and drizzle. But on the other hand, you may enjoy calm Mediterranean-like weather even in early spring and late fall.

Generally speaking, Scotland is three or four degrees cooler than southern England. The east is drier and colder than the west; Edinburgh's rainfall is comparable to Rome's, while Glasgow's is more like that in Vancouver—yet the cities are only 44 mi apart. Long summer evenings grow longer still as you travel north. Dawn in Orkney and Shetland in June is at around 1 AM, no more than an hour or so after sunset. Winter days are very short.

Scotland has few thunderstorms and little fog, except for local mists near coasts. But there are often variable winds that reach gale force even in summer. They blow away the hordes of gnats and midges, the curse of the western Highlands.

CLIMATE

What follows are average daily maximum and minimum temperatures for major cities in Scotland.

➤ FORECASTS: **Weather Channel Connection** (☎ 900/932–8437), 95¢ per minute from a Touch-Tone phone.

ABERDEEN

Jan.	43F	6C	May	54F	12C	Sept.	59F	15C
	36	2		43	6		49	9
Feb.	43F	6C	June	61F	16C	Oct.	54F	12C
	36	2		49	9		43	6
Mar.	47F	8C	July	63F	17C	Nov.	47F	8C
	36	2		52	11		40	4
Apr.	49F	9C	Aug.	63F	17C	Dec.	45F	7C
	40	4		52	11		36	2

EDINBURGH

Jan.	43F	6C	May	58F	14C	Sept.	61F	16C
	34	1		43	6		49	9
Feb.	43F	6C	June	63F	17C	Oct.	54F	12C
	34	1		49	9		45	7
Mar.	47F	8C	July	65F	18C	Nov.	49F	9C
	36	2		52	11		40	4
Apr.	52F	11C	Aug.	65F	18C	Dec.	45F	7C
	40	4		52	11		36	2

HIGHLANDS

Jan.	43F	6C	May	58F	14C	Sept.	61F	16C
	32	0		43	6		49	9
Feb.	45F	7C	June	63F	17C	Oct.	56F	13C
	34	1		49	9		43	6
Mar.	49F	9C	July	65F	18C	Nov.	49F	9C
	36	2		52	11		38	3
Apr.	52F	11C	Aug.	65F	18C	Dec.	45F	7C
	40	4		52	11		34	1

ORKNEY ISLANDS

Jan.	43F	6C	May	54F	12C	Sept.	58F	14C
	36	2		43	6		49	9
Feb.	43F	6C	June	58F	14C	Oct.	52F	11C
	36	2		47	8		45	7
Mar.	45F	7C	July	61F	16C	Nov.	47F	8C
	38	3		50	10		41	5
Apr.	49F	9C	Aug.	61F	16C	Dec.	45F	7C
	40	4		50	10		38	3

FESTIVALS AND SEASONAL EVENTS

➤ DEC. 30–JAN. 1: **Hogmanay** (Edinburgh Tourist Information, ☎ 0131/473–3838), Edinburgh's ancient, still-thriving alternative to Christmas.

➤ JAN. 25: **Burns Night** dinners and other events are held in memory of Robert Burns in Glasgow, Ayr, Dumfries, Edinburgh, and many other towns and villages.

➤ MID-JAN.–EARLY FEB.: **Celtic Connections** (✉ Glasgow Royal Concert Hall, 2 Sauchiehall St., Glasgow G2 3NY, ☎ 0141/332–6633), an ever-expanding annual homage to Celtic music, with musicians from all over the world, hands-on workshops, and much more.

➤ LAST TUESDAY IN JAN.: During **Up Helly Aa** (details from Shetland Tourist Board, ✉ Market Cross, Lerwick, Shetland ZE1 0LU, ☎ 01595/693434), Shetlanders celebrate their Viking heritage, culminating in the burning of a replica Viking long ship.

➤ EARLY APR.: **Edinburgh International Science Festival** (✉ 8 Lochend

Rd., Edinburgh EH6 8BR, ☎ 0131/530–2001, www.edinburghfestivals.co.uk) aims to make science accessible, interesting, and, above all, fun, especially—but not exclusively for children—at venues throughout the city.

➤ APR.: **Shetland Folk Festival** (details from Shetland Tourist Board; ☞ *above*) is one of the biggest folk gatherings in Scotland, set in the home of fiddle playing.

➤ EASTER: **Shoots and Roots** (☎ FAX 0131/557–1050), the Edinburgh Folk Festival, has an emphasis on folk, jazz, rock, and classical crossovers.

➤ MID-MAY: The **Perth Festival of the Arts** (☎ 01738/475295) offers orchestral and choral concerts, drama, opera, recitals, and ballet throughout Perth, Tayside.

➤ LATE MAY: **Orkney Folk Festival** (⊠ Box 4, Stromness, Orkney, ☎ 01856/851331) brings the folkies back up to the far north in the hundreds.

➤ JUNE–AUG.: **Highland Games,** held annually in many Highland towns, feature athletic and cultural events such as hammer throwing, caber tossing, Highland dancing, and pipe-band performances.

➤ THIRD WEEK IN JUNE: **St. Magnus Festival** (⊠ Strandal, Nicolson St., Kirkwall, Orkney, ☎ 01856/872669) is a feast of classical and modern music, often showcasing new vocal or orchestral compositions.

➤ MID-AUG.–EARLY SEPT.: The **Edinburgh International Festival** (⊠ Festival Centre, Castlehill, Edinburgh EH1 1ND, ☎ 0131/473–2099; tickets 0131/473–2001, FAX 0131/473–2003, www.edinburghfestivals.co.uk), which runs for three weeks, is the world's largest festival of the arts. The **Edinburgh International Film Festival** (⊠ Filmhouse, 88 Lothian Rd., Edinburgh EH3 9BZ, ☎ 0131/228–4051) concentrates on the best new films from all over the world. After dark is the **Edinburgh Military Tattoo** (⊠ 32 Market St., Edinburgh EH1 1QB, ☎ 0131/225–1188), a display of military expertise.

➤ SEPT.: The **Braemar Royal Highland Gathering** (⊠ Princess Royal and Duke of Fife Memorial Park, Braemar, Grampian, ☎ 01339/755377) hosts kilted clansmen from all over Scotland.

➤ OCT.: **Shetland Accordian and Fiddle Festival** (details from Shetland Tourist Board; ☞ *above*) concentrates on two of the most popular instruments of folk musicians in Scotland.

➤ THIRD WEEKEND IN NOV.: **Shoots and Roots** (☎ FAX 0131/557–1050), the second half of Edinburgh's annual folk jamboree, has a focus this time on traditional music.

INDEX

Icons and Symbols

★ Our special recommendations

✕ Restaurant

🏠 Lodging establishment

✕🏠 Lodging establishment whose restaurant warrants a special trip

☺ Good for kids (rubber duck)

☞ Sends you to another section of the guide for more information

✉ Address

☎ Telephone number

🕐 Opening and closing times

💷 Admission prices

🖰 Sends you to www.fodors.com/urls for up-to-date links to the property's Web site

Numbers in white and black circles ③ ❸ that appear on the maps, in the margins, and within the tours correspond to one another.

NOTES

NOTES

NOTES

NOTES

NOTES

FODOR'S SCOTLAND 2001

EDITORS: Beatrice Aranow, Christine Cipriani, Andrew Collins, Amy Karafin, Deborah Kaufman, Laura Kidder, and Matthew Lombardi

Editorial Contributors: Beth Ingpen, Stewart Hennessey, and Mark Porter

Editorial Production: Tom Holton

Maps: David Lindroth Inc., Mapping Specialists, *cartographers*; Rebecca Baer and Robert Blake, *map editors*

Design: Fabrizio La Rocca, *creative director*; Guido Caroti, *art director*; Jolie Novak, *photo editor*; Melanie Marin, *photo researcher*

Cover Design: Pentagram

Production/Manufacturing: Robert B. Shields

COPYRIGHT

ISBN 0–679–00626–5

ISSN 0743–0973

SPECIAL SALES

Fodor's Travel Publications are available at special discounts for bulk purchases for sales promotions or premiums. Special editions, including personalized covers, excerpts of existing guides, and corporate imprints, can be created in large quantities for special needs. For more information, contact your local bookseller or write to Special Markets, Fodor's Travel Publications, 280 Park Avenue, New York, NY 10017. Inquiries from Canada should be directed to your local Canadian bookseller or sent to Random House of Canada, Ltd., Marketing Department, 2775 Matheson Boulevard East, Mississauga, Ontario L4W 4P7. Inquiries from the United Kingdom should be sent to Fodor's Travel Publications, 20 Vauxhall Bridge Road, London, England SW1V 2SA.

PRINTED IN THE UNITED STATES OF AMERICA

10 9 8 7 6 5 4 3 2 1

IMPORTANT TIP

Although all prices, opening times, and other details in this book are based on information supplied to us at press time, changes occur all the time in the travel world, and Fodor's cannot accept responsibility for facts that become outdated or for inadvertent errors or omissions. So always confirm information when it matters, especially if you're making a detour to visit a specific place.

PHOTOGRAPHY

DIAF: *Giovanni Simeone, cover. (Glencoe)*

Aberdeen & Grampian Tourist Board: *16B. Anne Burgess, 16A.*

Abbotsford House, *2 top right, 11D, 28D.*

Clifton House, *30C.*

Kindra Clineff, *6B.*

Corbis: *26A. Roger Antrobus, 17E. MacDuff Everton, 18A. Dewitt Jones, 10A. Kevin Schafer, 25C. Roger Tidman, 24A, 25 bottom left. Adam Woolfitt, 30I.*

Cringletie House, *30H.*

DIAF: *Rosine Mazin, 23F. Daniel Faure, 15D, 20B. Pratt-Pries, 23D. Yvan Travert, 11C, 12B.*

Glamis Castle, *13D.*

Glasgow City Council, *3 bottom right, 8A.*

Glasgow School of Art, *9C.*

William Grant & Sons International, Ltd., *3 bottom left, 17D.*

Greater Glasgow & Clyde Valley Tourist Board, *8 top, 30F, 30G.*

Blaine Harrington III, *4–5, 23E.*

Her Majesty Queen Elizabeth II, *6C.*

Crown Copyright: *Historic Scotland, 2 bottom right, 10B, 19D, 27C, 29E.*

Robert Holmes Photography: *Robert Holmes, 13C, 22A, 22B. Dewitt Jones, 1, 10 bottom left, 15E.*

Houserstock: *Dave G. Houser, 18B.*

The Image Bank: *Gary Cralle, 8B, 9D, 17C, 30D.*

Catherine Karnow, *6A, 7E, 13E, 14A, 14B, 19E, 20A, 21D, 21E, 22C, 32.*

Liaison Agency: *Michael Lisnet, 24B.*

Libby Weir-Breen Public Relations, *30E.*

The National Trust for Scotland, *2 top left, 3 top left, 3 top right, 12A, 27B.*

PhotoDisc, *29F.*

Stone: *Laurie Campbell, 20 bottom left. Paul Harris, 11E. John Higginson, 21C. Chris Kapolka, 15C. John Lawrence, 7D, 19C. Kevin Schafer, 25D.*

Traquair House, *30A.*

The Witchery by the Castle, *2 bottom left, 2 bottom center, 30J.*

Yes, Glasgow, *30B.*

ABOUT OUR WRITERS

Every trip is a significant trip. Acutely aware of that fact, we've pulled out all stops in preparing this edition of *Fodor's Scotland*. To help you zero in on what to see, we've gathered some great color photos. To show you how to put it all together, we've created great itineraries and neighborhood walks. And to direct you to the places that are truly worth your time and money, we've rallied the team of endearingly picky know-it-alls we're pleased to call our writers. Having seen all corners of Scotland, they're real experts on the subjects they cover for us. If you knew them, you'd poll them for tips yourself.

The information in these pages is largely the work of **Beth Ingpen**. A longtime editorial contributor to *Fodor's Scotland*, Beth works as a freelance editor and writer. She was previously publishing manager with the Royal Society of Edinburgh, Scotland's premier learned society, and spent lunchtimes soaking up that city's culture, particularly in its art galleries and concert halls. Close to the sea, Beth's countryside house is set in the barley fields in the rural northeast.

Mark Porter, who updated this edition's Borders and the Southwest chapter, is a regular contributor to the *Sunday Times* and other national British newspapers, including *The Scotsman*. He is a seasoned travel writer and food critic, also writing for Britain's top food magazine, *Waitrose Food Illustrated*. A former political columnist and features, arts, travel, and books editor of the *Express on Sunday*, he lives and works in Scotland and London.

Stewart Hennessey, our Edinburgh updater, is a former journalist who contributed to various newspapers and magazines including *The Observer, The Independent, Scotland on Sunday, The Guardian, The Times, The Scotsman, GQ,* and *Time Out*. He currently lives in Edinburgh with his English wife, Maisie.

Don't Forget to Write

We love feedback—positive and negative—and follow up on all suggestions. So contact the Scotland editor at editors@fodors.com or c/o Fodor's, 280 Park Avenue, New York, NY 10017. Have a wonderful trip!

Karen Cure
Editorial Director